AMERICAN CONVERSATIONS

FROM THE CENTENNIAL THROUGH THE MILLENNIUM

AMERICAN CONVERSATIONS

FROM THE CENTENNIAL THROUGH THE MILLENNIUM

Volume 2

Volume 1 edited by *James H. Merrell*
Volume 2 edited by *Jerald Podair and Andrew Kersten*

James H. Merrell
Vassar College

Jerald Podair
Lawrence University

Andrew Kersten
University of Wisconsin—Green Bay

PEARSON

Boston   Columbus   Indianapolis   New York   San Francisco   Upper Saddle River
Amsterdam   Cape Town   Dubai   London   Madrid   Milan   Munich   Paris   Montréal   Toronto
Delhi   Mexico City   São Paulo   Sydney   Hong Kong   Seoul   Singapore   Taipei   Tokyo

Editorial Director: Craig Campanella
Editor in Chief: Dickson Musslewhite
Publisher: Charlyce Jones Owen
Editorial Assistant: Maureen Diana
Director of Marketing: Brandy Dawson
Senior Marketing Manager: Maureen Prado Roberts
Marketing Assistant: Christine Riva
Production Manager: Fran Russello
Art Director: Jayne Conte

Cover Designer: Suzanne Duda
Cover Art: Everett Collection Inc/Alamy
Media Director: Brian Hyland
Media Editor: Andrea Messineo
Supplements Editor: Emsal Hasan
Full-Service Project Management: George Jacob/ Integra
Printer/Binder: Edwards Brothers Malloy
Cover Printer: Lehigh Phoenix
Text Font: 10/12, Palatino

Credits and acknowledgments borrowed from other sources and reproduced, with permission, in this textbook appear on the appropriate page within text.

Library of Congress Cataloging-in-Publication Data
American conversations/edited by James H. Merrell, Jerald Podair, Andrew Kersten.

   p. cm.
ISBN-13: 978-0-13-158261-3
ISBN-10: 0-13-158261-5
1. United States—History—Sources. 2. United States—Civilization—Sources. I. Merrell, James Hart, 1953- II. Podair, Jerald E., 1953- III. Kersten, Andrew Edmund, 1969-
E173.A7235 2012
973—dc23

        2012020977

10 9 8 7 6 5 4 3 2 1

ISBN 10:   0-13-158261-5
ISBN 13: 978-0-13-158261-3

CONTENTS

PREFACE

American Conversations is a two-volume anthology of original sources treating U.S. history from early colonization through the turn of the millennium. Drawing upon our many decades of teaching and writing about American history, these books assemble on one stage a remarkable, colorful cast of characters that will captivate students of America's past. As the title suggests, our aim is to strike up a number of different conversations: between our readers and us, between the past and the present, and between the authors, painters, and photographers whose works fill these pages.

FEATURES

American Conversations includes a number of features that make it stand out from the many U.S. history readers on the shelf today:

1. **Primary sources.** Decades of teaching both original sources and scholarly works confirm our belief that history is most vividly and powerfully brought to life through texts composed in times past. Even the finest historical scholarship imposes a screen, a filter, between the reader and that past. Students respond well when brought face-to-face, as it were, with men and women who lived in bygone days.

2. **Longer excerpts.** Most primary-source anthologies contain many texts by many authors. It is common to have five or even ten brief excerpts in a single chapter, clamoring for the reader's attention. Whatever this approach gains by way of inclusion, the cacophony of voices breeds confusion rather than clarity. Instead, *American Conversations* offers lengthy excerpts of greater richness and substance. This enables readers to become more thoroughly acquainted with one person, one text, or one topic, to acquire a better sense of the flavor and feel of the American past. We are confident that the sources in *American Conversations* will become part of students' lifelong historical sensibility, challenging them to integrate the American history they learn into the America they experience.

3. **Texts by both famous and obscure Americans.** *American Conversations* reflects a commitment to bring forgotten Americans—Native Americans and African Americans, women and workers—out of the backwaters and into the historical mainstream where they belong. At the same time, however, we believe that all students of American history should be acquainted with certain leading figures and core texts. Accordingly, we juxtapose the forgotten and the famous. Volume 1 includes a West African creation story and Benjamin Franklin, a Revolutionary war soldier named Joseph Plumb Martin and Thomas Jefferson, the Pequot Indian William Apess and the abolitionist Frederick Douglass. Similarly, Volume 2 offers the Railroad Strike of 1877 and Andrew Carnegie, Japanese American war internee Charles Kikuchi and Norman Rockwell, and *Life* magazine's "American Women" of the 1950s and Elvis Presley. This combination offers a more robust understanding not only of hitherto unknown texts but also of documents and images that Americans think they already know well.

4. **Images.** On billboards and buses, on television and the Internet, Americans nowadays are bombarded with images, so much so that we tend to take them for granted and do not really "see" them as texts worthy of study. But examined with the same critical acumen devoted to written texts, images can be indispensable tools for illuminating the past. To sharpen the reader's eye, both volumes include

chapters devoted to visual texts. Volume 1 invites consideration of pictures of Native Americans in the 1580s, of nature and nationalism in nineteenth-century landscape art, and depictions of the Battle of Gettysburg. Volume 2 includes examples of the Great Depression photography of Dorothea Lange and Walker Evans, Norman Rockwell's "Four Freedoms" illustrations, and the Pop Art of Andy Warhol.

5. **Substantive head notes.** Accompanying the longer passages of primary sources are longer head notes introducing each chapter. These aspire to accomplish several things: capture the reader's interest and attention; tell the story of the text's author and its audience; shed light on the times that produced both author and audience; pose questions about the broader implications of the document; and ignite a conversation between the author and others in the book.

6. **Questions for Consideration and Conversation.** At the end of each head note are questions aimed at shaping the reader's experience without confining it to particular issues or particular answers. We have found over the years that students welcome having a few things in mind as they tackle a source—a few, but not too many. They can and will come up with other questions (and other answers) on their own.

7. **Genuine "conversation."** *American Conversations* is no mere catchy title: It conveys the volume's central purpose and carries several different meanings. The most obvious is the dialogue between reader and text, between now and then, today and yesterday. Then there is a running conversation between editors and reader as questions are raised to provoke thought and discussion. That discussion—with other readers and other students of history—is yet another form of conversation. Finally, there is the conversation across chapters, which the head notes promote. Rather than finishing one chapter, forgetting about it, and moving on to the next, students of American history will be able to give thought to time's cumulative power, to the ways different people in different eras speak to one another about common areas of interest and concern. The head notes invite these conversations between history's actors, between (for example) the aristocrat Dr. Hamilton and the democrat Thomas Paine, between the Puritan woman Mary Rowlandson in the 1670s and the Quaker women Angelina and Sarah Grimké in the 1830s, between railroad baron Thomas Scott in the 1870s and chronicler of the rural poor James Agee in the 1930s, and between the integrationist W. E. B. Du Bois in the 1900s and the separatist Malcolm X in the 1960s. This cross-fertilization profoundly enriches these volumes by helping to forge connections across chapters and centuries in important, illuminating ways. It makes for volumes that view the past not as static and divorced from the present but as the scene of dynamic and spirited conversations among Americans across generations, centuries, and eras.

American Conversations is, then, a guided tour through some fascinating precincts of this country's past. It aspires to tap into the very real, very powerful curiosity about American history that is evident in everything from the History Channel and Hollywood films to the streets of Williamsburg and the fields of Gettysburg. Channeling that curiosity, that energy, down a path we have marked out, it hopes to get readers to appreciate both the "pastness" of the past and its abiding hold on the present—and on the future.

ACKNOWLEDGMENTS

American Conversations is itself the product of many conversations over many years with friends, colleagues, students, and editors. Chats with Steve Forman, David Glassberg, Scott Moyers, and especially Clyde Griffen helped in the formative stages. Andrew Wylie and his staff at the Wylie Agency shepherded the project through many twists and turns on the way to publication. The Department of History and the Wilson Library at the University of Minnesota generously provided me space to work on the book during the many summers I spent in my home state. One August day on one of those Midwestern sojourns the university's Colonial History Workshop gathered to offer advice on my plans. John Howe and Jeani O'Brien, who arranged that session, went above and beyond the obligations of friendship to listen, each and every summer I spent in the Twin Cities, as I described the work's progress (or lack thereof).

Here at Vassar College I have benefited from generous funding and sabbatical leaves for scholarly pursuits such as this one. Generations of student research assistants—Matt Ambrose, Meghan Carey, Kate Collins, Carrie Maylor, Tawny Paul, Andrew Thibedeau, and Mariah Vitali—aided with various tasks. Even more generations of Vassar students—with others at the College of William & Mary (1982–84) and Northwestern University (1998–99)—helped by reading and discussing the texts in Volume 1. These chapters have been, as it were, "road tested" in classrooms across three decades: I have assigned nearly all of them in my courses, most of them many times.

Vassar colleagues, too, have been extraordinarily magnanimous with their time and knowledge. The Vassar History Department's administrative assistants, Norma Torney and Michelle Whalen, have helped in ways large and small. Bob Brigham, Miriam Cohen, and Rebecca Edwards offered their expertise in U.S. history and in teaching the American past. Ismail Rashid guided my thinking about West African history for Chapter 1. Leslie Offutt, hoping I would take a hint, presented me with not one or two but three different editions of Cabeza de Vaca's account of his adventures and misadventures (Chapter 2). Tony Wohl bestowed much-needed encouragement and good cheer early on in this work's life, and throughout the long gestation period; Bob DeMaria's friendship and scholarship have sustained me.

When I embarked on this long journey, my son Dave was in sixth grade and his brother Will was in nursery school. Both are now grown men. Over the years neither has supplied so much as a word, a source, or an idea to this volume; nonetheless, their contribution has been as profound as it is immeasurable. And the boys' contribution is nothing compared to that of their mother, my wife Linda Keiko-Yamane Merrell. Our conversations across almost forty years have been the most important and most deeply cherished of them all.

James H. Merrell
Poughkeepsie, New York

It has been a pleasure to work on this project with my coeditors, who are also my friends. Thanks to James Merrell for asking me to collaborate with him. His invitation gave me the opportunity to think about American history in novel and exciting ways. I'm grateful to Andrew Kersten for joining me on Volume 2, as well as for his support and loyalty over the years. I hope these volumes will justify the confidence Andrew Wylie and his staff have shown in us. Special thanks to Ekin Oklap in the Wylie Agency's London office for helping me out in a pinch.

Lawrence University is a model among liberal arts colleges in its encouragement of faculty scholarship. Thanks to Provost and Dean of the Faculty David Burrows for setting the institutional tone in this regard. Lawrence's Robert S. French Chair in American Studies has made it possible for me to live the life of the mind. Lawrence's generous faculty leave policies gave me the time and intellectual space to chart this volume's course. My experiences in London as Lawrence's London Centre Visiting Professor challenged many of my assumptions about American history and made me a better student of my own country's past. Wonderful student research assistants—Alyson Richey, Caitlin Gallogly, Hayley Vatch, and Jennifer Sdunzik—helped me translate my thoughts and ideas about this book to the printed page. Lori Rose, Valerie Carlow, and Maggie Marmor came through with their usual calm efficiency when I needed them most. My students in Lawrence's senior research seminar, "The Practice of History," inspire me year after year with their knowledge, ability, and enthusiasm for the best subject of all. Finally, I am proud to be a member of one of the finest liberal arts college history departments in the country at Lawrence University.

I am grateful to many fellow historians who have served as intellectual guides and role models, including James McPherson, Alan Brinkley, Gary Gerstle, Vernon Burton, and Daniel Rodgers. I became a historian because many years ago I fell under the spell of the master storytellers Walter Lord, William Manchester, Bruce Catton, and Jim Bishop. They took me to places I never forgot and made me want to tell great stories of my own.

My great friend Jerry Seaman has heard about this book for more years than he can count over lunches and dinners at our favorite Appleton diner; thanks for listening and for helping me settle the world's problems. Thanks also to Dr. Robert Klein, my old college roommate with whom I've laughed so often at life's inanities.

I owe most to my family. My late father, Simon Podair, taught me from an early age that books hold the world's riches, and of course, he was right. My late mother, Selma Podair, may not have loved history, but she certainly loved me. My daughter, Julie Podair, is a brilliant and courageous young woman, and I'm lucky to be her father. Speaking of luck, meeting Caren Benzer was, to borrow from Thomas Wolfe, "that dark miracle of chance which makes new magic in a dusty world." My world is a joyous place thanks to her.

Jerald E. Podair
Appleton, Wisconsin

I would like to thank James Merrell and Jerald Podair for inviting me to contribute to this project. I appreciate their generosity, patience, and creativity. Writing my chapters in the second volume of *American Conversations* reminded me of the tremendous diversity in the American experience. Despite the great investment of time and space in these chapters, I feel that we have only scratched the surface of the "conversations." And, yet, that is the genius of these books; these pages will foster more debate and discussions about the nature of the American past.

I would also like to thank my family, namely the three women with whom I live: Vickie, Bethany, and Emily, who were quite encouraging as I changed my sabbatical plans so that I could contribute to Volume 2. They were quite patient and attentive as I related all that I was learning about Elvis, the invention of the television, and various critical topics in modern U.S. history.

Andrew E. Kersten
Green Bay, Wisconsin

We wish to thank the following reviewers of *American Conversations* for their insightful comments in preparation for this first edition:

Stephen R. Boyd,
University of Texas, San Antonio;

James A. Hijiya,
University of Massachusetts Dartmouth;

Rebecca Hill,
Borough of Manhattan Community College;

Michael Hucles,
Old Dominion University;

Carol Sue Humphrey,
Oklahoma Baptist University;

Kevin Kern,
University of Akron;

Robert O'Brien,
Lone Star College—CyFair;

Linda K. Salvucci,
Trinity University;

Jeffrey G. Strickland,
Montclair State University; and

Ericka Kim Verba,
Santa Monica College.

ABOUT THE AUTHORS

James Merrell, editor of Volume 1 of *American Conversations*, is the Lucy Maynard Salmon Professor of History at Vassar College. He has been studying history for forty years, writing and publishing it for thirty, and teaching it for more than twenty-five—mostly at Vassar, with brief stints at Northwestern University and the College of William and Mary. Though he has taught everything from Machiavelli and Luther to McCarthy and LBJ, his main area of interest is American history from the opening of European colonization to the close of Reconstruction some three centuries later. Born and raised in Minnesota, Professor Merrell earned degrees at Lawrence University and Oxford University before receiving his M.A. and Ph.D. from the Johns Hopkins University. Prior to arriving at Vassar in 1984, he was a Fellow at the Newberry Library Center for the History of the American Indian (now the D'Arcy McNickle Center for American Indian and Indigenous Studies) at the Newberry Library in Chicago, and at the Institute of Early American History and Culture (now the Omohundro Institute of Early American History and Culture) in Williamsburg, Virginia. He has also received fellowships from the American Council of Learned Societies, the John Simon Guggenheim Memorial Foundation, and the National Endowment for the Humanities. Professor Merrell's research interests are in early American history in general and relations between Natives and newcomers in particular. Co-editor of three volumes (two anthologies by Routledge and one by Syracuse University Press) and author of numerous articles, his first book, *The Indians' New World: Catawbas and Their Neighbors from European Contact through the Era of Removal* (University of North Carolina Press, 1989; twentieth-anniversary edition, 2009), won the Frederick Jackson Turner Award and the Merle Curti Award from the Organization of American Historians as well as the Bancroft Prize. His second book, *Into the American Woods: Negotiators on the Pennsylvania Frontier* (W.W. Norton, 1999), was a finalist for the Pulitzer Prize and won Professor Merrell his second Bancroft Prize, making him one among the handful of historians ever to win that prestigious award twice.

Jerald Podair, coeditor of Volume 2 of *American Conversations*, is Professor of History and the Robert S. French Professor of American Studies at Lawrence University, in Appleton, Wisconsin. A native of New York City, and a former practicing attorney, he received his B.A. from New York University, a J.D. degree from Columbia University Law School, and a Ph.D. in American history from Princeton University. His research interests lie in the areas of American urban history and racial and ethnic relations. He is the author of *The Strike That Changed New York: Blacks, Whites, and the Ocean Hill-Brownsville Crisis*, published by Yale University Press, which was a finalist for the Organization of American Historians' Liberty Legacy Foundation Award for the best book on the struggle for civil rights in the United States, and an honorable mention for the Urban History Association's Book Award in North American urban history. *Bayard Rustin: American Dreamer*, his biography of the civil rights and labor leader, was published in 2009 by Rowman & Littlefield. His most recent book is a coedited volume entitled *The Struggle for Equality: Essays on Sectional Conflict, the Civil War, and the Long Reconstruction*, published in 2011 by the University of Virginia Press. His articles and reviews have appeared in *The American Historical Review*, *The Journal of American History*, *The Journal of Urban History*, *Reviews in American History*, *Radical History Review*, *Labor History*, and *American Studies*. He contributed an essay, " 'One City, One Standard': The Struggle for Equality in Rudolph Giuliani's New York," to *Civil Rights in New York City: From World War II to the Giuliani Era*, edited by Clarence Taylor, published by Fordham University

Press in 2011. At Lawrence University, he teaches courses on a variety of topics in nineteenth- and twentieth-century American history, including the Civil War and Reconstruction, the Great Depression and New Deal, the 1960s, and the Civil Rights Movement. He also teaches Lawrence's inaugural course in American Studies, which he introduced in 2007. He is the recipient of the Allan Nevins Prize, awarded by the Society of American Historians for "literary distinction in the writing of history," and a Fellow of the New York Academy of History. He was appointed by Wisconsin governor Jim Doyle to the state's Abraham Lincoln Bicentennial Commission, on which he served from 2008 to 2009. In 2010, he was honored by Lawrence University with its Award for Excellence in Scholarship, and in 2012 with its Faculty Convocation Award.

Andrew Kersten, coeditor of Volume 2 of *American Conversations*, is Frankenthal Professor of History in the Department of Democracy and Justice Studies at the University of Wisconsin–Green Bay. He teaches courses in U.S. history—the U.S. history survey, U.S. immigration history, and U.S. labor history—and interdisciplinary courses relating to his department. He researches and writes about American history since Reconstruction. His books include *Race, Jobs, and the War: The FEPC in the Midwest, 1941–46* (University of Illinois Press, 2000), which is an investigation of President Franklin D. Roosevelt's Fair Employment Practice Committee; *Labor's Home Front: The AFL during World War II* (New York University Press, 2006), which is a history of the American Federation of Labor during the war; *A. Philip Randolph: A Life in the Vanguard* (Rowman and Littlefield, 2006); and *Clarence Darrow: American Iconoclast* (Farrar, Straus, and Giroux, 2011). Currently, he is working on an online, digital database of A. Philip Randolph's writings, as well as an anthology of new historical interpretations about Randolph's life and legacy. He has two other professional passions. Kersten frequently collaborates with public historians and museums such as the National Railroad Museum and the Experimental Aircraft Association's Museum. He also enjoys working with K–12 history teachers. From 2003 to 2006, he led a Teaching American History Grant Program of his own design that offered intensive professional development for history teachers, and he continues to collaborate on curricular design and other educational issues.

AMERICAN CONVERSATIONS

FROM THE CENTENNIAL THROUGH THE MILLENNIUM

Introduction

"History is the memory of things said and done."

—Carl Becker

American Conversations, From the Centennial through the Millennium, Volume 2 begins in 1877, the tumultuous first year of the United States' second century of existence, and concludes as the world's most powerful nation enters a twenty-first century filled with new perils and opportunities. Like Volume 1, it offers an array of American voices, each seeking its place in a unique experiment in popular rule that Abraham Lincoln had called "the last best, hope of earth."[1] Taken together, their conversations would define that American experiment. This volume permits us to spend time as historical eavesdroppers, listening in on the American voices that matter most.

Not all of the voices you will hear are those with which you are acquainted. Some belonged to those who, like Lyndon Johnson and Elvis Presley, were indeed "famous." But it is our intention to present these familiar Americans in unfamiliar ways. You will hear Johnson, for example, in private Oval Office conversations, desperately searching for a way out of a deepening involvement in Vietnam that he fears will wreck his presidency. And you will see how newspaper reporters and reviewers, struck by a musical bolt from the blue—a young Elvis Presley—sought to explain an unprecedented cultural phenomenon. Others, like Charles Kikuchi, the Japanese American student caught up in the U.S. government's World War II internment net, and "A Striker" demanding his rights as a worker and a citizen during the Great Upheaval of 1877, were relatively—and in the case of the latter, literally—anonymous. But all of the voices we have selected share a connection to one or more of the defining issues of the American historical experience. They also connect to each other, making it possible to use their "smaller" (but never "small") stories to explore larger ones about our national past. We have deliberately chosen a limited number of longer texts to allow you to construct a narrative of that past for yourself. The historical personalities in this volume are important, then, not because they are all "famous" but because through them you can grasp the essential issues that undergird American history and understand their patterns of change and continuity as they travel across generations and eras. Once you begin to do this, you will be ready to join the community of historians and, along with them, build a "memory of things said and done" in the American past.[2]

A note on interpretation. We ask our students to approach historical subjects with what we call "critical sympathy." That is, a historian's job is to employ a critical eye—we wouldn't be of much use if we did not—but this alone is not enough. We also need a degree of sympathy for the men and women we study, an appreciation that, unlike us, they did not know how events would turn out, and that consequently they made choices that in retrospect seem misguided, wrongheaded, or even stupid. We also must resist the temptation to apply our current moral standards to the inhabitants of the past. When, for example, Abraham Lincoln said in 1858 that "I have no disposition to introduce political and social equality between the white and black races," he was reflecting the racial prejudices of his time.[3] That we do not share these prejudices in our own time does not make Lincoln any less legitimate as a subject of serious historical study. The man who would become our sixteenth president was flawed, as are all human beings. We can be critical of Lincoln's views while also having sympathy for him as one trapped within the confines of circumstances and attitudes, peering into a future with which we are familiar as "through a glass, darkly."[4] We hope, then, that you will engage the people and events in these volumes with as much critical sympathy as you can summon, trusting that future generations of historians will offer it to us as well.

The Civil War insured that the United States would be a nation and not merely a confederation of semi-autonomous states. But it did not decide what *kind* of nation it would be. A host of fundamental questions that had plagued, vexed, and divided Americans from their very beginnings were still unanswered: What did "equality" mean in American life? What was "freedom"? Were equality and freedom always complementary? When these two great American values conflicted, which took precedence? What did it mean to be a "citizen"? Who *was* a "citizen"? What was "American" identity? Who, and what, were "Americans"? Was there a distinctly "American" culture? Was America's essential element the individual or the group?

Americans also debated substantive issues that grew out of the aforementioned definitional ones. One such issue involved the part the federal government would play in the lives of Americans. What should be its objectives, its goals? How would it mediate disagreements between groups of Americans? To what degree would it be involved in managing the national economy? Another concerned the anticommunist impulse, which, during the Cold War, dominated American foreign policy and deeply influenced domestic politics and society. What were this impulse's implications? Its limits? A third issue related to the role of the United States in world affairs. What would its parameters be? What were the responsibilities—and constraints—of world leadership? Closer to home, how did the words "equality" and "freedom" define American gender relations? How "equal" and "free" were women in the United States? What of class relations? How "free" and "equal" were American workers? What were capitalism's implications for American class relations? For American politics and culture?

Americans—however they defined themselves—argued passionately, sometimes violently, over all of these questions after 1876. *American Conversations* tells the story of some of these arguments, and of how they resonated across time through the words and works of a wide variety of Americans, who, even if they were not personally acquainted, engaged and challenged each other.

Accordingly, we will see W. E. B. Du Bois and Malcolm X argue over whether, in Du Bois' words of 1903, it is "possible for a man to be both a Negro and an American." A participant in the Railroad Strike of 1877, the "individualist" Herbert Hoover, and Depression-era photographer Dorothea Lange, among others, will offer their understandings of what it means to be "equal" in America. Early twentieth-century cultural radical Crystal Eastman, *Life's* "American Woman" of the 1950s, and the 1960s feminist Jo Freeman will exchange views on the nature of gender equality in America. Excited observers of the young rock 'n' roll star Elvis Presley, anxious television critic Newton Minow, and celebrity artist Andy Warhol will debate the implications of the rise of popular media in modern America. Repentant Soviet spy Whittaker Chambers, members of the New Left group Students for a Democratic Society, and cold warrior Ronald Reagan will battle over the direction of American anti-communism and of American global power generally. Beat poet Allen Ginsberg, illustrator Norman Rockwell, and social scientist Robert Putnam will discuss the content and character of "American" culture. And World War I–era journalist Randolph Bourne and World War II–internee Charles Kikuchi will pose perhaps the most difficult question of all American conversations, that of the nature of "American" identity itself.

None of these issues were resolved during the nineteenth or twentieth centuries by these or any other American conversationalists, nor will they be in the twenty-first. And this, of course, is as it should be. American conversations are ongoing and open-ended. They link people and issues across history by the basic questions embedded in our democratic experiment. That there are no definitive answers to these questions is, in fact, a blessing. It forces each American generation to confront them in its own way and on its own terms, knowing that the reward lies in the journey itself, not in a preconceived final destination, in engaging, not concluding, the conversation. This volume invites you—as a reader, a historian, and a citizen,—to continue that journey by embarking on American conversations of your own.

Endnotes

1. Abraham Lincoln, Annual Message to Congress, December 1, 1862, in Don E. Fehrenbacher, ed., *Abraham Lincoln, Speeches and Writings, 1859–1865* (New York: Library of America, 1989), 415.
2. Carl Becker, "Everyman His Own Historian," *American Historical Review*, 37 (January 1932), 223.
3. Harold Holzer, ed., *The Lincoln-Douglas Debates: The First Complete, Unexpurgated Text* (New York: Harper Perennial, 1993), 63.
4. 1 *Corinthians* 13: 12.

CHAPTER 1

Workers and Owners Battle During the Great Railroad Strike of 1877

"We contend that the employer has no right to speculate on starvation..."

To Thomas Scott, it was an outrage. Scott was the president of the Pennsylvania Railroad, which in 1877 was not just the largest line in the United States, but the nation's largest corporation of any kind.[1] Although he was not the sole owner of the Pennsylvania—he drew a large salary as president—Scott thought of it as his own. He had helped build it, and now he ran it. Not with his hands, of course. That was for the laborers who laid the track out of Philadelphia, the Pennsylvania's hub, and the engineers, brakemen, firemen, and conductors who brought passengers, freight, and mail to their destinations. Scott and the men who managed the railroad's affairs from office buildings and terminal suites used the tools of the mind to create the Pennsylvania's transportation empire. Brain power, not physical power, was the coin of the realm in 1877, a new industrial age in which machines replaced bodies, and words and ideas substituted for sheer brawn as the mediums of power and success.

This new age suited men like Thomas Scott well. He was at home in a society which judged men on their wealth, knowledge, and power. In such a society, a man's property represented more than a measure of his finances. It was central to his self-worth. There was, of course, an established tradition in the United States of defending private property. The American Revolution itself had begun in large measure over the British crown's abrogation of the colonists' property rights through unrepresentative taxation. The Constitution was a document designed to defend private property, including slaves. The Fourteenth Amendment to the Constitution, ratified in 1868, had prohibited the taking of property without due process of law.

But beyond legal formalities lay an American culture of reverence for property, an impulse toward protecting owners from interference with what was theirs. This was why Thomas Scott was so angry in July 1877. That month, employees of the Pennsylvania and virtually every other major railroad in the country had struck in response to a unilateral 10% salary cut announced by Scott and his fellow operators. The strikers claimed they could not live on these reduced wages and that the railroads had an obligation to pay what could sustain them. Scott and his colleagues, however, believed that wages were set on the open market, through the forces of supply and demand. If an engineer, a brakeman, or a conductor was unhappy with his rate of pay, he was free to resign and allow the job to pass to another man willing to accept what the railroad was offering. He had no right—in Thomas Scott's mind, anyway—to interfere with these new hires, nor with the operation of the railroad itself. This the strikers had done, fighting off replacement workers, or "scabs," as they called them, engaging in acts of vandalism and arson, and blockading trains in their yards and terminals. Scott considered this intolerable. The Pennsylvania Railroad was his property. It did not belong to the workers. They were destroying what was not theirs, and Thomas Scott would not stand for it. He wired newly inaugurated president Rutherford B. Hayes, a man Scott had played a major role in putting in the White House, and asked him to send in federal troops to restore his property.

But to "A Striker," writing anonymously to avoid retribution at the hands of Thomas Scott and his fellow railroad barons, the situation was also an outrage. The 10% wage reduction imposed by the railways was only the latest in a series of cuts that began soon after the Panic of 1873 triggered the worst depression the nation had yet suffered. The investment house of Jay Cooke & Company had overextended itself financing railroad construction, and its bankruptcy in September of that year rippled through the American economy. By mid-decade, the number of unemployed Americans was estimated at between one and three million.[2] As one of America's few truly national economic institutions, the railroads were particularly vulnerable to severe changes in the business cycle. As prices fell, the rail lines resorted to wage-slashing and mass layoffs to stay afloat. Between 1873 and 1877, railway workers experienced pay cuts averaging 21–37% and the number of employees in the industry fell substantially.[3] Even those fortunate enough to keep their jobs were still forced to accept part-time service.

The railroad managers insisted these measures were the unavoidable consequences of financial austerity. Or were they? Thomas Scott's Pennsylvania and other carriers had issued bonds to raise the capital necessary for operations and expansion. These became debts owed to purchasers, payable with interest as they matured. Stockholders also demanded dividends on their investments. The railroads viewed these commitments as paramount to all others, including those involving their employees. Thus men like Thomas Scott believed it was proper to generate the cash they required by forcing men like "A Striker" to make do on less. Scott also thought it was proper to fix his costs by entering into "pooling" arrangements with other lines. The chief executives of the major railroads had, as part of such a pool, agreed in May 1877 to cut the wages of all employees earning more than one dollar per day by 10%.[4] This was the immediate impetus for the workers' violent actions in July. Times were hard, it was true, but most railroads were still rewarding their stockholders with dividends and paying off their bond obligations, not to mention offering their executives and managers generous salaries. It seemed to "A Striker" that the sacrifices attendant to "hard times" were not being shared equally.

There was, as well, the matter of unions. The railroad owners argued that the unfettered free market should govern labor relations. They viewed organizations through which workers banded together to increase their bargaining power as unwarranted interferences with the laws of supply and demand, as a form of socialism. Yet the same owners did not hesitate to band together themselves into pools to set fares, freight rates, and wages. Why, "A Striker" may have asked himself, was a union "socialistic" while a pooling arrangement was not?

The issue of government intervention in labor disputes also smacked of hypocrisy to "A Striker." Thomas Scott bristled at the thought of government authorities telling him how much to pay his workers, or limiting the freight rates he could charge on his railroad.[5] But he did not hesitate to call on state militias and federal soldiers to break strikes against "his" property. Why was one "socialism" but not the other?

And was there any limit to what a man could do with what he owned? Thomas Scott did not seem to think so. But shouldn't a private property owner have some public responsibilities? Just because a corporation like the Pennsylvania could take advantage of a labor surplus and pay their workers starvation-level wages, should it? "Law! What do I care about law? Hain't I got the power?" and "The public be damned!"—remarks imputed, respectively, to Cornelius Vanderbilt and his son William, owners of the New York Central Railroad—appeared to provide the answer.[6] It was this sentiment, common among the railroad barons, that may have angered men like "A Striker" most. Was there a moral and ethical "law" higher than that of simple supply and demand? Were there limits to private property rights in the United States? "A Striker" certainly thought so. To him, human needs outweighed the imperatives of profit. That is why he was as outraged at Thomas Scott as Scott was at him.

On May 15, 1877, the presidents of America's four major railroad lines—Thomas Scott's Pennsylvania, the Baltimore & Ohio (B & O), the Erie, and the New York Central & Hudson—convened in secrecy in Chicago and decided jointly on 10% salary cuts for virtually all of their men. The Pennsylvania was the first to make this public, on June 1, when it also served notice that it would be running what were known as "doubleheader" trains as a cost-saving device. Doubleheaders featured two locomotives, an inconvenience for engineers but a mortal danger for brakemen forced to couple and uncouple cars by hand. Twice the work meant twice the chance to be maimed—missing fingers were emblematic of this occupation—or crushed to death. The next day, a group of Pennsylvania employees met with Scott at the railroad's Philadelphia home office in an unsuccessful attempt to obtain a reversal of the salary reductions. It simply could not be done with the resources at hand, Scott told the men, neglecting to mention that the Pennsylvania had paid stockholder dividends throughout the depression years.

Some workers did not wait for Scott's answer. Across the state, just outside of Pittsburgh, the Trainmen's Union was being founded as Scott spoke to his aggrieved employees. The Union represented the first attempt to organize railroad employees on an industry-wide basis, regardless of skill or craft. In view of the lines' policy of firing and blacklisting those who joined unions, it was agreed that the group would be a secret one for the time being. Even this precaution did not prevent internal spies from reporting to management on the organizers, costing many their jobs.

By early July, all of the railroads had implemented the 10% wage reduction. The last to do so, the B & O, was the first struck, on July 11. That day, workers at the B & O's train yard in Martinsburg, West Virginia, spontaneously moved to stop trains from moving in and out. Martinsburg was a "railroad town." Most of its citizens had some connection to the B & O, and despised it. Low wages, dangerous working conditions, high freight rates and passenger fares, and exploitative landlord practices had led Martinsburg's citizens to feel a kinship with the strikers, many of whom were actual kin. Groups of supporters congregated around the train yard, a pattern that would be replicated wherever the strike spread. At the behest of B & O management, West Virginia's governor called out the state militia, but they too sympathized with the strikers. The governor and B & O's chief executive John Garrett then turned to President Hayes, demanding that he authorize the use of federal troops to protect railroad property. This Hayes agreed to almost immediately, and on July 20, U.S. Army regulars reopened Martinsburg's rail traffic.

But by then workers on other lines and in other cities and towns had joined the battle. At Cumberland, Maryland, strikers blocked freight trains, aided by townspeople and "tramps," jobless men who roamed the country in search of work. Maryland's governor called out the Baltimore-based state militia and ordered them to Cumberland. A crowd of some 15,000 working-class Baltimoreans—tramps, teenagers, women, and angry citizens—had other ideas. As the militia marched to the B & O's Camden Street depot on July 20, they were set upon by the mob, its anger stoked by class frustrations that had been building for decades. As one historian put it,

> (T)he emotion that fueled the crowd on Front Street was fury, engendered by the life sentence of toil and misery which the age had pronounced on them, turned against the great-bodied and soulless corporations, narrowed in this place to hatred of Maryland's dominant corporation (the B&O)... and bearing now upon the troops who defended its interests.[7]

Rocks, debris, and gunshots came from the crowd. Outnumbered and panicked, the militia opened fire. Within seconds, eleven men lay dead or dying. The enraged crowd then set fire to a locomotive, several passenger cars, and a portion of a platform at the Camden Street depot, as the governor, the mayor of Baltimore, and a militia regiment took cover inside. The mob trapped them in the depot overnight. The governor wired Hayes with an urgent appeal for federal troops, which the president quickly dispatched. By July 22, they had restored order in Baltimore. It would take more than another week, however, for the entire B & O line to be cleared of strikers' blockades and resume normal operations.

Meanwhile, in Pittsburgh, it was the Pennsylvania's turn. On July 19, rail workers of all job grades struck the line and prevented its trains from leaving the city. "It's a question of bread or blood," said a flagman, "and we're going to resist."[8] The strikers called on the rest of Pittsburgh's working class to join them. As in other cities, railroads—and especially the Philadelphia-based Pennsylvania—were scorned in Pittsburgh, and thousands rallied to the men. Even merchants, policemen, and local government officials were friendly to the strikers. Pennsylvania governor John Hartranft, however, was not. On July 19, he was on a western vacation, courtesy of Thomas Scott, who had provided a private railroad car for his convenience. By telegraph, Hartranft summoned a state militia regiment composed of Pittsburgh residents to quell the disturbance. But as had been the case in Martinsburg, some of the militiamen were relatives and friends of the railroad workers, and refused to use force against those they considered brethren. The strikers also helped their cause by ignoring passenger train traffic, thereby avoiding inconvenience to the general public.

With the city of Pittsburgh largely united behind the strikers, Governor Hartranft switched tactics. He called out a national guard unit from Philadelphia, which arrived on July 21. Without personal or community ties to the strikers, the guardsmen had no qualms about using force. During an altercation with the workers and their supporters, the Philadelphians opened fire, leaving ten dead. The mob counterattacked, rampaging through the Pennsylvania train yards and destroying engines, cars, and track. It forced the guardsmen into a roundhouse, a large structure in which railroad equipment was stored and repaired. The guardsmen did not escape until the next day, shooting twenty strikers and sympathizers to death as they did. The area in and around the Pennsylvania rail yards lay in pillage for almost two miles:

> In that bleak landscape of ashes and old iron rested the remains of 104 locomotives, and 2,152 cars of all sorts—passenger, Pullman, officers' and emigrants' coaches, baggage, paymaster, express, postal, refrigerator and stock cars, gondolas, coal cars, boxcars, and cabooses. If coupled into one ghostly train, they would have been strung out for eleven and a half miles.[9]

The damage had not been limited to railroad property. Anything associated with large-scale capital was a target. As the crowd set its sights on a grain elevator, an onlooker protested that it did not belong to the Pennsylvania. "It don't make a damned bit of difference," replied a strike sympathizer. "It's got to come down. It's a monopoly and we're tired of it."[10]

The mood in Pittsburgh mirrored that of other cities as the "Great Upheaval" spread through the nation. By the last week in July, America was closer to a mass working-class strike than at any time in its history. In a rare instance of interracial solidarity, virtually every worker in St. Louis left work for two days. Across the Mississippi River in East St. Louis, striking railroad workers captured the switching station that controlled movement in and out of the city and announced "General Order No. 1," stopping all freight traffic. Chicago spiraled into street violence as iron and steel workers, meat packers, and others joined railroad strikers in pitched battles with police. In Reading, Pennsylvania, a crowd of railroad men and their allies were fired on by state national guard units, killing eleven; miners in the coal country north of the city struck in solidarity.

By July 28, President Hayes had dispatched federal troops to West Virginia, Maryland, Pennsylvania, New York, Indiana, Illinois, and Missouri. Even this was not enough for Governor Hartranft and others, who demanded that the president raise a corps of volunteers and place the entire nation on a full war footing, much as Abraham Lincoln had done in 1861 after the Confederate attack on Fort Sumter. While Hayes wisely declined to take this drastic step, his use of army regulars to break the strikes and get the trains running again was an indication of his commitment to defending the rights of private property holders in the United States.

"We must have our property," a Pennsylvania railroad official exclaimed at the height of the disturbances.[11] The nation's property-holding classes reacted to the Great Upheaval with panic and hysteria. Until 1877, they were able to hold to the idea that the interests of capital and labor in America, while not identical, were at least compatible. The strikes put that notion to rest with brutal finality. Henceforth, the middle and upper classes in the United States would view the working class as a threat not only to property rights but also to the continued viability of American democracy. The violent uprisings of 1877 bore more than a passing resemblance in their eyes to the Paris Commune of 1871, a worldwide symbol of revolution and destruction. That year, working-class "communards" had seized control of that city and imposed a Marxist-inspired regime that confiscated property, abolished privileges based on wealth and status, and presided over the execution of the Archbishop of Paris. The Commune was overthrown by the French government after two months, but at the cost of thousands of lives lost during street battles.

Just six years later, similar scenes in the United States foretold an impending class war, and those who held property became more fearful than ever of losing it. Could there be class peace in America? Was there a "natural" enmity between workers and their bosses? Did "equality" in the United States mean an equal division of property? If so, would property need to be redistributed from those who had it to those who did not? And who would carry this out? The government? The workers themselves? The Great Upheaval raised more questions than it answered. One thing was certain, however. The propertied classes would never look at the American working class in the same way.

By late July, the strikes had essentially burned themselves out—with the assistance, of course, of federal troops, militia, guardsmen, and police. The final death toll was more than one hundred. There was a limit to the staying power of the raw emotions that had fired the strikes. They had been spontaneous and, with the exception of Allegheny City outside of Pittsburgh where leaders of the newly formed Trainmen's Union were briefly in control, established no institutional roots. They were not organized by a mass labor union that could have sustained them over time. This, however, did not prevent Thomas

Scott and other "respectable" Americans from blaming the disturbances on Marxists and foreigners. The Workingmen's Party, a small group with ties to the international socialist movement, came in for special attention. Many critics accused the Party of masterminding the strikes, ascribing an influence far beyond its numbers.

They also condemned the relatively weak labor movement. The Trainmen's Union, which had almost been destroyed by terminations and blacklistings of members before the strikes even began and played a relatively marginal role in them, was invested with the power to disrupt the entire American economic system. To prevent recurrences of the street violence that had so unnerved the property-holding classes, municipalities began constructing armories in which troops could be assembled and ammunition and supplies stored. Most states also improved the training of their militias and made more of an effort to recruit them from the "better" strata of society. The year 1877 also marked the first use of injunctions by federal courts to force the end of strikes. Some of the blocked railroad lines were bankrupt and in federal receivership, making interference with their operations a violation of federal law. In subsequent years, the courts would extend this injunctive policy to strikes against railroads that were not in receivership on the ground that they interfered with federally protected interstate commerce, and then to strikes generally, citing the Fourteenth Amendment's prohibition against the taking of property without due process of law.

The railroad workers did receive some concessions after the strikes ended. A few lines rescinded or scaled back their wage cuts—without recognizing their employees right to organize, of course—and instituted some rudimentary procedures whereby complaints could be brought to the attention of management. The New York Central's William Vanderbilt even made $100,000 available as a reward to his workers who had remained on the job. But the more prevalent reaction was fear and contempt, a sense that poorer Americans suffered from a want of character and wished to take what they had not earned. The aristocratic Reverend Henry Ward Beecher of Brooklyn's Plymouth Congregational Church, the nation's most celebrated minister in 1877, offered an example of this sentiment. He excoriated the railroad strikers for their "tyrannical opposition to all law and order." Sarcastically, he told his congregants "it is true that a dollar a day is not enough to support a man and five children, if the man insists on smoking and drinking beer. Is not a dollar a day enough to buy bread? Water costs nothing. Man cannot live by bread, it is true, but the man who cannot live on bread and water is not fit to live."[12]

The strikes of 1877 marked the emergence of what men like Beecher would come to call "the labor question" as the issue that would divide Americans most sharply for the remainder of the nineteenth century and the first half of the twentieth. With illusions of the harmony of class interests shattered, the nation braced for continued battle.

Thomas Scott and "A Striker" may as well have been describing two different nations when they wrote these pieces for the September 1877 edition of the *North American Review*, a leading opinion journal of the day. Scott's America is grounded in capitalism, competition, and individualism. It rewards those who take risks—business owners, financiers, and investors—with profits and material wealth. It is deeply imbued with the philosophy of "free labor," which first emerged in the antislavery North during the years preceding the Civil War and became one of the animating ideas of the new Republican Party. Free labor advocates, the most prominent of which was Abraham Lincoln, believed that America offered an open field of opportunity to the industrious, and that anyone with talent and a work ethic could achieve success. Although the emergence of what appeared to be a permanent working class in the United States during the nation's industrial takeoff after the Civil War called the free labor idea into question, its proponents continued to cling to it, arguing that poverty was the result of personal weakness and lack of initiative.

But the America of "A Striker" is the product of an economic system that offers few avenues for individual advancement. He writes that when his father emigrated from Sweden in the 1830s, the United States was still a land of opportunity and mobility for workingmen. Over the decades that followed, however, an aristocracy of wealth developed. The "moneyed men," typified by the railroad magnates, had destroyed the independence of the American worker. Wages were determined not through negotiations between equal parties, but by impersonal laws of supply and demand that invariably seemed to favor the employer. "A Striker" believes in moral laws that supersede those based on the market. He maintains that a worker is "entitled to wages sufficient to provide him with enough food, shelter, and clothing to sustain and preserve his health and strength," and that "the employer has no right to speculate on starvation when he reduces wages below a living figure, saying, if we refuse that remuneration, there are plenty of starving men out of work that will gladly accept half a loaf instead of no bread." Ultimately, large corporations, private as they might be, "are responsible to the state." It created them, and it thus "behooves the state to decide what the people are entitled to in return for all they have conceded to these companies...."

But for Thomas Scott, private property rights are sacrosanct. It is the state's primary responsibility to preserve property, not redistribute it. In his letter to the *Review*'s editor, Scott equates the interests of the railroads and those "of the government and society at large." Disgruntled men seeking to damage or take property lawfully belonging to others strike at the very foundation of American democratic life. When that property is that of the railroads, these unlawful actions post a special danger. Rail traffic, Scott argues, knits together the strands of the American economy. By 1877, the United States was no longer a series of isolated communities but an interconnected national market, requiring the "absolute and uninterrupted freedom of movement" that railroads alone could provide.[13] Halt railroad traffic, Scott argues, quoting Stephen Hurlbut, a former Civil War general then serving as a U.S. congressman from Illinois, "and in ten days many parts of the country would be near the starvation-point, and within a month there would be no hamlet in the vast territory drained by these channels, but would feel to the core of its business the effects of the stoppage of this regular and useful circulation." Scott also notes the "the absolute dependence of the whole community upon this great system of railways for almost its existence as a civilized body...."

Having ascribed life-and-death importance to the railroad industry, he takes the next logical step. Scott demands that the federal government intervene in strikes to protect essential national property from those bent on disruption and destruction. This would also include, in his view, federal protection of "the guaranty to every man of the right to work for such compensation as he may agree upon with other men free from interference or intimidation." Loyal to the free labor ideal, Scott remains confident that such "agreements" will be fair to both sides. He believes that railroad management has "always endeavored to treat the interests of employers and employed as identical." Indeed, he argues, most employers are keeping their doors open during the depression with little or no hope of profit only so workers can retain their jobs. Can those who own and run America's corporations be relied upon to protect the interests of their employees? Scott clearly believes they can. "A Striker" believes they cannot. There is a chasm between their perspectives on class relations, capitalism, the role of government, and the nature of "equality" and "freedom" in American life that will only widen in the coming years.

The Great Upheaval of 1877 dealt Thomas Scott a blow from which he would not recover. The financial losses the Pennsylvania had suffered forced him to abandon his challenge to John D. Rockefeller's Standard Oil Company for control of the petroleum refining and transportation market in the United States. Ultimately, the spoils of victory went neither to the railroads nor to the strikers but to the shrewd, opportunistic Rockefeller, who emerged as the nation's first true monopolist. Scott's health soon failed and he died in 1881, a casualty of the stress and turmoil of 1877. As for the anonymous "Striker," we know nothing of his end, of course. But we do know that the clashes of labor and capital at Baltimore, Pittsburgh, Martinsburg, and elsewhere initiated a violent conversation over the rules that would govern a new industrial society. Whether Thomas Scott's or "A Striker"'s version of those rules would prevail, only time would tell.

Questions for Consideration and Conversation

1. It is natural for many of us to sympathize with "A Striker" in this conversation. But can you make an argument for Thomas Scott's position?
2. As you can see, the Great Upheaval of 1877 was marked by violence on both sides. Is recourse to violence ever justified in a democracy?
3. What obligations do you think Thomas Scott owed to the American public? How would Herbert Hoover (Chapter 6) have answered this question? Dorothea Lange (Chapter 8)? The members of Students for a Democratic Society (Chapter 17)?
4. Scott argued that government regulation of his company's business affairs—his wage structure or freight rates, for example—was "socialistic" interference. But he did not hesitate to call on the federal government to employ troops to protect his property from strikers. Can a valid distinction be drawn between these positions?
5. The Great Upheaval came close to becoming a national working-class strike—what historians call a "general strike." What do you think would have happened if it had come to this? How would it have changed American history?
6. How did the Great Upheaval change class relations in the United States? How did it change the American conversation over the idea of "equality"?

Endnotes

1. Philip S. Foner, *The Great Labor Uprising of 1877* (New York: Monad Press, 1977), 13–14.
2. Ibid., 20; Robert V. Bruce, *1877: Year of Violence* (Chicago: Quadrangle Books, 1970), 19.
3. Foner, *The Great Labor Uprising*, 20.
4. Bruce, *1877*, 420.
5. The 1877 *Munn v. Illinois* Supreme Court decision had held that states could regulate railroad freight and storage fees. 94 U.S. 113 (1876).
6. John Steele Gordon, *The Scarlet Woman of Wall Street: Jay Gould, Jim Fisk, Cornelius Vanderbilt, the Erie Railway Wars, and the Birth of Wall Street* (New York: Weidenfeld & Nicolson, 1988), 123; H.W. Brands, *Masters of Enterprise: Giants of American Business from John Jacob Astor and J.P. Morgan to Bill Gates and Oprah Winfrey* (New York: Free Press, 1999), 23.
7. Bruce, *1877*, 104.
8. Ibid., 119.
9. Ibid., 180.
10. Ibid., 176.
11. Ibid., 142.
12. Ibid., 312–13.
13. See Robert H. Wiebe, *The Search for Order, 1877–1920* (New York: Hill and Wang, 1967) for an account of how this took place.

A Striker, "Fair Wages" (1877)

Source: The North American Review, Volume 125, Issue 258, September 1877, pp. 322–26.

The newspapers have fallen into line to defend the railway companies, who thus have brought all the great guns of public opinion to bear on one side of the fight, so the strikers have got the worst of it before the community. We have been so handled that if a workingman stands out to speak his mind, the public have theirs so full of pictures of him and his doings in the illustrated papers, that he is listened to as if he was a convicted rough pleading in mitigation of penalty, instead of an honest and sincere man asking for a fair show. I would not have any one mistake what my principles are and have been. I don't envy any man his wealth, whether it is ill-gotten or not. I am a workingman, therefore an honest one, and would refuse a dollar I did not earn, for I am neither a beggar to accept charity nor a thief to take what belongs to another, however he came by it. If it be his according to law, I, for one, am ready to protect him in his legal rights, and in return I want to be protected in what I believe to be mine.

Forty years ago my father came over to this country from Sweden. He had a small business and a large family. In Europe business does not grow as fast as children come, and poverty over there is an inheritance. He heard that North America was peopled and governed by workingmen, and the care of the States was mainly engaged in the welfare and prosperity of labor. That moved him, and so I came to be born here. He, and millions like him, made this country their home, and their homes have mainly made this country what it is. Until lately the States kept their faith and promise to the people, and we, the people, showed ours when trouble came; an assessment of blood was made on our shares of liberty, and we paid it. That is our record. We did not fight for this party or that party, but for the country and against all that were against the United States.

I am no politician, caring little whether one party or another holds the fort at Washington. My father, who, like me, was a workingman, used to say a country fared best where a strong and sound opposition party kept justice awake and made power behave.

So it was before the war, but since then, it seems to me, the power has got fixed so long in one set of hands that things are settling down into a condition like what my father left behind him in Europe forty years ago, and what stands there still. I mean the slavery of labor. The landed aristocracy over there made the feudal system, just as the moneyed men of this continent are now making a ruling class. As the aristocracy used to make war on each other, so in our time the millionaires live on each other's ruin. As the feudal lords hired mercenary soldiers to garrison their strongholds and to prey on the common people, so the railway lords and stock-exchange barons hire a mercenary press to defend their power, the object of both being the same: the spoils of labor. It looks very like as though this country was settling down into the form and system we fled from in Europe.

The rights and value of labor were acknowledged here forty years ago because the country wanted hands. Now we have made it rich, it turns our own earnings against us, and its prosperity becomes our disaster. We are told to look at Europe and perceive that this condition of affairs is the inevitable result of growth, of population, of wealth; but we look over there, and find that discontent, rebellion, and war are also the inevitable results, and it was to avoid such results these States declared themselves free, that Americans should have a government that was not a conspiracy.

That government has been regarded by the laboring classes of Europe and by our people as the stronghold of the workingman, and in this our present difficulty we are referred to its Constitution which should afford us a remedy for our grievances, the ballot-box is the panacea for all and every complaint. It is not so; and those who point to the remedy know it to be a sham, they know they can buy idlers and vagabonds enough to swell the ranks of wealth and run up a majority whenever a show of hands is required. They recruit the very men that wrecked Pittsburgh, and would pillage New York if they dared to face us, the workingmen, that fill the ranks of the militia.

We are sick of this game, we are soul-weary of looking around for some sympathy or spirit of justice, and, finding none, we turn to each other and form brotherhoods and unions, depots of the army of labor, officered by the skilled mechanic.

This organized force is now in process of formation, and prepared to meet the great questions of the age: Has labor any rights? If so, what are they? Our claim is simple. We demand *fair wages*.

We say that the man able and willing to work, and for whom there is work to do, is entitled to wages sufficient to provide him with enough food, shelter, and clothing to sustain and preserve his health and strength. We contend that the employer has no right to speculate on starvation when he reduces wages below a living figure, saying, if we refuse that remuneration, there are plenty of starving men out of work that will gladly accept half a loaf instead of no bread.

We contend that to regard the laboring class in this manner is to consider them as the captain of a slave-ship regards his cargo, who throws overboard those unable to stand their sufferings. Let those who knew the South before the war go now amongst the mining districts of Pennsylvania, and compare the home of the white laborer with the quarters of the slave; let them compare the fruits of freedom with the produce of slavery!

But we know the question is a difficult one to settle, we do not want to force it on with threats. The late strike was not intended to break out as it did; things broke loose and took a direction we regretted. We find ourselves answerable for results we had no share in or control over. Nevertheless we accept the event as a symptom of the disorder that is consuming our body and pray the country to look to it, it is not a passing complaint.

Let me put this matter in a plain way, as we understand it, and use round numbers instead of fractions, as we have to deal with hundreds of millions, dividing the subject into sections.

1. In the United States the amount of capital invested in railway property last year was $4,470,000,000, made up of $2,250,000,000 capital stock and $2,220,000,000 bonded debt. The gross earnings were $500,000,000, or about eight and a half per cent on the capital. The running expenses (of which the bulk was for labor) were $310,000,000, leaving $185,000,000 as interest to the capitalist, or barely four per cent on his investment.

   Labor is admitted into this enterprise as a preferential creditor, to be paid out of gross earnings before the most preferred mortgagee or bond holder receives a dollar. For as capital could not build the roads nor equip them without labor, so the enterprise, when complete, cannot be run without labor.

   Capital, therefore, takes a back seat when it comes to the push, and acknowledges not only that labor has the largest interest in the concern, but takes the first fruits.

I take the railroad as a sample out of all enterprises, and if we could get at figures, there is no doubt it is a fair sample of the crowd. If, then, labor is the more important and essential factor in the result, when it comes to the question which of the two shall suffer in moments of general distress, the capitalist in his pocket or the laborer in his belly, we think the answer has been already settled by the rights assumed by one and acknowledged by the other.

2. It is manifestly unjust that the workingman should be subject to under wages in bad times, if he has not the equivalent of over wages in good times. If railroad companies in concert with the laboring class had established a tariff of labor, and paid a bonus on wages at every distribution of dividends, that bonus being in proportion to the profits of the road, so that each man becomes a shareholder in his very small way, then he would have submitted to bear his share of distress when all were called on to share trouble, but to share it equally and alike.

3. When folks say that labor and capital must find, by the laws of demand and supply, their natural relations to each other in all commercial enterprises, and neither one has any rights it can enforce on the other, they take for granted that the labor market is, like the produce market, liable to natural fluctuations. If that were so, we should not complain. But it is not. The labor market has got to be like the stock and share market; a few large capitalists control it and make what prices they please. This sort of game may ruin the gamblers in stocks, and injure those who invest, but the trouble is confined mostly to those who deserve to lose or those who can afford it.

   But not so when the same practice operates in the labor market. The capitalist must not gamble with the bread of the workingman, or if he does, let him regard where that speculation led France one hundred years ago, when the financiers made a corner in flour, and the people broke the ring with the axe of the guillotine.

4. When the railway companies obtained privileges and rights over private property, and became by force of law the great landowners of the state, holding its movable property as well, and controlling every avenue and department of business, public and private, they became powerful monopolies. The state endowed them with powers to frame laws of their own and deprived

citizens of their property, means, facilities of transport, to vest it all in these corporations. Thus endowed, they cannot pretend they are no more than ordinary commercial enterprises. They are responsible to the state for the result of their operations, if they disturb fatally the order of our concerns. They are not independent. The state has claims upon them it has not on private concerns. They may not accept liabilities and then decline responsibility. It behooves the state to decide what the people are entitled to in return for all they have conceded to these companies, and to enforce such claims.

5. The English Parliament legislated on the question of the number of hours a working-man should labor. It limits them to so many.

It legislates for his health and supply of light and water. In all these matters the capitalist has an interest. (He does as much for his horse.) But when it comes to the question of a proper amount of food and clothing, of warmth and shelter, the government declines to interfere. It leaves the question of fair wages to be adjusted between employer and employed.

And so I leave it, fearing I have put the matter in rough language, but not intentionally rude, having a deep and loyal faith in the humanity and justice that abide in the hearts of all this community, and wishing that God had given me the power to touch them.

A "STRIKER."

THOMAS A. SCOTT, "THE RECENT STRIKES" (1877)

Source: The North American Review, Volume 125, Issue 258, September 1877, pp. 351–62.

Philadelphia, August 13, 1877.
Allen Thorndike Rice, Esq.,
Editor of the North American Review.

My DEAR SIR,

The request that you have done rue the honor to make, to give you for publication in the North American Review such results of my observation and experience during the recent disastrous disturbances in this country as may appear to have some bearing upon the general interests of the community, finds me absorbed in imperative duties which make it difficult for me to comply with your wishes. But the issues and results of these deplorable events are of such importance to the prosperity and happiness of the American people, without distinction of class, and to the very existence of our social and political institutions, that no one, perhaps, who happens, through whatever circumstances, to have been brought into immediate contact with these events, should allow any personal considerations to restrain him, when the proper occasion is presented, from expressing his candid and deliberate views in regard to them.

I therefore take pleasure in giving you the following statement, which must be taken for what it is worth by the thoughtful readers of the

North American Review, and my hope is that it may be found of some use in helping the public in this country to form just and practical conclusions on the subject.

On the 16th of July it became known that the firemen and freight brakemen of the Baltimore and Ohio Railroad were on a strike at Martinsburg, West Virginia, and that no freight trains were allowed to pass that point in either direction. This proved to be the beginning of a movement which spread with great rapidity from New York to Kansas, and from Michigan to Texas, which placed an embargo on the entire freight traffic of more than twenty thousand miles of railway, put passenger travel and the movement of the United States mails at the mercy of a mob, subjected great commercial centres like Chicago and St. Louis to the violent disturbance of all their business relations, and made the great manufacturing city of Pittsburgh for twenty-four hours such a scene of riot, arson, and bloodshed as can never be erased from the memory of its people.

In Baltimore, Reading, Scranton, Cleveland, Indianapolis, Fort Wayne, Columbus, Cincinnati, Louisville, and many points in New York and New Jersey, the laws were set at defiance, the property of the various railway companies seized, injured, or destroyed, the civil authorities overpowered or overawed, and in many cases compelled to call upon the military power of the States to protect persons and property. This call could not in all cases be fully met. The governors of West Virginia, Maryland, and Pennsylvania, acted with great promptness, but found the military organizations of their States, although very efficient for the suppression of any ordinary outbreak, unable to suppress what rapidly grew from a riot to an insurrection; and were compelled to invoke the aid of the United States government. To this the President at once responded to the extent of the forces at his command; and the presence of detachments of the regular army and navy hastily gathered from all quarters, and hurried to the points most seriously threatened, aided largely in securing the comparative quiet which now prevails within the borders of those States. Had it not been, however, that in many communities the municipal authorities acted with great nerve and efficiency, and were supported by organizations of citizens, and by a public sentiment determined to maintain law and order at any cost, the troubles to be encountered would no doubt have been much more serious.

I do not wish, and happily it is not necessary, to fill your pages with the mere recital of the distressing cases of violence and outrage which marked the course of these riots unexampled in American history. Suffice it to say that the conduct of the rioters is entirely inconsistent with the idea that this movement could have been directed by serious, right-minded men bent on improving the condition of the laboring classes. How wages could be improved by destroying property, the existence of which alone made the payment of any wages at all possible, it is difficult to understand. Nothing but the insanity of passion, played upon by designing and mischievous leaders, can explain the destruction of vast quantities of railroad equipment absolutely necessary to the transaction of its business, by men whose complaint was that the business done by the full equipment in possession of the railways did not pay them sufficient compensation for their labor.

During the greater part of our century of national existence we have enjoyed such unbroken prosperity that we had perhaps come to expect exemption from many of the worst problems which perplex other and older civilizations. The vast area of public land open to cultivation and settlement had steadily drained off not only our own surplus population, but that of other countries, and the rapid extension of our railway system, by furnishing markets for the productions of all parts of the country, had increased the national wealth and built up a general prosperity. But for the Civil War this state of things might have continued to exist; but the waste of human life and the destruction of property which accompanied that war, the loss of real productive power, and the creation of large debts, national, State, and municipal, involving heavy taxation to meet them, have entailed burdens upon us which were lightly felt during the feverish excitement of the civil conflict, but the weight of which became suddenly onerous and almost intolerable when the financial condition of the country was so seriously disturbed by the panic of 1873. In a few hours the credit upon which the fabric of our apparent prosperity rested was almost entirely destroyed, the capital which had been freely lent to all enterprises offering even a show of prospective profit was suddenly withdrawn. Since that time the country has been obliged to meet its debts, not by renewals, but by actual payments from its resources. Every important industry in the country has been compelled to practise the closest and most rigid economies, in order to escape marketing its products at an absolute loss. The cotton and woollen mills of New England, the furnaces and mines of Pennsylvania, Ohio, Indiana, Illinois, and Missouri, have all passed through the same experience, and have the same story to tell. The capital which communist orators so eloquently denounce has yielded such scant returns as the men who pretend to dictate the scale of adequate wages for labor would regard with disdain. In every manufacturing State in the country it is perfectly well known that many establishments have been kept in operation simply that the men might be employed. This has been done often without one iota of profit to the owners. During the last winter the large rolling-mills in Pennsylvania must have been closed, and thousands of laboring men reduced to idleness, and possibly want, had not the railroads which, during the recent madness that swept over the country, were selected for mob violence and opprobrium come to their relief by anticipating their wants, and by giving orders for rails months in advance of their actual requirements. Political economists may object that it was not an act of charity in which great corporations had any right to indulge, but it is certain that without this thousands of laboring men in the State of Pennsylvania alone would have suffered severely.

Not only this, but in order to aid the industries which are now so much depressed, and to enable manufacturers to continue business and thus keep their men steadily employed, the railways of the country have reduced their local freight charges to the lowest point ever known, and have moved the heavy materials used in making iron, steel, glass, and other products at rates barely above the actual cost of transportation; and yet, by a curiously inverted process of reasoning, the course thus pursued by the railways has been most bitterly denounced by the self-constituted mouthpieces of the very classes which have alone profited by it.

It is safe to assert that so far as the special class of railway employees, firemen and freight brakemen is concerned, there are, perhaps, but few railway companies in the United States which are not today employing a force of train-hands larger than their actual business requires. With the falling off of revenue from traffic, the question was presented at once to railway managers, whether the force employed on the lines should be reduced to that actually necessary for the work to be done, in which case greater compensation might have been paid to the men so retained while others equally deserving must have been turned adrift, or whether it would not be both wiser and kinder to retain as many men as possible in the service, by so allotting the work as to permit all to earn a sum, smaller indeed than in the past, yet it was hoped sufficient to support themselves and their families during the severe period of depression, to the near close of which railway managers, in common with all the business men of the country, perhaps too confidently looked forward. This course, as I have said, may be condemned by the hard rules of political economy. The experience of the past few weeks seems to show that it has commended itself as little to those whom it was intended to relieve, and to whom alone, if anybody, it has been beneficial.

It must not for a moment, however, be understood that the greatest portion, or, indeed, any considerable portion, of the outrages upon life and property which have disgraced our recent history were actually committed by railway employees. It is not true that the majority, or even any large portion, of these men have been disloyal to the trust reposed in them. Probably ninety per cent of the men on all the important lines of the country where strikes occurred were faithful to their duties, and either remained at work, or stood ready to resume it as soon as they were relieved from the actual intimidation to which they were subjected by the rioters and their leaders. It was the dissatisfied element which exists in that branch of industry as in all others which perpetrated or allowed the perpetration of most of the overt acts of violence, such as stopping trains, forcing men therefrom, uncoupling cars, disconnecting engines, and other lawless doings of the kind, and which made itself amenable also to the charge of directly attacking the interests of the government and society at large as well as of the railway companies.

As General Hurlbut of Illinois so forcibly expresses it, in a paper recently published, "they permitted themselves to be the nucleus around which the idle, vicious, and criminal element could gather. Reinforced by these dark and disreputable allies, they destroyed property, stopped commerce, deranged the mails, burned great public buildings, broke up tracks, and thus paralyzed the natural circulation of the Commonwealth." It is in the menace to the general interests of society involved in these disturbances that the real gravity of the situation with which this country is now called to deal exists. "The railroad system is to-day a supreme necessity to maintain life, furnish ready markets, and to bring about the enormous interchange of products which makes the country one. Stop it, and in ten days many parts of the country would near the starvation-point, and within a month there would be no hamlet in the vast territory drained by these channels but would feel to the core of its business the effects of the stoppage of this regular and usual circulation."

The enormous mechanical changes and progress of the past century have brought about a complete revolution, so gradual that perhaps it has not been generally apprehended, in the very condition of things in the United States. The water lines, which, at the date of the framing of the Constitution, were our important channels of internal commerce, have been almost superseded by the new iron highways. Upon these is borne a traffic so essentially national, so closely interwoven with the interests not only of our own but other countries, that it demands the most efficient and speedy protection against all unlawful interference. Grain and other agricultural products of Iowa, Minnesota, and Illinois, the wool, wine, and bullion of California, Nevada, and Utah, the cotton and other products of Texas, Louisiana, Mississippi, and Tennessee are largely carried over the railways to New York, Boston Philadelphia, Baltimore, and other Atlantic cities, much of it for, transshipment to Europe, while in return the manufactures of New England and the Middle States, with our importations from the various countries of the world, the basis of our national customs revenue, reach by the same railways all parts of the great West and the South. Certainly this great inland commerce, both in tonnage and value, is of such vast proportions, and requires for its successful management such absolute and uninterrupted freedom of movement, that the public to which the traffic belongs is entitled to instant and effective protection against all violent interruption, in the first place from the proper local authorities and the State itself, and in addition thereto, when their force is found inadequate, as it has been found in so many cases during the recent troubles, from the government of the United States.

It is well known that the government uses the railway lines of the country, both as postal and military highways, in such form as its interests may require. The Constitution of the United States imposes upon the government the duty of thoroughly protecting inter-State commerce. When it is considered that the stock and bond holders of the various railway companies, whenever the interests of the government required it, paid taxes upon their coupons, their dividends, and their gross receipts, that they promptly met every call made by the Federal authorities, and that the entire equipment of the various lines was often placed at the disposal of the government for the prompt movement of the national forces and their supplies, to the exclusion often of other and more profitable traffic, it would seem but a matter of equity that the government should insure such protection to these railways as would preserve their usefulness and keep them always in condition to render similar services when they may be required. But over and beyond such considerations as these, the absolute dependence of the whole community upon this great system of railways for almost its very existence as a civilized body would seem to impose upon the Federal government in the last resort the supreme duty of preventing any lawless and violent interference with the regular and certain operation of every railway in the United States.

This insurrection, which extended through fourteen States, and in many cases successfully defied the local authorities, presents a state of facts almost as serious as that which prevailed at the outbreak of the Civil War. Unless our own experience is to differ entirely from other countries, and it is not easy to see why it should, with the increasing population of our large cities and business centres, and the inevitable assemblage at such points of the vicious and evil-disposed, the late troubles may be but the prelude to other manifestations of mob violence, with this added peril, that now, for the first time in American history, has an organized mob learned its power to terrorize the law-abiding citizens of great communities. With our recent experience before us, it is believed that no thoughtful man can argue in favor of delay by the proper authorities in dealing with lawless and riotous assemblages. Delay simply leads to destruction of property, and may lead in the end to the destruction of life. The force used to repress such assemblages should be as prompt in its manifestation as the evil with which it deals. The interests concerned are too grave to admit of delay. The raising of the black flag and the stoppage of all vessels on the Great Lakes and on the Mississippi and Ohio rivers would not produce one tithe of the damage to the whole country that has resulted from the recent stoppage of the great trunk-lines. The burning of the vessels and their cargoes on these waters would raise a storm of wrath which no mob would dare to face, and would be visited by the United States government, under existing laws, with most exemplary punishment. But what distinction can be established between such a crime and the hideous destruction at Pittsburgh of over eighteen hundred cars laden with the products of the various States, together with the engines ready to move them to their destination, and the station buildings and machine-shops that were absolutely essential to their proper care and movement, and which with other like doings resulted in the stoppage of all commerce and business relations between the States, not only on one highway, but on many important lines, through the concerted action of the mob and its leaders? In the city of Pittsburgh much human life and many private dwellings and other property were sacrificed as the result of mob violence; indeed, it is almost a marvel that a large portion of that city was not destroyed by fire. Only the prevailing direction of the wind averted greater and more general disaster.

The authority of the United States, now potent to protect commerce moving upon the waters, should be equally potent when the same commerce is exposed to greater peril upon land. This brings us, then, to the practical question: In what shape can this protection be put so as to be extended most efficiently and with the least delay? The present regulations all favor, unintentionally, the rioters and the mob. In the first place the mayor of a city must exhaust his power, the sheriff of the county must essay his strength; then, while precious time is expending, for a mob constantly attracts dangerous elements and grows with impunity and success, the governor of the State must be called upon by the sheriff of a county. If the State happens to have an effective military organization, which at the present time is the case in perhaps not more than five out of the thirty-seven States of the Union, the governor can call out the military forces and suppress the riot. If the State has no such organization, or if the military forces of the State prove inadequate to the emergency, the governor is paralyzed and must call upon the United States for assistance. If the authorities of any State should, for any cause, fail or refuse to call upon the United States government, what possible remedy or protection is left to life and property within the limits of that Commonwealth?

It can readily be seen what frightful possibilities of mischief are afforded by the necessarily long interval which must elapse in the present state of our laws before the Federal authority can intervene in cases where its intervention is most imperative. In fact, as our recent experience has shown, the only roads which could

procure prompt protection and immunity from interference were those whose misfortunes had made them bankrupt and placed them in the direct custody of receivers appointed by United States courts. To the aid of these roads the United States Marshal could call United States troops, and no rioter dared to resist the power represented by the small but admirably disciplined detachments quartered near the scenes of the recent troubles. It will hardly be contended that the railway companies must become bankrupt in order to make secure the uninterrupted movement of traffic over their lines, or to entitle them to the efficient protection of the United States government. If a bondholder or other creditor is entitled to the protection of the Federal courts to prevent the threatened impairment of the value of a property through legal proceedings, he certainly should not be left without remedy against lawless violence which has actually destroyed the security for his investment, and has, as at Pittsburgh, converted millions of dollars into scrap-iron and ashes. The laws which give the Federal courts the summary process of injunction to restrain so comparatively trifling a wrong as an infringement of a patent-right certainly must have been intended or ought to give the United States authority to prevent a wrong-doing which not only destroys a particular road, but also paralyzes the entire commerce of the country and wastes the national wealth.

It is demonstrable that during the recent disturbances the government of the United States was itself a direct loser, and, through the government, the taxpayers of the whole country, to a very large amount by the diminution of the national revenues arising from the interruption of business and the interference with many of the operations on which the internal taxes of the country are levied, as well as by the diminution of the customs revenues; as all the imports during this period, instead of being forwarded to their destinations, were necessarily placed in store, of course without payment of any duty to the government for the time being. Suppose that this state of things had continued for sixty days, would not the United States government have been deprived of nearly all the revenues on which it relies to meet its current obligations?

Certainly it cannot have been contemplated in the formation of our government that the United States authorities should submit to see the transportation of the mails, covering the enormous financial and business transactions of the whole country, and the movement of the supplies required for its own various departments, made dependent upon the grace and favor of rioters, whose misconduct in almost any other form would have secured their immediate arrest and condign punishment. During the recent riots the movement of United States troops was impeded at several points, and large quantities of ammunition and other Federal stores, on their way to the Pacific coast, were forcibly detained for days. The operations of the national government in some parts of the country were as completely blocked as in the early days of the Civil War. There certainly should be a protection against such dangers and a remedy for such wrongs. If the government of the United States is to exercise its power of protection or of remedy, it perhaps can do so only through an adequate exhibition of the military force that may be given it for such purposes by Congress. The important question is to ascertain in what way the government can so exhibit its military force as to secure the utmost possible efficiency in the enforcement of law and order without jarring or disturbing the general framework of our institutions and our laws. It seems to be indispensable, in the light of recent events, that whatever force is to be used by the government in such emergencies should be so distributed and controlled that it may be concentrated upon any point or points that may be threatened within a few hours of any outbreak. Several companies of regular troops that were quartered at Baltimore, Philadelphia, Pittsburgh, Reading, Scranton, Louisville, Chicago, and other places, during the recent riots, had to be transported for such distances that, if they had been compelled to march instead of moving by rail, they would have been powerless to avert mischief. It was only by the fear or favor of the rioters that the United States were able to concentrate their forces where they did. In some cases formal resolutions were passed by the strikers that no troops should be allowed to pass over the lines. In Jersey City a mob endeavored to prevent the departure of a United States battery and the troops connected therewith. On the Erie Railway, between Cornell and Hornellsville, a few lawless men, by tearing up tracks, destroying bridges, and tampering with switches, were able seriously to retard the military forces of the State, which were there under the orders of the governor to reestablish law and order. What is needed, therefore, would clearly seem to be that proper forces should be so disposed at prominent points, large cities and other great business centres, in many of which the government has arsenals, custom-houses, mints, navy yards, and other property of its own to protect, that their movements can be combined rapidly, and they be directed against points of danger so as to be able to act effectively and with decision before violence can become triumphant.

With the experience of other countries to warn and guide us, and especially with the experience of England, where the rights of the people have for ages been guarded and asserted as jealously as they always have been and should be among ourselves, we shall have only ourselves to blame, if through apathy, demagoguism, or weakness we leave ourselves unprepared to meet an issue which from all the evidences of the times is only too likely again to be forced upon us. With the approach of winter, and the loss of outdoor employment which severe weather even in the most prosperous times entails, the country will have to deal not only with the deserving among the unemployed, who can be reached and helped through local organizations, but with vast numbers of idle, dangerous, and in many cases desperate men, who have been allowed unfortunately to catch a glimpse of their possible power for mischief. Such men, unless confronted by a thorough organization in the cities, States, and other communities, backed by the power of the Federal government and an unmistakable public opinion, will need but little urging to renew the scenes which have already brought such disgrace upon the American name.

It surely may be hoped that at the approaching session of Congress, the earnest, unprejudiced, and patriotic men of both Houses will discuss this grave subject independently of party lines, and with the united resolve to secure equity to all interests and to take all necessary measures to secure protection to life and property and the impartial enforcement of the laws, including the guaranty to every man of the right to work for such compensation as he may agree upon with other men, free from interference or intimidation. The able lawyers of the Senate and

House will perhaps frame a law which will give to the owners of every highway carrying inter-State commerce, whether by land or water, in which citizens of different States are interested, or carrying the United States mails or other government property, the right to appear by petition properly verified before the tribunals of the United States in order to show that the movement of such traffic has been interfered with by unlawful combinations, by threats, or by violence, and which upon such showing will give these tribunals the right, when necessary, to call upon the United States in the form now authorized by law to enforce their process by arresting the rioters and the suppression of all such unlawful combinations.

The magnitude of the evil to be met and dealt with can hardly be overstated. The remedy to be provided should be equally prompt and effective. It must be discussed and adopted in the interest of the whole country, and not of any particular class; for the interests of all classes of our citizens are the same in the maintenance of domestic peace and civil order.

But to no one class in the community is an absolute assurance of peace so important as to the men who have no capital but their labor. When the accumulations of labor are put in peril by lawlessness, capital may always protect itself by suspending the enterprises which give labor its value and insure it its reward. Anarchy not only deprives the laboring man of his present subsistence, but puts in jeopardy all his hopes of improvement for his own future and the future of his family.

My own railway experience, extending over a period of thirty years, leads me to believe that the managers of American railways in general may fearlessly appeal to their past relations with the faithful among their employees, to prove that they at least have always endeavored to treat the interests of employers and employed as identical, and have never failed to take into prompt and respectful consideration every grievance which has been fairly and properly presented to them. I am sure that it has been the purpose of the company with which I am connected to at all times pay its employees the best compensation that the business of the country would warrant; and I have no doubt that this will be the policy of the company for all future time, as it is founded on sound business principles no less than upon the instincts of humanity.

Very truly yours,
THOMAS A. SCOTT.

CHAPTER 2

Andrew Carnegie Counsels Class Cooperation

*"Today we find collisions between...capital and labor,
when there should be combination."*

The Great Upheaval of 1877 affected Andrew Carnegie, owner of the Carnegie Steel Company, deeply. He knew Thomas Scott well. Scott had, in fact, been the Scottish-born Carnegie's mentor when the younger man was getting his start in business at the Pennsylvania Railroad. Even after Carnegie left the Pennsylvania in 1865 to launch a career in the iron and steel industry that would reward him with fabulous wealth, he continued to regard Scott with affection and respect. No matter how successful he became, Carnegie never forgot his beginnings as "Mr. Scott's boy."

It saddened Carnegie to see his old patron devastated by the events of the great strikes, his reputation sullied, his finances threatened, and his health shattered. But Carnegie was even more disturbed by the implications of the strikes for class relations in the United States. Carnegie had spent his first thirteen years in the "Old World," and he feared that its strife and violence would eventually make its way across the Atlantic. In the wake of the Great Upheaval, he wondered if it had already done so.

By 1877, the Carnegie Steel Company was well on its way to a dominating position in the production of the world's most essential product. Steel locomotives and cars traveled on steel rails and over steel bridges, bringing steel-based products to urban centers whose skylines, streetcars, telegraph wires, and subterranean pipe systems were all girded by steel. Carnegie Steel was feeding the voracious appetite of an expanding American industrial economy, and making its owner rich in the process. Despite his own success, however, Carnegie worried that the country that had been so good to him was being torn to pieces by class-based jealousies and resentments.

Carnegie's personal story was the classic embodiment of the American dream.[1] He was born in Dunfermline, Scotland, on the cusp of the Industrial Revolution. His father, a hand weaver, was the victim of the mechanization of the linen manufacturing process that took hold almost immediately after Andrew's birth in 1835. Like so many others, the Carnegies emigrated to the United States in 1848 in search of a second chance. While the elder Carnegie could not adapt to the bustling industrial atmosphere of Pittsburgh, Pennsylvania, where the family settled, young Andrew thrived. He started out as a "bobbin boy" in a textile factory, responsible for the spindles through which thread was pulled during production, but kept his eye peeled for a better opportunity. Within a year, he was a telegraph messenger, so serious about his work that he learned by heart the addresses of the influential men he served. Soon Carnegie was promoted to telegraph operator, where his speed and efficiency caught the eye of Scott, a rising executive at the Pennsylvania Railroad, who hired him as his personal assistant.

As Scott moved up the ranks of the Pennsylvania, he took Carnegie with him. Carnegie became superintendent of the railroad's Pittsburgh line in 1856, when Scott was promoted from that position. During the Civil War, Scott was charged with coordinating the transport of Union troops, munitions, and supplies, and brought Carnegie along as his details man. By war's end Carnegie was financially secure, but he still worked for others. He longed to build a business on his own. The developing steel industry offered an intriguing opportunity. Leaving the Pennsylvania in 1865, Carnegie initially invested in the Keystone Bridge Company, which used iron to build its spans. Iron, while stronger than wood, was still prone to wear and breakage. Steel, fabricated from iron through the "Bessemer" process, was flexible and strong, and clearly represented a new technological frontier. Its possibilities dazzled Carnegie. In 1872, he established the Carnegie Steel Company.

The new venture was an immediate success, and Carnegie Steel plants soon dotted the industrial landscape of the East and Midwest. Carnegie believed the essential element of success in the steel business was controlling costs, and worked obsessively toward this goal. Wages were "costs," of course, and Carnegie wanted them as low as possible. At the same time, however, he prided himself on his benevolence toward his employees, and even claimed to support their right to unionize. He considered his workers to be invested in his enterprises and encouraged "a feeling of partnership between employers and employed."[2] Carnegie did not mean this in the literal sense, since he rejected the idea of cooperative ownership. But he believed there was a natural harmony of interests between owners and workers, that they were, in his words, "'in the same boat,' rejoicing together in their prosperity and calling into play their fortitude together in adversity."[3] Class conflict was unnecessary, Carnegie reasoned, as long as members of each knew their proper roles. After all, Carnegie himself had once been in the working class and had accepted its strictures and limits. He had respected his employers and sought to serve them well. He had learned from them, and now, thanks to his initiative, vision, and willingness to take risks, he had become one of them.

Carnegie understood that not every American worker could emulate his story. But even if his employees could not replicate the vast scale of his success, they could still earn good livings in one of his steel plants. Carnegie had come to the United States at a time when the influence of the free labor philosophy—that anyone willing to work hard could rise to respectability and security in an open American society and economy—was at its height. By the time of the Great Upheaval in 1877, however, the idea had lost much of its power to inspire and explain. A permanent, fixed-in-place working class now existed in the United States, as the railroad strikes illustrated so painfully. But like his mentor Tom Scott, Carnegie refused to let go of the remnants of the free labor doctrine, especially the aspect that promoted class peace. Carnegie loved the United States. Only in America, he would boast to the relatives he left behind in Scotland, could achievements such as his have been possible. What distinguished his adopted country from Europe, Carnegie believed, was its generally calm class relations, as well as the relative scarcity of "the blatant ignorant man, who regards capital as the natural enemy of labor, who does so much to embitter the relations between employer and employed."[4]

Or was the United States so different from Europe after all? In 1886, less than a decade after the Great Upheaval, the nation teetered on the brink of open class warfare as organized labor launched a campaign for an eight-hour workday. The Knights of Labor, composed largely of unskilled and semiskilled workers and the nation's largest union, was a prominent participant in this movement. Carnegie could tolerate the Knights, although he rejected the idea of an eight-hour day in his own plants. The group opposed violence, avoided strikes whenever possible, and sought to promote an image of respectability and moderation. But other elements of the campaign gave Carnegie pause. Socialists, communists, and anarchists, who believed in an ongoing struggle between the haves and have-nots in American life, were prominent in the eight-hour movement. Many were immigrants, lending their presence a sinister, alien quality in the eyes of the nation's native-born population.

The anarchists may have been the most threatening of all. Steeped in the traditions of revolutionary violence, they sought the overthrow of the government and the capitalist order by any means necessary. Anarchism was especially visible in Chicago, where Albert Parsons headed the International Working People's Association. Parsons did not fit the anarchist stereotype. He was native-born, a Southerner who had fought for the Confederacy during the Civil War, then recanted his racial views and joined the Reconstruction-era Republican Party in Texas. He embraced the cause of workers' rights in a post-war atmosphere of industrial expansion and labor repression. Like Carnegie, Parsons believed in free labor, but in its uncorrupted, pre-Civil War version, where men were not trapped in their places for life by the brutalities of capitalism. By 1886, after years spent fighting the employer class, enduring blacklisting and threats on his life, Parsons had given up on capitalism. He was an anarchist, calling on workers to wrest control of the means of production from owners like Andrew Carnegie and operate them for the good of all. Winning an eight-hour workday would represent a milestone on the road to that utopian goal.

On May 1, 1886, Parsons led a march of 80,000 on Chicago's Michigan Avenue, one of a series of such demonstrations that took place across America that day. On May 3, strikers at the McCormick Reaper plant in Chicago were attacked by police, and six workers shot to death. A protest rally was organized for the next evening, May 4, at Haymarket Square, one of the city's central gathering places. The rally was peaceful, although the speeches were militant. Parsons spoke, but left early. As the rally ended and the crowd began to break up, police moved in. Suddenly, a bomb exploded, killing a policeman. Authorities and workers began firing on each other. By the time order was restored, six more policemen and four demonstrators were mortally wounded.[5] Dozens more on both sides were injured. The identity of the bomb thrower was never established. Parsons had not been on the scene when the bombing occurred, but nonetheless was arrested and charged with murder. After a sensational trial that riveted the nation, he was convicted along with seven other anarchists. Parsons was executed in November 1887, amid an international outcry. To this day, the guilt of the "Haymarket martyrs" is vigorously disputed.[6]

It was in this charged atmosphere that Andrew Carnegie published two articles in *Forum*, a newly founded journal of current affairs, in which he set out his ideas on American class relations. The first, entitled "An Employer's View of the Labor Question," was written immediately before the Haymarket bombing; the other, "Results of the Labor Struggle," appeared in its aftermath. In both, Carnegie expresses his concern that tensions between employers and workers will get out of hand for no real purpose:

> Now, the poorest laborer in America...who can handle a pick or a shovel, stands upon equal terms with the purchaser of his labor. He sells it or withholds it as may seem best to him.... Not only has the laborer conquered his political and personal freedom: he has achieved industrial freedom as well, as far as the law can give it, and he now fronts his master, proclaiming himself his equal under the law.[7]

Yet despite these historic advances, Carnegie laments that "(t)oday we find collisions between these forces, capital and labor, when there should be combination."[8] Why couldn't workers and employers see that they needed each other, that "labor without his brother capital is helpless?"[9] Carnegie sought to put this adage to use in his relationships with his own men. He writes of his pleasure in making small accommodations for his workers, cementing their loyalty to him. "No man," he opines, "is a true gentleman who does not inspire the affection and devotion of his servants."[10] Carnegie seems confident that, even in the midst of the bitter argument over the eight-hour day, he enjoys the goodwill of his "servants." Yet his choice of words may reveal his true feelings about the structure of class relations in the United States. A "servant" is not an equal, or even an equal bargaining partner. He is the object of charity and paternalism—even pity—from his employer. As long as a servant knows his "place," harmony prevails. But what if a servant demands to sit at the same table as his master and to be treated with the respect that true equality commands? In a few years, during a bitter labor confrontation at his own factory, Carnegie would be forced to decide whether his workers were servants or equals.

Even after the Haymarket incident, Carnegie held to his faith in the inherent compatibility of labor-capital interests. In "The Results of the Labor Struggle," he cautions against the hysteria the bombing aroused among his fellow businessmen. The vast majority of American workers are not bomb-throwers or anarchists. Their goal is not to replace capitalism with some form of Marxism, but to provide for their families within the existing economic system. They are, Carnegie insists, "resolute for the maintenance of order."[11] They will respond to expressions of reason and kindness. "One hour of courtesy on the part of employers," he maintains, "would prevent many strikes."[12]

Strikes themselves need not be cataclysmic events on the model of the Great Upheaval of 1877. Carnegie argues that workers have the right to withhold their labor, and owners the right to withhold capital by closing their plants. In the event of a strike at one of his plants, Carnegie claims that he would not hire strikebreakers, bring in armed guards, or avail himself of the police, state militia, or federal troops. He would simply close down, wait for his employees to accept what he offered, and reopen when an agreement was reached. Carnegie is confident that conflicts between labor and capital will be rare if other owners adopt his practices. His two articles, in fact, are a set of blueprints for peaceful labor relations in the United States.

But things were not to be as simple as Carnegie imagined. The imperatives of profit—of keeping costs low—would overcome his benign instincts. In 1889, Carnegie appointed Henry Clay Frick chairman of his steel company. Frick was a hard-nosed, bottom line–oriented businessman with none of Carnegie's sense of paternalism for the hired help. With Carnegie's approval, Frick set out to break the union representing Carnegie Steel employees, the Amalgamated Association of Iron and Steel Workers. On Carnegie's instructions, he offered a wage cut during contract negotiations with the Amalgamated in 1892. In June of that year, with their existing contract about to expire, Frick locked workers out of Carnegie Steel's Homestead plant near Pittsburgh and began to hire strikebreakers. Carnegie left for a lengthy stay in Scotland so as to distance himself from the developing crisis.

On the morning of July 6, Frick attempted to land private Pinkerton guards, who would be used to protect the strikebreakers, from barges on the Ohio River. The locked-out workers, who were now considered strikers upon the expiration of their contract, attacked the guards. The Pinkertons fired on them, starting a wild gun battle. The guards were driven off. They made another unsuccessful effort to land later that morning, amid more violence. By noon, seven strikers and three Pinkertons lay dead or dying. The guards gave up in the afternoon. Disembarking from their barges, they were set upon by a mob of strikers and their supporters. Amid a fusillade of rocks and epithets, they marched to the town's opera house, where they took refuge as the crowd outside howled for their blood. Around midnight, they were evacuated to Pittsburgh and safety.[13]

The workers had won round one, but there were more to come. On July 12, Pennsylvania governor Robert Pattison, who had been elected with the help of Andrew Carnegie, sent the state militia to Homestead. Pushing aside the strikers milling outside the plant, they cleared the way for the entry of the strikebreakers. Within days the factory was up and running with new employees. Frustration soon set in among the strikers, as they realized that their absence was not affecting production. Frick and Carnegie had planned their strategy on the assumption that most of their employees could be easily replaced. The efficient operation of the Homestead plant with virtually a new workforce proved them correct.[14]

On July 23, the strikers suffered a huge blow in the court of public opinion when Alexander Berkman, an anarchist who supported the union, shot and stabbed Frick during an assassination attempt. The cold, aloof Frick—who survived—was transformed into an unlikely object of sympathy. By August, it was clear that the strike had failed. Humiliated workers began to apply for their old jobs, on Carnegie's terms. The Amalgamated Association, with only a fraction of its original members left, voted formally to end the strike in November.[15] The union's defeat at Homestead led to its decline at Carnegie's other plants, and it ceased to play a significant role in steel industry labor relations. Not until the 1930s and the rise of the United Steelworkers would there be a viable national steel union in America.

Carnegie kept a low profile at his castle in Scotland during the Homestead struggle, allowing Frick to act as the company's public face. Many in the labor movement branded Carnegie a coward and a hypocrite. He had boasted of his close relations with his men, of his concern for them, and of their mutual interest in making Carnegie Steel profitable. He had argued that class antagonisms in American society were "senseless."[16] He had supported his employees' right to join labor unions and even to strike. He had criticized the use of strikebreakers. Yet at Homestead, he had reduced wages, refused to bargain in good faith, locked his men out of his plant, hired private Pinkerton guards, called out the state militia, hired strikebreakers, and wrecked the union. Carnegie's need to control costs overrode the needs of his men. Capitalism, despite Carnegie's emphasis on its congenial virtues, was a system based not on harmony of interests, but self-interest. Albert Parsons died on the gallows in 1887 believing that workers and employers in the United States were inherently at odds, and that the American ideal of equality was incompatible with the vast disparities of wealth that capitalism produced. Had he been alive to see the events at Homestead in 1892, he would have viewed them as his vindication.

But Carnegie's later years would suggest that these issues were more complicated than men like Parsons imagined. In 1901, Carnegie sold his company to the financier J.P. Morgan, who used it to form the largest producer in the world, United States Steel. The purchase price was $480 million.[17] "Mr. Carnegie," Morgan told him when the sale was complete, "I want to congratulate you on being the richest man in the world."[18]

What would Carnegie do with this money? In "The Gospel of Wealth," an article he published in 1889, Carnegie had argued that the rich were obligated to employ their assets for the betterment of society.[19] By this Carnegie did not mean individual charity, which he dismissed as ineffectual and demeaning. He proposed instead the funding of libraries, universities, museums, concert halls, and parks in order to help Americans of limited means improve their lives through learning, culture, and healthful recreation. The massive concentrations of wealth decried by Albert Parsons and other radical critics of American capitalism were deemed a blessing by Carnegie, since only through the accumulation of great sums by a select few could the common good be advanced. The great industrialists and financiers were merely trustees for the public. The more money they made, the more money they would be in a position to donate. Capitalism, then, was not evil but a necessary and beneficial good.

By 1901, Carnegie was ready to put these ideas into practice. Between that year and his death in 1919, he gave away virtually his entire fortune. He built 3000 libraries, contributed to hundreds of educational institutions, founded the Carnegie Endowment for International Peace, and established the Carnegie Foundation as an ongoing source of support for research, learning, and the arts. In all, he gave some $350 million back to the country he loved.

But did this generosity justify Carnegie's business methods, his enormous economic power, or even his brutal actions during the Homestead strike? Did laudable ends excuse morally suspect means? These questions would provoke heated conversations between Americans, many of whom were the beneficiaries of Carnegie's largesse, over the value—and values—of capitalism in the United States. Carnegie's personal wealth, of course, was evidence of gross inequality in American society, but he had used it in ways that allowed Americans to become more equal. His ruthlessness at Homestead had made his workers less free, but his philanthropy offered countless Americans the opportunity for free and fulfilling lives. His argument that the interests of capital and labor were identical was belied by the events of the Homestead strike, but the institutions he funded helped calm class antagonisms by providing the descendents of the workers he attacked in 1892 a route to upward mobility without resort to Marxism. Andrew Carnegie's paradoxical life reminds us that it is possible for capitalism to be fair and unfair at the same time. American conversations over capitalism as an economic and social system would continue through the twentieth century, where they would be taken up by a diverse array of voices, including those of Herbert Hoover, Walker Evans, members of Students for a Democratic Society, and Ronald Reagan. Carnegie's American legacies are the steel he produced, the fortune he gave away, and the contradictions of the capitalist values he embodied.

Questions for Consideration and Conversation

1. Was Andrew Carnegie's idea of a "harmony of interests" between capital and labor realistic?
2. What did Carnegie's personal story—from bobbin boy to steel magnate—say about class structure and opportunity in America? How would Robert and Helen Lynd (Chapter 7) approach this question? Norman Rockwell (Chapter 10)?
3. Carnegie claimed to care deeply for the welfare of his workers. Why, then, did he seek to break the union at his Homestead steel plant?
4. Carnegie believed that American workers were "resolute for the maintenance of order." Was he correct?

5. How did the advent of professional corporate "managers" like Henry Clay Frick, who replaced Carnegie in the day-to-day administration of his company, change the relationship between "workers" and "bosses" in the United States?
6. Does Carnegie's philanthropic career, during which he gave virtually his entire fortune to charitable institutions, vindicate his career? Does it vindicate American capitalism? How would Herbert Hoover (Chapter 6), Walker Evans (Chapter 8), members of Students for a Democratic Society (Chapter 17), and Ronald Reagan (Chapter 21) respond to these questions?

Endnotes

1. A recent comprehensive biography of Carnegie is David Nasaw, *Andrew Carnegie* (New York: Penguin, 2006). See also Harold C. Livesay, *Andrew Carnegie and the Rise of Big Business*, 2nd ed. (New York: Longman, 2000).
2. Andrew Carnegie, ed. "An Employer's View of the Labor Question," in *The Gospel of Wealth* (Garden City, NY: Doubleday, 1933), 109.
3. Ibid., 108.
4. Ibid., 104.

5. James Green, *Death in the Haymarket: A Story of Chicago, the First Labor Movement and the Bombing That Divided Gilded Age America* (New York: Random House, 2006), 186–91.
6. See Green, *Death in the Haymarket*, and Paul Avrich, *The Haymarket Tragedy* (Princeton: Princeton University Press, 1984). Three other defendants were put to death alongside Parsons. Another cheated the gallows by committing suicide in his cell. Two others had their death sentences commuted to life

imprisonment, and were later pardoned. The last defendant received fifteen years in prison. Green, *Death in the Haymarket*, 264–71.

7. Carnegie, "An Employer's View of the Labor Question," 98.
8. Ibid.
9. Ibid., 104.
10. Ibid., 107.
11. Andrew Carnegie, ed., "Results of the Labor Struggle," *The Gospel of Wealth*, 132.
12. Ibid., 119.
13. William Serrin, *Homestead: The Glory and Tragedy of an American Steel Town* (New York: Random House,

1992), 75–82; Paul Krause, *The Battle for Homestead, 1880–1892: Politics, Culture, and Steel* (Pittsburgh: University of Pittsburgh Press, 1992), 12–43.
14. Serrin, *Homestead*, 82–87.
15. Ibid., 87–91; Krause, *The Battle for Homestead*, 315–57.
16. Carnegie, ed., "An Employer's View of the Labor Question," in *The Gospel of Wealth*, 99.
17. Livesay, *Andrew Carnegie*, 207.
18. Ibid.
19. See Andrew Carnegie, ed., "The Gospel of Wealth," in *The Gospel of Wealth*, 1–39.

ANDREW CARNEGIE, "AN EMPLOYER'S VIEW OF THE LABOR QUESTION" (1886)

Source: Andrew Carnegie, *The Gospel of Wealth*. Garden City, NY: Doubleday, 1933, pp. 107–21. Originally appeared in *Forum* 1 (April 1886): 114–25.

The struggle in which labor has been engaged during the past three hundred years, first against authority and then against capital, has been a triumphal march. Victory after victory has been achieved. Even so late as in Shakespeare's time, remains of villeinage or serfdom still existed in England. Before that, not only the labor but the person of the laborer belonged to the chief. The workers were either slaves or serfs; men and women were sold with the estate upon which they worked, and became the property of the new lord, just as did the timber which grew on the land. In those days we hear nothing of strikes or of trades unions, or differences of opinion between employer and employed. The fact is, labor had then no right which the chief, or employer, was bound to respect. Even as late as the beginning of this century, the position of the laborer in some departments was such as can scarcely be credited. What do our laboring friends think of this, that down to 1779 the miners of Britain were in a state of serfdom. They "were compelled by law to remain in the pits as long as the owner chose to keep them at work there, and were actually sold as part of the capital invested in the works. If they accepted an engagement elsewhere, their master could always have them fetched back and flogged as thieves for having attempted to rob him of their labor. This law was modified in 1779, but was not repealed till after the acts passed in 1797 and 1799" ("The Trades-Unions of England," p. 119). This was only ninety-seven years ago. Men are still

living who were living then. Again, in France, as late as 1806, every workman had to procure a license; and in Russia, down to our own days, agricultural laborers were sold with the soil they tilled.

Consider the change, nay, the revolution! Now the poorest laborer in America or in England, or indeed throughout the civilized world, who can handle a pick or a shovel, stands upon equal terms with the purchaser of his labor. He sells or withholds it as may seem best to him. He negotiates, and thus rises to the dignity of an independent contractor. When he has performed the work he bargained to do, he owes his employer nothing, and is under no obligation to him. Not only has the laborer conquered his political and personal freedom: he has achieved industrial freedom as well, as far as the law can give it, and he now fronts his master, proclaiming himself his equal under the law.

But, notwithstanding this complete revolution, it is evident that the permanent relations to each other of labor and capital have not yet evolved. The present adjustment does not work without friction, and changes must be made before we can have industrial peace. Today we find collisions between these forces, capital and labor, when there should be combination. The mill hands of an industrial village in France have just risen against their employers, attacked the manager's home and killed him. The streets of another French village are barricaded against the expected forces of order. The ship-builders of Sunderland, in

England, are at the verge of starvation, owing to a quarrel with their employers; and Leicester has just been the scene of industrial riots. In our country, labor disputes and strikes were never so numerous as now. East and West, North and South, everywhere, there is unrest, showing that an equilibrium has not yet been reached between employers and employed.

A strike or lockout is, in itself, a ridiculous affair. Whether a failure or a success, it gives no direct proof of its justice or injustice. In this it resembles war between two nations. It is simply a question of strength and endurance between the contestants. The gage of battle, or the duel, is not more senseless, as a means of establishing what is just and fair, than an industrial strike or lockout. It would be folly to conclude that we have reached any permanent adjustment between capital and labor until strikes and lockouts are as much things of the past as the gage of battle or the duel have become in the most advanced communities.

Taking for granted, then, that some further modifications must be made between capital and labor, I propose to consider the various plans that have been suggested by which labor can advance another stage in its development in relation to capital. And, as a preliminary, let it be noted that it is only labor and capital in their greatest masses which it is necessary to consider. It is only in large establishments that the industrial unrest of which I have spoken ominously manifests itself. The farmer who hires a man to assist him, or the gentleman who engages a groom or a butler, is not affected by strikes. The innumerable cases in which a few men only are directly concerned, which comprise in the aggregate the most of labor, present upon the whole a tolerably satisfactory condition of affairs. This clears the ground of much, and leaves us to deal only with the immense mining and manufacturing concerns of recent growth, in which capital and labor often array themselves in alarming antagonism.

Among the expedients suggested for their better reconciliation, the first place must be assigned to the idea of cooperation, or the plan by which the workers are to become part-owners in enterprises, and share their fortunes. There is no doubt that if this could be effected it would have the same beneficial effect upon the workman which the ownership of land has upon the man who has hitherto tilled the land for another. The sense of ownership would make of him more of a man as regards himself, and hence more of a citizen as regards the commonwealth. But we are here met by a difficulty which I confess I have not yet been able to overcome, and which renders me less sanguine

than I should like to be in regard to cooperation. The difficulty is this, and it seems to me to be inherent in all gigantic manufacturing, mining, and commercial operations. Two men or two combinations of men will erect blast-furnaces, iron-mills, cotton-mills, or piano manufactories adjoining each other, or engage in shipping or commercial business. They will start with equal capital and credit; and to those only superficially acquainted with the personnel of these concerns, success will seem as likely to attend the one as the other. Nevertheless, one will fail after dragging along a lifeless existence, and pass into the hands of its creditors; while the neighboring mill or business will make a fortune for its owners. Now, the successful manufacturer, dividing every month or every year a proportion of his profits among his workmen, either as a bonus or as dividends upon shares owned by them, will not only have a happy and contented body of operatives, but he will inevitably attract from his rival the very best workmen in every department. His rival, having no profits to divide among his workmen, and paying them only a small assured minimum to enable them to live, finds himself despoiled of foremen and of workmen necessary to carry on his business successfully. His workmen are discontented and, in their own opinion, defrauded of the proper fruits of their skill, through incapacity or inattention of their employers. Thus, unequal business capacity in the management produces unequal results.

It will be precisely the same if one of these manufactories belongs to the workmen themselves; but in this case, in the present stage of development of the workmen, the chances of failure will be enormously increased. It is, indeed, greatly to be doubted whether any body of working-men in the world could to-day organize and successfully carry on a mining or manufacturing or commercial business in competition with concerns owned by men trained to affairs. If any such cooperative organization succeeds, it may be taken for granted that it is principally owing to the exceptional business ability of one of the managers, and only in a very small degree to the efforts of the mass of workmen owners. This business ability is excessively rare, as is proved by the incredibly large proportion of those who enter upon the stormy sea of business only to fail. I should say that twenty cooperative concerns would fail to every one that would succeed. There are, of course, a few successful establishments, notably two in France and one in England, which are organized upon the cooperative plan, in which the workmen participate directly in the profits. But these were all created by the present owners, who now generously share the profits with their workmen, and are making the success of their manufactories upon the cooperative plan the proud work of their lives. What these concerns will become when the genius for affairs is no longer with them to guide, is a matter of grave doubt and, to me, of foreboding. I can, of course, picture in my mind a state of civilization in which the most talented business men shall find their most cherished work in carrying on immense concerns, not primarily for their own personal aggrandizement, but for the good of the masses of workers engaged therein, and their families; but this is only a foreshadowing of a dim and distant future. When a class of such men has evolved, the problem of capital and labor will be permanently solved to the entire satisfaction of both. But as this manifestly belongs to a future generation, I cannot consider cooperation, or common ownership, as the next immediate step in advance which it is possible for labor to make in its upward path.

The next suggestion is that peaceful settlement of differences should be reached through arbitration. Here we are upon firmer ground. I would lay it down as a maxim that there is no excuse for a strike or a lockout until arbitration of differences has been offered by one party and refused by the other. No doubt serious trouble attends even arbitration at present, from the difficulty of procuring suitable men to judge intelligently between the disputants. There is a natural disinclination among business men to expose their business to men in whom they have not entire confidence. We lack, so far, in America a retired class of men of affairs. Our vile practice is to keep on accumulating more dollars until we die. If it were the custom here, as it is in England, for men to withdraw from active business after acquiring a fortune, this class would furnish the proper arbitrators. On the other hand, the ex-presidents of trades-unions, such as Mr. Jarrett or Mr. Wihle, after they have retired from active control, would commend themselves to the manufacturers and to the men as possessed of the necessary technical knowledge, and educated to a point where commercial reasons would not be without their proper weight upon them. I consider that of all the agencies immediately available to prevent wasteful and embittering contests between capital and labor, arbitration is the most powerful and most beneficial.

The influence of trades-unions upon the relations between the employer and employed has been much discussed. Some establishments in America have refused to recognize the right of the men to form themselves into these unions, although

I am not aware that any concern in England would dare to take this position. This policy, however, may be regarded as only a temporary phase of the situation. The right of the working-men to combine and to form trades-unions is no less sacred than the right of the manufacturer to enter into associations and conferences with his fellows, and it must sooner or later be conceded. Indeed, it gives one but a poor opinion of the American workman if he permits himself to be deprived of a right which his fellow in England long since conquered for himself. My experience has been that trades-unions, upon the whole, are beneficial both to labor and to capital. They certainly educate the working-men, and give them a truer conception of the relations of capital and labor than they could otherwise form. The ablest and best workmen eventually come to the front in these organizations; and it may be laid down as a rule that the more intelligent the workman the fewer the contests with employers. It is not the intelligent workman, who knows that labor without his brother capital is helpless, but the blatant ignorant man, who regards capital as the natural enemy of labor, who does so much to embitter the relations between employer and employed; and the power of this ignorant demagogue arises chiefly from the lack of proper organization among the men through which their real voice can be expressed. This voice will always be found in favor of the judicious and intelligent representative. Of course, as men become intelligent more deference must be paid to them personally and to their rights, and even to their opinions and prejudices; and, upon the whole, a greater share of profits must be paid in the day of prosperity to the intelligent than to the ignorant workman. He cannot be imposed upon so readily. On the other hand, he will be found much readier to accept reduced compensation when business is depressed; and it is better in the long run for capital to be served by the highest intelligence, and to be made well aware of the fact that it is dealing with men who know what is due to them, both as to treatment and compensation.

One great source of the trouble between employers and employed arises from the fact that the immense establishments of to-day, in which alone we find serious conflicts between capital and labor, are not managed by their owners, but by salaried officers, who cannot possibly have any permanent interest in the welfare of the working-men. These officials are chiefly anxious to present a satisfactory balance-sheet at the end of the year, that their hundreds of shareholders may receive the usual dividends, and that they may therefore be secure in their positions, and be allowed to manage the business without unpleasant interference either by directors or shareholders. It is notable that bitter strikes seldom occur in small establishments where the owner comes into direct contact with his men, and knows their qualities, their struggles, and their aspirations. It is the chairman, situated hundreds of miles away from his men, who only pays a flying visit to the works and perhaps finds time to walk through the mill or mine once or twice a year, that is chiefly responsible for the disputes which break out at intervals. I have noticed that the manager who confers oftenest with a committee of his leading men has the least trouble with his workmen. Although it may be impracticable for the presidents of these large corporations to know the working-men personally, the manager at the mills, having a committee of his best men to present their suggestions and wishes from time to time, can do much to maintain and strengthen amicable relations, if not interfered with from headquarters. I, therefore, recognize in trades-unions, or, better still, in organizations of the men of each establishment, who select representatives to speak for them, a means, not of further embittering the relations between employer and employed, but of improving them.

It is astonishing how small a sacrifice upon the part of the employer will sometimes greatly benefit the men. I remember that at one of our meetings with a committee, it was incidentally remarked by one speaker that the necessity for obtaining credit at the stores in the neighborhood was a grave tax upon the men. An ordinary workman, he said, could not afford to maintain himself and family for a month, and as he only received his pay monthly, he was compelled to obtain credit and to pay exorbitantly for everything, whereas, if he had the cash, he could buy at twenty-five per cent less. "Well," I said, "why cannot we overcome that by paying every two weeks?" The reply was: "We did not like to ask it, because we have always understood that it would cause much trouble; but if you do that it will be worth an advance of five per cent in our wages." We have paid semi-monthly since. Another speaker happened to say that although they were in the midst of coal, the price charged for small lots delivered at their houses was a certain sum per bushel. The price named was double what our best coal was costing us. How easy for us to deliver to our men such coal as they required, and charge them cost! This was done without a cent's loss to us, but with much gain to the men. Several other points similar to these have arisen by which their labors might be lightened or products increased,

and others suggesting changes in machinery or facilities which, but for the conferences referred to, would have been unthought of by the employer and probably never asked for by the men. For these and other reasons I attribute the greatest importance to an organization of the men, through whose duly elected representatives the managers may be kept informed from time to time of their grievances and suggestions. No matter how able the manager, the clever workman can often show him how beneficial changes can be made in the special branch in which that workman labors. Unless the relations between manager and workmen are not only amicable but friendly, the owners miss much; nor is any man a first-class manager who has not the confidence and respect, and even the admiration, of his workmen. No man is a true gentleman who does not inspire the affection and devotion of his servants. The danger is that such committees may ask conferences too often; three or four meetings per year should be regarded as sufficient.

I come now to the greatest cause of the friction which prevails between capital and labor in the largest establishments, the real essence of the trouble, and the remedy I have to propose.

The trouble is that the men are not paid at any time the compensation proper to that time. All large concerns necessarily keep filled with orders, say for six months in advance, and these orders are taken, of course, at prices prevailing when they are booked. This year's operations furnish perhaps the best illustration of the difficulty. Steel rails at the end of last year for delivery this year were $29 per ton at the works. Of course the mills entered orders freely at this price, and kept on entering them until the demand growing unexpectedly great carried prices up to $35 per ton. Now, the various mills in America are compelled for the next six months or more to run upon orders which do not average $31 per ton at the seaboard and Pittsburg, and say $34 at Chicago. Transportation, ironstone, and prices of all kinds have advanced upon them in the meantime, and they must therefore run for the bulk of the year upon very small margins of profit. But the men, noticing in the papers the "great boom in steel rails," very naturally demand their share of the advance, and, under our existing faulty arrangements between capital and labor, they have secured it. The employers, therefore, have grudgingly given what they know under proper arrangements they should not have been required to give, and there has been friction, and still is dissatisfaction upon the part of the employers. Reverse this picture. The steel-rail market falls again. The mills have still six months' work at prices above the prevailing market, and can afford to pay men higher wages than the then existing state of the market would apparently justify. But having just been amerced in extra payments for labor which they should not have paid, they naturally attempt to reduce wages as the market price of rails goes down, and there arises discontent among the men, and we have a repetition of the negotiations and strikes which have characterized the beginning of this year. In other words, when the employer is going down the employee insists on going up, and vice versa. What we must seek is a plan by which the men will receive high wages when their employers are receiving high prices for the product, and hence are making large profits; and, *per contra*, when the employers are receiving low prices for product, and therefore small if any profits, the men will receive low wages. If this plan can be found, employers and employed will be "in the same boat," rejoicing together in their prosperity, and calling into play their fortitude together in adversity. There will be no room for quarrels, and instead of a feeling of antagonism there will be a feeling of partnership between employers and employed.

There is a simple means of producing this result, and to its general introduction both employers and employed should steadily bend their energies. Wages should be based upon a sliding scale, in proportion to the net prices received for product month by month. And I here gladly pay Mr. Potter, president of the North Chicago Rolling Mill Company, the great compliment to say that he has already taken a step in this direction, for to-day he is working his principal mill upon this plan. The result is that he has had no stoppage whatever this year, nor any dissatisfaction. All has gone smoothly along, and this in itself is worth at least as much to the manufacturer and to the men as the difference in wages one way or another which can arise from the new system.

The celebrated Crescent Steel Works of Pittsburg, manufacturers of the highest grades of tool steel, pay their skilled workmen by a sliding scale, based upon prices received for product—an important factor in the eminent success of that firm. The scale adopted by the iron manufacturers and workmen is only an approach to the true sliding scale; nevertheless it is a decided gain both to capital and labor, as it is adopted from year to year, and hence eliminates strikes on account of wages during the year, and limits these interruptions from that cause to the yearly negotiation as to the justice or injustice of the scale. As this scale, however, is not based upon the prices actually received for product, but upon the published list of prices, which should be received

in theory, there is not complete mutuality between the parties. In depressed times, such as the iron industry has been passing through in recent years, enormous concessions upon the published card prices have been necessary to effect sales, and in these the workmen have not shared with their employers. If, however, there was added to the scale, even in its present form, a stipulation that all causes of difference which could not be postponed till the end of the year, and then considered with the scale, should be referred to arbitration, and that, in case of failure of the owners and workmen to agree at the yearly conference, arbitration should also be resorted to, strikes and lockouts would be entirely eliminated from the iron business; and if the award of the arbitrators took effect from the date of reference the works could run without a day's interruption.

Dismissing, therefore, for the present all consideration of cooperation as not being within measurable distance, I believe the next steps in the advance toward permanent, peaceful relations between capital and labor are:

First. That compensation be paid the men based upon a sliding scale in proportion to the prices received for product.

Second. A proper organization of the men of every works to be made, by which the natural leaders, the best men, will eventually come to the front and confer freely with the employers.

Third. Peaceful arbitration to be in all cases resorted to for the settlement of differences which the owners and the mill committee cannot themselves adjust in friendly conference.

Fourth. No interruption ever to occur to the operations of the establishment, since the decision of the arbitrators shall be made to take effect from the date of reference.

If these measures were adopted by an establishment, several important advantages would be gained:

First. The employer and employed would simultaneously share their prosperity or adversity with each other. The scale once settled, the feeling of antagonism would be gone, and a feeling of mutuality would ensue. Capital and labor would be shoulder to shoulder, supporting each other.

Second. There could be neither strike nor lockout, since both parties had agreed to abide by a forthcoming decision of disputed points. Knowing that in the last resort strangers were to be called in to decide what should be a family affair, the cases would, indeed, be few which would not be amicably adjusted by the original parties without calling in others to judge between them.

Whatever the future may have in store for labor, the evolutionist, who sees nothing but certain and steady progress for the race, will never attempt to set bounds to its triumphs, even to its final form of complete and universal industrial cooperation, which I hope is some day to be reached. But I am persuaded that the next step forward is to be in the direction I have here ventured to point out; and as one who is now most anxious to contribute his part toward helping forward the day of amicable relations between the two forces of capital and labor, which are not enemies, but are really auxiliaries who stand and fall together, I ask at the hands of both capital and labor a careful consideration of these views.

ANDREW CARNEGIE, "RESULTS OF THE LABOR STRUGGLE" (1886)

Source: Andrew Carnegie, "Results of the Labor Struggle," in *The Gospel of Wealth.* Garden City, NY: Doubleday, 1933, pp. 115–33. Originally appeared in *Forum* 1 (August 1886): 538–51.

When "An Employer's View of the Labor Question" was written, labor and capital were at peace, each performing its proper function; capital providing for the wants of labor, and labor regularly discharging its daily task. But before that paper reached the public the most serious labor revolt that ever occurred in this country was upon us. Capital, frightened almost into panic, began to draw back into its strongholds, and many leaders of public opinion seemed to lose self-command. Among the number were not a few of our foremost political economists. These writers of the closet, a small but important class in this country, removed from personal contact with every-day affairs, and uninformed of the solid basis of virtue in the wage-receiving class upon which American society rests, necessarily regarded such phenomena from a purely speculative standpoint. Some of them apparently thought that the fundamental institutions upon which peaceful development depends had been, if not completely overthrown, at least gravely endangered, and that civilization itself had received a rude shock from the disturbance. More than one did not hesitate to intimate that the weakness of democratic institutions lay at the foundation of the revolt. Suggestions were made that the suffrage should be confined to the educated; that the masses might be held in stricter bonds. When we hear the cry of these alarmists we are tempted to reverse the rebuke of the sacred Teacher: they are always troubled more by the mote in their own country's eye than by the beam in the eye of other lands. They forget that not sixty days before monarchical Belgium was convulsed with labor revolts, compared with which ours were insignificant and practically harmless. That country, with its five and a half millions of inhabitants, had more rioters than the United States, with its fifty-six millions; and instead of restoring peace, as this country did, by means of the established forces of order, the Belgian government had to abandon, for a time, all law, and publicly authorize every citizen to wage private war against the insurgents.

Our magazines, reviews, and newspapers have been filled with plans involving radical changes considered necessary by these sciolists for the restoration and maintenance of proper relations between capital and labor. The pulpit has been equally prolific. Thirty days have not elapsed since the excitement was at its height, and yet to-day capital and labor are again cooperating everywhere, as at the date of my first paper, and we are now in position to judge of the extent of the disturbance and to reduce the specter to its real dimensions. It will soon be seen that what occurred was a very inadequate cause for the alarm created. The eruption was not, in itself, a very serious matter, either in its extent or in its consequences. Its lesson lay in the indications it gave of the forces underlying it. There are in the United States to-day a total of more than twenty millions of workers who earn their bread by the sweat of their brow; in trade and transportation alone there are more than seven millions. At the very height of the revolt, not more than 250,000 of these had temporarily ceased to labor. This was the estimate given by "Bradstreet's" on the 14th of May. Three days later it was 80,000, and four days after that only 47,000. The remaining millions continued to pursue their usual vocations in peace. It is fair to assume that the number reported on the 14th of May included all those who were dissatisfied and had requested advance of wages or redress of grievances, but were not really strikers at all. A demonstration that shrinks to one fourth its size from the 14th to the 17th of May, and then again to one half its remaining proportions in the next three days, can scarcely be called a contest. The number of those involved in a serious struggle with capital did not, therefore, at any one time exceed 50,000—not one per cent of the total wage-receiving class, in the branches where alone labor troubles occurred. How then, one is tempted to ask, did so small an interruption seem so great? Why was it taken for granted that a general revolt of labor had taken place, when not one worker in a hundred had really entered upon a contest? The reason for the delusion is obvious. The omnipresent press, with the electric telegraph at its command, spreads the report of a local disturbance in East St. Louis over the entire three million square miles of the land. It is felt almost as distinctly in New Orleans, Boston, and San Francisco as in the city of St. Louis itself, upon the opposite side of the river. The thoughts of men throughout the country concentrate upon this one point of outbreak. Excitable natures fancy the trouble to be general, and even imagine that the very ground trembles under their own feet. In this way the petty, local difficulty upon the Wabash system of railways, which involved only 3700 Knights of Labor, and a strike of a few hundred men on the Third Avenue Railway, New York, together with a few trifling and temporary disputes at other points, were magnified into a general warfare between capital and labor. There were but a few local skirmishes; peace already reigns; and our professors and political economists and the whole school of pessimists who tremble for the safety of human society in general, and of the Republic in particular, and the ministers that have bodily essayed to revolutionize existing conditions, are free to find another subject for their anxious fears and forebodings. The relations between capital and labor which have slowly evolved themselves in the gradual development of the race will not be readily changed. The solid walls with which humanity fortifies itself in each advanced position gained in its toilsome march forward will not fall to the ground at the blast of trumpets. Present conditions have grown up slowly, and can be changed for the better only slowly and by small, successive steps. A short history of the disturbances will, however, furnish many useful and needed lessons.

The trouble grew, as many serious troubles do grow, from a trifle. A leader of the Knights of Labor was dismissed. Whether the fact that he was a labor leader influenced his superior to dismiss him will probably never be known; but this much is to be said, that it was very likely to do so. Salaried officials in the service of large corporations are naturally disposed to keep under them only such men as give them no trouble.

On the other hand, the safety of its leaders is the key of labor's position. To surrender that is to surrender everything. Even if the leader in question had not been as regularly at work as other men, even if he had to take days now and then to attend to official duties for his brethren, the superior of that man should have dealt very leniently with him. The men cannot know whether their leader is stricken down for proper cause or not; but, at the same time, they cannot help suspecting. And here I call the attention of impartial minds to the elements of manhood and the high sense of honor and loyalty displayed upon the part of working men who sacrifice so much and throw themselves in the front of the conflict to secure the safety of their standard-bearers. Everything reasonable can be done with men of this spirit. The loyalty which they show to their leaders can be transferred to their employers by treating them as such men deserve. Society has nothing to fear from men so stanch and loyal to one another. Nor is the loyalty shown in this instance exceptional; it distinguishes working-men as a class. Mr. Irons has said that "one hour's gentlemanly courtesy on the part of the manager would have averted all this disaster." Whether this be true or not, the statement should not be overlooked, for it is true that one hour of courtesy on the part of employers would prevent many strikes. Whether the men ask in proper manner for interviews, or observe all the rules of etiquette, is immaterial. We expect from the presumably better-informed party representing capital much more in this respect than from labor; and it is not asking too much of men entrusted with the management of great properties that they should devote some part of their attention to searching out the causes of disaffection among their employees, and, where any exist, that they should meet the men more than half-way in the endeavor to allay them. There is nothing but good for both parties to be derived from labor teaching the representative of capital the dignity of man, as man. The working-man, becoming more and more intelligent, will hereafter demand the treatment due to an equal.

The strikers at first were excusable, even if mistaken, in imagining that their leader had been stricken down; but, under the excitement of conflict, violence was resorted to; and further, an attempt was made to drag into the quarrel railway lines that had nothing to do with it. The men took up these wrong positions and were deservedly driven from them. And labor here received a salutary lesson—namely, that nothing is to be gained by violence and lawlessness, nor by endeavoring to unjustly punish the innocent for the sins of the guilty. Public sentiment, always disposed to side with labor, was with the men at first, but soon finding itself unable to sanction their doings, it veered to the other side. When the strikers lost that indispensable ally they lost all.

The other branch of the revolt of labor occurred in New York city, where the employees of the Third Avenue Railway struck for fewer hours and better pay. If ever a strike was justifiable this one was. It is simply disgraceful for a corporation to compel its men to work fifteen or sixteen hours a day. Such was the verdict of the public, and the men won a deserved victory. Here again, as at St. Louis, for lack of proper leadership, they went too far; and in their demand for the employment of certain men and the dismissal of others they lost their only sure support—public sentiment. This was compelled to decide against their final demands, and consequently they failed, and deservedly failed. How completely public sentiment, when aroused, compels obedience, as we have seen it did both at St. Louis and in New York city, is further shown by the result of the order, issued June 6, requiring the men of all the city railroads in Brooklyn and New York to stop work until the striking employees of the Third Avenue line were reinstated. The edict was disregarded by the men themselves, who found that compliance would not be approved by the community, and that, therefore, the attempt would fail. It was an attempt that the worst foe of labor might have instigated.

These were the two chief strikes from which came the epidemic of demands and strikes throughout the country. None of these ebullitions proved of much moment. A rash had broken out upon the body politic, but it was only skin-deep, and disappeared as rapidly as it had come. At a somewhat later date the disturbance took a different form. A demand was made that the hours of labor should be reduced from ten to eight hours a day. To state this demand is to pronounce its fate. Existing conditions are not changed by twenty-per-cent leaps and bounds, and especially in times like these, when business is not even moderately profitable. Such a request simply meant that many employers of labor would not be able to keep their men at work at all. History proves, nevertheless, that the hours of labor are being gradually reduced. The percentage of men

working from ten to eleven hours in this country in 1830 was 29.7. These ten-hour workers increased in 1880 to 59.6 per cent of the whole; while the classes who in 1830 worked excessive hours—from twelve to thirteen—constituted 32.5 per cent. In 1880 they were only 14.6 per cent; while the number of men compelled to work between thirteen and fourteen hours, which was in 1830 13.5 per cent, had fallen in 1880 to 2.3 per cent. Those working twelve hours are generally employed in double shifts, night and day. I do not believe that we have reached the limit of this reduction, but I do believe that any permanent reduction will be secured only by the half-hour at a time. If labor be guided by wise counsel, it will ask for reductions of half-hours, and then wait until a reduction to this extent is firmly established, and surrounding circumstances have adjusted themselves to that.

In considering the reasonableness of the demand for fewer hours of labor, we must not lose sight of the fact that the American works more hours, on an average, than his fellow in Great Britain. Twenty-three trades in Massachusetts are reported as working sixty hours and seventeen minutes a week, on an average, while the same crafts in Great Britain work only fifty-three hours and fifty minutes, showing that the American works an hour a day longer than his English brother. In British textile factories, the number of working hours in a week ranges from fifty-four to fifty-six. In mines, foundries, and machine-shops, fifty-four hours make a week's work, which is equivalent to nine hours a day, six days a week; but the men, in all cases, work enough overtime each day to insure them a half-holiday on Saturday. In some districts, notably in Glasgow, the men prefer to work two weeks, and make every other Saturday a whole holiday. This gives them an opportunity to leave on early morning trains, on excursions, and to spend Saturday and Sunday with friends. The Allegheny Valley Railroad Company, under the management of my friend Mr. McCargo, introduced the half-Saturday holiday in the shops some time ago, with the happiest results. Mr. McCargo found, by years of experience, that working-men lose about half a day a week. Since the half-holiday was established no more time has been lost than before. The men work five and one half days a week regularly. While they are not paid, of course, for the half-holiday, they could not be induced to give it up. This example should be followed, not only by all the railroads of the country, but by every employer of labor, and should be supported by every man who seeks to improve the condition of the wage-receiving classes.

I venture to suggest to the representatives of labor, however, that before they demand any reduction upon ten hours per day, they should concentrate their efforts upon making ten hours the universal practice, and secure this. At present, every ton of pig-iron made in the world, except at two establishments, is made by men working in double shifts of twelve hours each, having neither Sunday nor holiday the year round. Every two weeks the day men change to the night shift by working twenty-four hours consecutively. Gasworks, paper-mills, flour-mills, and many other industries, are run by twelve-hour shifts, and breweries exact fifteen hours a day, on an average, from their men. I hold that it is not possible for men working ten hours a day to enlist public sentiment on their side in a demand for the shortening of their task, as long as many of their fellows are compelled to work twelve or more hours a day.

The eight-hour movement is not, however, without substantial foundation. Works that run day and night should be operated with three sets of men, each working eight hours. The steel-rail mills in this country are generally so run. The additional cost of the three sets of men has been divided between the workmen and the employers, the latter apparently having to meet an advance of wages to the extent of 16 per cent, but against this is to be placed the increased product which can be obtained. This is not inconsiderable, especially during the hot months, for it has been found that men working twelve hours a day continuously cannot produce as much per hour as men working eight hours a day; so that, if there be any profit at all in the business, the employer derives some advantage from the greater productive capacity of his works and capital, while the general expenses of the establishment remain practically as they were before. Since electric lighting has been perfected, many establishments which previously could not be run at night can be run with success. I therefore look for a large increase in the number of establishments working men only eight hours, but employing the machinery that now runs only ten hours the entire twenty four. Each shift, of course, takes turn of each of the three parts into which the twenty-four hours are divided, and thus the lives of the men are rendered less monotonous and many hours for recreation and self-improvement are obtained.

The literature called forth by the recent excitement is preponderatingly favorable to cooperation, or profit-sharing, as the only true remedy for all disputes between labor and capital. My April article has been criticized because it relegated that to the future. But the advocates of this plan should weigh well the fact that the majority of enterprises are not profitable; that most men who embark in business fail—indeed, it is stated that only five in every hundred succeed, and that, with the exception of a few wealthy and partially retired manufacturers, and a very few wealthy corporations, men engaged in business affairs are in the midst of an anxious and unceasing struggle to keep their heads above water. How to pay maturing obligations, how to obtain cash for the payment of their men, how to procure orders or how to sell product, and, in not a few instances, how to induce their creditors to be forbearing, are the problems which tax the minds of business men during the dark hours of night, when their employees are asleep. I attach less and less value to the teaching of those doctrinaires who sit in their cozy studies and spin theories concerning the relations between capital and labor, and set before us divers high ideals. The banquet to which they invite the working-man when they propose industrial cooperation is not yet quite prepared, and would prove to most of those who accepted the invitation a Barmecide feast. Taken as a whole, the condition of labor to-day would not be benefited, but positively injured, by cooperation.

Let me point out, however, to the advocates of profit-sharing that ample opportunity already exists for working-men to become part-owners in almost any department of industrialism, without changing present relations. The great railway corporations, in all cases, as well as the great manufacturing companies generally, are stock concerns, with shares of fifty or a hundred dollars each, which are bought and sold daily in the market. Not an employee of any of these but can buy any number of shares, and thus participate in the dividends and in the management. That capital is a unit is a popular error. On the contrary, it is made up of hundreds and thousands of small component parts, owned, for the most part, by people of limited means. The Pennsylvania Railway proper, for instance, which embraces only the 350 miles of line between Pittsburg and Philadelphia, is to-day owned by 19,340 shareholders, in lots of from one fifty-dollar share upward. The New York Central Railway, of 450 miles, between New York and Buffalo, belongs not to one, or two, or several capitalists, but to 10,418 shareholders, of whom about one third are women and executors of estates. The entire railway system of America will show a similar wide distribution of ownership among the people. There are but three railway corporations in which the great capitalists hold a considerable interest; and the interest in two of these is held by various members of a family, and in no case does it amount to the control of the whole. In one of these very cases, the New York Central, as we have seen, there are more than ten thousand owners.

Steel-rail mills, with only one exception, show a like state of affairs. One of them belongs to 215 shareholders; of whom 7 are employees, 32 are estates, and 57 are women. Another of these concerns is owned by 302 stockholders; of whom 101 are women, 29 are estates, representing an unknown number of individuals, and 20 are employees of the company. A large proportion of the remaining owners are small holders of comparatively limited means, who have, from time to time, invested their savings where they had confidence both as to certainty of income and safety of principal. The Merrimac Manufacturing Company (cotton), of Lowell, is owned by 2500 shareholders, of whom forty-two per cent are holders of one share, twenty-one per cent of two, and ten per cent of three shares. Twenty-seven per cent are holders of over three shares; and not less than thirty-eight per cent of the whole stock is held by trustees, guardians, and executors of charitable, religious, educational, and financial institutions.

I have obtained from other concerns similar statements, which need not be published. They prove without exception that from one fourth to one third of the number of shareholders in corporations are women and executors of estates. The number of shareholders I have given are those of record, each holding a separate certificate. But it is obvious, in the case of executors, that this one certificate may represent a dozen owners. Many certificates issued in the name of a firm represent several persons, while shares held by a corporation may represent hundreds; but if we assume that every certificate of stock issued by the Pennsylvania Railroad Company represents only two owners, which is absurdly under the truth, it follows that, should every employee of that great company quarrel with it, the contest would be not against a few, but against a much larger body than they themselves constitute. It is within the mark to say that every striking employee would oppose his personal interest against that of three or four other members of the community. The total number of men employed by the Pennsylvania Railroad Company is 18,911—not as many as there are shareholders of record. And what is true of the Pennsylvania Railway Company is true of the railway system as a whole, and, in a greater or less degree, of mining and manufacturing corporations generally. When one, therefore, denounces great corporations for unfair treatment of their men, he is not denouncing the act of some monster capitalist, but that of hundreds and thousands of small holders, scarcely one of whom would be a party to unfair or illiberal treatment of the working-man; the majority of them, indeed, would be found on his side; and, as we have seen, many of the owners themselves would be working-men. Labor has only to bring its just grievances to the attention of owners to secure fair and liberal treatment. The "great capitalist" is almost a myth, and exists, in any considerable number or degree, only in the heated imagination of the uninformed. Aggregate capital in railway corporations consists of many more individuals than it employs.

Following the labor disturbances, there came the mad work of a handful of foreign anarchists in Chicago and Milwaukee, who thought they saw in the excitement a fitting opportunity to execute their revolutionary plans. Although labor is not justly chargeable with their doings, nevertheless the cause of labor was temporarily discredited in public opinion by these outbreaks. The promptitude with which one labor organization after another not only disclaimed all sympathy with riot and disorder, but volunteered to enroll itself into armed force for the maintenance of order, should not be overlooked by the student of labor problems desirous of looking justly at the question from the laborer's point of view. It is another convincing proof, if further proof were necessary, that whenever the peace of this country is seriously threatened, the masses of men, not only in the professions and in the educated classes, but down to and through the very lowest ranks of industrious workers, are determined to maintain it. A survey of the field, now that peace is restored, gives the results as follows:

First. The "dead line" has been definitely fixed between the forces of disorder and anarchy and those of order. Bomb-throwing means swift death to the thrower. Rioters assembling in numbers and marching to pillage will be remorselessly shot down; not by the order of a government above the people, not by overwhelming standing armies, not by troops brought from a distance, but by the masses of peaceable and orderly citizens of all classes in their own community, from the capitalist down to and including the steady working-man, whose combined influence constitutes that irresistible force, under democratic institutions, known as public sentiment. That sentiment has not only supported the officials who shot down disturbers of the peace, but has extolled them in proportion to the promptitude of their action.

Second. Another proof of the indestructibility of human society, and of its determination and power to protect itself from every danger as it arises and to keep marching forward to higher states of development, has been given in Judge Mallory's words: "Every person who counsels, hires, procures, or incites others to the commission of any unlawful or criminal act, is equally guilty with those who actually perpetrate the act, though such person may not have been present at the time of the commission of the offense." The difference between liberty and license of speech is now clearly defined—a great gain.

Third. It has likewise been clearly shown that public sentiment sympathizes with the efforts of labor to obtain from capital a fuller recognition of its position and claims than has hitherto been accorded. And in this expression, "a fuller recognition," I include not only pecuniary compensation, but what I conceive to be even more important to-day—a greater consideration of the workingman as a man and a brother. I trust the time has gone by when corporations can hope to work men fifteen or sixteen hours a day. And the time approaches, I hope, when it will be impossible, in this country, to work men twelve hours a day continuously.

Fourth. While public sentiment has rightly and unmistakably condemned violence, even in the form for which there is the most excuse, I would have the public give due consideration to the terrible temptation to which the working-man on a strike is sometimes subjected. To expect that one dependent upon his daily wage for the necessaries of life will stand by peaceably and see a new man employed in his stead, is to expect much. This poor man may have a wife and children dependent upon his labor. Whether medicine for a sick child, or even nourishing food for a delicate wife, is procurable, depends upon his steady employment. In all but a very few departments of labor it is unnecessary, and, I think, improper, to subject men to such an ordeal. In the case of railways and a few other employments it is, of course, essential for the public wants that no interruption occur, and in such case substitutes must be employed; but the employer of labor will find it much more to his interest, wherever possible, to allow his works to remain idle and await the result of a dispute, than to employ the class of men that can be induced to take the place of other men who have stopped work. Neither the best men as men, nor the best men as workers, are thus to be obtained. There is an unwritten law among the best workmen: "Thou shalt not take thy neighbor's job."

No wise employer will lightly lose his old employees. Length of service counts for much in many ways. Calling upon strange men should be the last resort.

Fifth. The results of the recent disturbances have given indubitable proof that trades-unions must, in their very nature, become more conservative than the mass of the men they represent. If they fail to be conservative, they go to pieces through their own extravagance. I know of three instances in which threatened strikes were recently averted by the decision of the Master Workman of the Knights of Labor, supported by the best workmen, against the wishes of the less intelligent members of that organization. Representative institutions eventually bring to the front the ablest and most prudent men, and will be found as beneficial in the industrial as they have proved themselves to be in the political world. Leaders of the stamp of Mr. Powderly, Mr. Arthur, of the Brotherhood of Locomotive Engineers, and Messrs. Wihle and Martin, of the Amalgamated Iron and Steel Association, will gain and retain power; while such as the radical and impulsive Mr. Irons, if at first clothed with power, will soon lose it.

Thus, as the result of the recent revolt, we see advantages gained by both capital and labor. Capital is more secure because of what has been demonstrated, and labor will hereafter be more respectfully treated and its claims more carefully considered, in deference to an awakened public opinion in favor of the laborer. Labor won while it was reasonable in its demands and kept the peace; it lost when it asked what public sentiment pronounced unreasonable, and especially when it broke the peace.

The disturbance is over and peace again reigns; but let no one be unduly alarmed at frequent disputes between capital and labor. Kept within legal limits, they are encouraging symptoms, for they betoken the desire of the working-man to better his condition; and upon this desire hang all hopes of advancement of the masses. It is the stagnant pool of Contentment, not the running stream of Ambition, that breeds disease in the body social and political. The working-men of this country can no more be induced to sanction riot and disorder than can any other class of the community. Isolated cases of violence under strong provocation may break out upon the surface, but the body underneath is sound to the core, and resolute for the maintenance of order.

For the first time within my knowledge, the leading organs of public opinion in England have shown a more correct appreciation of the forces at work in the Republic than some of our own despondent writers. The London "Daily News" said truly that "the territorial democracy of America can be trusted to deal with such outbreaks"; and the "Daily Telegraph" spoke as follows:

> There is no need for any fear to be entertained lest the law-breakers of Chicago should get the better of the police, and, if it be necessary to invoke their aid, of the citizens of that astonishing young city. Frankly speaking, such

rioters would have a better chance of intimidating Birmingham than of overawing Chicago, St. Louis, or New York. In dealing with the insurgents of this class the record of the great Republic is singularly clear.

Not only the democracy, but the industrious working-men of which the democracy is so largely composed, have amply fulfilled the nattering predictions of our English friends, and may safely be trusted in the future to stand firmly for the maintenance of peace.

CHAPTER 3

W. E. B. Du Bois Calls for an American Pluralism

"How does it feel to be a problem?"

Unlike his great rival Booker T. Washington, W. E. B. Du Bois never made white Americans comfortable. He never intended to. Born William Edward Burghart Du Bois in Great Barrington Massachusetts in 1868, his career as a writer, activist, journalist, and scholar would span the better part of a century, ending during the height of the modern civil rights movement in 1963. In between, Du Bois's life embodied the black experience in America like no other. He was, at various times, an integrationist, a black nationalist, a socialist, and a Marxist—and ultimately, an expatriate, spending his last years in Africa. In all of his life's chapters, Du Bois wrestled with the issue of black identity. Were African Americans truly "American"? Did they want to be? Was it possible to be "black" and "American" at the same time? Du Bois answered these questions in different ways at different stages of his long career. But in 1903, as a relatively young man, he argued with passion and force in his greatest work, *The Souls of Black Folk*, that his people were not only part of the American conversation but at its center.

Du Bois wrote *The Souls of Black Folk* at the beginning of a century whose great unsolved issue, in his words, would be "the problem of the color-line."[1] Reversing "Jim Crow," the tide of legalized segregation that was sweeping through the South at the turn of the twentieth century, would only be part of the battle Du Bois hoped to wage and win. He also wished to forge a new relationship between the culture of black Americans and that of the nation as a whole. In 1903, it was incomprehensible to the vast majority of white Americans that the artistic output of the black community—its music, literature, poetry—was in any way worthy of its attention or respect. Du Bois was painfully aware of what he called the "all-pervading desire to inculcate disdain for everything black" that ran so deeply through white hearts and minds.[2] He knew that unless this attitude changed, even legal victories over Jim Crow would not be enough to make African Americans full-fledged participants in the nation's democratic undertaking. So he set out in *The Souls of Black Folk* to create an opportunity for African Americans to join their white brethren as "co-worker(s) in the kingdom of culture," building a uniquely American identity together.[3]

Du Bois understood how difficult a struggle—for understanding, for rights, for respect—this would be. Booker T. Washington (1856–1915) had avoided it, and had been rewarded for his forbearance. White support had made Washington the most powerful and influential man in the nation's black community at the turn of the twentieth century. The black college he founded, the Tuskegee Institute, was the object of largesse from white patrons, including Andrew Carnegie, who showered it with donations and scholarships. Thanks to Washington's connections in the Republican Party, he controlled African American patronage, doling out jobs to his allies in the manner of a political boss. It was small wonder that Washington's network of contacts and sympathizers was dubbed the "Tuskegee Machine."

Washington seemed content with black subservience, disenfranchisement, social marginalization, and exclusion from the power centers of American life. He had ingratiated himself among whites when, speaking before the Atlanta Cotton States and International Exposition in 1895, he counseled that "in all things that are purely social we can be as separate as the fingers, yet one as the hand in all things essential to mutual progress."[4] Washington maintained that black economic progress was more important than the right to vote or to use the same public facilities as whites. "The opportunity to earn a dollar in a factory just now," he told the Exposition delegates, "is worth infinitely more than the opportunity to spend a dollar in an opera house."[5] Equality under the law would come after blacks had proved their worth as men and women of sober industry. Once white Americans came to respect black conduct and values, and needed their skill and labor, Washington was confident that the rest would follow.

But Du Bois was uncomfortable with the idea that it was appropriate to judge his people by the standards of another race. By what right were whites the judges of black folk? Why did black folk have to "prove" themselves to whites? And why didn't whites view them as truly "American"? Du Bois resolved to articulate a new vision of black life in the United States, one that would offer an alternative to Washington's program. Doing so would not be easy. Washington was notoriously thin-skinned and jealous of his prerogatives. He had destroyed the careers of many who challenged his leadership in the black community. Indeed, Washington might even use his influence in black academic circles to harm Du Bois at Atlanta University, where by the turn of the twentieth century he was teaching history and economics. But Du Bois believed deeply enough in his vision to stake his professional life on it. In 1903, he published *The Souls of Black Folk.*

In truth, Du Bois had been preparing to write *The Souls of Black Folk* his entire life. His background could not have been more different from Washington's. Washington had been born a slave in the South, Du Bois free in the North. Washington received an "industrial" education at Hampton Institute in Virginia. There he learned the manual skills deemed appropriate for blacks in the post-Civil War South, a time when a skilled trade job was the best an African American could hope for. Du Bois earned a B.A. and a Ph.D. in history from Harvard and spent two years studying at the University of Berlin. Befitting his elite education, Du Bois had a polish and sophistication that bordered on haughtiness. Washington, a man of simple virtues, reflected the unpretentious straightforwardness of the rural South. Washington preached the virtues of patience, advising his people to build up economic capital in the form of small businesses and trades that would one day force whites to meet them on equal ground. But Du Bois was unsuited by education and temperament to wait for hearts and minds to change. From his first youthful encounters with whites in New England, he would write in *The Souls of Black Folk*, Du Bois realized that he was "shut out from their world by a vast veil."[6] He wished to pierce that veil, and join whites, not in "their" world, but in an America that would reflect the richness of both black and white identities.

Du Bois' vision could only be realized in an environment of legal and political equality. His agenda was thus vastly different from that of Washington. The Jim Crow laws enacted by most Southern state legislatures in the 1890s in order to segregate their public accommodations had to be repealed. Blacks had also lost the right to vote in the South during that decade, and this injustice also needed to be rectified. The 1896 *Plessy v. Ferguson* Supreme Court decision that upheld "separate but equal" facilities for blacks and whites—a direct product of Jim Crow laws itself—would consign blacks to a permanent inferior caste if not overturned. And the epidemic of lynching which had spread across the South after the end of Reconstruction in 1877 and reached a crescendo in the early years of the twentieth century threatened to trap African Americans in a vise of terror. Under such circumstances, thought Du Bois, how could Washington argue that black political equality was of secondary importance? How could blacks be expected to embrace the virtues of hard work, perseverance, and delayed gratification in a society that denied them the basic rights of citizenship? Washington's philosophy had gotten African Americans nowhere, and it was time to tell them—and white Americans—so.

Du Bois earned his Harvard Ph.D. in 1895, the same year Washington delivered his celebrated Atlanta Exposition speech. After teaching briefly at Wilberforce University, a black college in Ohio, Du Bois moved to Philadelphia, where he worked with a white sociologist at the University of Pennsylvania and conducted a ground-breaking study of the city's black community that he published as *The Philadelphia Negro* in 1899. By then, he had found his permanent intellectual home at Atlanta University, which was growing into one of the preeminent black institutions of higher learning in the United States. With its classical liberal arts curriculum, Atlanta was perfect for a man with Du Bois' perspective. He would teach at the university until 1909, when he became director of publicity and research of the newly founded National Association for the Advancement of Colored People (NAACP), and again between 1934 and 1944, when he headed Atlanta's sociology department.

Even as their diverging views drove them apart, Washington sought to draw Du Bois into the Tuskegee orbit, offering him a position at his school. Ever mindful of his independence, Du Bois kept his distance. By 1903, he had secured a publisher, A.C. McClurg and Company of Chicago, and assembled the essays for *The Souls of Black Folk*—including one that took direct aim at Booker T. Washington. The book appeared on April 18 of that year.

"How does it feel to be a problem?" Du Bois began "Of Our Spiritual Strivings," the first essay in *The Souls of Black Folk*, with this question.[7] It was implicit, he observed, in virtually every interaction he had with whites. He always seemed the object of special scrutiny. When Du Bois shook hands with a white man, he knew what was going through his mind. Not "I am shaking hands with a scholar, husband, and father"—all of which Du Bois was—but "I am shaking hands with a Negro." Du Bois was not just another human being, or just another American, to this white man, or to other white Americans. He was always a black man, an outsider, an "other." Whites, Du Bois wrote, permitted him:

> ...no true self-consciousness, but only (let) him see himself through the revelation of the other world. It is a peculiar sensation, this double-consciousness, this sense of always looking at one's self through the eyes of others, of measuring one's soul by the tape of a world that looks on in amused contempt and pity. One ever feels his two-ness—an American, a Negro; two souls, two thoughts, two unrecognized strivings, two warring ideals in one dark body, whose dogged strength alone keeps it from being torn asunder.[8]

But it would be too simple to ask merely to be viewed as an "American," and nothing more. Du Bois' vision was a more nuanced one. Long before the term "African American" became commonly accepted, he argued for its use in the nation's discourse. It captured perfectly the idea of "double-consciousness" that Du Bois introduced in "Of Our Spiritual Strivings." White society regarded Du Bois as both a black man of African descent and a black man living in America. This "double-consciousness" had certain advantages. It afforded Du Bois a unique outsider's perspective on white America. But beyond this, it offered only marginalization and isolation.

The solution for Du Bois was to permit blacks in the United States to retain their identity as a unique people while also identifying as Americans. This was a novel, even revolutionary, concept in 1903. Despite large-scale Catholic and Jewish immigration, the nation was still predominantly Protestant in both population and culture. Its power brokers—in politics, business, the professions, and academia—were overwhelmingly white Anglo-Saxon Protestants. Out of this dominance had come the assumption that Protestant culture was "American" culture, and that to be truly "American," one had to identify as a Protestant.

But in *The Souls of Black Folk* Du Bois was not only arguing against the predominance of white Protestantism but for the idea that dual or even multiple identities could still be considered distinctly "American" in character. He thus sought

> ...to merge his double self into a better and truer self. In this merging, he wishes neither of the older selves to be lost. He would not Africanize America, for America has too much to teach the world and Africa. He would not bleach his Negro soul in a flood of white Americanism, for he knows that Negro blood has a message for the world. He simply wishes to make it possible for a man to be both a Negro and an American, without being cursed and spit upon by his fellows, without having the doors of Opportunity closed roughly in his face.[9]

This was the first articulation of what would come to be known as "pluralism" in American culture. It represented a new approach to the question of American identity. Du Bois believed that the values of black Americans had much to offer the United States. In a nation obsessed with material gain—"a dusty desert of dollars and smartness," as he put it—blacks represented an "oasis of simple faith and reverence," a brake on capitalism's excesses.[10] Black culture, Du Bois argued, was "American" through and through. After all, blacks had been part of the American experience from the beginning, and both as slaves and free men, had influenced it profoundly. Black identity made one more "American," not less so. Du Bois envisioned

> ...the ideal of human brotherhood, gained through the unifying ideal of Race; the ideal of fostering and developing the traits and talents of the Negro, not in opposition to or contempt for other races, but rather in large conformity to the greater ideals of the American Republic, in order that some day on American soil two world-races may give each to each those characteristics both so sadly lack.[11]

Du Bois was thus calling for a new version of American identity, one that would not attack difference but celebrate it. Blacks could live as both blacks and Americans, free at last of the burdens and stigmas of double-consciousness. If, as Du Bois argued, the problem of the color-line would define the twentieth century, the survival of the nation itself hinged on realizing the American pluralist ideal. Later in the twentieth century, Randolph Bourne (see Chapter 4), Charles Kikuchi (see Chapter 9), Norman Rockwell (see Chapter 10), and Malcolm X (see Chapter 18) would take up the pluralist challenge that Du Bois posed. They too would confront the tensions between individual and group identities that lie at the heart of the ongoing struggle to define "America" as a nation and "Americans" as a people. But it was Du Bois who began this conversation, as America's first true pluralist.

Du Bois titled another chapter of *The Souls of Black Folk* "Of Mr. Booker T. Washington and Others." One can imagine Du Bois taking a deep breath before picking up his pen to write it. He knew that what he was about to say might cost him dearly. The reach of the "Tuskegee Machine" was long. But Du Bois was convinced that Washington's ideas had failed black Americans. Washington had advised them to accept segregation and second-class citizenship, and focus instead on the "accumulation of wealth" through "industrial education," and on the "conciliation of the South."[12] What had this gotten them? Disenfranchised? Jim Crowed? Lynched? And even assuming that black economic power could somehow compensate for political impotence, where was this power to come from? "Is it possible, and probable," Du Bois asked, "that nine millions of men can make effective progress in economic lines if they are deprived of political rights, made a servile caste, and allowed only the most meager chance for developing their exceptional men? If history and reason give any distinct answer to these questions, it is an emphatic *No*."[13]

How could a black artisan or small businessman defend his economic rights, Du Bois asked, without the right to vote? How could blacks be expected to develop "thrift and self-respect" when they were constantly reminded of their inequality before the law?[14] How could they ever hope to assume positions of responsibility in American society without the same liberal arts–based higher educations that whites were receiving? Washington had no answers to these questions, but Du Bois did. Voting rights, the end of Jim Crow, and the development of a "Talented Tenth" of classically educated African Americans would provide blacks with the political power, racial pride, and home-grown leadership to finally take true ownership of their nation's founding document, the Declaration of Independence.[15] All Washington's program offered was continued degradation, the bitter fruits of a "double-consciousness" made perpetual. It would ensure that Americans of African descent would always be asked the humiliating question with which *The Souls of Black Folk* began: "How does it feel to be a problem?" Du Bois' pluralist vision looked toward a day when they would transcend both this question and the double-consciousness that elicited it.

In the immediate aftermath of the appearance of *The Souls of Black Folk*, Du Bois felt Washington's wrath. The Tuskegee leader had never fully trusted the aloof, self-possessed Du Bois, one of the few men in the African American community that he could not co-opt or intimidate. Now the upstart had dared to challenge him in print, and he would have to pay for his indiscretion. Washington's initial line of attack was through the black newspapers whose editors he had cultivated. Hoping to blunt the force of the book's message, he made sure that most of them did not review *The Souls of Black Folk*. But there were enough editors willing to risk Washington's displeasure to give the book an audience in the black community, and by 1908, it had sold almost 10,000 copies. Washington also sought to discredit Du Bois among wealthy white racial liberals, some of whom, like Andrew Carnegie and John D. Rockefeller, had made substantial donations to black institutions like Tuskegee and Du Bois' own Atlanta University. And Washington induced African American notables who had indicated sympathy for Du Bois' positions to keep their opinions private. Nonetheless, in July 1905, Du Bois gathered twenty-nine of the most important black leaders in the country in Fort Erie, Ontario, on the Canadian side of Niagara Falls—the men had intended to meet in Buffalo but had been unable to locate a hotel that would accept blacks—to launch what became known as the "Niagara Movement."

Du Bois and his colleagues issued a demand for black legal equality that was guaranteed to ruffle the feathers of Washington, who had dispatched spies to Buffalo with instructions to report details of the meeting (unaware of the move to Canada, they searched in vain for the delegates). Under pressure from Washington, the Niagara Movement lasted only a few years, but it was succeeded by a more powerful and long-lived organization—the NAACP, which Du Bois helped organize in 1909 and 1910. The NAACP was composed primarily of wealthy whites—Du Bois was the new group's only black director—who had become disillusioned with Washington's cautious philosophy. Vicious race riots in Atlanta in 1906 and in Abraham Lincoln's hometown of Springfield, Illinois, in 1908 had convinced them that accommodation to Jim Crow offered few rewards. The NAACP would make full and immediate equality under the law its goal. The reversal of *Plessy v. Ferguson*, an end to Jim Crow, the enactment of anti-lynching legislation, black voter registration—these would motivate its leaders and members for the next sixty years. Leaving Atlanta University, Du Bois became the

NAACP's director of publicity and research, and the editor of its magazine, *The Crisis.* There, he found a platform for his vision of a pluralist America, as well as a degree of protection from Washington's attacks.

In any event, his rival had only a short time to live. Washington died in 1915. By then, the power of the Tuskegee Machine was ebbing. Woodrow Wilson, a Southern Democrat with no ties to Washington, had been elected president in 1912. He cut off the flow of patronage that had sustained the Machine during Republican administrations, and segregated the federal civil service. The year 1915 also marked the debut of the racist film *Birth of a Nation*, which not only romanticized the Ku Klux Klan of the nineteenth century, but helped spark a revived Klan that in the 1920s became as powerful in the North as in the South.

At the time of Washington's death, then, events had called into question the wisdom of his approach to race relations in the United States. But this was small consolation to Du Bois, who was beginning to reconsider his own philosophy in light of the same events. The 1920s and 1930s would mark his retreat from the pluralist vision of *The Souls of Black Folk*. Turning toward Marxism, Du Bois now viewed African Americans as members of an oppressed proletariat and part of a global class struggle. He resigned his position at the NAACP in 1934, disillusioned with the group's pro-integration stance, and resumed teaching at Atlanta University. In 1903, Du Bois had voiced the hope that "sometime, somewhere, men will judge men by their souls and not by their skins."[16] But now he wondered if it was possible to maintain an authentic black identity in an overwhelmingly white society. Could one indeed be both "Negro" and "American" after all? To Du Bois, being "American" now essentially meant being white.

As he moved more deeply into the Marxist orbit during the 1940s and 1950s, Du Bois linked the oppression of blacks in the United States to that of people of color worldwide. All, in his view, were colonized subjects, victims of European imperialism abroad and white racism at home. These sentiments made him increasingly unpopular with the federal government, which tried him for subversive activities in 1951. Found not guilty, Du Bois was nonetheless stripped of his passport, preventing him from travelling overseas until 1958. That year, he received the Lenin Peace Prize from the Soviet Union; he became an official member of the American Communist Party in 1961. From there, it was a short step to the final break with the nation whose promise Du Bois had embraced over a half-century earlier in *The Souls of Black Folk.* He emigrated to Ghana and gave up his United States citizenship in 1962. The next year, he took Ghanaian citizenship. On August 27, 1963, Du Bois passed away in Accra, Ghana, at the age of 95.

In an ironic coda to his long life, Du Bois' death came just one day before the March on Washington for Jobs and Freedom, the occasion for Dr. Martin Luther King, Jr.'s immortal "I Have a Dream" speech. King's dream for America in 1963 was remarkably close to the one Du Bois had offered sixty years earlier in *The Souls of Black Folk*. King too envisioned a nation in which it was possible to be both black and American, a pluralist society that took the best of what every racial, ethnic, and religious group had to offer. Indeed, King's famous declaration that he had "a dream that my four little children will one day live in a nation where they will not be judged by the color of their skin but by the content of their character" was an echo of Du Bois' "by their souls and not by their skins" dream of 1903.[17] Yet Du Bois died in a foreign country, having renounced both that dream and the nation in which he had pursued it.

W. E. B. Du Bois never solved the riddle of black identity in a white country. He was never able to merge the double-consciousness he described in *The Souls of Black Folk* into a pluralism that would redeem America's promise. At the end of his life, Du Bois believed that his people were still being forced to choose between being "black" and being "American." He no longer wished to be part of a country that made such a choice necessary. It is possible that had he lived as long as Du Bois, Washington would have reached the same conclusion. Malcolm X, as we will see (Chapter 18), sneered at the idea of a pluralist America. But to other Americans, it was a dream well worth pursuing. One of them was the white journalist and critic Randolph Bourne. Bourne's interests lay primarily with the European immigrants who had become such a large presence in American life by the 1910s, and not with African Americans per se. But like the younger Du Bois, he searched for ways to reconcile the "double selves" of the marginalized and fuse them into an American vision that recognized both. Bourne's pluralist dream would ignite a series of American conversations as charged and momentous as those that surrounded Du Bois.

Questions for Consideration and Conversation

1. How would Randolph Bourne (Chapter 4) have responded to the central question posed by Du Bois in *The Souls of Black Folk*: Was it possible to be "black" and "American" at the same time? What would Charles Kikuchi (Chapter 9) have said? How did Du Bois' own views on this question change over time?

2. Why did Du Bois believe that black cultural expressions—in music, art, and literature—were so important?

3. Why did Du Bois eventually lose faith in the idea of American pluralism? Was he justified?

4. How would Malcolm X (Chapter 18) have responded to the arguments of *The Souls of Black Folk*?

5. What did Du Bois mean when he wrote of black "double consciousness"? What were its disadvantages? Did it present any opportunities for black Americans?

6. Why did Du Bois feel Booker T. Washington's program had failed black Americans? Can anything be said in support of Washington's ideas?

7. Had Du Bois been alive to hear Martin Luther King, Jr.'s "I Have a Dream" speech at the March on Washington for Jobs and Freedom in August 1963, what might he have said about it?

Endnotes

1. W. E. B. Du Bois, *The Souls of Black Folk* (New York: Library of America, 1990), 3.
2. Ibid., 13.
3. Ibid., 9.
4. See Jacqueline M. Moore, *Booker T. Washington, W.E.B. Du Bois and the Struggle for Racial Uplift* (Wilmington, DE: Scholarly Resources, 2003), 127.
5. Ibid., 128.
6. Du Bois, *The Souls of Black Folk*, 8.
7. Ibid., 7.
8. Ibid., 8–9.
9. Ibid., 9.
10. Ibid., 14.
11. Ibid.
12. Ibid., 42–43.
13. Ibid., 43.
14. Ibid.
15. Du Bois' "Talented Tenth" referred to the elite intellectual class of black Americans, representing approximately 10% of their population in the United States.
16. Du Bois, *The Souls of Black Folk*, 188.
17. Clayborne Carson and Kris Shepard, eds., *A Call to Conscience: The Landmark Speeches of Dr. Martin Luther King, Jr.* (New York: Warner Books, 2001), 85.

W. E. B. Du Bois, "Of Our Spiritual Strivings" (1903)

Source: W. E. B. Du Bois, *The Souls of Black Folk.* Chicago: A.C. McClurg, 1903, pp. 7–15.

O water, voice of my heart, crying in the sand,
All night long crying with a mournful cry,
As I lie and listen, and cannot understand
The voice of my heart in my side or the voice of the sea,
O water, crying for rest, is it I, is it I?
All night long the water is crying to me.
Unresting water, there shall never be rest
Till the last moon droop and the last tide fail,
And the fire of the end begin to burn in the west;
And the heart shall be weary and wonder and cry like the sea,
All life long crying without avail,
As the water all night long is crying to me.

—Arthur Symons.

Between me and the other world there is ever an unasked question: unasked by some through feelings of delicacy; by others through the difficulty of rightly framing it. All, nevertheless, flutter round it. They approach me in a half-hesitant sort of way, eye me curiously or compassionately, and then, instead of saying directly, How does it feel to be a problem? they say, I know an excellent colored man in my town; or, I fought at Mechanicsville; or, Do not these Southern outrages make your blood boil? At these I smile, or am interested, or reduce the boiling to a simmer, as the occasion may require. To the real question, How does it feel to be a problem? I answer seldom a word.

And yet, being a problem is a strange experience,—peculiar even for one who has never been anything else, save perhaps in babyhood and in Europe. It is in the early days of rollicking boyhood that the revelation first bursts upon one, all in a day, as it were. I remember well when the shadow swept across me. I was a little thing, away up in the hills of New England, where the dark Housatonic winds between Hoosac and Taghkanic to the sea. In a wee wooden schoolhouse, something put it into the boys' and girls' heads to buy gorgeous visiting-cards—ten cents a package—and exchange. The exchange was merry, till one girl, a tall newcomer, refused my card,—refused it peremptorily, with a glance. Then it dawned upon me with a certain suddenness that I was different from the others; or like, mayhap, in heart and life and longing, but shut out from their world by a vast veil. I had thereafter no desire to tear down that veil, to creep through;

I held all beyond it in common contempt, and lived above it in a region of blue sky and great wandering shadows. That sky was bluest when I could beat my mates at examination-time, or beat them at a foot-race, or even beat their stringy heads. Alas, with the years all this fine contempt began to fade; for the words I longed for, and all their dazzling opportunities, were theirs, not mine. But they should not keep these prizes, I said; some, all, I would wrest from them. Just how I would do it I could never decide: by reading law, by healing the sick, by telling the wonderful tales that swam in my head,—some way. With other black boys the strife was not so fiercely sunny: their youth shrunk into tasteless sycophancy, or into silent hatred of the pale world about them and mocking distrust of everything white; or wasted itself in a bitter cry, Why did God make me an outcast and a stranger in mine own house? The shades of the prison-house closed round about us all: walls strait and stubborn to the whitest, but relentlessly narrow, tall, and unscalable to sons of night who must plod darkly on in resignation, or beat unavailing palms against the stone, or steadily, half hopelessly, watch the streak of blue above.

After the Egyptian and Indian, the Greek and Roman, the Teuton and Mongolian, the Negro is a sort of seventh son, born with a veil, and gifted with second-sight in this American world,—a world which yields him no true self-consciousness, but only lets him see himself through the revelation of the other world. It is a peculiar sensation, this double-consciousness, this sense of always looking at one's self through the eyes of others, of measuring one's soul by the tape of a world that looks on in amused contempt and pity. One ever feels his twoness,—an American, a Negro; two souls, two thoughts, two unreconciled strivings; two warring ideals in one dark body, whose dogged strength alone keeps it from being torn asunder.

The history of the American Negro is the history of this strife,—this longing to attain self-conscious manhood, to merge his double self into a better and truer self. In this merging he wishes neither of the older selves to be lost. He would not Africanize America, for America has too much to teach the world and Africa. He would not bleach his Negro soul in a flood of white Americanism, for he knows that Negro blood has a message for the world. He simply wishes to make it possible for a man to be both a Negro and an American, without being cursed and spit upon by his fellows, without having the doors of Opportunity closed roughly in his face.

This, then, is the end of his striving: to be a co-worker in the kingdom of culture, to escape both death and isolation, to husband and use his best powers and his latent genius. These powers of body and mind have in the past been strangely wasted, dispersed, or forgotten. The shadow of a mighty Negro past flits through the tale of Ethiopia the Shadowy and of Egypt the Sphinx. Through history, the powers of single black men flash here and there like falling stars, and die sometimes before the world has rightly gauged their brightness. Here in America, in the few days since Emancipation, the black man's turning hither and thither in hesitant and doubtful striving has often made his very strength to lose effectiveness, to seem like absence of power, like weakness. And yet it is not weakness,—it is the contradiction of double aims. The double-aimed struggle of the black artisan—on the one hand to escape white contempt for a nation of mere hewers of wood and drawers of water, and on the other hand to plough and nail and dig for a poverty-stricken horde—could only result in making him a poor craftsman, for he had but half a heart in either cause. By the poverty and ignorance of his people, the Negro minister or doctor was tempted toward quackery and demagogy; and by the criticism of the other world, toward ideals that made him ashamed of his lowly tasks. The would-be black savant was confronted by the paradox that the knowledge his people needed was a twice-told tale to his white neighbors, while the knowledge which would teach the white world was Greek to his own flesh and blood. The innate love of harmony and beauty that set the ruder souls of his people a-dancing and a-singing raised but confusion and doubt in the soul of the black artist; for the beauty revealed to him was the soul-beauty of a race which his larger audience despised, and he could not articulate the message of another people. This waste of double aims, this seeking to satisfy two unreconciled ideals, has wrought sad havoc with the courage and faith and deeds of ten thousand thousand people,—has sent them often wooing false gods and invoking false means of salvation, and at times has even seemed about to make them ashamed of themselves.

Away back in the days of bondage they thought to see in one divine event the end of all doubt and disappointment; few men ever worshipped Freedom with half such unquestioning faith as did the American Negro for two centuries. To him, so far as

he thought and dreamed, slavery was indeed the sum of all villainies, the cause of all sorrow, the root of all prejudice; Emancipation was the key to a promised land of sweeter beauty than ever stretched before the eyes of wearied Israelites.

In song and exhortation swelled one refrain—Liberty; in his tears and curses the God he implored had Freedom in his right hand. At last it came,—suddenly, fearfully, like a dream. With one wild carnival of blood and passion came the message in his own plaintive cadences:—

> *"Shout, O children!*
> *Shout, you're free!*
> *For God has bought your liberty!"*

Years have passed away since then,—ten, twenty, forty; forty years of national life, forty years of renewal and development, and yet the swarthy spectre sits in its accustomed seat at the Nation's feast. In vain do we cry to this our vastest social problem:—

> *"Take any shape but that, and my firm nerves*
> *Shall never tremble!"*

The Nation has not yet found peace from its sins; the freedman has not yet found in freedom his promised land. Whatever of good may have come in these years of change, the shadow of a deep disappointment rests upon the Negro people,—a disappointment all the more bitter because the unattained ideal was unbounded save by the simple ignorance of a lowly people.

The first decade was merely a prolongation of the vain search for freedom, the boon that seemed ever barely to elude their grasp,—like a tantalizing will-o'-the-wisp, maddening and misleading the headless host. The holocaust of war, the terrors of the Ku-Klux Klan, the lies of carpet-baggers, the disorganization of industry, and the contradictory advice of friends and foes, left the bewildered serf with no new watchword beyond the old cry for freedom. As the time flew, however, he began to grasp a new idea. The ideal of liberty demanded for its attainment powerful means, and these the Fifteenth Amendment gave him. The ballot, which before he had looked upon as a visible sign of freedom, he now regarded as the chief means of gaining and perfecting the liberty with which war had partially endowed him. And why not? Had not votes made war and emancipated millions? Had not votes enfranchised the freedmen? Was anything impossible to a power that had done all this? A million black men started with renewed zeal to vote themselves into the kingdom. So the decade flew away, the revolution of 1876 came, and left the half-free serf weary, wondering, but still inspired. Slowly but steadily, in the following years, a new vision began gradually to replace the dream of political power,— a powerful movement, the rise of another ideal to guide the unguided, another pillar of fire by night after a clouded day. It was the ideal of "book-learning"; the curiosity, born of compulsory ignorance, to know and test the power of the cabalistic letters of the white man, the longing to know. Here at last seemed to have been discovered the mountain path to Canaan; longer than the highway of Emancipation and law, steep and rugged, but straight, leading to heights high enough to overlook life.

Up the new path the advance guard toiled, slowly, heavily, doggedly; only those who have watched and guided the faltering feet, the misty minds, the dull understandings, of the dark pupils of these schools know how faithfully, how piteously, this people strove to learn. It was weary work. The cold statistician wrote down the inches of progress here and there, noted also where here and there a foot had slipped or some one had fallen. To the tired climbers, the horizon was ever dark, the mists were often cold, the Canaan was always dim and far away. If, however, the vistas disclosed as yet no goal, no resting-place, little but flattery and criticism, the journey at least gave leisure for reflection and self-examination; it changed the child of Emancipation to the youth with dawning self-consciousness, self-realization, self-respect. In those sombre forests of his striving his own soul rose before him, and he saw himself,—darkly as through a veil; and yet he saw in himself some faint revelation of his power, of his mission. He began to have a dim feeling that, to attain his place in the world, he must be himself, and not another. For the first time he sought to analyze the burden he bore upon his back, that dead-weight of social degradation partially masked behind a half-named Negro problem. He felt his poverty; without a cent, without a home, without land, tools, or savings, he had entered into competition with rich, landed, skilled neighbors. To be a poor man is hard, but to be a poor race in a land of dollars is the very bottom of hardships. He felt the weight of his ignorance,—not simply of letters, but of life, of business, of the humanities; the accumulated sloth and shirking and awkwardness of decades and centuries shackled his hands and feet. Nor was his burden all poverty and ignorance. The red stain of bastardy, which two centuries of systematic legal defilement of Negro women had stamped upon his race, meant

not only the loss of ancient African chastity, but also the hereditary weight of a mass of corruption from white adulterers, threatening almost the obliteration of the Negro home.

A people thus handicapped ought not to be asked to race with the world, but rather allowed to give all its time and thought to its own social problems. But alas! while sociologists gleefully count his bastards and his prostitutes, the very soul of the toiling, sweating black man is darkened by the shadow of a vast despair. Men call the shadow prejudice, and learnedly explain it as the natural defence of culture against barbarism, learning against ignorance, purity against crime, the "higher" against the "lower" races. To which the Negro cries Amen! and swears that to so much of this strange prejudice as is founded on just homage to civilization, culture, righteousness, and progress, he humbly bows and meekly does obeisance. But before that nameless prejudice that leaps beyond all this he stands helpless, dismayed, and well-nigh speechless; before that personal disrespect and mockery, the ridicule and systematic humiliation, the distortion of fact and wanton license of fancy, the cynical ignoring of the better and the boisterous welcoming of the worse, the all-pervading desire to inculcate disdain for everything black, from Toussaint to the devil,—before this there rises a sickening despair that would disarm and discourage any nation save that black host to whom "discouragement" is an unwritten word.

But the facing of so vast a prejudice could not but bring the inevitable self-questioning, self-disparagement, and lowering of ideals which ever accompany repression and breed in an atmosphere of contempt and hate. Whisperings and portents came home upon the four winds: Lo! we are diseased and dying, cried the dark hosts; we cannot write, our voting is vain; what need of education, since we must always cook and serve? And the Nation echoed and enforced this self-criticism, saying: Be content to be servants, and nothing more; what need of higher culture for half-men? Away with the black man's ballot, by force or fraud,—and behold the suicide of a race! Nevertheless, out of the evil came something of good,—the more careful adjustment of education to real life, the clearer perception of the Negroes' social responsibilities, and the sobering realization of the meaning of progress.

So dawned the time of Sturm und Drang: storm and stress to-day rocks our little boat on the mad waters of the world-sea; there is within and without the sound of conflict, the burning of body and rending of soul; inspiration strives with doubt, and faith with vain questionings. The bright ideals of the past,—physical freedom, political power, the training of brains and the training of hands,—all these in turn have waxed and waned, until even the last grows dim and overcast. Are they all wrong,—all false? No, not that, but each alone was over-simple and incomplete,—the dreams of a credulous race-childhood, or the fond imaginings of the other world which does not know and does not want to know our power.

To be really true, all these ideals must be melted and welded into one. The training of the schools we need to-day more than ever,—the training of deft hands, quick eyes and ears, and above all the broader, deeper, higher culture of gifted minds and pure hearts. The power of the ballot we need in sheer self-defence,—else what shall save us from a second slavery? Freedom, too, the long-sought, we still seek,—the freedom of life and limb, the freedom to work and think, the freedom to love and aspire. Work, culture, liberty,—all these we need, not singly but together, not successively but together, each growing and aiding each, and all striving toward that vaster ideal that swims before the Negro people, the ideal of human brotherhood, gained through the unifying ideal of Race; the ideal of fostering and developing the traits and talents of the Negro, not in opposition to or contempt for other races, but rather in large conformity to the greater ideals of the American Republic, in order that some day on American soil two world-races may give each to each those characteristics both so sadly lack. We the darker ones come even now not altogether empty-handed: there are to-day no truer exponents of the pure human spirit of the Declaration of Independence than the American Negroes; there is no true American music but the wild sweet melodies of the Negro slave; the American fairy tales and folklore are Indian and African; and, all in all, we black men seem the sole oasis of simple faith and reverence in a dusty desert of dollars and smartness. Will America be poorer if she replace her brutal dyspeptic blundering with light-hearted but determined Negro humility? or her coarse and cruel wit with loving jovial good-humor? or her vulgar music with the soul of the Sorrow Songs?

Merely a concrete test of the underlying principles of the great republic is the Negro Problem, and the spiritual striving of the freedmen's sons is the travail of souls whose burden is almost beyond the measure of their strength, but who bear it in the name of an historic race, in the name of this the land of their fathers' fathers, and in the name of human opportunity.

And now what I have briefly sketched in large outline let me on coming pages tell again in many ways, with loving emphasis and deeper detail, that men may listen to the striving in the souls of black folk.

W. E. B. Du Bois, "Of Mr. Booker T. Washington and Others" (1903)

Source: W. E. B. Du Bois, *The Souls of Black Folk.* Chicago: A.C. McClurg, 1903, pp. 36–48.

From birth till death enslaved; in word, in deed, unmanned!

Hereditary bondsmen! Know ye not
Who would be free themselves must strike the blow?

—Byron.

Easily the most striking thing in the history of the American Negro since 1876 is the ascendancy of Mr. Booker T. Washington. It began at the time when war memories and ideals were rapidly passing; a day of astonishing commercial development was dawning; a sense of doubt and hesitation overtook the freedmen's sons,—then it was that his leading began. Mr. Washington came, with a simple definite programme, at the psychological moment when the nation was a little ashamed of having bestowed so much sentiment on Negroes, and was concentrating its energies on Dollars. His programme of industrial education, conciliation of the South, and submission and silence as to civil and political rights, was not wholly original; the Free Negroes from 1830 up to war-time had striven to build industrial schools, and the American Missionary Association had from the first taught various trades; and Price and others had sought a way of honorable alliance with the best of the Southerners. But Mr. Washington first indissolubly linked these things; he put enthusiasm, unlimited energy, and perfect faith into his programme, and changed it from a by-path into a veritable Way of Life. And the tale of the methods by which he did this is a fascinating study of human life.

It startled the nation to hear a Negro advocating such a programme after many decades of bitter complaint; it startled and won the applause of the South, it interested and won the admiration of the North; and after a confused murmur of protest, it silenced if it did not convert the Negroes themselves. To gain the sympathy and cooperation of the various elements comprising the white South was Mr. Washington's first task; and this, at the time Tuskegee was founded, seemed, for a black man, well-nigh impossible. And yet ten years later it was done in the word spoken at Atlanta: "In all things purely social we can be as separate as the five fingers, and yet one as the hand in all things essential to mutual progress." This "Atlanta Compromise" is by all odds the most notable thing in Mr. Washington's career. The South interpreted it in different ways: the radicals received it as a complete surrender of the demand for civil and political equality; the conservatives, as a generously conceived working basis for mutual understanding. So both approved it, and to-day its author is certainly the most distinguished Southerner since Jefferson Davis, and the one with the largest personal following. Next to this achievement comes Mr. Washington's work in gaining place and consideration in the North. Others less shrewd and tactful had formerly essayed to sit on these two stools and had fallen between them; but as Mr. Washington knew the heart of the South from birth and training, so by singular insight he intuitively grasped the spirit of the age which was dominating the North. And so thoroughly did he learn the speech and thought of triumphant commercialism, and the ideals of material prosperity, that the picture of a lone black boy poring over a French grammar amid the weeds and dirt of a neglected home soon seemed to him the acme of absurdities. One wonders what Socrates and St. Francis of Assisi would say to this.

And yet this very singleness of vision and thorough oneness with his age is a mark of the successful man. It is as though Nature must needs make men narrow in order to give them force. So Mr. Washington's cult has gained unquestioning followers, his work has wonderfully prospered, his friends are legion, and his enemies are confounded. To-day he stands as the one recognized spokesman of his ten million fellows, and one of the most notable figures in a nation of seventy millions. One hesitates, therefore, to criticise a life which, beginning with so little, has done so much. And yet the time is come when one may speak in all sincerity and utter courtesy of the mistakes and shortcomings of Mr. Washington's career, as well as of his triumphs, without being thought captious or envious, and without forgetting that it is easier to do ill than well in the world.

The criticism that has hitherto met Mr. Washington has not always been of this broad character. In the South especially has he had to walk warily to avoid the harshest judgments,—and naturally so, for he is dealing with the one subject of deepest sensitiveness to that section. Twice—once when at the Chicago celebration of the Spanish-American War he alluded to the color-prejudice that is "eating away the vitals of the South," and once when he dined with President Roosevelt—has the resulting Southern criticism been violent enough to threaten seriously his popularity. In the North the feeling has several times forced itself into words, that Mr. Washington's counsels of submission overlooked certain elements of true manhood, and that his educational programme was unnecessarily narrow. Usually, however, such criticism has not found open expression, although, too, the spiritual sons of the Abolitionists have not been prepared to acknowledge that the schools founded before Tuskegee, by men of broad ideals and self-sacrificing spirit, were wholly failures or worthy of ridicule. While, then, criticism has not failed to follow Mr. Washington, yet the prevailing public opinion of the land has been but too willing to deliver the solution of a wearisome problem into his hands, and say, "If that is all you and your race ask, take it."

Among his own people, however, Mr. Washington has encountered the strongest and most lasting opposition, amounting at times to bitterness, and even today continuing strong and insistent even though largely silenced in outward expression by the public opinion of the nation. Some of this opposition is, of course, mere envy; the disappointment of displaced demagogues and the spite of narrow minds. But aside from this, there is among educated and thoughtful colored men in all parts of the land a feeling of deep regret, sorrow, and apprehension at the wide currency and ascendancy which some of Mr. Washington's theories have gained. These same men admire his sincerity of purpose, and are willing to forgive much to honest endeavor which is doing something worth the doing. They cooperate with Mr. Washington as far as they conscientiously can; and, indeed, it is no ordinary tribute to this man's tact and power that, steering as he must between so many diverse interests and opinions, he so largely retains the respect of all.

But the hushing of the criticism of honest opponents is a dangerous thing. It leads some of the best of the critics to unfortunate silence and paralysis of effort, and others to burst into speech so passionately and intemperately as to lose listeners. Honest and earnest criticism from those whose interests are most nearly touched,—criticism of writers by readers,—this is the soul of democracy and the safeguard of modern society. If the best of the American Negroes receive by outer pressure a leader whom they had not recognized before, manifestly there is here a certain palpable gain. Yet there is also irreparable loss,—a loss of that peculiarly valuable education which a group receives when by search and criticism it finds and commissions its own leaders. The way in which this is done is at once the most elementary and the nicest problem of social growth. History is but the record of such group-leadership; and yet how infinitely changeful is its type and character! And of all types and kinds, what can be more instructive than the leadership of a group within a group?—that curious double movement where real progress may be negative and actual advance be relative retrogression. All this is the social student's inspiration and despair.

Now in the past the American Negro has had instructive experience in the choosing of group leaders, founding thus a peculiar dynasty which in the light of present conditions is worth while studying. When sticks and stones and beasts form the sole environment of a people, their attitude is largely one of determined opposition to and conquest of natural forces. But when to earth and brute is added an environment of men and ideas, then the attitude of the imprisoned group may take three main forms,—a feeling of revolt and revenge; an attempt to adjust all thought and action to the will of the greater group; or, finally, a determined effort at self-realization and self-development despite environing opinion. The influence of all of these attitudes at various times can be traced in the history of the American Negro, and in the evolution of his successive leaders.

Before 1750, while the fire of African freedom still burned in the veins of the slaves, there was in all leadership or attempted leadership but the one motive of revolt and revenge,—typified in the terrible Maroons, the Danish blacks, and Cato of Stono, and veiling all the Americas in fear of insurrection. The liberalizing tendencies of the latter half of the eighteenth century brought, along with kindlier relations between black and white, thoughts of ultimate adjustment and assimilation. Such aspiration was especially voiced in the earnest songs of Phyllis, in the martyrdom of

Attucks, the fighting of Salem and Poor, the intellectual accomplishments of Banneker and Derham, and the political demands of the Cuffes.

Stern financial and social stress after the war cooled much of the previous humanitarian ardor. The disappointment and impatience of the Negroes at the persistence of slavery and serfdom voiced itself in two movements. The slaves in the South, aroused undoubtedly by vague rumors of the Haytian revolt, made three fierce attempts at insurrection,—in 1800 under Gabriel in Virginia, in 1822 under Vesey in Carolina, and in 1831 again in Virginia under the terrible Nat Turner. In the Free States, on the other hand, a new and curious attempt at self-development was made. In Philadelphia and New York color-prescription led to a withdrawal of Negro communicants from white churches and the formation of a peculiar socio-religious institution among the Negroes known as the African Church,—an organization still living and controlling in its various branches over a million of men. Walker's wild appeal against the trend of the times showed how the world was changing after the coming of the cotton-gin. By 1830 slavery seemed hopelessly fastened on the South, and the slaves thoroughly cowed into submission. The free Negroes of the North, inspired by the mulatto immigrants from the West Indies, began to change the basis of their demands; they recognized the slavery of slaves, but insisted that they themselves were freemen, and sought assimilation and amalgamation with the nation on the same terms with other men. Thus, Forten and Purvis of Philadelphia, Shad of Wilmington, Du Bois of New Haven, Barbadoes of Boston, and others, strove singly and together as men, they said, not as slaves; as "people of color," not as "Negroes." The trend of the times, however, refused them recognition save in individual and exceptional cases, considered them as one with all the despised blacks, and they soon found themselves striving to keep even the rights they formerly had of voting and working and moving as freemen. Schemes of migration and colonization arose among them; but these they refused to entertain, and they eventually turned to the Abolition movement as a final refuge.

Here, led by Remond, Nell, Wells-Brown, and Douglass, a new period of self-assertion and self-development dawned. To be sure, ultimate freedom and assimilation was the ideal before the leaders, but the assertion of the manhood rights of the Negro by himself was the main reliance, and John Brown's raid was the extreme of its logic. After the war and emancipation, the great form of Frederick Douglass, the greatest of American Negro leaders, still led the host. Self-assertion, especially in political lines, was the main programme, and behind Douglass came Elliot, Bruce, and Langston, and the Reconstruction politicians, and, less conspicuous but of greater social significance, Alexander Crummell and Bishop Daniel Payne.

Then came the Revolution of 1876, the suppression of the Negro votes, the changing and shifting of ideals, and the seeking of new lights in the great night. Douglass, in his old age, still bravely stood for the ideals of his early manhood,—ultimate assimilation through self-assertion, and on no other terms. For a time Price arose as a new leader, destined, it seemed, not to give up, but to re-state the old ideals in a form less repugnant to the white South. But he passed away in his prime. Then came the new leader. Nearly all the former ones had become leaders by the silent suffrage of their fellows, had sought to lead their own people alone, and were usually, save Douglass, little known outside their race. But Booker T. Washington arose as essentially the leader not of one race but of two,—a compromiser between the South, the North, and the Negro. Naturally the Negroes resented, at first bitterly, signs of compromise which surrendered their civil and political rights, even though this was to be exchanged for larger chances of economic development. The rich and dominating North, however, was not only weary of the race problem, but was investing largely in Southern enterprises, and welcomed any method of peaceful cooperation. Thus, by national opinion, the Negroes began to recognize Mr. Washington's leadership; and the voice of criticism was hushed.

Mr. Washington represents in Negro thought the old attitude of adjustment and submission; but adjustment at such a peculiar time as to make his programme unique. This is an age of unusual economic development, and Mr. Washington's programme naturally takes an economic cast, becoming a gospel of Work and Money to such an extent as apparently almost completely to overshadow the higher aims of life. Moreover, this is an age when the more advanced races are coming in closer contact with the less developed races, and the race-feeling is therefore intensified; and Mr. Washington's programme practically accepts the alleged inferiority of the Negro races. Again, in our own land, the reaction from the sentiment of war time has given impetus to race-prejudice against Negroes, and Mr. Washington withdraws many of the high demands of Negroes as men and American citizens. In other periods of intensified prejudice all the Negro's tendency to self-assertion has been called forth; at this period

a policy of submission is advocated. In the history of nearly all other races and peoples the doctrine preached at such crises has been that manly self-respect is worth more than lands and houses, and that a people who voluntarily surrender such respect, or cease striving for it, are not worth civilizing. In answer to this, it has been claimed that the Negro can survive only through submission. Mr. Washington distinctly asks that black people give up, at least for the present, three things,—

First, political power,

Second, insistence on civil rights,

Third, higher education of Negro youth,—

and concentrate all their energies on industrial education, and accumulation of wealth, and the conciliation of the South.

This policy has been courageously and insistently advocated for over fifteen years, and has been triumphant for perhaps ten years. As a result of this tender of the palm-branch, what has been the return? In these years there have occurred:

1. The disfranchisement of the Negro.
2. The legal creation of a distinct status of civil inferiority for the Negro.
3. The steady withdrawal of aid from institutions for the higher training of the Negro.

These movements are not, to be sure, direct results of Mr. Washington's teachings; but his propaganda has, without a shadow of doubt, helped their speedier accomplishment. The question then comes: Is it possible, and probable, that nine millions of men can make effective progress in economic lines if they are deprived of political rights, made a servile caste, and allowed only the most meagre chance for developing their exceptional men? If history and reason give any distinct answer to these questions, it is an emphatic NO. And Mr. Washington thus faces the triple paradox of his career:

1. He is striving nobly to make Negro artisans business men and property-owners; but it is utterly impossible, under modern competitive methods, for workingmen and property-owners to defend their rights and exist without the right of suffrage.
2. He insists on thrift and self-respect, but at the same time counsels a silent submission to civic inferiority such as is bound to sap the manhood of any race in the long run.
3. He advocates common-school and industrial training, and depreciates institutions of higher

learning; but neither the Negro common-schools, nor Tuskegee itself, could remain open a day were it not for teachers trained in Negro colleges, or trained by their graduates.

This triple paradox in Mr. Washington's position is the object of criticism by two classes of colored Americans. One class is spiritually descended from Toussaint the Savior, through Gabriel, Vesey, and Turner, and they represent the attitude of revolt and revenge; they hate the white South blindly and distrust the white race generally, and so far as they agree on definite action, think that the Negro's only hope lies in emigration beyond the borders of the United States. And yet, by the irony of fate, nothing has more effectually made this programme seem hopeless than the recent course of the United States toward weaker and darker peoples in the West Indies, Hawaii, and the Philippines,—for where in the world may we go and be safe from lying and brute force?

The other class of Negroes who cannot agree with Mr. Washington has hitherto said little aloud. They deprecate the sight of scattered counsels, of internal disagreement; and especially they dislike making their just criticism of a useful and earnest man an excuse for a general discharge of venom from small-minded opponents. Nevertheless, the questions involved are so fundamental and serious that it is difficult to see how men like the Grimkes, Kelly Miller, J. W. E. Bowen, and other representatives of this group, can much longer be silent. Such men feel in conscience bound to ask of this nation three things:

1. The right to vote.
2. Civic equality.
3. The education of youth according to ability.

They acknowledge Mr. Washington's invaluable service in counselling patience and courtesy in such demands; they do not ask that ignorant black men vote when ignorant whites are debarred, or that any reasonable restrictions in the suffrage should not be applied; they know that the low social level of the mass of the race is responsible for much discrimination against it, but they also know, and the nation knows, that relentless color-prejudice is more often a cause than a result of the Negro's degradation; they seek the abatement of this relic of barbarism, and not its systematic encouragement and pampering by all agencies of social power from the Associated Press to the Church of Christ. They advocate, with Mr. Washington, a broad system of Negro common schools supplemented by thorough industrial training; but they are surprised that a man of Mr. Washington's insight cannot see that no such educational system ever has rested or can rest on any other basis than that of the well-equipped college and university, and they insist that there is a demand for a few such institutions throughout the South to train the best of the Negro youth as teachers, professional men, and leaders.

This group of men honor Mr. Washington for his attitude of conciliation toward the white South; they accept the "Atlanta Compromise" in its broadest interpretation; they recognize, with him, many signs of promise, many men of high purpose and fair judgment, in this section; they know that no easy task has been laid upon a region already tottering under heavy burdens. But, nevertheless, they insist that the way to truth and right lies in straightforward honesty, not in indiscriminate flattery; in praising those of the South who do well and criticising uncompromisingly those who do ill; in taking advantage of the opportunities at hand and urging their fellows to do the same, but at the same time in remembering that only a firm adherence to their higher ideals and aspirations will ever keep those ideals within the realm of possibility.

They do not expect that the free right to vote, to enjoy civic rights, and to be educated, will come in a moment; they do not expect to see the bias and prejudices of years disappear at the blast of a trumpet; but they are absolutely certain that the way for a people to gain their reasonable rights is not by voluntarily throwing them away and insisting that they do not want them; that the way for a people to gain respect is not by continually belittling and ridiculing themselves; that, on the contrary, Negroes must insist continually, in season and out of season, that voting is necessary to modern manhood, that color discrimination is barbarism, and that black boys need education as well as white boys.

In failing thus to state plainly and unequivocally the legitimate demands of their people, even at the cost of opposing an honored leader, the thinking classes of American Negroes would shirk a heavy responsibility,—a responsibility to themselves, a responsibility to the struggling masses, a responsibility to the darker races of men whose future depends so largely on this American experiment, but especially a responsibility to this nation,—this common Fatherland. It is wrong to encourage a man or a people in evil-doing; it is wrong to aid and abet a national crime simply because it is unpopular not to do so. The growing spirit of kindliness and reconciliation between the North and South after the frightful difference of a generation ago ought to be a source of deep congratulation to all, and especially to those whose mistreatment caused the war; but if that reconciliation is to be marked by the industrial slavery and civic death of those same black men, with permanent legislation into a position of inferiority, then those black men, if they are really men, are called upon by every consideration of patriotism and loyalty to oppose such a course by all civilized methods, even though such opposition involves disagreement with Mr. Booker T. Washington. We have no right to sit silently by while the inevitable seeds are sown for a harvest of disaster to our children, black and white.

First, it is the duty of black men to judge the South discriminatingly. The present generation of Southerners are not responsible for the past, and they should not be blindly hated or blamed for it. Furthermore, to no class is the indiscriminate endorsement of the recent course of the South toward Negroes more nauseating than to the best thought of the South. The South is not "solid"; it is a land in the ferment of social change, wherein forces of all kinds are fighting for supremacy; and to praise the ill the South is today perpetrating is just as wrong as to condemn the good.

Discriminating and broad-minded criticism is what the South needs,—needs it for the sake of her own white sons and daughters, and for the insurance of robust, healthy mental and moral development. Today even the attitude of the Southern whites toward the blacks is not, as so many assume, in all cases the same; the ignorant Southerner hates the Negro, the workingmen fear his competition, the money-makers wish to use him as a laborer, some of the educated see a menace in his upward development, while others—usually the sons of the masters—wish to help him to rise. National opinion has enabled this last class to maintain the Negro common schools, and to protect the Negro partially in property, life, and limb. Through the pressure of the money-makers, the Negro is in danger of being reduced to semi-slavery, especially in the country districts; the workingmen, and those of the educated who fear the Negro, have united to disfranchise him, and some have urged his deportation; while the passions of the ignorant are easily aroused to lynch and abuse any black man. To praise this intricate whirl of thought and prejudice is nonsense; to inveigh indiscriminately against "the South" is unjust; but to use the same breath in praising Governor Aycock, exposing Senator Morgan, arguing with Mr. Thomas Nelson Page, and denouncing Senator Ben Tillman, is not only sane, but the imperative duty of thinking black men.

It would be unjust to Mr. Washington not to acknowledge that in several instances he has opposed movements in the South which were unjust to the Negro; he sent memorials to the Louisiana and Alabama constitutional conventions, he has spoken against lynching, and in other ways has openly or silently set his influence against sinister schemes and unfortunate happenings. Notwithstanding this, it is equally true to assert that on the whole the distinct impression left by Mr. Washington's propaganda is, first, that the South is justified in its present attitude toward the Negro because of the Negro's degradation; secondly, that the prime cause of the Negro's failure to rise more quickly is his wrong education in the past; and, thirdly, that his future rise depends primarily on his own efforts. Each of these propositions is a dangerous half-truth.

The supplementary truths must never be lost sight of: first, slavery and race-prejudice are potent if not sufficient causes of the Negro's position; second, industrial and common school training were necessarily slow in planting because they had to await the black teachers trained by higher institutions,—it being extremely doubtful if any essentially different development was possible, and certainly a Tuskegee was unthinkable before 1880; and, third, while it is a great truth to say that the Negro must strive and strive mightily to help himself, it is equally true that unless his striving be not simply seconded, but rather aroused and encouraged, by the initiative of the richer and wiser environing group, he cannot hope for great success.

In his failure to realize and impress this last point, Mr. Washington is especially to be criticised. His doctrine has tended to make the whites, North and South, shift the burden of the Negro problem to the Negro's shoulders and stand aside as critical and rather pessimistic spectators; when in fact the burden belongs to the nation, and the hands of none of us are clean if we bend not our energies to righting these great wrongs.

The South ought to be led, by candid and honest criticism, to assert her better self and do her full duty to the race she has cruelly wronged and is still wronging. The North—her co-partner in guilt—cannot salve her conscience by plastering it with gold. We cannot settle this problem by diplomacy and suaveness, by "policy" alone. If worse come to worst, can the moral fibre of this country survive the slow throttling and murder of nine millions of men?

The black men of America have a duty to perform, a duty stern and delicate,—a forward movement to oppose a part of the work of their greatest leader. So far as Mr. Washington preaches Thrift, Patience, and Industrial Training for the masses, we must hold up his hands and strive with him, rejoicing in his honors and glorying in the strength of this Joshua called of God and of man to lead the headless host. But so far as Mr. Washington apologizes for injustice, North or South, does not rightly value the privilege and duty of voting, belittles the emasculating effects of caste distinctions, and opposes the higher training and ambition of our brighter minds,—so far as he, the South, or the Nation, does this,—we must unceasingly and firmly oppose them. By every civilized and peaceful method we must strive for the rights which the world accords to men, clinging unwaveringly to those great words which the sons of the Fathers would fain forget: "We hold these truths to be self-evident: That all men are created equal; that they are endowed by their Creator with certain unalienable rights; that among these are life, liberty, and the pursuit of happiness."

CHAPTER 4

Randolph Bourne Transcends the "Melting-Pot" Idea

"The failure of the melting-pot, far from closing the great American democratic experiment, means that it has only just begun."

Between 1880 and 1929, some twenty-three million immigrants, mostly from eastern and southern Europe, came to the United States.[1] Pulled by job opportunities in American industry and pushed by economic stagnation and ethno-religious prejudice at home, they created a new America by the sheer weight of their numbers. The United States had been founded largely by Protestants of British descent. They made up the nation's ruling caste throughout the nineteenth century, dominating politics, business, the military, and the professions. But the Catholics and Jews who poured into the country during the latter part of that century and into the twentieth posed a challenge to that dominance. By 1915, most American cities were governed by "machines" that drew their power from Catholic, and sometimes Jewish, votes. Non-Protestants were beginning to wield significant economic power as well, both as entrepreneurs and consumers.

But it was in the area of culture—"American" culture—that the newcomers loomed largest. Could a man or a woman who was not a Protestant and not descended from British stock truly be "American"? Was the definition of an "American" inherently linked to Protestantism and Britishness? Would "America" lose its meaning if white Anglo-Saxon Protestants no longer constituted a majority of its population or ceased to control its institutions? By 1915, many old-stock American Protestants were asking these questions with special urgency, because the outbreak of World War I in Europe, and the likelihood that the United States would soon enter the conflict, made "preparedness" of the essence. A prepared nation was a united nation, with a united culture. But many Protestants believed that the new immigrants to the United States could not conform to such a culture. Many seemed inordinately attached to their countries of origin, maintaining their "old" customs, speaking their "old" languages, and even returning "home" periodically on sojourns financed with money earned in America. How, native-born Protestants wondered, could such people be considered "Americans"? And with war looming, how could their loyalty to their adopted country be trusted?

In 1908, a play entitled "The Melting Pot," written by a Jewish immigrant, had opened in New York. The title struck a chord with audiences and soon became part of the national lexicon. The idea of the "melting pot" appeared to offer a solution to the immigrant dilemma. If those from foreign lands could have their cultures, languages, and identities "melted down" into an Americanism that approximated white Protestantism, perhaps the nation's fractures could be healed. But the immigrants first needed to show they wanted to be "American," and to do so, they would need to give up their own cultures, languages, and identities. The ominous alternative, in the words of President Theodore Roosevelt, a strong proponent of the melting-pot idea, was "race suicide," in which an unassimilated immigrant population would overwhelm the native born and destroy "American" culture.[2] By the middle of the century's second decade, the United States seemed to be careening toward the precipice of cultural dissolution, a fragmented society without a core. Even as it prepared to confront enemies an ocean away, it seemed to many old-stock Protestants that the real threat to America's existence came from within.

But one American viewed the nation's identity catharsis not as a crisis but as an opportunity. Randolph Bourne had the sympathy for and understanding of the "outsider" that could only come from being one himself. He was born in 1886 in Bloomfield, New Jersey, a small town a few miles from New York City geographically, but separated from it by a vast gulf of worldliness and sophistication. Complications at birth left his face hideously misshapen, and attack of spinal tuberculosis when he was four rendered him a hunchback. He never grew over five feet tall. Bourne's alcoholic father dropped out of his life early on, and he was raised by his mother and a series of extended relations in an atmosphere of genteel poverty. Without funds after high school, he found work producing music rolls for player pianos in his hometown, dreaming of escape to the great city just across the river. His chance came in 1909, when he passed a scholarship examination and entered Columbia University as a twenty-three-year-old freshman. A voracious reader and brilliant conversationalist, Bourne quickly caught the eye of his professors, and even before his graduation in 1913 was producing reviews and criticism for national magazines.

At Columbia and in the city outside its gates, Bourne encountered an intoxicating array of peoples, languages, religions, and cultures. Many were exactly those that old-stock Protestants found so threatening. But Bourne, despite his own Anglo-Saxon background, viewed them differently. To him, they represented not the "end" of America, but its rebirth. Bourne began to believe that white Anglo-Saxon Protestants were holding the nation back. For too long, the United States had been gripped by a traditionalism that prevented it from finding its own voice. What old-stock Protestants called "American" was no more than a warmed-over version of British culture transplanted to new soil. American standards in literature, music, art, and architecture all came from across the Atlantic. Americans dismissed their own cultural products as inferior, second-rate. But Bourne sensed that the immigrant voices of New York and other large cities were authentically "American." The "real" America could be found in the streets—a youthful, urban, modern people looking not inward and to the past, but outward and to the future. The immigrants so loathed by the Protestant elites would not ruin America, but save it.

In 1914, fresh out of Columbia, Bourne became a contributor to a newly founded journal of ideas called *The New Republic*. The magazine was an apt vehicle for his developing sensibilities. Its editor, Herbert Croly, had written the founding text of modern American liberalism, *The Promise of American Life*, in 1909. In it, he argued for the acceptance of individuals "as they were" in an open, tolerant society that featured an expanded, activist federal government devoted to the interests of the weak and disadvantaged. Croly combined this concern for "the people"—including immigrants—with a faith in the power of the national state to make political and economic life more equal and fair. Croly intended *The New Republic* to be the medium for his liberal vision, and he hired some of the best young writers in the country, including Bourne, to bring it forth.

Bourne used the pages of the magazine over the next two years to articulate his developing view of American culture. He began to think beyond the idea of the melting pot, and beyond even the idea of what was known as "pluralism"—where immigrants would be accepted in the United States, but only through their group identity—to a more open and flexible formulation he called "cosmopolitanism." A cosmopolitan society would permit Americans, native-born and immigrant alike, to decide in their own way and on their own terms how they wished to "be" American. They could, if they so desired, leave their ethnic, religious, or racial affiliations behind, and identify instead with the nation and world. Alternatively, they could celebrate those inherited affiliations and define themselves primarily through them. They could even maintain attachments to their "old" countries by holding dual citizenships. Americans could thus be as "American" as they wished to be.

Bourne's cosmopolitanism surpassed even Du Bois' vision in its inclusiveness. In *The Souls of Black Folk*, Du Bois called for an America in which blacks could be both "Negroes" and "Americans" simultaneously, but still demanded that they retain a distinct racial identity. He argued that blacks were an essential part of the American pluralist experiment, but insisted on viewing them as a discrete group. Bourne took Du Bois' analysis a step further: Cosmopolitans were above all individuals and could negotiate their own societal positions free from any preconceived ideas as to how one with a particular ethnic, religious, or racial heritage "should" act. Would this rob the United States of a common culture, a civic "glue" to hold its people together? Would it mean that "America" was amorphous, adrift? Not at all, responded Bourne. The nation would still have a culture, but one that reflected the realities of a modern world. Thanks to the influence of immigrants, a dynamic and diverse "American" culture would open out to that world. While others despaired, Bourne looked confidently to America's cosmopolitan future.

By 1916, as the United States edged closer to entering World War I, Bourne was ready to articulate his idea of cosmopolitanism to a broad reading audience. The venue he chose, *The Atlantic Monthly*, was among the most prestigious and influential periodicals in the country, with a circulation that far outstripped that of *The New Republic*. Bourne published "Trans-national America" in *The Atlantic Monthly* in July 1916 despite the misgivings of its editor, Ellery Sedgwick. An old-stock Protestant "blue-blood," Sedgwick was uncomfortable with the essay's implications for his own social and economic class. He had good reason to be concerned. In "Trans-national America," Bourne launched an assault on the power and position of white Anglo-Saxon Protestants in national life and on their use of the melting-pot idea as an instrument of control. "American" culture, as old-stock Protestants defined it, was not "American" at all, but British. Bourne argued that Protestant elites had imposed a foreign Anglo-Saxonism on the nation, falsely labeling it "American." To make matters worse, they had spent the years since independence imitating the British in literature, art, music, and philosophy, instead of mining the cultural treasures of their own land for inspiration. And British culture, in Bourne's view, was stagnant, static, and insular.

But America could instead make use of the opportunities for the "cross-fertilization" of peoples and cultures that cosmopolitanism offered to reinvent the United States as "the first international nation."[3] The United States, Bourne maintained, "shall be what the immigrant shall have a hand in making it, and not what a ruling class, descendants of those British stocks which were the first permanent immigrants, decide that America shall be made."[4] The immigrant was essential "to save us from our own stagnation."[5] Tellingly, the most "British" region in the United States and the one most unaffected by immigrants was the South, and it was also the most "sterile" and backward, "having progressed scarcely beyond the early Victorian era."[6] While most native-born Protestants like Ellery Sedgwick feared that immigrants would not assimilate, Bourne feared on the other hand that they would, and that they were thus doomed to be "melted down into the indistinguishable dough of

Anglo-Saxonism."[7] Bourne envisioned instead "a cosmopolitan federation of national colonies, of foreign cultures" taking root in the United States, "from which the sting of devastating competition has been removed."[8] Across the Atlantic on the battlefields of Europe these cultures were intent on destroying each other, but in America they could not only coexist but form the world's first global society.

The cosmopolitan, Bourne wrote, "breathes a larger air."[9] What the cosmopolitan American would lose in cultural coherence—and Bourne conceded that "there is no distinctively American culture"—he would gain in becoming a "citizen of a larger world."[10] The United States, he predicted, "is coming to be, not a nationality but a transnationality, a weaving back and forth, with the other lands, of many threads of all sizes and colors."[11]

Bourne thus rejected the idea, put forth by proponents of the "melting pot," that Americans needed a commonly accepted culture to survive as a people. A transnational, cosmopolitan culture could offer an example to a world filled with petty prejudices. It could become the one place on earth where the chauvinisms of religion, ethnicity, and race did not hold sway. Trans-national America might not possess a definable core of, say, "Frenchness" or "Germanness," or for that matter, "Britishness," but it would not smash itself to pieces, as France, Germany, and Great Britain were then doing, in a futile attempt to impose its will on others. The United States, a global nation, would escape this fate. Instead, its "distinct but cooperating" cultures would ground a "Beloved Community," the most open and dynamic society the world had yet known.[12]

"Trans-national America" appalled Ellery Sedgwick. The editor could not understand how his young protégé could be so dismissive of the gifts of British culture. In Sedgwick's view, the qualities that made America unique—representative democracy, constitutional government, free enterprise—were all British in origin. The philosophy of "Trans-national America," if adopted, would cut the United States away from its unique heritage. Sedgwick believed that immigrants were an economic necessity as a source of cheap industrial labor. Their cultures deserved to be tolerated, but no more than this. To argue, as Bourne did, that these alien ways were somehow the basis of a new, rejuvenated American society was, from Sedgwick's Anglophilic perspective, akin to blasphemy. He did not publish Bourne's work again. At one time, Sedgwick had been convinced that this young Columbia graduate would be America's next great social critic; he now kept his distance. The two never reconciled.

Trouble was also brewing for Bourne at *The New Republic*. America's entry into World War I in April 1917 poisoned his relationships with the editors and writers at the magazine. Bourne had assumed that his *New Republic* colleagues would endorse his position that the war was incompatible with liberalism. He believed that they would understand that it ensnared the United States in the same web of blind nationalisms that were destroying Europe and that it was at odds with the cosmopolitan vision of an open and inclusive American society. But Bourne was mistaken. Most of the *New Republic* staff supported the war. They viewed it as a battle between democratic values, which they associated with Great Britain and France, and German autocracy. Nor were they immune from the temptations of jingoist nationalism. Like many European liberals and socialists, when their country went to war, they followed their flag. There was no room in their understanding of America's war mission for the coexistent cultures of Bourne's cosmopolitanism.

As Bourne criticized the war with more and more vehemence—protesting the "100% Americanism" campaigns, curtailments of civil liberties, and persecution of immigrants that were its byproducts—he became more and more estranged from the *New Republic*. By 1918 his work rarely appeared in the magazine. His outlets now were small-circulation antiwar journals watched closely by government officials seeking to ferret out seditious material; indeed, Bourne was being watched that summer by federal agents. Shunned by former friends, scrambling to make ends meet, he was at a dead end.

World War I killed Bourne's career as a writer, and tragically, it also killed him. A massive influenza epidemic swept through Europe in 1918, exacerbated by the fighting. By the fall, it had traveled with returning American soldiers across the Atlantic and begun to devastate the United States. Eventually, it would take 500,000 American lives, about ten times the number of soldiers the nation lost during the war itself.[13] Randolph Bourne's life was among them. Stricken in December 1918, just after the Armistice, his fragile constitution was no match for the spreading disease. He died in New York a few days before Christmas, at the age of 32.

Bourne's premature death left many unanswered questions. One of them concerned the place of African Americans in his cosmopolitan vision. Bourne spent most of his life thinking and writing about white immigrants and rarely touched on matters of race, but after a 1916 visit to Hampton Institute—Booker T. Washington's alma mater—he vowed to "unburden" himself on this subject in the future.[14] The influenza epidemic denied him that opportunity. It is possible that Bourne would not have been able to understand the unique position of African Americans in national life. He might have adopted the superficial perspective of many of his contemporaries, viewing race as simply another form of ethnic difference, and offering facile comparisons between blacks and white immigrants. But it is more likely that his nuanced mind would have grasped the special difficulties faced by African Americans in realizing W.E.B. Du Bois's hope of a nation in which it was "possible for a man to be both a Negro and an American."[15] Bourne would probably have understood that winning African Americans their place in a cosmopolitan national culture would require a sea change in the racial attitudes of white Americans, one that might be generations in the making.

Randolph Bourne's short life cast long shadows. He was at heart an optimist about America, believing deeply in its promise and possibility. He dreamed of a nation in which a man like Charles Kikuchi, who we will encounter later in this volume, would not be torn between his ethnic ties and allegiance to his country, and even a Malcolm X, another of our future subjects, who barely considered himself part of the American conversation at all, might nonetheless find space to be himself. Bourne's idea of America as a "Beloved Community," which we will see Students for a Democratic Society embrace in the 1960s, was unique in its broad-spiritedness and generosity toward those at the margins. But did Bourne's cosmopolitanism stretch the fabric of American culture too thin, replacing the exclusionary melting pot with a chaotic, antagonistic mix of cultures? Did the United States need a defining cultural core in order to survive? Americans would spend the decades after Bourne's death debating the questions his cosmopolitan vision raised and continue to do so in twenty-first-century arguments over the merits of multiculturalism and diversity. Bourne remains part of every American conversation about who we are and what—if anything—binds us together as a people.

Questions for Consideration and Conversation

1. Why did many Americans, including Theodore Roosevelt, subscribe so enthusiastically to the idea of the "melting pot"? Was there some validity to their argument that America required a unifying "core" culture?

2. Why did Randolph Bourne take such a dim view of Anglo-Saxon Protestant culture? Why did he think it was so harmful to America? Why did he feel that immigrants were more truly "American" than Anglo-Saxon Protestants?

3. How did Bourne's ideas about "American" identity transcend those of the "melting pot," and even those of Du Bois in *The Souls of Black Folk* (Chapter 3)?

4. Did Bourne's "cosmopolitan" ideas pose dangers to American cultural unity? Did they promise only a "chaotic, antagonistic mix of cultures"?

5. How would Charles Kikuchi (Chapter 9) have responded to Bourne's vision of "American" identity? Norman Rockwell (Chapter 10)? Allen Ginsberg (Chapter 12)? Malcolm X (Chapter 18)?

6. Why was World War I such a threat to Bourne's cosmopolitanism?

7. Had he lived, how might Bourne have analyzed the position of African Americans in the United States? Would he have been able to incorporate them into his cosmopolitan national identity?

Endnotes

1. John M. Murrin, et al., *Liberty, Equality, Power: A History of the American People*, 5th ed. (Boston: Thomson Wadsworth, 2008), 604.
2. Theodore Roosevelt, quoted in Bruce Clayton, *Forgotten Prophet: The Life of Randolph Bourne* (Baton Rouge and London: Louisiana State University Press, 1984), 189.
3. Randolph Bourne, "Trans-national America," *The Atlantic Monthly*, 118 (July 1916), 90, 93.
4. Ibid., 87.
5. Ibid.
6. Ibid., 90.
7. Ibid., 95.
8. Ibid., 93.
9. Ibid., 94.
10. Ibid., 91, 94.
11. Ibid., 96.
12. Ibid., 90, 97.
13. Clayton, *Forgotten Prophet*, 256, 257.
14. Randolph Bourne, quoted in Clayton, *Forgotten Prophet*, 200.
15. W. E. B. Du Bois, *The Souls of Black Folk* (New York: Library of America, 1990), 9.

RANDOLPH S. BOURNE, "TRANS-NATIONAL AMERICA" (1916)

Source: Randolph S. Bourne, "Trans-national America." *The Atlantic Monthly*, July 1916, Volume 118, No. 1, pp. 86–97.

No reverberatory effect of the great war has caused American public opinion more solicitude than the failure of the 'melting-pot.' The discovery of diverse nationalistic feelings among our great alien population has come to most people as an intense shock. It has brought out the unpleasant inconsistencies of our traditional beliefs. We have had to watch hard-hearted old Brahmins virtuously indignant at the spectacle of the immigrant refusing to be melted, while they jeer at patriots like Mary Antin who write about 'our forefathers.' We have had to listen to publicists who express themselves as stunned by the evidence of vigorous nationalistic and cultural movements in this country among Germans, Scandinavians, Bohemians, and Poles, while in the same breath they insist that the mien shall be forcibly assimilated to that Anglo-Saxon tradition which they unquestioningly label 'American.'

As the unpleasant truth has come upon us that assimilation in this country was proceeding on lines very different from those we had marked out for it, we found ourselves inclined to blame those who were thwarting our prophecies. The truth became culpable. We blamed the war, we blamed the Germans. And then we discovered with a moral shock that these movements had been making great headway before the war even began. We found that the tendency, reprehensible and paradoxical as it might be, has been for the national clusters of immigrants, as they became more and more firmly established and more and more prosperous, to cultivate more and more assiduously the literatures and cultural traditions of their homelands. Assimilation, in other words, instead of washing out the memories of Europe, made them more and more intensely real. Just as these clusters became more and more objectively

American, did they become more and more German or Scandinavian or Bohemian or Polish.

To face the fact that our aliens are already strong enough to take a share in the direction of their own destiny, and that the strong cultural movements represented by the foreign press, schools, and colonies are a challenge to our facile attempts, is not, however, to admit the failure of Americanization. It is not to fear the failure of democracy. It is rather to urge us to an investigation of what Americanism may rightly mean. It is to ask ourselves whether our ideal has been broad or narrow—whether perhaps the time has not come to assert a higher ideal than the 'melting-pot.' Surely we cannot be certain of our spiritual democracy when, claiming to melt the nations within us to a comprehension of our free and democratic institutions, we fly into panic at the first sign of their own will and tendency. We act as if we wanted Americanization to take place only on our own terms, and not by the consent of the governed. All our elaborate machinery of settlement and school and union, of social and political naturalization, however, will move with friction just in so far as it neglects to take into account this strong and virile insistence that America shall be what the immigrant will have a hand in making it, and not what a ruling class, descendant of those British stocks which were the first permanent immigrants, decide that America shall be made. This is the condition which confronts us, and which demands a clear and general readjustment of our attitude and our ideal.

I

Mary Antin is right when she looks upon our foreign-born as the people who missed the Mayflower and came over on the first boat they could find. But she forgets that when they did come it was not upon other Mayflower but upon a 'Fleur,' a 'Fleur de Mai,' a 'Fleur di Maggio,' a 'Majblomst.' These people were not mere arrivals from the same family, to be welcomed as understood and long-loved but strangers to the neighborhood, with whom a long process of settling down had to take place. For they brought with them their national and racial characters, and each new national quota had to wear slowly away the contempt with which its mere alienness got itself greeted. Each had to make its way slowly from the lowest strata of unskilled labor up to a level where it satisfied the accredited norms of social success.

We are all foreign-born or the descendants of foreign-born, and if distinctions are to be made between us, they should rightly be on some other ground than indigenousness. The early colonists came over with motives no less colonial than the later. They did not come to be assimilated in an American melting pot. They did not come to adopt the culture of the American Indian. They had not the smallest intention of 'giving themselves without reservation' to the new country. They came to get freedom to live as they wanted to. They came to escape from the stifling air and chaos of the old world; they came to make their fortune in a new land. They invented no new social framework. Rather they brought over bodily the old ways to which they had been accustomed. Tightly concentrated on a hostile frontier, they were conservative beyond belief. Their pioneer daring was reserved for the objective conquest of material resources. In their folkways, in their social and political institutions, they were, like every colonial people, slavishly imitative of the mother country. So that, in spite of the 'Revolution,' our whole legal and political system remained more English than the English, petrified and unchanging, while in England law developed to meet the needs of the changing times.

It is just this English-American conservatism that has been our chief obstacle to social advance. We have needed the new peoples—the order of the German and Scandinavian, the turbulence of the Slav and Hun—to save us from our own stagnation. I do not mean that the illiterate Slav is now the equal of the New Englander of pure descent. He is raw material to be educated, not into a New Englander, but into a socialized American along such lines as those thirty nationalities are being educated in the amazing school of Gary. I do not believe that this process is to be one of decades of evolution. The spectacle of Japan's sudden jump from medievalism to post-modernism should have destroyed the superstition. We are not dealing with individuals who are to 'evolve.' We are dealing with their children, who with that education we are about to have, will start level with all of us. Let us cease to think of ideals like democracy as magical qualities inherent in certain peoples. Let us speak, not of inferior races, but of inferior civilizations. We are all to educate and to be educated. These peoples in America are in a common enterprise. It is not what we are now that concerns us, but what this plastic next generation may become in the light of a new cosmopolitan ideal.

We are not dealing with static factors, but with fluid and dynamic generations. To contrast the older and the newer immigrants and see the one class as democratically motivated by love of liberty, and the other by mere money-getting, is not to illuminate the future. To think of earlier nationalities as culturally assimilated to America, while we picture the later as a sodden and resistive mass, makes only for bitterness and misunderstanding. There may be a difference between these earlier and these later stocks, but it lies neither in motive for coming nor in strength of cultural allegiance to the homeland. The truth is that no more tenacious cultural allegiance to the mother country has been shown by any alien nation than by the ruling class of Anglo-Saxon descendants in these American States. English snobberies, English religion, English literary styles, English literary reverences and canons, English ethics, English superiorities, have been the cultural food that we have drunk in from our mothers' breasts. The distinctively American spirit—pioneer, as distinguished from the reminiscently English—that appears in Whitman and Emerson and James, has had to exist on sufferance alongside of this other cult, unconsciously belittled by our cultural makers of opinion. No country has perhaps had so great indigenous genius which had so little influence on the country's traditions and expressions. The unpopular and dreaded German-American of the present day is a beginning amateur in comparison with those foolish Anglophiles of Boston and New York and Philadelphia whose reversion to cultural type sees uncritically in England's cause the cause of Civilization, and, under the guise of ethical independence of thought, carries along European traditions which are no more 'American' than the German categories themselves.

It speaks well for German-American innocence of heart or else for its lack of imagination that it has not turned the hyphen stigma into a 'Tu quoque!' If there were to be any hyphens scattered about, clearly they should be affixed to those English descendants who had had centuries of time to be made American where the German had had only half a century. Most significantly has the war brought out of them this alien virus, showing them still loving English things, owing allegiance to the English Kultur, moved by English shibboleths and prejudice. It is only because it has been the ruling class in this country that bestowed the epithet that we have not heard copiously and scornfully of 'hyphenated English Americans.' But even our quarrels with England have had the bad temper, the extravagance, of family quarrels. The Englishman of to-day nags us and dislikes us in that personal, peculiarly intimate way in which he dislikes the Australian, or as we may dislike our younger brothers. He still thinks of us incorrigibly as 'colonials.' America—official, controlling, literary, political America—is still, as a writer recently expressed it, 'culturally speaking, a self-governing dominion of the British Empire.'

The non-English American can scarcely be blamed if he sometimes thinks of the Anglo-Saxon predominance in America as little more than a predominance of priority. The Anglo-Saxon was merely the first immigrant, the first to found a colony. He has never really ceased to be the descendant of immigrants, nor has he ever succeeded in transforming that colony into a real nation, with a tenacious, richly woven fabric of native culture. Colonials from the other nations have come and settled down beside him. They found no definite native culture which should startle them out of their colonialism, and consequently they looked back to their mother-country, as the earlier Anglo-Saxon immigrant was looking back to his. What has been offered the newcomer has been the chance to learn English, to become a citizen, to salute the flag. And those elements of our ruling classes who are responsible for the public schools, the settlements, all the organizations for amelioration in the cities, have every reason to be proud of the care and labor which they have devoted to absorbing the immigrant. His opportunities the immigrant has taken to gladly, with almost pathetic eagerness to make his way in the new land without friction or disturbance. The common language has made not only for the necessary communication, but for all the amenities of life.

If freedom means the right to do pretty much as one pleases, so long as one does not interfere with others, the immigrant has found freedom, and the ruling element has been singularly liberal in its treatment of the invading hordes. But if freedom means a democratic cooperation in determining the ideals and purposes and industrial and social institutions of a country, then the immigrant has not been free, and Anglo-Saxon element is guilty of just what every dominant race is guilty of in every European country: the imposition of its own culture upon the minority peoples. The fact that this imposition has been so mild and, indeed, semi-conscious does not alter its quality. And the war has brought out just the degree to which that purpose of 'Americanizing,' that is, 'Anglo-Saxonizing,' the immigrant has failed.

For the Anglo-Saxon now in his bitterness to turn upon the other peoples, talk about their 'arrogance,' scold them for not being melted in a pot which never existed, is to betray the unconscious purpose which lay at the bottom of his heart. It betrays too the possession of a racial jealousy similar to that of which he is now accusing the so called 'hyphenates.'

Let the Anglo Saxon be proud enough of the heroic toil and heroic sacrifices which moulded the nation. But let him ask himself, if he had had to depend on the English descendants, where he would have been living to-day. To those of us who see in the exploitation of unskilled labor the strident red *leit-motif* of our civilization, the settling of the country presents a great social drama as the waves of immigration broke over it.

Let the Anglo-Saxon ask himself where he would have been if these races had not come? Let those who feel the inferiority of the non-Anglo-Saxon immigrant contemplate that region of the States which has remained the most distinctively 'American,' the South. Let him ask himself whether he would really like to see the foreign hordes Americanized into such an Americanization. Let him ask himself how superior this native civilization is to the great 'alien' states of Wisconsin and Minnesota, where Scandinavians, Poles, and Germans have self-consciously labored to preserve their traditional culture, while being outwardly and satisfactorily American. Let him ask himself how much more wisdom, intelligence, industry and social leadership has come out of these alien states than out of all the truly American ones. The South, in fact, while this vast Northern development has gone on, still remains an English colony, stagnant and complacent, having progressed culturally scarcely beyond the early Victorian era. It is culturally sterile because it has had no advantage of cross-fertilization like the Northern states. What has happened in states such as Wisconsin and Minnesota is that strong foreign cultures have struck root in a new and fertile soil. America has meant liberation, and German and Scandinavian political ideas and social energies have expanded to a new potency. The process has not been at all the fancied 'assimilation' of the Scandinavian or Teuton. Rather has it been a process of their assimilation of us—I speak as an Anglo-Saxon. The foreign cultures have not been melted down or run together, made into some homogeneous Americanism, but have remained distinct but cooperating to the greater glory and benefit not only of themselves but of all the native 'Americanism' around them.

What we emphatically do not want is that these distinctive qualities should be washed out into a tasteless, colorless fluid of uniformity. Already we have far too much of this insipidity—masses of people who are cultural half-breeds, neither assimilated Anglo-Saxons nor nationals of another culture. Each national colony in this country seems to retain in its foreign press, its vernacular literature, its schools, its intellectual and patriotic leaders, a central cultural nucleus. From this nucleus the colony extends out by imperceptible gradations to a fringe where national characteristics are all but lost. Our cities are filled with these half-breeds who retain their foreign names but have lost the foreign savor. This does not mean that they have actually been changed into New Englanders or Middle Westerners. It does not mean that they have been really Americanized. It means that, letting slip from them whatever native culture they had, they have substituted for it only the most rudimentary American—the American culture of the cheap newspaper, the 'movies,' the popular song, the ubiquitous automobile. The unthinking who survey this class call them assimilated, Americanized. The great American public school has done its work. With these people our institutions are safe. We may thrill with dread at the aggressive hyphenate, but this tame flabbiness is accepted as Americanization. The same moulders of opinion whose ideal is to melt the different races into Anglo-Saxon gold hail this poor product as the satisfying result of their alchemy.

Yet a truer cultural sense would have told us that it is not the self-conscious cultural nuclei that sap at our American life, but these fringes. It is not the Jew who sticks proudly to the faith of his fathers and boasts of that venerable culture of his who is dangerous to America, but the Jew who has lost the Jewish fire and become a mere elementary, grasping animal. It is not the Bohemian who supports the Bohemian schools in Chicago whose influence is sinister, but the Bohemian who has made money and has got into ward politics. Just so surely as we tend to disintegrate these nuclei of nationalistic culture do we tend to create hordes of men and women without a spiritual country, cultural outlaws, without taste, without standards but those of the mob. We sentence them to live on the most rudimentary planes of American life. The influences at the centre of the nuclei are centripetal. They make for the intelligence and the social values which mean an enhancement of life. And just because the foreign-born retains this expressiveness is he likely to be a better citizen of the American community. The influences at the fringe, however, are centrifugal, anarchical. They make for detached fragments of peoples. Those who came to find liberty achieve only license. They become the flotsam and jetsam of American life, the downward undertow of our civilization with its leering cheapness and falseness of taste and spiritual outlook, the absence of mind and sincere feeling which we see in our slovenly towns, our vapid moving pictures, our popular novels, and in the vacuous faces of the crowds on the city street. This is the cultural wreckage of our time, and it is from the fringes of the Anglo-Saxon as well as the other stocks that it falls. America has as yet no impelling integrating force. It makes too easily for this detritus of cultures. In our loose, free country, no constraining national purpose, no tenacious folk-tradition and folk-style hold the people to a line.

The war has shown us that not in any magical formula will this purpose be found. No intense nationalism of the European plan can be ours. But do we not begin to see a new and more adventurous ideal? Do we not see how the national colonies in America, deriving power from the deep cultural heart of Europe and yet living here in mutual toleration, freed from the age-long tangles of races, creeds, and dynasties, may work out a federated ideal? America is transplanted Europe, but a Europe that has not been disintegrated and scattered in the transplanting as in some Dispersion. Its colonies live here inextricably mingled, yet not homogeneous. They merge but they do not fuse.

America is a unique sociological fabric, and it bespeaks poverty of imagination not to be thrilled at the incalculable potentialities of so novel a union of men. To seek no other goal than the weary old nationalism—belligerent, exclusive, inbreeding, the poison of which we are witnessing now in Europe—is to make patriotism a hollow sham, and to declare that, in spite of our boastings, America must ever be a follower and not a leader of nations.

II

If we come to find this point of view plausible, we shall have to give up the search for our native 'American' culture. With the exception of the South and that New England which, like the Red Indian, seems to be passing into solemn oblivion, there is no distinctively American culture. It is apparently our lot rather to be a federation of cultures. This we have been for half a century, and the war has made it ever more evident that this is what we are destined to remain. This will not mean, however, that there are not expressions of indigenous genius that could not have sprung from any other soil. Music, poetry, philosophy, have been singularly fertile and new. Strangely enough, American genius has flared forth just in those directions which are least understood of the people. If the American note is bigness, action, the objective as contrasted with the reflective life, where is the epic expression of this spirit? Our drama and our fiction, the peculiar fields for the expression

of action and objectivity, are somehow exactly the fields of the spirit which remain poor and mediocre. American materialism is in some way inhibited from getting into impressive artistic form its own energy with which it bursts. Nor is it any better in architecture, the least romantic and subjective of all the arts. We are inarticulate of the very values which we profess to idealize. But in the finer forms—music, verse, the essay, philosophy—the American genius puts forth work equal to any of its contemporaries. Just in so far as our American genius has expressed the pioneer spirit, the adventurous, forward-looking drive of a colonial empire, is it representative of that whole America of the many races and peoples, and not of any partial or traditional enthusiasm. And only as that pioneer note is sounded can we really speak of the American culture. As long as we thought of Americanism in terms of the 'melting-pot,' our American cultural tradition lay in the past. It was something to which the new Americans were to be moulded. In the light of our changing ideal of Americanism, we must perpetrate the paradox that our American cultural tradition lies in the future. It will be what we all together make out of this incomparable opportunity of attacking the future with a new key.

Whatever American nationalism turns out to be, it is certain to become something utterly different from the nationalisms of twentieth-century Europe. This wave of reactionary enthusiasm to play the orthodox nationalistic game which is passing over the country is scarcely vital enough to last. We cannot swagger and thrill to the same national self-feeling. We must give new edges to our pride. We must be content to avoid the unnumbered woes that national patriotism has brought in Europe, and that fiercely heightened pride and self-consciousness. Alluring as this is, we must allow our imaginations to transcend this scarcely veiled belligerency. We can be serenely too proud to fight if our pride embraces the creative forces of civilization which armed contest nullifies. We can be too proud to fight if our code of honor transcends that of the schoolboy on the playground surrounded by his jeering mates. Our honor must be positive and creative, and not the mere jealous and negative protectiveness against metaphysical violations of our technical rights. When the doctrine is put forth that in one American flows the mystic blood of all our country's sacred honor, freedom, and prosperity, so that an injury to him is to be the signal for turning our whole nation into that clan-feud of horror and reprisal which would be war, then we find ourselves back among the musty schoolmen of the Middle Ages, and not in any pragmatic and realistic America of the twentieth century.

We should hold our gaze to what America has done, not what medieval codes of dueling she has failed to observe. We have transplanted European modernity to our soil, without the spirit that inflames it and turns all its energy into mutual destruction. Out of these foreign peoples there has somehow been squeezed the poison. An America, 'hyphenated' to bitterness, is somehow non-explosive. For, even if we all hark back in sympathy to a European nation, even if the war has set every one vibrating to some emotional string twanged on the other side of the Atlantic, the effect has been one of almost dramatic harmlessness.

What we have really been witnessing, however unappreciatively, in this country has been a thrilling and bloodless battle of Kulturs. In that arena of friction which has been the most dramatic—between the hyphenated German-American and the hyphenated English-American—there have emerged rivalries of philosophies which show up deep traditional attitudes, points of view which accurately reflect the gigantic issues of the war. America has mirrored the spiritual issues. The vicarious struggle has been played out peacefully here in the mind. We have seen the stout resistiveness of the old moral interpretation of history on which Victorian England thrived and made itself great in its own esteem. The clean and immensely satisfying vision of the war as a contest between right and wrong; the enthusiastic support of the Allies as the incarnation of virtue-on-a-rampage; the fierce envisaging of their selfish national purposes as the ideals of justice, freedom and democracy—all this has been thrown with intensest force against the German realistic interpretations in terms of the struggle for power and the virility of the integrated State. America has been the intellectual battleground of the nations.

III

The failure of the melting-pot, far from closing the great American democratic experiment, means that it has only just begun. Whatever American nationalism turns out to be, we see already that it will have a color richer and more exciting than our ideal has hitherto encompassed. In a world which has dreamed of internationalism, we find that we have all unawares been building up the first international nation. The voices which have cried for a tight and jealous nationalism of the European pattern are failing. From that ideal, however valiantly and disinterestedly it has been set

for us, time and tendency have moved us further and further away. What we have achieved has been rather a cosmopolitan federation of national colonies, of foreign cultures, from whom the sting of devastating competition has been removed. America is already the world-federation in miniature, the continent where for the first time in history has been achieved that miracle of hope, the peaceful living side by side, with character substantially preserved, of the most heterogeneous peoples under the sun. Nowhere else has such contiguity been anything but the breeder of misery. Here, notwithstanding our tragic failures of adjustment, the outlines are already too clear not to give us a new vision and a new orientation of the American mind in the world.

It is for the American of the younger generation to accept this cosmopolitanism, and carry it along with self-conscious and fruitful purpose. In his colleges, he is already getting, with the study of modern history and politics, the modern literatures, economic geography, the privilege of a cosmopolitan outlook such as the people of no other nation of to-day in Europe can possibly secure. If he is still a colonial, he is no longer the colonial of one partial culture, but of many. He is a colonial of the world. Colonialism has grown into cosmopolitanism, and his mother land is no one nation, but all who have anything life-enhancing to offer to the spirit. That vague sympathy which the France of ten years ago was feeling for the world—a sympathy which was drowned in the terrible reality of war— may be the modern American's, and that in a positive and aggressive sense. If the American is parochial, it is in sheer wantonness or cowardice. His provincialism is the measure of his fear of bogies or the defect of his imagination.

Indeed, it is not uncommon for the eager Anglo-Saxon who goes to a vivid American university to-day to find his true friends not among his own race but among the acclimatized German or Austrian, the acclimatized Jew, the acclimatized Scandinavian or Italian. In them he finds the cosmopolitan note. In these youths, foreign-born or the children of foreign-born parents, he is likely to find many of his old inbred morbid problems washed away. These friends are oblivious to the repressions of that tight little society in which he so provincially grew up. He has a pleasurable sense of liberation from the stale and familiar attitudes of those whose ingrowing culture has scarcely created anything vital for his America of to-day. He breathes a larger air. In his new enthusiasms for continental literature, for unplumbed Russian depths, for French clarity of thought, for

Teuton philosophies of power, he feels himself citizen of a larger world. He may be absurdly superficial, his outward-reaching wonder may ignore all the stiller and homelier virtues of his Anglo-Saxon home, but he has at least found the clue to that international mind which will be essential to all men and women of good-will if they are ever to save this Western world of ours from suicide. His new friends have gone through a similar evolution. America has burned most of the baser metal also from them. Meeting now with this common American background, all of them may yet retain that distinctiveness of their native cultures and their national spiritual slants. They are more valuable and interesting to each other for being different, yet that difference could not be creative were it not for this new cosmopolitan outlook which America has given them and which they all equally possess.

A college where such a spirit is possible even to the smallest degree, has within itself already the seeds of this international intellectual world of the future. It suggests that the contribution of America will be an intellectual internationalism which goes far beyond the mere exchange of scientific ideas and discoveries and the cold recording of facts. It will be an intellectual sympathy which is not satisfied until it has got at the heart of the different cultural expressions, and felt as they feel. It may have immense preferences, but it will make understanding and not indignation its end. Such a sympathy will unite and not divide.

Against the thinly disguised panic which calls itself 'patriotism' and the thinly disguised militarism which calls itself 'preparedness' the cosmopolitan ideal is set. This does not mean that those who hold it are for a policy of drift. They, too, long passionately for an integrated and disciplined America. But they do not want one which is integrated only for domestic economic exploitation of the workers or for predatory economic imperialism among the weaker peoples. They do not want one that is integrated by coercion or militarism, or for the truculent assertion of a medieval code of honor and of doubtful rights. They believe that the most effective integration will be one which coordinates the diverse elements and turns them consciously toward working out together the place of America in the world-situation. They demand for integration a genuine integrity, a wholeness and soundness of enthusiasm and purpose which can only come when no national colony within our America feels that it is being discriminated against or that its cultural case is being prejudged. This strength of cooperation, this feeling that all who are here may have a hand in the destiny of America, will

make for a finer spirit of integration than any narrow 'Americanism' or forced chauvinism.

In this effort we may have to accept some form of that dual citizenship which meets with so much articulate horror among us. Dual citizenship we may have to recognize as the rudimentary form of that international citizenship to which, if our words mean anything, we aspire. We have assumed unquestioningly that mere participation in the political life of the United States must cut the new citizen off from all sympathy with his old allegiance. Anything but a bodily transfer of devotion from one sovereignty to another has been viewed as a sort of moral treason against the Republic. We have insisted that the immigrant whom we welcomed escaping from the very exclusive nationalism of his European home shall forthwith adopt a nationalism just as exclusive, just as narrow, and even less legitimate because it is founded on no warm traditions of his own. Yet a nation like France is said to permit a formal and legal dual citizenship even at the present time. Though a citizen of hers may pretend to cast off his allegiance in favor of some other sovereignty, he is still subject to her laws when he returns. Once a citizen, always a citizen, no matter how many new citizenships he may embrace. And such a dual citizenship seems to us sound and right. For it recognizes that, although the Frenchman may accept the formal institutional framework of his new country and indeed become intensely loyal to it, yet his Frenchness he will never lose. What makes up the fabric of his soul will always be of this Frenchness, so that unless he becomes utterly degenerate he will always to some degree dwell still in his native environment.

Indeed, does not the cultivated American who goes to Europe practice a dual citizenship, which, if not formal, is no less real? The American who lives abroad may be the least expatriate of men. If he falls in love with French ways and French thinking and French democracy and seeks to saturate himself with the new spirit, he is guilty of at least a dual spiritual citizenship. He may be still American, yet he feels himself through sympathy also a Frenchman. And he finds that this expansion involves no shameful conflict within him, no surrender of his native attitude. He has rather for the first time caught a glimpse of the cosmopolitan spirit. And after wandering about through many races and civilizations he may return to America to find them all here living vividly and crudely, seeking the same adjustment that he made. He sees the new peoples here with a new vision. They are no longer masses of aliens, waiting to be 'assimilated,' waiting to be melted down into the indistinguishable dough of Anglo-Saxonism. They are rather threads of living and potent cultures, blindly striving to weave themselves into a novel international nation, the first the world has seen. In an Austria-Hungary or a Prussia the stronger of these cultures would be moving almost instinctively to subjugate the weaker. But in America those wills-to-power are turned in a different direction into learning how to live together.

Along with dual citizenship we shall have to accept, I think, that free and mobile passage of the immigrant between America and his native land again which now arouses so much prejudice among us. We shall have to accept the immigrant's return for the same reason that we consider justified our own flitting about the earth. To stigmatize the alien who works in America for a few years and returns to his own land, only perhaps to seek American fortune again, is to think in narrow nationalistic terms. It is to ignore the cosmopolitan significance of this migration. It is to ignore the fact that the returning immigrant is often a missionary to an inferior civilization.

This migratory habit has been especially common with the unskilled laborers who have been pouring into the United States in the last dozen years from every country in southeastern Europe. Many of them return to spend their earnings in their own country or to serve their country in war. But they return with an entirely new critical outlook, and a sense of the superiority of American organization to the primitive living around them. This continued passage to and fro has already raised the material standard of labour in many regions of these backward countries. For these regions are thus endowed with exactly what they need, the capital for the exploitation of their natural resources, and the spirit of enterprise. America is thus educating these laggard peoples from the very bottom of society up, awaking vast masses to a new-born hope for the future. In the migratory Greek, therefore, we have not the parasitic alien, the doubtful American asset, but a symbol of that cosmopolitan interchange which is coming, in spite of all war and national exclusiveness.

Only America, by reason of the unique liberty of opportunity and traditional isolation for which she seems to stand, can lead in this cosmopolitan enterprise. Only the American—and in this category I include the migratory alien who has lived with us and caught the pioneer spirit and a sense of new social vistas—has the chance to become that citizen of the world. America is coming to be, not a nationality but a trans-nationality, a weaving back and forth, with the other lands, of many threads of all sizes and colors. Any movement which attempts to thwart this weaving, or to dye the fabric any one color, or disentangle the threads of the strands, is false to this cosmopolitan vision. I do not mean that we shall necessarily glut ourselves with the raw product of humanity. It would be folly to absorb the nations faster than we could weave them. We have no duty either to admit or reject. It is purely a question of expediency. What concerns us is the fact that the strands are here. We must have a policy and an ideal for an actual situation. Our question is, What shall we do with our America? How are we likely to get the more creative America—by confining our imaginations to the ideal of the melting-pot, or broadening them to some such cosmopolitan conception as I have been vaguely sketching?

The war has shown America to be unable, though isolated geographically and politically from a European world-situation, to remain aloof and irresponsible. She is a wandering star in a sky dominated by two colossal constellations of states. Can she not work out some position of her own, some life of being in, yet not quite of, this seething and embroiled European world? This is her only hope and promise. A trans-nationality of all the nations, it is spiritually impossible for her to pass into the orbit of any one. It will be folly to hurry herself into a premature and sentimental nationalism, or to emulate Europe and play fast and loose with the forces that drag into war. No Americanization will fulfill this vision which does not recognize the uniqueness of this trans-nationalism of ours. The Anglo-Saxon attempt to fuse will only create enmity and distrust. The crusade against 'hyphenates' will only inflame the partial patriotism of trans-nationals, and cause them to assert their European traditions in strident and unwholesome ways. But the attempt to weave a wholly novel international nation out of our chaotic America will liberate and harmonize the creative power of all these peoples and give them the new spiritual citizenship, as so many individuals have already been given, of a world.

Is it a wild hope that the undertow of opposition to metaphysics in international relations, opposition to militarism, is less a cowardly provincialism than a groping for this higher cosmopolitan ideal? One can understand the irritated restlessness with which our proud pro-British colonists contemplate a heroic conflict across the seas in which they have no part. It was inevitable that our necessary inaction should evolve in their minds into the bogey of national shame and dishonor. But let us be careful about accepting their sensitiveness as final arbiter.

Let us look at our reluctance rather as the first crude beginnings of assertion on the part of certain strands in our nationality that they have a right to a voice in the construction of the American ideal. Let us face realistically the America we have around us. Let us work with the forces that are at work. Let us make something of this trans-national spirit instead of outlawing it. Already we are living this cosmopolitan America. What we need is everywhere a vivid consciousness of the new ideal. Deliberate headway must be made against the survivals of the melting pot ideal for the promise of American life.

We cannot Americanize America worthily by sentimentalizing and moralizing history. When the best schools are expressly renouncing the questionable duty of teaching patriotism by means of history, it is not the time to force shibboleth upon the immigrant. This form of Americanization has been heard because it appealed to the vestiges of our old sentimentalized and moralized patriotism. This has so far held the field as the expression of the new American's new devotion. The inflections of other voices have been drowned.

They must be heard. We must see if the lesson of the war has not been for hundreds of these later Americans a vivid realization of their trans-nationality, a new consciousness of what America meant to them as a citizenship in the world. It is the vague historic idealisms which have provided the fuel for the European flame. Our American ideal can make no progress until we do away with this romantic gilding of the past.

All our idealisms must be those of future social goals in which all can participate, the good life of personality lived in the environment of the Beloved Community. No mere doubtful triumphs of the past, which redound to the glory of only one of our trans-nationalities, can satisfy us. It must be a future America, on which all can unite, which pulls us irresistibly toward it, as we understand each other more warmly.

To make real this striving amid dangers and apathies is work for a younger *intelligentsia* of America. Here is an enterprise of integration into which we can all pour ourselves, of a spiritual welding which should make us, if the final menace ever came, no weaker, but infinitely strong.

CHAPTER 5

Crystal Eastman Reimagines the Institution of Marriage

"Women, more than men, succumb to marriage."

A product of the Victorian Age, Crystal Eastman spent her life in battle against its presumptions and constraints. She was born in 1881, a time of rigidly prescribed gender roles in the United States. By the time of her death in 1928, those prescriptions had been challenged in fundamental ways. Victorianism had begun to give way to modernism, thanks in large part to the efforts of the "New Woman" that Eastman epitomized. The birth of "the modern" in gender relations during the 1910s and 1920s settled some of the issues associated with Victorianism, but left others to persist through the 1950s (see Chapter 14, "*Life* Magazine Examines 'The American Woman' of the 1950s"), the 1960s (see Chapter 20, "Jo Freeman Redefines the American Woman"), and on into the twenty-first century. What were a wife's responsibilities to her husband? Was there only one way to be married? And were women to be considered equal to men in every respect, or viewed as requiring special protections? Crystal Eastman and her fellow New Women brought new perspectives to bear on these questions, but left their ongoing paradoxes to future generations of American men and women.

Crystal Eastman received early lessons in female empowerment. Her mother was an ordained Congregational minister, a rarity for a woman in the late nineteenth century. Crystal grew up in the small upstate New York town of Glenora, in a progressive atmosphere. The region was known as a hotbed of religious-centered reform activity, producing abolitionists, temperance crusaders, and women's rights activists; the Seneca Falls Woman's Rights Convention of 1848, the founding event of the women's movement, had been held nearby. Crystal's father, also a Congregational minister, was of this tradition. He encouraged his children, including Crystal's brother Max, who would become the editor of the socialist journal *The Masses*, to question authority and challenge injustice. The seeds of Crystal's lifelong commitment to pacifism, socialism, and feminism were planted here. This last fire burned especially brightly. At fifteen, already skeptical of traditional marriage arrangements, Eastman wrote that "no woman who allows husband and children to absorb her whole time and interest is safe against disaster."[1]

Crystal graduated from Vassar College in 1903 and headed for New York City, where she could put her ideas into practice. There, she cut a distinctive figure. An almost six-foot-tall blonde, she favored short dresses that marked her immediately as a cultural rebel. But there was much more to Eastman than outward appearance. A powerful intellect and penchant for fiercely expressed opinions ensured that few who met her forgot her. After obtaining a master's degree in sociology from Columbia University,

Eastman enrolled in New York University Law School as one of the institution's few female students. She graduated second in her class in 1907 and moved to Pittsburgh, where she conducted a year-long, Russell Sage Foundation–sponsored study of industrial accidents. Her findings were published in a pioneering volume, *Work Accidents and the Law*. Impressed by her Pittsburgh research, New York governor Charles Evans Hughes appointed Eastman to the State Employers' Liability Commission, the body's only female member. The commission drafted New York's first workman's compensation law, which became a model for similar legislation nationally.

In 1911, Eastman married Wallace Benedict, an insurance executive. Her New York friends viewed it as a strange match. Benedict was not of Eastman's world. A conventional businessman, he shared few of her radical passions. Nonetheless, Crystal cared for him enough to abandon New York for life in his hometown of Milwaukee, where she worked on an unsuccessful campaign for women's suffrage in Wisconsin. But by 1913, she had tired of life away from the open atmosphere of New York and was bored with Benedict. She left him and moved back East, settling in Greenwich Village, which by then had become the political and cultural heart of American radicalism. Lured by low rents, inexpensive restaurants, and a permissive social atmosphere, an overlapping group of young intellectuals, journalists, artists, socialists, and labor activists of both sexes gravitated to this lower Manhattan neighborhood and made it synonymous with "the modern."

The "bohemians" of Greenwich Village challenged every assumption of Victorian society. Victorian literature glorified "beauty" for its own sake; the modernists believed that art should represent not what was beautiful but what was real. Victorians accepted American political and economic institutions essentially as they were; the socialists and labor radicals of "The Village" advocated their root-and-branch transformation, with government action substituting for the workings of the free market. Victorian culture stressed self-control and respectability; bohemians prized freedom and unconventionality.

Perhaps most important, Victorian attitudes toward gender roles were rigidly traditional. Men were dominant. They were responsible for the economic support of their families and were to be obeyed to their husbands. Women were submissive. They were responsible for household upkeep and were to be obedient to their husbands. But the modernists of Greenwich Village embraced new possibilities in relations between the sexes—no prescribed gender roles, no duties of wifely obedience, no paralyzing dependencies. Their women worked for themselves, thought for themselves, and loved for themselves. Collectively, they were known by the 1910s as the "New Women." They did not ask politely for what they considered their rights. Instead, they demanded birth control, suffrage, and respect. More broadly, in the words of historian Christine Stansell, they sought "economic independence, sexual freedom, and psychological exemption from the repressive obligations of wifehood, motherhood, and daughterhood— a jettisoning of family duties for a heightened female individualism."[2]

It was this determination to live on their own terms that attracted Eastman most of all. Resettling in Greenwich Village, she joined her brother Max, who was then editing *The Masses*, and plunged into the free and uninhibited life of the New Woman. Eastman soon met Walter Fuller, a British labor radical and pacifist, and began living with him. She did not obtain a divorce from Benedict until 1916, when she and Fuller married. Flouting convention, she lived communally for a time with Fuller, Max, and a group of friends. These choices put her at odds with many of her allies in the women's suffrage and peace movements, such as the settlement house pioneer Jane Addams, who felt Eastman's personal life subverted her political goals. But Crystal believed in using that personal life as a new way of engaging in politics. In this she anticipated the feminist movement of the 1960s, and activists like Jo Freeman (see Chapter 20), who believed that "the personal is political." Eastman, described as the "newest of the New Women," was one of America's first "feminists," as that term came into widespread use in the 1910s.[3] The employment of culture as politics would come to mark the character of American feminism in the late twentieth century.

Reinstalled in Greenwich Village, Eastman plunged into the animating issues and causes of the day. After the outbreak of World War I in 1914, she worked with Jane Addams to form the Women's Peace Party, heading the group's New York chapter. She also became executive secretary of the American Union Against Militarism (AUAM), a national antiwar group. The AUAM gave birth to the American Civil Liberties Union, which protected the rights of war opponents after the United States joined the conflict in 1917. Along with Max, Eastman edited *The Liberator*, a socialist journal of ideas, and helped organize the National Labor Party to advocate for unions and government ownership of basic industries.

Eastman also sought to fuse the causes of peace and socialism with her greatest passion, women's rights. In 1913, Eastman was part of a breakaway from the established National American Woman Suffrage Association (NAWSA), which she viewed as insufficiently militant in pursuit of its goals. The Congressional Union, which Eastman organized along with fellow feminists Alice Paul and Lucy Burns, took the gloves off. Sponsoring mass protest meetings, blocking traffic, even demonstrating in front of the White House, its members shocked genteel opinion with their "unladylike" tactics, and were arrested by the hundreds. Renaming itself the National Woman's Party (NWP) in 1916, the group continued to bring pressure from outside the traditional political system at the same time the NAWSA worked from within it. The efforts of both were rewarded in 1920 with the ratification of the Nineteenth Amendment to the Constitution guaranteeing the right of women to vote in all elections.

In addition, Eastman was a strong supporter of the right to birth control and of its most prominent advocate, Margaret Sanger. To Crystal, the issue symbolized women's struggle for mastery over their own lives. Like Sanger, Eastman had seen too many married women—and married working-class women in particular—lose their personal independence to unwanted pregnancies. In Eastman's view, childbirth was often an instrument of male oppression, since wives who were constantly pregnant were forced to submit to their husbands. Eastman and Sanger believed that birth control was equally vital to young single women who toiled in factories and shops. It would liberate them from Victorian notions of sexual propriety and allow them to fully experience themselves as "New Women." In Sanger's words, they could "look the whole world in the face with a go-to-hell look in the eyes, to have an ideal, to speak and act in defiance of convention."[4] Eastman supported Sanger at her 1917 obscenity trial in Brooklyn for operating a birth control clinic, during which the basic principle of reproductive freedom was established. Afterward, Eastman continued as a vocal champion of a woman's right to determine when and under what circumstances she would become a mother.

Eastman believed that equal decision-making was at the heart of any relationship between a man and woman, and consciously structured her second marriage toward that end. She and Fuller raised their two children cooperatively. By 1918, Eastman was working at *The Liberator*, a job that would last until 1921, and Fuller continued writing and speaking on behalf of pacifism and socialism. Both opposed America's participation in World War I, and both suffered for their opinions. The war generated a wave of repression in the United States. The Espionage and Sedition Acts of 1917 and 1918 made it illegal to criticize the military or the war effort. The atmosphere of fear continued after the Armistice in a "Red Scare" that was less than discriminate in its targets; anyone who appeared to question the existing political, economic, or social system, as bohemians like Eastman and Fuller did, was under suspicion. The two were trailed by federal agents, and their speeches transcribed and reviewed by government authorities. They were blacklisted, and their job opportunities began to dry up. *The Liberator* was under the best of circumstances a marginally profitable enterprise. Now, with the government investigating it and its subscribers, the journal teetered on the brink of insolvency. Increasingly desperate for a means of earning a living, Fuller moved back to England in 1922 in search of steady work.

It was out of this shift in living arrangements that the idea for "Marriage Under Two Roofs," perhaps Eastman's best-known essay, grew. Crystal remained in the United States for a few months, then joined her husband in England, traveling back to America periodically over the next five years to look for employment. What today might be described as a "commuter marriage" was almost unheard of during the 1920s. Eastman decided to present it to a mainstream audience—earning some much-needed cash in the process—by writing a first-person article for *Cosmopolitan*, a popular women's magazine. The essay, which appeared in December 1923, somewhat embellished her own story, describing an arrangement with her husband under which they maintained separate residences in the same city; in reality, Eastman shuttled between countries. The point, however, was the same. She and her husband had been on the brink of divorce, Eastman informed her *Cosmopolitan* readers, when she made the suggestion that saved their marriage: They should live "under two roofs." She would rent an apartment on the outskirts of town where their children could enjoy the outdoors. He would live downtown near his office. At first, her husband protested: "You're breaking up our home."[5] Eastman countered that "we've had nothing worthy of the name of home for years, and the thing we have is going to pieces so fast that nothing but desperate measures will save it."[6]

Under what Crystal called her "two-roof scheme," she and her husband would plan their encounters to take advantage of marriage's benefits while minimizing its trials.[7] They might meet after work for dinner or a theatre performance and then decide to spend the rest of the evening separately, or he could return home with her and see their children. They would welcome their father's presence as a "treat."[8] No longer an active and often unappreciated supervisor of their daily activities, he would assume a new role as a kindly adviser, more like a beloved uncle than a traditional patriarch.

Eastman felt liberated by the new arrangement. It was, she explained, "a refreshment, a chance to be yourself for a while in a rich, free sense which nothing but a separate roof can give you."[9] This longing for the freedom to make even a married woman's life "an independent adventure" was at the heart of Eastman's vision of modern relations between the sexes.[10] She knew from bitter observation, not to mention her own experience with Wallace Benedict, that "women, more than men, succumb to marriage. They sink so easily into that fatal habit of depending on one person to rescue them from themselves. And this is the death of love."[11] Living apart from her husband thus did not diminish her, as traditionalists might charge; it permitted her to live fully and truly as a woman. Now that she and her husband lived apart, Eastman happily told her readers, the "more common type of married quarreling which resolves itself into being a little mean to each other all the time" was gone.[12] "There are no storms, no quarrels, no tears...criticisms and suggestions are made with the gentleness and reserve that is common between friends."[13] And, she added with evident satisfaction, "as for love, we seem to have found it again."[14]

Despite its tone of breezy self-assurance, "Marriage Under Two Roofs" begged several important questions. It appeared to place virtually the entire burden of child-rearing on the mother, with the father appearing at odd intervals to dispense genial wisdom and then vanishing conveniently from the scene. A household-role egalitarian in her own life, Eastman seemed unwilling to insist that her audience follow her example. Instead, she tacitly accepted the prevailing Victorian assumption that wives were responsible for the care of children. It is possible that the practical considerations of writing for a popular women's magazine prevailed over her true feelings. But for a woman who had spent most of her life struggling against entrenched gender stereotypes, her reluctance to challenge them in "Marriage Under Two Roofs" was puzzling.

Also perplexing was Eastman's blithe dismissal of the issue that must have been uppermost in the minds of her female readers: that of marital fidelity. Comparing marriage to a business relationship—a rather peculiar analogy coming from a socialist—Eastman counseled trust, while admitting that "in a literal and exact sense you don't know."[15] But even an increased risk of unfaithfulness, she argued, was worth the happiness that living separately would bring. It is doubtful this advice did much to reassure Eastman's audience. The gap between the open relationships of bohemian Greenwich Village and the traditionalism of Victorian Main Street may have been too wide to bridge. But whether or not she answered every question on marriage to the satisfaction of the purchasers of the December 1923 issue of *Cosmopolitan*, Eastman had presented a new, modern vision of domestic life that proposed to substantially alter prevailing norms. By daring her contemporaries to imagine gender configurations in which each partner enjoyed the freedom to define an identity and a marriage, Eastman began a conversation that extended into the 1950s (see Chapter 14), when even women who seemed content in the traditional home still harbored fears and doubts about the direction of their lives, and into the 1960s and 1970s, when women like Jo Freeman (see Chapter 20) questioned the validity of marriage itself.

Eastman also initiated a broader, century-long conversation over the nature and limits of gender equality. By the 1960s, feminists building on Eastman's ideas were arguing that differences based on sex were socially constructed and thus artificial, and that there were no "natural" roles for men and women apart from those associated with childbirth. A half-century after "Marriage Under Two Roofs" appeared, the heirs of the "New Women" of bohemian Greenwich Village transformed the foundations and assumptions of gender relations in the United States.

The 1920s were not kind to Crystal Eastman or to the women's movement generally. With the vote won, the movement lost its glue and broke into squabbling factions. The NWP, its membership rolls already declining in the wake of the suffrage victory, split over the Equal Rights Amendment. Introduced in 1923, the amendment mandated strict gender equality in all matters governed by law. It unintentionally threatened efforts to curb the exploitation of women in the workplace through what was known as "protective legislation." The Equal Rights Amendment thus alienated social reformers, like Jane Addams and the labor crusader Florence Kelley, who feared abuse of women on the factory and shop floors. If women were to be treated exactly the same as men, as Equal Rights Amendment supporters proposed, then all protective legislation would have to be repealed, and the clock turned back decades to a time when women were maimed or killed on dangerous jobs. On the other hand, the idea of women's supposed "weakness" had been at the core of Victorianism, serving as a badge of inferiority and a rationalization for discrimination at work and domination in the home. The Equal Rights Amendment issue crystallized the fundamental question of American gender relations—whether men and women were equal in all respects—and divided the women's movement.

Eastman had investigated women's working conditions in Pittsburgh and was familiar with their inequities. But she also believed deeply in gender equality and was suspicious of "protective" legislation that might keep women from more prestigious and well-paid "men's" work. Just as the NWP was torn over the implications of a constitutional amendment mandating strict gender equity, so was Eastman. She was also troubled by the narrow, legalistic focus of the Equal Rights Amendment. Its supporters seemed to have abandoned the causes of peace, socialism, labor rights, and sexual freedom that Eastman viewed as interrelated components of a broad agenda for societal change.

Nor did there appear to be a place for civil rights within the women's movement of the 1920s. Although W. E. B. Du Bois (see Chapter 3) worked for the National Association for the Advancement of Colored People (NAACP) in an office located a few blocks from Greenwich Village, feminists had virtually no contact with him. Eastman's friendship with the black writer and poet Claude McKay represented a rare exception to organized feminism's distance from the nation's African American community. Caught between the competing impulses in the women's movement and buffeted by her own personal troubles—she and Fuller continued to struggle financially and by the 1920s were in increasingly poor health—Eastman became, in one observer's words, "almost isolated even among her allies in the National Women's Party."[16]

In one last attempt to resolve her personal and political problems, Eastman left England without Fuller in August 1927 and found temporary work in America at *The Nation*, a leftist magazine. But Fuller died of a stroke only a month later, leaving Eastman on her own with two young children. Crystal herself did not have long to live. The kidney disorder from which she had suffered for almost a decade finally took her life on July 8, 1928. Her brother Max, who survived her by more than forty years, eventually repudiated his radical past and moved to the right.

Crystal Eastman's obituary in *The Nation* remarked that "she saw in the light of her faith a world in which men and women worked and played and loved as equals; nothing less than this would satisfy her."[17] Eastman had done much to make that world a reality. She had helped create the "New Woman" who liberated America from its Victorian straitjacket and made possible the freedom and openness of modernism. She helped women win the right to vote and more control over their bodies and marriages. But measured by the standards of her own obituary, Eastman could not have been satisfied at the time of her death. Even the marital balance-of-power described in "Marriage Under Two Roofs" tilted substantially toward the husband. Despite the efforts of the Greenwich Village bohemians, many of the barriers to honest, evenhanded relations between the sexes still existed. And the fundamental questions of gender equity in the United States remained unsettled within the women's movement itself, not to mention American society as a whole. How "equal" did women want to be? How equal did men want them to be? Crystal Eastman's answers, like those of her contemporaries, were incomplete. The conversation would continue.

Questions for Consideration and Conversation

1. How did Crystal Eastman's life epitomize the struggle between Victorianism and modernism in American society and culture?
2. What price did Eastman pay for challenging traditional American gender structures?
3. Why do you think the "New Women" arose when they did?
4. Eastman made her personal life a form of political expression. What might *Life's* "American Woman" of the 1950s (Chapter 14) and Jo Freeman (Chapter 20) have to say about this?
5. How were the causes of socialism, peace, and women's rights linked for Eastman?
6. How did Eastman define "equality" for women? What questions did the Equal Rights Amendment raise?
7. How was "Marriage Under Two Roofs" central to Eastman's vision of gender relations? She writes of its advantages. Are you convinced?
8. Why do you think Eastman neglected issues relating to racial equality? How might she explain this in a conversation with W. E. B. Du Bois (Chapter 3)?

Endnotes

1. Crystal Eastman, quoted in Blanche Wiesen Cook, ed., *Crystal Eastman on Women and Revolution* (New York: Oxford University Press, 1978), 4.
2. Christine Stansell, *American Moderns: Bohemian New York and the Creation of a New Century* (New York: Henry Holt, 2000), 227.
3. Ibid.
4. Margaret Sanger, quoted in Stansell, *American Moderns*, 238.
5. Crystal Eastman, "Marriage Under Two Roofs," in Cook, ed., *Crystal Eastman on Women and Revolution*, 76.
6. Ibid.
7. Ibid., 79.
8. Ibid.
9. Ibid., 80.
10. Ibid.
11. Ibid.
12. Ibid., 82.
13. Ibid., 81.
14. Ibid.
15. Ibid., 82.
16. Cook, ed., *Crystal Eastman on Women and Revolution*, 32.
17. Freda Kirchwey, "Crystal Eastman," in Cook, ed., *Crystal Eastman on Women and Revolution*, 373.

CRYSTAL EASTMAN, "MARRIAGE UNDER TWO ROOFS" (1923)

Source: Crystal Eastman, "Marriage Under Two Roofs," *Cosmopolitan*, December 1923.

"You're breaking up our home," my husband said.

"No I'm not. I'm trying to hold it together. You know we've had nothing worthy the name of home for years, and the thing we have is going to pieces so fast that nothing but desperate measures will save it. Try my scheme, then. Only try it, that's all I ask."

We tried it. And it has given us the one serene and happy period of all our married life. We no longer even think of separation, much less talk of it or threaten it. For the first time the fact that we love each other and have two splendid children is making us happy instead of miserable. My husband, who fought the scheme so bitterly, admits this now and often expatiates upon it.

Here is the story as well as I can tell it. To begin with, we had to move. The building in which we have lived for five years was to be torn down. Well, it just seemed to happen without our saying any more about it that we moved into two places instead of one. I took a small flat for myself and the children toward the edge of town where there are playgrounds and green spaces. My husband took a room in a clean rooming house within easy walking distance of his office. The two cost just a bit less than we had had to pay for a place large enough to hold us in reasonable comfort, all together. John's clothes and strictly personal possessions went to the room. Mine and the children's and our furniture, pictures and joint accumulations went to the flat. Technically he lives at one place and I at the other. But of course he keeps a change of clothes and all the essentials for night and morning comfort at my house, as might a favorite and frequent guest.

Every morning, like lovers, we telephone to exchange the day's greetings and make plans for the evening. Two or three times a week we dine together at my house and John stays all night. If we are to dine at a friend's house we usually arrange to meet there and at the end of the evening my husband may come home with me and he may not, according to our mood. If we are going to a theater I meet him in town for dinner, and after the show there are again always two possibilities—going home together like married lovers or parting on the street corner and going off in the night alone to our separate beds. And because neither course is inexorably forced upon us, either one is a bit of a lark. It is wonderful sometimes to be alone in the night and just know that someone loves you. In other moods you must have that lover in your arms. Marriage under two roofs makes room for moods.

Now about the children; for, paradoxical though it may seem, it is having children that complicates marriage so. Many pairs of lovers can have a house in common, a car, a cook, a club and all their Christmas presents; they can eat the same food, see the same plays, go to the same parties, cherish the same friends for years on end and enjoy it. But just introduce one or two children into that home, strong modern personalities, strange ebullient creatures neither his nor hers but mysteriously and indissolubly *theirs*—theirs to love, theirs to teach and train, theirs to be proud of, theirs to be ashamed of—and you have the material for tragedy. Obscure jealousies so often arise, deep resentments may be so long unspoken, rivers of cold misunderstanding may flow forever between the two who were at one before.

Perhaps I exaggerate the difficulty of bringing up children together. If the two parents come from an almost identical background, or if one has had a miserable childhood which he is glad to forget, there may be no difficulty at all. It is when, as in our case, both parents can claim a happy childhood but under totally different auspices, that their joint efforts to raise a family come so often to grief. I think my husband and I have quarreled with more anguish and bitterness over our children than over all other matters put together. But we quarrel no longer. The two-roof plan has made an end of quarreling.

"No wonder!" protests the indignant male. "You've got your way. You have the children, they live with you and you can bring them up as you like. But is that fair?"

Surely, as society is organized today, it is the mother's job to bring up the children. The father's job is to earn the living, and if he belongs as the father in our family does to the intellectual proletariat—people of education with expensive tastes and no capital, who must live by their wits—he will be hard at it for the first fifteen or twenty years of his married life. How can he be more than a "consulting partner" in the twenty-four hour a day job of bringing up children? He can criticize and interfere, or praise and suggest, according to his nature, be he cannot really do the job. Circumstances compel him to leave it to the mother. In big decisions about the children, of course, the father's will counts often more than the mother's, but in the everyday matter of training and association the most he can do is to "use his influence."

And in the usual American middle-class family, when is father's influence most often brought to bear? At breakfast! At breakfast of all times when everyone is already a little on edge from violating his natural instincts—children forced to "hurry up" and "be quiet" and "keep at it" when they long to dawdle and "fool"; mother forced to begin being patient and kind at a time in the day when it is against nature to be patient and kind; father, already heavy with his day's work, forced to spend his last precious half-hour in this crude confusion when his whole being cries out for solitude.

This at least can be said for the two-roof scheme: it automatically relieves father of the family breakfast, and the family breakfast of father! And no hard feelings anywhere. In our family father is now a treat. He might turn up some morning during the week, but if he does it is a surprise and everybody is so good that breakfast is almost a social occasion. Saturday afternoon father usually appears and takes you off for a lark somewhere, and Sunday he is just like a member of the family.

Is there really anything unfair in this arrangement? Are not the father's comments, criticisms and suggestions on the upbringing of his children apt to be better given and better received in the comparative leisure and freedom of Sunday than in the nagging, inescapable contact of a daily breakfast? Must a consulting partner review the raw, unfinished work every day?

At this point, I foresee, the passionate upholder of family life will try to compromise with me. "Why two roofs?" he will argue. "Why not a room for father at the top of the house and his breakfast served there? Is it necessary to drive him right out of the house?"

But I stand my ground. To begin with, for the type of family I am thinking of there seldom is a house. It is a flat, an apartment, a floor or two floors, at most a very small house. If father is lucky enough to have a room of his own it will not be out of hearing. He will always be acutely aware of the children in their noisy process of growing up. And mother will be aware of his presence in the house. The strain will still be there.

Moreover, even though you live in a palace, two rooms will not give you what two roofs will give you. Let us forget breakfast now—imagine it is evening, the long day's work is over, the children are asleep. Speaking from the woman's standpoint, can there be anything more irritating than a husband who shuts himself up in a room and says or intimates, "I want to be alone"? He is there with you in your common home. It is evening. You have been apart all day, and yet he wants to be alone! Outrageous! To sit and read in separate rooms under the same roof! Unnatural! Not to be borne! *Why did he come home if he wanted to be alone?*

Why?

Obviously because he had no home of his own to go to. Now put my scheme into operation. Give him a place of his own, completely outside of your jurisdiction, a place where he keeps his clothes, where he normally sleeps, to which he goes quite simply and naturally whenever he wants to, without explanations and without fear of reproach. At the morning telephone rendezvous you have agreed not to spend the evening together. You may be a little lonely the first few times this happens, but you soon get to like your "vacations" and to plan for them. You may have a friend in for dinner whom your husband takes no pleasure in. You may arrange for some kind of recreation, dancing, music, lecture or what-not for which he has no taste, or you may be tired enough to enjoy a few hours of solitude by your own hearth.

In any case, his absence is a refreshment, a chance to be yourself for a while in a rich, free sense which nothing but a separate roof can give you.

Women, more than men, succumb to marriage. They sink so easily into that fatal habit of depending on one person to rescue them from themselves. And this is the death of love.

The two-roof plan encourages a wife to cultivate initiative in rescuing herself, to develop social courage, to look upon her life as an independent adventure and get interested in it. And every Victorian tradition to the contrary, it is thus only that she can retain her charm down the years.

I wish I could set forth as freely and frankly my husband's feeling about this new scheme of life as I can my own. But he is not the sort of man who talks easily about himself. He is what the psychoanalysts call an "introvert." I know from a hundred signs that he likes it, but I can only guess why.

Most women tend to own and manage their husbands too much, and I am not free from that vice. Much of John's depression and irritability which used to be so baffling to me in the old days was due, I am sure, to his having no escape from me, no place where I did not come, no retreat from my influence. Now he has one. Often when we lived under the same roof he must have said to himself, "I love her but I can't stand her. She is too much for me." Now I know he never feels that.

People with very simple natures probably do not suffer from this pressure of one personality on the other in marriage. But for the usual modern type, the complex, sensitive, highly organized city dweller, man or woman, marriage can become such a constant invasion of his very self that it amounts sometimes to torture.

I am the last one to deny that there are successful marriages. I know ideally mated couples who can say to this argument with sincerity:

"But we don't want to get away from each other. We are perfectly happy as we are."

And I can answer only, "Bless you my children; there is nothing in this gospel for you."

Nor is there anything in it for young lovers in the first months of ecstasy and anguish, nor for parents, during the first baby's first year, nor for couples of whom one is a natural door-mat, nor for the excessively

domestic man who wants to know the price of everything to a penny, how often the baby falls down and what the cook does on her afternoon off. (Though in this case no doubt the wife needs a retreat.)

No, I am speaking only to those who are discouraged with marriage, who have given it a good trial and found it extremely difficult. But I am sure I shall have a large audience.

Our is not an extreme case. My husband is a bit temperamental but he has great charm. I am a "strong-minded" woman, perhaps, but not over-strong. We have hosts of friends who find us both good-natured, generous, easy to get along with. We are both of us intelligent. We can both take a joke. And I think we had more genuine love and respect for each other than is common.

Yet marriage was destroying us. We just lived from storm to storm, with tears, an emotional reconciliation and a brief lull of happiness between.

Now that we live under two roofs there are no storms, no quarrels, no tears. Our differences of opinion are not passionate and unbearable. They have an almost rational quality. Criticisms and suggestions are made with the gentleness and reserve that is common between friends. They are received with the open-minded forbearance of one who can be sure of the critic's early departure.

And as for love, we seem to have found it again. The hours we spend together have actually caught back some of the surprising gaiety and warm glow of sweetheart days.

What is the meaning of this all but universal habit of quarreling among the married?

When a friend irritates you or, as we say, gets on your nerves, you do not have to quarrel with her. You know she is going home pretty soon, or you are going home—a natural and inevitable separation will take place.

But with a husband or a wife there is no hope, nothing to look forward to. You cannot good-naturedly walk away, because you have no place to go. His *home*—or her home—is *your home*. This fact increases your irritation five hundredfold, and some outlet must be had.

Stormy quarrels, no matter how tender and intimate the interval between, are wearing to soul and body. But they are not nearly so devastating, I believe, as that much more common type of married quarreling which resolves itself into being a little mean to each other all the time.

Just who is there who does not know at least one couple like that—their conversations with each other made up almost entirely of small slighting remarks, each constantly belittling the achievements and enthusiasms of the other; kindly people in their relations with outsiders but always somewhat bitter and belligerent toward each other? Is anything less enjoyable than visiting such a home? Is it really good for children to grow up in such an atmosphere?

Perhaps divorce is the only remedy for difficult marriages. But if my theory is correct, if it is the too constant sharing of one home, with no easy and normal method of escape, which primarily makes them difficult, then some loosening of the time-and-space conventions so bound up with marriage is worth trying. Separate beds, separate rooms, have not done much to reconcile people to marriage. Why not take a bold romantic step and try separate roofs?

It will seem to many that in setting forth this new plan for achieving a happy marriage I have avoided the crucial test, that my argument can be challenged at its very heart.

Crudely put, the challenge is: "If my husband sleeps under a separate roof, how do I know that he is always alone?" or again: "If I don't go home every night, how do I know that some other man is not there in my place?" In a literal and exact sense you don't know. That is the answer.

But after all, marriage, like business, is founded on trust.

When a husband goes off to work in the morning, does he *know* that his wife is not going to neglect her children and make love to the plumber? He hopes she isn't, of course, but he cannot be absolutely sure. It would not be practical to ring her up every fifteen minutes to inquire; if he is to get on with his work, he must trust her.

And as for the poor wife, how can she know that her bread-winner is not spending the entire morning kissing the stenographer, unless she squanders what she saved up for the children's winter coats on a dictograph?

In the most conventional marriage there must be a considerable area of confidence as to the technical faithfulness of the parties. In marriage under two roofs you deliberately extend that area of confidence, that is all.

If one is of a very jealous disposition this may take some courage, but it is courage soon rewarded, for in this matter of marital faithfulness, as all wise women know, increasing the confidence usually lessens the risk. The two-roof scheme demands confidence during those very hours of ease when temptation is greatest; this cannot be denied.

But if it brings happiness where there was misery before, even that risk is well taken, for happiness is the only security.

CHAPTER 6

Herbert Hoover Champions Individualist Values

"I am an American individualist."

If Andrew Carnegie (see Chapter 2) epitomized the American self-made man of the late nineteenth century, Herbert Hoover was his early twentieth-century counterpart. Born in 1874 to a down-on-its-luck Iowa family, orphaned at nine, put to work at an early age, his youth bore many similarities to Carnegie's. Like Carnegie, Hoover was possessed of a driving ambition to rise in life, and to leave his humble origins far behind. Carnegie's great opportunity came through railroads and steel, Hoover's through mining and engineering, with an assist from the developing system of American higher education that by the 1890s had become an engine of upward mobility for those fortunate enough to enter its ranks.

After failing the entrance examination for admission to the newly established Stanford University, he redoubled his efforts and was accepted on his second try in 1891. He worked his way through, taking jobs few of his more well-off classmates would accept—launderer, newspaper seller, and clerk. Impressed with his determination and character, Hoover's Stanford classmates voted him student body treasurer during his junior year, the only elective office he would hold before becoming President of the United States in 1929. His orderly, rational mind gravitated toward engineering, and he graduated in 1895 with a degree in geology. Out of school, he once again started at the bottom, working as a manual laborer in a California mine before getting his break—a position as a mining "scout" in Australia. Hoover did his job so well that, again like Carnegie, he moved rapidly up the ladder of success. Posted to China and Burma, he built and operated profitable mines before starting his own company in 1908. It discovered and extracted valuable natural resources around the world, including coal, oil, zinc, silver, and gold. Everywhere Hoover traveled, his work ethic, organizational skills, and mastery of details won admirers and made him money. In 1914, aged forty, the impoverished orphan from Iowa was already a multimillionaire.

That same year, the outbreak of World War I led Hoover to direct his talents toward public service. The German invasion of Belgium had left its citizens near starvation. Aid officials aware of Hoover's reputation for getting things done, asked him to head the Commission for Relief in Belgium, charged with the task of getting food supplies through a war zone to reach the Belgian people. Hoover performed so effectively that he became an international hero, lauded as a humanitarian and, of all things for an administrator, a world celebrity. The word "Hooverize" found its way not only into the

English lexicon, but a number of European ones as well. It meant to conserve resources for the greater good. Some European cities named streets after Hoover.

When the United States joined the war in 1917, President Woodrow Wilson knew who to ask to serve as the nation's food administrator. Hoover used the power of his office to convince Americans to voluntarily limit their consumption in order to free up more resources for soldiers in the field. He coordinated everything—rationing quotas, promotional campaigns, production levels, and transportation and distribution protocols. By the time the war ended in November 1918, Hoover was being described in the American media as a miracle worker, and a possible presidential candidate in 1920. Hoover's partisan affiliations were unknown at this time; he might have argued that there was no "Republican" or "Democratic" way to feed the hungry. As a result, both major parties considered him for their tickets before settling on other candidates. One of them, Democratic vice presidential nominee Franklin D. Roosevelt (FDR), said of Hoover: "He is certainly a wonder, and I wish we could make him President of the United States. There could not be a better one."[1]

The victor in the 1920 presidential campaign, Republican Senator Warren G. Harding, brought Hoover into his administration as Secretary of Commerce. By this time, Hoover's reputation for efficient and effective humanitarianism had been further burnished by his service as chief of the American Relief Administration, during which he delivered billions of dollars of supplies to post-war Europe. In 1921, as he assumed his position in the Commerce Department, Herbert Hoover was arguably the most successful and respected public official in the United States. From the humblest of beginnings, he had become enormously wealthy. He had fed and clothed millions. He had also provided the organizational skills that enabled the United States to win the largest war in human history. What lessons did Hoover's triumphant American life hold for the nation as a whole? It was this question that he set out to address in *American Individualism*, which Hoover wrote in 1922 and published the following year.

Hoover understood, of course, that his was not the prototypical American life, any more than Carnegie's had been. But he believed that his success had been made possible by a uniquely American value—individualism—which afforded him the opportunity both to better himself and to serve others. Even if it was unrealistic to expect every American to become as rich and as renowned as Hoover, individualism still offered a surer route to economic security and personal fulfillment than any other idea or ideology.

Hoover took pains to differentiate American individualism from other systems, including communism, socialism, autocracy, and capitalism itself, which he dismissed as " 'every man for himself and the devil take the hindmost.' "[2] Hoover even distinguished American individualism from its European counterpart, which was characterized by impenetrable class barriers. American individualism was built on what Abraham Lincoln had called the "right to rise."[3] It stressed personal initiative and, in Hoover's words, "the emery wheel of competition."[4] These made it possible for those with talent to create wealth for both themselves and the greater American community. Equality of opportunity was central to Hoover's vision of American individualism. The fact that Hoover, a poor boy with no personal or professional connections, could nonetheless attend Stanford University and go on to a career filled with accomplishment and honor was symbolic of the ways in which America differed from other societies. In America, Hoover stated proudly, "we keep the social solution free from frozen strata of classes."[5] In other countries, being born on the bottom almost guaranteed staying there. In America, being born at the bottom, as Hoover's own life story illustrated, was no impediment to rising to the top.

But there was more to American individualism, Hoover argued, than the drive for wealth. It also contained spiritual and service-based elements that offered deeper rewards than a free market capitalism in which one's worth was measured solely by dollars and cents. Individualism, Hoover maintained, "alone admits the universal divine inspiration of every human soul."[6] It "aims to provide opportunity for self-expression, not merely economically, but spiritually as well."[7] This led in turn to the idea of service for the common good, illustrated again by Hoover's own life trajectory. Hoover urged "the embracement of the necessity of a greater and broader sense of service and a responsibility to others as a part of individualism."[8] American individualism did not connote heedless self-absorption. Its "variable mixtures of altruism and self-interest" had roots in America's early national period in the late eighteenth and early nineteenth centuries, and the idea of "republicanism."[9] Before industrialism and market capitalism robbed them of their independence and status, small and middling farmers and artisans comprised the backbone of the new nation. Hard-working, God-fearing, and economically self-sufficient, they also took seriously their obligations as citizens. As "republicans," they felt responsible to both their families and their neighbors. They did not hesitate to make personal sacrifices for their villages, towns, states, or, if need be, their country. Republicans were thus independent and interdependent.

Hoover's American individualism sought to replicate the republicanism of pre-industrial society in a modern nation, to restore a sense of interpersonal duty in an increasingly impersonal culture. Twentieth-century Americans too would look both inward and outward, combining autonomy and mutuality. It was this spirit, Hoover believed, that had won the World War, a victory of an inventive, imaginative, and courageous people working cooperatively for the betterment of all.

But were the tensions between individual and community in American society so easily resolved? Hoover did not apply the term "capitalist" to the United States in the pages of *American Individualism*. This was because Hoover understood that free market capitalism promoted acquisitiveness as its signal virtue and selfishness as a social good. These impulses were capable of producing wealth on a vast scale. But Hoover worried not only about wealth production but also about its distribution. Unregulated capitalism provided few solutions to this problem, so Hoover used the term "individualism" in its place. It became a way for him to combine capitalism's avaricious productiveness with the altruism and self-sacrifice associated with Marxism.

Yet who—or what—would ensure that Americans would live up to these standards of service to others? How would acquisitiveness and selfishness be controlled? Hoover did not offer a specific answer in *American Individualism*. Certainly he had faith in voluntarism; Americans, he believed, were naturally public-spirited. But, of course, voluntarism only went so far. Inevitably, government would need to play a role. *American Individualism* did not explicitly spell out what that role would be. Hoover excoriated the "ghastly failure" of communism in the Soviet Union as well as the inhumanities of unregulated capitalism in the United States.[10] What was government's part in resolving the tensions between the American individual and the American national community? Hoover's time as Secretary of Commerce between 1921 and 1929 would offer him the chance to implement his ideas in a cabinet department. His troubled years in the White House from 1929 to 1933 would force those ideas into practice on a national scale during the greatest economic crisis in the nation's history.

Hoover accepted President Harding's offer to join his cabinet on the condition that he would enjoy free rein for his ideas. Operating almost autonomously in a Harding administration mired in graft and scandal and after the president's death in August 1923, in a Calvin Coolidge administration noted for keeping its hands off subordinates, Hoover moved to realize the principles he articulated in *American Individualism*.

The Commerce Department traditionally had been a cabinet backwater, but the new secretary repositioned it at the intersection of American economic activity. Its role would be that of neither a heavy-handed regulator demoralizing private enterprise and destroying initiative, nor a passive bystander to the chaotic clash of inefficient and inequitable market forces. Instead, the Commerce Department would serve as a coordinator, mediator, and information source for American business. It would encourage the growth of trade associations, through which firms, while continuing to compete, could share ideas, coordinate strategies, and work together to minimize market disruptions. It would act as a facilitator, not a dictator. Its goal would be to keep economic traffic running fairly and smoothly, with active intervention only as a last resort.

This system of business–government collaboration, which came to be known as "associationalism," permitted Hoover to involve government in the affairs of business as an honest broker, preserving individual freedom of choice and action and the American system of competition and incentive. Yet at the same time, through a broad spirit of cooperation coordinated by a central authority sensitive to marketplace needs, the national economy could operate more efficiently than ever, producing more and more wealth for the American people. Associationalism thus gave Hoover the rational economic growth he desired, without the crushing statism that threatened individual freedom and initiative.

Hoover worked tirelessly at his idea throughout the 1920s, convening meetings of trade associations in Washington at which corporate officials discussed industry trends and shared news of advances in their fields. Without engaging in outright price or production-level fixing in violation of federal antitrust laws, Hoover encouraged the executives to reach general agreements on the direction of their business sectors. The trade associations then adopted their own internal mechanisms to enforce these agreements. This self-regulatory structure epitomized Hoover's idea of American individualism. It balanced personal liberty and rational management of the economy. While it was not clear if associationalism was the reason for the nation's generally prosperous economic atmosphere during the 1920s or merely its byproduct, Hoover's reputation as an innovative leader and public servant grew throughout the decade. It was as if this engineer had harnessed the technology to manage human beings in a complex economy just as he had the mining of gold or the distribution of food. A humanitarian who had saved lives in Europe was now bettering lives in America. If one name was linked with progress, ingenuity, and growth in the United States during the 1920s, it was Hoover's.

The next step was logical. Nominated by the Republican Party to succeed the retiring president Coolidge in 1928 without significant opposition, Hoover won an easy victory over Democratic candidate Governor Alfred E. Smith of New York, carrying almost 60% of the popular vote. Accepting the nomination, Hoover stated confidently that "We in America today are nearer to the final triumph over poverty than ever before in the history of any land."[11]

By the time Herbert Hoover ran for reelection against Franklin D. Roosevelt in 1932, events had taken a darker turn. The stock market crash of October 1929 and subsequent depression had severely tarnished Hoover's standing with an American public suffering an unemployment rate of one in four. As if to mock the prior use of his name, "Hoovervilles"—encampments of the destitute—sprang up in cities across the nation. Hoover was not responsible for the crash, but his American individualism seemed ill-suited to an economic landscape littered with bank failures and plant closings. True to his principles, President Hoover had tried to keep the federal government from intervening directly in the crisis. A national relief program for the unemployed and needy, he argued, would rob them of their dignity and sense of self-worth and eat away at the personal independence that was at the heart of American individualism.

It would also threaten the American virtue dearer to Hoover than any other: freedom. The president believed that economic and political liberty were related; once an intrusive governmental regulatory structure robbed Americans of control over their economic lives, political despotism was sure to follow. While Hoover believed in a rising standard of living for all Americans, he was not an egalitarian in the strict sense. His American individualism stressed the equal opportunity for Americans to become unequal based upon their attributes, talents, and drive. Freedom meant initiative and incentive, equality dependence and inertia. Hoover thus sought to confront the depression through a reassertion of an American individualism that prized freedom above all and dismissed federal assistance to individual Americans as a form of nascent tyranny.

But Franklin Roosevelt, Hoover's 1932 Democratic opponent and the man who had praised him so effusively only twelve years earlier, held to a different set of philosophical tenets. He promised a "New Deal" to the American people, one that in practical terms meant a redistribution of economic resources to what FDR called "the forgotten man" and an emphasis on equality as the nation's preeminent value. Unlike Hoover, Roosevelt believed America's resources were finite and its potential for further growth limited. In a well-publicized September 1932 San Francisco campaign speech, he declared that "our task now is not discovery or exploitation of natural resources, or necessarily producing more goods. It is the soberer, less dramatic business . . . . of distributing wealth and products more equitably, of adapting existing economic organizations to the service of the people."[12] Government would be the instrument of that process of economic equalization. To Hoover, this meant the heavy hand of central state authority stifling the freedom of the individual in the United States.

Hoover was also more optimistic than Roosevelt about the possibilities for growth in the American economy. Unlike FDR, he believed that the American frontier had not closed, but merely changed in character. "There will always be a frontier to conquer or hold as long as men think, plan, and dare," he wrote in *American Individualism*:

> . . . The days of the pioneer are not over. There are continents of human welfare of which we have penetrated only the coastal plain. The great continent of science is as yet explored only on its borders, and it is only the pioneer who will penetrate the frontier in the quest for new worlds to conquer.[13]

But this optimistic view was lost on the majority of presidential voters in 1932. Hoover lost the presidential election as badly as he had won four years earlier. In the midst of the worst depression in the nation's history, it may have been inevitable that the champion of the "forgotten man" would win out over that of the "American individual." The promise of equality was also more substantial and meaningful to suffering Americans than the more abstract and remote notion of freedom, especially when voters contrasted the ebullient Roosevelt with the dour Hoover. Convincing Americans that their nation's potential for growth was unlimited and that the individual and not the government was the instrument of that growth was virtually impossible under the conditions of 1932, and indeed, for the rest of the decade.

Nonetheless, Hoover continued to make the case for American individualism. Turned out of office on March 4, 1933, he watched as Roosevelt galvanized the nation with an inspiring inaugural address and then a torrent of "Hundred Days" New Deal legislation that included a massive program of direct relief payments to the poor and unemployed. After an initial experiment with a form of associationalism—Roosevelt's National Recovery Administration featured industry-wide codes of fair competition agreed upon by groups of producers but the agency was invalidated by the Supreme Court in 1935—FDR began to confront American business both rhetorically and with federal government power during what became known as the "Second New Deal." He won a massive reelection victory in 1936.

By then Hoover was deeply concerned about the implications of Roosevelt's philosophy. It appeared to the former president that American individualism had been supplanted by a statist regime barely distinguishable from socialism. The New Deal curtailed personal liberty, stifled initiative, and encouraged dependency, all for the promise of an equality of condition that could never be fulfilled in a stagnant economic environment. Hoover wondered if his own accomplishments would have been possible had he been born into Roosevelt's America. It certainly did not reward the creativity and risk-taking that had made Hoover so successful as a young man. But by the mid-1930s, fewer and fewer Americans were listening to Hoover. His own party had shunted him aside, and he was never again a serious candidate for national office. Although Hoover regained a measure of public respect in the late 1940s and 1950s as head of two widely praised governmental reorganization commissions—a return to his roots as a rational manager and efficiency expert—his name hung like an albatross on the Republican Party long after his death in 1964.

While there is no doubt that the American people repudiated Hoover the man, the ultimate fate of his ideas is more contested. Hoover joined a conversation with Roosevelt over the role of the federal government in national economic life, the nature and relative importance of America's core values of freedom and equality, and the meaning of individualism itself in American political culture. This conversation would engage Americans on all sides of the political spectrum—conservatives, liberals, radicals—in heated arguments for the rest of the twentieth century. In future chapters, we will see how Walker Evans and Dorothea Lange (Chapter 8), Whittaker Chambers (Chapter 11), members of Students for a Democratic Society (Chapter 17), and Ronald Reagan (Chapter 21) all drove and shaped this conversation.

"I am an American individualist," Herbert Hoover proclaimed at the height of his popularity and influence, offering his own individual journey to his countrymen as inspiration and example.[14] Certainly his journey had been a remarkable one. It shared much with that of Carnegie and even Lincoln in its triumph over obstacles that in other countries would have proved insurmountable. Hoover believed his journey could only have taken place in America. This may well be true. But was it "the" American journey or "an" American journey? While Hoover's insistence on "American individualism" as the nation's defining value destroyed his presidential career, the conversation he initiated was far from over.

Questions for Consideration and Conversation

1. Herbert Hoover and Andrew Carnegie (Chapter 2) were both self-made men and generous philanthropists. But was Carnegie the kind of "American individualist" of whom Hoover would have approved? What might Hoover have said about Carnegie's business methods?

2. How did Hoover's understanding of "individualism" extend beyond pure self-interest? What did he believe individuals owed the larger community? How did he distinguish his idea of "individualism" from capitalism?

3. Franklin Roosevelt (Chapter 10) once admired Hoover. What would FDR have said about Hoover and his individualist philosophy at the time of Roosevelt's "Four Freedoms" address in 1941?

4. Hoover believed that American individualism's "variable mixtures of altruism and self-interest" would resolve the tensions between individual and community in American society. Was he being realistic?

5. What was Hoover's view of the role of government in American economic and political life? What would

"A Striker" (Chapter 1), Dorothea Lange (Chapter 8), Ronald Reagan (Chapter 21), and Robert Putnam (Chapter 22) have to say about this issue?

6. Was "associationalism" as advocated and practiced by Hoover a viable way to run the American economy?

What would members of Students for a Democratic Society (Chapter 17) have said?

7. Why was "freedom," even more so than "equality," Hoover's preeminent American value?

Endnotes

1. Quoted in David Pietrusza, *1920: The Year of the Six Presidents* (New York: Basic Books, 2007), 112.
2. Herbert Hoover, *American Individualism* (Garden City, NY: Doubleday, Page & Company, 1923), 10.
3. See Gabor Boritt, *Lincoln and the Economics of the American Dream* (Urbana, IL: University of Illinois Press, 1994) and Scott Sandage, *Born Losers: A History of Failure in America* (Cambridge, MA: Harvard University Press, 2005), 218–25.
4. Hoover, *American Individualism*, 10.
5. Ibid., 9.
6. Ibid., 26.
7. Ibid., 37.
8. Ibid., 11.
9. Ibid., 12.
10. Ibid., 18.
11. Quoted in William A. DeGregorio, *The Complete Book of U.S. Presidents*, 4th ed. (New York: Barricade Books, 1993), 468.
12. Franklin D. Roosevelt, "Commonwealth Club Address," September 23, 1932, www.americanrhetoric.com/speeches/fdrcommonwealth.htm.
13. Hoover, *American Individualism*, 64.
14. Ibid., 8.

HERBERT HOOVER, *AMERICAN INDIVIDUALISM* (1923)

Source: Herbert Hoover, *American Individualism.* Garden City, NY: Doubleday, Page & Company 1923, pp. 1–47, 63–72.

We have witnessed in this last eight years the spread of revolution over one-third of the world. The causes of these explosions lie at far greater depths than the failure of governments in war. The war itself in its last stages was a conflict of social philosophies—but beyond this the causes of social explosion lay in the great inequalities and injustices of centuries flogged beyond endurance by the conflict and freed from restraint by the destruction of war. The urgent forces which drive human society have been plunged into a terrible furnace. Great theories spun by dreamers to remedy the pressing human ills have come to the front of men's minds. Great formulas came into life that promised to dissolve all trouble. Great masses of people have flocked to their banners in hopes born of misery and suffering. Nor has this great social ferment been confined to those nations that have burned with revolutions.

Now, as the storm of war, of revolution and of emotion subsides there is left even with us of the United States much unrest, much discontent with the surer forces of human advancement. To all of us, out of this crucible of actual, poignant, individual experience has come a deal of new understanding, and it is for all of us to ponder these new currents if we are to shape our future with intelligence.

Even those parts of the world that suffered less from the war have been partly infected by these ideas. Beyond this, however, many have had high hopes of civilization suddenly purified and ennobled by the sacrifices and services of the war; they had thought the fine unity of purpose gained in war would be carried into great unity of action in remedy of the faults of civilization in peace. But from concentration of every spiritual and material energy upon the single purpose of war the scene changed to the immense complexity and the many purposes of peace.

Thus there loom up certain definite underlying forces in our national life that need to be stripped of the imaginary—the transitory—and a definition should be given to the actual permanent and persistent motivation of our civilization. In contemplation of these questions we must go far deeper than the superficials of our political and economic structure, for these are but the products of our social philosophy—the machinery of our social system.

Nor is it ever amiss to review the political, economic, and spiritual principles through which our country has steadily grown in usefulness and greatness, not only to preserve them from being fouled by false notions, but more importantly that we may guide ourselves in the road of progress.

Five or six great social philosophies are at struggle in the world for ascendency. There is the Individualism of America. There is the Individualism of the more democratic states of Europe with its careful reservations of castes and classes. There are Communism, Socialism, Syndicalism, Capitalism, and finally there is Autocracy—whether by birth, by possessions, militarism, or divine right of kings. Even the Divine Right still lingers on although our lifetime has seen fully two-thirds of the earth's population, including Germany, Austria, Russia, and China, arrive at a state of angry disgust with this type of social motive power and throw it on the scrap heap.

All these thoughts are in ferment today in every country in the world. They fluctuate in ascendency with times and places. They compromise with each other in daily reaction on governments and peoples. Some of these ideas are perhaps more adapted to one race than another. Some are false, some are true. What we are interested in is their challenge to the physical and spiritual forces of America.

The partisans of some of these other brands of social schemes challenge us to comparison; and some of their partisans even among our own people are increasing in their agitation that we adopt one or another or parts of their devices in place of our tried individualism. They insist that our social foundations are exhausted, that like feudalism and autocracy America's plan has served its purpose—that it must be abandoned.

There are those who have been left in sober doubt of our institutions or are confounded by bewildering catchwords of vivid phrases. For in this welter of discussions there is much attempt to glorify or defame social and economic forces with phrases. Nor indeed should we disregard the potency of some of these phrases in their stir to action—"The dictatorship of the Proletariat," "Capitalistic nations," "Germany over all," and a score of others. We need only to review those that have jumped to horseback during the last ten years in order that we may be properly awed by the great social and political havoc that can be worked where the bestial instincts of hate, murder, and destruction are clothed by the demagogue in the fine terms of political idealism.

For myself, let me say at the very outset that my faith in the essential truth, strength, and vitality of the developing creed by which we have hitherto lived in this country of ours has been confirmed and deepened by the searching experiences of seven years of service in the backwash and misery of war. Seven years of contending with economic degeneration, with social disintegration, with incessant political dislocation, with all of its seething and ferment of individual and class conflict, could but impress me with the primary motivation of social forces, and the necessity for broader thought upon their great issues to humanity. And from it all I emerge an individualist—an unashamed individualist. But let me say also that I am an American individualist. For America has been steadily developing the ideals that constitute progressive individualism.

No doubt, individualism run riot, with no tempering principle, would provide a long category of inequalities, of tyrannies, dominations, and injustices. America, however, has tempered the whole conception of individualism by the injection of a definite principle, and from this principle it follows that attempts at domination, whether in government or in the processes of industry and commerce, are under an insistent curb. If we would have the values of individualism, their stimulation to initiative, to the development of hand and intellect, to the high development of thought and spirituality, they must be tempered with that firm and fixed ideal of American individualism—*an equality of opportunity*. If we would have these values we must soften its hardness and stimulate progress through that sense of service that lies in our people.

Therefore, it is not the individualism of other countries for which I would speak, but the individualism of America. Our individualism differs from all others because it embraces these great ideals: *that while we build our society upon the attainment of the individual, we shall safeguard to every individual an equality of opportunity to take that position in the community to which his intelligence, character, ability, and ambition entitle him; that we keep the social solution free from frozen strata of classes; that we shall stimulate effort of each individual to achievement; that through an enlarging sense of responsibility and understanding we shall assist him to this attainment; while he in turn must stand up to the emery wheel of competition.*

Individualism cannot be maintained as the foundation of a society if it looks to only legalistic justice based upon contracts, property, and political equality. Such legalistic safeguards are themselves not enough. In our individualism we have long since abandoned the laissez faire of the 18th Century—the notion that it is "every man for himself and the devil take the hindmost." We abandoned that when we adopted the ideal of equality of opportunity—the fair chance of Abraham Lincoln. We have confirmed its abandonment in terms of legislation, of social and economic justice—in part because we have learned that it is the hindmost who throws the bricks at our social edifice, in part because we have learned that the foremost are not always the best, nor the hindmost the worst—and in part because we have learned that social injustice is the destruction of justice itself. We have learned that the impulse to production can only be maintained at a high pitch if there is a fair division of the product. We have also learned that fair division can only be obtained by certain restrictions on the strong and the dominant. We have indeed gone even further in the 20th Century with the embracement of the necessity of a greater and broader sense of service and responsibility to others as a part of individualism.

Whatever may be the case with regard to Old World individualism and (we have given more back to Europe than we received from her) the truth that is important for us to grasp today is that there is a world of difference between the principles and spirit of Old World individualism and that which we have developed in our own country.

We have, in fact, a special social system of our own. We have made it ourselves from materials brought in revolt from conditions in Europe. We have lived it; we constantly improve it; we have seldom tried to define it. It abhors autocracy and does not argue with it, but fights it. It is not capitalism, or socialism, or syndicalism, nor a cross breed of them. Like most Americans, I refuse to be damned by anybody's word-classification of it, such as "capitalism," "plutocracy," "proletariat" or "middle class," or any other, or to any kind of compartment that is based on the assumption of some group dominating somebody else.

The social force in which I am interested is far higher and far more precious a thing than all these. It springs from something infinitely more enduring; it springs from the one source of human progress—that each individual shall be given the chance and stimulation for development of the best with which he has been endowed in heart and mind; it is the sole source of progress; it is American individualism.

The rightfulness of our individualism can rest either on philosophic, political, economic, or spiritual grounds. It can rest on the ground of being the only safe avenue to further human progress.

Philosophic Grounds

On the philosophic side we can agree at once that intelligence, character, courage, and the divine spark of the human soul are alone the property of individuals. These do not lie in agreements, in organizations, in institutions, in masses, or in groups. They abide alone in the individual mind and heart.

Production both of mind and hand rests upon impulses in each individual. These impulses are made of the varied forces of original instincts, motives, and acquired desires. Many of these are destructive and must be restrained through moral leadership and authority of the law and be eliminated finally by education. All are modified by a vast fund of experience and a vast plant and equipment of civilization which we pass on with increments to each succeeding generation.

The inherited instincts of self-preservation, acquisitiveness, fear, kindness, hate, curiosity, desire for self-expression, for power, for adulation, that we carry over from a thousand of generations must, for good or evil, be comprehended in a workable system embracing our accumulation of experiences and equipment. They may modify themselves with time—but in terms of generations. They differ in their urge upon different individuals. The dominant ones are selfish. But no civilization could be built or can endure solely upon the groundwork of unrestrained and unintelligent self-interest. The problem of the world is to restrain the destructive instincts while strengthening and enlarging those of altruistic character and constructive impulse—for thus we build for the future.

From the instincts of kindness, pity, fealty to family and race; the love of liberty; the mystical yearnings for spiritual things; the desire for fuller expression of the creative faculties; the impulses of service to community and nation, are moulded the ideals of our people. And the most potent force in society is its ideals. If one were to attempt to delimit the potency of instinct and ideals, it would be found that while instinct dominates in our preservation yet the great propelling force of progress is right ideals. It is true we do not realize the ideal; not even a single person personifies that realization. It is therefore not surprising that society, a collection of persons, a necessary maze of compromises, cannot realize it. But that it has ideals, that they revolve in a system that makes for steady advance of them is the first thing. Yet true as this is, the day has not arrived when any economic or social system will function and last if founded upon altruism alone.

With the growth of ideals through education, with the higher realization of freedom, of justice, of humanity, of service, the selfish impulses become less and less dominant, and if we ever reach the millennium, they will disappear in the aspirations and satisfactions of pure altruism. But for the next several generations we dare not abandon self-interest as a motive force to leadership and to production, lest we die.

The will-o'-the-wisp of all breeds of socialism is that they contemplate a motivation of human animals by altruism alone. It necessitates a bureaucracy of the entire population, in which, having obliterated the economic stimulation of each member, the fine gradations of character and ability are to be arranged in relative authority by ballot or more likely by a Tammany Hall or a Bolshevist party, or some other form of tyranny. The proof of the futility of these ideas as a stimulation to the development and activity of the individual does not lie alone in the ghastly failure of Russia, but it also lies in our own failure in attempts at nationalized industry.

Likewise the basic foundations of autocracy, whether it be class government or capitalism in the sense that a few men through unrestrained control of property determine the welfare of great numbers, is as far apart from the rightful expression of American individualism as the two poles. The will-o'-the-wisp of autocracy in any form is that it supposes that the good Lord endowed a special few with all the divine attributes. It contemplates one human animal dealing to the other human animals his just share of earth, of glory, and of immortality. The proof of the futility of these ideas in the development of the world does not lie alone in the grim failure of Germany, but it lies in the damage to our moral and social fabric from those who have sought economic domination in America, whether employer or employee.

We in America have had too much experience of life to fool ourselves into pretending that all men are equal in ability, in character, in intelligence, in ambition. That was part of the claptrap of the French Revolution. We have grown to understand that all we can hope to assure to the individual through government is liberty, justice, intellectual welfare, equality of opportunity, and stimulation to service.

It is in maintenance of a society fluid to these human qualities that our individualism departs from the individualism of Europe. There can be no rise for the individual through the frozen strata of classes, or of castes, and no stratification can take place in a mass livened by the free stir of its particles. This guarding of our individualism against stratification insists not only in preserving in the social solution an equal opportunity for the able and ambitious to rise from the bottom; it also insists that the sons of the successful shall not by any mere right of birth or favor continue to occupy their fathers' places of power against the rise of a new generation in process of coming up from the bottom. The pioneers of our American individualism had the good sense not to reward Washington and Jefferson and Hamilton with hereditary dukedoms and fixtures in landed estates, as Great Britain rewarded Marlborough and Nelson. Otherwise our American fields of opportunity would have been clogged with long generations inheriting their fathers' privileges without their fathers' capacity for service.

That our system has avoided the establishment and domination of class has a significant proof in the present Administration in Washington. Of the twelve men comprising the President, Vice-President, and Cabinet, nine have earned their own way in life without economic inheritance, and eight of them started with manual labor.

If we examine the impulses that carry us forward, none is so potent for progress as the yearning for individual self-expression, the desire for creation of something. Perhaps the greatest human happiness flows from personal achievement. Here lies the great urge of the constructive instinct of mankind. But it can only thrive in a society where the individual has liberty and stimulation to achievement. Nor does the community progress except through its participation in these multitudes of achievements.

Furthermore, the maintenance of productivity and the advancement of the things of the spirit depend upon the ever-renewed supply from the mass of those who can rise to leadership. Our social, economic, and intellectual progress is almost solely dependent upon the creative minds of those individuals with imaginative and administrative intelligence who create or who carry discoveries to widespread application. No race possesses more than a small percentage of these minds in a single generation. But little thought has ever been given to our racial dependency upon them. Nor that our progress is in so large a measure due to the fact that with our increased means of communication these rare individuals are today able to spread their influence over so enlarged a number of lesser capable minds as to have increased their potency a million-fold. In truth, the vastly greater productivity of the world with actually less physical labor is due to the wider spread of their influence through the discovery of these facilities. And they can arise solely through the selection that comes from the free-running mills of competition. They must be free to rise from the mass; they must be given the attraction of premiums to effort.

Leadership is a quality of the individual. It is the individual alone who can function in the world of intellect and in the field of leadership. If democracy is to secure its authorities in morals, religion, and states-manship, it must stimulate leadership from its own mass. Human leadership cannot be replenished by selection like queen bees, by divine right or bureau-cracies, but by the free rise of ability, character, and intelligence.

Even so, leadership cannot, no matter how bril-liant, carry progress far ahead of the average of the mass of individual units. Progress of the nation is the sum of progress in its individuals. Acts and ideas that lead to progress are born out of the womb of the individual mind, not out of the mind of the crowd. The crowd only feels: it has no mind of its own which can plan. The crowd is credulous, it destroys, it consumes, it hates, and it dreams—but it never builds. It is one of the most profound and important of exact psychological truths that man in the mass does not think but only feels. The mob functions only in a world of emotion. The demagogue feeds on mob emotions and his leadership is the leadership of emotion, not the leadership of intellect and progress. Popular desires are no criteria to the real need; they can be determined only by deliberative consideration, by education, by constructive leadership.

Spiritual Phases

Our social and economic system cannot march toward better days unless it is inspired by things of the spirit. It is here that the higher purposes of indi-vidualism must find their sustenance. Men do not live by bread alone. Nor is individualism merely a stimulus to production and the road to liberty; it alone admits the universal divine inspiration of every human soul. I may repeat that the divine spark does not lie in agreements, in organizations, in institutions, in masses or in groups. Spirituality with its faith, its hope, its charity, can be increased by each individu-al's own effort. And in proportion as each individual increases his own store of spirituality, in that propor-tion increases the idealism of democracy.

For centuries, the human race believed that divine inspiration rested in a few. The result was blind faith in religious hierarchies, the Divine Right of Kings. The world has been disillusioned of this belief that divinity rests in any special group or class whether it be through a creed, a tyranny of kings or of proletariat. Our individualism insists upon the divine in each human being. It rests upon the firm faith that the divine spark can be awakened in every heart. It was the refusal to compromise these things that led to the migration of those religious groups who so largely composed our forefathers. Our diversified religious faiths are the apotheosis of spiritual individualism.

The vast multiplication of voluntary organiza-tions for altruistic purposes are themselves proof of the ferment of spirituality, service, and mutual responsibility. These associations for advancement of public welfare, improvement, morals, charity, public opinion, health, the clubs and societies for recreation and intellectual advancement, represent something moving at a far greater depth than "joining." They represent the widespread aspiration for mutual advancement, self-expression, and neighborly help-fulness. Moreover, today when we rehearse our own individual memories of success, we find that none gives us such comfort as memory of service given. Do we not refer to our veterans as service men? Do not our merchants and business men pride themselves in something of service given beyond the price of their goods? When we traverse the glorious deeds of our fathers, we today never enumerate those acts that were not rooted in the soil of service. Those whom we revere are those who triumphed in service, for from them comes the uplift of the human heart and the uplift of the human mind.

While there are forces in the growth of our indi-vidualism which must be curbed with vigilance, yet there are no less glorious spiritual forces growing within that promise for the future. There is develop-ing in our people a new valuation of individuals and of groups and of nations. It is a rising vision of service. Indeed if I were to select the social force that above all others has advanced sharply during these past years of suffering, it is that of service—service to those with whom we come in contact, service to the nation, and service to the world itself. If we examine the great mys-tical forces of the past seven years we find this great spiritual force poured out by our people as never before in the history of the world—the ideal of service.

Just now we are weakened by the feeling of failure of immediate realization of the great ideas and hopes that arose through the exaltation of war. War by its very nature sets loose chaotic forces of which the resultants cannot be foretold or anticipated. The insensitiveness to the brutalities of physical violence, and all the spiritual dislocations of war, have left us, at the moment, poorer. The amount of serenity and content in the world is smaller.

The spiritual reaction after the war has been in part the fruit of some illusions during those five years. In the presence of unity of purpose and the mystic emotions of war, many men came to believe that salvation lay in mass and group action. They have seen the spiritual and material mobilization of nations, of classes, and groups, for sacrifice and service; they have conceived that real human progress can be achieved by working on "the psychology of the people"—by the "mass mind"; they yielded to leadership without reservation; they conceived that this leadership could continue without tyranny; they have forgotten that permanent spiritual progress lies with the individual.

Economic Phases

That high and increasing standards of living and comfort should be the first of considerations in public mind and in government needs no apology. We have long since realized that the basis of an advancing civilization must be a high and growing standard of living for all the people, not for a single class; that education, food, clothing, housing, and the spreading use of what we so often term nonessentials, are the real fertilizers of the soil from which spring the finer flowers of life. The economic development of the past fifty years has lifted the general standard of comfort far beyond the dreams of our forefathers. The only road to further advance in the standard of living is by greater invention, greater elimination of waste, greater production and better distribution of commodities and services, for by increasing their ratio to our numbers and dividing them justly we each will have more of them.

The superlative value of individualism through its impulse to production, its stimulation to invention, has, so far as I know, never been denied. Criticism of it has lain in its wastes but more importantly in its failures of equitable sharing of the product. In our country these contentions are mainly over the division to each of his share of the comforts and luxuries, for none of us is either hungry or cold or without a place to lay his head—and we have much besides. In less than four decades we have added electric lights, plumbing, telephones, gramophones, automobiles, and what not in wide diffusion to our standards of living. Each in turn began as a luxury, each in turn has become so commonplace that seventy or eighty per cent of our people participate in them.

To all practical souls there is little use in quarreling over the share of each of us until we have something to divide. So long as we maintain our individualism we will have increasing quantities to share and we shall have time and leisure and taxes with which to fight out proper sharing of the "surplus." The income tax returns show that this surplus is a minor part of our total production after taxes are paid. Some of this "surplus" must be set aside for rewards to saving for stimulation of proper effort to skill, to leadership and invention—therefore the dispute is in reality over much less than the total of such "surplus." While there should be no minimizing of a certain fringe of injustices in sharing the results of production or in the wasteful use made by some of their share, yet there is vastly wider field for gains to all of us through cheapening the costs of production and distribution through the eliminating of their wastes, from increasing the volume of product by each and every one doing his utmost, than will ever come to us even if we can think out a method of abstract justice in sharing which did not stifle production of the total product.

It is a certainty we are confronted with a population in such numbers as can only exist by production attuned to a pitch in which the slightest reduction of the impulse to produce will at once create misery and want. If we throttle the fundamental impulses of man our production will decay. The world in this hour is witnessing the most overshadowing tragedy of ten centuries in the heart-breaking life-and-death struggle with starvation by a nation with a hundred and fifty millions of people. In Russia under the new tyranny a group, in pursuit of social theories, have destroyed the primary self-interest impulse of the individual to production.

Although socialism in a nation-wide application has now proved itself with rivers of blood and inconceivable misery to be an economic and spiritual fallacy and has wrecked itself finally upon the rocks of destroyed production and moral degeneracy, I believe it to have been necessary for the world to have had this demonstration. Great theoretic and emotional ideas have arisen before in the world's history and have in more than mere material bankruptcy deluged the world with fearful losses of life. A purely philosophical view might be that in the long run humanity has to try every way, even precipices, in finding the road to betterment.

But those are utterly wrong who say that individualism has as its only end the acquisition and preservation of private property—the selfish snatching and hoarding of the common product. Our American individualism, indeed, is only in part an economic creed. It aims to provide opportunity for self-expression, not merely economically, but spiritually as well. Private property is not a fetish in America. The crushing of the liquor trade without a cent of compensation, with scarcely even a discussion of it, does not bear out the notion that we give property rights any headway over human rights. Our development of individualism shows an increasing tendency to regard right of property not as an object in itself, but in the light of a useful and necessary instrument in stimulation of initiative to the individual; not only stimulation to him that he may gain personal comfort, security in life, protection to his family, but also because individual accumulation and ownership is a basis of selection to leadership in administration of the tools of industry and commerce. It is where dominant private property is assembled in the hands of the groups who control the state that the individual begins to feel capital as an oppressor. Our American demand for equality of opportunity is a constant militant check upon capital becoming a thing to be feared. Out of fear we sometimes even go too far and stifle the reproductive use of capital by crushing the initiative that makes for its creation.

Some discussion of the legal limitations we have placed upon economic domination is given later on, but it is desirable to mention here certain potent forces in our economic life that are themselves providing their own correction to domination.

The domination by arbitrary individual ownership is disappearing because the works of today are steadily growing more and more beyond the resources of any one individual, and steadily taxation will reduce relatively excessive individual accumulations. The number of persons in partnership through division of ownership among many stockholders is steadily increasing—thus 100,000 to 200,000 partners in a single concern are not uncommon. The overwhelmingly largest portion of our mobile capital is that of our banks, insurance companies, building and loan associations, and the vast majority of all this is the aggregated small savings of our people. Thus large capital is steadily becoming more and more a mobilization of the savings of the small holder—the actual people themselves—and its administration becomes at once more sensitive to the moral opinions of the people in order to attract their support. The directors and managers of large concerns, themselves employees of these great groups of individual stockholders, or policy holders, reflect a spirit of community responsibility.

Large masses of capital can only find their market for service or production to great numbers of the same kind of people that they employ and they must therefore maintain confidence in their public responsibilities in order to retain their customers. In times when the products of manufacture were mostly luxuries to the average of the people, the condition of their employees was of no such interest to their customers as when they cater to employees in general. Of this latter, no greater proofs need exist than the efforts of many large concerns directly dependent upon public good will to restrain prices in scarcity—and the very general desire to yield a measure of service with the goods sold. Another phase of this same development in administration of capital is the growth of a sort of institutional sense in many large business enterprises. The encouragement of solidarity in all grades of their employees in the common service and common success, the sense of mutuality with the prosperity of the community are both vital developments in individualism.

There has been in the last thirty years an extraordinary growth of organizations for advancement of ideas in the community for mutual cooperation and economic objectives—the chambers of commerce, trade associations, labor unions, bankers, farmers, propaganda associations, and what not. These are indeed variable mixtures of altruism and self-interest. Nevertheless, in these groups the individual finds an opportunity for self-expression and participation in the moulding of ideas, a field for training and the stepping stones for leadership.

The number of leaders in local and national life whose opportunity to service and leadership came through these associations has become now of more importance than those through the direct lines of political and religious organization.

At times these groups come into sharp conflict and often enough charge each other with crimes against public interest. They do contain faults; if they develop into warring interests, if they dominate legislators and intimidate public officials, if they are to be a new setting of tyranny, then they will destroy the foundation of individualism. Our Government will then drift into the hands of timorous mediocrities dominated by groups until we shall become a syndicalist nation on a gigantic scale. On the other hand, each group is a realization of greater mutuality of interest, each contains some element of public service and each is a school of public responsibility. In the main, the same forces that permeate the nation at large eventually permeate these groups. The sense of service, a growing sense of responsibility, and the sense of constructive opposition to domination, constantly recall in them their responsibilities as well as their privileges. In the end no group can dominate the nation and a few successes in imposing the will of any group is its sure death warrant.

Today business organization is moving strongly toward cooperation. There are in the cooperative great hopes that we can even gain in individuality, equality of opportunity, and an enlarged field for initiative, and at the same time reduce many of the great wastes of over reckless competition in production and distribution. Those who either congratulate themselves or those who fear that cooperation is an advance toward socialism need neither rejoice nor worry. Cooperation in its current economic sense represents the initiative of self-interest blended with a sense of service, for nobody belongs to a cooperative who is not striving to sell his products or services for more or striving to buy from others for less or striving to make his income more secure. Their members are furnishing the capital for extension of their activities just as effectively as if they did it in corporate form and they are simply transferring the profit principle from joint return to individual return. Their only success lies where they eliminate waste either in production or distribution—and they can do neither if they destroy individual initiative. Indeed this phase of development of our individualism promises to become the dominant note of its 20th Century expansion. But it will thrive only in so far as it can construct leadership and a sense of service, and so long as it preserves the initiative and safeguards the individuality of its members.

The economic system which is the result of our individualism is not a frozen organism. It moves rapidly in its form of organization under the impulse of initiative of our citizens, of growing science, of larger production, and of constantly cheapening distribution.

A great test of the soundness of a social system must be its ability to evolve within itself those orderly shifts in its administration that enable it to apply the new tools of social, economic, and intellectual progress, and to eliminate the malign forces that may grow in the application of these tools. When we were almost wholly an agricultural people our form of organization and administration, both in the governmental and economic fields, could be simple. With the enormous shift in growth to industry and commerce we have erected organisms that each generation has denounced as Frankensteins, yet the succeeding generation proves them to be controllable and useful. The growth of corporate organizations, of our banking systems, of our railways, of our electrical power, of our farm cooperatives, of our trade unions, of our trade associations, and of a hundred others indeed develops both beneficent and malign forces. The

timid become frightened. But our basic social ideas march through the new things in the end. Our demagogues, of both radical and stand pat breed, thrive on demands for the destruction of one or another of these organizations as the only solution for their defects, yet progress requires only a guardianship of the vital principles of our individualism with its safeguard of true equality of opportunity in them....

The Future

Individualism has been the primary force of American civilization for three centuries. It is our sort of individualism that has supplied the motivation of America's political, economic, and spiritual institutions in all these years. It has proved its ability to develop its institutions with the changing scene. Our very form of government is the product of the individualism of our people, the demand for an equal opportunity, for a fair chance.

The American pioneer is the epic expression of that individualism, and the pioneer spirit is the response to the challenge of opportunity, to the challenge of nature, to the challenge of life, to the call of the frontier. That spirit need never die for lack of something for it to achieve. There will always be a frontier to conquer or to hold as long as men think, plan, and dare. Our American individualism has received much of its character from our contacts with the forces of nature on a new continent. It evolved government without official emissaries to show the way; it plowed and sowed two score of great states; it built roads, bridges, railways, cities; it carried forward every attribute of high civilization over a continent. The days of the pioneer are not over. There are continents of human welfare of which we have penetrated only the coastal plain. The great continent of science is as yet explored only on its borders, and it is only the pioneer who will penetrate the frontier in the quest for new worlds to conquer. The very genius of our institutions has been given to them by the pioneer spirit. Our individualism is rooted in our very nature. It is based on conviction born of experience. Equal opportunity, the demand for a fair chance, became the formula of American individualism because it is the method of American achievement. After the absorption of the great plains of the West came the era of industrial development with the new complex of forces that it has brought us. Now haltingly, but with more surety and precision than ever before and with a more conscious understanding of our mission, we are finding solution of these problems arising from new conditions, for the forces of our social system can compass and comprise these.

Our individualism is no middle ground between autocracy—whether of birth, economic or class origin—and socialism. Socialism of different varieties may have something to recommend it as an intellectual stop-look-and-listen sign, more especially for Old World societies. But it contains only destruction to the forces that make progress in our social system. Nor does salvation come by any device for concentration of power, whether political or economic, for both are equally reversions to Old World autocracy in new garments.

Salvation will not come to us out of the wreckage of individualism. What we need today is steady devotion to a better, brighter, broader individualism—an individualism that carries increasing responsibility and service to our fellows. Our need is not for a way out but for a way forward. We found our way out three centuries ago when our forefathers left Europe for these shores, to set up here a commonwealth conceived in liberty and dedicated to the development of individuality.

There are malign social forces other than our failures that would destroy our progress. There are the equal dangers both of reaction and radicalism. The perpetual howl of radicalism is that it is the sole voice of liberalism—that devotion to social progress is its field alone. These men would assume that all reform and human advance must come through government. They have forgotten that progress must come from the steady lift of the individual and that the measure of national idealism and progress is the quality of idealism in the individual. The most trying support of radicalism comes from the timid or dishonest minds that shrink from facing the result of radicalism itself but are devoted to defense of radicalism as proof of a liberal mind. Most theorists who denounce our individualism as a social basis seem to have a passion for ignorance of its constructive ideals.

An even greater danger is the destructive criticism of minds too weak or too partisan to harbor constructive ideas. For such, criticism is based upon the distortion of perspective or cunning misrepresentation. There is never danger from the radical himself until the structure and confidence of society has been undermined by the enthronement of destructive criticism. Destructive criticism can certainly lead to revolution unless there are those willing to withstand the malice that flows in return from refutation. It has been well said that revolution is no summer thunderstorm clearing the atmosphere. In modern society it is a tornado leaving in its path the destroyed homes of millions with their dead women and children.

There are also those who insist that the future must be a repetition of the past; that ideas are dangerous, that ideals are freaks.

To find that fine balance which links the future with the past, whose vision is of men and not of tools, that possesses the courage to construct rather than to criticize—this is our need. There is no oratory so easy, no writing so trenchant and vivid as the phrase-making of criticism and malice—there is none so difficult as inspiration to construction.

We cannot ever afford to rest at ease in the comfortable assumption that right ideas always prevail by some virtue of their own. In the long run they do. But there can be and there have been periods of centuries when the world slumped back toward darkness merely because great masses of men became impregnated with wrong ideas and wrong social philosophies. The declines of civilization have been born of wrong ideas. Most of the wars of the world, including the recent one, have been fought by the advocates of contrasting ideas of social philosophy. The primary safeguard of American individualism is an understanding of it; of faith that it is the most precious possession of American civilization, and a willingness courageously to test every process of national life upon the touchstone of this basic social premise. Development of the human institutions and of science and of industry have been long chains of trial and error. Our public relations to them and to other phases of our national life can be advanced in no other way than by a willingness to experiment in the remedy of our social faults. The failures and unsolved problems of economic and social life can be corrected; they can be solved within our social theme and under no other system. The solution is a matter of will to find solution; of a sense of duty as well as of a sense of right and citizenship. No one who buys "bootleg" whiskey can complain of gunmen and hoodlumism. Humanity has a long road to perfection, but we of America can make sure progress if we will preserve our individualism, if we will preserve and stimulate the initiative of our people, if we will build up our insistence and safeguards to equality of opportunity, if we will glorify service as a part of our national character. Progress will march if we hold an abiding faith in the intelligence, the initiative, the character, the courage, and the divine touch in the individual. We can safeguard these ends if we give to each individual that opportunity for which the spirit of America stands. We can make a social system as perfect as our generation merits and one that will be received in gratitude by our children.

CHAPTER 7

Robert and Helen Lynd Search for Modern America

"They're just working. They don't know what for.
They're just in a rut and keep on in it…"

Muncie is a small city in east-central Indiana, best known today as the college town of television talk show icon David Letterman. But in the 1920s and 1930s it was "Middletown," the fictional name given to it by two young researchers, Robert and Helen Lynd, who chose it as the subject of their study of the effects of modernization on a "typical" American locale.

We have already seen how the lives of Randolph Bourne and Crystal Eastman reflected the rise of modernism in large, cosmopolitan, and culturally diverse urban centers (see Chapters 4 and 5). Muncie represented an older, homogeneous, and more traditional America. Composed overwhelmingly of native-born Protestants, with relatively few blacks, Jews, or Catholics, it was spared the ethnic, religious, and racial angst of the major cities.

But Muncie was not immune to the transformations in work structure, home life, family relations, leisure activities, and community engagement brought forth by a rapidly modernizing nation. A sleepy, isolated town of 8,000 in 1890, Muncie's population had grown by the 1920s to almost 40,000. Once an agricultural hub attuned to the rhythms of the soil, it had become a manufacturing center, with glass and metal plants linked to the automobile industry of Detroit. During the last decades of the nineteenth century, Muncie had been a town of skilled, "republican" mechanics and craftsmen (see Chapter 6). By the 1920s it was a city teeming with unskilled and semiskilled factory hands working repetitive jobs under tight, arbitrary supervision, prisoners of the new economic order. The people of Muncie had once defined themselves by what they produced. Now their identity came from what they bought. Muncie's changes had been America's changes. The city's transition to modernity had reflected that of the nation as a whole. So Robert and Helen Lynd, searching for a locality through which to measure national social, cultural, economic, and technological change, found their way to Muncie. Its smaller story, they hoped, could help tell a larger American one.

It was fitting that the Lynds would gravitate to the Middle West. Both had begun their life journeys there. Robert was born in New Albany, Indiana, in 1892. New Albany was a small town, knit together by deep personal and community ties. He was thus acquainted with the simpler culture that predated the modern America he would examine in Muncie. Heading east for college, Robert graduated from Princeton University in 1914. After working in publishing for a few years, he returned to school at New York's Union Theological Seminary, where he was awarded a divinity degree in 1923.

By then he had met and married Helen Merrell, another displaced Midwesterner. The daughter of a Congregationalist church official, Helen grew up just outside Chicago in La Grange, Illinois. Like Robert, Helen also went to college in the East, attending Wellesley, after which she taught school and obtained a master's degree in history at Columbia University. In 1923, the newly married couple relocated to Wyoming, where Robert did missionary work among oil field workers. Outraged by the exploitative labor practices of their employers, he published an account of job conditions that attracted the attention of officials at the Rockefeller family–sponsored Institute of Social and Religious Research. They asked the Lynds to conduct a study of the religious practices of a "typical" American city. Robert and Helen accepted, but decided to expand their research to include all aspects of life in their subject city, a much more challenging undertaking.

The institute was taking a chance in hiring the young couple. What they were proposing was without precedent: No one had ever before attempted a comprehensive investigation of the daily practices of a single city. Moreover, this was a sociologically based inquiry, and neither Robert nor Helen possessed a sociology degree. There was even the question of whether Muncie's ethnic, racial, and religious homogeneity made it an appropriate subject for study. The Lynds wished to examine changes in work, leisure, family relationships, and community life, and a city with a diverse population would have made it difficult to obtain accurate measurements in these areas. They argued for a city like Muncie, located in what they called "that common-denominator of America, the Middle West."[1] But was Muncie truly "typical" of America in the 1920s? The Lynds were gambling that if race, religion, and ethnicity were taken out of the equation, the answer was yes. As they moved to Muncie in January 1924 to begin their work, it was far from assured that they would justify their sponsor's confidence.

The Lynds lived in Muncie for the next one and a half years. During that time they conducted interviews with residents, distributed surveys, compiled statistical profiles from public records, read local newspapers, and used their eyes and ears to take the pulse of the city. They approached the people of Muncie from the perspective of the anthropologist, who studies the everyday behaviors of members of an unfamiliar culture. Although the Muncie environment was not foreign to the Midwest-raised Lynds, they assumed for the purposes of their research that they were encountering it for the first time. This critical distance allowed them to build their study from the ground up.

Their Midwestern roots also helped the Lynds avoid the condescension often exhibited by the well-educated toward everyday folk. This attitude may have been typified by the novelist Sinclair Lewis, who had published the novel *Babbitt* two years before the Lynds arrived in Muncie. *Babbitt* was a scathing indictment of life in a provincial Midwestern city much like Muncie. Like Robert and Helen Lynd, Lewis was born in the Midwest and educated in the East, but the similarities ended there. Lewis was openly contemptuous of those he left behind. His portraits of the status-obsessed, work-alienated, spiritually barren residents of his fictional "Zenith" were designed to expose the narrow contours of life in cities like Muncie. But the Lynds were scholars, not novelists. They reported without editorializing. In so doing, these "amateurs" produced a classic of American social science literature.

Good researchers are good listeners, and the Lynds proved remarkably adept at drawing out their subjects. They also interviewed an impressively broad cross-section of "Muncians"—executives, factory hands, shopkeepers, teachers, politicians, clergymen, salesmen, housewives, and teenagers. Virtually everyone with whom they spoke agreed that Muncie was in the midst of a period of transformative change. Those old enough to remember the previous century felt the impact of these changes most deeply. To them, the modern city of Muncie was almost unrecognizable. The Lynds summarized what these "old-timers" had lived to see:

In the quiet county-seat of the middle eighties men lived relatively close to the earth and its products. In less than four decades, business class and working class, bosses and bossed, have been caught up by industry, this new trait in the city's culture that is shaping the pattern of the whole of living.[2]

The rise of a manufacturing economy in Muncie had fundamentally altered the relations of work. The power of the self-sufficient craftsman had been broken and the last vestiges of independent "republicanism" (see Chapter 6) destroyed. As the Lynds observed:

The shift from a system in which length of service, craftsmanship, and authority in the shop and social prestige among one's peers tended to go together to one which, in the main, demands little of a worker's personality save rapid, habitual reactions and an ability to submerge oneself in the performance of a few routinized easily learned movements seems to have wiped out many of the satisfactions that formerly accompanied the job.[3]

The inherent gratifications of production were now gone. "The work of a modern machine-tender," reported one Muncie factory employee, "leaves nothing tangible at the end of a day's work to which he can point with pride and say, 'I did that—it is the result of my own skill and my own effort.'"[4] A veteran worker was blunter: "You can take a boy fresh from the farm and in three days he can manage a machine as well as I can, and I've been at it twenty-seven years."[5]

What, then, had replaced the fulfillments of work for Muncians? The Lynds found they had taken refuge in buying, and in seeking identity through consumption. Muncie residents were now defining themselves through what they purchased, not what they produced. They had also embraced an unapologetic materialism in which one's standing and prestige was measured almost solely by money. "More and more of the activities of living," the Lynds reported, "are coming to be strained through the bars of the dollar sign.... There seems to be a constantly closer relation between the solitary factor of financial status and one's social status."[6]

In a class-stratified Muncie—the Lynds observed a sharp division of its residents into "business" and "working" classes—the common impulse was an obsession with money and what it could buy. A newspaper editorial titled "Your Bank Account Your Best Friend" declared, "if (money) doesn't answer all things, it at least answers more than 50 per cent of them."[7] While Muncie workers resented their employers, it was not in the classic Marxist sense of struggle over control of the means of production, but because they wanted what their bosses had. "Today," the Lynds wrote, "...every one lives on a slope from any point of which desirable things belonging to people all the way to the top are in view... Both business men and working men seem to be running for dear life in this business of making the money they earn keep pace with the even more rapid growth of their subjective wants."[8]

The most prominent of those "wants" was an automobile. There were two cars for every three families in the city.[9] The Lynds found that Muncians were attached to their autos to the virtual exclusion of all else. "We'd rather go without clothes than give up the car," said one.[10] "The car is the only pleasure we have."[11] Others were willing to forego indoor plumbing, and even food, for the sake of their automobiles. And no consumer product had a greater impact on life and leisure in Muncie. "Why on earth do you need to study what's changing this country?" a long-time resident asked the Lynds. "I can tell you what's happening in just four letters: 'A-U-T-O'!"[12]

If modernity had a tangible symbol in Muncie and elsewhere in the United States, it was the automobile. It changed everything. It altered residential patterns, permitting workers to live further from their places of employment and stimulating the beginnings of suburbanization. It transformed modes of socialization, ending the practice of "porch-visiting" that had defined Muncie neighborhood life for generations. It recast family relations by separating children from their parents, diminishing the latter's authority and control. It expanded leisure opportunities, allowing extended day excursions and vacation trips to hitherto inaccessible destinations. It chipped away at traditional moral codes by affording privacy for sexual encounters among the young. It even affected religious observance, as Muncians increasingly used their Sundays for motor trips instead of church services. The automobile had created a more mobile but less rooted society, with more room for individual choice but weaker connections to family and community.

The automobile-inspired transportation revolution described by the Lynds in Muncie was mirrored by one in communications. Here the cutting edges were the radio and the motion picture. By the mid-1920s, most Muncie households owned radios, which were inexpensive enough to fit within a working-class budget. Along with national magazines, nationally syndicated newspaper columns, and national advertising, the radio created a nationwide mass entertainment culture. Muncians could now hear the same programs as audiences in other parts of the United States, but at a price: National programming cut them off from the culture of their own community. Radio also isolated them from friends and neighbors in much the same way as the automobile, in this instance by sequestering them in their homes while they listened.

The third major item of leisure consumption discussed by the Lynds—the motion picture—worked a similar effect. Muncie was inundated with movies. There were nine movie theatres in town, presenting approximately 300 shows per week. Virtually every Muncie resident went to a performance during the course of a year, and a substantial percentage attended at least once a week. The movies were marketed as a form of escape. "All the adventure, all the romance, all the excitement you lack in your daily life," one newspaper advertisement proclaimed, "are in—pictures."[13] Like the automobile, the movies destabilized family relations, since parents and children attended separately. Sons and daughters would use film going, as they did the automobile, to define themselves against their fathers and mothers, weakening traditional family connections.

The Lynds also found that movie attendance hurt community engagement in Muncie, dampening interest in the civic institutions—including lodges, unions, clubs, leagues, and professional associations—that social scientists have come to call "civil society."[14] As early as the 1830s, Alexis de Tocqueville, the great French observer of democratic life in the United States, remarked on the tendency of Americans to form or join a wide variety of non-governmental associations.[15] These groups occupied a middle ground between the state and the family; through them, citizens could build democracy through active community participation. Without these organizations, De Tocqueville predicted, Americans would become passive and disengaged. Almost a century later, the Lynds could see De Tocqueville's fears realized, as a movie-obsessed population sought respite from drab work lives and unsatisfying personal relationships in an entertainment culture that tore at the roots of Muncie's civil society.

Taken as a whole, the automobile, radio, and motion picture exerted a centrifugal pull on Muncie, fraying its community ties and creating an atomized individualism that offered a richer material life but a poorer sense of identity and connection. In future chapters, we will see how Norman Rockwell in the 1940s (Chapter 10); Allen Ginsberg in the 1950s (Chapter 12); Andy Warhol in the 1960s (Chapter 16); and Robert Putnam in the 1990s (Chapter 22) sought to confront the loneliness and emptiness of a technologically advanced but soul-killingly impersonal modern American society.

Robert and Helen Lynd remained in Muncie until June 1925, when they returned East to compile and analyze their data. When they submitted their findings in manuscript form to the Institute of Social and Religious Research, its officials were not pleased. They believed the Lynds had paid too little attention to religious life in Muncie and were also uncomfortable with what they considered the report's overly negative tone. The institute reneged on its agreement to publish the Lynds' work, leaving them temporarily adrift. But they continued to shop the manuscript around, and misfortune turned to opportunity when Harcourt Brace & Company, a major commercial press, agreed to bring it out. With Muncie's identity disguised by a pseudonym, it was published in 1929 as *Middletown: A Study in Contemporary American Culture*. The book struck an immediate chord with both the academic community, which praised its rich social portrait of a "typical" American city, and the general reading public, which was drawn to its compelling personal narratives. *Middletown* was reprinted five times in 1929 and 1930 alone, and went on to become an American classic. It has never been out of print.

Middletown defined the rest of Robert and Helen Lynd's lives. Both used the book as springboards to long and distinguished academic careers. Robert received a Ph.D. in sociology from Columbia in 1931 using *Middletown* as his dissertation, and was then appointed by the school as a professor of sociology. He eventually received an endowed chair and remained a figure of prominence in his field until retiring in 1960. He died in 1970. Helen became a professor at Sarah Lawrence College, where she was a leader in the development of its innovative curricular and pedagogical system. At her death in 1982, she was lauded as a groundbreaker and role model for women in academia.

As for Muncie itself, its initial response to *Middletown* was marked by confusion and anger. Residents quickly discovered that "Middletown" was Muncie, and took offense at the Lynds' characterizations. An administrator at the city's Ball State Teachers College charged that the book was "cynical."[16] A newspaper demanded the removal of a copy of *Middletown* that had been deposited in the cornerstone of a local church.[17] But Muncie eventually came to terms with the book and its authors. The Lynds returned there in 1935 to research a successor volume—published in 1937 as *Middletown in Transition*—and were well-received, perhaps in gratitude for the boost in name recognition the city now enjoyed. From then on, Muncie's image was inseparable from *Middletown*, and a source of identity for an otherwise unremarkable venue. Today, at the renamed Ball State University, a Center for Middletown Studies carries on the work the Lynds began and preserves their pioneering legacy.

"They're just working. They don't know what for. They're just in a rut and keep on in it, doing the same monotonous work every day…"[18] The Muncie factory executive who thus described his employees to the Lynds in *Middletown* was also describing the new America that modernity had spawned. It was a nation whose people struggled to reconcile the idea of individualism celebrated by Herbert Hoover (see Chapter 6) with the harsh realities of an impersonal society and culture. Alienated from deadening industrial jobs, unable to take pride in their work, Americans increasingly used consumption and leisure to give their lives meaning and direction.

But were automobiles, radios, movies, and other symbols of the material benefits of modernity enough? Was "America" no more than the sum of what its people purchased? These questions hung in the air throughout the 1920s, but a low unemployment rate, easy credit, and rising stock prices confined the ranks of the disillusioned to fringe radicals and intellectuals like Sinclair Lewis. The free enterprise system was the source of the products that Middletowners so eagerly consumed. They accepted that system almost reflexively, "a partially understood but earnestly followed scheme of getting a living," as the Lynds put it.[19] But with the stock market crash of 1929 and the advent of the Great Depression, these questions of American identity in a modern age, along with even more basic ones of the viability of American capitalism itself, presented themselves with new urgency. The Lynds had quoted a Muncie newspaper editorial arguing that "the American citizen's first importance to his country is no longer that of citizen but that of consumer."[20] *Middletown*'s implication was that American identity had no meaning apart from the ability to spend. Could the United States survive without mass consumption? The 1930s would put the modern idea of America as a nation of buyers to the test.

Questions for Consideration and Conversation

1. How would Randolph Bourne (Chapter 4) have described "Middletown"? Crystal Eastman (Chapter 5)? Norman Rockwell (Chapter 10)? Andy Warhol (Chapter 16)? Would he have considered it an example of his "American individualism"?

2. Had "modernity" robbed Middletowners of their individualism? Why did consumption rather than production now hold the key to a "new" American identity?

3. Do you think that a study of a city with the racial, religious, and ethnic homogeneity of "Middletown" offers valid insights on the nation as a whole? What is this study's value?

4. What would Herbert Hoover say about the obsessive materialism he would have observed in "Middletown" had he visited it during the 1920s?

5. How did the automobile "change everything" in "Middletown"? The radio? The motion picture?

6. Robert Putnam (Chapter 22) undoubtedly read *Middletown* as part of his training as a sociologist. How do you think it influenced his thinking?

7. *Middletown*'s implicit conclusion was "American identity had no meaning apart from the ability to spend." Do you agree? How did the 1930s in America (see Chapter 8) challenge this conclusion? The 1960s (see Chapters 15, 16, and 17)?

Endnotes

1. Robert S. Lynd and Helen Merrell Lynd, *Middletown: A Study in Contemporary American Culture* (New York: Harcourt Brace & Company, 1929), 8.
2. Ibid., 87.
3. Ibid., 75.
4. Ibid., 76.
5. Ibid., 74.
6. Ibid., 80–81.
7. Ibid., 84.
8. Ibid., 87.
9. Ibid., 253.
10. Ibid., 255.
11. Ibid., 256.
12. Ibid., 251.
13. Ibid., 265.
14. Robert Putnam, who we will encounter in Chapter 22, will have more to say on civil society's role in promoting community engagement in American democratic life.
15. See Alexis de Tocqueville, *Democracy in America* (New York: Penguin, 2003), 595–600.
16. *New York Times*, November 3, 1970, 38.
17. Ibid.
18. Robert S. Lynd and Helen Merrell Lynd, *Middletown*, 75.
19. Ibid., 89.
20. Ibid., 88.

ROBERT AND HELEN LYND, *MIDDLETOWN* (1929)

Source: Robert S. Lynd and Helen Merrell Lynd, *Middletown*. New York: Harcourt, 1929, pp. 73–89, 251–65, 267–71.

Why Do They Work So Hard?

One emerges from the offices, stores, and factories of Middletown asking in some bewilderment why all the able-bodied men and many of the women devote their best energies for long hours day after day to this driving activity seemingly so foreign to many of the most powerful impulses of human beings. Is all this expenditure of energy necessary to secure food, clothing, shelter, and other things essential to existence? If not, precisely what over and beyond these subsistence necessaries is Middletown getting out of its work?

For very many of those who get the living for Middletown the amount of robust satisfaction they derive from the actual performance of their specific jobs seems, at best, to be slight. Among the business men the kudos accruing to the eminent in getting a living and to some of their minor associates yields a kind of incidental satisfaction; the successful manufacturer even tends today to supplant in local prestige and authority the judge, preacher, and "professor" of thirty-five to forty years ago. But for the working class both any satisfactions inherent in the actual daily doing of the job and the prestige and kudos of the able worker among his associates would appear to be declining.

The demands of the iron man for swiftness and endurance rather than training and skill have led to the gradual abandonment of the apprentice-master craftsman system; one of the chief characteristics of Middletown life in the nineties, this system is now virtually a thing of the past. The master mechanic was the aristocrat among workmen of 1890—"one of the noblest of God's creatures," as one of them put it. But even in the nineties machinery was beginning to undermine the monopolistic status of his skill; he was beginning to feel the ground shifting under his feet. The State Statistician recorded uneasy protests of men from all over the State. Today all that is left of the four-year apprentice system among 9,000 workers in the manufacturing and mechanical industries is three or four score apprentices scattered through the building and molding trades. "It's 'high speed steel' and specialization and Ford cars that's hit the machinist's union," according to a skilled Middletown worker. "You had to know how to use the old carbon steel to keep it from gettin' hot and spoilin' the edge. But this 'high speed steel' and this

new 'stelite' don't absorb the heat and are harder than carbon steel. You can take a boy fresh from the farm and in three days he can manage a machine as well as I can, and I've been at it twenty-seven years."

With the passing of apprenticeship the line between skilled and unskilled worker has become so blurred as to be in some shops almost non-existent. The superintendent of a leading Middletown machine shop says, "Seventy-five per cent. of our force of 800 men can be taken from farm or high school and trained in a week's time." In the glass plant whose shift in processes is noted in Chapter VI, 84 per cent. of the tool-using personnel, exclusive of foremen, require one month or less of training, another 4 per cent. not more than six months, 6 per cent. a year, and the remaining 6 per cent. three years. Foundry workers have not lost to the iron man as heavily as machinists, but even here the trend is marked. In Middletown's leading foundry in the early nineties, 47 per cent. of the workers (including foremen) had three to six years' training. This trained group today is half as great (24 per cent.) and 60 per cent. of all the castings produced are made by a group of newcomers who cast with the help of machines and require only a fortnight or so of training.

"Do you think the man who runs a complicated machine takes pride in his work and gets a feeling of proprietorship in his machine?" a responsible executive in charge of personnel in a large machine shop was asked.

"No, I don't," was his ready reply. "There's a man who's ground diameters on gears here for fifteen years and done nothing else. It's a fairly highly skilled job and takes more than six months to learn. But it's so endlessly monotonous! That man is dead, just dead! And there's a lot of others like him, and I don't know what to do for them."

"What," asked the questioner, "do you think most of the men in the plant are working for?—to own a car, or a home, or just to keep their heads above water?"

"They're just working. They don't know what for. They're just in a rut and keep on in it, doing the same monotonous work every day, and wondering when a slump will come and they will be laid off."

"How much of the time are your thoughts on your job?" an alert young Middletown bench molder was asked.

"As long as there happens to be any new problem about the casting I'm making, I'm thinking about it, but as soon as ever I get the hang of the thing there isn't 25 per cent. of me paying attention to the job."

The shift from a system in which length of service, craftsmanship, and authority in the shop and social prestige among one's peers tended to go together to one which, in the main, demands little of a worker's personality save rapid, habitual reactions and an ability to submerge himself in the performance of a few routinized easily learned movements seems to have wiped out many of the satisfactions that formerly accompanied the job. Middletown's shops are full of men of whom it may be said that "there isn't 25 per cent. of them paying attention to the job." And as they leave the shop in the evening, "The work of a modern machine-tender leaves nothing tangible at the end of the day's work to which he can point with pride and say, 'I did that—it is the result of my own skill and my own effort.'"

The intangible income accruing to many of the business group derives in part from such new devices as membership in Rotary and other civic clubs, the Chamber of Commerce, Business and Professional Women's Club, and the various professional clubs. But among the working class not only have no such new groups arisen to reward and bolster their work, but the once powerful trade unions have for the most part either disappeared or persist in attenuated form.

By the early nineties Middletown had become "one of the best organized cities in the United States." By 1897, thirty "locals" totaling 3,766 members were affiliated with the A. F. of L. and the city vied with Detroit and other cities as a labor convention city. In 1899 the first chapter of a national women's organization, the Women's Union Label League, was launched in Middletown. At this time organized labor formed one of the most active coördinating centers in the lives of some thousands of Middletown working class families, touching their getting-a-living, educational, leisure-time, and even in a few cases religious activities. On the getting-a-living sector the unions brought tangible pressure for a weekly pay law, standardized wage scales, factory inspection, safety devices and other things regarded as improvements, and helped in sickness or death, while crowded mass meetings held in the opera house collected large sums for the striking workers in Homestead and else where. A special Workingmen's Library and Reading Room, with a paid librarian and a wide assortment of books, was much frequented. Undoubtedly the religious element

in the labor movement of this day was missed by many, but a Middletown old-timer still refers enthusiastically to the Knights of Labor as a "grand organization" with a "fine ritual," and a member of both iron and glass unions during the nineties is emphatic regarding the greater importance of the ceremonial aspects of the unions in those days, particularly when new members were received, as compared with the bald meetings of today. As centers of leisure time the unions ranked among the important social factors in the lives of a large number of workers. Such items as these appear in the Middletown press all through the nineties:

A column account of the Ball and Concert given by Midland Lodge No. 20, Amalgamated Association of Iron and Steel Workers in Shirk's Hall, described it as "the largest event of its kind ever given in [Middletown] or the Gas Belt...1,200 to 1,500 present."

An account of the installation of officers and banquet of the Painters' and Decorators' Union records the presence of 200 visitors, including wives and children. A "fine literary program was rendered." The Chief of Police was the guest of honor, and the ex-president and secretary of the Middletown Trades Council spoke. Nearly every member of the police force was present. The hall was decorated with American flags. There was singing, and the new invention, the gramophone, was featured. After the literary program came dancing.

"The Cigar Makers' 'Blue Label' nine played a very hotly contested game with union barbers' nine yesterday [Sunday] P.M."

"Yesterday P.M. [Sunday] the Bakers met at Hummel's Hall on invitation of Aug. Waick, our president, who set up a keg and lunch. We had a meeting, installed officers, then a good time."

Labor Day, a great day in the nineties, is today barely noticed.

From the end of the nineties such laconic reports as "Strike defeated by use of machinery" mark increasingly the failing status of organized labor in Middletown. According to the secretary of one national union, "the organized labor movement in [Middletown] does not compare with that of 1890 as one to one hundred." The city's civic clubs boast of its being an "open shop town."

The social function of the union has disappeared in this day of movies and automobile, save for sparsely attended dances at Labor Hall. The strong molders' union, e.g., has to compel attendance at its meetings by making attendance at one or the other of the two monthly meetings compulsory under a penalty of a dollar fine. There is no longer a Workingmen's Library or any other educational activity. Multiple lodge memberships, occasional factory "mutual welfare associations," the diffusion of the habit of carrying life insurance, socialized provision of workmen's compensation, and the beginning of the practice in at least three factories of carrying group life-insurance for all workers, are slowly taking over the insurance function performed by the trade unions. Of the 100 working class families for whom income distribution was secured, only eleven contributed anything to the support of labor unions; amounts contributed ranged from $18.00 to $60.00.

Likewise, public opinion is no longer with organized labor. In the earlier period a prominent Middletown lawyer and the superintendent of schools addressed an open meeting of the Knights of Labor, and the local press commended the "success of the meeting of this flourishing order." When Samuel Gompers came to town in ninety-seven he was dined in the mayor's home before addressing the great crowd at the opera house. The press carried daily items agitating for stricter local enforcement of the weekly pay law, or urging public support of union solicitations for funds for union purposes, or calling speeches at labor mass-meetings "very able and enjoyable addresses." The proceedings of the Glass Workers' Convention in Baltimore in 1890 were reported in full on the first page. Such a note as this was common: "During the last few months there have been organized in this city several trade organizations and labor unions...and much good has resulted there from." At a grand Farmers and Knights of Labor picnic in 1890, "a perfect jam, notwithstanding the rain," the speaker "ably denounced trusts, Standard Oil, etc.," according to the leading paper. The largest men's clothing firm presented a union with a silk parade-banner costing nearly $100. Today the Middletown press has little that is good to say of organized labor. The pulpit avoids such subjects, particularly in the churches of the business class, and when it speaks it is apt to do so in guarded, equivocal terms. A prevalent attitude among the business class appears in the statement of one of the city's leaders, "Working men don't need unions nowadays. There are no great evils or problems now as there were fifty years ago. We are much more in danger of coddling the working men than abusing them. Working people are just as well off now as they can possibly be except for things which are in the nature of industry and cannot be helped."

This decrease in the psychological satisfactions formerly derived from the sense of craftsmanship and in group solidarity, added to the considerations adduced in the preceding chapters, serves to strengthen the impression gained from talk with families of the working class that, however it may be with their better-educated children, for most of the present generation of workers "there is no break through on their industrial sector." It is important for the consideration of other life-activities to bear in mind this fact, that the heavy majority of the numerically dominant working class group live in a world in which neither present nor future appears to hold as much prospect of dominance on the job or of the breaking through to further expansion of personal powers by the head of the family as among the business group.

Frustrated in this sector of their lives, many workers seek compensations elsewhere. The president of the Middletown Trades Council, an alert and energetic molder of thirty and until now the most active figure in the local labor movement, has left the working class to become one of the minor office-holders in the dominant political machine. Others who do not leave are finding outlets, if no longer in the saloon, in such compensatory devices as hooking up the radio or driving the "old bus." The great pressure toward education on the part of the working class is, of course, another phase of this desire to escape to better things.

For both working and business class no other accompaniment of getting a living approaches in importance the money received for their work. It is more this future, instrumental aspect of work, rather than the intrinsic satisfactions involved, that keeps Middletown working so hard as more and more of the activities of living are coming to be strained through the bars of the dollar sign. Among the business group, such things as one's circle of friends, the kind of car one drives, playing golf, joining Rotary, the church to which one belongs, one's political principles, the social position of one's wife apparently tend to be scrutinized somewhat more than formerly in Middletown for their instrumental bearing upon the main business of getting a living, while, conversely, one's status in these various other activities tends to be much influenced by one's financial position. As vicinage has decreased in its influence upon the ordinary social contacts of this group, there appears to be a constantly closer relation between the solitary factor of financial status and one's social status. A leading citizen presented this matter in a nutshell to a member of the research staff in discussing the almost universal local custom of "placing" new comers in terms of where they live, how they live, the kind of car they drive, and similar externals: "It's perfectly natural. You see, they know money, and they don't know you."

This dominance of the dollar appears in the apparently growing tendency among younger working class men to swap a problematic future for immediate "big money." Foremen complain that Middletown boys entering the shops today are increasingly less interested in being moved from job to job until they have become all-round skilled workers, but want to stay on one machine and run up their production so that they may quickly reach a maximum wage scale.

The rise of large-scale advertising, popular magazines, movies, radio, and other channels of increased cultural diffusion from without are rapidly changing habits of thought as to what things are essential to living and multiplying optional occasions for spending money. Installment buying, which turns wishes into horses overnight, and the heavy increase in the number of children receiving higher education, with its occasions for breaking with home traditions, are facilitating this rise to new standards of living. In 1890 Middletown appears to have lived on a series of plateaus as regards standard of living; old citizens say there was more contentment with relative arrival; it was a common thing to hear a remark that so and so "is pretty good for people in our circumstances." Today the edges of the plateaus have been shaved off, and every one lives on a slope from any point of which desirable things belonging to people all the way to the top are in view.

This diffusion of new urgent occasions for spending money in every sector of living is exhibited by such new tools and services commonly used in Middletown today, but either unknown or little used in the nineties, as the following:

In the home—furnace, running hot and cold water, modern sanitation, electric appliances ranging from toasters to washing machines, telephone, refrigeration, green vegetables and fresh fruit all the year round, greater variety of clothing, silk hose and underwear, commercial pressing and cleaning of clothes, commercial laundering or use of expensive electrical equipment in the home, cosmetics, manicuring, and commercial hair-dressing.

In spending leisure time—movies (attendance far more frequent than at earlier occasional "shows"), automobile (gas, tires, depreciation, cost of trips), phonograph, radio, more elaborate children's playthings, more club dues for more members of the family, Y.M.C.A. and Y.W.C.A., more formal dances and banquets, including a highly competitive series of "smartly appointed affairs" by high school clubs; cigarette smoking and expensive cigars.

In education—high school and college (involving longer dependence of children), many new incidental costs such as entrance to constant school athletic contests.

In the face of these rapidly multiplying accessories to living, the "social problem" of "the high cost of living" is apparently envisaged by most people in Middletown as soluble if they can only inch themselves up a notch higher in the amount of money received for their work. Under these circumstances, why shouldn't money be important to people in Middletown? "The Bible never spoke a truer word," says the local paper in an editorial headed "Your Bank Account Your Best Friend," "than when it said: 'But money answereth all things.'... If it doesn't answer all things, it at least answers more than 50 per cent. of them." And again, "Of our happy position in world affairs there need be no...further proof than the stability of our money system." One leading Middletown business man summed up this trend toward a monetary approach to the satisfactions of life in addressing a local civic club when he said, "Next to the doctor we think of the banker to help us and to guide us in our wants and worries today."

Money being, then, so crucial, how much money do Middletown people actually receive? The minimum cost of living for a "standard family of five" in Middletown in 1924 was $1,920.87. A complete distribution of the earnings of Middletown is not available. Twelve to 15 per cent. of those getting the city's living reported a large enough income for 1923 to make the filing of a Federal income tax return necessary. Of the 16,000–17,000 people gainfully employed in 1923—including, however, somewhere in the neighborhood of a thousand married women, some of whom undoubtedly made joint returns with their husbands—210 reported net incomes (i.e., minus interest, contributions, etc.) of $5,000 or over, 999 more net incomes less than $5,000 but large enough to be taxable after subtracting allowed exemptions ($1,000 if single, $2,500 if married, and $400 per dependent), while 1,036 more filed returns but were not taxable after subtracting allowed deductions and exemptions. The other 85–88 per cent. of those earning the city's living presumably received either less than $1,000 if single or less than $2,000 if married, or failed to make income tax returns. A cross section of working class earnings is afforded by the following distribution of 100 of the working class families interviewed according to their earnings in the preceding twelve months:

	Distribution of Families by Fathers' Earnings Only	Distribution of Families by Total Family Earnings
Total number of families...	100	100
Earning less than minimum standard of $1,920.87		
Families of 5 members or more	42	39
Families of 4 or 3 members (including families of 2 foremen)...	35	35
Earning more than minimum standard of $1,920.87		
Families of 5 members or more (including one foreman)...	10	13
Families of 4 or 3 members (including 6 foremen)...	13	13

The incomes of these 100 families range from $344.56 to $3,460.00, with the median at $1,494.75 and the first and third quartiles respectively at $1,193.63 and $2,006.00.

The relative earning power of males and females in Middletown is indicated by the fact that in a characteristic leading Middletown plant during the first six months of 1924 the weighted average hourly wage of all females (excluding office force and forewomen) was $0.31 and of all males (excluding office force and foremen) $0.55. The bulk of this plant is on a ten-hour basis, fifty-five hours per week, making the average annual income for fifty-two weeks, provided work is steady, $886.60 for females and $1,573.00 for males. In three other major plants similar average wages for males were $0.55, $0.54 and $0.59. In general, unskilled female labor gets $0.18 to $0.28 an hour and a few skilled females $0.30 to $0.50. Unskilled males receive $0.35 to $0.40 an hour and skilled males from $0.50 to $1.00 and occasionally slightly more.

As over against these wages of women in industry in Middletown in 1924, ranging from $10.00 to $18.00 a week in the main, the younger clerks in the leading department store received $10.00 a week, and more experienced clerks a flat rate from $8.00 to $17.00 a week plus a bonus, if earned—the whole amounting occasionally "when times are good" for a veteran clerk to $30.00 to $40.00 a week.

A detailed calculation of a cost of living index for Middletown in 1924 on the basis of the cost of living in 1891 reveals an increase of 117 per cent. A comparison of the average yearly earnings of the 100 heads of families in 1924 with available figures for 439 glass, wood, and iron and steel workers in Middletown in 1891 reveals an average of $1,469.61 in the former case and $505.65 in the latter, or an increase of 191 per cent.

today. Or if we take the earnings of school teachers as an index, probably conservative, of the trend in earnings, as against this rise of 117 per cent. in the cost of living, it appears that the minimum salary paid to grade school teachers has risen 143 per cent. and the maximum 159 per cent. and the minimum salary paid to high school teachers 134 per cent. and the maximum 250 per cent. The median salary for grade school teachers in 1924 was $1,331.25, with the first and third quartiles at $983.66 and $1,368.00 respectively. The median salary for high school teachers was $1,575.00, with the first and third quartiles at $1,449.43 and $1,705.50 respectively. Substantial increases in the incomes of persons in certain other representative occupations are suggested by the fact that the salary of a bank teller has mounted from $50.00 or $65.00 a month in 1890 to $166.67 a month in 1924, that of an average male clerk in a leading men's clothing store from $12.00 a week in 1890 to $35.00 today; a doctor's fee for a normal delivery with the same amount of accompanying care in both periods has risen from $10.00 to $35.00, and for a house call from $1.00 to $3.00.

Thus this crucial activity of spending one's best energies year in and year out in doing things remote from the immediate concerns of living eventuates apparently in the ability to buy somewhat more than formerly, but both business men and working men seem to be running for dear life in this business of making the money they earn keep pace with the even more rapid growth of their subjective wants. A Rip Van Winkle who fell asleep in the Middletown of 1885 to awake today would marvel at the change as did the French economist Say when he revisited England at the close of the Napoleonic Wars; every one seemed to run intent upon his own business as though fearing to stop lest those behind trample him down. In the quiet county-seat of the middle eighties men lived relatively close to the earth and its products. In less than four decades, business class and working class, bosses and bossed, have been caught up by Industry, this new trait in the city's culture that is shaping the pattern of the whole of living. According to its needs, large numbers of people anxious to get their living are periodically stopped by the recurrent phenomenon of "bad times" when the machines stop running, workers are "laid off" by the hundreds, salesmen sell less, bankers call in loans, "credit freezes," and many Middletown families may take their children from school, move into cheaper homes, cut down on food, and do without many of the countless things they desire.

The working class is mystified by the whole fateful business. Many of them say, for instance, that they went to the polls and voted for Coolidge in November, 1924, after being assured daily by the local papers that "A vote for Coolidge is a vote for prosperity and your job"; puzzled as to why "times" did not improve after the overwhelming victory of Coolidge, a number of them asked the interviewers if the latter thought times would be better "after the first of the year"; the first of the year having come and gone, their question was changed to "Will business pick up in the spring?"

The attitude of the business men, as fairly reflected by the editorial pages of the press which today echo, the sentiments heard at Rotary and the Chamber of Commerce, is more confident but confusing. Within a year the leading paper offered the following prescriptions for local prosperity: "The first duty of a citizen is to produce"; and later, "The American citizen's first importance to his country is no longer that of citizen but that of consumer. Consumption is a new necessity." "The way to make business boom is to buy." At the same time that the citizen is told to "consume" he is told, "Better start saving late than never. If you haven't opened your weekly savings account with some local bank, trust company, or building and loan, today's the day." Still within the same year the people of Middletown are told: "The only true prosperity is that for which can be assigned natural reasons such as good crops, a demand for building materials,... increased need for transportation," and "...advancing prices are due to natural causes which are always responsible for prices.... As all wealth comes from the soil, so does all prosperity, which is only another way of saying so does all business." But again, "natural causes" are apparently not the chief essential: "There can be no greater single contribution to the welfare of the nation than the spirit of hopefulness...." "[This] will be a banner year because the people believe it will be, which amounts to the determination that it shall be...." Still another solution for securing "good times" appears: "The most prosperous town is that in which the citizens are bound most closely together.... Loyalty to the home town...is intensely practical.... The thing we must get into our heads about this out-of-town buying business is that it hurts the individual who does it and his friends who live here. Spending your money at home in the long run amounts practically to spending it upon yourself, and buying away from home means buying the comforts and luxuries for the other fellow." "A dollar that is spent out of town never returns." One looking on at this procedure may begin to wonder if the business men, too, are not somewhat bewildered.

Although neither business men nor working men like the recurring "hard times," members of both groups urge the maintenance of the present industrial system. The former laud the group leaders who urge "normalcy" and "more business in government and less government in business," while the following sentences from an address by a leading worker, the president of the Trades Council, during the 1924 political campaign, sets forth the same faith in "free competition" on the part of the working class: "The important issue is the economic issue. We can all unite on that. We want a return to active free competition, so that prices will be lower and a man can buy enough for himself and his family with the money he makes." Both groups, as they order a lay-off, cut wages to meet outside competition, or, on the other hand, vote for La Follette in the hope of his being able to "do something to help the working man," appear to be fumbling earnestly to make their appropriate moves in the situation according to the rules of the game as far as they see them; but both appear to be bound on the wheel of this modern game of corner-clipping production. The puzzled observer may wonder how far any of them realizes the relation of his particular move to the whole function of getting a living. He might even be reminded of a picture appearing in a periodical circulated in Middletown during the course of the study: A mother leans over her two absorbed infants playing at cards on the floor and asks, "What are you playing, children?"

"We're playing 'Putcher,' Mamma. Bobby, putcher card down."

In the midst of such a partially understood but earnestly followed scheme of getting a living, the rest of living goes on in Middletown....

Although lectures, reading, music, and art are strongly intrenched in Middletown's traditions, it is none of these that would first attract the attention of a newcomer watching Middletown at play.

"Why on earth do you need to study what's changing this country?" said a lifelong resident and shrewd observer of the Middle West. "I can tell you what's happening in just four letters: A-U-T-O!"

In 1890 the possession of a pony was the wildest flight of a Middletown boy's dreams. In 1924 a Bible class teacher in a Middletown school concluded her teaching of the Creation: "And how, children, is there any of these animals that God created that man could have got along without?" One after another of the animals from goat to mosquito was mentioned and for some reason rejected; finally, "The horse!" said one boy triumphantly, and the rest of the class agreed. Ten or twelve years ago a new horse fountain was installed at the corner of the Courthouse square; now it remains dry during most of the blazing heat of a Mid-Western summer, and no one cares. The "horse culture" of Middletown has almost disappeared.

Nor was the horse culture in all the years of its undisputed sway ever as pervasive a part of the life of Middletown as is the cluster of habits that have grown up overnight around the automobile. A local carriage manufacturer of the early days estimates that about 125 families owned a horse and buggy in 1890, practically all of them business class folk. "A regular sight summer mornings was Mrs. Jim B____ [the wife of one of the city's leading men] with a friend out in her rig, shelling peas for dinner while her horse ambled along the road." As spring came on each year entries like these began to appear in the diaries:

"April 1, '88. Easter. A beautiful day, cloudy at times but very warm, and much walking and riding about town."

"May 19, '89. Considerable carriage riding today."

"July 16, '89. Considerable riding this evening. People out 'cooling off.' "

"Sept. 18, '87. Wife and myself went to the Cemetery this afternoon in the buggy. Quite a number of others were placing flowers upon the graves of their dear ones...."

But if the few rode in carriages in 1890, the great mass walked. The Sunday afternoon stroll was the rule.

Meanwhile, in a Middletown machine shop a man was tinkering at a "steam wagon" which in September, 1890, was placed on the street for the first trial....

"The vehicle has the appearance of an ordinary road wagon, when put in motion," said the newspaper, "though there is no tongue attached. It is run on the principle of a railroad locomotive, a lever in front which guides the vehicle being operated by the person driving. The power is a small engine placed under the running gears and the steam is made by a small gasoline flame beneath a fuel tank. Twenty-five miles an hour can be attained with this wonderful device. The wagon will carry any load that can be placed on it, climbing hills and passing over bad roads with the same ease as over a level road. The wagon complete cost nearly $1,000."

In other cities other men were also working at these "horseless wagons." As late as 1895 Elwood Haynes of Kokomo, Indiana, one of the early tinkerers, was stopped by a policeman as he drove his horseless car into Chicago and ordered to take the thing off the streets. In 1896 the resplendent posters of the alert P. T. Barnum featured in the foreground a "horseless carriage to be seen every day in the new street parade"—with elephants, camels and all the rest of the circus lost in the background while the crowd cheers "the famous Duryea Motorwagon or Motorcycle."

The first real automobile appeared in Middletown in 1900. About 1906 it was estimated that "there are probably 200 in the city and county." At the close of 1923 there were 6,221 passenger cars in the city, one for every 6.1 persons, or roughly two for every three families. Of these 6,221 cars, 41 per cent. were Fords; 54 per cent. of the total were cars of models of 1920 or later, and 17 per cent. models earlier than 1917. These cars average a bit over 5,000 miles a year. For some of the workers and some of the business class, use of the automobile is a seasonal matter, but the increase in surfaced roads and in closed cars is rapidly making the car a year-round tool for leisure-time as well as getting-a-living activities. As, at the turn of the century, business class people began to feel apologetic if they did not have a telephone, so ownership of an automobile has now reached the point of being an accepted essential of normal living.

Into the equilibrium of habits which constitutes for each individual some integration in living has come this new habit, upsetting old adjustments, and blasting its way through such accustomed and unquestioned dicta as "Rain or shine, I never miss a Sunday morning at church"; "A high school boy does not need much spending money"; "I don't need exercise, walking to the office keeps me fit"; "I wouldn't think of moving out of town and being so far from my friends"; "Parents ought always to know where their children are." The newcomer is most quickly and amicably incorporated into those regions of behavior in which men are engaged in doing impersonal, matter-of-fact things; much more contested is its advent where emotionally charged sanctions and taboos are concerned. No one questions the use of the auto for transporting groceries, getting to one's place of work or to the golf course, or in place of the porch for "cooling off after supper" on a hot summer evening; however much the activities concerned with getting a living may be altered by the fact that a factory can draw from workmen within a radius of forty-five miles, or however much old labor union men resent the intrusion of this new alternate way of spending an evening, these things are hardly major issues. But when auto riding tends to replace the traditional call in the family parlor as a way of approach between the unmarried, "the home is endangered," and all-day Sunday motor trips are a "threat against the church"; it is in the activities concerned with the home and religion that the automobile occasions the greatest emotional conflicts.

Group-sanctioned values are disturbed by the inroads of the automobile upon the family budget A case in point is the not uncommon practice of mortgaging a home to buy an automobile. Data on automobile ownership were secured from 123 working class families. Of these, sixty have cars. Forty-one of the sixty own their homes. Twenty-six of these forty-one families have mortgages on their homes. Forty of the sixty-three families who do not own a car own their homes. Twenty-nine of these have mortgages on their homes. Obviously other factors are involved in many of Middletown's mortgages. That the automobile does represent a real choice in the minds of some at least is suggested by the acid retort of one citizen to the question about car ownership: "No, sir, we've *not* got a car. *That's* why we've got a home." According to an officer of a Middletown automobile financing company, 75 to 90 per cent. of the cars purchased locally are bought on time payment, and a working man earning $35.00 a week frequently plans to use one week's pay each month as payment for his car.

The automobile has apparently unsettled the habit of careful saving for some families. "Part of the money we spend on the car would go to the bank, I suppose," said more than one working class wife. A business man explained his recent inviting of social oblivion by selling his car by saying: "My car, counting depreciation and everything, was costing mighty nearly $100.00 a month, and my wife and I sat down together the other night and just figured that we're getting along, and if we're to have anything later on, we've just got to begin to save." The "moral" aspect of the competition between the automobile and certain accepted expenditures appears in the remark of another business man, "An automobile is a luxury, and no one has a right to one if he can't afford it. I haven't the slightest sympathy for any one who is out of work if he owns a car."

Men in the clothing industry are convinced that automobiles are bought at the expense of clothing, and the statements of a number of the working class wives bear this out:

"We'd rather do without clothes than give up the car," said one mother of nine children. "We used to go to his sister's to visit, but by the time we'd get the children shoed and dressed there wasn't any money left for carfare. Now no matter how they look, we just poke 'em in the car and take 'em along."

"We don't have no fancy clothes when we have the car to pay for," said another. "The car is the only pleasure we have."

Even food may suffer:

"I'll go without food before I'll see us give up the car," said one woman emphatically, and several who were out of work were apparently making precisely this adjustment.

Twenty-one of the twenty-six families owning a car for whom data on bathroom facilities happened to be secured live in homes without bathtubs. Here we obviously have a new habit cutting in ahead of an older one and slowing down the diffusion of the latter.

Meanwhile, advertisements pound away at Middletown people with the tempting advice to spend money for automobiles for the sake of their homes and families:

"Hit the trail to better times!" says one such advertisement.

Another depicts a gray-haired banker lending a young couple the money to buy a car and proffering the friendly advice: "Before you can save money, you first must make money. And to make it you must have health, contentment, and full command of all your resources.... I have often advised customers of mine to buy cars, as I felt that the increased stimulation and opportunity of observation would enable them to earn amounts equal to the cost of their cars."

Many families feel that an automobile is justified as an agency holding the family group together. "I never feel as close to my family as when we are all together in the car," said one business class mother and one or two spoke of giving up Country Club membership or other recreations to get a car for this reason. "We don't spend anything on recreation except for the car. We save every place we can and put the money into the car. It keeps the family together," was an opinion voiced more than once. Sixty-one per cent. of 337 boys and 60 per cent. of 423 girls in the three upper years of the high school say that they motor more often with their parents than without them.

But this centralizing tendency of the automobile may be only a passing phase; sets in the other direction are almost equally prominent. "Our daughters [eighteen and fifteen] don't use our car much because they are always with somebody else in their car when we go out motoring," lamented one business class mother. And another said, "The two older children [eighteen and sixteen] never go out when the family motors. They always have something else on." "In the nineties we were all much more together," said another wife. "People brought chairs and cushions out of the house and sat on the lawn evenings. We rolled out a strip of carpet and put cushions on the porch step to take care of the unlimited overflow of neighbors that dropped by. We'd sit out so all evening. The younger couples perhaps would wander off for half an hour to get a soda but come back to join in the informal singing or listen while somebody strummed a mandolin or guitar." "What on earth *do* you want me to do? Just sit around home all evening!" retorted a popular high school girl of today when her father discouraged her going out motoring for the evening with a young blade in a rakish car waiting at the curb. The fact that 348 boys and 382 girls in the three upper years of the high school placed "use of the automobile" fifth and fourth respectively in a list of twelve possible sources of disagreement between them and their parents suggests that this may be an increasing decentralizing agent.

An earnest teacher in a Sunday School class of working class boys and girls in their late teens was winding up the lesson on the temptations of Jesus: "These three temptations summarize all the temptations we encounter today: physical comfort, fame, and wealth. Can you think of any temptation we have today that Jesus didn't have?" "Speed!" rejoined one boy. The unwanted interruption was quickly passed over. But the boy had mentioned a tendency underlying one of the four chief infringements of group laws in Middletown today, and the manifestations of Speed are not confined to "speeding." "Auto Polo next Sunday!!" shouts the display advertisement of an amusement park near the city. "It's motor

insanity—too fast for the movies!" The boys who have cars "step on the gas," and those who haven't cars sometimes steal them: "The desire of youth to step on the gas when it has no machine of its own," said the local press, "is considered responsible for the theft of the greater part of the [154] automobiles stolen from [Middletown] during the past year."

The threat which the automobile presents to some anxious parents is suggested by the fact that of thirty girls brought before the juvenile court in the twelve months preceding September 1, 1924, charged with "sex crimes," for whom the place where the offense occurred was given in the records, nineteen were listed as having committed the offense in an automobile. Here again the automobile appears to some as an "enemy" of the home and society.

Sharp, also, is the resentment aroused by this elbowing new device when it interferes with old-established religious habits.

The minister trying to change people's behavior in desired directions through the spoken word must compete against the strong pull of the open road strengthened by endless printed "copy" inciting to travel. Preaching to 200 people on a hot, sunny Sunday in midsummer on "The Supreme Need of Today," a leading Middletown minister denounced "automobilitis—the thing those people have who go off motoring on Sunday instead of going to church. If you want to use your car on Sunday, take it out Sunday morning and bring some shut-ins to church and Sunday School; then in the afternoon, if you choose, go out and worship God in the beauty of nature—but don't neglect to worship Him indoors too." This same month there appeared in the *Saturday Evening Post*, reaching approximately one family in six in Middletown, a two-page spread on the automobile as an "enricher of life," quoting "a bank president in a Mid-Western city" as saying, "A man who works six days a week and spends the seventh on his own doorstep certainly will not pick up the extra dimes in the great thoroughfares of life." "Some sunny Sunday very soon," said another two-page spread in the *Post*, "just drive an Overland up to your door—tell the family to hurry the packing and get aboard—and be off with smiles down the nearest road—free, loose, and happy—bound for green wonderlands." Another such advertisement urged Middletown to "Increase Your Week-End Touring Radius." If we except the concentrated group pressure of war time, never perhaps since the days of the camp-meeting have the citizens of this community been subjected to such a powerfully focused stream of habit diffusion. To get the full force of this appeal, one must remember that the nearest lakes or hills are one hundred miles from Middletown in either direction and that an afternoon's motoring brings only mile upon mile of level stretches like Middletown itself.

"We had a fine day yesterday," exclaimed an elderly pillar of a prominent church, by way of Monday morning greeting. "We left home at five in the morning. By seven we swept into ____. At eight we had breakfast at ____, eighty miles from home. From there we went on to Lake ____, the longest in the state. I had never seen it before, and I've lived here all my life, but I sure do want to go again. Then we went to ____ [the Y.M.C.A. camp] and had our chicken dinner. It's a fine thing for people to get out that way on Sundays. No question about it. They see different things and get a larger outlook."

"Did you miss church?" he was asked.

"Yes, I did, but you can't do both. I never missed church or Sunday School for thirteen years and I kind of feel as if I'd done my share. The ministers ought not to rail against people's driving on Sunday. They ought just to realize that they won't be there every Sunday during the summer, and make church interesting enough so they'll want to come."

But if the automobile touches the rest of Middletown's living at many points, it has revolutionized its leisure; more, perhaps, than the movies or any other intrusion new to Middletown since the nineties, it is making leisure-time enjoyment a regularly expected part of every day and week rather than an occasional event. The readily available leisure-time options of even the working class have been multiplied many-fold. As one working class housewife remarked, "We just go to lots of things we couldn't go to if we didn't have a car." Beefsteak and watermelon picnics in a park or a near-by wood can be a matter of a moment's decision on a hot afternoon.

Not only has walking for pleasure become practically extinct, but the occasional event such as a parade on a holiday attracts far less attention now.

"Lots of noise on the street preparing for the 4th," reports the diary of a Middletown merchant on July 3, 1891. And on the 4th: "The town full of people—grand parade with representatives of different trades, an ox roasted whole, four bands, fire-works, races, greased pig, dancing all day, etc." An account in '93 reports: "Quite a stir in town. Firecrackers going off all night and all this day—big horse racing at the Fair Ground. Stores all closed this afternoon. Fireworks at the Fair Ground this evening."

Today the week before the Fourth brings a pale edition of the earlier din, continuing until the night before. But the Fourth dawns quietly on an empty city; Middletown has taken to the road. Memorial Day and Labor Day are likewise shorn of their earlier glory.

Use of the automobile has apparently been influential in spreading the "vacation" habit. The custom of having each summer a respite, usually of two weeks, from getting-a-living activities, with pay unabated, is increasingly common among the business class, but it is as yet very uncommon among the workers. "Vacations in 1890?" echoed one substantial citizen. "Why, the word wasn't in the dictionary!" "Executives of the 1890 period *never* took a vacation," said another man of a type common in Middletown thirty-five years ago, who used to announce proudly that they had "not missed a day's work in twenty years." Vacations there were in the nineties, nevertheless, particularly for the wives and children of those business folk who had most financial leeway. Put-In Bay, Chautauqua, country boarding-houses where the rates were $5.00 a week for adults and $3.00 for children, the annual conference of the State Baptist Association, the Annual National Christian Endeavor Convention, the annual G.A.R. encampment, all drew people from Middletown. But these affected almost entirely business class people. A check of the habits of the parents of the 124 working class wives shows that summer vacations were almost unknown among this large section of the population in the nineties. In lieu of vacations both for workers and many of the business class there were excursions: those crowded, grimy, exuberant, banana-smelling affairs on which one sat up nights in a day coach, or, if a "dude," took a sleeper, from Saturday till Monday morning, and went back to work a bit seedy from loss of sleep but full of the glamour of Petoskey, or the ball game at Chicago. Two hundred and twelve people from Middletown went to Chicago in one week-end on one such excursion. One hundred and fifty journeyed to the state capital to see the unveiling of a monument to an ex-governor—"a statesman," as they called them in those days. Even train excursions to towns fifteen, twenty, and forty miles away were great events, and people reported having "seen the sights" of these other Middletowns with much enthusiasm.

Today a few plants close for one or two weeks each summer, allowing their workers an annual "vacation" without pay. Others do not close down, but workers "can usually take not over two weeks off without pay and have their jobs back when they return." Foremen in many plants get one or two weeks with pay. Of the 122 working class families giving information on this point, five families took one week off in 1923 and again in 1924, seven others took something over a week in each year, twelve took a week or more in only one of the two years. No others had as extensive vacations as these twenty-four, although other entire families took less than a week in one or both years, and in other cases some members of the families took vacations of varying lengths. Of the 100 families for whom income distribution was secured, thirty-four reported money spent on vacations; the amounts ranged from $1.49 to $175.00, averaging $24.12.

But even short trips are still beyond the horizon of many workers' families, as such comments as the following show:

"We haven't had a vacation in five years. He got a day off to paint the house, and another year they gave him two hours off to get the deed to the house signed."

"Never had a vacation in my life, honey!"

"Can't afford one this year because we're repairing the house."

"I don't know what a vacation is—I haven't had one for so long."

"We like to get out in the car each week for half a day but can't afford a longer vacation."

But the automobile is extending the radius of those who are allowed vacations with pay and is putting short trips within the reach of some for whom such vacations are still "not in the dictionary."

"The only vacation we've had in twenty years was three days we took off last year to go to Benton Harbor with my brother-in-law," said one woman, proudly recounting her trip. "We had two Fords. The women slept in the cars, the men on boards between the two running boards. Here's a picture of the two cars, taken just as the sun was coming up. See the shadows? And there's a *hill* back of them."

Like the automobile, the motion picture is more to Middletown than simply a new way of doing an old thing; it has added new dimensions to the city's leisure. To be sure, the spectacle-watching habit was strong upon Middletown in the nineties. Whenever they had a chance people turned out to a "show," but chances were relatively fewer. Fourteen times during January, 1890, for instance, the Opera House was opened for performances ranging from *Uncle Tom's Cabin* to *The Black Crook*, before the paper announced that "there will not be any more attractions at the Opera House for nearly two weeks." In July there were no "attractions"; a half dozen were scattered through August and September; there were twelve in October.

Today nine motion picture theaters operate from 1 to 11 P.M. seven days a week summer and winter; four of the nine give three different programs a week, the other five having two a week; thus twenty-two different programs with a total of over 300 performances are available to Middletown every week in the year. In addition, during January, 1923, there were three plays in Middletown and four motion pictures in other places than the regular theaters, in July three plays and one additional movie, in October two plays and one movie.

About two and three-fourths times the city's entire population attended the nine motion picture theaters during the month of July, 1923, the "valley" month of the year, and four and one-half times the total population in the "peak" month of December. Of 395 boys and 457 girls in the three upper years of the high school who stated how many times they had attended the movies in "the last seven days," a characteristic week in mid-November, 30 per cent. of the boys and 39 per cent. of the girls had not attended, 31 and 29 per cent. respectively had been only once, 22 and 21 per cent. respectively two times, 10 and 7 per cent. three times, and 7 and 4 per cent. four or more times. According to the housewives interviewed regarding the custom in their own families, in three of the forty business class families interviewed and in thirty-eight of the 122 working class families no member "goes at all" to the movies. One family in ten in each group goes as an entire family once a week or oftener; the two parents go together without their children once a week or oftener in four business class families (one in ten), and in two working class families (one in sixty); in fifteen business class families and in thirty-eight working class families the children were said by their mothers to go without their parents one or more times weekly.

In short, the frequency of movie attendance of high school boys and girls is about equal, business class families tend to go more often than do working class families, and children of both groups attend more often without their parents than do all the individuals or other combinations of family members put together. The decentralizing tendency of the movies upon the family, suggested by this last, is further indicated by the fact that only 21 per cent. of 337 boys and 33 per cent. of 423 girls in the three upper years of the high school go to the movies more often with their parents than without them. On the other hand, the comment is frequently heard in Middletown that movies have cut into lodge attendance, and it is probable that time formerly spent in lodges, saloons, and unions is now being spent in part at the movies, at least occasionally with other members of the family. Like the automobile and radio, the movies, by breaking up leisure time into an individual, family, or small group affair, represent a counter movement to the trend toward organization so marked in clubs and other leisure-time pursuits.

How is life being quickened by the movies for the youngsters who bulk so large in the audiences, for the punch press operator at the end of his working day, for the wife who goes to a "picture" every week or so "while he stays home with the children," for those business class families who habitually attend?

"Go to a motion picture...and let yourself go," Middletown reads in a *Saturday Evening Post* advertisement. "Before you know it you are *living* the story-laughing, loving, hating, struggling, winning! All the adventure, all the romance, all the excitement you lack in your daily life are in—Pictures. They take you completely out of yourself into a wonderful new world.... Out of the cage of everyday existence! If only for an afternoon or an evening—escape!"...

Some high school teachers are convinced that the movies are a powerful factor in bringing about the "early sophistication" of the young and the relaxing of social taboos. One working class mother frankly welcomes the movies as an aid in child rearing, saying, "I send my daughter because a girl has to learn the ways of the world somehow and the movies are a good safe way." The judge of the juvenile court lists the movies as one of the "big four" causes of local juvenile delinquency, believing that the disregard of group mores by the young is definitely related to the witnessing week after week of fictitious behavior sequences that habitually link the taking of long chances and the happy ending. While the community attempts to safeguard its schools from commercially intent private hands, this powerful new educational instrument, which has taken Middletown unawares, remains in the hands of a group of men—an ex-peanut-stand proprietor, an ex-bicycle racer and race promoter, and so on— whose primary concern is making money.

Middletown in 1890 was not hesitant in criticizing poor shows at the Opera House. The "morning after" reviews of 1890 bristle with frank adjectives: "Their version of the play is incomplete. Their scenery is limited to one drop. The women are ancient, the costumes dingy and old. Outside of a few specialties, the show was very 'bum.'" When *Sappho* struck town in 1900, the press roasted it roundly, concluding, "[Middletown] has had enough of naughtiness of the stage.... Manager W——will do well to fumigate his pretty playhouse before one of the clean, instructive, entertaining plays he has billed comes before the footlights." The newspapers of today keep their hands off the movies, save for running free publicity stories and cuts furnished by the exhibitors who advertise. Save for some efforts among certain of the women's clubs to "clean up the movies" and the opposition of the Ministerial Association to "Sunday movies," Middletown appears content in the main to take the movies at their face value—"a darned good show"—and largely disregard their educational or habit-forming aspects.

Though less widely diffused as yet than automobile owning or movie attendance, the radio nevertheless is rapidly crowding its way in among the necessities in the family standard of living. Not the least remarkable feature of this new invention is its accessibility. Here skill and ingenuity can in part offset money as an open sesame to swift sharing of the enjoyments of the wealthy. With but little equipment one can call the life of the rest of the world from the air, and this equipment can be purchased piecemeal at the ten-cent store. Far from being simply one more means of passive enjoyment, the radio has given rise to much ingenious manipulative activity. In a count of representative sections of Middletown, it was found that, of 303 homes in twenty-eight blocks in the "best section" of town, inhabited almost entirely by the business class, 12 per cent. had radios; of 518 workers' homes in sixty-four blocks, 6 per cent. had radios.

As this new tool is rolling back the horizons of Middletown for the bank clerk or the mechanic sitting at home and listening to a Philharmonic concert or a sermon by Dr. Fosdick, or to President Coolidge bidding his father good night on the eve of election, and as it is wedging its way with the movie, the automobile, and other new tools into the twisted mass of habits that are living for the 38,000 people of Middletown, readjustments necessarily occur. Such comments as the following suggest their nature:

"I use time evenings listening in that I used to spend in reading."

"The radio is hurting movie going, especially Sunday evening." (From a leading movie exhibitor.)

"I don't use my car so much any more. The heavy traffic makes it less fun. But I spend seven nights a week on my radio. We hear fine music from Boston." (From a shabby man of fifty.)

"Sundays I take the boy to Sunday School and come straight home and tune in. I get first an eastern service, then a Cincinnati one. Then there's nothing doing till about two-thirty, when I pick up an eastern service again and follow 'em across the country till I wind up with California about ten-thirty. Last night I heard a ripping sermon from Westminster Church somewhere in California. We've no preachers here that can compare with any of them."

"One of the bad features of radio," according to a teacher, "is that children stay up late at night and are not fit for school next day."

"We've spent close on to $100 on our radio, and we built it ourselves at that," commented one of the worker's wives. "Where'd we get the money? Oh, out of our savings, like everybody else."

In the flux of competing habits that are oscillating the members of the family now towards and now away from the home, radio occupies an intermediate position. Twenty-five per cent. of 337 high school boys and 22 per cent. of 423 high school girls said that they listen more often to the radio with their parents than without them, and, as pointed out above, 20 per cent. of 274 boys in the three upper years of the high school answered "radio" to the question, "In what thing that you are doing at home this fall are you most interested?"—more than gave any other answer. More than one mother said that her family used to scatter in the evening—"but now we all sit around and listen to the radio."

Likewise the place of the radio in relation to Middletown's other leisure habits is not wholly clear. As it becomes more perfected, cheaper, and a more accepted part of life, it may cease to call forth so much active, constructive ingenuity and become one more form of passive enjoyment. Doubtless it will continue to play a mighty role in lifting Middletown out of the humdrum of every day; it is beginning to take over that function of the great political rallies or the trips by the trainload to the state capital to hear a noted speaker or to see a monument dedicated that a generation ago helped to set the average man in a wide place. But it seems not unlikely that, while furnishing a new means of diversified enjoyment, it will at the same time operate, with national advertising, syndicated newspapers, and other means of large-scale diffusion, as yet another means of standardizing many of Middletown's habits. Indeed, at no point is one brought up more sharply against the impossibility of studying Middletown as a self-contained, self-starting community than when one watches these space-binding leisure-time inventions imported from without—automobile, motion picture, and radio—reshaping the city.

CHAPTER 8

Walker Evans and Dorothea Lange Photograph the Great Depression

"Let us now praise famous men…"

In a migrant labor camp outside Nipomo, California, a woman sits gazing into the distance. Her clothing is threadbare. She holds an infant in her arms. Two other children press against her, heads turned away. The woman's face is drawn and careworn, devoid of hope. She appears utterly alone in her despair.

Eighteen hundred miles to the east in a Hale County, Alabama, tenant farmer's shack, the Woods family sits before a camera. They are painfully thin, their garments little more than rags. All but one are barefoot. Like her counterpart in California, the mother holds an infant in her arms. The family stares into the camera, the pain of their lives etched on their faces.

These images were the work of two great American photographers. The first, which has come to be known as "Migrant Mother," was taken by Dorothea Lange. The second, published in the book *Let Us Now Praise Famous Men*, was from the lens of Walker Evans. They were produced within months of each other in 1936, as the Great Depression raged across the United States. Both images mocked the idea of "American individualism" that Herbert Hoover championed and the consumerism and materialism that the men and women of *Middletown* personified. The poverty portrayed in these images is more than material. "Migrant Mother" and the Woods family seem spiritually bereft. American capitalism appears to have failed them. The world of Andrew Carnegie, which rewarded those who were industrious and imaginative with wealth and honor, bears no resemblance to theirs. Any hope for their deliverance lies not in the individual but the group, not in competition but cooperation, and not through self-help but government assistance.

In this sense "Migrant Mother" and the Woods family represented millions of Americans during the nation's most catastrophic depression, to whom group solidarity in the form of New Deal programs, labor unions, and even the Communist Party meant security, hope, and dignity. Dorothea Lange and Walker Evans gave these men and women a voice and an identity through the power of the visual image. While both found expression primarily through art and not politics, each raised a series of political questions essential to the American conversation, rendered all the more immediate by the nation's dire economic straits. What did the federal government owe its citizens? Did Americans have the right to an income? A job? Health care? Who bore the responsibility for poverty and want—the state or the individual? What was the meaning of "individualism" in American life? What obligations did Americans have toward each other? Lange and Evans used their cameras to set these questions before the American people. In their hands, photographs became forceful rhetorical devices, potent tools of conversation, argument, and persuasion.

Dorothea Lange was born Dorothea Nutzhorn in Hoboken, New Jersey, in 1895 and grew up on New York City's Lower East Side. When she was seven, she suffered an attack of polio that damaged her right leg and caused her to walk with a limp for the rest of her life. Her illness, she later observed, "formed me, guided me, instructed me, helped me, and humiliated me."[1] Ridiculed by other children and abandoned by her father at age twelve—she adopted her mother's maiden name to avoid association with him—Dorothea developed a sympathy and appreciation for the struggles of the marginalized and dispossessed. After working as an apprentice in various New York photography studios, she opened one of her own in San Francisco in 1919. During the 1920s, Lange lived conventionally, establishing a successful portrait business while marrying and raising two children. Everything changed, however, with the advent of the Great Depression. Lange was deeply affected by the suffering around her. One day in 1933 she saw a breadline in downtown San Francisco. Instinctively, she snapped a photograph. The resulting image altered the path of her life. Studio portraiture now seemed empty and meaningless compared to the plight of starving men and women. Lange began to photograph the victims of the Great Depression, hoping her art would put a human face on the grim statistics of economic disaster.

In 1935, Lange found an outlet for her new direction when she was hired by the California Rural Rehabilitation Administration to photograph migrants fleeing the "Dust Bowls" of the Plains states in search of agricultural work in the West. The people Lange encountered as she traveled California with her camera were in dire circumstances. They had been uprooted from their farms in Oklahoma, Kansas, Texas, Colorado, and New Mexico by a natural catastrophe—a lethal combination of drought and wind that blew away topsoil, destroyed livestock, and rendered land unusable. Packing their possessions into family jalopies, they drove west. But California was to be no promised land. Derided as "Okies" by locals, forced into backbreaking field work, penned into squalid labor camps that were little more than prisons, the migrants epitomized the inequity and brutality of a capitalist system gone awry. This was what Lange saw through her viewfinder.

There seemed only one force strong enough to right these wrongs, to bring its weight to bear on behalf of these wounded souls: the federal government. The programs of Franklin D. Roosevelt's New Deal offered help to what the president called "the forgotten man." They also gave Lange an opportunity to realize her social vision through photography. The Resettlement Administration, later renamed the Farm Security Administration, was a New Deal agency established to aid the very people Lange was photographing, a federal version of the California Rural Rehabilitation Administration for which she already worked. She joined it as a staff photographer in 1935, part of its mission to galvanize public support for the migrant poor.

In March of the next year, Lange was returning home to the San Francisco Bay area from a Southern California field trip when she saw a sign for a pea pickers' camp near Nipomo, about 150 miles northwest of Los Angeles. Exhausted after a month on the road, she drove on. But a few miles later, she had second thoughts. Turning her car around, she drove back to the camp. Almost immediately, she saw the woman who would come to represent the ravages of the Great Depression for millions of

Americans—"Migrant Mother"—sitting in a tent with her children. Lange quickly took a series of photographs, and then returned to the road.

On the other side of the country, Walker Evans was preparing to take important photographs of his own. Like Lange, Evans was an artist with a social conscience, although their personal backgrounds could not have been more different. Born into a well-to-do family in 1903, Evans grew up as a child of privilege. After graduating from Phillips Academy Andover in Massachusetts, he attended Williams College for a year, then lived in Paris and worked in New York as a stockbrokerage clerk. By the early 1930s he had found his voice in photography, illustrating a volume of poetry by Hart Crane with images of the Brooklyn Bridge, traveling to Cuba to document political repression, and contributing to experimental art journals. His career path intersected with Lange's when he too began to work for the Resettlement Administration in 1935.

Evans' interests lay primarily in the rural South, where the impact of the Depression was particularly acute. In the 1930s, the region was still coping with the political, social, and economic aftereffects of the Civil War. Chronically cash-poor and debt-ridden, technologically underdeveloped, shackled to money crops such as cotton and tobacco on increasingly exhausted soil, the Southern farmer recreated feudalism in a twentieth-century setting. Evans was drawn to the South's tenant farmers as Lange was to the migrant workers of the West. He made a number of trips south from New York in 1935 and early 1936 on assignment from the Resettlement Administration, and was deeply affected by the privation and hopelessness he encountered. By this time Evans had become a close friend of James Agee, a brilliant young writer and critic who worked for *Fortune* magazine. Agee also wished to use his gifts—in his case literary ones—to capture the human tragedy unfolding around him. Agee and Evans convinced *Fortune* to commission an article on the lives of Southern tenant farmers. In July 1936 they traveled to Hale County in west-central Alabama to observe three families who eked out an existence growing cotton on rented land.

Evans and Agee could scarcely believe what they saw that summer. These men, women, and children were bound to the land like serfs. Their houses were ramshackle and threadbare. Virtually everything they wore was hand-made. They were thin and worn, old before their time. Their life possibilities were as shrunken as their bodies. The cotton field imprisoned them. Cotton, Agee wrote, "demands more work of a tenant family and yields less reward than all the rest.... (It) is the central leverage and symbol of his privation and of his wasted life...(I)n hour upon hour, it is speechless, silent, serious, ceaseless and lonely work along the great silence of the unshaded land..."[2]

Evans' photographs reflect this despair. One of the farmers, Thomas Woods, poses with his wife Ivy, two of their children, Ivy's daughter from another relationship, and his mother-in-law.[3] They stare into the distance in fearful anticipation of what is to come, their expressions resembling that of "Migrant Mother." Their home is barren. Battered objects hang on splintered wooden walls. They sit uneasily on uneven floorboards. A broom, a straight-backed chair, and an improvised towel rack occupy a lonely corner of their kitchen. In contrast to "Migrant Mother," the Woods family is rooted to one spot of ground, having worked the same plot of land for generations. But they share "Migrant Mother's" sense of desolation and hopelessness. Together, the images of the Woods family and "Migrant Mother" created a powerful visual record of the Great Depression's human cost, and an equally powerful indictment of the individualism that only a few years earlier appeared to offer the American people so much. For Lange, Evans, and Agee, the question hung in the air: Is an economic system capable of producing scenes like these worth supporting? At a time when the American Communist Party was making substantial gains in popular opinion, their voices resonated deeply. "Migrant Mother" and the Woods family spoke for millions of Americans without saying a word.

Lange gave one of the photographs she had taken of "Migrant Mother" to her superiors at the Resettlement Administration. She also showed it to editors at her local newspaper, the *San Francisco News.* They saw the dramatic potential of the image and rushed it into print. On March 11, 1936, it appeared on the editorial page of the *News* with the heading "What Does the 'New Deal' Mean to this Mother and Her Child?"[4]

"Migrant Mother" quickly helped the migrants in the Nipomo camp. Officials in Washington, alerted by the Resettlement Administration and galvanized by the photograph's publication, sent a massive food shipment to them. But by then "Migrant Mother" herself was no longer in the camp. She and her family had left almost immediately, driving north in search of work. They had stayed, in fact, for less than a day. The brief time she spent with Lange, however, immortalized her. Almost overnight, "Migrant Mother" became an iconic American image.

She also made a profound contribution to the American conversation. "Migrant Mother's" appearance challenged the individualist ideal on which American capitalism was grounded, and offered an alternative: that of America as a community, with mutual obligations flowing between citizens and their government. A new society could rise out of the ashes of the Great Depression in which Americans "looked out" for each other and the government "looked out" for them. The clear message of Lange's photograph was that "Migrant Mother" could not help herself and it was up to others to do so. Equally clear was its endorsement of the policies of the New Deal, of which the Resettlement and Farm Security Administrations were integral parts. "Migrant Mother" answered critics of government-sponsored relief programs like Herbert Hoover who argued that they sapped initiative and threatened individual freedom, arguing instead that "freedom" to starve was no freedom at all and even suggesting that the paramount "American" value was not freedom but equality. "Migrant Mother" did not seek the "freedom" to earn more than her neighbor. All she asked was enough food, shelter, and work to give her an equal standard of life. She desired security, not riches. Through the cooperative community of the New Deal, "Migrant Mother" could get what she needed and deserved.

"Migrant Mother" helped both the New Deal and Dorothea Lange. The image established her as a major American artist. Lange worked for the Resettlement Administration—renamed the Farm Security Administration in 1937—for the rest of the decade. During World War II, she served as a photographer for the War Relocation Authority, which interned some 120,000 Japanese Americans by order of President Roosevelt. This controversial measure itself stimulated a series of heated American conversations; we will visit them in Chapter 9 through the story of Charles Kikuchi, who spent almost a year in a War Relocation Authority camp. Lange sought to use her photographs to expose what she considered gross violations of the internees' constitutional and human rights, only to have the images impounded by the military.

But Lange's growing reputation transcended the work she did for the federal government. She continued to make social issues the center of her photography, including a study of the life of a public defender in Oakland and a project on rural American women. She founded the photography magazine *Aperture* and taught at the California School of Fine Arts. At her death in 1965, she was regarded as an exemplar of the photographer as artist and social critic. Frequent retrospective exhibits and publications have added to her reputation in recent decades. "Migrant Mother," however, towers over her other achievements. Simultaneously the defining image of Great Depression despair and a compelling articulation of New Deal promise, it is a testament to the power of the visual to define and affect the American conversation.

Walker Evans' photographs also altered the trajectory of the American conversation, but not with the immediacy of Lange's work. *Fortune* editors rejected the article he and Agee submitted based on their stay in Hale County. The authors then decided to try to publish an expanded version of the piece as a book. This too proved difficult. It took until 1938 to obtain a contract with Harper & Brothers, but the company ultimately declined the finished manuscript. After more disappointments, Boston-based Houghton Mifflin Company agreed to bring it out. It was finally published in 1941 as *Let Us Now Praise Famous Men*, the title a reference to a portion of the Book of Ecclesiastes. By then the depression was coming to an end, hastened by the upsurge in government spending occasioned by America's pre-World War II military buildup. The impending conflict, and not the plight of tenant farmers, now dominated national discourse; the book sold only 600 copies. But critics hailed it as an innovative and moving account of the inequities of rural American life, and their praise kept it in the public eye.

Over the next two decades its reputation continued to grow. A contributing factor was the aura that had developed around Agee, whose career as a critic, screenwriter, and novelist offered enough glimpses of his prodigious lyrical talents to make him an object of intense fascination in the American literary community. Agee's premature death in 1955 stimulated further interest, and in 1960 Houghton Mifflin reissued *Let Us Now Praise Famous Men*. The book's rich prose and vivid imagery struck a chord during America's most populist and anti-authoritarian decade since the 1930s themselves, and it became a commercial success.

By the 1960s Evans had established his reputation as a great American photographer, earning critical praise for his work at *Fortune* as well as his portraits of people and scenes on the New York City subways. He also taught photography at Yale in the decade before his death in 1975. Like Lange, Evans' social conscience drove his work without dominating it. He was an artist, not an ideologue. But at the same time, Evans felt a deep need to describe social realities in the United States, and his photography thrust his audience into uncomfortable proximity with want and despair. He thus used art to question the verities and assumptions of American capitalism.

In 1962, as *Let Us Now Praise Famous Men* enjoyed its new-found popularity, the New Left group Students for a Democratic Society released its founding document, the Port Huron Statement (see Chapter 17). It raised the same questions as had Evans and Agee about the fairness of an economic system that could produce the Woods family. Students for a Democratic Society members also challenged the ethos of American individualism, substituting a vision of a community of equals—what the group called the "beloved community"—in its place. During the 1960s, Students for a Democratic Society would continue the conversation over "American" values that *Let Us Now Praise Famous Men* had joined.

Neither "Migrant Mother" nor *Let Us Now Praise Famous Men* escaped controversy. Lange had spent only a few minutes with "Migrant Mother." She had not ascertained crucial aspects of her story. Indeed, she had not even asked her name. The real "Migrant Mother" was Florence Owens Thompson, an Oklahoman of Native American descent who had moved to California in 1926. A series of jobs in mills, restaurants, and the fields brought her and her family to the Nipomo migrant camp in March 1936. Unbeknownst to Lange, however, Thompson did not live there, nor was she starving. She owned an automobile, which had broken down near the camp. Thompson was waiting there while two of her children took the car's radiator into Nipomo for repair. Lange stumbled upon her near the camp's entrance. The rushed photographer got much of Thompson's story wrong. "Migrant Mother" had not, as Lange reported, sold the tires off her automobile for food. Nor was she "desperate," as Lange described her.[5] Thompson and her family were poor, but not helpless. They worked, put food on the table, and eventually survived the depression.

In fact, what seemed to anger Thompson most when she came forward to reveal her identity in the 1970s was Lange's portrayal of her as a victim. Thompson viewed herself instead as a strong, resourceful "survivor" who refused to allow the Great Depression to destroy her spirit. She may have possessed more of the attributes of Hoover's American individualism than Lange would have cared to admit. To some degree, the photographer's interests and those of her subject ran at cross purposes. In order to rally public support for New Deal initiatives such as the Resettlement and Farm Security Administrations, Lange was impelled to accentuate "Migrant Mother's" dependence and need. But Thompson sought dignity and respect even in the face of hardship and injustice. Lange and Thompson themselves represented the tensions between community and individual that animated so many American conversations.

Evans and Agee also were objects of criticism. Their decision to study white tenant families excluded African Americans, who made up a huge portion of the South's rural poor. Their absence from a volume purporting to expose the conditions of the exploited and oppressed was striking. Southern racism—and African Americans themselves—received only passing mention in *Let Us Now Praise Famous Men*. Both Evans and Agee were socially engaged artists and would have deeply resented any imputation of racism. But by choosing to ignore black tenants, they missed an opportunity to present a complete view of Southern injustice as a system of class and racial servitude that entrapped both whites and blacks. This omission diminished the moral force of their work. While their "praise" of the Woods family was justifiable, Evans and Agee may have overreached in placing the mantle of biblical martyrdom on Southern whites who shared the virulent racial attitudes of the region. Neither the Woods family nor Florence Thompson, then, were the perfect victims of their authors' imaginations. In their zeal to mythologize their subjects, Lange, Evans, and Agee rendered them less human, robbing them of the complexities and paradoxes of real people.

Nonetheless, "Migrant Mother" and *Let Us Now Praise Famous Men* endure as forceful rejoinders to America's individualist impulse. During the 1920s, *Middletown* defined the United States in terms of materialism. Americans, it suggested, were what they purchased. Herbert Hoover combined this definition with a celebration of self-reliance and personal autonomy and a view of government as a threat to initiative and independence. But by the 1930s, as the Great Depression destroyed Americans' ability to purchase, and "individuals" like "Migrant Mother" and the members of the Woods family suffered, Evans, Agee, and Lange were rejecting this idea. Even after jobs and purchasing power had returned, a prosperous 1960s generation represented by Students for a Democratic Society continued to voice its dissatisfaction with an America that appeared to place consumer wants before human needs.

In this they continued a conversation over the nature and efficacy of American individualism that linked Carnegie, Hoover, and the Lynds, as well as Evans, Agee, and Lange. Individualism's critics searched for an "American" identity that embodied more than consumerism. "Migrant Mother" and *Let Us Now Praise Famous Men* envisioned instead an America grounded in cooperation and community, a nation that relied on government not only to right social and economic injustices but to bind individuals together in a network of mutual responsibility and service.

The twentieth century would witness a battle between individualist and communitarian understandings of American identity. Each such understanding was based on a different interpretation of the New Deal and its legacy. Were New Deal programs examples of compassionate government action on behalf of the poor and dispossessed? Or were they a misguided assault on personal initiative and free enterprise? The work of Lange, Evans, and Agee offered arguments for the first perspective. Ronald Reagan (see Chapter 21), who early in life was a New Deal supporter, eventually came to advocate the latter view. Unresolved, this deeply contested issue would drive American conversations for years to come.

Questions for Consideration and Conversation

1. What arguments do "Migrant Mother" and the Woods family make against "American individualism" and in favor of government intervention in the American economy?

2. How does Herbert Hoover's argument (Chapter 6) that government assistance saps initiative and creates dependency relate to programs like the Resettlement and Farm Security Administrations?

3. Dorothea Lange, Walker Evans, and James Agee clearly believed America's most important value was equality, not freedom. How would Andrew Carnegie (Chapter 2), Whittaker Chambers (Chapter 11), and Ronald Reagan (Chapter 21) respond?

4. Why do you think *Let Us Now Praise Famous Men* became so popular during the 1960s? How did Students for a Democratic Society (Chapter 17) continue the conversation over the issues Agee and Evans had raised?

5. Lange, Evans, and Agee were all driven by social conscience and as such, were "political" artists. Should art be "political"? Is art's power enhanced or diminished by its association with politics?

6. How does "Migrant Mother's" reappearance in the 1970s as the real-life Florence Thompson resentful of her portrayal as a helpless "victim" challenge Lange's broader arguments about the role of government and the responsibilities of the "community" in American life?

7. Does the fact that Lange got important elements of "Migrant Mother's" story wrong change your reaction to her photograph? What about Evans and Agee's neglect of African American experiences in their work?

Endnotes

1. http://www.getty.edu/education/for_teachers/curricula/dorothea_lange/background1.html

2. James Agee and Walker Evans, *Let Us Now Praise Famous Men* (Boston: Houghton Mifflin, 1941), 326, 344.

3. Evans and Agee assigned the tenant families pseudonyms to afford them some degree of privacy. Thomas Woods' real name was Bud Fields; his wife's name was Lily Fields.

4. Geoffrey Dunn, "Photographic License," *New Times: San Luis Obispo*, January 17, 2002, http://archive.newtimesslo.com/archive/2004-01-21/archives/cov_stories_2002/cov_01172002.html

5. Quoted in Ibid.

JAMES AGEE, *LET US NOW PRAISE FAMOUS MEN* (1941)

Source: James Agee and Walker Evans, *Let Us Now Praise Famous Men*. Boston: Houghton Mifflin, 1941, pp. 257–86, 319–48.

Cotton

Cotton is only one among several crops and among many labors: and all these other crops and labors mean life itself. Cotton means nothing of the sort. It demands more work of a tenant family and yields less reward than all the rest. It is the reason the tenant has the means to do the rest, and to have the rest, and to live, as a tenant, at all. Aside from a few negligibilities of minor sale and barter and of out-of-season work, it is his one possible source of money, and through this fact, though his living depends far less on money than on the manipulations of immediate nature, it has a certain royalty. It is also that by which he has all else besides money. But it is also his chief contracted obligation, for which he must neglect all else as need be; and is the central leverage and symbol of his privation and of his wasted life. It is the one crop and labor which is in no possible way useful as it stands to the tenant's living; it is among all these the one which must and can be turned into money; it is among all these the one in which the landowner is most interested; and it is among all these the one of which the tenant can hope for least, and can be surest that he is being cheated, and is always to be cheated. All other tasks are incidental to it; it is constantly on everyone's mind; yet of all of them it is the work in which the tenant has least hope and least interest, and to which he must devote the most energy. Any less involved and self-contradictory attempt to understand what cotton and cotton work "means" to a tenant would, it seems to me, be false to it. It has the doubleness that all jobs have by which one stays alive and in which one's life is made a cheated ruin, and the same sprained and twilight effect on those who must work at it: but because it is only one among the many jobs by which a tenant family must stay alive, and deflects all these others, and receives still other light from their more personal need, reward, and value, its meanings are much more complex than those of most jobs: it is a strong stale magnet among many others more weak and more yielding of life and hope. In the mind of one in whom all these magnetisms are daily and habituated from his birth, these meanings are one somber mull: yet all their several forces are pulling at once, and by them the brain is quietly drawn and quartered. It seems to me it is only through such a complex of meanings that a tenant can feel, toward that crop, toward each plant in it, toward all that work, what he and all grown women too appear to feel, a particular automatism, a quiet, apathetic, and inarticulate yet deeply vindictive hatred, and at the same time utter hopelessness, and the deepest of their anxieties and of their hopes: as if the plant stood enormous in the unsteady sky fastened above them in all they do like the eyes of an overseer. To do all of the hardest work of your life in service of these drawings-apart of ambiguities; and to have all other tasks and all one's consciousness stained and drawn apart in it: I can conceive of little else which could be so inevitably destructive of the appetite for living, of the spirit, of the being, or by whatever name the centers of individuals are to be called: and this very literally: for just as there are deep chemical or electric changes in all the body under anger, or love, or fear, so there must certainly be at the center of these meanings and their directed emotions; perhaps most essentially, an incalculably somber and heavy weight and dark knotted iron of subnausea at the peak of the diaphragm, darkening and weakening the whole body and being, the literal feeling by which the words a broken heart are no longer poetic, but are merely the most accurate possible description.

Yet these things as themselves are withdrawn almost beyond visibility, and the true focus and right telling of it would be in the exact textures of each immediate task.

Of cotton farming I know almost nothing with my own eyes; the rest I have of Bud Woods. I asked enough of other people to realize that every tenant differs a little in his methods, so nothing of this can be set down as "standard" or "correct"; but the dissonances are of small detail rather than of the frame and series in the year. I respect dialects too deeply, when they are used by those who have a right to them, not to be hesitant in using them, but I have decided to use some of Woods' language here. I have decided, too, to try to use my imagination a little, as carefully as I can. I must warn you that the result is sure to be somewhat inaccurate: but it is accurate anyhow to my ignorance, which I would not wish to disguise.

From the end of the season and on through the winter the cotton and the corn stand stripped and destroyed, the cotton black and brown, the corn gray and brown and rotted gold, much more shattered, the banks of woodland bare, drenched and black, the clay dirt sombered wet or hard with a shine of iron, peaceful and exhausted; the look of trees in a once full-blown country where such a burning of war has gone there is no food left even for birds and insects, all now brought utterly quiet, and the bare homes dark with dampness, under the soft and mourning mid-winter suns of autumnal days, when all glows gold yet lifeless, and under constrictions of those bitter freezings when the clay is shafted and sprilled with ice, and the aching thinly drifted snows which give the land its shape, and, above all, the long, cold, silent, inexhaustible, and dark winter rains:

In the late fall or middle February this tenant, which of the three or of the millions I do not care—a man, dressed against the wet coldness, may be seen small and dark in his prostrated fields, taking down these sometimes brittle, sometimes rotted forests of last year's crops with a club or with a cutter, putting death to bed, cleaning the land: and late in February, in fulfillment of an obligation to his landlord, he borrows a second mule and, with a two-horse plow, runs up the levees,* that is, the terraces, which shall preserve his land; this in a softening mild brightness and

---

*These farms are the width of a state and still more from the river. Is levee originally a land or a river word? It must be a river word, for terracing against erosion is recent in America. So the Mississippi has such power that men who have never seen it use its language in their work.

odoriferousness of presaging spring, and a rustling shearing apart of the heavy land, his mules moving in slow scarce-wakened method as of work before dawn, knowing the real year's work to be not started yet, only made ready for. It is when this is done, at about the first of March, that the actual work begins, with what is planted where, and with what grade and amount of fertilizer, determined by the landlord, who will also, if he wishes, criticize, advise, and govern at all stages of planting and cultivation. But the physical work, and for that matter the knowledge by which he works, is the tenant's, and this is his tenth or his fortieth year's beginning of it, and it is of the tenant I want to tell.

How you break the land in the first place depends on whether you have one or two mules or can double up with another tenant for two mules. It is much better to broadcast if you can. With two mules you can count on doing it all in that most thorough way. But if you have only one mule you break what you have time for, more shallowly, and, for the rest, you bed, that is, start the land.

To broadcast, to break the land broadcast: take a twister, which is about the same as a turning plow, and, heading the mule in concentrics the shape of the field, lay open as broad and deep a ribbon of the stiff dirt as the strength of the mule and of your own guidance can manage: eight wide by six deep with a single-horse plow, and twice that with a double, is doing well: the operation has the staggering and reeling yet steady quality of a small sailboat clambering a storm.

Where you have broadcast the land, you then lay out the furrows three and a half feet apart with a shovel plow; and put down fertilizer; and by four furrows with a turning plow, twist the dirt back over the fertilized furrow. But if, lacking mule power, you have still land which is not broken, and it is near time to plant, you bed the rest. There are two beddings. The first is hard bedding: breaking the hard pan between the rows.

Hard bedding: set the plow parallel to the line of (last year's) stalks and along their right, follow each row to its end and up the far side. The dirt lays open always to the right. Then set the plow close in against the stalks and go around again. The stubble is cleaned out this second time round and between each two rows is a bed of soft dirt: that is to say, the hard pan is all broken. That is the first bedding.

Then drop guano along the line where the stalks were, by machine or by horn. Few tenants use the machine; most of them either buy a horn, or make it,

as Woods does. It is a long tin cone, small and low, with a wood handle, and a hole in the low end. It is held in the left hand, pointed low to the furrow, and is fed in fistfuls, in a steady rhythm, from the fertilizer sack, the incipient frock, slung heavy along the right side.

After you have strowed the gyewanner you turn the dirt back over with two plowings just as before: and that is the second bedding. Pitch the bed shallow, or you won't be able to work it right.

If you have done all this right you haven't got a blemish in all your land that is not broke: and you are ready to plant.

But just roughly, only as a matter of suggestion, compute the work that has been done so far, in ten acres of land, remembering that this is not counting in ten more acres of corn and a few minor crops: how many times has this land been retraced in the rolling-gaited guidance and tensions and whippings and orderings of plowing, and with the steadily held horn, the steady arc of the right arm and right hand fisting and opening like a heart, the heavy weight of the sack at the right side?

Broadcasting, the whole unbroken plaque slivered open in rectilinear concenters, eight inches apart and six deep if with one mule, sixteen apart and twelve deep if with two: remember how much length of line is coiled in one reel or within one phonograph record: and then each furrow, each three and a half feet, scooped open with a shovel plow: and in each row the fertilizer laid: and each row folded cleanly back in four transits of its complete length: or bedding, the first bedding in four transits of each length; and then the fertilizer: and four more transits of each length: every one of the many rows of the whole of the field gone eight times over with a plow and a ninth by hand; and only now is it ready for planting.

Planting

There are three harrs you might use but the spring-toothed harr is best. The long-toothed section harrow tears your bed to pieces; the short-toothed is better, but catches on snags and is more likely to pack the bed than loosen it. The springtooth moves lightly but incisively with a sort of knee-action sensitiveness to the modulations of the ground, and it jumps snags. You harrow just one row at a time and right behind the harrow comes the planter. The planter is rather like a tennis-court marker: a seed bin set between light wheels, with a little plow protruded from beneath it like a foot from under a hoopskirt. The little beak of the plow slits open the dirt; just at its lifted heel the seed thrills out in a spindling stream; a flat wheel flats the dirt over: a light-traveling, tender, iron sexual act entirely worthy of setting beside the die-log and the swept broad-handed arm.*

Depending on the moisture and the soil, it will be five days to two weeks before the cotton will show.

Cultivating begins, as soon as it shows an inch.

Cultivation:

Barring off: the sweepings: chopping: laying by:

The first job is barring off.

Set a five- to six-inch twister, the smallest one you have, as, close in against the stalks as you can get it and not damage them, as close as the breadth of a finger if you are good at it, and throw the dirt to the middle. Alongside this plow is a wide tin defender, which doesn't allow a blemish to fall on the young plants.

Then comes the first of the four sweepings. The sweeps are blunt stocks shaped a good deal like sting-rays. Over their dull foreheads and broad shoulders they neither twist nor roll the dirt, but shake it from the middle to the beds on either side.

For the first sweeping you still use the defender. Use a little stock, but the biggest you dare to; probably the eighteen-inch.

Next after that comes the chopping, and with this the whole family helps down through the children of eight or seven, and by helps, I mean that the family works full time at it. Chopping is a simple and hard job, and a hot one, for by now the sun, though still damp, is very strong, hot with a kind of itchy intensity that is seldom known in northern springs. The work is, simply, thinning the cotton to a stand; hills a foot to sixteen inches apart, two to four stalks to the hill. It is done with an eight to ten-inch hoeblade. You cut the cotton flush off at the ground, bent just a little above it, with a short sharp blow of the blade of which each stroke is light enough work; but multiplied into the many hundreds in each continuously added hour, it aches first the forearms, which so harden they seem to become one bone, and in time the whole spine.

The second sweeping is done with the twenty to twenty-two-inch stock you will use from now on; then comes hoeing, another job for the whole family; then you run the middles; that is, you put down soda by hand or horn or machine; soda makes the weed, guano puts on the fruit; then comes the third sweeping; and then another hoeing. The first and second sweepings you have gone pretty deep. The stuff is small and you want to give loose ground to your feed roots. The third sweeping is shallow, for the feed roots have extended themselves within danger of injury.

The fourth sweeping is so light a scraping that it is scarcely more than a ritual, like a barber's last delicate moments with his muse before he holds the mirror up to the dark side of your skull. The cotton has to be treated very carefully. By this last sweeping it is making. Break roots, or lack rain, and it is stopped dead as a hammer.

This fourth sweeping is the operation more properly known as laying by. From now on until picking time, there is nothing more a farmer can do. Everything is up to the sky, the dirt, and the cotton itself; and in six weeks now, and while the farmer is fending off such of its enemies as he can touch, and, lacking rations money to live on, is desperately seeking and conceivably finding work, or with his family is hung as if on a hook on his front porch in the terrible leisure, the cotton is making, and his year's fate is being quietly fought out between agencies over which he has no control. And in this white midsummer, while he is thus waiting however he can, and defending what little he can, these are his enemies, and this is what the cotton is doing with its time:

Each square points up. That is to say: on twig-ends, certain of the fringed leaves point themselves into the sharp form of an infant prepuce; each square points up: and opens a flat white flower which turns pink next day, purple the next, and on the next day shrivels and falls, forced off by the growth, at the base of the bloom, of the boll. The development from square to boll consumes three weeks in the early summer, ten days in the later, longer and more intense heat. The plants are well fringed with pointed squares, and young cold bolls, by the time the crop is laid by; and the blooming keeps on all summer. The development of each boll from the size of a pea to that point where, at the size of a big walnut, it darkens and dries and its white contents silently explode it, takes five to eight weeks and is by no means ended when the picking season has begun.

And meanwhile the enemies: bitterweed, rag-weed, Johnson grass; the weevil, the army worm; the

---

*I am unsure of this planting machine; I did not see one there; but what Woods described to me seemed to tally with something I had seen, and not remembered with perfect clearness, from my childhood. The die-log is still used, Woods says, by some of the older-fashioned farmers and by some negroes. I'm not very clear about it either, but I am interested because according to Woods its use goes a *way* on back. My "impression" is that it's simple enough: a hollow homemade cylinder of wood with a hole in it to regulate and direct the falling stream of seed as would be more difficult by hand.

slippery chances of the sky. Bitterweed is easily killed out and won't come up again. Ragweed will, with another prong every time. That weed can suck your crop to death. Johnson grass, it takes hell and scissors to control. You can't control it in the drill with your plowing. If you just cut it off with the hoe, it is high as your thumb by the next morning. The best you can do is dig up the root with the corner of your hoe, and that doesn't hold it back any too well.

There is a lot less trouble from the weevils* than there used to be, but not the army worms. Army worms are devils. The biggest of them get to be the size of your little finger. They eat leaves and squares and young bolls. You get only a light crop of them at first. They web up in the leaves and turn into flies, the flies lay eggs, the eggs turn into army worms by the millions and if they have got this good a start of you you can hear the sound of them eating in the whole field and it sounds like a brushfire. They are a bad menace but they are not as hard to control as the weevil. You mix arsenic poison with a sorry grade of flour and dust the plants late of an evening (afternoon) or soon of a morning (pre-morning); and the dew makes a paste of it that won't blow off.

It is only in a very unusual year that you do well with both of the most important crops, the two life mainly depends on, because they need rain and sun in such different amounts. Cotton needs a great deal less rain than corn; it is really a sun flower. If it is going to get a superflux of rain, that will best come before it is blooming; and if it has got to rain during that part of the summer when a fairsized field is blooming a bale a day, it had best rain late in the evening when the blooms are shutting or at night, not in the morning or the mid day: for then the bloom is blared out flat; rain gets in it easy and hangs on it; it shuts wet, sours, and sticks to the boll; next morning it turns red and falls. Often the boll comes off with it. But the boll that stays on is sour and rotted and good for nothing. Or to put it the other way around, it can take just one rain at the wrong time of day at the wrong time of summer to wreck you out of a whole bale.

It is therefore not surprising that they are constant readers of the sky; that it holds not an ounce of "beauty" to them (though I know of no more magnificent skies than those of Alabama); that it is the Iodestone of their deepest pieties; and that they have, also, the deep stormfear which is apparently common

to all primitive peoples. Wind is as terrifying to them as cloud and lightening and thunder: and I remember how, sitting with the Woods, in an afternoon when George was away at work, and a storm was building, Mrs. Gudger and her children came hurrying three quarters of a mile beneath the blackening air to shelter among company. Gudger says: "You never can tell what's in a cloud."

Picking season

Late in August the fields begin to whiten more rarely with late bloom and more frequently with cotton and then still thicker with cotton, a sparkling ground starlight of it, steadily bursting into more and more millions of points, all the leaves seeming shrunken smaller; quite as at night the whole frontage of the universe is more and more thoroughly printed in the increasing darkness; and the wide cloudless and tremendous light holds the earth clamped and trained as beneath a vacuum bell and burningglass; in such a brilliance that half and two thirds of the sky is painful to look into; and in this white maturing oven the enlarged bolls are streaked a rusty green, then bronze, and are split and splayed open each in a loose vomit of cotton. These split bolls are now *burrs*, hard and edged as chiseled wood, pointed nearly as thorns, spread open in three and four and five gores or cells. It is slow at first, just a few dozen scattered here and there and then a few tens of dozens, and then there is a space of two or three days in which a whole field seems to be crackling open at once, and at this time it seems natural that it must be gone into and picked, but all the more temperate and experienced tenants wait a few days longer until it will be fully worth the effort: and during this bursting of bolls and this waiting, there is a kind of quickening, as if deep under the ground, of all existence, toward a climax which cannot be delayed much longer, but which is held in the tensions of this reluctance, tightening, and delay: and this can be seen equally in long, sweeping drivings of a car between these spangling fields, and in any one of the small towns or the county seats, and in the changed eyes of any one family, a kind of tightening as of an undertow, the whole world and year lifted nearly upon its crest, and soon beginning the long chute down to winter: children, and once in a while a very young or a very old woman or man, whose work is scarcely entered upon or whose last task and climax this may be, are deeply taken with an excitement and a restlessness to begin picking, and in the towns, where it is going to mean money, the towns whose existence is for it and depends on it, and which

---

*If I remember rightly, people never learned any successful method against him, and it is some insect, whose name and kind I forget, who holds him in check.

in most times of year are sunken in sleep as at the bottom of a sea: these towns are sharpening awake; even the white hot streets of a large city are subtly changed in this season: but Gudger and his wife and Ricketts and Woods, and most of the heads of the million and a quarter families who have made this and are to do the working of taking it for their own harm and another's use, they are only a little more quiet than usual, as they might be if they were waiting for a train to come in, and keep looking at the fields, and judging them; and at length one morning (the Ricketts women are already three days advanced in ragged work), Gudger says, Well:

Well; I reckin tomorrow we'd better start to picking:

And the next morning very early, with their broad hats and great sacks and the hickory baskets, they are out, silent, their bodies all slanted, on the hill: and in every field in hundreds of miles, black and white, it is the same: and such as it is, it is a joy which scarcely touches any tenant; and is worn thin and through in half a morning, and is gone for a year.

It is simple and terrible work. Skill will help you; all the endurance you can draw up against it from the roots of your existence will be thoroughly used as fuel to it: but neither skill nor endurance can make it any easier.

Over the right shoulder you have slung a long white sack whose half length trails the ground behind. You work with both hands as fast and steadily as you can. The trick is to get the cotton between your fingertips at its very roots in the burr in all three or four or five gores at once so that it is brought out clean in one pluck. It is easy enough with one burr in perhaps ten, where the cotton is ready to fall; with the rest, the fibers are more tight and tricky. So another trick is, to learn these several different shapes of burr and resistance as nearly as possible by instinct, so there will be no second trying and delay, and none left wasted in the burr; and, too, as quickly to judge what may be too rotted and dirtied to use, and what is not yet quite ready to take: there are a lot suspended between these small uncertainties, and there should be no delay, no need to use the mind's judgement, and few mistakes. Still another trick is, between these strong pulls of efficiency, proper judgement, and maximum speed, not to hurt your fingers on the burrs any worse than you can help. You would have to try hard, to break your flesh on any one burr, whether on its sharp points or its edges; and a single raindrop is only scarcely instrumental in ironing a mountain flat; but in each plucking of the hand the fingers are searched deep in along these several sharp, hard edges. In two hours' picking the hands are just well limbered up. At the end of a week you are favoring your fingers, still in the obligation of speed. The later of the three to five times over the field, the last long weeks of the season, you might be happy if it were possible to exchange them for boils. With each of these hundreds of thousands of insertions of the hands, moreover, the fingers are brought to a small point, in an action upon every joint and tendon in the hand. I suggest that if you will try, three hundred times in succession, the following exercise: touch all five fingertips as closely as possible into one point, trying meanwhile to hold loose cotton in the palm of the hand: you will see that this can very quickly tire, cramp and deteriorate the whole instrument, and will understand how easily rheumatism can take up its strictures in just this place.

Meanwhile, too, you are working in a land of sunlight and heat which are special to just such country at just that time of year: sunlight that stands and stacks itself upon you with the serene weight of deep sea water, and heat that makes the jointed and muscled and fine-structured body glow like one indiscriminate oil; and this brilliant weight of heat is piled upon you more and more heavily in hour after hour so that it can seem you are a diving bell whose strained seams must at any moment burst, and the eyes are marked in stinging sweat, and the head, if your health is a little unstable, is gently roaring, like a private blow torch, and less gently beating with aching blood: also the bag, which can hold a hundred pounds, is filling as it is dragged from plant to plant, four to nine burrs to a plant to be rifled swiftly, and the load shrugged along another foot or two and the white row stretched ahead to a blur and innumerably manifolded in other white rows which have not yet been touched, and younger bolls in the cleaned row behind already breaking like slow popcorn in the heat, and the sack still heavier and heavier, so that it pulls you back as a beast might rather than a mere dead weight: but it is not only this: cotton plants are low, so that in this heat and burden of the immanent sun and of the heavying sack you are dragging, you are continuously somewhat stooped over even if you are a child, and are bent very deep if you are a man or a woman. A strong back is a godsend, but not even the strongest back was built for that treatment, and there combine at the kidneys, and rill down the thighs and up the spine and athwart the shoulders the ticklish weakness of gruel or water, and an aching that is increased in geometric progressions, and at length, in the small of the spine, a literal and persistent sensation of yielding, buckling, splintering, and breakage: and all of this, even though the mercy of nature has hardened your flesh and has anesthetized your nerves and your powers of reflection and of imagination, yet reaches in time the brain and the more mirror-like nerves, and thereby is redoubled upon itself much more powerfully than before: and this is all compounded upon you during each successive hour of the day and during each successive day in a force which rest and food and sleep only partly and superficially refresh: and though, later in the season, you are relieved of the worst of the heat, it is in exchange at the last for a coolness which many pickers like even less well, since it so slows and chills the lubricant garment of sweat they work in, and seriously slows and stiffens the fingers which by then at best afford an excruciation in every touch.

The tenants' idiom has been used ad nauseam by the more unspeakable of the northern journalists but it happens to be accurate: that picking goes on each day from can to can't: sometimes, if there is a feeling of rush, the Ricketts continue it by moonlight. In the blasting heat of the first of the season, unless there is a rush to beat a rain or to make up an almost completed Wagonload, it is customary to quit work an hour and a half or even two hours in the worst part of the day and to sit or lie in the shade and possible draft of the hallway or porch asleep or dozing after dinner. This time narrows off as the weeks go by and a sense of rush and of the wish to be done with it grows on the pickers and is tightened through from the landlord. I have heard of tenants and pickers who have no rest-period and no midday meal,* but those I am acquainted with have it. It is of course no parallel in heartiness and variety to the proud and enormous meals which farm wives of the wheat country prepare for harvest hands, and which are so very zestfully regarded by some belated virgilians as common to what they like to call the American Scene. It is in fact the ordinary every day food, with perhaps a little less variety than in the earlier summer, hastily thrown

together and heated by a woman who has hurried in exhausted from the field as few jumps as possible ahead of her family, and served in the dishes she hurriedly rinsed before she hurried out on the early morning as few jumps as possible behind them. When they are all done, she hurries through the dish washing and puts on her straw hat or her sun-bonnet and goes on back into the field, and they are all at it in a strung-out little bunch, the sun a bitter white on their deeply bent backs, and the sacks trailing, a slow breeze idling in the tops of the pines and hickories along the far side but the leaves of the low cotton scarcely touched in it, and the whole land, under hours of heat still to go, yet listed subtly forward toward the late end of the day. They seem very small in the field and very lonely, and the motions of their industry are so small, in range, their bodies so slowly moving, that it seems less that they are so hard at work than that they are bowed over so deeply into some fascination or grief, or are as those pilgrims of Quebec who take the great flights of stairs upon their knees, slowly, a prayer spoken in each step. Ellen lies in the white load of the cotton-basket in the shade asleep; Squinchy picks the front of his dress full and takes it to his mother; Clair Bell fills a hat time after time in great speed and with an expression of delight rushes up behind her mother and dumps the cotton on all of her she can reach and goes crazy with laughter, and her mother and the girls stop a minute and she is hugged, but they talk more among themselves than the other families, they are much more quiet than is usual to them, and Mrs. Ricketts only pauses a minute, cleaning the cotton from her skirts and her hair and putting it in her sack, and then she is bowed over deeply at work again. Woods is badly slowed by weakness and by the pain in his shoulder; he welcomes any possible excuse to stop and sometimes has to pause whether there is any excuse or not, but his wife and her mother are both strong and good pickers, so he is able to get by without a hired hand. Thomas is not old enough yet to be any use. Burt too is very young for it and works only by fits and starts; little is expected of children so small, but it is no harm what little they do; you can't learn them too young. Junior is not very quick with it at best. He will work for a while furiously hard, in jealousy of Louise, and then slacken up with sore hands and begin to bully Burt. Katy is very quick. Last summer, when she was only eight, she picked a hundred and ten pounds in a day in a race with Flora Merry Lee. This summer she has had runarounds and is losing two fingernails but she is picking steadily. Pearl Woods is big for her age and

---

*On the big plantations, where a good deal of the picking is done by day labor and is watched over by riding bosses, all the equations of speed and unresting steadiness are of course intensified; the whole nature of the work, in the men and women and their children, is somewhat altered. Yet not so much as might at first seem. A man and his family working alone are drawn narrowly together in these weeds even within themselves, and know they are being watched: from the very first, in town, their landlords are observant of which tenants bring their cotton first to gin and of who is slow and late; also, there is nearly always, in the tenant's family, the exceedingly sharp need of cottonseed money.

is very steadily useful. Louise is an extraordinarily steady and quick worker for her age; she can pick a hundred and fifty pounds in a day. The two Ricketts boys are all right when their papa is on hand to keep them at their work; as it is, with Ricketts at the sawmills they clown a good deal, and tease their sisters. Mrs. Gudger picks about the average for a woman, a hundred and fifty to two hundred pounds a day. She is fast with her fingers until the work exhausts her; "last half of the day I just don't see how I can keep on with it." George Gudger is a very poor picker. When he was a child he fell in the fireplace and burnt the flesh off the fiat of both hands to the bone, so that his fingers are stiff and slow and the best he has ever done in a day is a hundred and fifty pounds. The average for a man is nearer two hundred and fifty. His back hurts him badly too, so he usually picks on his knees, the way the others pick only when they are resting. Mrs. Ricketts used to pick three hundred and three hundred and fifty pounds in a day but sickness has slowed her to less than two hundred now. Mrs. Ricketts is more often than not a fantast, quite without realizing, and in all these figures they gave me there may be inaccuracy—according to general talk surrounding the Rust machine a hundred pounds a day is good picking—but these are their own estimates of their own abilities, on a matter in which tenants have some pride, and that seems to me more to the point than their accuracy. There are sometimes shifts into gayety in the picking, or a brief excitement, a race between two of the children, or a snake killed; or two who sit a few moments in their sweat in the shaded clay when they have taken some water, but they say very little to each other, for there is little to say, and are soon back to it, and mainly, in hour upon hour, it is speechless, silent, serious, ceaseless and lonely work along the great silence of the unshaded land, ending each day in a vast blaze of dust on the west, every leaf sharpened in long knives of shadow, the clay drawn down through red to purple, and the leaves losing color, and the wild blind eyes of the cotton staring in twilight, in those odors of work done and of nature lost once more to night whose sweetness is a torture, and in the slow, loaded walking home, whose stiff and gentle motions are those of creatures just awakened.

The cotton is ordinarily stored in a small structure out in the land, the cotton house; but none of these three families has one. The Gudgers store it in one of the chambers of their barn, the Woods on their front porch, raising planks around it, the Ricketts in their spare room. The Ricketts children love to play in it, tumbling and diving and burying each other; sometimes, it is a

sort of treat, they are allowed to sleep in it. Rats like it too, to make nest-es* in, and that draws ratsnakes. It is not around, though, for very long at a time. Each family has a set of archaic iron beam scales, and when these scales have weighed out fourteen hundred pounds of cotton it is loaded, if possible during the first of the morning, onto the narrow and high-boarded wagon, and is taken into Cookstown to gin.

It is a long tall deep narrow load shored in with weathered wagonsides and bulged up in a high puff above these sides, and the mule, held far over to the right of the highway to let the cars go by, steps more steadily and even more slowly than ordinary, with a look almost of pomp, dragging the hearse-shaped wagon: its iron wheels on the left grince in the slags of the highway, those on the right in clay: and high upon the load, the father at the reins, the whole of the family is sitting, if it is a small family, or if it is a large, those children whose turn it is, and perhaps the mother too. The husband is dressed in the better of his work clothes; the wife, and the children, in such as they might wear to town on Saturday, or even, some of them, to church, and the children are happy and excited, high on the soft load, and even a woman is taken with it a little, much more soberly, and even the man who is driving, has in the tightness of his jaws, and in his eyes, which meet those of any stranger with the curious challenging and protective, fearful and fierce pride a poor mother shows when her child, dressed in its best, is being curiously looked at; even he who knows best of any of them, is taken with something of the same: and there is in fact about the whole of it some raw, festal quality, some air also of solemn grandeur, this member in the inconceivably huge and slow parade of mule-drawn, crawling wagons, creaking under the weight of the year's bloodsweated and prayed-over work, on all the roads drawn in, from the utmost runners and ramifications of the slender red roads of all the south and into the southern highways, a wagon every few hundred yards, crested this with a white and this with a black family, all drawn toward those little trembling lodes which are the gins, and all and in each private and silent heart toward that

---

*Mrs. Gudger's word. Her saying of it was, "rats likes it to make nest-es in." It is a common pluralization in the south. There is no Cuteness in it, of speaking by diminutives, and I wonder whether this is not Scottish dialect, and whether they, too, are not innocent of the "itsybitsying" which the middle-class literacy assumes of them. *Later.* On the proof-sheets is the following note, which I use with thanks: "Isn't it the Middle-English plural? Chaucer used it for this same word and as a usual plural ending."

climax of one more year's work which yields so little at best, and nothing so often, and worse to so many hundreds of thousands:

The gin itself, too, the wagons drawn up in line, the people waiting on each wagon, the suspendered white-shirted men on the platform, the emblematic sweep of the grand-shouldered iron beam scales cradling gently on the dark doorway their design of justice, the landlords in their shirt-sleeves at the gin or relaxed in swivels beside the decorated safes in their little offices, the heavy-muscled and bloodfaced young men in baseball caps who tumble the bales with short sharp hooks, the loafers drawn into this place to have their batteries recharged in the violence that is in process here in the bare and weedy outskirts of this bare and brutal town; all this also in its hard, slack, nearly speechless, sullen-eyed way, is dancelike and triumphal: the big blank surfaces of corrugated metal, bright and sick as gas in the sunlight, square their darkness round a shuddering racket that subsumes all easy speaking: the tenant gets his ticket and his bale number, and waits his turn in the long quiet line; the wagon ahead is emptied and moves forward lightly as the mule is cut; he cuts his own load heavily under as the gin head is hoisted; he reaches up for the suction pipe and they let it down to him; he swings and cradles its voracity down through the crest of and round and round his stack of cotton, until the last lint has leapt up from the wagon bed; and all the while the gin is working in the deafening appetites of its metals, only it is his work the gin is digesting now, and standing so close in next its flank, he is intimate with this noise of great energy, cost and mystery; and out at the rear, the tin and ghostly interior of the seed shed, against whose roof and rafters a pipe extends a steady sleet of seed and upon all whose interior surfaces and all the air a dry nightmare fleece like the false snows of Christmas movies hangs shuddering as it might in horror of its just accomplished parturition: and out in front, the last of the cotton snowlike relaxing in pulses down a slide of dark iron into the compress its pure whiteness; and a few moments merely of pressure under the floor level, the air of an off-stage strangling; and the bale is lifted like a theater organ, the presses unlatched, the numbered brass tag attached, the metal ties made fast: it hangs in the light breathing of the scales, his bale, the one he has made, and a little is slivered from it, and its weight and staple length are recorded on his ginning slip, and it is caught with the hooks and tumbled out of the way, his bale of cotton, depersonalized forever now, identical with all others, which shall be melted indistinguishably into an oblivion of fabrics, wounds, bleedings, and wars; he takes his ginning slip to his landlord, and gets his cottonseed money, and does a little buying; and gathers his family together; and leaves town. The exodus from town is even more formal than the parade in was. It has taken almost exactly eighteen minutes to gin each bale, once the waiting was over, and each tenant has done almost exactly the same amount of business afterward, and the empty, light grinding wagons are distributed along the roads in a likewise exact collaboration of time and space apart, that is, the time consumed by ginning plus business, and the space apart which, in that time, a mule traverses at his classic noctambular pace. It is as if those who were drawn in full by the sun and their own effort and sucked dry at a metal heart were restored, were sown once more at large upon the slow breadths of their country, in the precisions of some mechanic and superhuman hand.

That is repeated as many times as you have picked a bale. Your field is combed over three, four or five times. The height of the ginning season in that part of the country is early October, and in that time the loaded wagons are on the road before the least crack of daylight, the waiting is endless hours, and the gin is still pulsing and beating after dark. After that comes hog-killing, and the gristing of the corn and milling of the sorghum that were planted late to come ready late; and more urgent and specific meditation of whether or not to move to another man, and of whether you are to be kept; and settlement time; and the sky descends, the air becomes like dark glass, the ground stiffens, the clay honeycombs with frost, the corn and the cotton stand stripped to the naked bone and the trees are black, the odors of pork and woodsmoke sharpen all over the country, the long dark silent sleeping rains stream down in such grieving as nothing shall ever stop, and the houses are cold, fragile drums, and the animals tremble, and the clay is one shapeless sea, and winter has shut.

WALKER EVANS, PHOTOGRAPHS FROM *LET US NOW PRAISE FAMOUS MEN* (1936)

FIGURE 8-1 Fields' family at home.   *Source*: Library of Congress.

FIGURE 8-2 Fields' family home—corner of kitchen.   *Source*: Library of Congress.

DOROTHEA LANGE, "MIGRANT MOTHER" (1936)

FIGURE 8-3 "Migrant Mother."   *Source*: Library of Congress.

CHAPTER 9

Charles Kikuchi Copes with War Relocation

"They are now at the crossroads."

Like W. E. B. Du Bois (see Chapter 3) and Randolph Bourne (see Chapter 4), Charles Kikuchi sought to negotiate his "American" identity from the position of an outsider. Unlike his predecessors, however, Kikuchi had to do this as a prisoner in an internment camp. Immediately after the start of World War II, Kikuchi, along with over 100,000 other Japanese Americans living on the West Coast, was uprooted from his home and placed in a war relocation camp by order of President Franklin D. Roosevelt. Approximately two-thirds of those removed were American citizens.

Defenders of the president's action argued that it was justified by military necessity. In the unsettled atmosphere following Japan's December 1941 attack on Pearl Harbor, many believed that Americans of Japanese descent in Oregon, Washington State, and especially California, posed an imminent threat to the security of the nation. Military authorities claimed that they had neither the time nor the manpower to draw distinctions between the loyal and disloyal, and that the entire Japanese American population thus required relocation. As a result, Charles Kikuchi and thousands of others spent a substantial portion of the war years in barbed wire-enclosed camps in remote desert locations with primitive food and sanitary facilities. Although the U.S. Supreme Court upheld the registration and relocation provisions of the Japanese removal program, it remains one of the most controversial measures ever enacted by the federal government.

That the internees were victims is beyond dispute. Even the government has acknowledged the injustice of its actions. History has tended to regard those affected by the internment as faceless symbols, not fully realized human beings. But each of their stories was personal as well as political. Examining one such personal story allows us to see the Japanese internment as more than a simple morality play with clearly demarcated lines of innocence and guilt, but as a series of complex and unsettling questions. Can one be a citizen of the United States but not completely "American"? Is it ever justifiable to restrict the liberties of members of an ethnic group because the United States is at war with their country of origin, or is this an impermissible form of "racial profiling"? If barred from becoming a U.S. citizen on the basis of ethnic origin, how does one become "American"? And even if one is an American citizen, is it possible to honor both national and ethnic ties simultaneously? Every Japanese American, whether citizen or alien, had to answer these questions during the internment years. Given the adverse circumstances, it is not surprising that some rejected American identity altogether, even to the point of renouncing their citizenship. Most, however, struggled to define themselves as Americans even as America segregated and stigmatized them. We are fortunate that one such American chose to record the details of that struggle.

Charles Kikuchi was born in Vallejo, California, north of San Francisco, in 1915. His father was an "Issei"—an immigrant from Japan, who was ineligible for American citizenship under the terms of a 1798 federal law limiting eligibility for naturalization to Caucasians. His son was a "Nisei," born in the United States and thus automatically a citizen by virtue of the Fourteenth Amendment to the Constitution. Charles' early life was tumultuous. His parents quarreled frequently and were unable to give him the attention he needed. They placed him in a Salvation Army home at the age of eight, and he remained there through high school. Most of the home's residents were Caucasian, exposing Charles to non-Japanese for the first time. As a result, he learned to move between the world of his ancestry and that of the white majority, at once an "outsider" and an "insider," much like Du Bois had been.

In the California of the 1930s, however, it was difficult for a young man of Japanese descent to move very far up the American ladder of success. The only jobs open to Kikuchi after high school were in a Japanese-owned grocery or farm or as a domestic servant. He obtained work in San Francisco as a houseboy for a well-to-do white family while he studied at San Francisco State University, from which he graduated in 1939. During this period, Kikuchi found himself drawn to the middle-class values of his employer, who considered him part of his family. Kikuchi began to think of his Japanese ancestry as a burden, and even investigated the feasibility of a medical procedure that would render his facial appearance more "Caucasian" in character, much as Malcolm X would alter his hair style for the same purpose (see Chapter 18).

But Kikuchi discovered that he could not escape his heritage when, even with a college degree in hand, he struggled in the prejudiced atmosphere of the day to find a job appropriate to his level of education. He spent part of the summer of 1940 as a farm laborer in rural California under grueling conditions. Here Kikuchi experienced racism and exploitation of an unexpected nature. Tensions between Japanese and Filipinos in the fields spilled into violence, and the two groups self-segregated. Kikuchi aroused the ire of "his own" people by befriending a Filipino. The farm owners were largely Japanese; Kikuchi learned that summer that greed and brutality were not the sole provinces of white employers.

Kikuchi also learned that racial and class oppression were often interconnected. He asked himself if the Filipinos were treated inhumanely by the Japanese growers because they were of a different race, or because they were workers. Kikuchi's summer of farm labor deepened his anxieties about his own place in America as an impoverished member of a minority group. What was his "American" identity? Kikuchi decided to pursue graduate studies in social work at the University of California at Berkeley in part to answer this question. He was there on December 7, 1941, when news of Pearl Harbor reached him. Kikuchi knew immediately that his life as a Japanese American was about to change. Earlier that year, in a class paper, Kikuchi had written: "torn between two cultures, the Nisei finds no place or security in either."[1] Now he would have to find his own place in an altered American landscape rife with hostility and danger.

Kikuchi had good reason to fear the reaction of white Americans—and especially white Californians—to Pearl Harbor. Even before December 1941, Japanese in the United States had lived on the margins, viewed as the alien "other." In an American culture containing strong impulses toward nativism and white supremacy, they were burdened not only with the stigma of the immigrant but also that of the "yellow" race. Japanese began to arrive in the United States in the late 1800s, drawn by economic opportunities, especially the possibility of land ownership. Most settled in California, where by 1920 they comprised about 2% of the state's population.[2] Despite their relatively small numbers, whites felt threatened by the Japanese, and mounted campaigns to exclude and restrict them. In 1907 and 1908, under pressure from California public officials, President Theodore Roosevelt entered into "Gentleman's Agreements" with the government of Japan under which the flow of Japanese laborers into the United States was virtually cut off. The Immigration Act of 1924 ended legal Japanese entry entirely. California whites also attempted to deny the Japanese access to land through a 1913 law that banned aliens who could not become citizens—meaning all Issei—from owning real property used for commercial agriculture, forcing them into sham transactions involving their Nisei children or Caucasian stand-ins.

Despite this atmosphere of prejudice and hostility, Japanese Americans had achieved an impressive measure of economic success by 1941 in California and on the West Coast generally, operating small businesses and farms. By the eve of Pearl Harbor, a sharp cultural divide had developed between non-citizen Issei and their Nisei offspring. Many of the latter, like Charles Kikuchi, were college educated and more willing to engage "America"—which, given their dominant position in virtually every aspect of national life, essentially meant white Caucasian America. Events would soon strain both the Issei and Nisei versions of the "American" experience to the breaking point.

On December 7, 1941, Charles Kikuchi wrote in his diary:

Pearl Harbor. We are at war! Jesus Christ, the Japs bombed Hawaii...I think of the Japs coming to bomb us, but I will go and fight even if I think I am a coward and I don't believe in war but this time it has to be....I think not of California and America, but I wonder what is going to happen to the Nisei and to our parents. They may lock up the aliens. How can one think of the future? We are behind the eightball, and that question for the California Nisei "whither Nisei?" (is) so true. The next five years will determine the future of the Nisei. They are now at the crossroads. Will they be able to take it or will they go under? If we are ever going to prove our Americanism, this is the time.[3]

Kikuchi was in conflict, as the sometimes contradictory elements of his diary entry attested. On one hand, he wrote of offering the ultimate demonstration of his "Americanism" by fighting for the United States against Japan. He even adopted the anti-Japanese slur employed by many white Americans: "Japs." On the other hand, Kikuchi was acutely aware of his status as an outsider, and of the dangers he and his people now faced. By 1941, Kikuchi was close to embodying the "cosmopolitanism" that Randolph Bourne (see Chapter 4) had championed a quarter-century earlier. He moved in a social circle at Berkeley that included students and faculty from a variety of ethnic and racial backgrounds—what we would today call "diverse." But after December 7, 1941, this cosmopolitan identity was denied him. To a traumatized West Coast white population fearful of disloyal elements, military officials worried about the possibility of attack, and government authorities sensitive to aroused public opinion, Kikuchi was simply a "Japanese," or even a "Jap."

On February 19, 1942, President Roosevelt signed Executive Order 9066, authorizing the War Department to remove "any and all persons" from areas deemed essential to national security. General John L. DeWitt, in charge of western military operations, wasted no time in designating California, Oregon, and Washington State as "military areas" and ordering the evacuation of all Japanese, regardless of citizenship status, from them. In March, another executive order created the War Relocation Authority (WRA) to coordinate Japanese removal. Kikuchi was completing his studies at Berkeley in the spring of 1942 when he and his family were ordered to report to Tanforan Assembly Center near San Bruno, south of San Francisco. There, on the site of a racetrack, they would await relocation inland while living in a horse stable. By April, General DeWitt had ordered all Japanese living on the West Coast to report to designated assembly centers. Due to the short notice, many evacuees had to sell their property at distress prices or abandon it altogether; dollar estimates of losses ranged between $67 and $116 million.[4]

As the relocation orders took effect, constitutional challenges began to work their way through the federal judicial system. It would take until 1943 and 1944, however, for the Supreme Court to finally decide them.

Charles Kikuchi's diary for his time at Tanforan Assembly Center from May to August 1942 reveals a man torn by conflicting impulses—between a proud identification with America and its democratic promise and anger at his country's betrayal of its own ideals. He also oscillates between disgust with Issei detainees who denounce American racism and support Japan in the war, and a discomforting sense that they are correct. Kikuchi admits that while "outwardly I try to pass off as adjusted to this setup," he finds that "waves of resentment come over me at the funniest times."[5] He avers that "Americanization of the group" is "the thing I want to do." But then, "doubts about the Caucasian-American good faith" cloud his thoughts. He concludes—correctly—that "in short, I am a very confused young man."[6]

Perhaps adding to Kikuchi's confusion was the mundane quality of everyday camp life at Tanforan. He was living with his family for the first time since his youth, and even as he debated the merits of American democracy with his father—the elder Kikuchi viewed it as irredeemably racist—his childhood wounds were healing. By the end of his time at Tanforan, Kikuchi wrote that "the chief value I got out of this forced evacuation was the strengthening of the family bonds. I never knew my family before this...."[7] His new attitude was largely a function of time—there was plenty of it in the assembly center. Kikuchi worked on the camp newspaper and served as a liaison between the internees and the Tanforan administration. But most of his days were spent reading, writing, and thinking. Kikuchi's conversations with friends mixed ruminations on the nature of racism and authoritarianism with the casual and banal. One diary entry on a discussion that touched on the destruction of democracy in France, the need for equal rights for African Americans, and the impact of economics on the war closes with the observation that "Jack ate almost a whole box of crackers during the conversation."[8]

Kikuchi's diary offers no sense of menace or danger in camp life. Evacuees are free to walk about, socialize, and organize community activities. But they are not free to leave, and this eats at Kikuchi most. He knows that no similar internment program exists for Americans of German and Italian descent. There was virtually no pro-Japanese espionage or sabotage on the West Coast; even J. Edgar Hoover of the Federal Bureau of Investigation was satisfied that there was no danger in this regard. It is obvious to Kikuchi that his people are being singled out on the basis of race. He worries that disillusioned Nisei will abandon their loyalty to the United States. "How can we fight fascism," he asks in a diary entry, "if we allow its doctrines to become part of government policy?....Many of the Nisei are getting more race conscious than ever before....(W)e are all lumped together as disloyal Japs. And I wonder how the Nisei soldier feels? This is one hell of a way to create national unity."[9]

Kikuchi's frustrations were well grounded. In 1943, the U.S. military attempted to recruit Japanese American internees; a substantial number, estimated at 10–15% of the total, refused to serve.[10] Some detainees also renounced their American citizenship.[11] Approximately 18,000 Japanese classified as "disloyal" were interned at a camp at Tule Lake, California, for the duration of the war, and about 9,000 of these asked to be repatriated to Japan upon their release.[12] Kikuchi never abandoned his own effort to define an "American" identity, but he could also understand why others did. He saw what the men responsible for the internment could not: that in the midst of a war for national survival, the most important question America faced was the nature and quality of the "America" that would emerge from it.

In September 1942, Charles Kikuchi was transferred with his family from Tanforan Assembly Center to the Gila River Relocation Center in Arizona. Gila was one of ten such camps established by the WRA to house Japanese internees on a more permanent basis. Most were situated in remote locations with inhospitable climates. Like the Resettlement and Farm Security Administrations (see Chapter 8), the WRA commissioned photographers to document the internees' experiences in the camps, hoping to create a visual record that would justify their existence. Among them was Dorothea Lange, whose "Migrant Mother" had done so much to generate public support for the programs of the New Deal (see Chapter 8).

At first the WRA gave Lange full access to registration centers and assembly and relocation camps. But this was not the benevolent government presence that Lange had observed in the fields and farms of California a few years earlier. She was appalled by the treatment accorded the internees, most of whom, she pointed out repeatedly, were American citizens. In May 1942, Lange appealed directly to President Roosevelt to issue a proclamation endorsing the patriotism of the Japanese Americans in the camps, but was rebuffed.[13] Lange then decided to present the internment as it really was, and not the whitewashed version offered by the other WRA photographers. She spent five months in 1942 taking unguarded photographs of the evacuees' lives (see Figures 9-1–9-5). The dehumanizing atmosphere and demoralizing conditions recorded in her images were not what WRA officials had in mind, and they impounded many of her photographs. Lange considered her work on the Japanese internment among the most important of her career. If "Migrant Mother" represented her commitment to economic equality, her camp photographs were a call for racial justice in the United States. Like Kikuchi, Lange felt deeply the contradictions of a nation fighting a war against racism abroad while practicing it at home. It would take until after the war and the advent of the modern civil rights movement to begin the process of resolving this contradiction.

Charles Kikuchi was released from the Gila River Relocation Center in April 1943, on the condition that he not move back to California. The WRA gradually furloughed a substantial number of internees and resettled them east of the Rocky Mountains, but did not permit the Japanese to return to the West Coast until January 1945. Kikuchi headed to Chicago, where he worked for the Berkeley-sponsored Japanese Evacuation and Relocation Study of resettled Nisei. Drafted into the Army in mid-1945, he served briefly, then enrolled at New York University's Graduate School of Social Work, from which he received a master's degree in 1947. Kikuchi spent the remainder of his life in New York as a Veterans' Administration social worker. He was largely able to resume his pre-war "cosmopolitan" life, moving in a diverse circle of friends and colleagues, and was especially active in the struggle for African American civil rights.

It is difficult to judge the effect of Kikuchi's wartime internment. He argued in his New York University master's thesis that the WRA's post-internment resettlement program helped Nisei by exposing them to a variety of "American" races and cultures: "(F)or most resettlers, the wide opportunities of working with Americans of different racial stock was a completely new experience.... and on the whole they adjusted in a positive manner to it."[14] In 1973, from a distance of three decades, he maintained that "on the whole the Nisei group didn't get too damaged" by the resettlement, and that "generally, we probably gained as a result."[15]

Here, however, Kikuchi may have been speaking more as a social observer than an individual. World War II was a philosophical victory for the United States as well as a military one. The defeat of the racist ideology of Nazi Germany—and to some degree, that of Imperial Japan—could not help but discredit the internment, not to mention the oppression of African Americans in the South and elsewhere. Thus it is not surprising that the postwar era spawned a new "pluralist" American ideology, which endorsed ethnic, racial, and religious "difference" under a broad umbrella of "American" identity. Japanese in the United States benefited from this more flexible and expansive approach to being "American," and Kikuchi's successful and fulfilling life after his release provides at least one example of its achievements.

But the fact that Charles Kikuchi was afforded the opportunity to effectively merge his "double selves" as a man of Japanese ancestry and an American—realizing at least in part the dream of W. E. B. Du Bois a half century earlier (see Chapter 3)—does not mitigate the damage done to the Japanese, citizens and aliens alike, by the internment. And even the more open and inclusive "pluralist" approach to national identity that came out of World War II did not permanently fix its meaning and resolve the conversation over who and what was "American," as we will see when we encounter Malcolm X (see Chapter 18), Jo Freeman (see Chapter 20), Robert Putnam (see Chapter 22), and Samuel Huntington (see Chapter 23). Ultimately, the price paid by Japanese Americans for the birth of American pluralism was unnecessarily high.

It took over forty years after the WRA camps were closed in 1946 for the internees to obtain redress from the U.S. government. The Supreme Court had initially upheld the constitutionality of the registration and evacuation requirements for Japanese American citizens in *Hirabayashi v. U.S.* (1943) and *Korematsu v. U.S.* (1944), respectively, ruling that they were justifiable wartime emergency measures under Roosevelt's Executive Order 9066. But in *Ex Parte Endo* (1944), the Court held that American citizens of Japanese descent who the government conceded were loyal to the United States could not be detained in internment camps, leading to the release of virtually all Nisei. The *Endo* decision forced the WRA to reopen the West Coast for resettlement and close the last of the camps.

Most Japanese, however, could not simply pick up where they had left off before Pearl Harbor. The emotional and economic costs of their ordeal were heavy, and at first it seemed that little in the way of compensation would be forthcoming. But during the 1970s and 1980s, a "Redress Movement" began to take shape and bear fruit. President Gerald Ford officially revoked Executive Order 9066 in 1976, and in 1983 a federal commission established to investigate the internment ruled that "E.O. 9066 was not justified by military necessity.... The broad historical causes that shaped these decisions were race prejudice, war hysteria, and a failure of political leadership."[16] Federal courts also vacated the convictions that underlay the *Hirabayashi* and *Korematsu* Supreme Court decisions, ruling that the government had used false and misleading evidence at the original trials. Finally, in 1988, the year Charles Kikuchi died, President Ronald Reagan signed a redress act providing for an official apology and a payment of $20,000 to each internee.

By then the Issei and Nisei had been succeeded by the Sansei, third-generation Japanese Americans born after World War II, as well as their children, the Yonsei. Their memories of the internment, of course, were secondhand. They were also the beneficiaries of post-war American pluralism, encountering few—or fewer—of the obstacles faced by their parents and grandparents. For them, there was no question of their "Americanism," as there had been for Charles Kikuchi. Still, the question of "American" identity with which Kikuchi had wrestled was theirs as well, and the Sansei and Yonsei carried on a conversation that Du Bois and Bourne had helped initiate earlier in the twentieth century.

But one did not need to be on the margins to participate in this conversation. In 1942, as the Japanese internment program proceeded, Norman Rockwell, then America's most popular illustrator, began work on a set of paintings dramatizing the nation's war aims as articulated by President Roosevelt. The resulting "Four Freedoms" series said much about why Americans fought in World War II, as well as revealing a great deal about how they understood themselves as Americans. In giving life to the democratic and egalitarian vision of the president whose executive order robbed Charles Kikuchi of his freedom, Rockwell thus joined the conversation over the meaning of American identity in a postwar world.

Questions for Consideration and Conversation

1. What might Randolph Bourne (Chapter 4) have made of Charles Kikuchi's story? What conclusions would he have drawn from it? How would it have affected Bourne's "cosmopolitan" idea?

2. W. E. B. Du Bois (Chapter 3) was a witness to the Japanese American internment and relocation during World War II. What do you think he said about it? How would it have affected his ideas about "double consciousness" and American pluralism?

3. Was the relocation an instance of what we would today call "racial profiling"? Can you mount an argument in favor of the relocations?

4. Despite his travails, Kikuchi still considered himself "American." How did he justify this view? What was his "American" identity? Can one "honor both national and ethnic ties simultaneously"?

5. Does the idea of American "citizenship" need to be redefined in the light of Kikuchi's story? What does "citizenship" mean?

6. In May 1942, Dorothea Lange (Chapter 8) appealed to President Roosevelt for a public endorsement of the patriotism of the interned Japanese Americans. What do you think she said?

7. How did the Japanese American relocation hurt American pluralism? Did it help it?

Endnotes

1. John Modell, ed., *The Kikuchi Diary: Chronicle from an American Concentration Camp* (Urbana: University of Illinois Press, 1973), 22.
2. Ibid., 5.
3. Ibid., 42–43.
4. Greg Robinson, *By Order of the President: FDR and the Internment of Japanese Americans* (Cambridge: Harvard University Press, 2001), 144.
5. Modell, ed., *The Kikuchi Diary*, 187.
6. Ibid.
7. Ibid., 252.
8. Ibid., 184.
9. Ibid., 117.
10. Robinson, *By Order of the President*, 183.
11. Modell, ed., *The Kikuchi Diary*, 36.
12. Ibid.
13. Robinson, *By Order of the President*, 171.
14. Modell, ed., *The Kikuchi Diary*, 26.
15. Ibid.
16. Quoted in Robinson, *By Order of the President*, 251.

CHARLES KIKUCHI, *THE KIKUCHI DIARY: CHRONICLE FROM AN AMERICAN CONCENTRATION CAMP* (1942)

Source: John Modell, ed., *The Kikuchi Diary: Chronicle from an American Concentration Camp.* Urbana and Chicago: University of Illinois Press, 1973, pp. 51–53, 55–60, 66–67, 70–72, 113–19, 148, 152–53, 156–58, 164–65, 183–84, 187–88, 196–99, 217–19, 223, 252–53.

April 30, 1942, Berkeley

Today is the day that we are going to get kicked out of Berkeley. It certainly is degrading. I am down here in the control station and I have nothing to do so I am jotting down these notes! The Army Lieutenant over there doesn't want any of the photographers to take pictures of these miserable people waiting for the Greyhound bus because he thinks that the American public might get a sympathetic attitude towards them.

I'm supposed to see my family at Tanforan as Jack told me to give the same family number. I wonder how it is going to be living with them as I haven't done this for years and years? I should have gone over to San Francisco and evacuated with them, but I had a last final to take. I understand that we are going to live in the horse stalls. I hope that the Army has the courtesy to remove the manure first.

This morning I went over to the bank to close my account and the bank teller whom I have never seen before solemnly shook my hand and he said, "Goodbye, have a nice time." I wonder if that isn't the attitude of the American people? They don't seem to be bitter against us, and I certainly don't think I am any different from them. That General De Witt certainly gripes my ass because he has been listening to the Associated Farmers too much.

Oh, oh, there goes a "thing" in slacks and she is taking pictures of that old Issei lady with a baby. She says she is the official photographer, but I think she ought to leave these people alone. The Nisei around here don't seem to be so sad. They look like they are going on a vacation. They are all gathered around the bulletin board to find out the exact date of their departure. "When are you leaving?" they are saying to one another. Some of those old Issei men must have gone on a binge last night because they smell like *sake*.

Mitch just came over to tell us that I was going on the last bus out of Berkeley with him. Oh, how lucky I am! The Red Cross lady just told me that she would send a truck after my baggage and she wants the phone number. I never had a phone in that dump on Haste Street.

I have a queer sensation and it doesn't seem real. There are smiling faces all around me and there are long faces and gloomy faces too. All kinds of Japanese and Caucasian faces around this place. Soon they will be neurotic cases. Wang thinks that he has an empty feeling in his stomach and I told him to go get a hamburger upstairs because the Church people are handing out free food. I guess this is a major catastrophe so I guess we deserve some free concessions.

The Church people around here seem so nice and full of consideration saying, "Can we store your things?" "Do you need clothes?" "Sank you," the Issei smile even now though they are leaving with hearts full of sorrow. But the Nisei around here seem pretty bold and their manners are brazen. They are demanding service. I guess they are taking advantage of their college educations after all. "The Japs are leaving, hurrah, hurrah!" some little kids are yelling down the street but everybody ignores them. Well, I have to go up to the campus and get the results of my last exam and will barely be able to make it back here in time for the last bus. God, what a prospect to look forward to living among all those Japs!...

May 4, 1942 Monday

There are such varied reactions to the whole thing: some are content and thankful; others gush "sank you" but are full of complaints within their own circles. Still others are bolder and come right out with it. We thought that we would not have any dinner tonight because the cooks went on a strike. They really are overworked—preparing 3000 meals. Then there have been considerable "personality difficulties." The battle for prestige here is terrific—everyone wants to be a somebody, it seems—any kind of work will do as long as they get the official badges that distinguish them. The waiters also joined the strike because they only have 1000 dishes to feed 3000 people and they really have to get them out in a rush. I saw one Issei dishwasher slap a Nisei girl because she complained that the cups were so dirty. Their nerves are on edge in the cooking division because they are the target for many complaints when it really is not their fault. They are going to open up the new messhalls for sure tomorrow so a great deal of the overload rush will be cut down. The electricians are also griped because they have to replace so many fuses. The wiring system in the stables is very poor and with all the extra lights needed, the system has broken down. Because of the cold, many of the people use cooking heaters to keep warm with. They brought in 50 kerosene heaters today for the aged, ill, and the babies, but this is by no means sufficient.

Oh, I sure could go for a hamburger now: the big juicy kind. I've eaten so much canned food the past week that it becomes tasteless. Many of the boys are worried about being fed saltpetre because they think it will ruin their manhood.

A contrasting reaction is the number of victory gardens that are being planted; these industrious Japanese! They just don't seem to know how to take it easy—they've worked so hard all of their lives that they just can't stand idleness—or waste. They are so concerned that water is not left running or that electricity is not being wasted. Today many of the smaller family units were asked to move to make room for the new evacuees and they certainly did squawk. Here they have their places all fixed up nice and cozy and then they have to start all over again. But they will take it without too much fuss. I wonder if it is because they feel thankful for any treatment that they get regardless of what it is or whether they still are full of unnecessary fears about how the government is going to treat them. Sometimes I get tired of hearing all these "sank you's" which certainly is not the real feeling in so many cases.

I ran across an interesting restroom today. Down by the stables there is an old restroom which says "Gents" on one side and "Colored Gents" on the other! I suppose it was for the use of the stable-boys.

To think that such a thing is possible in California is surprising. I guess class lines and the eternal striving for status and prestige exist wherever you go, and we are still in need of a great deal of enlightenment.

About 20 of us met tonight to really get the Camp paper going because we really do need some source of information. Most of the group were represented and they are all behind the movement. Taro Katayama was elected Temporary Editor so that the policy setting will at least be liberal and outspoken. We plan to distribute the papers through the mail service. All the Nisei lads want to be postmen because they feel that it will be a good opportunity to get to know the girls. The postoffice, next to the Employment Department, is the most rushed place in camp right now. The Clerk there said he sold over 1500 one cent cards today and you should have seen the stack of mail that already has been received by the postoffice.

Some of the UC boys have a "U.C. Extension" sign posted up, but they don't seem to be doing much studying. They sit around and gab and listen to the records. One can't blame them for not studying at a time like this...

May 5, 1942 Tuesday

Today I ran across the first Japan nationalist who reacted violently. He said that Japan "requested" that we be put into a concentration camp so that we have to do it for the sake of Japan. The man seemed pleasant and harmless enough at first, but when he started to talk on this subject, I was amazed to see the bitter look of hatred in his eyes and face. He asked us point-blank whether we were for Japan or America and we said "America" on the basis of our beliefs and education. He got extremely angry and pounded on the table while shouting that we Nisei were fools and that we had better stick by Japan because we could never be Americans; only "Ketos" [white men, literally, hairy people] could be Americans. Since we had Japanese faces we should be for Japan because she would always protect us and not treat us like dogs, etc. We argued for a while but apparently it is no use trying to reason with a person of this type who thinks emotionally. I get fearful of this attitude sometimes because it has been this very thing that makes Americanization so difficult, especially if there is a general tendency to get it from both sides. And I still am not convinced that it is impossible to educate the Issei, although the argument that we are in camp just like them and therefore not Americans is beginning to influence many Nisei. It's a good thing perhaps that I don't understand Japanese because

I am not exposed so much to this sort of talk. It makes me feel so uneasy and mad. It gripes me no end to think of being confined in the same place with these Japanists. If they could only realize that in spite of all their past mistreatments, they have not done so bad in America because of the democratic traditions—with its faults. It may be a sense of personal frustration which is projected to a hatred of all "Keto" and deep resentment towards America. I hope we are able to counteract this sort of thing among the young kids. Prof. Obata was in today and he was worried by this same thing—he is an Issei so there are many of them that live by the American way. He wants to direct a camp art class in order to raise the morale—this point needs to be stressed over and over.

...

The War goes on; men are killed, but this camp is not much aware of that. The Germans have not started the spring offensive although they are challenging the British fleet in the North Sea. Japan is still making gains and is about to cut the China lifeline in Burma, but the Allies are rapidly gaining power. I hope it is not too late.

May 6, 1942 Wednesday

Jack [Charles's brother John] and I were talking about the War. Sometimes, I wonder whether he really believes what he says or whether he is merely trying to get a rise out of me. He says a Japanese victory is the only solution to the Asiatic problem since the "Keto" will continue to exploit these people regardless of what we may claim about democracy. Could be. However, I said that under a democratic tradition there was more hope for the majority than under a militant nationalistic policy. And I wonder if he ever [would] "kow tow" to one of those officious "Japs" who has obtained a little power. Then a little later, he turns right around and condemns the lack of community spirit among the Japanese here and that he would not be able to adjust himself permanently to a Japanese community.

...

May 6, 1942 Wednesday

Mario and Helen came to visit today and Jack sneaked them off to our stable, which is illegal. He told the M.P. that they were going to see "Mr. Johnson" in the Employment office, and the M.P. came in mad as anything looking for the Japanese with the varsity sweater. I told him that there were 4000 Japanese here and that he would have to give a better description.

Later I sent one of our messenger boys down and told them to be "on alert." Helen flirted with the guard and so things turned out "ok."

Corregidor fell yesterday; overheard an Issei remark: "About time, no?" I feel so much like telling them off sometimes, but I guess this should be done in a more diplomatic way. To think that those soldiers are dying off like that, and then to have their efforts passed off like that. It makes me boil.

My first few days only make me feel like an American more, but that's something that you can't go "parading off." I just feel that way, I guess. It may be an overdefensive reaction, but I think it goes deeper than that. Mitch and I are speaking only English to all applicants in the employment office as any large segregation of Japanese will easily drift into speaking only Japanese. It's very interesting to talk to the young Nisei that come in; they are so Americanized. I think that we should start some sort of discussion groups or something so that they won't lose contact with the outside influences. They are all fairly ambitious and think in terms of going on to school and then adjusting themselves here in the U.S. after the war. The more conservative ones invariably have fathers who were engaged in some business with Japan. I guess they get more of the "old country" influence from their parents.

...

I feel like trying to join the Army also, but that's being heroic. I still can't decide whether I would be more useful doing service work among the Japanese here. I think I will be able to adjust myself easily enough although not knowing the language may be a handicap but not necessarily too big to overcome. At least I no longer feel apologetic about it. I guess it has been my emotional reactions against political Japan that have blocked my learning the language in the past few years.

Today they have started to put Nisei police to patrol the barracks and the messhall. There have been several cases of theft reported and the kitchen has been raided a number of times. One woman reported a fur coat stolen, but she may have just lost it as I don't see why anyone would want a fur coat in a place like this. A more serious problem is the reported solicitations by Japanese prostitutes up in the single men's dormitory. The Army M.P. are on their trails and Nisei police have been stationed to intercept them if they show up at night. (And Mr. Greene thinks we don't need social workers!) This is not so bad; but if this sort of thing starts among the young Nisei, it will be very difficult to control. This camp has a sort of pioneer atmosphere

about it and if the kids are left in idleness, trouble could easily develop. Already some of the so called "rowdy Nisei" are shooting craps so that they can get money to spend in the canteen. The development of a well balanced recreational program will be a good influence. I sound like a moralist, but I am thinking more in terms of future social adjustments of the Japanese here, which will be difficult, and morale will have to be kept at a high level if we expect progress to be made.

...

May 8, 1942 Friday

Some of the Issei are sore because they think Mitch and I are too fresh because we don't speak Japanese to them [at the employment bureau] and act on a master and slave basis instead of frankly speaking man to man. It's all right to respect the client, but I think the time for "coddling" them passed after December 7. Most of them can understand and speak English, surprisingly enough, and they should be made to use it more. A lot of Nisei kids come in and mix their Japanese in with their English. Now that we are cut off from the Caucasian contacts, there will be a greater tendency to speak more and more Japanese unless we carefully guard against it. Someday these Nisei will once again go out into the greater American society and it is so important that they be able to speak English well—that's why education is so important. I still think it is a big mistake to evacuate *all* the Japanese. Segregation is the least desirable thing that could happen and it certainly is going to increase the problem of future social adjustments. How can we expect to develop Americanization when they are all put together with the stigma of disloyalty pointed at them? I am convinced that the Nisei could become good Americans, and will be, if they are not treated with such suspicion. The presence here of all those pro-Japan Issei certainly will not help things out any.

The house manager of the men's barracks told some of the single Nisei up there not to speak English because the Issei did not like it. This kind of thing makes me boil; after all, we are in America. It's a good thing that we have a number of family units here or social disorganization would develop at a much faster rate. These parents more or less realize that the Nisei are going through a difficult period and they keep quiet, except in a few cases where they just can't resist the "I told you so's." Pop and Mom rarely talk about the war; they seem to feel that we are of America and I just don't know how to figure them out. They may sincerely believe that Japan is in the right; but they have come to accept the democratic way and more or less live by it. It's a good thing that they are not rabid nationalists; I'm afraid that I would not be able to stand it. Our family probably is not typical because all of us are more outspoken and liberal in our ways—Alice is about the most conservative, or conventional, person in the family. A lot of the Nisei tell me that I'm different because I was reared in an American home, but I just can't see that. It encourages me to see the number of Nisei around here who really feel and live by the democratic way.

The Japanese are known for their politeness and honesty, but if they stay here long, they certainly will degenerate. Because of the inadequacy of facilities they take everything in sight. Some of the things they have done have been downright stupid—such as breaking up the coal bin for lumber and taking linoleum from the other stables. The manners will not improve either. I hate to think of seeing them eat in a restaurant after they eat in those messhalls for a year or so! They will be so coarse and vulgar; under frontier conditions, one could not expect to hope for any better. One Japanese woman remarked that the "honest" Japanese were no better than the Filipinos in this camp—they took everything!

...

I was up in the Grandstands and had a good view of the outside; maybe I was depressed, but a funny feeling of loneliness and of being out of place swept over me. Perhaps this was due to the fact that I walked through the men's dormitory where all those Japanese old men were jabbering away in their conversations about the war. These type of people should be evacuated, but why put all the innocent Nisei—99½%—in with them? This burns me up no end.

May 11, 1942 Monday

During the heaviest rush in mid-morning Mr. Greene called Mitch out and had a long talk with him. When he came back he told me that Greene told him to tell me that he did not wish me to work in the office for a while, because they had received complaints that we were too fresh and that we did not speak Japanese to the clients. But it is strange that Mr. Greene would not tell me himself. According to Mitch, the girls in the inner office were the ones to pass these complaints on to Mr. Greene. It seems that Mr. Greene does not like social workers. He told Mitch that the "U.C. Social Welfare" students have a bad reputation. So there must be some deeper reason for Mr. Greene's actions. I don't know the man, having only spoken to

him slightly on a couple of occasions about the possibilities of a social welfare department—which he was definitely not receptive to. It can't be that he doesn't need extra help in the office, we had more applicants than we could handle. Naturally, I was resentful of the superficial reasons that were given without even having a chance to defend myself; in fact, I was plenty burned up. Why couldn't he have told me those things to my face? Mr. Greene stated that the Issei were not coming in to apply because we did not speak Japanese to them. But why coddle them?

If the solution is either Americanization or deportation, they must be made to realize that they are in America—not Japan. In the week that I have been working voluntarily, I had only one or two cases who could not understand English and they could all speak it in a way. If they had some definite policy about wages, etc., I am sure that they would come in and apply regardless of who was taking the interview.

And Mitch has been much more blunt and frank than I have, yet I am made the scapegoat for some unknown reason. Mr. Greene must have had some conflict with social workers in the past, otherwise why should he make such remarks about them to Mitch and Ann. He is not a profound man; this I can believe without prejudice. All he wants to do is to keep the Japanese busy and happy for the moment. He doesn't seem too concerned about the future. I was so mad that I had to go up to Taro's room and cool off a couple of hours. If I have a run-in with Mr. Greene now, I will be finished as far as this camp is concerned. Yet I cannot let this go by without defending myself. I had an appointment to see him this afternoon but he was too busy so I will see him tomorrow and find out what it is all about.

I am deeply disturbed about these events. I'm not trying to spy or anything; all I want to do is to be of service. But as things have gone, being an American is a handicap around here. Will I still have to continue bumping my head against a stone wall? Maybe I am not diplomatic enough, but I just can't stand kowtowing to a person just because he has a white face. I won't put myself in an inferior position for anyone. I wonder what Mr. Greene has against social workers. There doesn't seem to be any other reason for his actions because I haven't had but few contacts with him, and Mrs. E. of the placement division definitely dislikes Mitch because of his frankness. I certainly have cooperated with her. This morning she came out and started to speak to the Nisei in Japanese and Mitch remarked that they could understand English. She responded with a look that could have killed. I was an innocent bystander.

I wish I wasn't so set on being a social worker. By now I could have worked into something else here; but it's not what I want. I still think I could be of service in spite of not knowing Japanese, if only given a chance. I want to be doing something that has implications for the future. I thought Mari was stubborn in wanting a medical social worker job and nothing else, but now I can see her motivations. I feel the same way about this mess—for personal as well as social reasons. It gets to be a sort of frustrating thing and I still don't want to give up—why should I? I've been here only a week yet I can catch myself getting extremely anti-Japanese again. I'm being forced to live by Japanese ways and I rebel inwardly and outwardly. And I'm not the only one. I have noticed this same reaction among several of my progressive friends—one symptom of this is that they refuse to talk Japanese among themselves and they use the term "Japs" more often when they feel disgusted with the people. I hope this camp doesn't make us conform to the standard Japanese ways. But we may become disillusioned and maladjusted if we fight against it. I think the principles are worth fighting for and I, furthermore, do not have any other choice than Americanization. Ann suggests that I work into the Education department when it is organized. This may be one of the ways that I could be of use. I don't know.

...

Another police was put on to patrol the hospital because so many things such as thermometers have been stolen. A girl was taking a shower and somebody walked off with her bathrobe. Everyone is beginning to put locks on their doors. These things must indicate something, but it will take a sociologist to figure it out. An Issei and a Nisei got in a fight today because one claimed the other had stolen some lumber from him and the other did not like the idea of being called a thief and so he took a swing.

The Issei barracks busybody is going all around with a clipping of "Terry and the Pirates." He claims that the Japanese are insulted with these drawings of buck teeth. I think they are very realistic. The Issei man who is protesting has the biggest set of buck teeth that I have ever seen! Such is life.

...

June 7, 1942 Sunday

Went to the College Fellowship tonight to hear the panel discussion on "What Should the Nisei Attitude as Christians Be towards the U.S. Government?" The messhall was jammed with college students from the Bay Area. As usual no questions were raised from the floor, except for the ones I asked. I felt silly and was disgusted at the same time.... None of the four [speakers] probed into the real reasons. They completely ignored the economic basis and stressed the opinion that Christianity would right all wrongs. I am afraid that this is not a very practical approach and I told them that they should fight for real democracy with the liberal elements, but they would not see it. Many of this group are pacifists and they don't feel that they can do anything in the direct war efforts, which I think is very harmful. If Americanization is the only answer for us, we must fight the vicious forces seeking to disfranchise and deport us. Bill Sasagawa, who testified on the Tolan Committee in Los Angeles, was the only other person to speak up. He pointed out that the group was too complacent and that religion was not the only answer. He said that the Negroes only get things because they fought for their rights and we should do the same. He even went as far as to tell them about the Negroes who came back from the last war and returned to Chicago just in time to bear the brunt of discrimination which became bitter due to the fact that the Negroes had been brought in from the South during the war to handle defense jobs. After the war the Caucasians made a determined effort to drive all Negroes out. The returning Negroes refused to turn in their guns, but used them instead to stand for their rights. Bill did not mean to say that we should use guns, but that we should fight for what was ours and we would if we really felt like Americans and believed in the democratic principles. An outsider might have thought that Bill was telling us to fight the government orders with physical actions, but this is not what he meant. What a story this would have made for the Joint Immigration Committee and the American Legion to use as an argument for deportation! T. H. told me after the meeting that he now feels that we should join the liberals of this country and fight the thing out, and he hopes that the government will follow its program of fair treatment out. Emiko finally got interested because she came home and started to read the Tolan Reports. M. Y. was so worked up that she kept saying, "I hate the Japs." She thinks they (Nisei) are getting too Japanese in the concentration camp.

June 8, 1942 Monday 11:00 P.M.

Cast my absentee ballot today for the S. F. special elections. Voted yes on both measures to increase the bond debt for no special reason. The only reason I voted today was to protect my voting privileges for the important elections which will come up in the fall. The man elected at that time will shape the post war policies for the world. A special deputy came in and notarized our ballots. I counted about 630 Nisei voters in the room while I was there. Lily T. said that she was voting just to show the American Legion that we were interested in our franchise even in times like these. Grace S. said that she was voting because this was one way of showing our loyalty and interests in America. Taro W. voted because this was one privilege which he would fight to retain because it was a symbol of his Americanism. James O. cast his ballot because the JACL told him to. He didn't think it was worth anything anymore. Nobu T. thought that voting was one of the few civil rights left to us. The general opinion was that the Nisei should take advantage of his voting privilege in view of the fact that there were forces that want to take this right away from us. None of them thought that the two issues on the question of county bonds was the important thing. And I doubt if the majority of eligible S. F. Nisei voters even went to the trouble to send for their absentee ballots.

Family difficulties again. Bette and Emiko just don't seem to get along with Alice and the rift is getting wider. Emiko and Alice had a nasty spat this afternoon and all of us tended to take Emiko's side. Alice was not completely to blame because Emiko is very touchy these days. We have been picking on Alice too much. She was very quiet this evening and she has the idea that we are all turning against her. This must have hurt her deeply because she went to bed and cried a little, according to Emiko. All of us will have to quit picking on her; she takes the brunt of the criticisms for some reason or other. And Jack bawled Mom out tonight because she was going to take a shower at 10:00 with a cold wind blowing outside and her with her cold. Miyako had been patiently waiting to go with Mom to the showers and when she found that she could not go, she became very disturbed. Jack started to tease her by saying we were going to send Mom back to Japan and what would Miyako do about it. Miyako took this very seriously and she kept saying, "I want to go with Mom." We said she was an American and would not get along in Japan because she was not a Jap, but Miyako said she didn't care because she was going with Mom. Finally Mom got mad and she came out and told us that she had no hopes of ever going to Japan and to stop teasing Miyako. Pop has long ago given up any idea of returning to Japan. Mom borrowed a Japanese magazine this morning and we ridiculed it as Jap propaganda, but she didn't mind. She just smiled and said, "Just a story book that I read. No can read American

papers." Although she does not realize it fully, she is closer to America than Japan. The family has completely democratized her. We have much more freedom in our stable than in some of the other family units where the older generation still reign supreme. Mom is prepared for anything as long as she has her children about. All of the little children seem to make our rooms the general headquarters and Mom is good-natured about the noise and rarely rebukes them. And she is always giving them things to eat. It's no wonder our family never saved any money; Mom used to spend it all for food for the kids. Pop finally finished Tom's sailboat today, but Mom would not let him and Tom go down to Lake Tanforan to test it out because it was too windy. They were both disappointed. The boat is quite an artistic work of art. Pop never says anything about family affairs any more. He has left the policy making up to Mom and us older ones. Jack makes most of the important decisions as I still don't feel that it is up to me. I can't assume the privilege without taking the responsibility.

...

At present the government objectives are broad but indefinite. We must keep pushing for the widest policy, along with the progressive liberals, so that such anti-democratic moves like the NSGW disfranchisement and deportation program does not succeed. If we were certain, as a group, just what the Federal settlement policy would be, then the morale would take an upward swing and the Japanese [evacuee group] would be more positive in its actions. Yesterday Bendetsen of the Army came out with a statement trying to justify the evacuation. Last week Olson roars about the "Jap" threats in California. Such statements are bound to instill fears, especially when the newspapers give such things wide publicity.

But no federal policy can be complete unless it is made in terms of the worldwide issues of this war. Although we are a drop in the bucket as far as numbers are concerned, the social implications and significance are of fundamental importance to this country as well as to the rest of the democratic world. How can we fight Fascism if we allow its doctrines to become a part of government policies? The contradiction would be too obvious to ignore. Many of the American Chinese, Negroes, and Jews can see that a dangerous precedent can be set, which could easily include them later if this thing is not handled democratically. Already my Chinese, Negro, and Jewish friends have made remarks about the possibility. Perhaps we don't get enough of the other side of the picture, seeing that we are out here in California, in the hotbed of the greatest agitation. I can't blame the Nisei for being resentful when they read about "Jap soldier in U.S. uniform arrested!" I do so myself. One of the dangers of this is that many of the Nisei are getting more race conscious than even before because of this very thing—we are all lumped together as disloyal Japs. And I wonder how the Nisei soldier feels? This is one hell of a way to create national unity.

Furthermore, the growing Japanese attitudes among some of the Nisei are unhealthy. It leaves me with an uneasy feeling. The more liberal Nisei have the same reaction; some are bitter in denouncing it; some feel helpless and wonder if the Nisei are really Americanized. There seems to be a definite split between these groups. The Kibei forms yet another separate group. The only time I see them in large numbers is at the *Sumo* matches. And the present administration actually is hampering Americanization. Greene told McQueen today that the "Town Hall" writing incident would not happen again! This extreme shortsightedness makes our work very difficult. And we just cannot carry out a successful Americanization program without Caucasian leadership. We lack it among ourselves. A well-defined governmental policy would help the liberal cause greatly. One of the things about the Nisei liberals is that they have more Caucasian contacts, judging from the visitors that come in. They have not been so closely tied down to the Japanese community in the past as the small-time businessmen who represent the JACL clique. Many of the liberals are now fearful of the program being allowed to continue under Army control. This is only supposed to be a temporary center; it may become a permanent one. This would hamper the WRA efforts enormously. The army is a military machine and not equipped to handle the social problems which have resulted from the evacuation, such as health, sex, personality adjustments, family problems, education, occupations, etc.

…

Relocation, thus, becomes very significant to the Japanese and the Nisei. After the war, the government will have to continue handling the problem wisely; the Japanese just can't be dumped out to shift for themselves. It's much better that they remain wards of the government until individual adjustments are made. But this may mean permanent segregation. Resettlement of small groups seems to be the most feasible program, but we would then have the problem of social isolation. In any event we have to be given a chance to contribute directly to this country. If the war lasts long enough the Nisei manpower can become very important in the war effort, given the right kind of training. The meeting of the WRA officials with the Advisory Council last Friday is a good sign.

We are not war prisoners, yet our constitutional rights have been taken from us, namely fundamental civil liberties. Viewed from this angle, it is no more than right that the government sees us through this mess. And a complete agricultural relocation is not the answer. Neither can it be on the basis of the former Jap towns which could not give economic opportunities for the college Nisei who usually ended up on Grant Avenue. That is out. Eisenhower and the sociologists must have a headache trying to get a long-range program with a wise social goal. As time goes on, the picture will become clearer.

…

June 24, 1942 Wednesday

All of the [Town Hall] speakers dodged the main issue, except Vic. The Issei are not all loyal, that is foolish. All of the people I have spoken to state that the Issei still feel for Japan. Cannot blame them in a way but the future must be left in Nisei hands, sink or swim. Pre-evacuation days did not show Americanization of the Issei. They clung to their old traditions, had language schools, and even praised Japan. We can't wait until they become Americanized, if ever. We have to work right now. The Army is wise in forbidding Japanese in public meetings; this only encourages them to be more Japanese. I feel sorry for the Issei fighting for their former positions, but they are too pro-Japan to be trusted with our future. The break with the past must be clean.

June 27, 1942 Saturday

Today was one of those real hot days. We all sweltered in the heat. Saw the first shorts on girls, aside from the baseball field. The light, pale S. F. Nisei are certainly getting dark in this open air life. Soon it will be difficult to distinguish them from their country cousins. The girls are going in for sun baths and dark tans. They wear dark glasses to shade their eyes and go out in the grass in the infield to sun themselves. I don't know whether I prefer this heat to the wind. It seems so confined here. We just can't jump into a car and go swimming out at the beach or go into a nice air cooled theater. About all the people can do is go sit in the grandstands and watch the heat waves in the distance. They must really suffer in some of the other centers like Fresno and Merced. The infield barracks get very hot.

June 29, 1942 Monday

Heard over the radio this morning that 100 of the former restricted areas around power plants, etc., have now been reopened to the Germans and Italians under orders from De Witt. Implying that the danger of sabotage is now gone with the Japanese evacuated. The liberals around camp are disgusted as hell. They said that this action proves that evacuation was only on a racial basis, and De Witt's order is rank as hell. And just yesterday five German spies set ashore from a submarine on the Florida coast were caught along with some American-born agents who are being rounded up by the FBI. It doesn't make much sense. I believe the assembly centers should all be closed up and the government should give us a hearing right away and if found "loyal" be helped back into private life where we can be of some use instead of a financial burden on the government.

...

The 50 constitutional delegates met in the House Managers' meeting tonight and it was well conducted. Guy Ueyama was chosen chairman and he conducted it according to parliamentary rules. The best organized group were the politically-minded liberals from Ernie's precinct.... The struggle for power was again evident. The liberals had skeleton outlines all planned from which they made suggestions. Katayama was there blowing his own horn as usual. The Issei are strong for an assembly to act as the legislative body and want to give it most of the power. This doesn't give much for the councilmen to do. Tod Fujita spoke in defense of the house managers who have been doing much of the administrative tasks in nature. Roberts' rules of order were followed so that the group could not get too far off the track. The Issei in back rows never said a word during the meeting, letting Ikeda be their champion. All of the Nisei spoke in English except Katayama who spoke of us as "Japanese" and the Caucasians as "Americans." The nerve of the guy; he should be in a camp for having such reactionary views, according to Jack. Three representatives from the administration and the internal police came in to see that nothing subversive was said.

...

July 1, 1942 Wednesday 1:45

Outside I can hear the swish of the cars as they go by down the highway. The barbed wire fence way below us reminds us that we are on the inside. On the other side of the highway there is a huge glass hothouse where they raise chrysanthemums and dahlias. The tiny men working hard way in the distance look like ants, but they are free men. The armed soldier, some lonely boy from the middle west, paces back and forth up by the main gate. In the sentry boxes, the soldiers look bored. They probably are more bored than the residents here.

Eight men came back from North Dakota to rejoin their families yesterday and their collective families greeted them with buckets of tears. Everyone was trying to tell each other how bad it was in a concentration camp—in North Dakota and at Tanforan. Lorraine's father was one of them. He was some sort of a merchant who did a lot of traveling around the country and in the deep south. As one of the "big shots" in the Japanese Association, he was picked up when war broke out and shipped to N. D. Lorraine did not think that she would see him again as he was so old, so was greatly overjoyed when he got back.

In checking up on the number of visitors at the gate, I was burned up by a notice I saw on the wall. The police chief has ordered that all Negro visitors be checked closely and their slips be kept in a separate file. Evidently they think that there is a great danger of the Japanese stirring up the Negroes. (They call it race hatred.) Another list is kept separately for people that they want watched for one reason or another. People as they drive by look at us as if we were some sort of caged monstrosity. Over 7000 visitors have been here since May 14th and they include many professors from U. C., Stanford, Mills, S. F. State, and other Bay Area colleges. Many church and Y people also come down. The peak of the visitor rush has probably been reached and there has been a drop in the number in the past few days. A new system is being set up. Visitors are to be given blue badges when they come in and a previous application has to be made before they are allowed to come in through the gates.

Mom and Pop went up to interview for the barber shop, but Greene told Pop that he was a little too old. Pop protested that age did not make any difference because he was a "first class" barber. Greene told Mom that she could work if she wanted to on the girls' hair, but she did not want to do it alone. Besides, she felt that she had too much to do at home. We told Pop that he could concentrate on his English lessons now. For the past few days he has not taken out his razors to sharpen them. We bring a few fellows home for haircuts occasionally just to keep him in practice. He took it surprisingly well; perhaps he is not saying what he must really feel. Being cast aside is not easy to take. It is fortunate that he has another interest to keep him occupied now.

Draft registration for the 18–20 years olds took place during the past few days, and 271 signed up from here. I asked the member of the Burlingame [California] draft board just what our status would be but he would not commit himself. He said that a ruling would have to be made by the federal government on the matter. Right now most of the Nisei have been placed in 4-C: aliens ineligible to citizenship.

...

July 6, 1942 Monday

Taro and I talked to Greene for 45 minutes today and he is not such a bad guy. He has the right attitude towards the Japanese even though many of his ideas are a bit distorted. Greene feels that the Issei are a millstone around our necks. He feels that it is up to the Nisei now and blames much of the lack of assimilation on the Japanese alone. "You are Americans, but you have not entirely worked into our melting pot, but preferred to stay in your isolated communities. Things are not so bad here and you can contribute to the war effort by not causing too much trouble. You can handle your educational and recreational system completely. And you Nisei have a large task ahead of you to keep the young ones Americanized and not fall under the first-generation influence. The Issei are hopeless." Some of his illogic brought faint glimmers of smiles to Taro's face. But Greene is better than some. He was sympathetic about the whole paper mess and was a little griped at Davis. The whole thing probably goes back to the WPA politics. Greene should have been made center manager (God forbid) or assistant, but both Davis and Estes got placed ahead of him. Greene says the welfare division has been started but all they will do is to take applications for clothes. "No case work is involved because it is not based upon need. Later I plan to put the division in with the barbers, beauty operators, and shoemakers down in mess-hall 19"! (This is his idea of social work—a clerical stooge.)

McQueen came up while we were talking to Greene and censored some of my stuff on "Your Opinion." He marked out fight fascism "from within as well as out" and Jimmy says that he is more anti-Communist than [anti-] fascist and considers Communism as the greater danger. It's not any use in bucking the army and I may as well take Taro's advice and become less excited about the whole thing.

...

July 14, 1942 Tuesday

Marie, Ann, Mitch, Jimmy, Jack, and myself got into a long discussion about how much democracy meant to us as individuals. Mitch says that he would even go in the army and die for it, in spite of the fact that he knew he would be kept down. Marie said that although democracy was not perfect, it was the only system that offered any hope for a future, if we could fulfill its destinies. Jack was a little more skeptical. He even suggested that we [could] be in such grave danger that we would then realize that we were losing something. Where this point was he could not say. I said that this was what happened in France and they lost all. Jimmy suggested that the colored races of the world had reason to feel despair and mistrust the white man because of the past experiences. The treatment of minority groups even in this country is contradictory to democracy. Jack thought this was the reason why so many minority groups did not feel for democracy, because they have never had it. He said that before we could do anything, race prejudice had to be eliminated, and he did not see how this was possible. Marie said this feeling of hopelessness was one of the reasons why many Nisei were rejecting patriotism. But this was a negative approach. A lot of things would be cleared up if the Caucasian Americans showed their good faith by letting the bars of immigration down and by giving the Negro a democratic chance. Asia would never trust the U.S. unless we showed good faith at home first. Ann thought that it was worth the fight to make democracy right and eliminate the patronizing attitude of the white man. Whether America could shake off the stupid mistakes of prejudices was something that none of us could make a definite answer upon. We did not know whether economic greed would still be the dominant end of these nations at war. We hoped and believed that the world would be changed for the better, under a democratic system. Jack thought that this was not being practical enough, but the rest of us could not agree to that. Jack ate almost a whole box of crackers during the conversation.

...

July 21, 1942 Tuesday 12:30

It seems that my week will be very full. Sunday night: party; Monday: folk dancing; tonight: precinct meeting for nomination of Congressmen; Wednesday: Town Hall; Thursday: lecture; Friday: invited to party held by the file clerk girls or work on paper; Saturday: dance; Sunday: invited to party. And yet the social activities are meaningless—they seem so unreal. But it is so difficult to read. Somehow, it seems that nothing matters any more except the war and the future. I know I am disturbed. On top of that I resent this unreal environment and the people who look like they accept it. I also know that adjustments would be more difficult on the outside. I'm trying to escape reality at the same time I face it. It doesn't make sense. Sometimes I get such an awful empty feeling; my nerves are so jangled. Waves of resentment come over me at the funniest times. Outwardly, I try to pass off as adjusted to this setup, but things happen or I read something which brings almost a violent reaction. The psychologists would call it frustration, I suppose. The only stabilizing thing in this whole mess is the family. I am afraid that I would go to pieces except for them, in spite of arguments. Other people I have talked to say much the same thing. It may be due to an unconscious feeling of loss so we clutch on to what we do have. Fear of the future?

Yet I don't honestly say that I am unhappy here; but here is only a short time. We still have a long future. My self-confidence has taken a jolt. I'm not really doing what I had hoped to do. And the Japanese language looms up as an inescapable obstacle. Will it always be my Waterloo? Every time some Issei addresses me with the lingo, I feel like a damn foreigner. It should be the other way round, but that is intolerance. Friends from the outside say that I will be of great use to the Nisei, but I sometimes doubt that. The thing I want to do—Americanization of the group—is not going fast enough. I get so impatient. Then I have to catch myself or else assume a smug feeling of superiority over those "Japs." But pointing the finger of scorn is not the answer. I think I can see the road clear ahead of me; then doubts about the Caucasian-American good faith enters. In short, I am a very confused young man.

...

July 29, 1942 Wednesday 11:25

Jack was baiting Pop and Mom about the war today. It all started when he was making out Red Cross messages to Mom's relatives in Tokyo. He made a remark that they may have been wiped out by the bombing of Tokyo. Pop said that this was a lie and that Tokyo was not bombed. From there they went into the war situation and Jack said that more Jap and German soldiers were killed in battle than American and Russian ones. Pop said that both sides were sending out a lot of propaganda. He believed that Japan was fighting for the equality of races. I was left to argue with him and it distressed me very much to see how restricted in thinking many of the Issei have made themselves. Pop recognizes the fact that the war was brutal and he said that it was hard for the Nisei because they did not understand things so well and that much of their book learning did not give them the true facts. He gave the typical Issei argument that we did not have much chance in a democracy. I pressed the point and showed how much better off we were here and why we could never go any place else. He granted this point, but said that I should not get caught up in the war hysteria and hate all Japanese. Mixed with this sound logic were many limited views about how honorable the Japanese soldiers were and that he did not like to see them fight America because they were only protecting themselves. He blamed it on both governments and not the people although he resented the idea that the white people wished to "stamp on the necks of the yellow man." I said that the Japs were more notorious for this, citing the cases of Manchuria and Korea. Pop said he did not wish to have arguments splitting the family up and that we should wait and see after the war who was right. He doubted the promises of the Allies to give more equality to all races. He based this conclusion on the results of the last war, plus the treatment of the Japanese and the Negroes in the U.S. We just don't think from the same basis, and if I admit the defects of democracy, it gives him a winning point. Pop and Mom would rather have us put wars out of our minds, but this very camp makes us aware that a war is going on now. I am afraid I was a bit irritated.

What the Issei should do is to realize how they are benefiting by democracy right now, even in this camp to a limited extent. Since they are not well acquainted with the wider issues, they tend to formulate their opinions from limited personal experiences or from rumors. At the same time they forget that it was a minority group that treated the Issei so harshly and that this treatment was not based on democratic practices. But there would be more possibilities if they realized that this was not a race war but a war of principles arising from world economic problems. Pop believes in democratic practices, only he mistakes the fallacies of democracy as the real thing and therefore would not label these beliefs as such. The way we bait them naturally puts them on an extreme defensive as any references to the bad qualities of a Japanese soldier are taken on a personal basis as a reflection on their own characters.

Pop holds the capitalistic idea. He is prejudiced against the Russians because they are "bullshee-veesky." He says that if a man makes a million dollars, the government takes 90% away and gives it to a lazy person. I asked him what was wrong with that, pointing out how he had to charge 35 cents for haircuts when he was a better barber than the Caucasian that charged 65 cents. He said "no," a man should get what he could. This led to a discussion of prejudices. Pop thinks Hitler is a sourfish and distrusts the Germans; Koreans are not the same as Japanese. A Jew is a cheating kike, a Filipino goes around raping women, and the Japanese in the U.S. are cutthroats (only when I am not arguing with him). Pop is a mixture of past fears and frustrations.

...

It's a funny thing that the Nisei will give great talks about democracy. Although we may not have much chance at self-government here, the right to vote is important. We should be laying the basis for self-government in the relocation areas right here. Much will depend upon the Nisei and the present apathy is not a good start even though the elected persons are comparative greenhorns. We have to develop leadership gradually and not expect it to turn up suddenly. At least they can gather a little experience in the procedures of self-government here, although the practice of it will probably be denied by our WRA administrators.

July 30, 1942 Thursday

The radio announced this morning that General De Witt had ordered the clearance of all assembly centers (including Tanforan) to relocation centers by August 7th. Everyone got greatly excited and the news spread around camp like wildfire. I saw a couple of kids getting boxes to pack. Taro wanted to check on the story so I went up to see Davis. I couldn't get by the secretary so I sent the message in. He said that there was absolutely no basis to the story and that he had received no news of it. So I guess that we will be here for a little while. The favorite pastime is speculating where to go next. There is a mass dread of going to Arizona and the people are willing to believe the worst about it. Letters written by people who have been sent there paint a black picture of the place. The place seems to be unbearable. It won't be long now before we are all moved and there is an increasing tension among the people. The attached letter was received by one of the Issei. K., a Councilman, got a hold of it and made a translation. He showed it to me yesterday and at that time planned to carbon copy a lot of them and pass them out. Today about 15 Nisei showed me the letter and hundreds in camp already know about it. I heard about 8 different oral versions and each was exaggerated a little more.

...

August 10, 1942 Monday

[The house managers] don't think much of Greene either, as they had some not so complimentary things to say about him. The same steam was blown off about Davis and all of the administrative staff, except a few. The root of these feelings is the recent denial of self-government. The house managers are particularly wrought up about it and a spirit of resentment has been growing. They are in a fix about the coming elections because they will be called upon to whip up interest, but the general opinion of the fellows was that the whole thing was a joke and an insult to the group. So in making messhall announcements, they plan to read it hurriedly in English only and they have quietly been spreading the word around that it doesn't mean a thing. Gandhi was arrested yesterday in India and T. S. said that J. H. should lead the movement for passive resistance here.

The fellows (about 8 of the house managers) were bitter in some of their attitudes. I told them that this was no excuse for just lying down and quitting because we still had a long future to work out. J. H. was of the opinion that we should put up a fight now, but the others told him that he would only be jeopardizing his chances by making a "big noise" here when we were only going to be here for another month or so anyway. J. was not so sure that the WRA would be able to do much because of the financial limitations. I told him that getting all excited about little things was a short-sighted approach. Toby came in and he started to tell us about the meeting with the WRA and how he would try to get a representative committee together to propose plans if Davis would recognize us. If not, he planned to have various people in camp work as individuals.

We got back to attitudes of the Nisei and I questioned if all of them were sincere in their manifestations at the same time expecting all the rights and privileges of a democracy. One fellow made the startling statement that Japan was responsible for our good treatment and we should communicate with the Spanish Embassy. I reminded him that we were Americans and our only recourse was with our government. I did not like the remark that we were Japanese and whatever side won, we were a hopeless case. I told the fellow that now more than ever we should take a positive stand for the U.S. and work for democracy as our only hope. He said that this was a "race war" and that four out of five Nisei would agree with him. This disturbed me: I didn't know what to say. Here, they are taking up the very propaganda of the Axis nations while fighting for their "democratic rights" in these Centers. It would indicate that we are still confused, full of uncertain fears. J. cited the example that he had said "good morning" to Mr. D.—and had received a sneering "what of it?" for an answer. This infuriated him. J. T. said that small-minded people existed no matter where we were and we should be intelligent enough not to let emotional experiences of this sort prevent us from thinking clearly.

A more constructive discussion was then entered upon. We said that America was the only answer—right or wrong—and we had to make the best of it. I claimed that all the pro-nationalist Japanese already had returned to Japan, which drew a laugh. John was worried that we may develop inferiority complexes when we go back into the American life. Tomoto said we would either come out fighting and full of guts or else become a weak bunch of sissies, afraid of life and forever expecting handouts from the government. I said that there was a definite chance that we (the children especially) would have "messhall manners"—getting into long lines for everything. The whole group said that this should be prevented at all costs and that the leadership within the group would determine a lot of the attitudes. It was agreed that the sudden release of 120,000 Issei and Nisei into the American community after the war would be tragic. We hoped that the government would carry the program through right to the final resettlement of the people, not forgetting the possibility that many may stay on in the relocation areas if they were made a success. T. said that we would be lucky to make enough for the bare necessities and we could expect many days eating beans. They thought that if the Tanforan group went together progress could be made, but were not so sure about the "backwoods" country people.

…

August 15, 1942 Saturday 10:45

Nobby was very proud this afternoon because one of his high school teachers had written an article for *Freedom* magazine (a new one) in which he discussed some hardship cases of evacuees. One of his illustrations was Nobby "who came to high school and was so American in everything he did." Nobby was the water boy for the football team and an enthusiast of American jazz, movies, and comic strips. "When Pearl Harbor came, he became quiet and subdued with a personal sense of tragedy." When Nobby left for camp, his teacher told him that he was a good loyal American and that he should never lose faith in his ideals.

I am afraid that the fellows in the office ribbed him a little too much and deflated his egotist conceit, which has become more and more evident lately. Nobby left us very irritated. I told him that he should not let these little things bother him because he has the possibilities to achieve much in life. Nobby is so advanced for his age that it irritates his high school friends when he consciously attempts to show them up. So he goes around with much older boys, a sort of hanger-on around the fringes. They are inferior to him intellectually, but they jitterbug and make a lot of noise, which is the badge of success for the younger kids. We in the office sort of deflate him at times so that he won't get too objectionable to everyone for his own good. Nobby has not said anything about the progress of his parents' repatriation lately. He has milked the last ounce of sympathy from us on this matter.

…

August 31, 1942 Monday

In reviewing the four months here, the chief value I got out of this forced evacuation was the strengthening of the family bonds. I never knew my family before this and this was the first chance that I have had to really get acquainted. There is something wholesome about it and with the unity which it presents, one does not feel alone, knowing that there are some who will back one up in moments of crisis. It sort of binds strength to an individual thrown into a completely strange group. We have had our arguments and bickerings, but this has been a normal process which only lasts for a little while. This family is composed of very strong individualists, but the right of the individual in the family is respected by the others if it does not conflict with the whole group and is [not] harmful to it.

Because the older children are around, the family is more advanced as far as Americanization is concerned. We were pretty far advanced even before our arrival in Tanforan in this respect, coming from a community where there were very few Japanese.

I don't quite know how to explain the growth of family unity rather than disorganization. One thing may be that it never was an economic bond since we never did have much money. Mom and Pop have conceded a lot to their children and they don't expect us to be anything else but American. The personalities of all the family are good. I certainly was not that way when I was of high-school age. Even now, the majority of the young Nisei that I see around seem rather reserved. It must be due to their wider contacts with Caucasian children. Emiko and Bette are much maturer than most of the other Nisei girls their age in this camp.

Pop and Mom have come through a difficult adjustment period. Now I believe that they actually like it here since they don't have any economic worries. Mom still has not realized that the children have grown up, but she is strongly aware of it. Most of the family decisions are now made by the older children. They [Mom and Pop] are naturally consulted and an effort is made to believe that it came from them.

Of course, we have only had four months of this life and things may be different after we have been in a camp for a much longer period. But we always manage to get along in a fair way. I wonder what will happen if we all suddenly rebelled against this kind of living? The postwar period is going to be trying no matter which way we look at it. I may do further graduate work or else try to get into Civil Service. The latter is the only future for me that I can see at this time.

Well, the new chapter starts tomorrow. I don't feel up to the effort to attempt a review of the camp now. I'm sleepy and I have to get up at 3 o'clock!

DOROTHEA LANGE, PHOTOGRAPHS OF THE JAPANESE INTERNMENT (1942)

FIGURE 9-1 Japanese assemble at Control Station, San Francisco, for evacuation to Santa Anita Assembly Center Camp.   *Source:* Library of Congress.

FIGURE 9-2 Civilian exclusion order #5, posted at First and Front streets, directing removal by April 7 of persons of Japanese ancestry, from the first San Francisco section to be affected by evacuation.   *Source:* Library of Congress.

FIGURE 9-3 Japanese American boarding up store prior to evacuation.   *Source:* Library of Congress.

FIGURE 9-4 Relocated Japanese American family.   *Source:* Library of Congress.

FIGURE 9-5 Tanforan Assembly Center, San Bruno, California, June 16, 1942.   *Source:* National Archives and Records Administration.

CHAPTER 10

Norman Rockwell Sees America as It Sees Itself

"Freedom of Speech...Freedom to Worship...Freedom from Want... Freedom from Fear..."

Norman Rockwell answered the question, "What is America?" with deceptive simplicity. At first glance, his illustrations, which appeared on the covers and in the pages of *The Saturday Evening Post* between 1916 and 1963, seem light and sentimental, advertisements for an America that did not actually exist. By his own admission, Rockwell painted "life as I would like it to be."[1] His illustrations were populated almost exclusively by whites. He avoided controversial political subjects, notably civil rights, until the last years of his career. He told stories, some humorous, others evocative, still others bittersweet, but none freighted with the pain and complexity of life as it was.

Yet it would be a mistake to dismiss or underestimate Rockwell, as so many cultural critics have done over the years. "I was showing the America I knew and observed to others who might not have noticed," Rockwell once said about his work. "My fundamental purpose is to interpret the typical American."[2] While it can be argued that the white, small-town, middle-class Americans that Rockwell painted for over half of the twentieth century were not "typical," it is also true that there were millions of them, as his phenomenal popularity attested. Indeed, for the purposes of history, the issue of whether Rockwell's subjects were "typical" Americans may be beside the point. He portrayed generations of Americans as they imagined themselves to be. Even if this is not as they "really" were, history is about perceptions of reality as much as it is about reality itself. Rockwell's view of "American" identity may have been based on myth, but the enormous power and influence of that myth makes it an essential part of the American conversation.

Politics and war are also the stuff of myth, and here Rockwell was able to make his most significant contribution to America's conversation about itself. In January 1941, President Franklin D. Roosevelt set forth four goals for which America would fight if it entered World War II—what became known as the "Four Freedoms." Inspired, Rockwell set out to illustrate each of them, and they appeared on the covers of *The Saturday Evening Post* in February and March 1943, in support of what by then had become the nation's war effort. His depictions of "Freedom of Speech," "Freedom to Worship," "Freedom from Want," and "Freedom from Fear" transformed Roosevelt's words into vivid visual symbols of national purpose and promise, as millions fought and won the most important war in world history. Rockwell accomplished this, as was his custom, by reflecting Americans' self-image back at them, reinforcing the beliefs—or myths—they already held. Myths have their uses, and Rockwell's familiar visual language sustained an ideal of national unity and common purpose at a time when Americans needed it most. Nonetheless, the relative homogeneity of Rockwell's images, and their awkward juxtaposition with the internment of Japanese Americans taking place at roughly the same time as the publication of the "Four Freedoms" series (see Chapter 9), underscored the contradictions between myth and reality in American life. Rockwell offered a comforting American identity, but not a definitive one.

Norman Rockwell hailed from a most unlikely place for someone who would go on to depict the everyday lives of small-town Americans. He was born in New York City in 1894 and grew up there in a middle-class household. His interest in art started early. After dropping out of high school to enroll in the Art Students League, he began selling commercial illustrations. His breakthrough came in 1916, when he sold his first cover to *The Saturday Evening Post*, a general interest weekly magazine that during the first half of the twentieth century was one of the most widely read in the United States. Rockwell's work would appear on the *Post*'s cover 320 more times, creating an indelible association between artist and venue in the public mind.[3] For most Americans, Norman Rockwell *was The Saturday Evening Post.*

During the 1910s, 1920s and 1930s, Rockwell developed the illustrative style that made him famous. He painted "average" Americans—or those he believed to be "average" Americans—in situations and poses that were calculated to elicit a smile or nod of recognition. Boys run from a pond, a "No Swimming" sign prominent in the background. A kindly doctor pretends to examine a young girl's doll with a stethoscope while she looks on apprehensively. A family returning from vacation slumps in exhaustion on a bench. Rockwell used these and other images to evoke a common American language of experience and memory. He especially touched those in rural areas, and even urbanites who located the "real" America in small towns.

Rockwell's art thus served as both reality and myth, affirming the values and virtues of what we would today call "Middle America" to people who feared they were losing them. As a commercial illustrator, Rockwell could reach a broader audience than an artist who exhibited in galleries and museums. He did not produce abstract compositions demanding sophisticated interpretive skills. Rockwell's work was clear, direct, and designed to be reproduced and seen by millions. Critics may have denied him the more prestigious title of "artist," but Rockwell was content to be known as a "mere" illustrator. He enjoyed greater influence—not to mention a higher income—drawing magazine covers than he ever would as a critically lionized artist.

During the first half of the twentieth century, Rockwell epitomized the rise of the "middlebrow," a way station between the "high" culture that critics celebrated and the "low," vulgar culture of the masses. *The Saturday Evening Post* itself was a middlebrow publication, with features on politics and lifestyles designed to appeal to a middle-income, middle-class reader who was educated but not an intellectual. Critics may have sneered at "middlebrow" Americans, but their numbers grew rapidly in the twentieth century. Rockwell's work spoke powerfully to them, and they rewarded him handsomely. In 1939, when he left the New York City area to live with his family in rural Arlington, Vermont, he was the most popular illustrator in the United States.

That year, World War II began in Europe. Despite strong isolationist sentiment, which was especially prevalent in the Midwest, President Roosevelt knew that America would eventually have to confront Nazi Germany and Imperial Japan. FDR understood that even Americans who did not consider themselves isolationists were disillusioned with the results of World War I, in which the United States lost 116,000 men, only to see the European powers revert to the same imperialist and militarist policies that had caused the conflict in the first place. The Paris Peace Conference of 1919 had degenerated into a ruthless land and money grab, as victorious Great Britain and France expanded their colonial empires at the expense of defeated Germany and saddled it with reparation obligations so onerous that they made another world conflict almost inevitable. The rise of Nazism in Germany, fascism in Italy, and Stalinism in the Soviet Union were all direct results of World War I. Now, with World War II underway, Roosevelt faced the challenge of defining America's potential involvement in a way that would justify its accompanying sacrifices to a skeptical public.

In 1940, the Nazi blitzkrieg swallowed up most of Europe. France fell in June, leaving Great Britain alone and isolated against Hitler's onslaught. Despite the inspirational leadership of the new prime minister Winston Churchill, England faced a grave existential threat. Its cities bombed nightly by the Luftwaffe, its shipping lanes disrupted by German battleships and U-boats, and desperately in need of war material, Great Britain was strangling. What if England fell? Obviously the United States was Hitler's next target, but the likelihood of a direct attack thousands of miles across the Atlantic seemed remote. Leading American isolationists, including celebrated aviator Charles Lindbergh, argued that the U.S. mainland was impregnable to attack, and there was thus no reason to intervene in a European war. But Roosevelt knew that however distant the actual battlefield, this was America's war as well. Nazism, fascism, and Japanese militarism imperiled democracy, equality, and freedom all over the world. Unlike the isolationists, FDR viewed these fundamental American principles as universally applicable. But the president needed to articulate his message to the American people convincingly, with a simplicity and clarity accessible to the average citizen. To accomplish this, he would need Norman Rockwell.

After winning reelection to an unprecedented third presidential term in November 1940, FDR focused his attention on his State of the Union message to Congress, scheduled for January 6, 1941. Roosevelt decided to use the speech to lay out his vision of a just America and world, and in so doing make the case both for intervention in the war and for a strong international role afterwards. He would employ the idea of "freedom" as a unifying theme, because it was freedom that distinguished democratic nations like the United States and Great Britain from the totalitarian dictatorships plotting world conquest. On January 6, before a packed House of Representatives, FDR rejected both isolationism and the appeasement of the nation's enemies. "No realistic American," he warned, "can expect from a dictator's peace international generosity, or return of true independence, or world disarmament, or freedom of expression, or freedom of religion—or even good business. Such a peace would bring no security for us or for our neighbors. Those who would give up essential liberty to purchase a little temporary safety deserve neither liberty nor safety."[4]

Roosevelt then told the American people that the war was one for "a world founded upon four essential freedoms," which he enumerated in spare, dramatic language:

> The first is freedom of speech and expression—everywhere in the world. The second is freedom of every person to worship God in his own way—everywhere in the world. The third is freedom from want...—everywhere in the world. The fourth is freedom from fear....—anywhere in the world.[5]

The thunderous applause that greeted these words was not confined to the halls of Congress. The president had succeeded in distilling his understanding of national meaning and purpose into clear, vivid, and evocative language. FDR reminded Americans of who they were and what they would need to defend. Public support for Roosevelt rose dramatically after the "Four Freedoms" speech. In August 1941, the president met with Churchill off the coast of Newfoundland, Canada, and reiterated the principles of the Four Freedoms in the Atlantic Charter, which framed the war—one that America had not yet entered—in terms of universal human freedom. By the time the December 7, 1941,

Japanese attack on Pearl Harbor propelled the United States into a two-front, global conflict, the Four Freedoms had provided the emotional underpinnings for a popular, sustained war effort that reached the grassroots of American society.

Roosevelt had succeeded in presenting the war in a manner that Norman Rockwell would have found familiar. The Four Freedoms, however, were only words. To have their intended effect, they would have to be translated into images. The most logical person to produce those images was Rockwell himself, although this was not immediately apparent to the U.S. government. After Pearl Harbor, Rockwell searched for a way to aid the war effort. Like many Americans, he had been deeply affected by Roosevelt's "Four Freedoms" speech. Rockwell decided to illustrate each of the Freedoms and donate them to the War Department to generate positive publicity and raise funds. But he struggled over the artwork. How could he cast FDR's language in visual terms? After weeks of agonizing, he had a brainstorm at three in the morning. As Rockwell later recounted in his autobiography:

> I suddenly remembered how (his neighbor) Jim Edgerton had stood up in town meeting and said something that everybody else disagreed with. But they let him have his say. No one had shouted him down. My gosh, I thought, that's it. There it is. Freedom of Speech. I'll illustrate the Four Freedoms using my Vermont neighbors as models. I'll express the ideas in simple, everyday scenes. Freedom of Speech—a New England town meeting. Freedom from Want—a Thanksgiving dinner. Take them out of the noble language...and put them in terms everybody can understand.[6]

What Roosevelt had done with words, then, Rockwell would do with images. He would articulate American values for a vast middlebrow audience that was the bellwether of national public opinion. He worked up some preliminary sketches and took them to Washington in the spring of 1942, offering his services for free. To his disappointment, officials in the Office of War Information were not interested. Some judged his ideas unsophisticated and obvious, almost cartoonish. Others felt that "real" artists, rather than mere illustrators like Rockwell, should be in charge of publicizing the war. Discouraged, Rockwell boarded a train for home. But he decided to get off in Philadelphia, where *The Saturday Evening Post* was headquartered. He showed the sketches to his editor, whose reaction was instantaneous: He asked Rockwell to draw the "Four Freedoms" for the *Post*.

Rockwell worked on the project for the next six months. "Freedom of Speech," which went through five versions, and "Freedom to Worship," which alone consumed two months, were the most challenging pieces. When he was finally done, Rockwell had produced a series of indelible American images. A lone dissenter has his say at a town meeting. Men and women of a variety of faiths pray under a heading that reads, "each according to the dictates of his own conscience." A happy, prosperous family enjoys a Thanksgiving meal. A father and mother watch over their sleeping children. Rockwell's illustrations were so powerful they did not require captions. Indeed, the essays that accompanied each of the "Four Freedoms" when they were published in consecutive issues of *The Saturday Evening Post* between February 20 and March 13, 1943 were almost superfluous, and quickly forgotten. The images themselves were a national sensation. Even though they appeared inside the magazines and not on the covers, they generated huge sales, as well as a large demand for reprints.

At this point War Department officials, realizing their error in rejecting Rockwell's sketches the previous year, asked to use the illustrations as the centerpiece of the government's Second War Loan Drive. The Treasury Department put the originals on tour and distributed millions of "Four Freedoms" posters captioned "Ours...To Fight For" and "Buy War Bonds." Thanks to Rockwell's work, the drive was a great success, traveling to sixteen cities and raising over $130 million.[7] Eventually, the government produced four million "Four Freedoms" posters.[8]

Rockwell's illustrations came to embody the war effort to the American people. As he had throughout his career, he led his audience to identify personally with his images. Americans could imagine themselves in each scene. The genius of the "Four Freedoms" series was its linkage of the familiar and everyday with larger issues of what it meant to be an American. Most of Rockwell's viewers had attended Thanksgiving dinners with their families, put their children to bed at night, bowed their heads in prayer, or voiced their disagreement with majority opinion. The "Four Freedoms" illustrations showed that these were political gestures as well as personal ones. Rockwell's intention was to offer more than comfort and security to a people at war. He wished to transcend immediate events to define the American conversation for all.

President Roosevelt was thrilled by the nation's response to the "Four Freedoms" series and wrote Rockwell, "I think you have done a superb job in bringing home to the plain, everyday citizen the plain, everyday truths behind the Four Freedoms...."[9] Rockwell's work continued to inspire Americans on the battlefield and home front until victory was won in 1945. That year, a profile of Rockwell in *The New Yorker* described the "Four Freedoms" as "received by the public with more enthusiasm, perhaps, than any other paintings in the history of American art."[10]

Yet despite the acclaim they generated, the "Four Freedoms" left many issues unaddressed. The illustrations were undoubtedly "American" symbols, but what "America" did they symbolize? Rockwell's critics complained that his work only scratched the surface of his subjects. Consider, for example, "Freedom from Want." Roosevelt's speech had identified economic security as a fundamental right, yet nowhere in the U.S. Constitution was there any mention of the "right" to an income, a job, medical care, housing, or an education. The family depicted in "Freedom from Want" was clearly well fed, but was FDR or Rockwell suggesting that all Americans were entitled to what this family enjoyed?

In 1944, Roosevelt delivered what became known as his "Second Bill of Rights" speech, in which he argued that economic rights should be considered an essential element of American citizenship, and a complement to the original Bill of Rights and its procedural guarantees. FDR died before he could turn the words of this speech into action, but the debate over how "equal" Americans were to be and what role the federal government would play in making them so continued long after the war fought to achieve "Freedom from Want" ended. The meaning of Rockwell's portrait of a bountiful Thanksgiving meal was thus not as clear as it seemed.

Rockwell raised the same issues about economic justice in the United States as had Lange and Evans a few years earlier (see Chapter 8). He painted "Freedom from Want" to lend a human face to Roosevelt's vision of a nation and world without hunger and need. But his ends were more clearly articulated than his means. Rockwell traced only the bare outlines of American identity, leaving deeper and potentially divisive questions unanswered.

So it was with his other illustrations. "Freedom of Speech" avoided the issue of war dissent, as well as that of views that could not be contained within the parameters of Rockwell's New England town meeting. Doubtless there was a consensus in Rockwell's Arlington, Vermont, on the governing principles of political, social, and economic life. Jim Edgerton, Rockwell's neighbor and model for "Freedom of Speech," was in all likelihood not a Marxist demanding a radical redistribution of the town's resources. But what if he was? Neither Roosevelt's formulation nor Rockwell's illustration offered much guidance as to the limits of "Freedom of Speech" when consensus broke down.

"Freedom to Worship" was also problematic. Was the United States a Christian, or even a Protestant nation? Non-Protestants had made progress since Randolph Bourne had championed their culture during World War I (see Chapter 4), and certainly since the days of Tom Scott (see Chapter 1), but White Anglo-Saxon Protestants (WASPs) still controlled most of the avenues to power in America at the time Rockwell painted "Freedom to Worship." Indeed, most of his neighbors in Arlington, not to mention his editors at *The Saturday Evening Post*, were Protestants. President Roosevelt himself was a member of the WASP elite. Did "Freedom to Worship" mean merely that every American was free "to worship God in his own way," or did it envision an equitable distribution of societal resources—power, money, influence—regardless of religious affiliation? As long as Protestants had more of these than non-Protestants, did true "Freedom to Worship" exist in the United States? Again, Roosevelt's words and Rockwell's images offered no sure answers.

Even "Freedom from Fear," which of all the Freedoms seemed most directly related to the war, raised as many questions as it resolved. There was, of course, the glaring counterexample of the Japanese American internment, ordered by the same president who had authored the "Four Freedoms." Rockwell did not speak to this issue, or to that of the treatment of African Americans, in his work. Weren't all Americans entitled to "Freedom from Fear"?

In addition, the use of American power to create a world order in which, as Roosevelt described it, "no nation will be in a position to commit an act of physical aggression against any neighbor," was laudable in principle, but presented issues of American global power that extended well beyond the ability of parents to protect their sleeping children.[11] Was it appropriate, or even feasible, for the United States to impose its understanding of "Freedom from Fear" in places where it was not desired? Did America have the right to force its culture, its values, its version of freedom "anywhere in the world"?[12] During the half-century following the end of World War II, these questions would become prominent in the American conversation, and Whittaker Chambers (see Chapter 11), Lyndon Johnson (see Chapter 19), Ronald Reagan (see Chapter 21), and Samuel Huntington (see Chapter 23) would offer their own understandings of the nature, reach, and limits of America's global mission. Rockwell's and Roosevelt's vision of a world "without fear" would prove to be more complicated and filled with unanticipated consequences than either could have imagined.

The certitudes of the "Four Freedoms" in word and image would thus be clouded by the complexities lurking beneath them. This does not lessen the impact of Norman Rockwell's work. Like a self-fulfilling prophecy, his art reinforced the "average American's" view of his country. But in the post–World War II decades, it would become less clear who the "average American" was, and what he—or she—believed (see Chapter 17 on Students for a Democratic Society; Chapter 18 on Malcolm X; and Chapter 20 on Jo Freeman). By the mid-1960s, even Rockwell had come to understand this; he left *The Saturday Evening Post* in 1963 and spent the last decade of his career at *Look* magazine, where he took on more controversial subjects, including civil rights.

Rockwell is best remembered, however, for a perspective on American identity that aimed to reassure, inspire, and unite. Not until Ronald Reagan—who, fittingly, wrote the foreword to a collection of Rockwell illustrations that appeared after his death in 1978—did an American public figure appear so convinced of the justness of his nation's cause, both at home and "everywhere in the world."[13] The World War II years that Rockwell's work defined were a moment of consensus on the worth of American institutions and values. Rockwell helped create that consensus through the power of his visual imagery. The "Four Freedoms" may indeed have been myth, but they were crucial to the survival of both the American nation and the American conversation itself.

Questions for Consideration and Conversation

1. Can President Franklin Roosevelt's Japanese American relocation order be squared with his "Four Freedoms" address (see Chapter 9)?
2. Does the fact that Rockwell's subjects are not "typical" Americans detract from his message?
3. Why do you think Americans who did not live in small towns still accepted Rockwell's view of America?
4. Even though the United States was virtually impregnable to foreign attack, President Roosevelt believed America needed to intervene in World War II. Why?
5. Why did Roosevelt's "Four Freedoms" speech generate so much support for America's war effort?
6. Why were Rockwell's "Four Freedoms" illustrations so popular with the American people?
7. What questions did Rockwell's "Four Freedoms" illustrations leave unanswered?
8. What might members of Students for a Democratic Society (Chapter 17) have said about the implications of Rockwell's "Freedom From Fear"? Whittaker Chambers (Chapter 11)? Samuel Huntington (Chapter 23)?
9. Why do you think it was fitting for Ronald Reagan (Chapter 21) to write the forward to a collection of Rockwell's work?

Endnotes

1. http://www.normanrockwell.com/about/quotes.htm
2. Ibid.
3. http://www.normanrockwell.com/about/biography2.htm
4. John Grafton, ed., *Great Speeches: Franklin Delano Roosevelt* (Mineola, NY: Dover Publications, Inc., 1999), 94.
5. Ibid., 99.
6. Norman Rockwell, *My Adventures as an Illustrator: An Autobiography* (Indianapolis: Curtis Publishing Company, 1979), 339.
7. Ibid., 343.
8. Maureen Hart Hennessey, "The Four Freedoms," in Maureen Hart Hennessey and Anne Knutson (eds.), *Norman Rockwell: Pictures for the American People* (New York: Harry N. Abrams, Inc., 1999), 102.
9. http://www.best-norman-rockwell-art.com/four-freedoms.html
10. Quoted in Hennessey, "The Four Freedoms," 102.
11. Grafton, ed., *Great Speeches: Franklin Delano Roosevelt*, 99.
12. Ibid.
13. Ronald Reagan, "Foreword," in George Mendoza, *Norman Rockwell's Patriotic Times* (New York: Viking Penguin, Inc., 1985).

NORMAN ROCKWELL, FOUR FREEDOMS POSTER (1943)

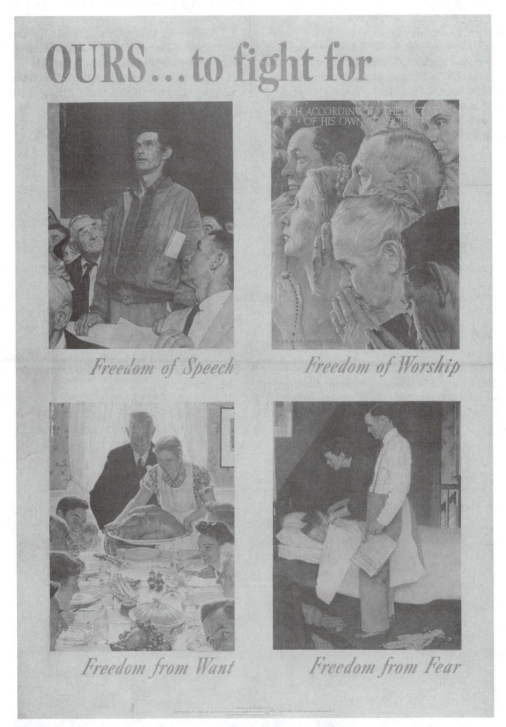

FIGURE 10-1 U.S. Treasury Department, "Ours...to fight for" poster, 1943, used in Second War Loan Drive.   *Source:* Library of Congress/Printed by permission of the Norman Rockwell Family Agency Copyright © 1943 The Norman Rockwell Family Entities.

CHAPTER 11

Whittaker Chambers Defends the Anticommunist Impulse

"God or Man?"

T he names "Whittaker Chambers" and "Alger Hiss" are linked forever in American history. The two could not have been more different. Hiss was sophisticated and well connected. He was a brilliant student at Harvard Law School, a law clerk for a Supreme Court justice, a high-ranking State Department official, and a close adviser to President Franklin D. Roosevelt. In 1945, he helped found the United Nations. Chambers was an awkward, overweight loner, a college dropout who worked in relative obscurity as a magazine editor. In appearance and demeanor, he was as forgettable as Hiss was striking. But when on August 3, 1948, Chambers appeared before the House Committee on Un-American Activities (HUAC) and identified Alger Hiss as a member of the American Communist Party, Chambers instantly became one of the most famous—or infamous—men in the United States. This was largely due to the stature of the man Chambers had accused. By 1948, Hiss was the president of the Carnegie Endowment for International Peace, which was a prominent instrument of Andrew Carnegie's philanthropy (see Chapter 2), and one of the world's most important conflict management organizations outside the United Nations itself.

Chambers' sudden notoriety was also a function of the nature of his charges. Allies during much of World War II but bitter rivals in its immediate aftermath, by 1948 the United States and the Soviet Union were locked in the early stages of the Cold War. At the Yalta Conference in February 1945— at which Hiss had been an aide to FDR—Soviet dictator Joseph Stalin had promised to permit free elections in Poland, which he was in the process of capturing from the Germans. Breaking his word, Stalin established a puppet regime there. He also sponsored Marxist dictatorships in East Germany and seven Eastern European nations on the Soviet Union's borders, a so-called "Iron Curtain" of rigged elections, secret police, thought control, and economic collectivism. In 1948 he cut off ground access to the American-administered sector of Berlin, forcing the United States to airlift food and supplies into the city. Thanks in part to a series of espionage agents in the United States, Stalin's nuclear program was proceeding rapidly. The program would produce an atomic bomb in 1949. Despite American efforts to bolster Western European democracies through the 1947 Marshall Plan, which provided much needed economic assistance, communist parties in France, Italy, and West Germany were making substantial electoral gains. It was possible to envision popular mandates for Marxist regimes in those countries.

But the Cold War atmosphere in which Whittaker Chambers made his accusations was shaped by more than external political events. Americans were shaken by the idea that Communism itself was on the march, and in Chambers' ominous words, "the winning side." It seemed as if Marxism was riding the tide of history, sweeping aside all in its wake. It claimed to offer certainties that democratic capitalism could not: economic security for all, employment for all, adequate housing for all, a decent education for all, and medical care for all. Marxism appeared to speak to mankind's hopes, capitalism to its fears. The idea of "materialism"—that human history consisted of the struggle between classes for control of material resources, or the "means of production"—was immensely attractive to men and women who sought explanations for poverty and oppression. Marxism placed human beings in control of their own destinies. It dispensed with the idea of religion, since God was irrelevant to material life. There was no hereafter, but only the iron laws of history, which led toward human liberation not in the afterlife but here on earth.

To an American people steeped in the innocent and comforting imagery of Norman Rockwell (see Chapter 10), Marxism appeared sinister, aggressive, and profoundly unsettling. It was thus not surprising that when Chambers linked Hiss to Communism, he sparked a national outcry. Hiss, for his part, was indignant. He vehemently denied ever being a communist. Hiss claimed, in fact, that he did not even know Chambers. Chambers, however, knew Alger Hiss and identified him as the man from whom he had received classified State Department documents in the 1930s, when both were members of a spy ring sponsored by the Soviet Union. Chambers maintained that Hiss had been a valuable source of information for the USSR. He had provided Chambers with important secrets that he had in turn passed on to the Soviets. Hiss called Chambers a liar.

Which man was telling the truth? By implicating Hiss, Chambers was also implicating himself, admitting his own communist ties and espionage activities. But he was willing to hold his past up to scrutiny as a warning against the dangers of Marxism. Chambers had once been so loyal to Communism that he betrayed his country. But now, he was a fervent anticommunist, a committed Christian who viewed his former life with remorse and shame. Chambers believed that the most important question facing the United States was not the direction of the class struggle, as Marxists argued, but "the absolutely fundamental struggle between the primacy of God or man, between God and no God, between soul and soul.... These issues are the real line of cleavage in the modern world between conservative and revolutionary, cutting across all lines of economic class and political party."[1] Chambers had once thought that America's defining value was equality, and that the nation's deliverance lay in an equitable distribution of material resources. But by the time he testified before HUAC, he had come to regard freedom as even more precious and meaningful. Marxism promised equality, but at the price of freedom. From Chambers' new perspective, even the New Deal was suspect in its use of government power to restrict individual initiative and choice. This view aligned him with one of the New Deal's most prominent critics, Herbert Hoover (see Chapter 6).

Chambers' anticommunism, fueled both by personal disillusionment and religious passion, was almost apocalyptic in its intensity. His purpose in accusing Hiss went beyond the immediate goal of exposing a threat to national security. Chambers wished to present the American people with a stark moral choice. Would they be indifferent to Marxism's assault on individual freedom? Would they choose materialism over faith? Man over God? Chambers meant the stakes to be high when he offered his testimony to HUAC in August 1948. His intentions were not lost on Hiss or those who rushed to his defense.

Hiss and his supporters also knew that at issue were a host of crucial American questions. There was the matter of the New Deal, with which Hiss, who had served in the Roosevelt Administration for almost its entire duration, was closely associated. The argument over the New Deal's legacy continued after FDR's death in 1945. Harry Truman, who succeeded Roosevelt in the White House, was a strong proponent of its philosophy and sought to continue New Deal policies through what he called the "Fair

Deal." What were the consequences of an expanded federal government role in the nation's political, social, and economic life? Was equality or freedom America's preeminent value? The New Deal featured much less government intrusiveness than Marxism, of course, as well as a less literal approach to equality. But even in a capitalist democracy like the United States, the fundamental issue was the same as in the Soviet Union. Was state power benign or malign? Did it promote equality or threaten freedom? Were America's problems material or spiritual, of the body or the soul? Whittaker Chambers' charges and Alger Hiss's denials thrust these questions into the American conversation, in an atmosphere filled with Cold War suspicion and paranoia.

Whittaker Chambers was an unlikely communist and an even more unlikely spy. Born in 1901, he was raised in the Long Island, New York suburb of Lynbrook by a troubled family. His father left the household when Whittaker was a young boy, and although he eventually returned, the older man's distant personality created a lifelong barrier between father and son. Chambers' dominating mother was instead the major influence in his life. Intelligent and bookish, Chambers grew up with few friends and profound feelings of isolation and apartness. He entered Columbia University in 1920, where he studied literature and languages, attracting attention as a writer. But the sad memories of his early years continued to haunt him. Acquaintances at Columbia described him as appearing alienated and lost. Chambers' family life continued to be chaotic. His younger brother suffered from alcoholism and depression, and committed suicide in 1926. Chambers' grandmother, who lived in Lynbrook with his parents, exhibited signs of serious mental illness. His father remained remote. Whittaker was also struggling with his sexual identity. He began to be drawn to men as well as women, and given the social strictures of the day, felt compelled to keep his feelings secret.

What was not secret during Chambers' Columbia years was his growing attraction to Marxism. Reflecting on his decision to become a communist, Chambers remarked on the sense of security and certainty it offered. Not only did it promise economic justice in a nation marred by extremes of wealth and poverty, but also human redemption on earth. In this sense, it resembled a religious faith. Marxism was a belief system with clear appeal to a marginalized young man like Chambers, and he embraced it with zeal. He dropped out of Columbia and in 1925 joined the Communist Party of the United States. Moving quickly upward in its ranks, he served on the staff of the Party's newspaper, *The Daily Worker*, and later became editor of its literary magazine, *The New Masses*.

In 1932, newly married, Chambers was faced with a life-altering decision. Communist Party leaders demanded that he go "underground" and become a spy, a liaison between American government officials who were engaged in espionage and the Soviet Union. This was a formidable test of Chambers' loyalty. It would require him to quit his job, drop his friends, and even disassociate from the Communist Party itself in order to make his activities more difficult to trace. It was dangerous work that could cost him his life. It was also, of course, illegal and would require him to betray his country. Despite these risks, Chambers chose to obey his leaders and become a spy. Over the next six years, Chambers served as a "courier," receiving stolen government documents and turning them over to Soviet representatives in the United States. It was during this time that he became acquainted with Alger Hiss.

A rising star in the Roosevelt Administration, Hiss worked for both the Agricultural Adjustment Administration—a New Deal agency created to control the prices of farm products—and the State Department. Hiss believed deeply in the Soviet Union, as did many on the American left during the Depression years. At a time when the United States was wracked by class tensions and labor strife, and when it seemed that its economy could not feed, clothe, house, and employ its own people, the USSR stood as a beacon of hope. The Soviet Union was dedicated to human needs and material equality. There, men like Hiss believed, all were fed, all were housed, all received adequate medical care, and all were given the opportunity to work productively. To Hiss, the Soviet system appeared to be a more ambitious and effective version of the American New Deal. During the 1930s, few Soviet sympathizers were aware of the extent of the brutality of dictator Joseph Stalin, who was in the process of murdering millions of his own citizens in purges and massacres. In the wake of the full revelation of Stalinist atrocities, as well as the cynical Hitler–Stalin Pact of 1939 in which the USSR allied with a Nazi regime that was its mortal ideological enemy, much of this support melted away. But there were still some who continued to admire the Soviet Union, including Alger Hiss. His brand of Marxism, like that of Chambers during his time as a spy, was a true faith, a secular religion.

Born in 1904 in Baltimore, Hiss built a successful career as a lawyer, diplomat, and presidential aide. Few would have believed that the elegant, urbane Hiss could be a Soviet espionage agent. He was the epitome of the Eastern Establishment, with Ivy League credentials and links to the highest reaches of government, academia, and professional life. On the surface, it seemed he had too much to lose as a spy. But like Chambers, Hiss was drawn to Communism's promise of a just and equal world, and to the Soviet Union as its embodiment. Hiss began making copies of State Department documents and giving them to Chambers, who would pass them on to his Soviet contacts for transmission to Moscow. During this time, Hiss and Chambers became personally close. Hiss even sublet his apartment to Chambers and gave him a car. Chambers admired Hiss, who appeared to be everything the self-conscious, withdrawn "courier" was not.

After Chambers made his accusations in 1948, some Hiss supporters intimated that Chambers may have developed a romantic attraction to Hiss and fabricated his charges after he was rebuffed. Whether or not this was true, Chambers was unquestionably a man of passionate attachments, whether personal or ideological, and they waxed and waned with great force. By the late 1930s, Chambers' allegiance to Communism, which had dominated his life for over a decade, began to weaken. He was appalled by the ferocity of the Stalinist purges, which commenced in earnest in 1936. News of staged "show" trials and mass executions of so-called "counterrevolutionaries" and "capitalist spies" seeped out of the Soviet Union and into the American communist underground. Some, like Alger Hiss, chose to ignore the reports. Chambers could not bring himself to do so. The violence and inhumanity of the purges seemed to contradict everything for which Marxism claimed to stand. Chambers had also moved closer to Christianity, no doubt influenced by the irreligious nature of his ebbing Marxist faith. In 1938, he decided to leave both the communist underground and the Party itself.

These moves would be as dangerous as his espionage activities. The Soviets were notorious for retaliating against defectors. Chambers knew of some who had been murdered. Fearing for his safety, Chambers fled with his family to an isolated farm outside Westminster, Maryland, about twenty-five miles northwest of Baltimore. For protection, he had made microfilm copies of some of the documents he received from Hiss before delivering them to his Soviet contacts. He hid these for possible future use. Chambers now viewed himself as a "radical" Christian, and joined a Quaker congregation, or Meeting, in the Westminster area. He had travelled a long distance—from a deep faith in man and materialism to an equally intense devotion to God and freedom. Chambers now believed that America faced a spiritual crisis. He would spend the rest of his life warning of Communism's corrosive effect on the soul.

Out of the communist orbit and on his own, Chambers now faced the task of earning a living. In 1939, he found employment at *Time* magazine, where he wrote and edited until his appearance before HUAC in August 1948. During World War II, Chambers made sporadic attempts to alert Roosevelt administration officials to the existence of a Soviet spy ring that had infiltrated the government, but was rebuffed. The USSR was then an American ally and revelations of espionage activity could have disrupted the relationship between the two countries. But there was no need for forbearance after the world war ended and the Cold War began. Richard Nixon, a young congressman from California serving on HUAC, launched an investigation of Chambers' August 1948 testimony and was quickly convinced of its veracity.

Others were less impressed. President Harry Truman, whose administration Hiss had represented at the United Nations Charter Conference in 1945, called Chambers' story a "red herring," by which he meant an exaggerated, hysterical story employed for partisan political purposes. Nixon was a Republican, and his party had not occupied the White House in sixteen years. It had lost four consecutive presidential elections since Herbert Hoover's 1932 defeat, and was about to lose a fifth in November 1948 when Truman won reelection. Alger Hiss was by all surface appearances a loyal Democrat and New Deal supporter. Chambers and Nixon were Republican critics of Roosevelt and Truman. What quickly became known as the Hiss–Chambers case, then, was both a partisan battle between Democrats and Republicans and an argument over the New Deal and its legacy. But Chambers also conceived it as a deeper struggle for America itself. Were the American people on the road to a form of serfdom at the hands of a government that encroached on freedom at home and lacked the will to confront Marxism abroad? Chambers intended his HUAC testimony to force Americans to answer that question.

During his initial appearance before HUAC, Chambers had linked Hiss only to the Communist Party and not to espionage activities. But after Hiss had come before the Committee and swore not only that he had never been a communist but that he had never even met Chambers, his accuser was compelled to produce evidence to support his claims. Chambers and Hiss met face to face before HUAC members. Hiss now said that he recognized Chambers, but under another name, "George Crosley." He had known "Crosley" casually in Washington during the 1930s, but had never engaged in espionage with him and had had no contact with him after 1936. Chambers stuck to his story: Hiss had been a communist. When Chambers repeated it on the radio program "Meet the Press"—Congressional testimony was immune from slander actions—Hiss sued him for defamation. Chambers refused to back down and broadened his charges to include espionage.

The documents that Chambers had secreted a decade earlier now came into play. On November 17, 1948, he produced sixty-five pages of State Department reports and papers that he claimed Hiss had stolen, retyped, and replaced, and four pages of secret cables handwritten by Hiss. Then, on December 2, 1948, Chambers led HUAC representatives to a pumpkin he had hollowed out on his Maryland farm, opened it, and produced four microfilm rolls he had hidden there.

It was the Hiss–Chambers case's most dramatic moment. The so-called "Pumpkin Papers" contained, along with some innocuous material, documents stolen from State Department files. The circumstances surrounding the papers' production drove the public mood. Chambers' eccentricities—only a man with deeply paranoid tendencies would hide evidence in a pumpkin and take investigators into his fields under cover of night to retrieve them—made the case fodder for tabloid newspapers and the popular media. With public opinion shifting in Chambers' favor, pressure mounted on the government to bring Hiss to trial. Since the federal statute of limitations for espionage was five years and Chambers' allegations went back to the 1930s, Hiss was instead indicted for perjury; he had told a grand jury that he had not seen Chambers after 1936 and had never given him any State Department material.

It would take two trials, consuming much of 1949, to convict Hiss. At his first trial, which ended in a hung jury, Chambers was forced to recount his own espionage activities, as well as to admit that he too had perjured himself by altering aspects of his story during his HUAC testimony. But the government used expert witnesses to show that some of the documents produced by Chambers had been typed on a typewriter once owned by Hiss. At his first trial, Hiss' claim that these documents were forgeries, combined with the impressive character testimony introduced on his behalf by a series of respected public officials, convinced enough jurors of his innocence to prevent a verdict from being reached. But on January 21, 1950, a second jury convicted Hiss of perjury. He spent three-and-a-half years in federal prison.

On this level, of course, the outcome was a victory for Chambers. However, many Americans, a disproportionate number of whom occupied positions of influence and power in Eastern Establishment circles, not only remained convinced of Hiss' innocence but also believed that the cause of anticommunism was unsavory and dishonest. There was ample justification for this belief. Senator Joseph McCarthy, who came to prominence just after the second Hiss trial ended and created a sensation with his indiscriminate and frequently inaccurate charges of communist subversion in the U.S. State Department, was only the most well-known of a series of demagogues whipping up "Red Scare" hysteria for partisan purposes; Richard Nixon, Chambers' HUAC ally, was another. Chambers realized that he needed to explain to the American people why he had accused Hiss. Leaving *Time*, he set to work on a book about the case.

Witness was published in 1952. As he had promised his publishers at Random House, it was an exhaustive account of his activities as a Soviet spy, his relationship with Hiss, and the events of the controversy itself. But *Witness* did more than this. It argued passionately against Marxism and against an American liberalism that shrank from confronting it. Chambers wrote that in what he called the "Great Case," "the two irreconcilable faiths of our time—Communism and Freedom—came to grips in the persons of two conscious and resolute men."[2] Chambers saw Communism as representing "the focus of the concentrated evil of our time."[3]

Why, then, did so many intelligent, compassionate men and women, including both Chambers and Hiss, become communists? Chambers linked Marxism's appeal to both humanitarian and religious impulses. Communists wished to help the weak, the poor, and the defenseless. This, of course, did not differentiate them from liberals. But unlike liberals, Marxists did not trust the compromises, half-measures, and delays of the democratic process. They offered instead the hope of rapid, decisive, and transformative change. This vision was immensely attractive to those, like Chambers and Hiss, who dreamed of a just and equal America. Marxism fused this immediatism with a powerful faith in the future that resembled a religion in its depth and intensity. By replacing traditional religious belief, Marxism gave good-hearted and well-meaning men and women a way to "change the world."[4] There would be no need to wait for God's work to reveal itself.

But Chambers argued that this secular faith exacted its pound of flesh. Communism exalted mankind in the abstract but degraded it in practice. It destroyed the freedom of the individual to speak, to criticize, and to worship God. The United States had just fought a world war to secure those freedoms, as Norman Rockwell had illustrated so powerfully (see Chapter 10). Marxism promised "Freedom from Want," but at the price of the other three Freedoms, especially "Freedom from Fear." In *Witness*, Chambers told the story of a woman he knew who had learned this bitter truth:

> The daughter of a former German diplomat was trying to explain to me why her father, who, as an enlightened modern man, had been extremely pro-communist, had become an implacable anti-communist. It was hard for her because, as an enlightened modern girl, she shared the communist vision without being a communist. But she loved her father and the irrationality of his defection embarrassed her. 'He was immensely pro-Soviet,' she said, 'and then—you will laugh at me— but you must not laugh at my father—and then—one night—in Moscow—he heard screams. That's all. Simply one night he heard screams.'[5]

"What communist," Chambers asked, "has not heard those screams?"[6]

Chambers was prone to dramatic gestures and exaggerated emotions, and the United States was obviously not the Soviet Union. But having observed the workings of Communism from close range, he feared that Americans did not understand its insidious quality, seducing with a promise of material security for all while eating away at initiative, choice, and personal autonomy. The New Deal was not Stalinism, but Chambers—like Hoover—believed its centralized power structures and bureaucratic controls represented steps in that direction (see Chapter 6). What kind of nation did Americans want? What was "American" identity? Chambers' answers differed markedly from those offered by Dorothea Lange and Walker Evans, and even from the optimistic prescriptions of Norman Rockwell (see Chapters 8 and 10). Chambers imagined an America full of temptations and snares, in which the promise of a benign government protecting its citizens and fulfilling their economic needs masked the dangers of an overreaching central state endangering individual freedom. *Witness* warned Americans that as they became more dependent on government—for jobs, income, housing, medical care—they risked their essential quality *as* Americans.

Chambers' dark anticommunist vision would haunt the American conversation for the next forty years. In future chapters we will see how from markedly different perspectives, Ronald Reagan (Chapter 21) and members of Students for a Democratic Society (Chapter 17) sought to address the question of the compatibility of a strong national state and American freedom.

Witness was a critical and commercial triumph for Chambers. Reviewers praised its literary quality and emotional depth, and it spent over a year on the bestseller list. Its stature also grew after Hiss' book on the case, *In the Court of Public Opinion*, was published in 1957. Unlike *Witness, In the Court of Public Opinion* was dry and distant in tone, offering few insights into Hiss' thoughts and motivations. It reiterated his charge that the State Department documents used to convict him at his second trial were forgeries. Hiss' cause nonetheless remained popular in many liberal and leftist circles. The hysterical red baiting of Joe McCarthy had created a group of "anti-anticommunists" who were appalled by his tactics. In an environment rife with personal smears, blacklistings, and guilt-by-association, it was natural to believe that Hiss was a victim of the Red Scare. In the decades before his death in 1996, Hiss successfully cast himself as a symbol of Cold War excess. At first disbarred in the wake of his felony conviction for perjury, he was readmitted to law practice in Massachusetts in 1975. Hiss died at the age of ninety-two, insisting on his innocence to the end. His supporters regarded him as a martyr.

But by 1996, that group of supporters had diminished substantially, thanks to the release of what were known as the "Venona Papers." Venona was a secret U.S. government project that had intercepted and decoded messages sent by Soviet officials to Moscow in the 1940s. One such message identified a State Department official who had attended the Yalta Conference in February 1945 as a Soviet espionage agent. His code name was "Ales." Of the four members of the State Department who were at Yalta, three had unimpeachable credentials; one was the Secretary of State himself. The fourth was Alger Hiss.[7] Thus, the Soviets' own internal communications identified Hiss as a spy with a reasonable degree of certainty.

Chambers' vindication came too late for him to enjoy. After the publication of *Witness* he lived mainly on his Westminster farm and wrote for *National Review*, a new conservative magazine that would become the voice of a revitalized American right in the 1970s and 1980s (see Chapter 21 on Ronald Reagan). Chambers died of heart failure in Westminster in 1961. He was posthumously awarded the Presidential Medal of Freedom, the nation's highest civilian award, by President Ronald Reagan in 1984.

It was easy for Hiss supporters, as well as Americans justifiably concerned about the dangers posed by the crude McCarthyite version of anticommunism, to dismiss

Whittaker Chambers as another representative of those low impulses. But Chambers was not Joe McCarthy or even Richard Nixon. He was a principled opponent of Marxism who believed that its materialism and statism, elevation of man over God, and insistence that laudable ends justified the most ruthless of means endangered America's most precious value—individual freedom. By arguing that the nation's problems were not primarily material in nature but instead bound up with values and principles, Chambers challenged the work of the New Deal. Dorothea Lange and Walker Evans, after all, viewed "Migrant Mother" and the Woods family as victims of an inequitable economic system, not a soul-deadening central state (see Chapter 8). They saw government as a solution, while Chambers saw it as a problem.

Thirty years after the Hiss–Chambers case, Americans would elect as their president a man who also considered an activist state a threat to individual liberty. One of his heroes, fittingly, was Whittaker Chambers. That president, Ronald Reagan, would continue a conversation over the federal government's proper role in American life that grew out of the New Deal and which propelled Whittaker Chambers and Alger Hiss on their different journeys to the same HUAC hearing room in August 1948. Equality or freedom? Government or individual? God or man? Whittaker Chambers intended these questions to outlive him. *Witness* ensured they would.

Questions for Consideration and Conversation

1. Why was Marxism so attractive to the young Whittaker Chambers? Why did he become disillusioned with it?
2. What motivated Alger Hiss to spy for the Soviet Union?
3. How did arguments over the Hiss–Chambers case reflect larger disagreements over the direction of the New Deal and the role of government in American life?
4. Why was it so difficult for many Democrats and liberals to believe in Hiss' guilt?
5. In emphasizing America's spiritual crisis over its material inequalities, and the American value of freedom over that of equality, was Chambers making a mistake? How would Dorothea Lange and Walker Evans (Chapter 8) have responded to Chambers' position? Herbert Hoover (Chapter 6)? Members of Students for a Democratic Society (Chapter 17)?
6. How might Chambers have argued that Marxism compromised the "Four Freedoms" (Chapter 10)?
7. Do you believe Chambers? Hiss? Both?

Endnotes

1. Sam Tanenhaus, *Whittaker Chambers: A Biography* (New York: Random House, 1997), 171.
2. Whittaker Chambers, *Witness* (Chicago: Henry Regnery, 1952), 4.
3. Ibid., 8.
4. Karl Marx, quoted in Ibid., 9.
5. Ibid., 13–14.
6. Ibid., 14.
7. See Tanenhaus, *Whittaker Chambers*, 519–20.

WHITTAKER CHAMBERS, *WITNESS* (1952)

Source: Whittaker Chambers, *Witness*. Chicago: Henry Regnery, 1952, pp. 3–22.

Foreword in the form of a Letter to my Children

Beloved Children,

I am sitting in the kitchen of the little house at Medfield, our second farm which is cut off by the ridge and a quarter-mile across the fields from our home place, where you are. I am writing a book. In it I am speaking to you. But I am also speaking to the world. To both I owe an accounting.

It is a terrible book. It is terrible in what it tells about men. If anything, it is more terrible in what it tells about the world in which you live. It is about what the world calls the Hiss-Chambers Case, or even more simply, the Hiss Case. It is about a spy case. All the props of an espionage case are there—foreign agents, household traitors, stolen documents, microfilm, furtive meetings, secret hideaways, phony names, an informer, investigations, trials, official justice.

But if the Hiss Case were only this, it would not be worth my writing about or your reading about. It would be another fat folder in the sad files of the police, another crime drama in which the props would be mistaken for the play (as many people have consistently mistaken them). It would not be what alone gave it meaning, what the mass of men and women instinctively sensed it to be, often without quite knowing why. It would not be what, at the very beginning, I was moved to call it: "a tragedy of history."

For it was more than human tragedy. Much more than Alger Hiss or Whittaker Chambers was on trial in the trials of Alger Hiss. Two faiths were on trial. Human societies, like human beings, live by faith and die when faith dies. At issue in the Hiss Case was the question whether this sick society, which we call Western civilization, could in its extremity still cast up a man whose faith in it was so great that he would voluntarily abandon those things which men hold good, including life, to defend it. At issue was the question whether this man's faith could prevail against a man whose equal faith it was that this society is sick beyond saving, and that mercy itself pleads for its swift extinction and replacement by another. At issue was the question whether, in the desperately divided society, there still remained the will to recognize the issues in time to offset the immense rally of public power to distort and pervert the facts.

At heart, the Great Case was this critical conflict of faiths; that is why it was a great case. On a scale personal enough to be felt by all, but big enough to be symbolic, the two irreconcilable faiths of our time—Communism and Freedom—came to grips in the persons of two conscious and resolute men. Indeed, it would have been hard, in a world still only dimly aware of what the conflict is about, to find two other men who knew so clearly. Both had been schooled in the same view of history (the Marxist view). Both were trained by the same party in the same selfless, semi-soldierly discipline. Neither would nor could yield without betraying, not himself, but his faith; and the different character of these faiths was shown by the different conduct of the two men toward each other throughout the struggle. For, with dark certitude, both knew, almost from the beginning, that the Great Case could end only in the destruction of one or both of the contending figures, just as the history of our times (both men had been taught) can end only in the destruction of one or both of the contending forces.

But this destruction is not the tragedy. The nature of tragedy is itself misunderstood. Part of the world supposes that the tragedy in the Hiss Case lies in the acts of disloyalty revealed. Part believes that the tragedy lies in the fact that an able, intelligent man, Alger Hiss, was cut short in the course of a brilliant public career. Some find it tragic that Whittaker Chambers, of his own will, gave up a $30,000-a-year job and a secure future to haunt for the rest of his days the ruins of his life. These are shocking facts, criminal facts, disturbing facts: they are not tragic.

Crime, violence, infamy are not tragedy. Tragedy occurs when a human soul awakes and seeks, in suffering and pain, to free itself from crime, violence, infamy, even at the cost of life. The struggle is the tragedy—not defeat or death. That is why the spectacle of tragedy has always filled men, not with despair, but with a sense of hope and exaltation. That is why this terrible book is also a book of hope. For it is about the struggle of the human soul—of more than one human soul. It is in this sense that the Hiss Case is a tragedy. This is its meaning beyond the headlines, the revelations, the shame and suffering of the people involved. But this tragedy will have been for nothing unless men understand it rightly, and from it the world takes hope and heart to begin its own tragic struggle with the evil that besets it from within and from without, unless it faces the fact that the world, the whole world, is sick unto death and that, among other things, this Case has turned a finger of fierce light into the suddenly opened and reeking body of our time.

My children, as long as you live, the shadow of the Hiss Case will brush you. In every pair of eyes that rests on you, you will see pass, like a cloud passing behind a woods in winter, the memory of your father—dissembled in friendly eyes, lurking in unfriendly eyes. Sometimes you will wonder which is harder to bear: friendly forgiveness or forthright hate. In time, therefore, when the sum of your experience of life gives you authority, you will ask yourselves the question: What was my father?

I will give you an answer: I was a witness. I do not mean a witness for the Government or against Alger Hiss and the others. Nor do I mean the short, squat, solitary figure, trudging through the impersonal halls of public buildings to testify before Congressional committees, grand juries, loyalty boards, courts of law. A man is not primarily a witness *against* something. That is only incidental to the fact that he is a witness *for* something. A witness, in the sense that I am using the word, is a man whose life and faith are so completely one that when the challenge comes to step out and testify for his faith, he does so, disregarding all risks, accepting all consequences.

One day in the great jury room of the Grand Jury of the Southern District of New York, a juror leaned forward slightly and asked me: "Mr. Chambers, what does it mean to be a Communist?" I hesitated for a moment, trying to find the simplest, most direct way to convey the heart of this complex experience to men and women to whom the very fact of the experience was all but incomprehensible. Then I said:

"When I was a Communist, I had three heroes. One was a Russian. One was a Pole. One was a German Jew.

"The Pole was Felix Djerjinsky. He was ascetic, highly sensitive, intelligent. He was a Communist. After the Russian Revolution, he became head of the Tcheka and organizer of the Red Terror. As a young man, Djerjinsky had been a political prisoner in the Paviak Prison in Warsaw. There he insisted on being given the task of cleaning the latrines of the other prisoners. For he held that the most developed member of any community must take upon himself the lowliest tasks as an example to those who are less developed. That is one thing that it meant to be a Communist.

"The German Jew was Eugen Leviné. He was a Communist. During the Bavarian Soviet Republic in 1919, Leviné was the organizer of the Workers and Soldiers Soviets. When the Bavarian Soviet Republic was crushed, Leviné was captured and court-martialed. The court-martial told him: 'You are under sentence of death.' Leviné answered: 'We Communists are always under sentence of death.' That is another thing that it meant to be a Communist.

"The Russian was not a Communist. He was a pre-Communist revolutionist named Kalyaev. (I should have said Sazonov.) He was arrested for a minor part in the assassination of the Tsarist prime minister, von Plehve. He was sent into Siberian exile to one of the worst prison camps, where the political prisoners were flogged. Kalyaev sought some way to protest this outrage to the world. The means were few, but at last he found a way. In protest against the flogging of other men, Kalyaev drenched himself in kerosene, set himself on fire and burned himself to death. That also is what it meant to be a Communist."

That also is what it means to be a witness.

But a man may also be an involuntary witness. I do not know any way to explain why God's grace touches a man who seems unworthy of it. But neither do I know any other way to explain how a man like myself—tarnished by life, unprepossessing, not brave—could prevail so far against the powers of the world arrayed almost solidly against him, to destroy him and defeat his truth. In this sense, I am an involuntary witness to God's grace and to the fortifying power of faith.

It was my fate to be in turn a witness to each of the two great faiths of our time. And so we come to the terrible word, Communism. My very dear children, nothing in all these pages will be written so much for you, though it is so unlike anything you would want to read. In nothing shall I be so much a witness, in no way am I so much called upon to fulfill my task, as in trying to make clear to you (and to the world) the true nature of Communism and the source of its power, which was the cause of my ordeal as a man, and remains the historic ordeal of the world in the 20th century. For in this century, within the next decades, will be decided for generations whether all mankind is to become Communist, whether the whole world is to become free, or whether, in the struggle, civilization as we know it is to be completely destroyed or completely changed. It is our fate to live upon that turning point in history.

The world has reached that turning point by the steep stages of a crisis mounting for generations. The turning point is the next to the last step. It was reached in blood, sweat, tears, havoc and death in World War II. The chief fruit of the First World War was the Russian Revolution and the rise of Communism as a national power. The chief fruit of the Second World War was our arrival at the next to the last step of the crisis with the rise of Communism as a world power. History is likely to say that these were the only decisive results of the world wars.

The last war simplified the balance of political forces in the world by reducing them to two. For the first time, it made the power of the Communist sector of mankind (embodied in the Soviet Union) roughly equal to the power of the free sector of mankind (embodied in the United States). It made the collision of these powers all but inevitable. For the world wars did not end the crisis. They raised its tensions to a new pitch. They raised the crisis to a new stage. All the politics of our time, including the politics of war, will be the politics of this crisis.

Few men are so dull that they do not know that the crisis exists and that it threatens their lives at every point. It is popular to call it a social crisis. It is in fact a total crisis—religious, moral, intellectual, social, political, economic. It is popular to call it a crisis of the Western world. It is in fact a crisis of the whole world. Communism, which claims to be a solution of the crisis, is itself a symptom and an irritant of the crisis.

In part, the crisis results from the impact of science and technology upon mankind which, neither socially nor morally, has caught up with the problems posed by that impact. In part, it is caused by men's efforts to solve those problems. World wars are the military expression of the crisis. World-wide depressions are its economic expression. Universal desperation is its spiritual climate. This is the climate of Communism. Communism in our time can no more be considered apart from the crisis than a fever can be acted upon apart from an infected body.

I see in Communism the focus of the concentrated evil of our time. You will ask: Why, then, do men become Communists? How did it happen that you, our gentle and loved father, were once a Communist? Were you simply stupid? No, I was not stupid. Were you morally depraved? No, I was not morally depraved. Indeed, educated men become Communists chiefly for moral reasons. Did you not know that the crimes and horrors of Communism are inherent in Communism? Yes, I knew that fact. Then why did you become a Communist? It would help more to ask: How did it happen that this movement, once a mere muttering of political outcasts, became this immense force that now contests the mastery of mankind? Even when all the chances and mistakes of history are allowed for, the answer must be: Communism makes some profound appeal to the human mind. You will not find out what it is by calling Communism names. That will not help much to explain why Communism whose horrors, on a scale unparalleled in history, are now public knowledge, still recruits its thousands and holds its millions—among them some of the best minds alive. Look at Klaus Fuchs, standing in the London dock, quiet, doomed, destroyed, and say whether it is possible to answer in that way the simple question: Why?

First, let me try to say what Communism is not. It is not simply a vicious plot hatched by wicked men in a sub-cellar. It is not just the writings of Marx and Lenin, dialectical materialism, the Politburo, the labor theory of value, the theory of the general strike, the Red Army, secret police, labor camps, underground conspiracy, the dictatorship of the proletariat, the technique of the coup d'état. It is not even those chanting, bannered millions that stream periodically, like disorganized armies, through the heart of the world's capitals: Moscow, New York, Tokyo, Paris, Rome. These are expressions of Communism, but they are not what Communism is about.

In the Hiss trials, where Communism was a haunting specter, but which did little or nothing to explain Communism, Communists were assumed to be criminals, pariahs, clandestine men who lead double lives under false names, travel on false passports, deny traditional religion, morality, the sanctity of oaths, preach violence and practice treason. These things are true about Communists, but they are not what Communism is about.

The revolutionary heart of Communism is not the theatrical appeal: "Workers of the world, unite. You have nothing to lose but your chains. You have a world to gain." It is a simple statement of Karl Marx, further simplified for handy use: "Philosophers have explained the world; it is necessary to change the world." Communists are bound together by no secret oath. The tie that binds them across the frontiers of nations, across barriers of language and differences of class and education, in defiance of religion, morality, truth, law, honor, the weaknesses of the body and the irresolutions of the mind, even unto death, is a simple conviction: It is necessary to change the world. Their power, whose nature baffles the rest of the world, because in a large measure the rest of the world has lost that power, is the power to hold convictions and to act on them. It is the same power that moves mountains; it is also an unfailing power to move men. Communists are that part of mankind which has recovered the power to live or die—to bear witness—for its faith. And it is a simple, rational faith that inspires men to live or die for it.

It is not new. It is, in fact, man's second oldest faith. Its promise was whispered in the first days of the Creation under the Tree of the Knowledge of Good and Evil: "Ye shall be as gods." It is the great alternative faith of mankind. Like all great faiths, its force derives from a simple vision. Other ages have had great visions. They have always been different versions of the same vision: the vision of God and man's relationship to God. The Communist vision is the vision of Man without God.

It is the vision of man's mind displacing God as the creative intelligence of the world. It is the vision of man's liberated mind, by the sole force of its rational intelligence, redirecting man's destiny and reorganizing man's life and the world. It is the vision of man, once more the central figure of the Creation, not because God made man in His image, but because man's mind makes him the most intelligent of the animals. Copernicus and his successors displaced man as the central fact of the universe by proving that the earth was not the central star of the universe. Communism restores man to his sovereignty by the simple method of denying God.

The vision is a challenge and implies a threat. It challenges man to prove by his acts that he is the masterwork of the Creation—by making thought and act one. It challenges him to prove it by using the force of his rational mind to end the bloody meaninglessness of man's history—by giving it purpose and a plan. It challenges him to prove it by reducing the meaningless chaos of nature, by imposing on it his rational will to order, abundance, security, peace. It is the vision of materialism. But it threatens, if man's mind is unequal to the problems of man's progress, that he will sink back into savagery (the A and the H bombs have raised the issue in explosive forms), until nature replaces him with a more intelligent form of life.

It is an intensely practical vision. The tools to turn it into reality are at hand—science and technology, whose traditional method, the rigorous exclusion of all supernatural factors in solving problems, has contributed to the intellectual climate in which the vision flourishes, just as they have contributed to the crisis in which Communism thrives. For the vision is shared by millions who are not Communists (they are part of Communism's secret strength). Its first commandment is found, not in the *Communist Manifesto*, but in the first sentence of the physics primer: "All of the progress of mankind to date results from the making of careful measurements." But Communism, for the first time in history, has made this vision the faith of a great modern political movement.

Hence the Communist Party is quite justified in calling itself the most revolutionary party in history. It has posed in practical form the most revolutionary question in history: God or Man? It has taken the logical next step which three hundred years of rationalism hesitated to take, and said what millions of modern minds think, but do not dare or care to say: If man's mind is the decisive force in the world, what need is there for God? Henceforth man's mind is man's fate.

This vision *is* the Communist revolution, which, like all great revolutions, occurs in man's mind before it takes form in man's acts. Insurrection and conspiracy are merely methods of realizing the vision; they are merely part of the politics of Communism. Without its vision, they, like Communism, would have no meaning and could not rally a parcel of pickpockets. Communism does not summon men to crime or to Utopia, as its easy critics like to think. On the plane of faith, it summons mankind to turn its vision into practical reality. On the plane of action, it summons men to struggle against the inertia of the past which, embodied in social, political and economic forms, Communism claims, is blocking the will of mankind to make its next great forward stride. It summons men to overcome the crisis, which, Communism claims, is in effect a crisis of rending frustration, with the world, unable to stand still, but unwilling to go forward along the road that the logic of a technological civilization points out—Communism.

This is Communism's moral sanction, which is twofold. Its vision points the way to the future; its faith labors to turn the future into present reality. It says to every man who joins it: the vision is a practical problem of history; the way to achieve it is a practical problem of politics, which is the present tense of history. Have you the moral strength to take upon yourself the crimes of history so that man at last may close his chronicle of age-old, senseless suffering, and replace it with purpose and a plan? The answer a man makes to this question is the difference between the Communist and those miscellaneous socialists, liberals, fellow travelers, unclassified progressives and men of good will, all of whom share a similar vision, but do not share the faith because they will not take upon themselves the penalties of the faith. The answer is the root of that sense of moral superiority which makes Communists, though caught in crime, berate their opponents with withering self-righteousness.

The Communist vision has a mighty agitator and a mighty propagandist. They are the crisis. The agitator needs no soap box. It speaks insistently to the human mind at the point where desperation lurks.

The propagandist writes no Communist gibberish. It speaks insistently to the human mind at the point where man's hope and man's energy fuse to fierceness.

The vision inspires. The crisis impels. The workingman is chiefly moved by the crisis. The educated man is chiefly moved by the vision. The workingman, living upon a mean margin of life, can afford few visions—even practical visions. An educated man, peering from the Harvard Yard, or any college campus, upon a world in chaos, finds in the vision the two certainties for which the mind of man tirelessly seeks: a reason to live and a reason to die. No other faith of our time presents them with the same practical intensity. That is why Communism is the central experience of the first half of the 20th century, and may be its final experience—will be, unless the free world, in the agony of its struggle with Communism, overcomes its crisis by discovering, in suffering and pain, a power of faith which will provide man's mind, at the same intensity, with the same two certainties: a reason to live and a reason to die. If it fails, this will be the century of the great social wars. If it succeeds, this will be the century of the great wars of faith.

You will ask: Why, then, do men cease to be Communists? One answer is: Very few do. Thirty years after the Russian Revolution, after the known atrocities, the purges, the revelations, the jolting zigzags of Communist politics, there is only a handful of ex-Communists in the whole world. By ex-Communists I do not mean those who break with Communism over differences of strategy and tactics (like Trotsky) or organization (like Tito). Those are merely quarrels over a road map by people all of whom are in a hurry to get to the same place.

Nor, by ex-Communists, do I mean those thousands who continually drift into the Communist Party and out again. The turnover is vast. These are the spiritual vagrants of our time whose traditional faith has been leached out in the bland climate of rationalism. They are looking for an intellectual night's lodging. They lack the character for Communist faith because they lack the character for any faith. So they drop away, though Communism keeps its hold on them.

By an ex-Communist, I mean a man who knew clearly why he became a Communist, who served Communism devotedly and knew why he served it, who broke with Communism unconditionally and knew why he broke with it. Of these there are very few—an index to the power of the vision and the power of the crisis.

History very largely fixes the patterns of force that make men Communists. Hence one Communist conversion sounds much like another—rather impersonal and repetitious, awesome and tiresome, like long lines of similar people all stolidly waiting to get in to see the same movie. A man's break with Communism is intensely personal. Hence the account of no two breaks is likely to be the same. The reasons that made one Communist break may seem without force to another ex-Communist.

It is a fact that a man can join the Communist Party, can be very active in it for years, without completely understanding the nature of Communism or the political methods that follow inevitably from its vision. One day such incomplete Communists discover that the Communist Party is not what they thought it was. They break with it and turn on it with the rage of an honest dupe, a dupe who has given a part of his life to a swindle. Often they forget that it takes two to make a swindle.

Others remain Communists for years, warmed by the light of its vision, firmly closing their eyes to the crimes and horrors inseparable from its practical politics. One day they have to face the facts. They are appalled at what they have abetted. They spend the rest of their days trying to explain, usually without great success, the dark clue to their complicity. As their understanding of Communism was incomplete and led them to a dead end, their understanding of breaking with it is incomplete and leads them to a dead end. It leads to less than Communism, which was a vision and a faith. The world outside Communism, the world in crisis, lacks a vision and a faith. There is before these ex-Communists absolutely nothing. Behind them is a threat. For they have, in fact, broken not with the vision, but with the politics of the vision. In the name of reason and intelligence, the vision keeps them firmly in its grip—self-divided, paralyzed, powerless to act against it.

Hence the most secret fold of their minds is haunted by a terrifying thought: What if we were wrong? What if our inconstancy is our guilt? That is the fate of those who break without knowing clearly that Communism is wrong because something else is right, because to the challenge: *God or Man?*, they continue to give the answer: *Man.* Their pathos is that not even the Communist ordeal could teach them that man without God is just what Communism said he was: the most intelligent of the animals, that man without God is a beast, never more beastly than when he is most intelligent about his beastliness. *"Er nennt's Vernunft,"* says the Devil in Goethe's *Faust, "und braucht's allein, nur tierischer als jedes Tier zu sein"*— Man calls it reason and uses it simply to be more beastly than any beast. Not grasping the source of the evil they sincerely hate, such ex-Communists in general make ineffectual witnesses against it. They are witnesses against something; they have ceased to be witnesses for anything.

Yet there is one experience which most sincere ex-Communists share, whether or not they go only part way to the end of the question it poses. The daughter of a former German diplomat in Moscow was trying to explain to me why her father, who, as an enlightened modern man, had been extremely pro-Communist, had become an implacable anti-Communist. It was hard for her because, as an enlightened modern girl, she shared the Communist vision without being a Communist. But she loved her father and the irrationality of his defection embarrassed her. "He was immensely pro-Soviet," she said, "and then—you will laugh at me—but you must not laugh at my father—and then—one night—in Moscow—he heard screams. That's all. Simply one night he heard screams."

A child of Reason and the 20th century, she knew that there is a logic of the mind. She did not know that the soul has a logic that may be more compelling than the mind's. She did not know at all that she had swept away the logic of the mind, the logic of history, the logic of politics, the myth of the 20th century, with five annihilating words: one night he heard screams.

What Communist has not heard those screams? They come from husbands torn forever from their wives in midnight arrests. They come, muffled, from the execution cellars of the secret police, from the torture chambers of the Lubianka, from all the citadels of terror now stretching from Berlin to Canton. They come from those freight cars loaded with men, women and children, the enemies of the Communist State, locked in, packed in, left on remote sidings to freeze to death at night in the Russian winter. They come from minds driven mad by the horrors of mass starvation ordered and enforced as a policy of the Communist State. They come from the starved skeletons, worked to death, or flogged to death (as an example to others) in the freezing filth of sub-arctic labor camps. They come from children whose parents are suddenly, inexplicably, taken away from them—parents they will never see again.

What Communist has not heard those screams? Execution, says the Communist code, is the highest measure of social protection. What man can call himself a Communist who has not accepted the fact that Terror is an instrument of policy, right if the vision is right, justified by history, enjoined by the balance of forces in the social wars of this century? Those screams

have reached every Communist's mind. Usually they stop there. What judge willingly dwells upon the man the laws compel him to condemn to death—the laws of nations or the laws of history?

But one day the Communist really hears those screams. He is going about his routine party tasks. He is lifting a dripping reel of microfilm from a developing tank. He is justifying to a Communist fraction in a trade union an extremely unwelcome directive of the Central Committee. He is receiving from a trusted superior an order to go to another country and, in a designated hotel, at a designated hour, meet a man whose name he will never know, but who will give him a package whose contents he will never learn. Suddenly, there closes around that Communist a separating silence, and in that silence he hears screams. He hears them for the first time. For they do not merely reach his mind. They pierce beyond. They pierce to his soul. He says to himself: "Those are not the screams of man in agony. Those are the screams of a soul in agony." He hears them for the first time because a soul in extremity has communicated with that which alone can hear it—another human soul.

Why does the Communist ever hear them? Because in the end there persists in every man, however he may deny it, a scrap of soul. The Communist who suffers this singular experience then says to himself: "What is happening to me? I must be sick." If he does not instantly stifle that scrap of soul, he is lost. If he admits it for a moment, he has admitted that there is something greater than Reason, greater than the logic of mind, of politics, of history, of economics, which alone justifies the vision. If the party senses his weakness, and the party is peculiarly cunning at sensing such weakness, it will humiliate him, degrade him, condemn him, expel him. If it can, it will destroy him. And the party will be right. For he, has betrayed that which alone justifies its faith—the vision of Almighty Man. He has brushed the only vision that has force against the vision of Almighty Mind. He stands before the fact of God.

The Communist Party is familiar with this experience to which its members are sometimes liable in prison, in illness, in indecision. It is recognized frankly as a sickness. There are ways of treating it—if it is confessed. It is when it is not confessed that the party, sensing a subtle crisis, turns upon it savagely. What ex-Communist has not suffered this experience in one form or another, to one degree or another? What he does about it depends on the individual man. That is why no ex-Communist dare answer for his sad fraternity the question: Why do men break with Communism? He can only answer the question: How did you break with Communism? My answer is: Slowly, reluctantly, in agony.

Yet my break began long before I heard those screams. Perhaps it does for everyone. I do not know how far back it began. Avalanches gather force and crash, unheard, in men as in the mountains. But I date my break from a very casual happening. I was sitting in our apartment on St. Paul Street in Baltimore. It was shortly before we moved to Alger Hiss's apartment in Washington. My daughter was in her high chair. I was watching her eat. She was the most miraculous thing that had ever happened in my life. I liked to watch her even when she smeared porridge on her face or dropped it meditatively on the floor. My eye came to rest on the delicate convolutions of her ear—those intricate, perfect ears. The thought passed through my mind: "No, those ears were not created by any chance coming together of atoms in nature (the Communist view). They could have been created only by immense design." The thought was involuntary and unwanted. I crowded it out of my mind. But I never wholly forgot it or the occasion. I had to crowd it out of my mind. If I had completed it, I should have had to say: Design presupposes God. I did not then know that, at that moment, the finger of God was first laid upon my forehead.

One thing most ex-Communists could agree upon: they broke because they wanted to be free. They do not all mean the same thing by "free." Freedom is a need of the soul, and nothing else. It is in striving toward God that the soul strives continually after a condition of freedom. God alone is the inciter and guarantor of freedom. He is the only guarantor. External freedom is only an aspect of interior freedom. Political freedom, as the Western world has known it, is only a political reading of the Bible. Religion and freedom are indivisible. Without freedom the soul dies. Without the soul there is no justification for freedom. Necessity is the only ultimate justification known to the mind. Hence every sincere break with Communism is a religious experience, though the Communist fail to identify its true nature, though he fail to go to the end of the experience. His break is the political expression of the perpetual need of the soul whose first faint stirring he has felt within him, years, months or days before he breaks. A Communist breaks because he must choose at last between irreconcilable opposites—God or Man, Soul or Mind, Freedom or Communism.

Communism is what happens when, in the name of Mind, men free themselves from God. But its view of God, its knowledge of God, its experience of God, is what alone gives character to a society or a nation, and meaning to its destiny. Its culture, the voice of this character, is merely that view, knowledge, experience, of God, fixed by its most intense spirits in terms intelligible to the mass of men. There has never been a society or a nation without God. But history is cluttered with the wreckage of nations that became indifferent to God, and died.

The crisis of Communism exists to the degree in which it has failed to free the peoples that it rules from God. Nobody knows this better than the Communist Party of the Soviet Union. The crisis of the Western world exists to the degree in which it is indifferent to God. It exists to the degree in which the Western world actually shares Communism's materialist vision, is so dazzled by the logic of the materialist interpretation of history, politics and economics, that it fails to grasp that, for it, the only possible answer to the Communist challenge: Faith in God or Faith in Man? is the challenge: Faith in God.

Economics is not the central problem of this century. It is a relative problem which can be solved in relative ways. Faith is the central problem of this age. The Western world does not know it, but it already possesses the answer to this problem—but only provided that its faith in God and the freedom He enjoins is as great as Communism's faith in Man.

My dear children, before I close this foreword, I want to recall to you briefly the life that we led in the ten years between the time when I broke with Communism and the time when I began to testify—the things we did, worked for, loved, believed in. For it was that happy life, which, on the human side, in part made it possible for me to do later on the things I had to do, or endure the things that happened to me.

Those were the days of the happy little worries, which then seemed so big. We know now that they were the golden days. They will not come again. In those days, our greatest worry was how to meet the payments on the mortgage, how to get the ploughing done in time, how to get health accreditation for our herd, how to get the hay in before the rain. I sometimes took my vacation in hay harvest so that I could help work the load. You two little children used to trample the load, drive the hay truck in the fields when you could barely reach the foot pedals, or drive the tractor that pulled up the loaded harpoons to the mow. At evening, you would break off to help Mother milk while I went on haying. For we came of age on the farm when we decided not to hire barn help, but to run the herd ourselves as a family.

Often the ovenlike heat in the comb of the barn and the sweet smell of alfalfa made us sick. Sometimes we fell asleep at the supper table from fatigue. But the hard work was good for us; and you knew only the peace of a home governed by a father and mother whose marriage the years (and an earlier suffering which you could not remember) had deepened into the perfect love that enveloped you.

Mother was a slight, overalled figure forever working for you in the house or beside you in the barns and gardens. Papa was a squat, overalled figure, fat but forceful, who taught John, at nine, the man-size glory of driving the tractor; or sat beside Ellen, at the wheel of the truck, an embodiment of security and power, as we drove loads of cattle through the night. On summer Sundays, you sat between Papa and Mama in the Quaker meeting house. Through the open doors, as you tried not to twist and turn in the long silence, you could see the far, blue Maryland hills and hear the redbirds and ground robins in the graveyard behind.

Only Ellen had a vague, troubled recollection of another time and another image of Papa. Then (it was during the years 1938 and 1939), if for any reason she pattered down the hall at night, she would find Papa, with the light on, writing, with a revolver on the table or a gun against the chair. She knew that there were people who wanted to kill Papa and who might try to kidnap her. But a wide sea of sunlight and of time lay between that puzzling recollection and the farm.

The farm was your kingdom, and the world lay far beyond the protecting walls thrown up by work and love. It is true that comic strips were not encouraged, comic books were banned, the radio could be turned on only by permission which was seldom given (or asked), and you saw few movies. But you grew in the presence of eternal wonders. There was the birth of lambs and calves. You remember how once, when I was away and the veterinarian could not come, you saw Mother reach in and turn the calf inside the cow so that it could be born. There was also the death of animals, sometimes violent, sometimes slow and painful—nothing is more constant on a farm than death.

Sometimes, of a spring evening, Papa would hear that distant honking that always makes his scalp tingle, and we would all rush out to see the wild geese, in lines of hundreds, steer up from the southwest, turn over the barn as over a landmark, and head into the north. Or on autumn nights of sudden cold that set the ewes breeding in the orchard, Papa would call you out of the house to stand with him in the now celebrated pumpkin patch and watch the northern lights flicker in electric clouds on the horizon, mount, die down, fade and mount again till they filled the whole northern sky with ghostly light in motion.

Thus, as children, you experienced two of the most important things men ever know—the wonder of life and the wonder of the universe, the wonder of life within the wonder of the universe. More important, you knew them not from books, not from lectures, but simply from living among them. Most important, you knew them with reverence and awe—that reverence and awe that has died out of the modern world and been replaced by man's monkeylike amazement at the cleverness of his own inventive brain.

I have watched greatness touch you in another way. I have seen you sit, uninvited and unforced, listening in complete silence to the third movement of the Ninth Symphony. I thought you understood, as much as children can, when I told you that that music was the moment at which Beethoven finally passed beyond the suffering of his life on earth and reached for the hand of God, as God reaches for the hand of Adam in Michelangelo's vision of the Creation.

And once, in place of a bedtime story, I was reading Shakespeare to John—at his own request, for I never forced such things on you. I came to that passage in which Macbeth, having murdered Duncan, realizes what he has done to his own soul, and asks if all the water in the world can ever wash the blood from his hand, or will it not rather

The Multitudinous Seas Incarnadine?

At that line, John's whole body twitched. I gave great silent thanks to God. For I knew that if, as children, you could thus feel in your souls the reverence and awe for life and the world, which is the ultimate meaning of Beethoven and Shakespeare, as man and woman you could never be satisfied with less. I felt a great faith that sooner or later you would understand what I once told you, not because I expected you to understand it then, but because I hoped that you would remember it later: "True wisdom comes from the overcoming of suffering and sin. All true wisdom is therefore touched with sadness."

If all this sounds unduly solemn, you know that our lives were not; that all of us suffer from an incurable itch to puncture false solemnity. In our daily lives, we were fun-loving and gay. For those who have solemnity in their souls generally have enough of it there, and do not need to force it into their faces.

Then, on August 3, 1948, you learned for the first time that your father had once been a Communist, that he had worked in something called "the underground," that it was shameful, and that for some reason he was in Washington telling the world about it. While he was in the underground, he testified, he had worked with a number of other Communists. One of them was a man with the odd name of Alger Hiss. Later, Alger Hiss denied the allegation. Thus the Great Case began, and with it our lives were changed forever.

Dear children, one autumn twilight, when you were much smaller, I slipped away from you in play and stood for a moment alone in the apple orchard near the barn. Then I heard your two voices, piping together anxiously, calling to me: "Papa! Papa!" from the harvested cornfield. In the years when I was away five days a week in New York, working to pay for the farm, I used to think of you both before I fell asleep at night. And that is how you almost always came to me—voices of beloved children, calling to me from the gathered fields at dusk.

You called to me once again at night in the same orchard. That was a good many years later. A shadow deeper and more chilling than the autumn evening had closed upon us—I mean the Hiss Case. It was the first year of the Case. We had been doing the evening milking together. For us, one of the few happy results of the Case was that at last I could be home with you most of the time (in life these good things usually come too little or too late). I was washing and disinfecting the cows, and putting on and taking off the milkers. You were stripping after me.

In the quiet, there suddenly swept over my mind a clear realization of our true position—obscure, all but friendless people (some of my great friends had already taken refuge in aloofness; the others I had withdrawn from so as not to involve them in my affairs). Against me was an almost solid line-up of the most powerful groups and men in the country, the bitterly hostile reaction of much of the press, the smiling skepticism of much of the public, the venomous calumnies of the Hiss forces, the all but universal failure to understand the real meaning of the Case or my real purpose. A sense of the enormous futility of my effort, and my own inadequacy, drowned me. I felt a physical cold creep through me, settle around my heart and freeze any pulse of hope. The sight of you children, guiltless and defenseless, was more than I could bear. I was alone against the world; my longing was to be left completely alone, or not to be at all. It was that death of the will which Communism, with great cunning, always tries to induce in its victims.

I waited until the last cow was stripped and the last can lifted into the cooler. Then I stole into the upper barn and out into the apple orchard. It was a very dark night. The stars were large and cold. This cold was one with the coldness in myself. The lights of the barn, the house and the neighbors' houses were warm in the windows and on the ground; they were not for me. Then I heard Ellen call me in the barn and John called: "Papa!" Still calling, Ellen went down to the house to see if I were there. I heard John opening gates as he went to the calf barn, and he called me there. With all the longing of my love for you, I wanted to answer. But if I answered, I must come back to the living world. I could not do that.

John began to call me in the cow stable, in the milk house. He went into the dark side of the barn (I heard him slide the door back), into the upper barn, where at night he used to be afraid. He stepped outside in the dark, calling: "Papa! Papa!"—then, frantically, on the verge of tears: "Papa!" I walked over to him. I felt that I was making the most terrible surrender I should have to make on earth. "Papa!," he cried and threw his arms around me, "don't ever go away." "No," I said, "no, I won't ever go away." Both of us knew that the words "go away" stood for something else, and that I had given him my promise not to kill myself. Later on, as you will see, I was tempted, in my wretchedness, to break that promise.

My children, when you were little, we used sometimes to go for walks in our pine woods. In the open fields, you would run along by yourselves. But you used instinctively to give me your hands as we entered those woods, where it was darker, lonelier, and in the stillness our voices sounded loud and frightening. In this book I am again giving you my hands. I am leading you, not through cool pine woods, but up and up a narrow defile between bare and steep rocks from which in shadow things uncoil and slither away. It will be dark. But, in the end, if I have led you aright, you will make out three crosses, from two of which hang thieves. I will have brought you to Golgotha—the place of skulls. This is the meaning of the journey. Before you understand, I may not be there, my hands may have slipped from yours. It will not matter. For when you understand what you see, you will no longer be children. You will know that life is pain, that each of us hangs always upon the cross of himself. And when you know that this is true of every man, woman and child on earth, you will be wise.

Your Father

CHAPTER 12

Allen Ginsberg Begins the Counterculture

"I saw the best minds of my generation destroyed by madness, starving hysterical naked...."

A llen Ginsberg and Whittaker Chambers (see Chapter 11) were both outsiders who believed deeply in the idea of American freedom, but their similarities ended there. Chambers, a former Marxist, believed that communism destroyed the human soul. Ginsberg, the son of a communist, believed that capitalism was the soul-destroyer. Chambers stood for middle-class respectability. Ginsberg, born into the middle class, rejected its values outright and spent his life in flight from them. Chambers viewed "freedom," in political terms, as a wall of protection between the individual and an intrusive, bureaucratic central state. Ginsberg's vision of "freedom" was cultural, offering an opportunity for individual expression and fulfillment. If Chambers altered the political landscape of the nation, facilitating the election of Ronald Reagan as president in 1980 (see Chapter 21), Ginsberg effected a transformation that was no less profound. As the acknowledged founder of what became known as the "Beat Generation" of poets, he helped define American culture in new ways.

Until Ginsberg and the Beats burst onto the scene in the mid-1950s, there was little disagreement on the trajectory of the "American Dream." Get an education. Learn a skill. Obey authority. Get a job. Get married. Have children. Buy a home. Purchase consumer products. Get a promotion. Get a better job. Make more money. Have more children. Buy a better house. Buy more consumer products. Retire. Ginsberg set this American edifice of materialism and conformity afire, and if he was not successful in burning it to the ground, he did construct the foundation of a new American Dream, and a new way to live an American life. Question authority. Satisfy yourself, not others. Follow your own moral code. Be an individual. Spurn materialism and its entanglements. Express yourself without inhibition. Love freely. Live peacefully.

In time, the alternative American culture championed by Ginsberg and the Beats would grow into the "counterculture" of the 1960s, a rejection of traditional American values built around music, dress, drugs, sexual liberty, inclusiveness, peace, and anti-materialism. By the latter decades of the twentieth century, it would influence "mainstream" American culture to the point of supplanting it. America's contemporary cultural landscape, with its celebration of individual expression, choice, and conscience, can trace its roots to Allen Ginsberg and a Beat Generation of outcasts who first questioned the worth—and even the sanity—of the Cold War version of the American Dream.

Allen Ginsberg was born to be a cultural rebel. His father Louis was a noted poet in Paterson, New Jersey, where Allen grew up and attended high school. His mother Naomi was an outspoken political activist and lifelong communist. She was also mentally unstable, and Allen's childhood was deeply affected by her prolonged absences while receiving hospital treatment. Young Allen had a profound feeling of apartness, of living outside the American mainstream. His parents' intellectual backgrounds and radical politics were reasons for this. So too was his Jewish heritage, which especially during the 1930s and 1940s forced him to the margins. His physical attraction to men also marked him as one who did not "belong." He sensed that the America in which he lived was mad. Part of this came from his hostility to capitalism as an economic system. Like Lange and Evans (see Chapter 8), Ginsberg was a firsthand observer of the miseries of the Great Depression.

But Ginsberg's alienation went deeper than anger at the inequitable distribution of wealth in the United States. To him, the idea of American capitalism itself was madness. It forced men and women into stunted and foreshortened lives, robbing them of the opportunity to make independent decisions about who they would be and the paths they would follow. It produced a society of the regimented and the repressed, working at repetitive, unfulfilling jobs to feed both their lust for material possessions and the machine of capitalism itself. Ginsberg would later refer to this oppressive, life-denying force as "Moloch" in his greatest poem, "Howl."

Ginsberg entered Columbia University in 1942. There he lived an intellectual double life. He studied with some of the great figures of traditional American literary criticism, including the renowned Lionel Trilling. But at the same time, Ginsberg associated with a group of young men who shared his outsider sensibilities and cultural rebelliousness. These included Jack Kerouac, a former Columbia football player, and William Burroughs, a drug-addicted product of a wealthy St. Louis family. Along with Ginsberg, they would become the central figures of the Beat Generation, Kerouac for his stream-of-consciousness novel *On the Road* (1957), and Burroughs for *Naked Lunch* (1959), an account of the hipster underworld.

As his college career progressed, Ginsberg's defiant nature won out over whatever careerist impulses he may have possessed. Columbia suspended him in 1945 for tracing the words "Butler (the university president) has no balls" and "Fuck the Jews" (ironic in view of his own heritage) on the window of his dormitory room. Ginsberg's rebellion extended beyond the realm of personal behavior. His writing and critical perspective also moved away from established forms. Turning his back on his mentor Trilling, Ginsberg rejected traditional poetry, with its regular meter, prescribed structure, and detached viewpoint. Instead, he adopted a style that mirrored the patterns of his own life.

By 1948, the year he completed his Columbia education, that life was chaotic, mystical, and as far as those in positions of legal authority were concerned, touched by madness. One day that year, Ginsberg claimed that he had heard the voice of the English Romantic poet William Blake (1757–1827) and experienced a joyous and peaceful vision, akin to a religious awakening. Ginsberg would seek to capture the emotion of that vision in his poetry, often with the aid of hallucinogenic drugs. In 1949, he was arrested after police discovered property stolen by a friend in his apartment. Admitting his homosexuality to the authorities, Ginsberg was adjudged mentally ill and institutionalized at the New York State Psychiatric Institute in Upper Manhattan. There, he met Carl Solomon, who shared his interest in unstructured poetic expression, as well as his alienated worldview. The two became close friends, and Solomon would appear prominently in Ginsberg's "Howl" a few years later.

Released from the Psychiatric Institute in February 1950, Ginsberg resumed his life on the margins. He rented cheap apartments in areas of New York City shunned by "respectable" people, including Greenwich Village, which since the time of Crystal Eastman (see Chapter 5) had been associated with cultural rebellion. He wrote poetry, although without much public recognition. And he continued to associate with an expanding group of fellow refugees from "straight" society that now had a name: "Beats." Ginsberg's friend Jack Kerouac had so named them as an allusion to their "beatific" natures, which transcended the numbing conformity and competitive acquis- itiveness of modern American life.

"Beats" formed a kind of religious community, albeit a secular one, in which God and heaven were to be found on earth through the power of the human mind and soul rather than the traditional bible and church. Drug use in such circumstances was not self-indulgence but a means to opening "the doors of perception," as Ginsberg's inspiration William Blake once wrote.[1] This, of course, was not how "straight" society viewed drugs, and during the early 1950s, in a Cold War–influenced atmosphere of anticommunist paranoia and nuclear fear, the Beats—to the extent they were noticed at all—appeared to symbolize everything that mainstream America found disturbing and threatening.

In 1954, Ginsberg left New York for San Francisco, a move that would change both the direction of his career and the trajectory of the Beat movement. To support himself, Ginsberg took a job as a market researcher for an advertising firm, working in the very system whose values he abhorred. But the paychecks subsidized his writing, and in 1955 Ginsberg began to compose "Howl," the poem that would define him and the Beat Generation. He wrote in an apartment on Montgomery Street in the North Beach section of San Francisco, an area similar to New York's Greenwich Village in its atmosphere of artistic, political, and personal experimentation and ferment. Reflecting on "Howl's" origins, Ginsberg later remarked: "I was curious to leave behind after my generation an emotional time bomb that would continue exploding in U.S. conscious- ness in case our military-industrial-nationalist complex solidified into a repressive police bureaucracy."[2] "Howl" would be his "American Scream," a cry of pain against the ravages of the conventional American Dream.[3]

As he labored over "Howl," Ginsberg envisioned an American nightmare. Cold War repression extended beyond the hunt for communists. Anyone considered a "deviant" was a target, and homosexuals were particularly vulnerable, as Ginsberg himself had discovered in 1949. As Ginsberg worked at his San Francisco advertising firm, dressed incongruously for the day in a sober suit and tie, he was reminded of the millions of Americans who, similarly attired, toiled at mind-numbing occupations where they learned above all to "go along to get along" for the sake of a bigger house, a better car, or a fatter paycheck.

Hovering over everything was the specter of nuclear Armageddon, the product of a geopolitical rivalry between the United States and the Soviet Union that Ginsberg viewed as without purpose. Unlike Whittaker Chambers (see Chapter 11), who inter- preted the Cold War as an elemental struggle between good and evil, Ginsberg saw the competing sides as moral equivalents. Both were violent, repressive, and inhumane. Both, in the word Ginsberg would employ in "Howl," were "Moloch," a reference to the ancient God who demanded to be worshipped by the sacrifice of children—the Soviet Union for its crushing bureaucracy and the United States for its exploitative capitalism. Both "Molochs" strangled the human spirit. But, of course, Ginsberg lived in the United States and not in the Soviet Union, so it was with his own country that he was most preoccupied. And the only possible response to the American Moloch was, in Ginsberg's words, "orphic creativeness, juvenescent savagery, primitive aban- don"—what middle-class Americans understood as madness.[4] It was in this spirit that Ginsberg composed "Howl."

On October 7, 1955, Ginsberg read from "Howl" for the first time in public. The occasion was a poetry reading organized by Ginsberg at the Six Gallery, an art space frequented by Beats and others in San Francisco's cultural underground. Jack Kerouac attended, as did Lawrence Ferlinghetti, owner of the nearby City Lights Bookstore and a

Beat poet himself. Ferlinghetti had begun to publish inexpensive paperback collections of local poetry under the "City Lights Books" imprint. Ginsberg used his background in advertising to publicize the event in North Beach and in the culturally radical university community of Berkeley across San Francisco Bay, and at 8 P.M. on the evening of October 7 the Six Gallery was packed with an audience curious to hear a "new" form of poetry. As jugs of cheap wine were passed around, the reading began with work from other young poets. By 11 P.M., when Ginsberg himself took the stage, the alcohol had gone to everyone's heads, and the scene was raucous, a perfect atmosphere for the most raucous American poem of the twentieth century.

The version of "Howl" Ginsberg read that night was still a work in progress and was missing what would become its Parts II and III. Nonetheless, what he was able to deliver electrified the crowd. With an ecstatic Kerouac leading the way, shouts of "Go! Go!" filled the room.[5] Ginsberg concluded to a frenzied ovation.[6] The next day he received a telegram from Ferlinghetti. It echoed the words written by the philosopher and essayist Ralph Waldo Emerson to the poet Walt Whitman upon the publication of his *Leaves of Grass* in 1855, exactly a century earlier: "I greet you at the beginning of a great career."[7] Ferlinghetti wished to do more than congratulate Ginsberg; he intended to publish him. "Howl and Other Poems" appeared in 1956 as part of City Lights Books' Pocket Poets Series. By the end of the twentieth century, it had been reissued fifty-six times and was approaching 900,000 copies in print.[8]

From his famous first lines, "I saw the best minds of my generation destroyed by madness, starving hysterical naked," Ginsberg served notice that he intended to challenge every American verity and violate every American taboo.[9] He referred directly and unapologetically to drug use ("...looking for an angry fix, angel headed hipsters burning for the ancient heavenly connection to the starry dynamo in the machinery of night...").[10] He praised the delights of both homosexual eroticism ("...who let themselves be fucked in the ass by saintly motorcyclists, and screamed with joy...") and heterosexual sex ("...joy to the memory of his innumerable lays of girls in empty lots & diner backyards, movie houses' rickety rows, on mountaintops in caves or with gaunt waitresses in familiar roadside lonely petticoat upliftings...").[11] He invoked jazz ("...sat up smoking in the supernatural darkness of cold-water flats floating across the tops of cities contemplating jazz...") and the emerging musical form of rock 'n roll (see Chapter 13) ("...who scribbled all night rocking and rolling over lofty incantations which in the yellow morning were stanzas of gibberish...").[12] He warned of nuclear war ("...listening to the crack of doom on the hydrogen jukebox...") and the Red Scare ("...who reappeared on the West Coast investigating the F.B.I. in beards and shorts."), materialism ("...who burned cigarette holes in their arms protesting the narcotic tobacco haze of Capitalism..."), and conformity ("...who were burned alive in their innocent flannel suits on Madison Avenue...").[13] And he wrote of madness ("...presented themselves on the granite steps of the madhouse with shaven heads and harlequin speech of suicide, demanding instantaneous lobotomy...") as the only sane response to an American society that was itself touched by insanity.[14]

Ginsberg's public reading of "Howl" represented the coming of age of an alternative vision of American life that would find expression not only in the Beat Generation but also in a growing youth culture built around music and film (see Chapter 13 on Elvis Presley) and, in the 1960s, both a revitalized left-wing movement (see Chapter 17 on Students for a Democratic Society) and what became known as the "counterculture." By the late twentieth century, the values of that counterculture would shift "mainstream" American culture toward the individual expression, personal fulfillment and freedom of choice that Ginsberg had celebrated in "Howl." What began as a gathering of Beat poets and their followers in a San Francisco art gallery eventually changed the shape and direction of American life.

During the remainder of 1955 and on into 1956, Ginsberg worked on Parts II and III of "Howl," as well as on a "Footnote" to the poem. Part II employed the word "Moloch," repeated as a refrain, to describe an America built around militarism ("Moloch the vast stone of war!"), capitalism ("Moloch whose blood is running money!"), sexual repression ("lacklove and manless in Moloch!"), and alienation ("Moloch who entered my soul early! Moloch in whom I am a consciousness without a body! Moloch who frightened me out of my natural ecstasy!").[15] Condemned by Moloch to "Robot apartments! invisible suburbs!", Americans lived amid madness.[16] In Part III of "Howl," Ginsberg personalized this madness in the figure of Carl Solomon, whom he had befriended during his time at the New York State Psychiatric Institute in 1949. Fictionalizing the institute as "Rockland," he placed Solomon at the vortex of a hurricane of American insanity, with "twenty-five thousand mad comrades all together singing the final stanzas of the Internationale," and "where we wake up electrified out of the coma by our own souls' airplanes roaring over the roof…"[17] Only those who were themselves mad, like Solomon and Ginsberg, could see America as it truly was and pierce the veil of smug self-delusion that lay at the heart of national identity.

American values had been questioned before, of course—by Du Bois (see Chapter 3), Bourne (see Chapter 4), Eastman (see Chapter 5), and Lange and Evans (see Chapter 8), among others, but never with such directness and candor. Prior critics had asked the United States to live up to its ideals: racial equality, economic justice, gender equity, and cultural pluralism. But Ginsberg appeared to argue that even if the nation did so, there still would be an emptiness at its core and meaninglessness to its life that was almost irredeemable. Did "America"—however one defined it—work? This question, raised by "Howl" in the 1950s, would develop a life of its own, influencing the New Left (see Chapter 17), radical feminism (see Chapter 20), and the counterculture during the 1960s, and even the work of Robert Putnam (see Chapter 22) as late as the 1990s. The ongoing American obsession with personal meaning and fulfillment would be "Howl's" legacy.

"Howl" was praised in a September 1956 *New York Times* review as a "most remarkable poem," containing "a redemptive quality of love."[18] The newspaper's prestigious endorsement made Ginsberg a literary star. He also received crucial support from an unlikely source: the California state court system, where during the summer and fall of 1957, "Howl" was prosecuted as "obscene." The trial provided the opportunity for a series of literary scholars to testify to the poem's social importance and artistic merit, and since the proceedings received national attention, they substituted for an expensive advertising campaign. When the presiding judge held that "Howl" had "some redeeming social importance" and cleared it of obscenity charges, he made it the most famous poem in America.[19] He also turned the Beats into a national phenomenon. In 1958, a San Francisco journalist bent on linking them with communism labeled them "beatniks," after the recently launched Soviet space satellite "Sputnik." While the attempt at red baiting largely failed, the name stuck and entered American popular culture; it even inspired characters on television situation comedies, including "Maynard G. Krebs" in "The Many Loves of Dobie Gillis" (1959–63).

While average Americans came to know them for their drug use and styles of speech and dress, the Beats had by the late 1950s and early 1960s become respected members of the American literary community. Kerouac's *On the Road* (1957) and Burroughs' *Naked Lunch* (1959) joined "Howl" as the founding texts of a new expressive form that celebrated spontaneity, instinct, and the self, and exhibited a skeptical attitude toward established American institutions. None of the Beats were "political" in the traditional sense of seeking to affect elections or legislation. But by exposing the materialism, conformity, and violence in the American bloodstream, they employed culture as a potent tool of political change. Those who followed in their wake—New Leftists, women's movement activists, hippies, and rock musicians, among others—would also make culture the cutting edge of an attack on mainstream American values.

The Beat Generation delivered a hard slap to the face of a self-satisfied society. Their message that birth/school/job/house/family/children/better job/larger house/retirement was a march to oblivion would resonate with future American generations, notably the youth of the 1960s, who looked upon Ginsberg and the Beats as heroes and role models, and the so-called "Me Generation" of the 1980s, whose focus on individual expression also owed much to their example. Just over half a century after Ginsberg read "Howl" for the first time at San Francisco's Six Gallery, a volume of essays entitled *The Poem That Changed America* was published to commemorate the event.[20] The book's title did not exaggerate. The American culture of the twenty-first century that for better or worse celebrates the self above all else owes its existence in large measure to a bearded, bespectacled poet with a radical new message.

Allen Ginsberg went on to have one of the most distinguished careers in the history of American letters. Critics hailed his "Kaddish," written as he struggled to come to grips with the death of his mother and published in 1961, as a deeply moving account of personal grief. It took its place alongside "Howl" as a classic of Beat poetic form. In January 1967, Ginsberg helped organize the "Human Be-In," the San Francisco gathering of hippies, rock musicians, and poets regarded as the birthplace of the American counterculture. He became a leading figure in the counterculture, a living link between the Beats and the new generation. He traveled and performed with Bob Dylan and became known for public readings of his poetry. Ginsberg also made widely distributed recordings of his poems, one of the first artists to utilize modern technology to disseminate his work. After Kerouac's death in 1969, Ginsberg established the Jack Kerouac School of Disembodied Poetics in Boulder, Colorado, to support and sustain the traditions of Beat literature. In 1973 he became a member of the National Institute of Arts and Letters, a sign that he was now considered part of the literary establishment he once challenged. The following year, his *The Fall of America* won the National Book Award. During the last decade of his life, Ginsberg returned to the academic life he had shunned as a young man, as Distinguished Professor of English at Brooklyn College. Recognition and honors poured in until his death from liver cancer in 1997.

Ginsberg had helped engineer an American cultural transformation as profound as any involving traditional politics. Revolutionaries need not carry guns or control governments, as Ginsberg's life and career illustrated. Sometimes words are like weapons. And as the subject of our next chapter will show, sometimes revolutionaries carry guitars.

Questions for Consideration and Conversation

1. To Allen Ginsberg, what was "mad" about America in the 1950s?
2. What would Whittaker Chambers (Chapter 11) have said about Ginsberg and "Howl"? What were the differences between their visions of "freedom"?
3. How did Ginsberg and the "Beats" challenge the "American Dream"?
4. How did the Cold War influence Ginsberg's poetry?
5. What did rock 'n roll (see Chapter 13) have in common with Beat poetry?
6. "Howl" makes it clear that Ginsberg believes culture is a more effective instrument of change in America than traditional politics. Do you agree with him?

Endnotes

1. William Blake, *The Marriage of Heaven and Hell* (Coral Gables, FL: University of Miami Press, 1963), 14.
2. Allen Ginsberg, "I've Lived with and Enjoyed 'Howl,'" in Jason Shinder, ed., *The Poem That Changed America: "Howl" Fifty Years Later* (New York: Farrar, Straus and Giroux, 2006), 146.
3. See Jonah Raskin, *American Scream: Allen Ginsberg's "Howl" and the Making of the Beat Generation* (Berkeley: University of California Press, 2004).
4. Quoted in Ibid., 68.
5. Ibid., 18.
6. Ibid.
7. Quoted in Ibid., 19.
8. See Allen Ginsberg, *Howl and Other Poems* (San Francisco, CA: City Lights Books, 2000).
9. Ibid., 9.
10. Ibid.
11. Ibid., 13–15.
12. Ibid., 9, 16.
13. Ibid., 11–13, 16.
14. Ibid., 18.
15. Ibid., 21–22.
16. Ibid., 22.
17. Ibid., 25–26.
18. Quoted in Raskin, *American Scream*, 186–187.
19. Quoted in Ibid., 202.
20. See Shinder, ed., *The Poem That Changed America*.

ALLEN GINSBERG, *HOWL* (1956)

Source: Allen Ginsberg, "Howl," from *Howl and Other Poems.* San Francisco: City Lights Books, 1956, pp. 9–20.

For Carl Solomon

I

I saw the best minds of my generation destroyed by madness, starving hysterical naked,
dragging themselves through the negro streets at dawn looking for an angry fix,
angelheaded hipsters burning for the ancient heavenly connection to the starry dynamo in the machinery of night,
who poverty and tatters and hollow-eyed and high sat up smoking in the supernatural darkness of cold-water flats floating across the tops of cities contemplating jazz,
who bared their brains to Heaven under the El and saw Mohammedan angels staggering on tenement roofs illuminated,
who passed through universities with radiant cool eyes hallucinating Arkansas and Blake-light tragedy among the scholars of war,
who were expelled from the academies for crazy & publishing obscene odes on the windows of the skull,
who cowered in unshaven rooms in underwear, burning their money in wastebaskets and listening to the Terror through the wall,
who got busted in their pubic beards returning through Laredo with a belt of marijuana for New York,
who ate fire in paint hotels or drank turpentine in Paradise Alley, death, or purgatoried their torsos night after night
with dreams, with drugs, with waking nightmares, alcohol and cock and endless balls,
incomparable blind streets of shuddering cloud and lightning in the mind leaping toward poles of Canada & Paterson, illuminating all the motionless world of Time between,
Peyote solidities of halls, backyard green tree cemetery dawns, wine drunkenness over the rooftops, storefront boroughs of teahead joyride neon blinking traffic light, sun and moon and tree vibrations in the roaring winter dusks of Brooklyn, ashcan rantings and kind king light of mind,
who chained themselves to subways for the endless ride from Battery to holy Bronx on benzedrine until the noise of wheels and children brought them down shuddering mouth-wracked and battered bleak of brain all drained of brilliance in the drear light of Zoo,
who sank all night in submarine light of Bickford's floated out and sat through the stale beer afternoon in desolate Fugazzi's, listening to the crack of doom on the hydrogen jukebox,
who talked continuously seventy hours from park to pad to bar to Bellevue to museum to the Brooklyn Bridge,

*a lost battalion of platonic conversationalists jumping
down the stoops off fire escapes off windowsills
off Empire State out of the moon,*

*yacketayakking screaming vomiting whispering facts
and memories and anecdotes and eyeball kicks
and shocks of hospitals and jails and wars,*

*whole intellects disgorged in total recall for seven days
and nights with brilliant eyes, meat for the
Synagogue cast on the pavement,*

*who vanished into nowhere Zen New Jersey leaving a
trail of ambiguous picture postcards of Atlantic
City Hall,*

*suffering Eastern sweats and Tangerian bone-grind-
ings and migraines of China under junk-with-
drawal in Newark's bleak furnished room,*

*who wandered around and around at midnight in the
railroad yard wondering where to go, and went,
leaving no broken hearts,*

*who lit cigarettes in boxcars boxcars boxcars racketing
through snow toward lonesome farms in grand-
father night,*

*who studied Plotinus Poe St. John of the Cross telep-
athy and bop kabbalah because the cosmos instinctively vibrated at their feet in Kansas,*

*who loned it through the streets of Idaho seeking vis-
ionary indian angels who were visionary indian
angels,*

*who thought they were only mad when Baltimore
gleamed in supernatural ecstasy,*

*who jumped in limousines with the Chinaman of Okla-
homa on the impulse of winter midnight street
light smalltown rain,*

*who lounged hungry and lonesome through Houston
seeking jazz or sex or soup, and followed the
brilliant Spaniard to converse about America
and Eternity, a hopeless task, and so took ship
to Africa,*

*who disappeared into the volcanoes of Mexico leaving
behind nothing but the shadow of dungarees
and the lava and ash of poetry scattered in fire
place Chicago,*

*who reappeared on the West Coast investigating the
F.B.I. in beards and shorts with big pacifist
eyes sexy in their dark skin passing out incomprehensible leaflets,*

*who burned cigarette holes in their arms protesting
the narcotic tobacco haze of Capitalism,*

*who distributed Supercommunist pamphlets in Union
Square weeping and undressing while the sirens
of Los Alamos wailed them down, and wailed
down Wall, and the Staten Island ferry also
wailed,*

*who broke down crying in white gymnasiums naked
and trembling before the machinery of other
skeletons,*

*who bit detectives in the neck and shrieked with delight
in policecars for committing no crime but their
own wild cooking pederasty and intoxication,*

*who howled on their knees in the subway and were
dragged off the roof waving genitals and manu-
scripts,*

*who let themselves be fucked in the ass by saintly
motorcyclists, and screamed with joy,*

*who blew and were blown by those human seraphim,
the sailors, caresses of Atlantic and Caribbean
love,*

*who balled in the morning in the evenings in rose
gardens and the grass of public parks and
cemeteries scattering their semen freely to
whomever come who may,*

*who hiccuped endlessly trying to giggle but wound up
with a sob behind a partition in a Turkish Bath
when the blond & naked angel came to pierce
them with a sword,*

*who lost their loveboys to the three old shrews of fate
the one eyed shrew of the heterosexual dollar
the one eyed shrew that winks out of the womb
and the one eyed shrew that does nothing but
sit on her ass and snip the intellectual golden
threads of the craftsman's loom,*

*who copulated ecstatic and insatiate with a bottle of
beer a sweetheart a package of cigarettes a can-
dle and fell off the bed, and continued along
the floor and down the hall and ended fainting
on the wall with a vision of ultimate cunt and
come eluding the last gyzym of consciousness,*

*who sweetened the snatches of a million girls trembling
in the sunset, and were red eyed in the morning
but prepared to sweeten the snatch of the sun
rise, flashing buttocks under barns and naked
in the lake,*

*who went out whoring through Colorado in myriad
stolen night-cars, N.C., secret hero of these
poems, cocksman and Adonis of Denver-joy
to the memory of his innumerable lays of girls
in empty lots & diner backyards, moviehouses'
rickety rows, on mountaintops in caves or with
gaunt waitresses in familiar roadside lonely petticoat upliftings & especially secret gas-station
solipsisms of johns, & hometown alleys too,*

*who faded out in vast sordid movies, were shifted in
dreams, woke on a sudden Manhattan, and
picked themselves up out of basements hung
over with heartless Tokay and horrors of Third*

Avenue iron dreams & stumbled to unemploy-
    ment offices,
who walked all night with their shoes full of blood on
    the snowbank docks waiting for a door in the
    East River to open to a room full of steamheat
    and opium,
who created great suicidal dramas on the apartment
    cliff-banks of the Hudson under the wartime
    blue floodlight of the moon & their heads shall
    be crowned with laurel in oblivion,
who ate the lamb stew of the imagination or digested
    the crab at the muddy bottom of the rivers of
    Bowery,
who wept at the romance of the streets with their
    pushcarts full of onions and bad music,
who sat in boxes breathing in the darkness under the
    bridge, and rose up to build harpsichords in
    their lofts,
who coughed on the sixth floor of Harlem crowned
    with flame under the tubercular sky surrounded
    by orange crates of theology,
who scribbled all night rocking and rolling over lofty
    incantations which in the yellow morning were
    stanzas of gibberish,
who cooked rotten animals lung heart feet tail borsht
    & tortillas dreaming of the pure vegetable
    kingdom,
who plunged themselves under meat trucks looking for
    an egg,
who threw their watches off the roof to cast their ballot
    for Eternity outside of Time, & alarm clocks
    fell on their heads every day for the next decade,
who cut their wrists three times successively unsuccess-
    fully, gave up and were forced to open antique
    stores where they thought they were growing
    old and cried,
who were burned alive in their innocent flannel suits
    on Madison Avenue amid blasts of leaden verse
    & the tanked-up clatter of the iron regiments
    of fashion & the nitroglycerine shrieks of the
    fairies of advertising & the mustard gas of sinis-
    ter intelligent editors, or were run down by the
    drunken taxicabs of Absolute Reality,
who jumped off the Brooklyn Bridge this actually hap-
    pened and walked away unknown and forgotten
    into the ghostly daze of Chinatown soup alley
    ways & firetrucks, not even one free beer,
who sang out of their windows in despair, fell out of
    the subway window, jumped in the filthy Pas-
    saic, leaped on negroes, cried all over the street,
    danced on broken wineglasses barefoot smashed
    phonograph records of nostalgic European

1930s German jazz finished the whiskey and
    threw up groaning into the bloody toilet, moans
    in their ears and the blast of colossal steam
    whistles,
who barreled down the highways of the past journeying
    to each other's hotrod-Golgotha jail-solitude
    watch or Birmingham jazz incarnation,
who drove crosscountry seventytwo hours to find out
    if I had a vision or you had a vision or he had
    a vision to find out Eternity,
who journeyed to Denver, who died in Denver, who
    came back to Denver & waited in vain, who
    watched over Denver & brooded & loned in
    Denver and finally went away to find out the
    Time, & now Denver is lonesome for her heroes,
who fell on their knees in hopeless cathedrals praying
    for each other's salvation and light and breasts,
    until the soul illuminated its hair for a second,
who crashed through their minds in jail waiting for
    impossible criminals with golden heads and the
    charm of reality in their hearts who sang sweet
    blues to Alcatraz,
who retired to Mexico to cultivate a habit, or Rocky
    Mount to tender Buddha or Tangiers to boys
    or Southern Pacific to the black locomotive or
    Harvard to Narcissus to Woodlawn to the
    daisychain or grave,
who demanded sanity trials accusing the radio of hyp-
    notism & were left with their insanity & their
    hands & a hung jury,
who threw potato salad at CCNY lecturers on Dadaism
    and subsequently presented themselves on the
    granite steps of the madhouse with shaven heads
    and harlequin speech of suicide, demanding in-
    stantaneous lobotomy,
and who were given instead the concrete void of insulin
    Metrazol electricity hydrotherapy psycho-
    therapy occupational therapy pingpong &
    amnesia,
who in humorless protest overturned only one symbolic
    pingpong table, resting briefly in catatonia,
returning years later truly bald except for a wig of
    blood, and tears and fingers, to the visible mad-
    man doom of the wards of the madtowns of the
    East,
Pilgrim State's Rockland's and Greystone's foetid
    halls, bickering with the echoes of the soul, rock-
    ing and rolling in the midnight solitude-bench
    dolmen-realms of love, dream of life a night-
    mare, bodies turned to stone as heavy as the
    moon,
with mother finally ******, and the last fantastic book

*flung out of the tenement window, and the last
door closed at 4. A.M. and the last telephone
slammed at the wall in reply and the last furnished room emptied down to the last piece of
mental furniture, a yellow paper rose twisted
on a wire hanger in the closet, and even that
imaginary, nothing but a hopeful little bit of
hallucination-*

*ah, Carl, while you are not safe I am not safe, and
now you're really in the total animal soup of
time-*

*and who therefore ran through the icy streets obsessed
with a sudden flash of the alchemy of the use
of the ellipse the catalog the meter & the vibrating plane,*

*who dreamt and made incarnate gaps in Time & Space
through images juxtaposed, and trapped the
archangel of the soul between 2 visual images
and joined the elemental verbs and set the noun*

*and dash of consciousness together jumping
with sensation of Pater Omnipotens Aeterna
Deus*

*to recreate the syntax and measure of poor human
prose and stand before you speechless and intelligent and shaking with shame, rejected yet con-
fessing out the soul to conform to the rhythm
of thought in his naked and endless head,*

*the madman bum and angel beat in Time, unknown,
yet putting down here what might be left to say
in time come after death,*

*and rose reincarnate in the ghostly clothes of jazz in
the goldhorn shadow of the band and blew the
suffering of America's naked mind for love into
an eli eli lamma lamma sabacthani saxophone
cry that shivered the cities down to the last radio*

*with the absolute heart of the poem of life butchered
out of their own bodies good to eat a thousand
years.*

CHAPTER 13

Elvis Presley Shakes Up America

*"A big-shouldered youth with sideburns and a full-lipped
face wandered slowly on stage…"*

Elvis was the revolution; he was a tidal wave, which forever reshaped America's cultural shorelines. There were those who preceded Elvis; he did not invent rock and roll. But social critics who derided the musical trend before Elvis burst onto the scene had to admit afterward that it was a fad no longer. Rock music had millions of devotees, and by the late 1950s they had crowned their king: Elvis A. Presley. His meteoric rise to cultural royalty was awe-inspiring. In 1956, the year he became known nationally and internationally, Elvis had ten songs on *Billboard*'s Top 100. His record sales that year alone accounted for two-thirds of the Radio Corporation of America's (RCA) output. Elvis maintained his cultural hegemony through the early 1970s. As many viewers watched his 1973 television special as did the Apollo moon landing four years earlier. By the time of his death on August 16, 1977, however, the forty-two-year-old had lost much of his cultural cache and his career had lost its luster. He nonetheless remains a global icon as well as a global industry.

Elvis Aaron Presley and his twin brother (Jesse Garon), who was stillborn, were born on January 8, 1935. His father, Vernon, and his mother, Gladys, were poor, eking out a meager existence in Tupelo, Mississippi. Vernon drove a milk truck and worked as a sharecropper. Elvis was closest to his mother. The Presleys knew much misery growing up in a racially segregated, poverty-struck part of the country. In 1937, Vernon Presley was convicted for check fraud and sent to the infamous Parchman prison. Religious faith, dancing, and music were the joys that kept the family together through this and other rough patches. Elvis was particularly interested in music; he sought it out everywhere, even ignoring the customary racial boundaries. He was as addicted to the gospel music of his all-white Assembly of God Holiness church as to the rhythm-and-blues that he heard in the black section of town. He loved listening to the *Grand Ole Opry* on the radio and dreamed of singing country songs on that magical platform. His first public appearance came in 1945 when he sang at the Mississippi-Alabama Fair and Dairy Show. He came in fifth place. The next year, his mother gave him his first guitar. Elvis poured all his nervous energy into the instrument. It was the perfect outlet for a sensitive boy whom the neighborhood toughs teased for his unusually close relationship with his mother.

In the summer of 1954, Elvis caught his big break. His family had moved to Memphis, Tennessee, so his father could escape prosecution for some other illegal scam. By day, Elvis worked odd jobs and went to high school; by night he immersed himself in the musical Mecca of the South. He had refined his tastes and among his idols were Mississippi Slim (with whom he had met and sung), Johnny Lee Hooker, B. B. King, Big Bill Broonzy, and Jimmie Rodgers. In Memphis, he not only sang in the high school musicals and entered various talent contests but also was on the lookout for prospects to make it big. In 1954, he walked into Sam Phillips's Memphis Recording Service (soon to be renamed Sun Studio) and took a chance. Phillips, whose business recorded mostly African American artists, was looking for a crossover singer, someone who sounded black but was white. Elvis had two sessions there that fateful summer. The first fizzled as Elvis was nervous, hesitant, and jittery. The second session, recorded on July 5, 1954, made history. His song "That's All Right" hit the airwaves as soon as Phillips could get it out of the studio. A white DJ on WHBQ known for spinning "race records" first played it for his listeners. They began calling in immediately asking for more. The DJ played Elvis' record an astonishing fourteen times in a row and even managed to get Elvis into the studio for a live interview. Significantly, the DJ asked him where he had gone to school. Elvis answered Humes High; everyone knew what that meant. Humes was an all-white school.

Elvis became an overnight success in the Memphis music scene. No one was quite sure how to categorize his music. Was it rock and roll? Was it country? Was it hill-billy? Soon the sound was labeled rockabilly, an amalgam of styles. Regardless, it was clear that Elvis was breaking boundaries. His music also crossed a racial barrier. That was revolutionary—if not insurrectionary—for a white male Southerner. Elvis learned a great deal from black musicians, and it was quite evident that he drew inspiration from gospel, jazz, and rhythm-and-blues. But it was more than just upsetting the taboos about whites singing and dancing to African American music. Elvis broke proper class etiquette, too. His sound and his dancing represented the angst, anxiety, aspirations, and energy of the Southern working class. That terrified the guardians of propriety and attracted throngs of followers.

In the fall of 1954, Sam Phillips helped Elvis score a coup by getting the nineteen-year-old star on the *Grand Ole Opry* in Nashville. Elvis and his band of Scotty Moore and Bill Black played a rocking version of "Blue Moon of Kentucky," Bill Monroe's classic bluegrass hit. Monroe professed to liking Elvis' rendition, but the powers behind the *Opry* did not, allegedly chastising the upstart for bringing "nigger music" to their program. Nevertheless, the appearance on Nashville's marquee stage quickly led to a tour of the South. His barn-burning successes caught the eye of Colonel Tom Parker, a country-music promoter. Within two years, Parker was running the show. He made all the business deals for music, movies, appearances, endorsements, and merchandising. Under the Colonel's tutelage Elvis became incredibly wealthy, as did his manager. Critics have charged that Colonel Parker—whose rank was hon-orific in the Southern tradition; whose name was really Andreas Cornelis van Kuijk; and whose nativity was Denmark, not the United States—took advantage of Elvis. That might be so, but their collaboration made it possible for Elvis to take his family out of poverty. In 1957, he purchased a mansion on thirteen acres, which he called Graceland. It was large enough to accommodate his parents, his growing entou-rage, and guests. Further, during the late 1950s, Elvis had a string of monstrous hits: "Heartbreak Hotel," "Don't Be Cruel," "Hound Dog," "Teddy Bear," and "Jailhouse Rock." Parker managed to get Elvis on *The Milton Berle Show*, *The Steve Allen Show*, and *The Ed Sullivan Show*. Those gigs were not entirely all-conquering. For example, Allen made Elvis out to be a rube. But American viewers watched in record numbers. Elvis had reached a national audience and his music sales soared. Colonel Parker built upon the momentum with a series of films: *Love Me Tender* (1956), *Loving You* (1957), *Jailhouse Rock* (1957), and *King Creole* (1958). As the 1950s came to a close, there seemed no part of the cultural geography that the King of rock and roll and his man-ager could not conquer.

After an amazing four hectic years, in 1958, Elvis' career was sidetracked. This band, known as the Blue Moon Boys, left him, angry that they had not received the salaries or credit due them. Then he received his draft notice. Overnight, the King of rock and roll became Private Presley of A Company, Second Medium Tank Battalion, Second Armored Division. In July, his beloved mother passed away. In 1960, Elvis returned to civilian life. But those two years seemed so much longer. Although he was ready to resume his fast-paced career at the top of the music and movie industries, American fickle tastes had changed. Increasingly Elvis seemed out of touch. He made over two dozen films in the 1960s, all but a few were not memorable or financially successful. In a musical era known for its singer/songwriters, he seemed less than genuine and not as gifted. Further, he had an increasingly difficult time relating to teenagers, once the bread and butter of his record buyers. His once-supreme position was challenged by a vast array of artists such as the Beatles, whose music seemed in tune with the cultural and political transformations. Elvis had not been a beatnik in the 1950s and was decidedly not a hippie of the 1960s. If anything, publicly, he became more staid, marrying his long-time girlfriend Priscilla Beaulieu in 1967, starting a family, and appearing more middle-aged. Elvis had developed a considerable paunch. He was terribly unhappy. In 1968, in an attempt to recapture the magic of his musical career, Elvis staged a special on NBC; it was a sensation. Elvis had lost a considerable amount of weight and was clad in black leather. "The Comeback Special" as it became known was a springboard to new albums and a long-running show in Las Vegas and sold-out performances at such places as Madison Square Garden in New York. Elvis was back on top, now bejeweled in his larger-than-life rhinestone-studded jumpsuits with matching cape.

The superhero of American music remained miserable. In the 1970s, his world began to fall apart. His behavior which had always been a little odd became even more so. In 1970, he arranged a meeting with President Richard M. Nixon and offered his services to become an agent for the Bureau of Narcotics and Dangerous Drugs. By that time, Elvis himself was hopelessly addicted to a wide array of legal and illicit drugs. His marriage failed as Elvis' dalliances with other women became unbearable for Priscilla. Professionally, Elvis was cracking, too. In 1973, the year he and Priscilla divorced, he fired the Colonel. Lawsuits followed. Elvis' stage show suffered mightily, as the drugs hindered and disrupted his performances. He kept up a breakneck pace, however. In 1976, despite being obese and strung-out, he gave 130 concerts. He endured a scaled-back schedule in 1977, giving fifty-six in the first six months. On August 16, 1977, Elvis was found dead of a drug overdose on a bathroom floor in his Graceland mansion. The King had died.

Long live the King. He has had a wacky posthumous career. Elvis sightings and tales of UFO abductions became commonplace by the 1980s. Yet, there is no denying Elvis' incredible influence on popular music. From 1958 to 1977, he garnered seventy-seven gold records. Twenty-five of his albums and fifty-four of his singles were top-ten *Billboard* releases. Dozens of musicians from Little Richard to John Lennon credited Elvis for opening the door to their musical careers. Radical civil rights activist Eldridge Cleaver maintained that Elvis' willingness to embrace black culture laid the groundwork for the social and political revolutions of the 1960s. Finally, Elvis documentaries and compilation records have done exceedingly well. His last number one album was in 2002.

The following newspaper articles provide a glimpse into Elvis' enduring legacy, allowing one to listen in on that decades-long musical and cultural conversation that he had with his devotees and his detractors. Above all else, Elvis was known for the close, personal relationships that he built with the fans, particularly with his female ones. Collectively these articles witness a typical Elvis concert. Let's go!

Weeks before any of the events—whether the performance in Orlando or Portland or New York City or San Francisco—DJs and record store managers built momentum for Elvis' arrival. Playing and selling his music created a deep yearning in his fans, an insatiable desire to see the sensational young artist that scared the parents and other guardians of proper behavior. As tour dates were announced there was no stopping young people from shelling out the $2.50 ($20.00 in today's dollars) to see their new idol (*San Francisco Chronicle*, June 4, 1956). At first, when Elvis broke onto the scene, small venues like Oakland's Auditorium Arena, which sat 3,500, housed plenty of room. But by 1957—two years into the Elvis craze—much larger places were needed. On August 31, in Spokane, Washington, 12,000 came out to see him at Memorial Stadium; and two days later he sang in front of 14,600 at Portland, Oregon's city stadium. Elvis' concerts were big events, one building upon the other.

Word of mouth spread the excitement, too. It also spread concern about this Mississippian whose hypnotic control over young girls was astounding. Entering the stadiums and large arenas, fans felt the anticipation as well as the anxiety, which was only heightened by the cordon of one hundred policemen who were there to protect the innocent from unruly behavior. Sitting jammed one against another, it was as one reporter put it, "it was impossible to sort out individualized rights" (*The Spokesman-Review*, August 31, 1957). After listening patiently and appreciatively through the one hour of opening acts, the lights reset, signaling their King's imminent arrival.

Elvis had been backstage talking with fans wanting a personal audience with rock and roll royalty, reporters who wanted know more about this cultural tornado, and critics who wished to shake him up. In June 1956, Sandra McCune, head of the brand-new Oakland Elvis Presley fan club, got a backstage pass. The fourteen-year-old wanted Elvis' approval for the group's new official dress: a quilted skirt with the hero's name "emblazoned in red" across the front (*The San Francisco Chronicle*, June 4, 1956). Journalists quizzed Elvis about his instant fame. How long do you think you'll last? Do you consider your act vulgar? Do you like girls? Do you plan to marry? Do you sleep in pajamas? If reporters expected to find a "Rube from Ruberville," they were sadly mistaken (*The Spokesman-Review*, August 31, 1957). Elvis had the newspapers eating from his hands. He had a smart answer to every question. One non-believer asked what will he do once "this rock 'n roll fad passes?" Elvis did not miss a beat: "I'll probably sit back and think about what I once had…with no regrets. Right now, I don't think about that" (*St. Petersburg Times*, August 6, 1956). It was all great fun. When the time neared, police ushered everyone away and escorted Elvis to the restroom.

While Elvis was busying himself backstage, the opening acts had succeeded in building a "nervous tension" (*The Oregonian*, September 3, 1957). There was a ten-minute intermission during which gleeful fans bought up all the Elvis memorabilia, which cost nearly as much as the tickets (*San Francisco Chronicle*, June 4, 1956). Screams signaled that the King approached. Riding in on one of his Cadillacs or his Lincoln Continental, sometimes accompanied by dignitaries such as Portland mayor Terry Schrunk who gave the crowd a seal of approval, bedlam broke loose as Elvis took the stage (*The Oregonian*, September 3, 1957). If the audience had wanted to hear Elvis sing, "they were defeating themselves" by screaming and stamping their feet (*The Oregonian*, September 3, 1957). Perhaps they wanted to *see* him more than *hear* him. For the controversy about Elvis was not merely about the music. It was about his moves: that nervous sneer, his thumb wiggling, his loose uncontrollable knees, and that gyrating hip. Truly he lived up to that sexually charged cognomen: Elvis the Pelvis (*The Orlando Sentinel*, August 8, 1956). All that strutting and all that crawling and all that swooning created quite a stir. Young women—reporters consistently noted that the crowd was mostly female and mostly around the age of fourteen—lost all self-restraint. "Fast-moving policemen," a newspaperman for the Spokane Daily Chronicle reported, "kept several girls from tumbling over the front rail of the grandstand as they almost swooned during a Presley number" (*The Spokane Daily Chronicle*, August 31, 1957). Many of those who did not faint kept shrieking, yelling, and jumping during Elvis' eighteen-song set which ended with his smash hit "Hound Dog." The fifty-minute show left the audience wanting more. But they'd have to buy more records or come back another day. Some adoring fans hung out by Elvis' car, hoping to see one last glimpse. Elvis never left without signing autographs, hugging, and smooching the fifty "assorted fans [who] managed to grab him and shouted and screamed as he drove away" (*San Francisco Chronicle*, June 5, 1956).

In each town, a post-performance community conversation raged. Was Elvis' concert good? Was Elvis a charlatan? Was he indecent? Was he dangerous? There seemed to be a definite age-gap in the answers to those questions. Those under the age of twenty were unanimous: Elvis was great! Pat Hix, who had a front-row seat at Elvis' 1956 Orlando concert, loved every second. "I like his style of singing and his flashy clothes best about him" (*Orlando Sentinel*, August 9, 1956). According to cub reporter, fourteen-year-old Holly Johnson of Portland, Oregon, the city's 1957 concert was spectacular: "he sounded as good as his records, even better." Moreover, in her view, the show created no disorder as "the teen-agers were quite well-behaved considering the large crowd" (*The Oregonian*, September 3, 1957).

Adults were divided. One mother who had chaperoned her daughter to a concert was not high on the King. "Look at him. He looks just like a hound dog in heat and sounds like a sick cat" (*Orlando Sentinel*, August 9, 1956). The *San Francisco Chronicle*'s arts reporter, Ralph J. Gleason was similarly unimpressed. The effect that Elvis had on his female fans was in a word "frightening" (*San Francisco Chronicle*, June 5, 1956). The hysteria and fainting was abnormal and perhaps anti-social. It reminded Gleason not merely of Frank Sinatra and Johnnie Ray—two crooners who also made women swoon—but of the Sportspalast in Berlin, where Nazis gathered to "chant in unison during the Third Reich." "His emotional power is frightening," Gleason remarked (*San Francisco Chronicle*, June 5, 1956).

Few were as petrified as Gleason. Robert Brumblay, Spokane's city juvenile probation officer, went to Elvis' 1957 concert to watch his influence on teenagers. Brumblay told reporters that he was nervous beforehand, fearing a revolt of youthful exuberance. But "nothing out line happened." "Almost all the city could complain of was a few youngsters who were stealing soil from the stadium infield. Presley's feet had touched it" (*The Spokesman-Review*, August 31, 1957). Elvis clearly changed the minds of some critics who were ready to pan him as so many others had. But in interviews, he was so captivating and charming that many found him just a "regular guy" and dismissed any notion that he contributed "anything to juvenile delinquency," then a national concern (*St. Peterburg Times*, August 6, 1957). There were even a few mothers who changed their tune. Phyilis Lauritz had expected to hate the Elvis concert she attended in Portland in 1957 but had to admit publicly that "he really isn't horrible" (*The Oregonian*, September 3, 1957). He was talented, genuine, patriotic, and to some degree clean cut. Could a mother ask for more?

Elvis' first fans were in their thirties when they heard the news that he had died. But the rapport—that musical conversation—continues. They still buy his records. Over 600,000 make the trip to Graceland each year. Elvis impersonators can be found nearly in every city across the globe. Over forty-two million websites mention his name. He remains an international icon a half a century after he burst into American consciousness and three decades after his death. Elvis was nevertheless a cultural radical, pushing America in new directions and changing concepts of race and class. He was a part of those mid-century movements such as the feminist and civil rights movements that redefined postwar America. What Elvis had to say and how he said it left an indelible impression on history.

Questions for Consideration and Conversation

1. Elvis seemingly drove people crazy when he appeared before them. What do you think caused people to have this strong reaction to him?
2. Elvis drew inspiration from African American music. What effects do you think that this had on American culture and politics?
3. Elvis was a crossover star in many ways, topping the music and cinema charts. What other stars—both then and now—had such success?
4. Over time, Elvis' personal life became increasingly troubled. What do you think that says about fame in America? How might have Andy Warhol answered this question (Chapter 16)?
5. Was Elvis as important an artist as Norman Rockwell (Chapter 10) or Allen Ginsberg (Chapter 12)?
6. Given that his career has been over for decades, why do you think Americans still think about Elvis?

JEAN YOTHERS, PRESLEY MAKES 'EM SHRIEK, YELL, JUMP (1956)

Source: Orlando Sentinel Star, August 9, 1956.

A big-shouldered youth with sideburns and a full-lipped face wandered slowly on stage and thousands of adoring teenage girls went wild. They shrieked. They screamed. They jumped up in their seats. And they gazed at their idol as though transported into a state of ecstatic bliss.

Subject of this mass hysteria was Elvis Aaron Presley, 21-year-old singer and hero of the nation's teenagers who purely fractured two full houses at Municipal Auditorium last night with his unique actions and sensational style. Wearing a bright green coat, black trousers and white shoes, the heavy-lidded, touseled-haired Elvis surveyed his audience with a half-smile on his lips and then cut loose with a three-piece band backing him up.

When he moaned out Heartbreak Hotel, his first number, the auditorium was filled with piercing, ear-splitting screams. When he jumped around the stage to Long Tall Sally, fans rushed up to the rail to snap pictures, and as he twisted his hips suggestively to the rhythm, they yelled like dying cats, "Oh Elvis."

Four Policemen were posted at both stage entrances to hold back the crowds, but still they milled about the auditorium taking photographs of the gyrating Elvis at all angles.

When he removed his green coat to throw himself into Hound Dog, his current record, a delighted squeal erupted from the house that could've blown the top from Vesuvius. He then wiggled and switched his hips passionately, dragging the microphone. He was gone, man, gone.

"What do you think of this guy?" a mother-spectator was asked. "I just came cause the kids wanted to," she said "I was curious. Now I know. Look at him. He looks just like a hound dog in heat and sounds like a sick cat." First-row sitter Pat Hix, a teenage girl, had a different slant. She adores Elvis. "I like his style of singing and his flashy clothes best about him," she said with reverence. Backstage in the Pelvis' dressing room, he was a different person. Relaxed and friendly, he answered in his slow, southern drawl.

Q. "How long do you think you'll stay on top in show business?
A. Ah wish ah knew ma'am. People change a lot.
Q. Do you consider your gyrations vulgar?
A. No ma'am. Ah don't. Ah don't feel sexy when Ah'm on stage.
Q. What kind of girl do you want to marry?
A. [with a sight] Ah've never thought much about it.
Q. Do you sleep in pajamas?
A. No ma'am. Ah sleep in my shorts.
Q. Do you kiss all those girls you read about in the papers?
A. Only upon special request."

RALPH J. GLEASON, PRESLEY LEAVES YOU IN A BLUE SUEDE FUNK (1956)

Source: San Francisco Chronicle, June 5, 1956.

Elvis Presley doesn't wear blue suede shoes. He wears black pumps and when he goes on stage to sing he removes his cream-colored striped jacket with the black velvet collar and puts a blood-red one.

Prior to his appearance on the stage, he chats quietly with former schoolmates, acquaintances and musicians in the dressing room. Sunday night in Oakland, he poked his head outside and occasionally yelled at the audience which earlier that afternoon had done its best to step on his black pumps.

He is afraid of the crowd. Perhaps "afraid" is not exactly the right word—he says he loves them. But he wouldn't pay a visit to the men's room Sunday night without a police escort.

The reaction of the audience, which was mainly teenage girls, is simply frightening. At the afternoon performance, one of the ushers claimed an impromptu, voluntary panty raid disrupted proceedings for a while and at the evening show two young ladies collapsed with a mild case of hysteria and another fainted clear away at the mere prospect of owning an autograph from the Presley pen.

Presley's reaction to the crowd is unusual. He plays to it constantly on stage with a performance that it is earthy and extremely direct and you won't see it on the Milton Berle show tonight when he makes his appearance. It's a bit rugged for TV. "Ah thunk they're wunnerful." Presley says in a thick southern drawl, of the audience. "It makes muh want to live up to their opinion of muh."

After the show, Presley stayed in the dressing room for almost half an hour until a squad of Oakland police could safely escort him to his car. As it was, 50 assorted fans managed to grab him and shouted and screamed as he drove away. To the few who were able to crash the police line and actually get near to him. Presley was casual, friendly and seemed to make it a habit to give each a quick peck on the cheek.

As to performance itself, there were several interesting things. He apparently doesn't play the guitar at all, uses it merely as a prop. He is obviously either a trained showman or a natural one. His entire performance, grotesque as it may be, was deftly aimed at his own fans whom he deliberately raised to an emotional pitch that bears no little resemblance to the effect of Johnnie Ray, Frank Sinatra and, even, to those thousands who crowded the Sportspalast in berlin to chant in unison during the Third Reich, his emotional power is frightening.

But his musical performance is as elemental as the gyrations of an "exotic" dancer in a Tenderloin joint.

WILLIAM McPHILLIPS, ELVIS HITS TOWN AND TEENAGERS TURN OUT (1956)

Source: San Francisco Chronicle, June 4, 1956.

A young man with a virile voice and twitching hip muscles yesterday supplied what was apparently a notable lack for a segment of Bay Area teen-agers: an idol.

Sort of between gods since Eddie married Debbie, 3500 squealing school kids found their man in Mississippi's gift to the arts, 21 year-old Elvis Presley.

It was only after one of the most elaborate warm-ups in local show business that they saw him performing on the stage of Oakland's Auditorium Arena.

Presley Was Plenty

But once he got there, they found Presley was everything they hoped for—and a lot more.

Frank Sinatra, who went on to gain weight in his roles if not his physique, and Johnnie Ray, who sobbed his heart out on order, both appealed to an awakening maternal instinct.

Presley, 180 pounds of undeniably male characteristics built in a six-foot frame, appealed to something else.

Cop Off The Beat

Said a disgusted Oakland cop, one of a dozen detailed to guard RCA Victor's new find from possible harm at the hands of autograph seekers:

"If he did that same stuff on the streets, we'd lock him up."

Dubbed "Elvis the Pelvis" by some critics, Presley stalked glowering out onto the stage for a mere 20 minutes after other performers teased the audience for an hour and a half.

The roar that met him subsided only when he launched his almost powerful baritone into "Heartbreak Hotel," which under his handling has become the Nation's top-selling record.

Black Denim Knees

The crowd was quiet as he sang, in lyrics verging on the unintelligible—until one of his black-denim-clad knees shot out.

When the screams subsided, the right knee picked up where the other left off and gradually, as the movement spread upward, the famous voice was lost in bedlam.

Presley, his ducktailed lawny hair now hanging in his eyes, grabbed the microphone as if it were alive and dragged it around the stage, now petting it now turning upon it the full vent of his manly wrath.

Every song sounded much the same almost identical as the reactions of the audience which paid up to $2.50 to see his writhings.

Mostly Girls

Composed mostly of teen-aged girls, the audience contained some oldsters and a sprinkling of weird-looking young men.

During a ten-minute intermission—after the build-up and before Presley's appearance—they had ample time to pick up a few souvenirs as provided by Presley's manager, former Tennessee carnival worker Colonel Tom Parker.

There were "programs" for 50 cents—which contained ten pages of pictures and a space for autographs.

There were song books which at $1 a copy contained words and music of the rock-and-roll hillbilly tunes Presley has made famous.

Or there were autographed pictures of the singer, which sold at either 50 cents or a dollar, depending on the customer's emotional pitch.

In the lobby, the day was dedicated to teenagers, with soft drinks replacing the sandwich stand's usual beer and coffee menu.

In his dressing room, both before and after his performances, Presley, who two years ago drove a truck in Memphis for $35 a week, was surrounded by budding beauties.

One was 14-year-old Sandra McCune, who as president of newly formed Oakland chapter of the Elvis Presley Fan Club wanted to know if he approved of their official dress—a quilted skirt with his name emblazoned in red.

Over the Heart

It was worn, she explained breathlessly, only with a locket containing his picture, which by club rules must be placed over the heart.

Presley absently put his arm around her and confided to reporters that he wanted to be an actor.

"But all this wild emotion in me," he said. "I've got to sing and I think I do it well."

A lone music critic in the audience agreed with him, at least partially.

"He's is wonderful I guess," he said. "From the hips down, anyway".

ANNE ROWE, BROOM-SWEEPING ELVIS A REGULAR GUY (1956)

Source: St. Petersburg Times, August 6, 1956.

Dressed as sharp as a cat in black pegged pants, striped belt, blue shirt, white tie, maroon jacket and white buck shoes, the king of rock n' roll picked up a broom and started sweeping out his dressing room.

This was my fabulous introduction to the four-caddie Elvis Presley, whose reputation had given this reporter reason "to proceed with caution" in his presence.

No need for alarm, though, for Presley posed willingly for press photographers, answered questions

without hesitation and seemed to us like a real regular guy during the hour we spent with him in his dressing room before the first appearance at the Ft. Homer Hesterly Armory in Tampa yesterday. Presley will appear at the Florida Theatre here Tuesday for three performances.

Appearing just a little bit nervous, Elvis swept the floor clear of cigarette butts, and then transformed the broom into a microphone crooning "Don't Be Cruel" into the handle.

Putting the broom aside, he walked outside, where it was only slightly cooler than the stifling heat in his dressing room, surveyed the curiosity seekers lined up at the gate, laughed and hollered, "I'll be right with you"—with NO obvious southern accent.

Elvis gave me the impression that he would have enjoyed going over to the gate and talking with his fans. He signed autographs of those who were permitted to talk with him and seemed to enjoy playing with a couple of tots nearby who were observing the commotion with wide-eyed wonder.

Favorite Song

Returning to his dressing room Elvis picked up his leather-bound guitar, plucked a few strings and began singing "Don't Be Cruel" once again...his favorite of all the songs he's recorded because "it has the most meaning." Soon he was joined by the Jordenaires, the boys who back Elvis on many of his records. Elvis' nervousness apparently left him. He was doing what he loves best...singing. He sang the song through, put down his guitar and when asked for an interview, was more than willing to submit to questions. Asked what he thought of those who imitate him, he said "I think it's good. It shows I'm doing well enough, otherwise, why would they want to imitate me?"

Naturally we asked him if he was interested in girls. To this he replied with a wink, a smile and a mere "yes", said he had a "steady at one time," but hasn't given much thought to marriage or the type of girl he would choose.

Like James Dean

Queried on his recent motion picture pact with Hal Wallis, Elvis replied, "I won't give up singing for acting. I think I'll make about one picture a year and whether I like it or not depends on how well I do." Elvis also said his screen favorites are the late James Dean and Marlon Brando.

What will he do when this rock 'n roll "fad" passes? "I'll probably sit back and think about what I once had...with no regrets. Right now, I don't think about that." Presley retorted.

Apparently Presley wasn't pleased with his much publicized performance on the Steve Allen show, when he appeared in a dinner suit and was forced to stand still while going through his act. "All I thought about that suit," said Elvis, "was gettin' out of it."

No Quarrel with Critics

He has no quarrel with the critics who've panned him since he first won not only the admiration, but the hearts of almost every teenager in the country. "Those people have a job to do just like me. I think when you're in this business you've got to expect that sort of treatment. Some people wouldn't pay a nickel to see me. But as long as my records keep selling and these folks keep turning out to hear me sing. I'm happy."

Elvis is amazed at his sudden success, but is enjoying every minute of it. He does feel bad that his busy schedule get him home only about once a month. He is very close to his parents who live in the $40,000 air conditioned ranch home he bought for them in Memphis. He says his mother and father encourage his career, feel he is not contributing anything to juvenile delinquency and accept his absence from home as a matter of course.

"I used to travel by plane all the time," replied Presley when we asked him how he commuted, "but once I got scared flying so now I travel down here on the ground in a car." Elvis did not arrive in one of his four Cadillac's, but instead propelled a slinky, white $10,000 Lincoln Continental which he purchased in Miami because "I couldn't very will appear on Ed Sullivan's show if I wasn't driving his sponsor's product, could I?"

Loves that Lincoln

Like a little boy with a new toy, he lifted the hood of his newest purchase, displayed the engine to several onlookers and when asked how fast the car could go, laughed "You mean how fast can it FLY?" Touching the hood ornament fondly he said "This thing cost $350."

Besides his cars, Elvis is an avid motorcycle fan, although he has little time to ride his own.

Our interview came to halt when a knock on the door informed Presley that it was time for him to go on.

He thanked me for taking time out to talk to him and hurried out to the crowd eagerly awaiting his appearance.

He was greeted with deafening screams from the audience of about 1,000 teen-agers, which oddly enough was sprinkled liberally with adults.

In His Glory

Now Presley was in his glory. He rocked 'n rolled his way through seven numbers, laughing, winking, pointing and wriggling in the well-known Presley manner.

While his fans yelled, cried, pulled their hair, held their ears, jumped clapped and laughed, Elvis displayed his terrific showmanship. It was more than obvious that he loved every scream and yell and...every minute on that stage. He wrestled with the mike, breaking two apart in his frenzy, and finally, with perspiration pouring down his face, he practically tore his jacket off and let go on two more numbers.

He may be an ex-truck driver from Mississippi, a rockabilly whose "gimmick" has carried him to success, but the ovation he received yesterday proves that Presley is the biggest thing in show business today.

HOLLY JOHNSON, 14,600 FANS SQUEAL, JUMP AS ELVIS SHAKES, GYRATES (1957)

Source: The Oregonian, September 3, 1957.

All Shook up.

That's putting it mild.

But there wasn't anything mild about the reaction of some 14,600 fans who cut their touches Monday night in Multnomah stadium when Elvis Presley took over.

Stadium officials, special policemen and civic dignitaries alike mopped their brows and said they'd never seen anything like it.

And maybe they never will again. There those who might hope so.

Elvis was spirited to the stadium by some means known only to his managers and appeared garbed in a conservative light jacket and jeweled belt, at a press conference hand by the shower rooms in the Multnomah club.

There, he answered questions put to him by fan clubs members contest winners, press and radio representatives, and then was whisked away to do the gold lame and brilliant-studded jacket that has become one of his trademarks.

Fans Scream Up Storm

Mayor Terry Schrunk was seated in the front of a waiting white Lincoln convertible. Elvis was assisted to a perch on the back, someone gave a secret signal, and the panic was on.

Around the stadium floor he rode, waving and shaking his clasped hands and the kids—and the adults too—in the stands screamed up a storm.

It was bedlam, noise-wise but physically it was the true Portland conservative tradition.

Maybe they would have liked to, but no one swarmed out of the stands and onto the stadium ground as has happened in other cities and as is feared and guarded against by the Presley entourage.

The fans were primed. They had been listening for more than an hour to other entertainers who helped build up the beat. And when Elvis finally appeared, they cut loose.

They Scream and Jump

They screamed and they stamped their feet and they jumped and they swayed from side to side.

As one of the 100 police reserves called to special duty observed, if they came to hear him sing, they were defeating themselves. But they were having a wonderful time. You could see that in the rapt faces and hear it in their screams.

Elvis himself wasn't on stage very long. But he worked like a hound dog while he was. He sang most of the songs that have made him famous, starting with "Heartbreak Hotel" and then working through "Don't Be Cruel" and "Loving You".

He clowned and he hammed it up and he seemed to be having as good a time as his audience obviously was. Sure he shook and gyrated and every time he did it, 14,600 people let out a whoop.

CHAPTER 14

Life Magazine Examines "The American Woman" of the 1950s

*"[A] secure and reasonably happy household, a contented and proud husband…
(T)hese creations call for the distinctive talents of women"*

No matter what class, race, or ethnicity, World War II transformed American women's lives. During the Great Depression, women—especially those who were married—had great difficulty finding work. With defense mobilization, however, came new opportunities for women in civilian and the military life. Women entered the factories in unprecedented numbers. And, they joined unions, both the American Federation of Labor and the Congress of Industrial Organizations. Women served in all branches of service. They became the symbol of American might on the home front. Rosie the Riveter was the iconic working-class hero that helped win the war. After V-E and V-J days, Americans pounded swords back into ploughshares. And, in the public discussions about the peacetime transition, they debated their fears and aspirations. Would the Great Depression return? Would the old mores about race, class, and gender remain? Concerning the latter, Americans wondered aloud what was the proper role for women. In 1956, ten years after the end of World War II, *Life* magazine, that quintessential American middle-class periodical, entered the fray with a special double issue on the American woman. Typical of the mainstream conservativism of the early Cold War, the issue acknowledged the social, political, and economic challenges that had been identified by women's rights activists. Yet while exposing the problems for American women, the magazine simultaneously sought to limit the radical potential of what became known as feminism's second wave.

The editors of *Life* selected Catherine Marshall (1914–1983), an author who was known for her popular biography of her late husband, Peter Marshall, who had been a prominent Presbyterian and Chaplain of the U.S. Senate. Marshall set the conservative tone for the issue. She began with a keen observation: "Caught as she is in conflicting currents, the American woman of today finds herself being analyzed and admired, envied and criticized as never before." Americans still held those Rosies who had come to the nation's aid during the war in high esteem. However, many women workers had been booted from the factories after the war. From factory-owners to union officials, the message was generally consistent: Women should return to more domestic labors. However, they faced criticism there, too. In 1955, Phillip Wylie published an expanded edition of his 1942 best seller, *A Generation of Vipers*, which had launched a devastating critique of American women, particularly mothers, who Wylie claimed were overbearing, suffocating, and emasculating. Marshall offered her criticisms of American women, too. Women "have won their rights—the right to bring home a pay check, to enter business, industry or politics." "Freedom always seems like fun," she commented, "duties and responsibilities not so." Marshall asserted that as women have taken advantage of new opportunities, they have become dissatisfied with their lives. "Can it be that many of woman's current troubles began with the period of her preoccupation with her 'right'?" Marshall certainly thought so, and yet she fully acknowledged that in this age of the "feminist revolution" there was no returning to the status quo ante. The authors of the following articles—and perhaps their readers as well—did not necessarily share that view.

In "She Misses Some Goals," Mary Ellen Chase (1887–1973), a significant author of the first half of the twentieth century and a pioneering educator at the University of Minnesota and Smith College who had just retired from academia the previous year, acknowledged that women were "discontented, restive, and even complaining" but argued that they had no reason to do so. Chase agreed with her friend, a foreign visitor, who concluded that "as a whole, American women are just not doing their part in keeping your country where it has to be for the sake of the world." A decade into the Cold War with the Soviet Union, Chase was forced to agree. The feminist movement had opened new doors of opportunity for American women. Many had taken advantage of going to college, earning degree, and taking jobs in places previously closed to women. But as a group, they "are *not* living up to their responsibilities." "They are *not* contributing their necessary part to the common welfare." For Chase, the root of the problem was not that women were not applying their advanced degrees in order to become the next Jane Austens or George Eliots. Was it "too early marriage"? No. Rather, it was that they were not using their creative genius to produce: "a well-ordered home, a secure and reasonably happy household, a contented and proud husband, an atmosphere within her family of intelligent companionship in those values which at once delight, amuse and nourish the human mind and spirit." Chase maintained that women were not utilizing their "distinctive talents." Instead, they were spending their time on "nonsense" such as do-good organizations or worse. Too many women spent their time buying household appliances from blenders to televisions. Not only did the family not need these items, but this craven lust for material goods put the family on the road to bankruptcy. It also masked a deeper problem: a "poverty of mind and imagination." Presaging Betty Friedan's exploration of a "problem with no name," Chase criticized women for seeking psychological refuge in department stores as well as alcohol. Unlike Friedan, Chase told women to pull themselves together and accept their lives and gendered social roles. Otherwise, the results would be devastating. "Unless we shortly take strict account of our mental, moral and spiritual stock by examining ourselves with that common sense, integrity and wholesome fear of failure which apparently our mothers and grandmothers employed without the help of a psychiatrist, we are surely headed for far worse troubles than those which so many of us are so unprofitably imagining."

Unlike Mary Ellen Chase, Emily Kimbrough (1899–1989), another popular author who had also written for the *Ladies Home Journal*, called on critics to give American women a break. Rather than excoriate them for their failings, Kimbrough wanted "conceded" to women "those graces she offers" and "granted to her years of grace in which to bring to a final fitting the pattern for her life." More than Chase, Kimbrough celebrated women's advances, though she offered a strange historical perspective. Instead of acknowledging the efforts, pains, and achievements of the first wave of the feminist movement, she credits "vacuum cleaners and other mechanical devises" that delivered "women from a large part of household drudgery." "I doubt that the doctors, scientists, inventors and manufacturers, pouring over their microscopes and blueprints, set as their goal the emancipation of women. But emancipation is what they produced." Despite this totally erroneous and fallacious interpretation of history, Kimbrough does state that no one can "turn back this tide now." That being the case, she urged Americans to recognize that women had double duty as professionals and as mothers who had to put careers on hold, sometimes for an hour or a day or even longer, in order to tend to family needs and domestic crises. No doubt, Kimbrough added, that this "double life" creates stresses inside and outside the family. Significantly, she did not call for women to return home or for fathers to take on an expanded role. Rather, "if a woman is given years of grace in which to become similarly organized, I believe many difficulties within herself and many criticisms from the world around her will level off."

The award-winning American poet Phyllis McGinley (1905–1978) also rebutted the criticisms of women, but in a slightly more tongue-in-cheek manner. Adeptly, she poked fun at a handful of hackneyed prejudices against women. Dispensing with that old pernicious myth, she declared that "women like women just fine." There was one exception, she mentioned jokingly: "the hunting season" when looking for "a man for our hearth." Where some saw rivals, McGinley observed a kind of sisterhood among women who exchange loaves of bread, recipes, and sympathy. There were several other reasons why McGinley championed women. In an age concerned with Communist spies, they were "the secret-keepers" quite unlike the "kiss and tell" men. They were dependable; they repaired any and all household gadgets; they had stamina and were the "unfragile sex"; and they were better drivers. Here, she had the accident statistics to back her up. Further, she asserted that men's failures behind the wheel had as much to do with recklessness as with their innate sense of intuition. Unlike women who liked "to be guided by fact," men used their fabled intuition to get around when they were lost. Just as she would consult a doctor to help a sick child, she was not above asking for directions. McGinley did not hold it against men. They might not have been good at many things, but "how splendid that they aren't!" "Expendable they may be. But into our hard, practical lives they bring tenderness and sentiment." "And," she jabbed, "Who better graces a drawing room? What prettier a sight can one see at evening under the soft glow of the lamp than a man dressed in his old tweed jacket and lounging slippers?" Given their abilities, McGinley wondered what would happen if women assumed the occupations of government and trade and thus "gave men their freedom." But in the end, undercutting her poetic rhapsody, she wrote that perhaps the status quo was better; at least, women avoided "thrashing around in the very masculine morasses" of world affairs.

In her essay, Cornelia Otis Skinner (1899–1979), an actress, author, and friend of Emily Kimbrough, did not pull any punches and bluntly wrote that women were misguided in their "shrill, ridiculous war over the dead issue of feminism." Skinner was particularly upset with those pioneers who broke barriers to enter new professions previously closed to women. For instance, she recalled her female doctor as a child who "had crashed the gates of the medical profession." Although Skinner's mother thought the general practitioner to be excellent, the woman whom the young Skinner labeled "Dr. Spook" scared the girl with her mannish ways and appearance. "She was one of the Emancipated Women all right," Skinner wrote, "the first shackle from which she had emancipated herself was charm." Skinner believed that women had no reason to break out of their station in American life. They should not take up unwomanly pursuits. Should a female musician, for example, take up unwomanly instruments like the bassoon or kettledrum or tuba? No, stick to the dainty sounds of the piano, harp, violin, and flute. She ratified the English conductor Sir Thomas Beecham, who likened women in the symphony to vultures on the battlefield: "They appear after everyone else is dead...The sooner they're allowed to run their course, the sooner the present era will blow up in ineptitude, inefficiency and incompetence. There will be five years of no music, and at the end people will say, 'Now we'll start over.' " To Skinner, that sentiment ranged far beyond the concert hall. She wanted all those anachronistic feminists to stop their efforts to become carpenters, mechanics, boxers, doctors, and locomotive engineers. "The day I look through the cab window of [the New York Central's Twentieth Century Limited] and see, seated behind the throttle, a woman wearing goggles...I will take a plane." Skinner saw no use in breaking barriers for the sake of advancing the equality of women. The only true achievements were those gained by *citizens*. "Ladies, we have won our case," Skinner concluded, "but for heaven's sake let's stop trying to prove it over and over again."

After breezing through these articles, the reader might have been left with a negative view of the American movement to establish equality of opportunity and equity between the genders. They might have been left with the question: Who then is the typical and proper American woman? What does she look like? What does she do? A photo-essay by Ralph Crane offered some answers. The editors at *Life* chose Marge Sutton of Los Angeles as their representative American woman. The photographs showed Sutton in her spacious, suburban L. A. kitchen talking on the phone, wrestling a dirty shirt off her son while minding her daughter and a neighborhood friend. Married when she was sixteen, the thirty-two-year-old Sutton was a "happy, successful housewife and useful civic worker." She embodied the ideals implicated in Skinner's article. With the help of her gardener and full-time maid, she devoted all her waking hours to her family, her husband, and his career. She hosted an astonishingly large number of parties to advance their business and social agenda. Sutton estimated that she entertained 1,500 people a year and that her grocery bill was roughly $100 per week ($800 in today's dollars). The photographs show the many ways in which Sutton gives her time and effort to her family and friends. She was perfectly content within those confines.

In the special issue of *Life*, the editors put weight on primarily one side of the conversation about women in the United States of the 1950s. Taken together, these articles seem to promote the postwar American domestic ideal. Women's lives were located primarily in the home and seen through the context of their families. Social expectations of them appear to involve accepting those roles as wife, mother, and homemaker as well as excelling at them. Mary Ellen Chase seemed to suggest that the fate of the non-Communist West hinged on women's abilities to foster a happy, secure home. The women's issue of *Life* also defined the domestic ideal as particularly suburban, white, native-born, and middle class. Women belonging to different races or recent immigrants were not mentioned explicitly in the text or in the photographs. These suburban women were seen more as nurturers, caregivers, and consumers. They were also supposed to be the heterosexual partners of their husbands. Like suburban life, marriage was at the center of the postwar proscription for women. They were expected to remain alluring to men at all times. At various points, almost every article made reference to their attractiveness, charm, beauty, appeal, and prettiness. The editors of *Life* magazine seemed to be saying that to be an ideal American woman, she had to be a matronly domestic goddess, cheerily making order and happiness out of a disorderly Cold War world.

In the main, these articles appear to toe an anti-feminist line. Catherine Marshall's introduction, Mary Ellen Chase's jeremiad, Emily Kimbrough's plea for grace, Ralph Crane's myopic photo-essay, Phyllis McGinley's tongue-in-cheek analysis of women's attributes, and Cornelia Otis Skinner's rant all mention the feminist movement directly or refer to it indirectly. Clearly, it was on these authors' minds. And, yet, it is significant that none of the authors, with the exception of Kimbrough, who became involved with the civil rights movement and the National Urban League in the 1960s, were very involved in politics or social movements. Many if not all the authors would have agreed with Mary Ellen Chase's British friend who was astonished at her discontented American counterparts since "they have just everything that every woman wants." But comments like this might have opened up another line of thought for readers, especially female ones: What were these complaints of American women and did they match their own? Although the *Life* issue mirrors the conservative politics of the time, the magazine did not have a fixed meaning for all readers, and some might have read other ideas into and out of the articles.

The only feminist to write for this issue of *Life* was Margaret Mead (1901–1978), whose article focused on American women pioneers of the West in the nineteenth century. It did have a feminist message, but it was quite muted. No other feminists contributed to the issue or were photographed or profiled. Nevertheless, readers of the magazine might have identified with the brief discussions of the great dissatisfaction some had with domestic life. The authors tried to argue that feminism itself was the cause of the unhappiness. As Catherine Marshall wrote, "Can it be that many women's current troubles began with the period of her preoccupation with her 'rights'? Perhaps, so...." Leaving off the issue of causation, Mary Ellen Chase also noted that many women were miserable. Moreover, participation in social groups such as the Junior League or the local PTA did not create "stability or contentment." Further, Chase sounded about women's abuse of alcohol and vaguely alluded to the growing problem of overuse of prescription drugs to relieve women's anxieties.

Other authors in the magazine also touched on feminist issues by either advancing nondomestic roles for women or making the reader aware of them, if only to criticize them. Of course, all the writers for this special issue had careers, and significant life experiences, outside the home—some famously so, like Emily Kimbrough and her one-time literary collaborator Cornelia Otis Skinner, who wrote together *Our Hearts Were Young and Gay* (1942), a remembrance of their travels together in Europe in the 1920s. Chase made reference to traditional but important careers such as librarians, nurses, and office clerks. Kimbrough carried this quite a bit further in her discussion of women as business executives, and the photographs that accompanied her article introduced readers to women who had become geneticists, mechanical engineers, doctors, general managers, and federal government officials like Pat Byrne, who was then running the U.S. State Department's Laos desk and had already done extensive work in Saigon. Later she became the U.S. ambassador to Mali (1976–1979) and Burma (1979–1983) and the Deputy Ambassador to the United Nations (1985–1989). Even the true anti-feminist of the issue, Cornelia Otis Skinner, brought up female job pioneers in music and entertainment. Certainly, she wanted readers to join in her castigation of them, but arguably not everyone did. Yet, one message was clear throughout the issue: Not all women in postwar America measured themselves and their aspirations against the Cold War domestic ideal.

Regardless of the many readings, the special women's issue of *Life* magazine did not adequately represent the larger public conversation of the status of women in American society. Far from it. The 1950s were the seedtime for the modern women's rights movement. By the early 1960s, the so-called second wave of feminism was rolling. During the first wave, activists successfully won property rights, educational opportunities, and most significantly the vote for women. After the Great Depression, women's issues turned toward securing an end to discrimination in employment, equality in education, maternity leave and child care, a women's right to control her fertility, and passage of the Equal Rights Amendment. Additionally, second-wave feminists fought for advances for unions, immigrants, and civil rights. By the 1950s, the movement for women's rights was a cross-class, multi-ethnic, and multi-racial movement of women and men joined with other organizations to make the United States live up to the ideals expressed in the Declaration of Independence and take on all social issues from discrimination to juvenile delinquency to the banality of gendered stereotypes found on American television programs. Not all women and not all groups worked harmoniously together. There were splits over politics and sexuality. Organizations such as the

Daughters of Bilitis and the Women Strike for Peace pushed those in the center of American political culture to deal with issues of homosexuality and Cold War militarism. Yet another split in the women's movement of the 1950s and 1960s concerned the emergence of younger activists like Jo Freeman who were more strident in their opposition to what they termed "sexism." They did not merely want accommodation within the social system but "women's liberation." The work of these women would lead to new debates and eventually to yet another feminist wave.

Questions for Consideration and Conversation

1. It is sometimes said that *Life* magazine represented the American middle class in terms of social norms, economic lifestyles, and political tendencies. In what ways did this issue portray middle-class concerns, as opposed to working-class concerns or even elite concerns?

2. This issue of *Life* magazine ignores issues of race and ethnicity. How does this strengthen or weaken the arguments in the magazine's essays?

3. In what ways do you think that the authors in this special issue of *Life* magazine got it right? In what ways do you think that these authors were off base?

4. How do you think Crystal Eastman would have responded after reading these articles (Chapter 5)? How about Jo Freeman (Chapter 20)?

5. Do you think that these views on women's proper roles continue to influence and inform our own culture today?

6. What do you think is propelling the changes that these authors are discussing? Is it social change? Is it political change? Is it economic change? Or, is it some combination of these changes?

AN INTRODUCTION BY MRS. PETER MARSHALL (1956)

Source: "The American Woman: Her Achievements and Troubles," *Life*, Special Issue, December 24, 1956 (Volume 41, No. 26), pp. 2–3, 23–25, 28–29, 41–43, 72–76, 109–18, 150–51.

To be an American woman today is to be cast in an exciting, challenging and difficult role—exciting because the sky seems to be the limit in education, work and freedom; challenging because the whole concept of "woman's rights" is still relatively new—scarcely more than 50 years old; and difficult because the new freedom has produced a backwash of unforeseen emotional and psychological problems for the emancipated woman. Caught as she is in conflicting currents, the American woman of today finds herself being analyzed and admired, envied and criticized as never before.

The Editors of LIFE have devoted this special issue to the achievements and troubles of this fascinating, puzzling, eminently noticeable figure, the American woman. It is an appropriate time for such an issue because woman today is in a time of transition.... [S]he is still torn between using her freedom wisely and using it wastefully.

The case of the woman and the automobile may be a sort of parable for our day. Men invented the horseless carriage. Women, wearing coquettish dusters, were at first only eager passengers. To them the actual mechanics of the car were an enigma. Not for the world would a woman have tried to crank the thing or change a tire.

Then the car grew more attractive. Self-starters replaced cranks, and tires did not have to be changed so often. Women found that they, too, could handle a car. Right away they wanted to drive. Soon many of them had permits, and for a while driving was heady wine. They did not have to be beholden to any male for transportation. It was sweet release to go where they wanted whenever they wanted. But even in the transportation field rights inevitably have duties and responsibilities attached. In our day many a suburban housewife finds that the wonderful "freedom to drive" means that she is chained to the family car, beholden indeed, serving continually every member of her family....

This same pattern applies to any area in which women have won their rights—the right to bring home a pay check, to enter business, industry or politics. In each of these fields all the steps have seemed exciting and enjoyable—until the last one. Freedom always seems like fun; duties and responsibilities not always so.

In addition to her new responsibilities this present-day woman finds that she has certain strong urges and instinctive needs. If she is to be a truly happy person, these needs must be met. Ask any thoughtful, honest woman what the most satisfying moments of her life have been, and she will never mention the day she got her first job or the day she outwitted her boss on his ground. But she will always speak of the night when, as a teen-ager, she wore her first formal... and twirled in the arms of a not-so-bad date to tingly music. Or the night the man she loved took her in his arms, bringing a special look to her face.... Then there was the moment when she held her first baby in her arms. It was not just releasing, it was completely fulfilling....

When women do *not* have the deep satisfaction of these experiences, their troubles begin.... Can it be that many of woman's current troubles began with the period of her preoccupation with her "rights"? Perhaps so, for there are only two basic approaches to any aspect of human life: one approach sees life as a "right," the other as a "privilege."

We women have always had certain privileges that no man could take from us: our differentness; our unique femininity; the prerogative of bearing children, our devotion to beauty in ourselves and our environment. But privileges no longer cherished have a way of disappearing. It is possible that the difficulties in which we women now find ourselves are but another manifestation of that ancient but inexorable law: "Whosoever will save his life shall lose it."

Historians of the future may speak of the 20th Century as "the era of the feminist revolution." As in all revolutions, there have been many worthwhile gains, some agonizing losses, and no possibility of returning to the status quo. To be sure, the modern woman has no desire to surrender a single gain she has made. Today she is healthier, loses fewer babies in infancy, is more attractive than ever before.... Indeed, she is something of a phenomenon. Hence the Editors of LIFE have attempted in this, the second of LIFE's memorable double issues on a single topic, to pull together the different strands that make up the American woman's world and to present a kaleidoscope of opinions about her, her successes and her problems.

In so doing they may have rendered us women a very real service. For woman has shown through the ages that though she has limitations, she also has resilience. She has lived out revolutions before. With the kind of information implicit in this kind of thoughtful journalism, plus a new kind of dedication to the task before her, the modern American woman will yet be grateful to be herself, proud to be a woman.

MARY ELLEN CHASE, SHE MISSES SOME GOALS (1956)

Source: "The American Woman: Her Achievements and Troubles," *Life*, Special Issue, December 24, 1956 (Volume 41, No. 26), pp. 2–3, 23–25, 28–29, 41–43, 72–76, 109–18, 150–51.

A year ago in London I talked at length with a distinguished English woman just returned from an extensive lecture tour in America. She had spoken in some 20 of our states before audiences ranging from women's clubs to our leading colleges and universities. She had talked with numberless American women of every age and condition in life, and often she had been a guest in their homes. She had had a marvelous time and made the usual remarks about "that incredible American kindness and hospitality," but then she came to the thing which was puzzling her:

"Whatever is the matter with your American women? Everywhere I went I got the distinct impression that far too many of them are discontented, restive, and even complaining. They seem to me to have just everything that every woman wants. They have beauty and brains, husbands who evidently adore them and are proud of them, more freedom of every sort than any other women in the world. They have opportunities for creative and constructive work which no other women in any other country could possibly have, and yet they don't seem to be making use of them. In comparison, our British women are surely dowdy and maybe dull, but I honestly believe they've got more staying power than yours have, and even more resources within themselves. I can't help thinking that, as a whole, American women are just not doing their part in keeping your country where it has to be for the sake of the world. Am I right or wrong?"

I am afraid she is right. But I say this with definite reservations, for in 35 years as a college teacher and also as a lecturer throughout the country I have known and still know thousands of American women who are clearly happy and contented, whether married or unmarried. If married, they are having fun with their children, helping their husbands to achieve recognition and success, doing housework which their astonished mothers could never have accomplished without a servant or two, and directing their still-unspent energies in any number of constructive ways in their communities.

Last winter, which I spent in one of our largest university towns, I knew dozens of young college graduates, recently married to boys still studying for advanced degrees. These girls are surely neither dissatisfied nor grumbling. Instead, they are cheerfully working in bookshops or libraries, business firms or hospitals, or even in part-time domestic service, to help pay the bills until their husbands can finish their study or research. I know, too, any number of girls still unmarried, but wasting no time either in feminine wiles or in destructive anxiety. They are teaching, or studying, or working at all manner of jobs, managing to look alive and charming as only the American girl can look, having a wonderful time and, in consequence, giving others a wonderful time as well.

This is the brighter side of the American picture. It gives one hope and arouses unqualified admiration. But alas! It throws the darker side into even more pronounced relief. My English friend was right: American women, as a whole, are not making full use of their privileges or their powers. They are not living up to their responsibilities. They are not contributing their necessary part to the common welfare.

Why is it that, with their vast new freedom of opportunity, with time, talents and encouragement, our women, with rare and notable exceptions, are not becoming great scientists, doctors, musicians, artists and writers? The best of the girls in our colleges display remarkable mental grasp and ability, do a very high grade of work and are potentially brilliant scholars and thinkers.

What becomes of these abilities after those degrees are taken? Too early marriage, either immediately after graduation from college or even while in college, may be the answer, but I seriously doubt if it is. American husbands, in the main, do not offer insuperable objections to their wives pursuing their own intellectual interests. In fact, they are almost pathetically proud of the rare outside achievements of the distaff side of the household. If a girl marries early and has her family, the children are in school or college or themselves married while she is still relatively young. At 40, or 45, or even 50 the American woman has years ahead for study, or for scientific, or business or artistic pursuits. Why doesn't she pursue them? What becomes of that power and drive so evident in her earlier years?

Let us even suggest for a moment that a woman's mind, in general, may lack those qualities which produce great books, great music, great works of art. Perhaps her more subjective, sentimental nature stands in the way of masterpieces. A glance at, say, literary achievement might force one to concede that Jane Austens and George Eliots are not only fewer in number among the great novelists than are their male rivals, but that their work at its best lacks the scope and strength of the Fieldings, the Flauberts and the Dostoevskis of the world.

But if this is true, and I am not at all prepared to grant that it is, what about those masterpieces which a woman can create, and she alone? A well-ordered home, a secure and reasonably happy household, a contented and proud husband, an atmosphere within her family of intelligent companionship in those values which at once delight, amuse and nourish the human mind and spirit. All these creations call for the distinctive talents of women. They are beyond those of men.

The Need for Leadership

Countless American communities and neighborhoods would like to rely upon women for leadership in all sorts of necessary and productive activities: educational, social, political and religious. Schools desperately need the American woman's common sense and judgment, perhaps even her help as the teacher she once planned to be. Hospitals could use her in a far more important capacity than trundling a book wagon once a week through the wards. Political organizations need her well-informed sanity, her fresh ideas, her innate good taste. Churches are waiting to enlist her mind and devotion in more necessary and dignified service than dispensing coffee and salad at social affairs. Why aren't more thousands of American women seizing the opportunities open to them and employing their evident talents in an intelligent, eager and constructive way?

For the fact remains that a vast amount of nonsense is bolstering up the confused egos of a vast multitude of a women. They dabble at volunteer charitable work. Junior Leagues in dozens of cities supply the comfortable illusion that they are "doing good" in some cause or another. Women justify their existence, even while they deplore their wasted lives, by frenzied participation in church gatherings, in "social service," in many other pastimes. If such activities resulted in stability and contentment, one would not raise a voice against them. But quite clearly they do not, in general, either quell restiveness and dissatisfaction or demand the best that American women have to give.

The longing after *things* enters into this dreary picture, especially in the case of younger women in the early years of marriage. And unfortunately they long for things neither advisable nor possible on the average family income. These possessions, which apparently offer magic to subdue discontent and boredom, must in many cases be bought on the installment plan: television sets, new cars, all manner of those household appliances which often only make possible a dangerous amount of added and misdirected leisure. The payments for them, with skyrocketing interest, certainly increase the anxiety and uncertainty which the things themselves hopefully promised to assuage. I cannot think it unfair to suggest that in nine out of 10 of these cases of wobbling credit and rising debt women bear most of the initial responsibility.

There is also a sinister implication latent in this craving for mere *things*, a discomfiting suggestion that this need for material possessions betrays a poverty of imagination, a lack of aspiration. The overwhelming desire for them may arise from a reluctance, perhaps half-unconscious, to aim for those immaterial possessions which are far harder to achieve, those intellectual and spiritual values and activities which alone give meaning to one's life.

There are other disturbing symptoms of this poverty of mind and imagination among too many of our American women. A larger number of them than one likes to contemplate, of all ages, are spending huge sums in the hope that psychiatrists can unearth the source of their discontent or of their apathy and set them straight again.

Too much alcohol has become another uneasy and perilous refuge for an increasing number of restless and unhappy women. These, as I have observed in many places over recent years, are quite as likely to be of middle age as younger. This senseless and deplorable excess in a social habit otherwise genial and pleasant is clearly yet another sign of disquietude and disappointment. It is surely not adding to the initiative, vitality and ambition of our women, and it is just as surely lowering their stature in the eyes of their

sons and daughters, as I myself have had ample occasion to know from the sorry confidences of embarrassed and distressed young people of college age.

Rationalization inevitably plays a leading part in this human tragedy of misdirected or undirected energies: "Life's just become too complicated, I've given up trying to understand what it's all about." "What can we do in this neighborhood except go along with every-body else?" "Men never understand what women are up against. I'd like to see them get three meals a day and still keep on the top of the wave." "I'm worried sick about my children. Just think what they're facing in this crazy world," "I'm actually dead tired of cocktail parties, but, of course, we have to go."

The Disaster of Anxiety

Anxiety has a subtle and disastrous way of breeding anxiety. A troubled woman not only wrecks herself but carries others along with her. This truth was borne in upon me recently by a conversation which I had with an anxious young man.

"No, I'm not thinking of getting married yet awhile." he said. "It's hard to explain why without seeming disloyal, but you've known our family for years so maybe you'll get what I mean. You know how wonderful mother really is, what a good head she has, and how attractive she can be. But something's wrong somewhere. Dad and I have spent years trying to find out, ever since I was old enough to see that things weren't right. Mother's just not contented. There's always something wrong with us, or the world, or things as they are. She claims that most women feel as she does, sort of at loose ends, not knowing what to do with their lives. If the girl I married turned out to be at loose ends, too, I couldn't take it. I want to be proud of my wife."

Many years ago the poet Wordsworth had something to say about the right sort of woman which all of us might well seriously take to heart. To him she was

nobly planned
To warn, to comfort, and command.

His definition is doubtless sentimental and perhaps outdated, but it still has appeal, and not to men only. Such a woman is all too rare a creature in our society today. Thousands of us American women, young, middle-aged and even elderly, are not merely wasting our time and disregarding our opportunities, which would be bad enough in all conscience. We are actually strewing destruction in our wake. Unless we shortly take strict account of our mental, moral and spiritual stock by examining ourselves with that common sense, integrity and wholesome fear of failure which apparently our mothers and grandmothers employed without the help of a psychiatrist, we are surely headed for far worse troubles than those which so many of us are so unprofitably imagining. Our powers of warning will be directed largely against ourselves; we shall comfort no one; and instead of that respect and admiration which we must still want and ought to deserve, we shall command only disparagement and censure.

Emily Kimbrough, She Needs Some Years of Grace (1956)

Source: "The American Woman: Her Achievements and Troubles," *Life*, Special Issue, December 24, 1956 (Volume 41, No. 26), pp. 2–3, 23–25, 28–29, 41–43, 72–76, 109–18, 150–51.

Since the rise and fall of Eve, women have not "had it so good" as American women are having it today. And since the wrath of fell upon Eve, women have not been so excoriated as the American woman is today. She is an easy mark for the slings and arrows other critics simply because she is so conspicuous. She has asked for what she gets. She has pushed, shoved, shrilled her way into the open, demanding recognition. The banner she carries reads, "Better to be kicked than not noticed," and the skill of a sharpshooter is not required to hit that kind of target.

To reach the open spaces where she is so vulnerable to criticism, she began less than a century ago with a siege on what had been impregnable male fortresses, the private universities. The men thought they could keep the doors barred tight against female intruders, but the women made them surrender. Some of them withstood the siege longer than others. Schools of architecture took a great deal of battering: Harvard, for example, did not give way until 1912. In the current list of registered architects in this country, a list that totals 24,756, there are only 933 women. Yet I wonder, as I set down these figures, if a woman had participated in the design of the Forrest Theater in Philadelphia, would the dressing rooms for actors have been omitted? It was male architects who omitted them—and yet a frequently repeated gibe at women from business executives is, "Women are too fussy about details."

Having once got into universities, women burst out the door at the far end, one hand clasping a degree, the other compressed into a fist for knocking at other gates. It is this energetic and sometimes militant female, lighting for all the things she thinks she deserves, who is today labeled if not libeled as "spoiled, arrogant, restless, dissatisfied, a misfit equally in the home and the business world."

Although there is justification for some of these accusations, I believe they are neither accurate nor constructive. Margaret Ayer Barnes called her Pulitzer prize-winning novel *Years of Grace*, and I have borrowed her title because I think it defines both the age in which the American woman is now living and the attitude I should like to see adopted by her critics. I should like conceded to her those graces she offers, and I should like granted to her years of grace in which to bring to a final fitting the pattern for her life.

In the last 50 years the American woman has truly blazed a trail. Her severest critics cannot dispute this. Women from every part of the world have followed her. She was the first to be heeded and acknowledged as a social leader in her community, the first to gain wide freedom and recognition, the first to reach the stratum of business executives. Most of her rights she had won by herself, frequently without approval from men, sometimes against their active opposition.

In this struggle, however, she has had certain reinforcements which were provided, paradoxically and unwittingly, by men. Until this century childbearing and her gynecological problems drained many women of strength and resilience. Until this century there were no vacuum cleaners and other mechanical devices to deliver women from a large part of household drudgery. I doubt that the doctors, scientists, inventors and manufacturers, poring over their microscopes and blueprints, set as their goal the emancipation of women. But emancipation is what they produced. Thanks to the medical profession, which has made physiological ordeals less taxing, and thanks to the mechanical inventiveness which substituted the vacuum cleaner for the broom, the 20th-Century American woman has had more energy and more time to devote to trail-blazing.

This trail-blazing has undoubtedly unsettled a great many people, including the American woman herself, but it has also accomplished something. Perhaps the clearest single example of the problems and achievements that go hand in hand with trail-blazing is in the business world. No one can deny that the American woman has become an important and valuable force in business.

There is still, admittedly, an opposition group, declaring that if women would retrace their steps along the trail, go back home and stay there, they would again become serene, contented, more "womanly"—whatever that nebulous adjective implies. This is a declaration impossible to substantiate. Too many women have come too far from the home. All the Canutes in the world, lined up shoulder to shoulder, could not turn back this tide now.

It is more pertinent to consider, therefore, the persistence of the qualifying phrase used by men about women, "remarkable for a woman." Why should it be remarkable that a woman can be successful in business? It seems to me far more remarkable that she is so seldom in the top position. Why is she, instead, many times only next to the top? Vice president but not president, member of the executive board but not its chairman. Is it because the topmost positions represent the last stand of all the Custers in America? I think not. I do not believe there would be a Custer left standing if he were the only obstacle.

Alterations in a Pattern

I think the explanation is to be found in the American woman's pattern of living. And I think this same explanation accounts for many of the criticisms directed not only at the career woman but at the whole female society. The American woman has cut out her pattern during the last 50 years of endeavor, but she is still having to make alterations in it. She is not yet able to pull the basting threads because she is not yet sure of how she wants it to fit. She cannot, for one thing, sew up the seam between her house and her outside activities. She must leave it partly open in order to deal with a sick child crying or a telephone call that will summon her home to cope with a domestic crisis.

A man's pattern does not require such alteration. It was cut and fitted so long ago that now it is custom-made. A man is given an education commensurate with his own mental, and his father's financial, capacity. He is expected to marry, produce a family, provide shelter, food, clothing and, when the time comes, education for his children. Home life, business life and responsibilities in his community are placed by this tailoring in widely separate pockets. In short, man is organized.

If a woman is given years of grace in which to become similarly organized, I believe many difficulties within herself and many criticisms from the world around her will level off, though organization will not solve all the difficulties.

Of those problems that might be surmounted, I have some personal knowledge. One of my daughters after her marriage taught school in a large city. After the birth of a baby she was forced to give up the job she loved because her salary was considerably less than the standard wages of a general houseworker who would mind the child. Had there been in this large city some means of organizing the women of her age and similar purpose so that one baby tender could have been employed by a group of mothers, she might have continued her life outside the home.

My other daughter is a member of a mother pool in a small community. The operation of the pool is both simple and effective. Each mother in turn takes on the care of the children in the group for one morning a week at her own house. This arrangement leaves the other members free for whatever occupation they wish during that period. Such an organization could be expanded to permit each mother four or five half-days or even full days of outside activity every week.

Some women who would prefer to lead a double life, running their households and also participating in outside activities, give in to the difficulties caused by a lack of organization or by special circumstances. They close the door to the outside and stay at home. But does that satisfy the critics? Not for a minute. "She is restless" they say reproachfully. "She does not convey serenity to her husband or her children because she herself has no peace of mind." She is, in short, classified as a failure both as wife and mother.

This is, of course, too wide a generalization. There are many women who, having to make *a* choice, are happy to stay at home. They have tried combining domestic life with outside activity and been swamped in confusion. They are only too thankful to slam the door and settle down by the fireside. The restless ones are those who teeter on the doorstep, not really sure they want to go out, nor for how much time.

When a woman does step outside the front door, she is, of course, even more exposed as a target. If she tries to take up a career, she is told that "women are not trained properly" or that "women don't like responsibility."

Once again, it is largely the newness and incompleteness of the pattern that provokes these criticisms. If she has set her sights on law, medicine or a similar formal profession, she receives the training required. But many women do not know, until an occasion or a need arises, what activities outside the home they are going to follow. It is difficult to train properly when you don't know what job you are training for. As for the critics who say that women don't like to assume responsibility, they are forgetting that a housewife is not even considered extraordinary when she deals, singlehandedly, with all the varied responsibilities of the home.

I would not for a moment suggest that all women should or could be successful jugglers of two careers. But when opportunity or inclination beckons, the American woman has shown repeatedly that she can handle responsibilities outside the home. The list is long of women in the business and political world who have taken over a husband's work at the time of his death and carried it on to even greater success. Research has disclosed few instances of a man's taking over in an emergency, as a career for any length of time, a woman's program, either professional or domestic.

I believe that the American woman has flexibility and imagination to contribute to all worlds, including especially the world of the home. This flexibility is an attribute produced by her unsettled pattern. What other qualities are hers by very reason of her difficulties? Why, an ability to make decisions quickly, a sharpened imagination, an adaptability to change, a willingness to compromise and a shrewd but warm perceptiveness in human relations. Surely these are useful and needed qualities in every area of activity.

Therefore, gentlemen and other critics, acknowledge what she has gained and grant her a few more years of grace for fittings on her pattern. When the last basting threads are drawn, and it sits as easily on her shoulders as yours fits you, she will not strain or fret. And it might come to pass, gentlemen, that when her tailoring is as well fashioned as yours, you will find yourselves asking grace of her.

Ralph Crane, Busy Wife's Achievements (1956)

Source: "The American Woman: Her Achievements and Troubles," *Life*, Special Issue, December 24, 1956 (Volume 41, No. 26), pp. 2–3, 23–25, 28–29, 41–43, 72–76, 109–18, 150–51.

Marjorie Sutton is home manager, mother, hostess and useful civic worker

At the kitchen counter which doubles as her office, Marjorie Sutton of Los Angeles for a brief moment… straddles her two equally busy lives as a happy, successful housewife and as a useful civic worker.

At 32, Mrs. Sutton is admittedly lucky. She is pretty and popular. Her husband earns an average of $25,000. She has a spacious home, a gardener and a full-time maid. Thus freed of much of a housewife's drudgery, she has a unique opportunity to work for her community—and she does. She is a sponsor of the Campfire Girls, serves on P.T.A. committees, helps raise funds for Centinela Hospital and Goodwill Industries, sings in the choir at Hollywood's First Presbyterian, and inevitably is drawn into many of her husband's civic interests.

But Marge Sutton thinks of herself primarily as a housewife and, having stepped from high school into marriage, has made a career of running her home briskly and well. She does much of the cooking, makes clothes for her four children (ages 6–14) and for herself and, as a hostess, she entertains an endless stream of guests—1,500 a year, she estimates.

Marjorie Hayworth and George Sutton were married when he was 17 and she 16 and both were in high school. George rejected a football scholarship to go to work at his father's Ford agency (he took it over in 1948) and Marge left school to set up housekeeping.

With great understatement, George says, "Marge likes to keep busy." In her daily round she attends club or charity meetings, drives the children to school, does the weekly grocery shopping (average bill: $100), makes ceramics and is planning to study French. A conscientious mother, she spends a lot of time with her children, helping with homework and on costumes for parties, listening to their stories and problems. Her husband comes home for lunch almost every day and Marge makes it a point, whatever her schedule, to be there too. She shares his enthusiasm for driving their Model T. "She'd be a racer if I'd let her," says George.

Many evenings the Suttons entertain two to 200 guests—church groups, their children's clubs, business friends. This leaves little time for reading or solitude but they try to arrange a few evenings alone. "We're a big family," says George, "and it's nice to have a quiet meeting of the board of directors now and then."

PHYLLIS MCGINLEY, WOMEN ARE WONDERFUL (1956)

Source: "The American Woman: Her Achievements and Troubles," *Life*, Special Issue, December 24, 1956 (Volume 41, No. 26), pp. 2–3, 23–25, 28–29, 41–43, 72–76, 109–18, 150–51.

They like each other for all the sound, sturdy virtues that men do not have

Woman today is in danger of being so completely analyzed and discovered that she will soon have lost much of her allure and a good deal of her armor. Medicine measures her astonishing strength. Anthropology discusses her adaptability. Philip Wylie attacks her for being too aggressive and Ashley Montagu says she belongs to a superior race. In the open arenas of business, sports, day labor and the arts, she has been cajoled into demonstrating competencies she had managed to conceal for centuries, even from herself. So I expect I won't he read out of the Female Party if I smash one more dearly held belief—the belief that women dislike other women.

For quite the contrary is true. Women like women fine. The more feminine she is, the more comfortable a woman feels with her own gender. It is only the occasional and therefore noticeable rake or adventuress among our sex who refuses to make friends with us. I speak now merely of genuine friendship. Our love we reserve for its proper object, Man. How could we help loving men, the dear, romantic, illogical, timid, sentimental things? Their hearts are so tender, their trusts so deep; and they are often such good cooks too! Uncertain, coy and hard to please they may be, but it is woman's duty to cosset and protect them. And she has done so to the best of her considerable ability for a long, long while. In addition, men make the best possible fathers for our children.

What man has misconstrued, perhaps, is woman's behavior during what I must bluntly call the hunting season. We are immensely practical. If the race is to continue, we like to provide a second parent. So we go about the serious business of finding husbands in a serious manner which allows no time for small luxuries like mercy toward competitors. Nature turns red in tooth and claw, every method is fair and rivals get no quarter.

Once triumphant, however, with a man for our hearth, a fresh generation on its way, we sheathe our swords. We lay aside, as it were, certain secret weapons, and reaccept the company of our own kind.

We choose each other for neighbors. We dress for one another's approval. We borrow loaves of bread, exchange recipes and sympathy, talk over our problems together. Watch women at cocktail parties. All eyes and smiles for the gentlemen at first, the safe (by which I mean the satisfactorily married) ladies begin gradually to drift away from the bantering males. They do it tactfully. The fiction must be maintained that men are their sole concern. But by almost imperceptible degrees, women edge toward some sofa where another woman is ensconced. There, while the talk seethes and bubbles around them, they whisper cozily together of truly important things like baby-sitters and little dressmakers.

Do I imply by this that women are as frivolous and unintellectual as they have been accused of being in other eras? Or that the larger issues do not concern them and that maybe old theologians were justified in debating whether or not they had souls? Far from it. I am simply trying to convey the natural attraction that binds us together. Those two women on the sofa might well go on from household problems to the lesser topics of literature, space-rockets or politics. I know. For I am frequently one of the ladies on the sofa. In other words, I like women.

Shoe Trees and Knobless Knees

My reasons are many and sufficient. I like them for their all-around, all-weather dependability. I like them because they are generally so steady, realistic and careful about tidying up after a hot shower, I admire them for their prudence, thrift, gallantry, common sense and their knob-less knees, and because they are neither so vain nor so given to emotion as their opposite numbers. I like the way they answer letters promptly, put shoe trees in their shoes at night and are so durable physically. Their natures may not be so fine or their hearts so readily touched as man's, but they are not so easily imposed on either. And then they own all those basic manual skills like repairing gadgets and replacing tops on toothpaste tubes. I respect them, too, because they are such good drivers.

Say what you will, the male operator of a car is not in a class with his female counterpart. Statistics show a greater ratio of fatal accidents for the man. At long last there has been official recognition of male incompetence by insurance companies in 45 states, where a car can be insured at a greatly lowered rate if there are no male drivers in the family under 25. Don't misunderstand me. I'm not blaming men. It is in their natures in dream greatly, even amid traffic. The young ones cannot help showing off to their dates and the older ones must not be held culpable for a tendency to compete with the sedan in front.

In spite of knowing several men who really handle an automobile very well, I somehow always feel safer when a woman is at the wheel. For one thing, she has had such a lot of experience. There is not a man in a thousand who has spent so much time playing chauffeur as the average housewife, urban, country or suburban. What's more, a woman gets where she is going with a minimum of fuss and temper. She is not too proud to inquire directions and when they are being given to her, she listens. Men would rather pore endlessly over maps, however inadequate, or else make out by intuition.

Now I have nothing against intuition. It is one of men's inborn and most endearing qualities. But their trust in it baffles the ordinary straight-thinking woman. In every field from horse racing to national politics we prefer to marshal facts, estimate them calmly and then make our choice, rather than rely on some sixth sense. Something is always telling a man some peculiar inner voice—that Senator Humphrey Crough is really going to solve the farm problem, or that the storm windows don't need to go up this weekend because we're certain to have a mild November, or that tonight is his lucky night and he's bound to fill that inside straight.

There are, I admit, areas where intuition pays off. If Columbus hadn't had a hunch that he could sail to India by way of the Atlantic Ocean, he'd never have bumped into San Salvador. Wellington felt in his bones that he could stop Napoleon at Waterloo, just as those prospectors in California felt there was gold lying around the vicinity; and their bones were speaking true. Moreover, few businesses could burgeon or stock markets flourish or plays get produced without the impulsiveness of Adam's heir.

Just the same, women choose to proceed less rashly. They know that if their hunches go astray, they will have to pick up the pieces. Even in small things a woman likes to be guided by fact. Let her loose in a delicatessen and she comes out with the loaf of rye bread and the half pint of cream which she had put down on her list instead of the olives stuffed with anchovies, the assorted cheeses, pumpernickels, pickles, herring, potato salad, breast of turkey, pastes, spreads and relishes which her husband dreamed the larder might need over the weekend. And if she has a sore throat she does not ignore it completely on the theory that rude germs go away if one doesn't speak to them, or else take, groaning, to her bed because she has an intuition she will die before nightfall. She consults her doctor or a thermometer.

The Unfragile Sex

Of course women can keep calm about illnesses because, as a sex, we are so much less fragile than men—a point which scarcely needs belaboring. Again, statistics prove it. Wives consistently outlive their husbands. If one of a pair of twins succumbs in infancy, it is nearly always the delicate boy rather than the sturdy girl. Despite the severer tensions of a woman's life (and what hard-driven executive would exchange his routine for the soul-lacerating vexations of a housewife's day?) we are not so prone to ulcers, alcoholism or gout. We survive shipwreck, bankruptcy and childbirth with notorious aplomb.

Even the small ordeals find us less vulnerable. We are brave at the dentist's, self-possessed in the doctor's office and disinclined to faint while being vaccinated. Again, we deserve no credit. Providence simply has provided us with that extra bit of stamina.

Providence has indeed, almost made men expendable—or is trying to. I read with apprehension last spring that scientists had found they could raise turkeys from unfertilized eggs without benefit of a male turkey. They called it parthenogenesis. The scientists when last heard from were dubiously experimenting with some of the higher vertebrates such as rabbits. It gives one to think.

Extra stamina accounts for much. It explains why, no matter how they may clamor for equality, men can never hope to compete with women in certain sports and occupations. Men may do well enough in less demanding fields. They can throw a ball overhand, hurl a discus about, climb an unimportant mountain. But put them down in a crowded department store at holiday time for some jolly scrimmage and they collapse at the first counter. A woman in three-inch heels, with a tote bag weighing 10 pounds on her arm as handicap, can out walk a man on a shopping expedition any day and out dance him again at night. In one morning she can wash iron turn mattresses, wrestle with the sweeper, paper the ceiling of the dinette, and do it on black coffee and a slice of toast.

Which brings me to another admirable female trait: the ability to get along on a restricted diet. A husband before breakfast is more terrible than an army with banners. Deprive him of his lunch and he wilts like a plucked dandelion. And the dinnerless male is something too dismal to contemplate. So, when undertaking a vital mission, women like to have women for companions. They are not always having to be stoked with food. If they *must* stop along the line of march for sustenance, they are willing to settle for a teashop instead of the most expensive cafe in town, and to divide the bill fairly afterwards. This I find consoling. One of man's most exasperating qualities is his insistence on lavish gestures when he is settling a restaurant charge.

Notice what happens when two couples are dining out. Mr. and Mrs. Whitehouse, an unextravagant pair, have taken the $3.50 blue plate special with a martini apiece. Mr. and Mrs. Blair have each downed two or three cocktails and gone on to beef tenderloin, asparagus hollandaise and for dessert something flaming in a silver dish. But when the bill is brought, Mr. Whitehouse says expansively. "We'll just split it," and pays his unequal share without a murmur.

You won't catch us ladies behaving so. When we lunch or dine together we tot up every item ("Marge, you had the chicken sandwich on nut-and-raisin bread, and Evelyn, did you order two cups of coffee with that lemon-sponge?"), figure how the cost should fall and even divide the tip in proper ratio.

It's this no-nonsense side of women that is pleasant to deal with. They are the real sportsmen. They don't constantly have to be building up frail egos by large public performances like over tipping the hatcheck girl, speaking fluent French to the Hungarian waiter and sending back the wine to be re-cooled. They are neither too proud to carry packages nor too timid to ask a dilatory clerk for service.

What I enjoy, too, about my feminine friends is their downright honesty. Ask a woman if she likes your hairdo and she tells you. Make a small bet with her and she expects to be paid. And when she passes on a bit of scandal, she doesn't call it "shop talk," thus lending it a spurious moral air. Of course we women gossip on occasion. But our appetite for

it is not so avid as a man's. It is in the boys' gyms, the college fraternity houses, the club locker rooms, the paneled offices of business that gossip reaches its luxuriant flower. More tidbits float around the corridors of one major advertising firm in an afternoon than Louella Parsons ever matched in a year's output. Commuting trains buzz with it. The professions grow fat on it. The fluffiest blonde of a private secretary locks more secrets in her chic head than the granite-jawed tycoon who employs her. Women, in fact, are the secret-keepers. Forced by biological circumstance to live a subtler life than their brothers, they have learned to hold their tongues. "Kiss and tell" is a male and not a female slogan. There is something about man's naive character, something less than flintlike in his soul, which makes him a poor risk for a confidence.

That additional flint in a woman helps her, moreover, to keep her head. She is not always out on some rash adventure—leading a lost cause, buying shares in El Dorado or lending money to a brave little widow with nine famishing and nonexistent children. If we have not man's compassion, we also lack his gullibility.

And then from the purely technical point of view. I do like women's mechanical handiness. They are so reassuringly clever about mending things—about fixing locks on doors and putting in new fuses and repairing leaky faucets and stopping windows from rattling. What's more, they do it with no fuss and just a piece of string or old wire.

Now and then a gifted man sets out to be his own plumber or carpenter or electrician. But did you ever watch him at his work? To begin with, he must first invest in an elaborate set of tools, expensive as Russian sable. These he brings out lovingly, one by one, fondling them as a hunter does his rifles. Then he commandeers as helpers anyone unfortunate enough to be within earshot. People must hold things. Someone must hand him things. The ladder has to be supported. He has to have fetched to him intermittently sharpeners for his chisels, cloths for wiping his hands, hot water from the sink and cups of coffee or cold drinks at frequent intervals. Papers must be laid down around him and the entire household must listen to his exhortations, arguments and complaints. Particularly, there must be some obliging menial to look on, admire and deposit the laurel wreath on his brow when the job, as it sometimes does, gets finished. But I've seen women merely give a sharp slap to a reluctant washing machine or a dig in the ribs to a sulky toaster, and off it goes.

Mechanically deft as they are, not to speak of honest, clean, courteous, brave, reverent and loyal, women are the proper objects of woman's admiration. Oh why, I often wonder, in defiance of Henry Higgins, can't men be more like us!

But I always hear myself answering, "How splendid that they aren't!" Expendable they may be. But into our hard, practical lives they bring tenderness and sentiment. They give existence its meaning, its essential élan. They encourage our better natures. And they are esthetically so appealing too! Who better graces a drawing room? What prettier sight can one see at evening under the soft glow of the lamp than a man dressed in his old tweed jacket and lounging slippers?

No, without men we should be the poorer. Brightness would fall from the air, life would lose most of its color and all of its romance. And there would be no one to help us lift our monotonous daily burdens. Besides having to go to the office every morning, we would also have to write all the novels, paint all the pictures, start all the wars; and we have better business than that already. Women are the fulfilled sex. Through our children we are able to produce our own immortality, so we lack that divine restlessness which sends men charging off in pursuit of fortune or fame or an imagined Utopia. That is why we number so few geniuses among us. The wholesome oyster wears no pearl, the healthy whale no ambergris, and as long as we can keep on adding to the race, we harbor a sort of health within ourselves.

Sometimes I have a notion that what might improve the situation is to have women take over the occupations of government and trade and to give men their freedom. Let them do what they are best at. While we scrawl interoffice memos and direct national or extra national affairs, men could spend all their time inventing wheels, peering at stars, composing poems, carving statues, exploring continents— discovering, reforming or crying out in a sacramental wilderness. Efficiency would probably increase and no one would have to worry so much about the Suez Canal or an election.

On the other hand, though, I like our status too much to make the suggestion seriously. For everybody knows it's a man's world and they have not managed it very well, but at least it's their baby. If women took over, we might find ourselves thrashing around in the very masculine morasses we have so far managed to avoid.

CORNELIA OTIS SKINNER, WOMEN ARE MISGUIDED (1956)

Source: "The American Woman: Her Achievements and Troubles," *Life*, Special Issue, December 24, 1956 (Volume 41, No. 26), pp. 2–3, 23–25, 28–29, 41–43, 72–76, 109–18, 150–51.

They are still waging a shrill, ridiculous war over the dead issue of feminism

I happen not to be what is known as a "woman's woman." The female who is proud of the fact that she is a "woman's woman" is as ludicrous to me as the manhood-triumphant male who boasts of being a "man's man." I am quite content to be a woman but I don't regard my state as a remarkable accomplishment. I am not inordinately proud of my sex any more than I am inordinately proud of mankind as a whole. And I am anything but proud of the unwomanly way in which women's women are behaving these days.

Being completely nonpartisan when it comes to the comparative merits and superiorities of the two sexes, I am always astonished when I run across the earnestly vigorous partisans, those "what-women-are-doing" enthusiasts who still go under the outdated term of feminists. There are still an astonishing number of American women who get all worked up over American women, hailing each new distinction of any member of the sisterhood as one more goal for their team. And often as not, the more unfeminine the achievement, the more rapturous the cheers.

I have been exposed to this attitude all my life, for my mother was awfully impressed by the emancipated female "who did things." To be sure, when I was a child women had not been doing things for too many years as far as the professions or civic affairs were concerned, and my mother thought those who did were wonderful. There was a female general practitioner that mother thought was especially wonderful—only, I'm sure, because she had crashed the gates of the medical profession, for as a person she was fright, resembling a tweed-clad horse with a definite mustache and smelling of leather and disinfectant. I called her "Dr. Spook." She was one of the Emancipated Women all right, and the first shackle from which she had emancipated herself was charm.

I had to put up with Dr. Spook because she was the first woman doctor in our neighborhood. To be the *first* woman to accomplish any unusual feat has always been heralded, especially by other women, as being something remarkably splendid. Woman will go to all lengths in her incomprehensible scuffle to prove herself the equal of man. In 1901 Mrs. Anna Edson Taylor had herself nailed into a steel-bound barrel, shoved out into the rapids of the Niagara River and swept down over the falls. She goes down in the pages of history as the first person to survive this idiotic act. Whether or not it proved women to be the equal of men in courage and shock absorption, it certainly proved that they can be equally asinine.

A surprising number of women in this country still maintain that they can do anything better than a man can. This is a pity, for if a woman *can* do a man's job better than he, and if she lets him know it, she is no true woman. It is certainly not to be questioned that in many fields women are on a par of excellence with men. In others, their excellence might he summed up by the words of Dr. Samuel Johnson; "Sir, a woman preaching is like a dog's walking on his hind legs. It is not done well: but you are surprised to find it done at all."

Whether they do them well or not, there are certain trades I wish the girls had not taken up. For instance, that of the hospital technician. I have never had a blood count taken or other medical tests performed upon me by anyone but a very brisk, very terrifying, young Miss Efficiency, smugly competent, aloofly impersonal and about as compassionate as an armadillo.

Funereal Hostesses

Then there are those lady headwaiters who go by the euphemistic title of "hostesses." For me they strike a chilling note. A headwaiter leads one directly to a table with an anticipatory flourish that whets the appetite. A head waitress, after considerable hesitancy, takes a mysteriously circuitous route to what proves to be the most distant table, as though she thought it best not to let one be seen. It is rather like being shown to a pew at a funeral.

I also feel curiously uncomfortable about all-girl orchestras. I am ready to grant that the female musician can be every inch the equal of the male artist, if not occasionally the superior. But the sight of a woman playing a peculiarly unwomanly instrument is so distracting that one spends the time watching her instead of listening to the sounds she produces. There is no logical reason why female musicians should be confined to the piano, the harp, the violin, the viola and an occasional flute. And there are no logical grounds, artistic or physical, for objection to a woman's playing on a bassoon or pounding a kettledrum or venting interesting sounds by means of a tuba. But she looks ridiculous. The English conductor Sir Thomas Beecham apparently shares my dim view of lady musicians. When, on a guest tour of this country, he discovered women in the symphony orchestras, he fulminated: "Women are like the vultures on the battlefield: they appear after everyone else is dead.... The sooner they're allowed to run their course, the sooner the present era will blow up in ineptitude, inefficiency and incompetence. There will be five years of no music, and at the end people will say 'Now we'll start over.'"

Actually there was recently a talented young female bassoonist who gave up a promising career on that sturdy instrument, not to do something more feminine but to take up bullfighting. This is Patricia Hayes of San Angelo, Texas, who has had spectacular success in the arenas of Mexico and Portugal. Unfortunately she is not America's only matadoress. Pat McCormick (also from Texas) has slaughtered more than 125 bulls since 1952, and Bette Ford, a former model front McKeesport, Pa., has accounted for more than 53 bulls since 1954.

It is obvious that in time there will hardly be a job that women will not try to tackle. I don't know if as yet the carpenter's union has admitted any women to their ranks, and so far we do not employ many lady paper hangers, plumbers or garage mechanics. As far as I know, the Brotherhood of Locomotive Engineers is still a brotherhood. Trains are my favorite means of transportation, but the day I look through the cab window of the Century and see, seated behind the throttle, a woman wearing goggles and one of those caps made of bed-ticking. I will take a plane.

And the day a woman wins a heavyweight or even a bantamweight championship over a male pugilist (and there have been lady boxers), I will take up lavender and lace.

Women have plenty of champions among the sociologists and anthropologists who have proved her equality to man. If she is equal, the fact is not too disturbing. What is disturbing is the inordinate pride we flaunt in our accomplishments, a sort of we-are-the-leaders girls' college attitude—which is okay as long as one is a girl in college. If a woman can do a job as well as a man, so what? As for all those women's groups and committees, I think they are fine if they are accomplishing fine things. They are to be commended for proving themselves constructive, valuable *citizens* but not for proving themselves constructive, valuable *women*. Any step toward the betterment of this sorry world is a splendid thing. But the fact that the public benefactor is a woman doesn't make it any more splendid.

Ladies, we have won our case, but for heaven's sake let's stop trying to prove it over and over again. By setting ourselves up as a race apart and special we lose many of the delights and fulfillments of being women. In the long run, we cannot do without men and men cannot do without us—not unless we drive them to it with our shrill cheering for our own accomplishments. If ever the day approaches when men *can* do without us, I will take out citizenship papers in another and more agreeable planet.

CHAPTER 15

Newton Minow Takes On Television's "Wasteland"

*"I invite you to sit down in front of your television set . . .
I can assure you that you will observe a vast wasteland"*

If he was nervous, it did not show a bit. As Newton Minor (b. 1926), the thirty-five–year-old, newly appointed Chairman of the Federal Communication Commission (FCC), rose to the podium of the grand ballroom of the Sheraton-Park hotel in Washington, D.C., he calmly looked out at the sea of 2000 television executives and managers and delivered a blistering rebuke of the American television industry. Just the previous day, May 8, 1961, President John Kennedy, who had not even been in office for four months, had taken part in the jocose opening ceremonies of the three-day National Broadcasters Association "new frontiers" convention. All pleasantries, which had produced that mimetic conference slogan, were soon long forgotten. They were replaced by the hard feelings caused by Minow's stern upbraiding. His speech, titled "Television and the Public Interest" (the young bureaucrat's first public address), attacked not only the greed and monopolistic ways of the barons of broadcasting but also severely criticized American broadcasters for the programs that they aired, challenging them to devise shows that met the challenges that Americans faced at home and abroad. Minow charged that television had become nothing more than "a vast wasteland" with little to no redeeming cultural or political value. It had been that way for some time, but Minow signaled a sea change in the relationship between broadcasters and the public interest. Like it or not, the federal government in the form of the FCC was going to make TV culturally and politically responsible. These words set off a very public debate about the role of television in American society, one that seemingly has had no end.

The two thousand TV businessmen in the audience were not taken completely by surprise at Minow's words. They had heard rumblings that President Kennedy was critical of the state of television and film. But, such political claptrap had become regular election-season fare. Nevertheless, more than any of his thirteen predecessors, Minow's speech drew a clear line between past and future practices, and television executives were not pleased. Since TV's inception, they—particularly the bosses at the three major networks ABC, CBS, and NBC—had enjoyed a virtual free reign. The federal government had essentially treated their empires of airwaves with salutatory neglect. Though they would complain, that era was quickly coming to an end.

Nearly a century before Minow assumed his government post and gave that unprecedented tongue-lashing, futurists dreamed about sending images across wired and wireless communication devises. In 1880, scientists began theorizing about a device that would allow seeing by telegraph. Such televisionaries were not engaged in mere fantasy. Beginning in 1883, several technological advances, such as Paul Nipkow's "electronic telescope," made a televised future closer than many thought possible. Initially, the development of television was an international affair as Germans such as Nipkow and Russians such as Constantin Perskyi led the way. In 1900, at the International Electricity Conference in Paris, France, Perskyi named the device he and others were working on: television, a word which superseded all others. Before the end of the decade, no one would remember the older quaint labels: electric telescope, seeing-by-telegraph, telephonography, or audiovision.

When the idea of the television settled into the United States sometime following World War I, American inventors pursued it like electronic technology's Holy Grail. By the early 1920s, C. Francis Jenkins had created a prototype of a mechanical television that relayed images sent by a wireless transmitter. The resolution was an amazing forty-eight parallel lines of definition (consider that today's televisions have hundreds of lines). Jenkins and his rivals Herbert Ives of American Telephone and Telegraph (AT&T) and Ernst F. W. Alexanderson of General Electric (GE) made strides during the 1920s, and in 1928, the Federal Radio Commission (which was rechristened the Federal Communications Commission in 1934) granted the first television station license. Though promising, Jenkins' work was a victim of the stock market crash of 1929, which robbed him of funds, and the ensuing Great Depression, which deprived him of consumers.

For five years, television was submerged in the economic morass of Depression-era America. But in 1934, it emerged once again. This period of television history took on a David versus Goliath quality. That year, a young, brilliant, and brash inventor, Philo T. Farnsworth first introduced to the world an all-electric television, which quickly replaced the mechanical TV that depended on a moving disk to create images. It brought him fame, a small fortune, and also a dramatic fight with the most powerful television mogul of the period: David Sarnoff. At the time, Sarnoff's company, the Radio Corporation of America (RCA), was among the most powerful in the United States if not the world, having close business partnerships with several key enterprises including AT&T, GE, and Westinghouse. Sarnoff was an unflagging advocate of electronic television, and he had the capability to deliver not only the televisions to the masses but also provide content on his National Broadcasting Company (NBC) network. In 1930, Sarnoff had launched NBC's and RCA's first experimental television station. Initial successes encouraged him to invest more resources into the medium. Farnsworth's big announcement only encouraged Sarnoff to redouble his efforts. By 1939, when Sarnoff bought Farnsworth out, RCA had its own reliable all-electronic system, with an innovative cathode-ray tube created by Vladimir Kosma Zworykin. Sarnoff first unveiled his television to a curious public at the beginning of the 1939 World's Fair in New York City. NBC's broadcast featured both Franklin D. Roosevelt and his wife Eleanor. It was the first time that the president and the first lady appeared on television. People were fascinated, but the television era suffered yet another false start. No average American could afford a TV set; there were only a handful of stations with limited range; and significantly there were hardly any programs on television, yet alone worth watching. Making matters worse for commercial television, the onset of World War II delayed all timelines for creating and marketing new televisions as well as for the development of new stations and programs.

During the war, neither Sarnoff nor his rivals at other networks stood still. While working for the U.S. Army and Navy, RCA's engineers made several breakthroughs in electronic technology, producing night scopes for rifles, radar, and the first video-guided ordnance. Sarnoff's scientists improved the television as well. By 1940, RCA's black-and-white television had 441 lines of resolution at 30 frames per second. This was good but behind DuMont's TV, which offered 625 lines at 15 frames per second. And, the Columbia Broadcasting Company was already selling a rudimentary color set. RCA might not have made the best TV, but they had the most affordable ones. Its low-cost 630 TS model dominated the market following the war. Priced at $385 ($4,600 in today's dollars), the set was pricey but within reach. In 1945, RCA sold 10,000 units. The next year it sold 250,000. The television era had finally dawned in earnest.

Television companies had little trouble marketing the sets. Whether consumers actually believed the advertisers' claims that those glowing tubes constituted electronic hearths which warmed American homes during the chilliest phase of the Cold War or not, people rushed to make the investment. It had taken fifty years for radio to be adopted by fifty million American households; it took only twenty years for television. The tipping point was 1950, when nearly 10 percent of the nation or about 4 million households owned a TV and watched about three and a half hours of programming a day. Five years later ten times as many Americans had televisions. The number of stations had grown from 6 in 1946 to 458 in 1955.

Americans tuned in mainly to watch sporting events (the first World Series was televised in Jackie Robinson's rookie year of 1947), radio comedies that had found new life on TV such as *Amos 'n' Andy*, and the networks' stock fare: variety shows. Drawing inspiration from the vaudeville era of American entertainment, the live variety show was enormously popular. Americans' seeming insatiable appetite for that format produced the first king of television: Milton Berle, who at one time commanded nearly 70% of the audience while his show was on. Imitations—many of them quite good—followed including Ed Sullivan's show. Situational comedies created some of the most influential actors in American history including Lucille Ball and Jackie Gleason. Dramas, especially spaghetti westerns, drew large audiences as well.

While television succeeded financially due to ever-increasing revenues from advertisements and while the network shows created a new kind of common American culture, there were some voices of dissent. Some claimed that television presented a serious danger to children. The glorification of gun violence and the endless parade of giggly showgirls on variety shows left some wondering about the medium's impact on young minds. Others complained that television was too vacuous. Edward R. Murrow, whose own hard-hitting news programs set industry standards, bemoaned the programming of the 1950s for its heavy emphasis on entertainment and for its unwillingness to detract Americans from the vital issues of the day. Television executives rebuffed the criticisms. Their goal was to air the "least offensive program," and this "LOP" imperative made lots of money and made TV as ubiquitous as the radio it replaced.

Politicians seeking national office were among the first to realize the importance of the new media. It allowed them to reach large audiences quickly. Master TV, and one could master the electorate. Both Dwight D. Eisenhower and Richard M. Nixon had used television quite successfully in the 1950s as they built their political empires. At the same time, TV could bring down politicians. In 1954, Wisconsin Senator Joseph McCarthy embarrassed himself during his public investigation of the U.S. Army. He never recovered politically. Further, some politicians found it useful to develop a critical view of television, often while on TV, to advance their careers. It was a way to tempt voters some relief from the constant fear that television was somehow a corrupting influence upon the culture. Both John Kennedy and his main political advisor, his brother Robert, talked frequently during the 1960s presidential campaign about the need to reform television. Once in office, they appointed Newton Minow, a former law partner and political ally of Illinois Governor Adlai E. Stevenson, to the FCC in hopes of using the White House's bully pulpit to cajole TV's bosses into cleaning up their industry.

President Kennedy wasted no time in laying out his administration's priorities and desires regarding television. This was essentially Minow's mission at the National Association of Broadcasters convention in May 1961. He did his job well. Some thought too well as no one could remember any head of a federal regulatory agency taking such a stern tone with industry representatives. He began the speech by removing—at least rhetorically—the broadcasters' sense of entitlement. The airwaves themselves were a part of the public trust. "You earn your bread by using public property," he reminded his audience. For too long, television had only worried about their stockholders while ignoring their true beneficiaries: the American people. Minow vowed to rectify that. Perhaps sounding a bit like a Roman orator, he claimed, "I am in Washington to help broadcasting, not to harm it; to strengthen it, not weaken it; to reward it, not to punish it; to encourage it, not threaten it; and to stimulate it, not censor it." "Above all, I am here to uphold and protect the public interest."

To date, Minow asserted, television programming simply had not been "good enough." There had been some good shows. He listed his favorites: *The Fred Astaire Show*, *Twilight Zone*, and *The Nation's Future*. But the rest was bunk: "totally unbelievable families, blood and thunder, mayhem, violence, sadism, murder, western bad men, gangsters, cartoons, and endless commercials." In a phrase, TV was "a vast wasteland." The prime time lineups were bad enough for adults, but for children, Minow maintained, the effects of bad TV were pernicious. Already by the 1960s, the young were spending as much time in front of the television as they were in school. According to Minow, the shows directed at younger audiences had no redeeming value. Broadcasting executives had long defended their children's programming by claiming that they needed to maintain high ratings. "If parents, teachers, and ministers conducted their responsibilities by following the ratings," the FCC chairman retorted, "children would have a steady diet of ice cream, school holidays, and no Sunday school." It was not enough "to cater to the nation's whims," Minow charged, "you must also serve the nation's needs."

Finally, Minow issued his challenge and his threat. To serve the public in the midst of the Cold War, Minow demanded that broadcasters attend to the intellectual health of the American public by airing educational, religious, and instructive programming. He urged them to focus on the national issues as well as international and local. Minow was particularly interested in local news coverage and programming, claiming that "too many local stations operate with one hand on the network switch and the other on a projector loaded with old movies." Whatever the truth to that assertion, he expressed clearly his deep concern that too much power was concentrated in the hands of too few networks. Taking action against monopoly was no idle threat. He promised thorough license renewal hearings and announced that the FCC was approving a UHF broadcasting which would open up more bandwidth for television broadcasters, large and small, local and national. In closing, Minow paraphrased his political mentor saying: "Ask not what broadcasting can do for you; ask what you can do for broadcasting. And ask what broadcasting can do for America."

There was a mixed reaction to Minow's speech. Citizens, it seemed, highly approved. Over the next few days, as newspapers carried the text and analysis of his words, hundreds of people telephoned their approval directly to his office in Washington, D.C. Many more sent telegrams and letters thanking him for his courageous stand. Reporters generally responded favorably to Minow's attempt to create new broadcasting standards, or as one put it: "a flooring under the house of broadcasting."[1] Nearly a week after the convention, the *New York Times* printed a laudatory editorial, which in part stated that "it is for free enterprise to demonstrate that it has the restraint, good sense and elasticity not to let the furies of competition debase values of taste and awareness."[2] Some within the industry were also happy. In a moment of *schadenfreude*, advertisement executives, who normally bore the brunt of the public's scorn over television, rejoiced that the FCC recognized how a small group of network executives had cornered the market on broadcast content. Unsurprisingly, television industry insiders were angry. LeRoy Collins, head of the National Association of Broadcasters and an ally of President Kennedy, thought that Minow's remarks were "extreme" and had gone too far. "You can't blame us," one executive said, "no one likes to be spanked in public by a child."[3] A few years later, CBS executives allegedly tried to get even with Minow. Their 1964 hit sitcom, *Gilligan's Island*, featured an unseaworthy, unreliable, diminutive boat, which sank and ran aground on an uncharted island, named the *S. S. Minnow*, the name perhaps changed to defend against lawsuits.

Chairman Minow lived up to his words, and by the end of the 1960s, television had indeed changed. The sixties' civil rights movements and the war in Vietnam were both televised, raising American consciousness. New educational programming, including the extraordinarily successful shows from the Children's Television Workshop, became staples in American homes. Yet, despite these changes, critics still charged that American television remained a wasteland. Drawing inspiration from Marshall McLuhan, Neil Postman wrote that Americans were amusing themselves to death. Everything in American life—politics, religion, news, athletics, and education—had been reduced to televised entertainment. The result was that Americans were losing the capacity for deep, critical, and creative thought. Postman was not talking about the shows to which Minow objected. Writing in the 1980s, Postman had no problem with guns, violence, and silliness. *The A-Team, Cheers, Fantasy Island*, and *The Love Boat* posed no threat aside from boredom. The inanity of television, if not American culture, had become something Americans learned to live with if not love as the artist Andy Warhol so memorably illustrated. Rather it was the news and educational programming that was inimitable to public health. *60 Minutes*, local news, and *Sesame Street*—all products of that post-Wasteland Speech era— robbed Americans of independent thought. "The problem," wrote Postman, "does not reside in *what* people watch." "The problem," he explained, "is in *that* we watch."[4] Corporations were doing the investigating and thinking for us. Postman expressed the fears of some Americans that the televised future that some had prophesied at the dawn of the twentieth century had become the hedonistic, anti-intellectual anti-utopia predicted by Aldous Huxley.

Questions for Consideration and Conversation

1. What did Newton Minow say that made the television executives so upset? Why would it matter what a federal bureaucrat felt about the status of TV in America?

2. Try to find some old television shows from the 1950s and early 1960s. Do you think that Minow was right in saying that these shows produced a cultural "wasteland"?

3. What role do you think the federal government should have in relation to our mass media, such as television broadcasting or radio or even the Internet?

4. Minow pushed for better television that might make citizens smarter and more engaged. Should television broadcasting serve the needs of the people or should it serve the needs of those who make profits from advertising and from the production of the "least offensive program"?

5. Television and other forms of mass culture were essential in the rise to prominence for some Americans. Discuss the ways in which Elvis (Chapter 13) as well as Allen Ginsberg (Chapter 12) benefited from the growth of television in the 1950s.

6. If television programming in the late 1950s and early 1960s was a "vast wasteland," what would Minow have said about our TV landscape today?

Endnotes

1. Jack Gould, "TV: Withering Critique," *New York Times*, May 10, 1961.
2. "The Wasteland," *New York Times*, May 14, 1961.
3. Jack Gould, "TV: At the Wailing Wall," *New York Times*, May 11, 1961.

4. Neil Postman, *Amusing Ourselves to Death: Public Discourse in the Age of Show Business* (New York: Penguin, 1986), 160.

NEWTON MINOW, TELEVISION AND THE PUBLIC INTEREST (1961)

Source: Newton Minow, "Television and the Public Interest" (delivered to National Association of Broadcasters, Chicago, IL, May 9, 1961). Lester Thonssen, *Representative American Speeches, 1961–1962*. New York: H.W. Wilson Company, 1962.

Governor Collins, distinguished guests, ladies and gentlemen. Governor Collins you're much too kind, as all of you have been to me the last few days. It's been a great pleasure and an honor for me to meet so many of you. And I want to thank you for this opportunity to meet with you today.

As you know, this is my first public address since I took over my new job. When the New Frontiersmen rode into town, I locked myself in my office to do my homework and get my feet wet. But apparently I haven't managed yet to stay out of hot water. I seem to have detected a very nervous apprehension about what I might say or do when I emerged from that locked office for this, my maiden station break.

So first let me begin by dispelling a rumor. I was not picked for this job because I regard myself as the fastest draw on the New Frontier. Second, let me start a rumor. Like you, I have carefully read President Kennedy's messages about the regulatory agencies, conflict of interest, and the dangers of *ex parte* contacts. And, of course, we at the Federal Communications Commission will do our part. Indeed, I may even suggest that we change the name of the FCC to The Seven Untouchables.

It may also come as a surprise to some of you, but I want you to know that you have my admiration and my respect. Yours is a most honorable profession. Anyone who is in the broadcasting business has a tough row to hoe. You earn your bread by using public property. When you work in broadcasting you volunteer for public service, public pressure, and public regulation. You must compete with other attractions and other investments, and the only way you can do it is to prove to us every three years that you should have been in business in the first place.

I can think of easier ways to make a living.

But I cannot think of more satisfying ways.

I admire your courage—but that doesn't mean that I would make life any easier for you. Your license lets you use the public's airwaves as trustees for 180 million Americans. The public is your beneficiary. If you want to stay on as trustees, you must deliver a decent return to the public—not only to your stockholders. So, as a representative of the public, your health and your product are among my chief concerns.

Now as to your health, let's talk only of television today. 1960 gross broadcast revenues of the television industry were over 1,268,000,000 dollars. Profit before taxes was 243,900,000 dollars, an average return on revenue of 19.2 per cent. Compare these with 1959, when gross broadcast revenues were 1,163,900,000 dollars, and profit before taxes was 222,300,000, an average return on revenue of 19.1 per cent. So the percentage increase of total revenues from '59 to '60 was 9 per cent, and the percentage increase of profit was 9.7 per cent. This, despite a recession throughout the country. For your investors, the price has indeed been right.

So I have confidence in your health, but not in your product. It is with this and much more in mind that I come before you today.

One editorialist in the trade press wrote that "the FCC of the New Frontier is going to be one of the toughest FCC's in the history of broadcast regulation." If he meant that we intend to enforce the law in the public interest, let me make it perfectly clear that he is right: We do. If he meant that we intend to muzzle or censor broadcasting, he is dead wrong. It wouldn't surprise me if some of you had expected me to come here today and say to you in effect, "Clean up your own house or the government will do it for you." Well, in a limited sense, you would be right because I've just said it.

But I want to say to you as earnestly as I can that it is not in that spirit that I come before you today, nor is it in that spirit that I intend to serve the FCC. I am in Washington to help broadcasting, not to harm it; to strengthen it, not weaken it; to reward it, not to punish it; to encourage it, not threaten it; and to stimulate it, not censor it. Above all, I am here to uphold and protect the public interest.

Now what do we mean by "the public interest?" Some say the public interest is merely what interests the public. I disagree. And so does your distinguished president, Governor Collins. In a recent speech—and of course as I also told you yesterday—In a recent speech he said, *Broadcasting to serve the public interest, must have a soul and a conscience, a burning desire to excel, as well as to sell; the urge to build the character, citizenship, and intellectual stature of people, as well as to expand the gross national product....By no means do I imply that broadcasters disregard the public interest....But a much better job can be done, and should be done.*

I could not agree more with Governor Collins. And I would add that in today's world, with chaos in Laos and the Congo aflame, with Communist tyranny on our Caribbean doorstep, relentless pressures on our Atlantic alliance, with social and economic problems at home of the gravest nature, yes, and with the technological knowledge that makes it possible, as our President has said, *not only to destroy our world but to destroy poverty around the world*—in a time of peril and opportunity, the old complacent, unbalanced fare of action-adventure and situation comedies is simply not good enough.

Your industry possesses the most powerful voice in America. It has an inescapable duty to make that voice ring with intelligence and with leadership. In a few years, this exciting industry has grown from a novelty to an instrument of overwhelming impact on the American people. It should be making ready for the kind of leadership that newspapers and magazines assumed years ago, to make our people aware of their world.

Ours has been called the jet age, the atomic age, the space age. It is also, I submit, the television age. And just as history will decide whether the leaders of today's world employed the atom to destroy the world or rebuild it for mankind's benefit, so will history decide whether today's broadcasters employed

their powerful voice to enrich the people or to debase them.

If I seem today to address myself chiefly to the problems of television, I don't want any of you radio broadcasters to think that we've gone to sleep at your switch. We haven't. We still listen. But in recent years most of the controversies and cross-currents in broadcast programming have swirled around television. And so my subject today is the television industry and the public interest.

Like everybody, I wear more than one hat. I am the chairman of the FCC. But I am also a television viewer and the husband and father of other television viewers. I have seen a great many television programs that seemed to me eminently worthwhile and I am not talking about the much bemoaned good old days of "Playhouse 90" and "Studio One."

I'm talking about this past season. Some were wonderfully entertaining, such as "The Fabulous Fifties," "The Fred Astaire Show," and "The Bing Crosby Special"; some were dramatic and moving, such as Conrad's "Victory" and "Twilight Zone"; some were marvelously informative, such as "The Nation's Future," "CBS Reports," "The Valiant Years." I could list many more—programs that I am sure everyone here felt enriched his own life and that of his family. When television is good, nothing—not the theater, not the magazines or newspapers—nothing is better.

But when television is bad, nothing is worse. I invite each of you to sit down in front of your television set when your station goes on the air and stay there, for a day, without a book, without a magazine, without a newspaper, without a profit and loss sheet or a rating book to distract you. Keep your eyes glued to that set until the station signs off. I can assure you that what you will observe is a vast wasteland.

You will see a procession of game shows, formula comedies about totally unbelievable families, blood and thunder, mayhem, violence, sadism, murder, western bad men, western good men, private eyes, gangsters, more violence, and cartoons. And endlessly, commercials—many screaming, cajoling, and offending. And most of all, boredom. True, you'll see a few things you will enjoy. But they will be very, very few. And if you think I exaggerate, I only ask you to try it.

Is there one person in this room who claims that broadcasting can't do better? Well a glance at next season's proposed programming can give us little heart. Of 73 and 1/2 hours of prime evening time, the networks have tentatively scheduled 59 hours of categories of action-adventure, situation comedy, variety, quiz, and movies. Is there one network president in this room who claims he can't do better? Well, is there at least one network president who believes that the other networks can do better? Gentlemen, your trust accounting with your beneficiaries is long overdue. Never have so few owed so much to so many.

Why is so much of television so bad? I've heard many answers: demands of your advertisers; competition for ever higher ratings; the need always to attract a mass audience; the high cost of television programs; the insatiable appetite for programming material. These are some of the reasons. Unquestionably, these are tough problems not susceptible to easy answers. But I am not convinced that you have tried hard enough to solve them.

I do not accept the idea that the present over-all programming is aimed accurately at the public taste. The ratings tell us only that some people have their television sets turned on and of that number, so many are tuned to one channel and so many to another. They don't tell us what the public might watch if they were offered half-a-dozen additional choices. A rating, at best, is an indication of how many people saw what you gave them. Unfortunately, it does not reveal the depth of the penetration, or the intensity of reaction, and it never reveals what the acceptance would have been if what you gave them had been better—if all the forces of art and creativity and daring and imagination had been unleashed. I believe in the people's good sense and good taste, and I am not convinced that the people's taste is as low as some of you assume.

My concern with the rating services is not with their accuracy. Perhaps they are accurate. I really don't know. What, then, is wrong with the ratings? It's not been their accuracy—it's been their use.

Certainly, I hope you will agree that ratings should have little influence where children are concerned. The best estimates indicate that during the hours of 5 to 6 P.M. sixty per cent of your audience is composed of children under twelve. And most young children today, believe it or not, spend as much time watching television as they do in the schoolroom. I repeat—let that sink in, ladies and gentlemen—most young children today spend as much time watching television as they do in the schoolroom. It used to be said that there were three great influences on a child: home, school, and church. Today, there is a fourth great influence, and you ladies and gentlemen in this room control it.

If parents, teachers, and ministers conducted their responsibilities by following the ratings, children would have a steady diet of ice cream, school holidays, and no Sunday school. What about your responsibilities? Is there no room on television to teach, to inform, to uplift, to stretch, to enlarge the capacities of our children? Is there no room for programs deepening their understanding of children in other lands? Is there no room for a children's news show explaining something to them about the world at their level of understanding? Is there no room for reading the great literature of the past, for teaching them the great traditions of freedom? There are some fine children's shows, but they are drowned out in the massive doses of cartoons, violence, and more violence. Must these be your trademarks? Search your consciences and see if you cannot offer more to your young beneficiaries whose future you guide so many hours each and every day.

Now what about adult programming and ratings? You know, newspaper publishers take popularity ratings too. And the answers are pretty clear: It is almost always the comics, followed by advice to the lovelorn columns. But, ladies and gentlemen, the news is still on the front page of all newspapers; the editorials are not replaced by more comics; and the newspapers have not become one long collection of advice to the lovelorn. Yet newspapers do not even need a license from the government to be in business; they do not use public property. But in television, where your responsibilities as public trustees are so plain, the moment that the ratings indicate that westerns are popular there are new imitations of westerns on the air faster than the old coaxial cable could take us from Hollywood to New York. Broadcasting cannot continue to live by the numbers. Ratings ought to be the slave of the broadcaster, not his master. And you and I both know—You and I both know that the rating services themselves would agree.

Let me make clear that what I am talking about is balance. I believe that the public interest is made up of many interests. There are many people in this great country and you must serve all of us. You will get no argument from me if you say that, given a choice between a western and a symphony, more people will watch the western. I like westerns too, but a steady diet for the whole country is obviously not in the public interest. We all know that people would more often prefer to be entertained than stimulated or informed. But your obligations are not satisfied if you look only to popularity as a test of what to broadcast. You are not only in show business; you are free to communicate ideas as well as relaxation.

And as Governor Collins said to you yesterday when he encouraged you to editorialize—as you know the FCC has now encouraged editorializing for years. We want you to do this; we want you to editorialize, take positions. We only ask that you do it in a fair and a responsible manner. Those stations that have editorialized have demonstrated to you that the FCC will always encourage a fair and responsible clash of opinion.

You must provide a wider range of choices, more diversity, more alternatives. It is not enough to cater to the nation's whims; you must also serve the nation's needs. And I would add this: that if some of you persist in a relentless search for the highest rating and the lowest common denominator, you may very well lose your audience. Because, to paraphrase a great American who was recently my law partner, the people are wise, wiser than some of the broadcasters—and politicians—think.

As you may have gathered, I would like to see television improved. But how is this to be brought about? By voluntary action by the broadcasters themselves? By direct government intervention? Or how?

Let me address myself now to my role not as a viewer but as chairman of the FCC. I could not if I would, chart for you this afternoon in detail all of the actions I contemplate. Instead, I want to make clear some of the fundamental principles which guide me.

First: the people own the air. And they own it as much in prime evening time as they do at six o'clock Sunday morning. For every hour that the people give you—you owe them something. And I intend to see that your debt is paid with service.

Second: I think it would be foolish and wasteful for us to continue any worn-out wrangle over the problems of payola, rigged quiz shows, and other mistakes of the past. There are laws on the books which we will enforce. But there is no chip on my shoulder. We live together in perilous, uncertain times; we face together staggering problems; and we must not waste much time now by rehashing the clichés of past controversy. To quarrel over the past is to lose the future.

Third: I believe in the free enterprise system. I want to—I want to see broadcasting improved, and I want you to do the job. I am proud to champion your cause. It is not rare for American businessmen to serve a public trust. Yours is a special trust because it is imposed by law.

Fourth: I will do all I can to help educational television. There are still not enough educational stations, and major centers of the country still lack usable educational channels. If there were a limited number of printing presses in this country, you may be sure that a fair proportion of them would be put to educational use. Educational television has an enormous contribution to make to the future, and I intend to give it a hand along the way. If there is not a nationwide educational television system in this country, it will not be the fault of the FCC.

Fifth: I am unalterably opposed to governmental censorship. There will be no suppression of programming which does not meet with bureaucratic tastes. Censorship strikes at the tap root of our free society.

Sixth: I did not come to Washington to idly observe the squandering of the public's airwaves. The squandering of our airwaves is no less important than the lavish waste of any precious natural resource. I intend to take the job of chairman of the FCC very seriously. I happen to believe in the gravity of my own particular sector of the New Frontier. There will be times perhaps when you will consider that I take myself or my job *too* seriously. Frankly, I don't care if you do. For I am convinced that either one takes this job seriously—or one can be seriously taken.

Now how will these principles be applied? Clearly at the heart of the FCC's authority lies its power to license, to renew or fail to renew, or to revoke a license. As you know, when your license comes up for renewal, your performance is compared with your promises. I understand that many people feel that in the past licenses were often renewed *pro forma*. I say to you now: renewal will not be *pro forma* in the future. There is nothing permanent or sacred about a broadcast license.

But simply matching promises and performance is not enough. I intend to do more. I intend to find out whether the people care. I intend to find out whether the community which each broadcaster serves believes he has been serving the public interest. When a renewal is set down for a hearing, I intend, whenever possible, to hold a well-advertised public hearing, right in the community you have promised to serve. I want the people who own the air and the homes that television enters to tell you and the FCC what's been going on. I want the people—if they're truly interested in the service you give them—to make notes, document cases, tell us the facts. And for those few of you who really believe that the public interest is merely what interests the public, I hope that these hearings will arouse no little interest.

The FCC has a fine reserve of monitors—almost 180 million Americans gathered around 56 million sets. If you want those monitors to be your friends at court, it's up to you.

Now some of you may say, "Yes, but I still do not know where the line is between a grant of a renewal and the hearing you just spoke of." My answer is: Why should you want to know how close you can come to the edge of the cliff? What the Commission asks of you is to make a conscientious, good-faith effort to serve the public interest. Everyone of you serves a community in which the people would benefit by educational, and religious, instructive and other public service programming. Every one of you serves an area which has local needs—as to local elections, controversial issues, local news, local talent. Make a serious, genuine effort to put on that programming. And when you do, you will not be playing brinkmanship with the public interest.

Now what I've been saying applies to the broadcast stations. Now a station break for the networks—and will last even longer than 40 seconds: Your networks know your importance in this great industry. Today, more than one half of all hours of television station programming comes from the networks; in prime time, this rises to more than three fourths of the available hours.

You know that the FCC has been studying network operations for some time. I intend to press this to a speedy conclusion with useful results. I can tell you right now, however, that I am deeply concerned with concentration of power in the hands of the networks. As a result, too many local stations have foregone any efforts at local programming, with little use of live talent and local service. Too many local stations operate with one hand on the network switch and the other on a projector loaded with old movies. We want the individual stations to be free to meet their legal responsibilities to serve their communities.

I join Governor Collins in his views so well expressed to the advertisers who use the public air. And I urge the networks to join him and undertake a very special mission on behalf of this industry. You can tell your advertisers, "This is the high quality we are going to serve—take it or other people will. If you think you can find a better place to move

automobiles, cigarettes, and soap, then go ahead and try." Tell your sponsors to be less concerned with costs per thousand and more concerned with understanding per millions. And remind your stockholders that an investment in broadcasting is buying a share in public responsibility. The networks can start this industry on the road to freedom from the dictatorship of numbers.

But there is more to the problem than network influences on stations or advertiser influences on networks. I know the problems networks face in trying to clear some of their best programs—the informational programs that exemplify public service. They are your finest hours, whether sustaining or commercial, whether regularly scheduled or special. These are the signs that broadcasting knows the way to leadership. They make the public's trust in you a wise choice.

They should be seen. As you know, we are readying for use new forms by which broadcast stations will report their programming to the Commission. You probably also know that special attention will be paid in these forms to reports of public service programming. I believe that stations taking network service should also be required to report the extent of the local clearance of network public service programs, and when they fail to clear them, they should explain why. If it is to put on some outstanding local program, this is one reason. But if it is simply to run an old movie, that's an entirely different matter. And the Commission should consider such clearance reports carefully when making up its mind about the licensee's over-all programming.

We intend to move—and as you know, and as I want to say publicly, the FCC was rapidly moving in other new areas before the new Administration arrived in Washington. And I want to pay my public respects to my very able predecessor, Fred Ford, and to my colleagues on the Commission, each of whom has welcomed me to the FCC with warmth and cooperation.

We have approved an experiment with pay TV, and in New York we are testing the potential of UHF broadcasting. Either or both of these may revolutionize television. Only a foolish prophet would venture to guess the direction they will take, and their effect. But we intend that they shall be explored fully, for they are part of broadcasting's New Frontier. The questions surrounding pay TV are largely economic. The questions surrounding UHF are largely technological. We are going to give the infant—the infant pay TV a chance to prove whether it can offer a useful service; we are going to protect it from those who would strangle it in its crib.

As for UHF, I'm sure you know about our test in the canyons of New York City. We will take every possible positive step to break through the allocations barrier into UHF. We will put this sleeping giant to use and in the years ahead we may have twice as many channels operating in cities where now there are only two or three. We may have a half dozen networks instead of three.

I have told you that I believe in the free enterprise system. I believe that most of television's problems stem from lack of competition. This is the importance of UHF to me: with more channels on the air, we will be able to provide every community with enough stations to offer service to all parts of the public. Programs with a mass market appeal required by mass product advertisers certainly will still be available. But other stations will recognize the need to appeal to more limited markets and to special tastes. In this way, we can all have a much wider range of programs. Television should thrive on this competition, and the country should benefit from alternative sources of service to the public. And, Governor Collins, I hope the NAB will benefit from many new members.

Another and perhaps the most important frontier: Television will rapidly join the parade into space. International television will be with us soon. No one knows how long it will be until a broadcast from a studio in New York will be viewed in India as well as in Indiana, will be seen in the Congo as it is seen in Chicago. But as surely as we are meeting here today, that day will come; and once again our world will shrink.

What will the people of other countries think of us when they see our western bad men and good men punching each other in the jaw in between the shooting? What will the Latin American or African child learn of America from this great communications industry? We cannot permit television in its present form to be our voice overseas.

There is your challenge to leadership. You must reexamine some fundamentals of your industry. You must open your minds and open your hearts to the limitless horizons of tomorrow. I can suggest some words that should serve to guide you:

Television and all who participate in it are jointly accountable to the American public for respect for the special needs of children, for community responsibility, for the advancement of education and culture, for the acceptability of the program materials chosen, for decency and decorum in production, and for propriety in advertising. This responsibility cannot be discharged by any given group of programs, but can be discharged only through the highest standards of respect for the American home, applied to every moment of every program presented by television.

Program materials should enlarge the horizons of the viewer, provide him with wholesome entertainment, afford helpful stimulation, and remind him of the responsibilities which the citizen has towards his society.

Now those are not my words. They are yours. They are taken literally, verbatim, from your own Television Code. They reflect the leadership and aspirations of your own great industry. I urge you to respect them as I do. And I urge you to respect the intelligent and farsighted leadership of Governor LeRoy Collins, and to make this meeting a creative act. I urge you at this meeting and, after you leave, back home, at your stations and your networks, to strive ceaselessly to improve your product and to better serve your viewers, the American people.

I hope that we at the FCC will not allow ourselves to become so bogged down in the mountain of papers, hearings, memoranda, orders, and the daily routine that we close our eyes to this wider view of the public interest. And I hope that you broadcasters will not permit yourselves to become so absorbed in the daily chase for ratings, sales, and profits that you lose this wider view. Now more than ever before in broadcasting's history the times demand the best of all of us.

We need imagination in programming, not sterility; creativity, not imitation; experimentation, not conformity; excellence, not mediocrity. Television is filled with creative, imaginative people. You must strive to set them free.

Television in its young life has had many hours of greatness—its "Victory at Sea," its Army-McCarthy hearings, its "Peter Pan," its "Kraft Theaters," its "See It Now," its "Project 20," the World Series, its political conventions and campaigns, and the Great Debates. And it's had its endless hours of mediocrity and its moments of public disgrace. There are estimates today that the average viewer spends about 200 minutes daily with television, while the average reader spends 38 minutes with magazines, 40 minutes with newspapers. Television has grown faster than a teenager, and now it is time to grow up.

What you gentlemen broadcast through the people's air affects the people's taste, their knowledge, their opinions, their understanding of themselves and of their world—and their future.

Just think for a moment of the impact of broadcasting in the past few days. Yesterday was one of the great days of my life. Last week the President asked me to ride over with him when he came to speak here at the NAB. And when I went to the White House he said, "Do you think it would be a good idea to take Commander Shepard?" And, of course, I said it would be magnificent. And I was privileged to ride here yesterday in a car with the President and the Vice President, Commander and Mrs. Shepard. This was an unexpected, unscheduled stop. And Commander Shepard said to me, "Where are we going?" "What is this group?" And I said, "This is the *National Association of Broadcasters* at its annual convention."

This is the group, this is the industry that made it possible for millions of Americans to share with you that great moment in history; that his gallant flight was witnessed by millions of anxious Americans who saw in it an intimacy which they could achieve through no other medium, in no other way. It was one of your finest hours. The depth of broadcasting's contribution to public understanding of that event cannot be measured. And it thrilled me—as a representative of the government that deals with this industry—to say to Commander Shepard the group that he was about to see.

I say to you ladies and gentlemen—I remind you what the President said in his stirring inaugural. He said: "Ask not what America can do for you; ask what you can do for America." I say to you ladies and gentlemen: Ask not what broadcasting can do for you; ask what you can do for broadcasting. And ask what broadcasting can do for America.

I urge you, I urge you to put the people's airwaves to the service of the people and the cause of freedom. You must help prepare a generation for great decisions. You must help a great nation fulfill its future.

Do this! I pledge you our help.

Thank you.

CHAPTER 16

Andy Warhol Celebrates the Mundane

"In the future everyone will be famous for fifteen minutes."

Allen Ginsberg (see Chapter 12) believed rampant commercialism and materialism had turned the American Dream into a nightmare. Andy Warhol shrugged and said, "so what?" Indeed, Warhol used American commercialism and materialism as the foundation of his art, which from the early 1960s until his death in 1987 recorded and reflected the nation's obsession with consumerism, media, and celebrity. Warhol pioneered "Pop Art," in which everyday objects, artifacts, and images became the subjects of artistic production.

For Warhol, "production" was at the heart of the creative process. He made "factory" art for a mass society, devoid of personal touch, reproduced again and again. Norman Rockwell's *Saturday Evening Post* work was also mass-produced, of course, but Rockwell never considered himself anything more than an illustrator (see Chapter 10). Warhol legitimized reproduction as "fine" art, with a meaning deeper than its surface appearance.

Unlike many "instinctive" artists, Warhol had a well-thought out idea of what he wanted to say, as well as a clear vision of the "America" his art embodied. Material objects, the fruit of a capitalism unmatched in its ability to make "things," defined Warhol's America. Warhol loved "things." His home and workplace were crowded with boxes—Warhol called them "time capsules"—filled with his acquisitions, large and small. He found as much meaning in the mundane as in the exceptional. He marveled, for example, at the simplicity of the Coca-Cola bottle, reproducing its image as iconic art. It has been said that all of Warhol's work was "based on repetitions," and the endlessly repeating image, whether of Coca-Cola bottles, the face of Marilyn Monroe, or cans of Campbell's Soup, was the vehicle through which he presented himself to his audience.[1]

It was also the way in which Warhol presented America itself—as an endless series of standardized images, representing familiar products, objects, and people. Warhol constructed "American" identity through commodities and celebrities. His vision resembled that of Allen Ginsberg (see Chapter 12). But unlike Ginsberg, Warhol did not consider American society "mad." He viewed consumerism and commoditization not as evidence of sickness and decay, but as "American" traits to be explored in the name of art.

Moreover, in an impersonal, mass-produced American society, Warhol understood the deep American need for individuality. Hence the attraction to celebrity, a shallow, often fleeting form of notoriety based not on actual achievement but self-promotion and exhibitionism. While Ginsberg rejected the idea of celebrity as meaningless and empty, Warhol embraced it for just these qualities. What could be more "American," he argued, than the fixation on celebrity or the desire of anonymous

Americans for a taste of it themselves? When Warhol said, "in the future everyone will be famous for fifteen minutes," he was describing the America he saw before him in the second half of the twentieth century, a coldly efficient producing machine in which consumption offered the only route to personal identity and meaning.[2]

Was a society based on such principles healthy? Decades earlier, the Lynds had expressed their doubts (see Chapter 7). But Warhol was more sanguine. He believed that there was nothing inherently wrong with such a society. Warhol was one of the rare post–World War II cultural figures who did not scold the act of mass consumption. Instead, he gloried in it. "What's great about this country," he wrote in 1975,

> is that America started the tradition where the richest consumers buy essentially the same things as the poorest. You can be watching TV and see Coca-Cola, and you can know that the President drinks Coke, Liz Taylor drinks Coke, and just think, you can drink Coke too. A Coke is a Coke and no amount of money can get you a better Coke than the one the bum on the corner is drinking. All the Cokes are the same and all the Cokes are good. Liz Taylor knows it, the President knows it, the bum knows it, and you know it.[3]

Warhol transformed consumer items into objects of art and the act of consumption itself into a symbol of mass American egalitarianism.

Andy Warhol was born in 1928 as Andrew Warhola. His parents were immigrants from the present-day Slovakia who settled in Pittsburgh in search of economic opportunity, much as Andrew Carnegie's had come from Scotland three-quarters of a century earlier (see Chapter 2). When he was nine, Andy suffered an attack of St. Vitus Chorea, which caused fits of uncontrollable shaking and left unsightly blotches on his skin. Out of school and at home for months, he passed the time sketching and looking at photographs of screen stars, perhaps the genesis of his later preoccupation with celebrities.

Andy's father died in 1942, but left enough money for his son to go to college, and in 1945 he enrolled at Carnegie Institute of Technology (now Carnegie Mellon University). Studying painting and design, Andy became known on campus for his quirky mannerisms and innovative artistic techniques, notably the "blotted line," where he would transfer an image on which the ink was still wet to another piece of paper, creating a blurred, exaggerated "look." Andy's work appeared in student art exhibitions, although his portrayal of a nose-picking, entitled "Why Pick on Me?" was considered too risqué for the Associated Artists of Pittsburgh show, then the most prestigious in the city. Even as he experimented with new approaches, Andy received a solid grounding in traditional art forms at Carnegie and, upon graduation in 1949, was prepared to try his hand in the world of commercial art. That meant only one place: New York City.

Soon after Andy arrived in New York, he took a new name to mark his new life: Andy Warhol. He quickly climbed the ladder of success as a commercial illustrator. Art directors at major advertising firms came to admire his spontaneous and vibrant work, which often featured variations on the "blotted line." During the 1950s, Warhol earned a comfortable living and considerable professional respect, winning a number of awards from the influential Art Directors Club. Between 1955 and 1957, his illustrations for the I. Miller Shoe Company attracted national attention and gave him star status in his world.

That world, however, had become increasingly limiting for Warhol. His real interests lay not in advertising, but in "serious" art. "Fine" artists produced their work individually. Warhol's "ads" were turned out mechanically. But why, he asked, did this make them any less worthy of critical appreciation? Warhol employed assistants in his advertising work. Despite their role in creating the final "product," it was understood that Warhol was the "author." Why couldn't the same rule apply to "fine" art? The line between an illustrator like Norman Rockwell and a serious artist could thus be erased.

Further, why couldn't the subject matter of commercial art—consumer goods and celebrity images—also be considered appropriate for "important" art? By the early 1960s a small but growing group of artists, including Robert Rauschenberg, Jasper Johns, and Roy Lichtenstein, were already employing reproduction techniques and well-known likenesses in the developing field of "Pop Art." Warhol wished to join them and have his work accorded the respect due meaningful art. He wanted his paintings to appear in museum and gallery shows and be reviewed by influential critics. Shoe advertisements were fleeting, but "serious" art had staying power. Art touched deeper and more profound truths than illustrations, which held no meaning apart from the objects they portrayed. Warhol resolved to cross from the literal to the metaphorical without altering the essential nature of his work.

To do this, he would have to market himself as a serious artist in a manner reminiscent of the advertising agencies whose products he helped sell, and create his own unique image. Soon, Warhol was a "persona." Attired in a blond—and sometimes silver—wig, wearing sunglasses indoors, saying little in public, he cultivated an enigmatic air that attracted attention and interest. Adding to Warhol's mystery was his ambiguous sexuality. Warhol was a homosexual, but used professional and personal connections with women to hint that he was bisexual. Who *was* Andy Warhol? Andy set out to force members of the New York art world to ask this question without being able to answer it definitively, which of course would lead to more questions and his ultimate goal of more attention.

But if surface appearances would get him noticed, the quality of his art would determine his enduring reputation. And by the early 1960s, Andy Warhol was attracting serious attention in the New York art world. His entrée was an artistic technique known as silk screening. Related to the "blotted line," silk screening involved printing a photograph on a screen and applying paint to "colorize" the image, often with garish and exaggerated hues. The technique allowed Warhol to create art objects quickly, and his use of assistants further expedited the process. In August 1962, just after the death of movie star and celebrity icon Marilyn Monroe, Warhol silkscreened one of her photographs, creating a series of gold-tinted images meant to accentuate her tragic glamour. "Marilyn Diptych" was part of Warhol's first New York solo show at the Stable Gallery on November 6, 1962. Also featured were images of another "pop" celebrity, Elvis Presley, and of a series of disasters, including a newspaper photograph of a plane crash.

A few months earlier, at a show in Los Angeles, Warhol had exhibited a painting of what would become his most famous subject: Campbell Soup cans, thirty-two varieties in all, a familiar sight directly out of the average American supermarket aisle. Warhol's immediate inspiration for the cans was relatively prosaic. His mother, with whom he now shared his New York apartment, had made Campbell's soups a staple of the meals she cooked for her son. But the cans were meant to represent more than mere advertisement or family memory. The mechanical, impersonal way in which they were produced mirrored the American society in which they were consumed. Warhol used Campbell's cans as he did Marilyn Monroe, Elvis Presley, and even plane crash images—to portray an America whose essence was consumption, celebrity, and tabloid-style disaster and violence.

This "Pop" approach to art, in Warhol's hands, was a method of representation and description, and not a form of social criticism. The shallowness and ephemerality of the America his art explored did not concern him. The fact that his fellow Americans devoured consumer goods, violent images, and lurid accounts of the lives of entertainers was to Warhol neither good nor evil. Celebrity itself, in fact, was to Warhol a type of consumer product, akin to Campbell's Soup or Coca-Cola. Like soup or soda, celebrity was a widely available and disposable commodity. It made fame more egalitarian—"commonism," Warhol called it—and put it within reach of every American.[4] Warhol's art was democratic because it promised the same experiences, including the same Coca-Cola, the same Campbell's Soup, and the same fifteen minutes in the spotlight, to all.

No one pursued fame in America more obsessively than Warhol himself. The critical and commercial successes of his 1962 exhibitions were sources of tremendous personal gratification. He was now a "star" in the serious art world. Warhol's breakthrough was an instance of man and moment coinciding. By 1962, American culture was opening up to new modes of expression. In part this was a result of the work of the Beat Generation poets and writers (see Chapter 12), who had imagined new cultural directions and possibilities. In addition, two decades of prosperity were by the early 1960s allowing Americans to examine their lives *as* Americans in an atmosphere free from economic insecurity. An art that was self-referential and ironic, that made the American way of life itself its subject, was well suited for a society enjoying the luxury of self-examination. There was now a market for Warhol's work and message.

He set out to meet that market with production techniques borrowed from American industrial capitalism. In 1963, Warhol opened the "Factory," which would be his artistic and social headquarters in various Manhattan locations for the rest of his life. The Factory served many purposes for Warhol. It was his workplace, where he and an array of assistants mass-produced silkscreened art. Warhol's customers would purchase paintings that his hands had not touched, often a series of identical colorized reproductions of familiar photographs or product images. He thus melded his two professional lives, using the perspective of the commercial illustrator to make a serious artistic statement.

But the Factory was more than a production studio. It also functioned as a gathering place for a circle of designers, actors, models, musicians, and filmmakers brought together by Warhol as a "salon" of cutting-edge tastes and trends. The Factory was thus both social and artistic space. In Warhol's mind, the two overlapped. Celebrity was an art form, and he used the Factory to locate, refine, and display it.

One of the ways in which he did so was through film. Warhol felt compelled to document everything he observed, and film lent itself perfectly to his ambitions. Beginning in 1963, Warhol produced a series of films that, like his paintings, pushed the boundaries of the form. In "Sleep" (1963), he recorded a sleeping man for five hours. "Empire" (1964) employed a lone camera trained on New York's Empire State Building for eight hours, the "action" consisting of the onset of night.

His most commercially successful film was "The Chelsea Girls" (1966), set in the Chelsea Hotel on Manhattan's West Side. The hotel was a display case for the city's underground and alternative culture, and drew Warhol like a magnet. The film starred the model known as "Nico," one of a group of women Warhol "discovered" at the Factory and dubbed a "superstar" in a deliberate attempt to play on the idea of "celebrity" by creating one from scratch. "The Chelsea Girls" contained two simultaneously presented film reels, which Warhol employed to create a jarring effect. The themes of Warhol's paintings—celebrity, consumption, and impersonality—were also present in his films, and enabled him to become even more famous himself. Warhol explored yet another medium when he managed and produced the experimental rock group the "Velvet Underground" between 1965 and 1967.

But there was a dark side to the celebrity that Warhol pursued, documented, and worshipped. Befitting a man who believed that everyone deserved fifteen minutes of fame, Warhol had a habit of discarding friends and collaborators like empty soup cans or soda bottles when he believed their time had expired. One such discard was a sometime Factory employee and hanger-on named Valerie Solanas, who was out of favor with Warhol and whose proposed screenplay he had casually brushed aside. On June 3, 1968, an incensed Solanas shot Warhol, damaging his stomach, lungs, and liver and almost killing him. In an ironic confirmation of Warhol's own ideas about the power of celebrity in the United States, emergency room doctors initially pronounced him dead, but made another attempt to revive the artist after a colleague identified him.[5]

To Warhol even the shooting itself was a form of art, since it became grist for the tabloid press, generating headlines similar to those featured in his "disaster" paintings. But artistic pretense could not alleviate the ongoing effects of Warhol's injuries, from which he never fully healed. He was forced to wear a corset for the rest of his life to hold his body together, and the unsightly scars left by his wounds served as ongoing reminders of his vulnerability.

Professionally, Warhol responded to his shooting by making the Factory more exclusive, restricting access to those he knew—which by the late 1960s and 1970s meant other celebrities. He also retreated into the world of Manhattan glitter, becoming a fixture during the late 1970s at the legendary disco Studio 54, where he mingled with the "beautiful people" who congregated there. He now was known more for his paintings of the wealthy and well-known than for productions of "Pop" images. By accepting portrait assignments on commission, Warhol was becoming more of a mainstream artist, relying on "patrons" for a living. His other pursuits, which included the celebrity gossip magazine *Interview* as well as television programs and modeling assignments, further diminished his "cutting edge" reputation. A humiliating incident in 1985, when a woman ripped off his wig during a book signing, may have symbolized his descent into the mundane. Obsessed by image, Warhol was now losing control over his own. With his weaknesses exposed, the pretense of celebrity and glamour disappeared. Warhol became merely a balding middle-aged man who wore a corset.

His end was equally mundane. On February 20, 1987, Warhol entered New York Hospital for a routine gallbladder operation. The surgery was successful, but while recuperating he suddenly went into cardiac arrest and died on the morning of February 22 at the age of fifty-eight. He was buried beside his parents in a Pittsburgh cemetery; a friend dropped a bottle of Estee Lauder perfume and copies of *Interview* into his grave.[6]

Warhol also returned home to Pittsburgh in another sense. In 1994, the Andy Warhol Museum opened in the city. It has become not only the largest Warhol repository in the world but also America's largest museum devoted to one artist. The paintings, illustrations, photographs, films, videos, and recordings it contains, along with the trove of "objects" he acquired throughout his life, commemorate both Warhol and the America of his imagination. Warhol's America was defined by what it produced and consumed. It was a place where everything, including celebrity, was an object to be admired and possessed. Both Whittaker Chambers and Allen Ginsberg worried—from different perspectives—about America's soul (see Chapters 11 and 12). Warhol harbored no such concerns. He showed America as it was, with no remonstrance or apology.

Warhol never expressed an interest in politics and it did not play a major role in his work. Nonetheless, his art raised serious questions about America's political culture. Did a nation that offered only "fifteen minutes of fame" to each of its citizens offer enough? Was individual identity possible in a modern mass society? Could a people who measured their worth almost exclusively in terms of material possessions and "objects" be considered "equal" and "free"? Did America's meaning lie solely in its capacity to produce and consume? Without this, did "American" identity exist? And did the average American's comfortable material life come at the price of injustice and exploitation? Warhol did not come to grips with these questions, but a group of young radicals forming at roughly the same time Warhol was ascending the ladder of the American art world confronted them head on. That group, Students for a Democratic Society, or SDS, would seek to use its answers to remake the American conversation over the course of the tumultuous 1960s.

Questions for Consideration and Conversation

1. What was Andy Warhol's vision of the "America" his art captured?
2. How was Warhol's American vision the same as Allen Ginsberg's (Chapter 12)? How was it different?
3. What did Warhol's well-known remark that "in the future everyone will be famous for fifteen minutes" say about individual identity in modern America? Had celebrity become America's defining "product"?
4. How did Warhol and Robert and Helen Lynd (Chapter 7) interpret American consumerism and materialism in different ways? What might Whittaker Chambers (Chapter 11) have said about Warhol's art?
5. Was Warhol an egalitarian? Or an elitist? Or both?
6. Why were the 1960s a perfect time for Warhol's art, and Pop Art generally?
7. What might members of Students for a Democratic Society (Chapter 17) have said if they attended an exhibition of Warhol's work?

Endnotes

1. Wayne Koestenbaum, *Andy Warhol* (New York: Viking Penguin, 2001), 10.
2. Justin Kaplan, ed., *Bartlett's Familiar Quotations*, 16th ed. (Boston: Little Brown, 1992), 758.
3. Andy Warhol, *The Philosophy of Andy Warhol: From A to B and Back Again* (New York: Harcourt Brace Jovanovich, 1977), 100–01.
4. Koestenbaum, *Andy Warhol*, 63.
5. Ibid., 149.
6. Ibid., 214.

ANDY WARHOL, *TWO HUNDRED CAMPBELL'S SOUP CANS* (1962)

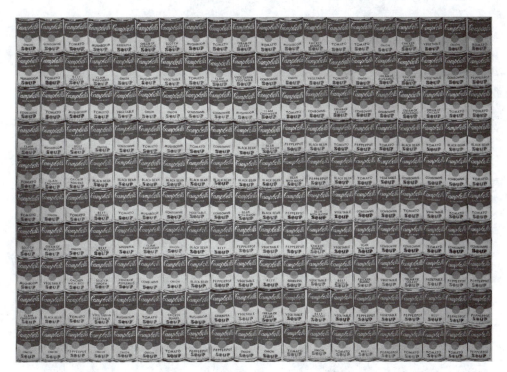

Source: © 2012 The Andy Warhol Foundation for the Visual Arts, Inc./Artists Rights Society (ARS), New York.

ANDY WARHOL, *FIVE COKE BOTTLES* (1962)

Source: © 2012 The Andy Warhol Foundation for the Visual Arts, Inc. / Artists Rights Society (ARS), New York.

CHAPTER 17

Students for a Democratic Society Revives American Radicalism

"We regard men as infinitely precious and possessed of unfulfilled capacities for reason, freedom, and love."

Early in the morning of June 16, 1962, the members of a fledgling youth group called Students for a Democratic Society (SDS) stood on the banks of Lake Huron and watched the sun rise over the Michigan shore. After an all-night debate, they had adopted a manifesto, titled the "Port Huron Statement," that they believed would change the course of American history. As they stood in the gathering light, some holding hands, emotions ran high. "It was exalting," one recalled. "We felt that we were different, and that we were going to do things differently....It felt like the dawn of a new age."[1]

SDS was the most visible manifestation of what was known as the "New Left" in the United States during the 1960s. The word "new," of course, implies the existence of an "old," and the students who gathered in Port Huron, Michigan, were well aware of what had come before them. Many were the children of socialists, communists, unionists, and liberals who had come of age during the New Deal and who were referred to as the "Old Left." The Old Left's concerns were with class issues, the labor movement, and the Soviet Union. By the 1950s, most Old Leftists had in fact become as obsessed with the USSR, and Communism generally, as Whittaker Chambers (see Chapter 11). Sectarian disputes over whether communists should be allowed to participate in political life and whether alliances with them were productive or foolhardy dominated discussion to the virtual exclusion of all else. As a result, by the beginning of the 1960s, Old Leftists occupied a narrow corner of the American political landscape. Some worked within the Democratic Party, settling for the incremental changes that traditional politics offered. Others retained affiliations with socialist groups whose miniscule memberships rendered them virtually powerless. There was little room for the young in the Old Left.

This is what brought the members of SDS to Port Huron in June 1962. Almost two centuries earlier, the revolutionary pamphleteer Thomas Paine wrote: "We have it in our power to begin the world over again."[2] The young leftists of SDS felt the same way. They wished to create a new, revitalized left in America, unencumbered by the preoccupations of past generations and armed with the power to speak to new American constituencies in the cause of transformative change. Like the Beats, whom they admired (see Chapter 12), SDS activists sought to use close interpersonal relationships—what they called "the beloved community"—as an instrument of that change.

But SDS also employed politics in ways the Beats could never have imagined. They broadened the scope of "politics" beyond the traditional areas of voting, lobbying, and legislation to include direct action, including demonstrations, sit-ins, and civil disobedience. In this, they drew inspiration from the civil rights movement and the Student Nonviolent Coordinating Committee (SNCC). SNCC grew out of the February 1960 lunch counter sit-ins conducted by black students in Greensboro, North Carolina, and along with Dr. Martin Luther King, Jr.,'s Southern Christian Leadership Conference, became the civil rights movement's driving force. SNCC members were known for taking direct action against racial segregation by deliberately violating unjust laws and accepting harsh punishments with courage and dignity. Thus, armed with a transformative vision, a new perspective on politics, and an inspirational example, SDS set out to shake America to its roots.

Given its youthful orientation, there was some irony in the fact that SDS's origins lay in the Old Left. SDS began its existence as the student wing of the League for Industrial Democracy (LID), a labor-oriented group with ties to the Socialist Party. LID was composed of aging veterans of the labor organizing wars of the 1930s and 1940s who were now militant anticommunists. In 1958, Al Haber, a student and activist at the University of Michigan at Ann Arbor, became the leader of the local branch of the Student League for Industrial Democracy. Haber renamed the group "Students for a Democratic Society" in early 1960 and began to reshape it as an independent organization, the voice of the alienated and disaffected on campus.

Haber had less faith in unions as agents of change than he did in universities. The years following the end of World War II had seen an upsurge in college enrollments and a massive expansion of university resources. Much of this growth was a result of government defense contracts. By the early 1960s the Cold War had built what was labeled the "multiversity." Massive, impersonal, and bureaucratic, the multiversity rewarded conformity in the classroom and obedience in campus behavior. It seemed designed to crush imagination and creativity. But in the midst of this unpromising environment, Haber saw hope, in the form of the students themselves. Their growing influence and sheer weight of numbers held the potential for massive societal change—if their energy could be harnessed and channeled.

Haber soon had a crucial ally, a SDS recruit named Tom Hayden, who would become the principal author of the Port Huron Statement and the public voice of the group through most of the 1960s. Hayden was precisely the kind of student Haber wished SDS to attract. A senior at Michigan in 1961 and the editor of the campus newspaper, Hayden was a brilliant writer, charismatic speaker, and natural leader. Born in 1939 to working-class Catholic parents, Hayden grew up near Detroit. Imbued with a strong sense of social justice, he was influenced by Beat writer Jack Kerouac's *On the Road* (see Chapter 12) and its powerful depiction of an alternative set of personal relationships based on community and love. Hayden was also inspired by the moral example of Martin Luther King, Jr., who he interviewed for the Michigan student newspaper in 1960. King's philosophy was: "Stop writing, start acting."[3] Hayden resolved to take it to heart.

Hayden came to SDS with a dream of a regenerated American democracy. What if Americans could create a "beloved community" built around trust, empathy, and kindness, instead of competition, materialism, and envy? What if individuals could participate directly in the decisions that determined their lives, rather than ceding authority to politicians, businessmen, and bureaucrats? What if students could be the driving force of a movement that would put an end to racial injustice, poverty, nuclear fear, imperialism, and the Cold War? Hayden began to recruit students who shared these dreams, first at Michigan and then at chapters that he and Haber helped form on other campuses.

At first progress was slow. A planning conference in December 1961 drew only forty-five delegates to Ann Arbor. But at the conference, a decision was made that would change SDS. Hayden was selected to draft an organizational manifesto, containing principles, goals, and strategies. It would be presented to the group at its convention in Port Huron the following June. Working steadily through the winter and spring of 1962, Hayden finished his draft just in time for the convention.

Hayden constructed the manifesto around the idea of "participatory democracy," which he borrowed from Arnold Kaufman, one of his University of Michigan professors. Hayden dedicated the manifesto—which SDS renamed a less doctrinaire sounding "statement"—to "the ancient, still unfulfilled conception of man attaining determining influence over his circumstances of life."[4] Hayden distinguished "participatory" from "representative" democracy, in which elected officials made decisions on behalf of "the people." Hayden instead envisioned "the people" themselves making these decisions through "face-to-face" discussions among equal citizens.[5] The mass society that was post–World War II America precluded true democracy. Only by bringing power back to the grassroots and allowing all to participate could the nation's democratic promise be realized. Hayden coupled this idea with a related one: the perfectibility of mankind. "We regard *men* as infinitely precious and possessed of unfulfilled capacities for reason, freedom, and love," he wrote (with the casual attitude toward women customary for the day even among radicals). "...Men have unrealized potential for self-cultivation, self-direction, self-understanding, and creativity."[6] Hayden believed that participatory democracy would encourage these qualities, bringing out the best in man and freeing him to create a new America.

Hayden then described that new America. Politically, it would guarantee that every individual voice be heard and accounted for. No longer would "power elites"—governmental authorities, businessmen, bureaucrats, the military—dominate public discourse. In a participatory democracy, "politics has the function of bringing people out of isolation and into community," as a "means of finding meaning in personal life."[7] In Hayden's view, political activity did more than affect policy. It also promoted the discovery of the authentic self, an almost mystical goal not far removed from that of Ginsberg and the Beats (see Chapter 12).

Hayden's economic program was socialist in orientation. It involved what he termed "democratic social regulation" of industry and business that would remedy modern American capitalism's inequities. "Although our technology is destroying old and creating new forms of social organization," Hayden wrote, referring to the growing trend of automation, "men still tolerate meaningless work and idleness."[8] Economic life, he argued, "should involve incentives worthier than money or survival. It should be educative, not stultifying; creative, not mechanical; self-directed, not manipulated, encouraging independence, a respect for others, a sense of dignity, and a willingness to accept social responsibility...."[9] Hayden envisioned a sweeping redefinition of work in American society, echoing the classic Marxist critique of capitalist labor relations. He rejected the idea of a materially rich but spiritually barren economic system, much as did the Lynds, Ginsberg, and Chambers, challenging America to leaven its massive productivity with human values (see Chapters 7, 11–12).

Hayden applied his faith in human potential and in democracy to the specific problems confronting the United States in 1962. He argued for a reduction of Cold War tensions with the Soviet Union, viewing the two sides as equally complicit in a race to nuclear Armageddon. He criticized an unreasoning anticommunism that stifled domestic political discussion and hurt the cause of peace. Hayden advocated a massive war on poverty using monies saved from reductions in military spending, and the creation of a "public sector" of the economy devoted expressly to human needs.[10] He called on unions to transcend narrow wage-and-hour concerns to achieve a "synthesis of the civil rights, peace, and economic reform movements."[11] He identified the "military-industrial complex"—a term coined by President Dwight Eisenhower to denote the mutually beneficial economic relationship between the business sector and the armed services—as the driving force behind an American imperialism that exploited poor and non-white people around the world.

Hayden also criticized the role played by major American universities in the military–industrial complex through research contracts awarded by the Department of Defense. He linked SDS and the student generation to anticolonialism abroad and civil rights at home. Hayden placed students at the center of the revolution he hoped to inspire. He understood that universities, as repositories of knowledge in a modern, information-based society, were immensely potent and influential. Controlling the university meant controlling the levers and gears of American power. Students were future leaders. What began on college campuses would eventually transform the nation. Universities, Hayden concluded, were the incubators of revolt and change.

Fifty-nine delegates gathered at Port Huron on June 12, 1962, to debate the draft of Hayden's statement. They took SDS's core principle of participatory democracy to heart, dividing the document into sections and assigning small groups to work on revisions and additions. The delegates would then meet as a whole to approve the final version. A controversy over SDS's position on anticommunism developed on the convention's second day, when the delegates discussed whether to seat a member of a Communist Party youth group as an observer. This aroused the ire of SDS's sponsors at LID, which had sent representatives to insure that the students followed their "line." They objected to any association with communists, as well as to what they considered Hayden's moral equation of the United States and the Soviet Union in Cold War politics. In a gesture of defiance, the SDS delegates voted to seat the communist-affiliated observer, symbolizing their break with the Old Left and its ideological fixations.

The small groups charged with revising Hayden's draft changed some of his language and rearranged the order of some sections. On the morning of Friday, June 15, the Port Huron Statement was brought before the entire body. The discussion lasted through the day and into the night, as the delegates argued over concrete issues (what would be the statement's position on Communism?) and those of a more abstract nature (is man perfectible?). Finally, at five o' clock on the morning of Saturday, June 16, the final touches were added and the statement adopted by the convention. Tom Hayden was elected SDS president, and the delegates, their work done, walked down to the shore of Lake Huron to greet the sunrise. They were ready to make history.

SDS's prospects, however, were far from certain. In 1962, the United States was not involved in a major land war. It was relatively prosperous. It was also generally supportive of the policies of President John F. Kennedy (JFK), whose image was that of a youthful and vigorous reformer. But the national landscape would change rapidly. Just two years later in 1964, SDS's outlook was more favorable. By then the charismatic JFK was dead. The new president was Lyndon Johnson (see Chapter 19), a drawling, lumbering Texan who appeared to represent an earlier political generation. The civil rights movement was moving from integration to confrontation. In Mississippi, the Freedom Summer voter registration drive, in which both SDS and SNCC participated, was marred by the murder of three civil rights workers by white vigilantes and by strife between black and white activists over leadership of the project. At the 1964 Democratic National Convention, the Mississippi Freedom Democratic Party, an interracial group formed to challenge the segregated regular Mississippi delegation, was denied official seating status on Johnson's orders, souring SNCC and SDS on the possibilities of change through traditional electoral politics. Also that year, the first wave of what would become a series of racially charged civil disturbances rolled through urban ghettos.

Above all, there was Vietnam. On August 7, 1964, President Johnson secured the Gulf of Tonkin Resolution from Congress in response to an alleged attack by North Vietnamese gunboats on patrolling American ships. The resolution permitted Johnson to drastically increase the number of U.S. ground troops in Vietnam, as well as launch large scale, systematic bombing raids on North Vietnamese targets (see Chapter 19). The troop escalations and bombings would continue over the next four years. In 1968 there were over 500,000 Americans serving in Vietnam, and the United States had dropped more bombs on the country than it deployed in all of World War II.

By the mid-1960s, the war was a looming presence in university life. While student deferments were available, draft notices awaited once college was done. SDS's antiwar message, which it had crafted before the Vietnam conflict escalated, now gained traction on American campuses. SDS was "out front" on Vietnam, protesting the Gulf of Tonkin resolution as soon as it was adopted, and taking ownership of the issues of war and imperialism. It sponsored the initial "teach-in" against the war in March 1965, staging an all-night occupation of a University of Michigan building. On April 17 of that year, SDS led the nation's first major antiwar demonstration, rallying in front of the White House and the Washington Monument. Paul Potter, who had succeeded Hayden as SDS president, addressed the crowd of over 15,000:

> What we must do is begin to build a democratic and humane society in which human life and initiative are precious...What kind of system is it that justifies the United States or any country seizing the destinies of the Vietnamese people and using them callously for its own purpose? What kind of system is it that....creates faceless and terrible bureaucracies and makes those the place where people spend their lives and do their work, that consistently puts material values before human values?....What place is there for ordinary men in that system, and how are they to control it, make it bend itself to their wills rather than bending them to its? We must name that system. We must name it, describe it, analyze it, understand it and change it.[12]

Potter's words drew a standing ovation from the protesters. Inspired, they marched en masse on the Capitol.

SDS had become the vanguard of the antiwar movement and the campus organization of choice for the politically engaged on American campuses. By late 1965 it had 10,000 members in chapters across the country, a number that would grow to some 100,000 by 1968.[13] But with that growth came strains that exposed contradictions that the group's founders had been able to ignore at Port Huron in 1962. "Participatory democracy" was a workable idea for fifty-nine men and women who were personal friends and shared a commitment to open, inclusive deliberation. It was considerably more problematic in a mass organization with a far-flung membership that bore some resemblance to the clogged bureaucracies SDS leaders purported to oppose. Beginning in 1965 the SDS national office was wracked by bitter disputes between participatory democracy literalists who demanded that every question be debated exhaustively and those who believed that an effective organization required strong central leadership. As the anticentralizers gained sway, membership applications piled up unanswered and local chapters were left to drift without direction. In one extreme example of participatory democracy run amok, a group of SDSers working on an antipoverty project in Cleveland held a twenty-four-hour meeting to decide whether to take a day off and go to the beach.[14]

By the late 1960s, SDS was factionalized and divided, much like any mass organization with multiple constituencies. The antiwar movement had given SDS impressive membership numbers but no coherent direction. Should SDS move off college campuses and attempt to organize white workers? Or were working-class whites too conservative to be reached by appeals to interracial class solidarity? What about the black poor? Could they ally with students in common cause against the War in Vietnam or would racial barriers stand in the way? Was SDS's true home on college campuses among white middle-class students who had developed their own culture of music, dress, drugs, and personal behavior—what became known as the "counterculture"? Did this new culture have the power to influence those residing beyond university walls? Opinion within SDS on these questions varied widely, and without a strong central leadership no core policy emerged on any of them.

Tension also existed within SDS between individual and group prerogatives. "The goal of man and society," Hayden had argued in the Port Huron Statement, "should be human independence: a concern...with finding a meaning in life that is personally authentic."[15] Yet Hayden had also written that "human interdependence is contemporary fact; human brotherhood must be willed....Personal links between man and man are needed...."[16] How could the "beloved community" be squared with "personal authenticity"? Hayden knew that only through group solidarity and sacrifice could SDS accomplish its goals. But he also knew that individuals in SDS were free only insofar as they could follow their own moral guides. Forced "interdependence" smacked of totalitarianism. The extremes of personal "independence" bred self-indulgence and anarchy. Hayden had put his faith in human perfectibility. Perhaps, he ruefully admitted years later, he had hoped for too much.[17]

By the time he participated in the August 1968 antiwar demonstrations at the Democratic National Convention in Chicago, Tom Hayden was one of the most well-known radical leaders in the United States. As such, he was an obvious target for the city's police, who arrested him twice and threatened to kill him. Hayden was forced to don a disguise on the demonstration's climactic night, when Chicago officers unleashed a vicious assault on the protesters in what later would be described in a government-sponsored report as a "police riot."[18] Hayden was nonetheless indicted and tried for inciting violence as part of a group of radicals popularly known as the "Chicago Seven." He was found guilty in February 1970 and sentenced to a five-year prison term, which he never served; his conviction was overturned on appeal due to judicial and prosecutorial bias. Hayden went on to a career in the representative democracy he had disdained in the Port Huron Statement, becoming active in California Democratic Party politics. He served as a state assemblyman and senator between 1982 and 2000 and ran unsuccessfully for mayor of Los Angeles in 1997.

SDS, in which Hayden had invested so much hope, imploded from within in 1969. That year, a faction affiliated with the Progressive Labor Party (PLP), a Marxist group that supported the violent rising of the international proletariat and regarded Chinese dictator Mao Tse-tung as a hero and role model, took control of the organization. In the hands of the PLP zealots, SDS became the totalitarian caricature that its initial Old Left sponsors in LID had feared, and that the young idealists who had adopted the Port Huron Statement had vowed to reject. SDS meetings degenerated into propaganda sessions with ritualized slogan chanting and displays of Mao's "Little Red Book" of revolutionary quotations. An even more extreme faction that called itself the "Weathermen"—so named after a line from a Bob Dylan song that proclaimed, "you don't need a weatherman to know which way the wind blows"—left SDS in the wake of the PLP takeover and engaged in a series of attacks on government buildings and installations that traumatized the nation. In 1970, a Weathermen explosives "factory" in a Greenwich Village townhouse blew up, killing three members and sending the survivors into hiding. As the "Weather Underground," the group dodged authorities for over a decade, becoming notorious for bombings of the Capitol Building in 1971 and the Pentagon in 1972, as well as for a 1981 robbery of a Brinks security truck that left three dead. Eventually all members surrendered or were captured. Some continue to serve time in prison.

SDS's end was a mockery of its beginnings. Authoritarian, rigid, violent, and ideologically fanatical, it bore no resemblance to the group whose members held hands on the shore of Lake Huron in June 1962. Needless to say, many of SDS's dreams went unrealized. The group never broadened its reach beyond its campus constituency. Intent on creating a "new" left in America that would be distinct from the "old," it rejected opportunities for beneficial coalitions with liberals, socialists, and labor groups. Determined to remain "authentic," SDS spurned the compromises and bargains of traditional party politics. Its attempts to reach out to white workers fell victim to class and cultural differences. Despite its overtures to the black poor— SDS sponsored a community-organizing program in urban ghettos—racial tensions and misunderstandings sabotaged any opportunities for lasting alliances. Its devotion to forging "personal links between man and man" did not extend to women, who rarely attained positions of power within the organization.[19] SDS did not even achieve its primary goal of ending the War in Vietnam, which ground on for years after the group's demise.

But in spite of its failings and disappointments, SDS changed the American conversation. Like the Declaration of Independence and the Gettysburg Address, the Port Huron Statement articulated a set of ideals that while not completely fulfilled were notable for their very existence. The Port Huron Statement is best viewed as a series of American challenges. Can America offer individual citizens a truly participatory voice in their democracy? Can it give them a meaningful identity in a mass society? Can it break down bureaucratic walls to foster a more humane society? Can it create a "beloved community"? Can it rid itself of poverty and want? Can it accord African Americans full equality? Can it live in peace with its ideological rivals? The Port Huron Statement asked Americans to imagine new possibilities for themselves and their country. It shifted the ground under Lyndon Johnson (see Chapter 19) and Ronald Reagan (see Chapter 21), forcing both to conduct the American conversation on altered terrain. It made Robert Putnam (see Chapter 22) think about the nature of civic engagement in the United States and the ways in which engaged citizens can create true American communities. It even prompted feminist writer and activist Jo Freeman (see Chapter 20) to consider how women could use the politics of participatory democracy to gain personal freedom. Like a stone thrown in a pool, the Port Huron Statement produced ripples that carried to far shores. It stands as one of the most successful "failures" in American history.

Questions for Consideration and Conversation

1. Why were New Leftists, like the members of Students for a Democratic Society (SDS), so contemptuous of the "Old Left"? Did they have a right to be?

2. How did SDS members resemble the "Beats" (Chapter 12)? How were they different?

3. How was SDS inspired by the civil rights movement?

4. Why did Tom Hayden and his fellow SDS members believe so strongly in the idea of "participatory democracy"? What did it mean to them? Did they expect too much of it?

5. Why did SDS members argue that students and universities could be the engines of transformative change in America? Do you think they were correct?

6. Why couldn't SDS, and the New Left generally, construct a lasting alliance with white workers? African Americans? Women?

7. Why was Vietnam the "perfect issue" for SDS?

8. Why did SDS fail? *Did* it fail?

Endnotes

1. Sharon Jeffrey, quoted in James Miller, *"Democracy Is in the Streets": From Port Huron to the Siege of Chicago* (New York: Simon and Schuster, 1987), 125.
2. Thomas Paine, "Common Sense" in Philip S. Foner, ed., *The Complete Writings of Thomas Paine*, Vol. I (New York: The Citadel Press, 1945), 45.
3. See Miller, *"Democracy Is in the Streets,"* 48.
4. Port Huron Statement, in Miller, *"Democracy Is in the Streets,"* 331.
5. C. Wright Mills, quoted in Miller, *"Democracy Is in the Streets,"* 84.
6. Port Huron Statement, in Miller, *"Democracy Is in the Streets,"* 332.
7. Ibid., 333.
8. Ibid., 330.
9. Ibid., 333.
10. Ibid., 363.
11. Ibid., 371.
12. Paul Potter, quoted in Miller, *"Democracy Is in the Streets,"* 232–33.
13. Miller, *"Democracy Is in the Streets,"* 259.
14. Ibid., 207.
15. Port Huron Statement, in Miller, *"Democracy Is in the Streets,"* 332.
16. Ibid.
17. See Miller, *"Democracy Is in the Streets,"* 325.
18. See National Commission on the Causes and Prevention of Violence ("Walker Commission"), *Rights in Conflict: Convention Week in Chicago, August 25–29, 1968* (New York: E.P. Dutton, 1968).
19. Port Huron Statement, in Miller, *"Democracy Is in the Streets,"* 332.

STUDENTS FOR A DEMOCRATIC SOCIETY, PORT HURON STATEMENT (1962)

Introduction: Agenda For a Generation

We are people of this generation, bred in at least modest comfort, housed now in universities, looking uncomfortably to the world we inherit.

When we were kids the United States was the wealthiest and strongest country in the world: the only one with the atom bomb, the least scarred by modern war, an initiator of the United Nations that we thought would distribute Western influence throughout the world. Freedom and equality for each individual, government of, by, and for the people—these American values we found good, principles by which we could live as men. Many of us began maturing in complacency.

As we grew, however, our comfort was penetrated by events too troubling to dismiss. First, the permeating and victimizing fact of human degradation, symbolized by the Southern struggle against racial bigotry, compelled most of us from silence to activism. Second, the enclosing fact of the Cold War, symbolized by the presence of the Bomb, brought awareness that we ourselves, and our friends, and millions of abstract "others" we knew more directly because of our common peril, might die at any time. We might deliberately ignore, or avoid, or fail to feel all other human problems, but not these two, for these were too immediate and crushing in their impact, too challenging in the demand that we as individuals take the responsibility for encounter and resolution.

While these and other problems either directly oppressed us or rankled our consciences and became our own subjective concerns, we began to see complicated and disturbing paradoxes in our surrounding America. The declaration "all men are created equal..." rang hollow before the facts of Negro life in the South and the big cities of the North. The proclaimed peaceful intentions of the United States contradicted its economic and military investments in the Cold War status quo.

We witnessed, and continue to witness, other paradoxes. With nuclear energy whole cities can easily be powered, yet the dominant nation states seem more likely to unleash destruction greater than that incurred in all wars of human history. Although our own technology is destroying old and creating new forms of social organization, men still tolerate meaningless work and idleness. While two-thirds of mankind suffers undernourishment, our own upper classes revel amidst superfluous abundance. Although world population is expected to double in forty years, the nations still tolerate anarchy as a major principle of international conduct and uncontrolled exploitation governs the sapping of the earth's physical resources. Although mankind desperately needs revolutionary leadership, America rests in national stalemate, its goals ambiguous and tradition-bound instead of informed and clear, its democratic system apathetic and manipulated rather than "of, by, and for the people."

Not only did tarnish appear on our image of American virtue, not only did disillusion occur when the hypocrisy of American ideals was discovered, but we began to sense that what we had originally seen as the American Golden Age was actually the decline of an era. The worldwide outbreak of revolution against colonialism and imperialism, the entrenchment of totalitarian states, the menace of war, overpopulation, international disorder, super technology—these trends were testing the tenacity of our own commitment to democracy and freedom and our abilities to visualize their application to a world in upheaval.

Our work is guided by the sense that we may be the last generation in the experiment with living. But we are a minority—the vast majority of our people regard the temporary equilibriums of our society and world as eternally functional parts. In this is perhaps the outstanding paradox: we ourselves are imbued with urgency, yet the message of our society is that there is no viable alternative to the present. Beneath the reassuring tones of the politicians, beneath the common opinion that America will "muddle through", beneath the stagnation of those who have closed their minds to the future, is the pervading feeling that there simply are no alternatives, that our times have witnessed the exhaustion not only of Utopias, but of any new departures as well. Feeling the press of complexity upon the emptiness of life, people are fearful of the thought that at any moment things might thrust out of control. They fear change itself, since change might smash whatever invisible framework seems to hold back chaos for them now. For most Americans, all crusades are suspect, threatening. The fact that each individual sees apathy in his fellows perpetuates the common reluctance to organize for change. The dominant institutions are complex enough to blunt the minds of their potential critics, and entrenched enough to swiftly dissipate or entirely repel the energies of protest and reform, thus limiting human expectancies. Then, too, we are a materially improved society, and by our own improvements we seem to have weakened the case for further change.

Some would have us believe that Americans feel contentment amidst prosperity—but might it not better be called a glaze above deeply felt anxieties about their role in the new world? And if these anxieties produce a developed indifference to human affairs, do they not as well produce a yearning to believe there is an alternative to the present, that something can be done to change circumstances in the school, the workplaces, the bureaucracies, the government? It is to this latter yearning, at once the spark and engine of change, that we direct our present appeal. The search for truly democratic alternatives to the present, and a commitment to social experimentation with them, is a worthy and fulfilling human enterprise, one which moves us and, we hope, others today. On such a basis do we offer this document of our convictions and analysis: as an effort in understanding and changing the conditions of humanity in the late twentieth century, an effort rooted in the ancient, still unfulfilled conception of man attaining determining influence over his circumstances of life.

Values

Making values explicit—an initial task in establishing alternatives—is an activity that has been devalued and corrupted. The conventional moral terms of the age, the politician moralities—"free world", "people's democracies"—reflect realities poorly, if at all, and seem to function more as ruling myths than as descriptive principles. But neither has our experience in the universities brought as moral enlightenment. Our professors and administrators sacrifice controversy to public relations; their curriculums change more slowly than the living events of the world; their skills and silence are purchased by investors in the arms race; passion is called unscholastic. The questions we might want raised—what is really important? can we live in a different and better way? if we wanted to change society, how would we do it?—are not thought to be questions of a "fruitful, empirical nature", and thus are brushed aside.

Unlike youth in other countries we are used to moral leadership being exercised and moral dimensions being clarified by our elders. But today, for us, not even the liberal and socialist preachments of the past seem adequate to the forms of the present. Consider the old slogans; Capitalism Cannot Reform Itself, United Front Against Fascism, General Strike, All Out on May Day. Or, more recently, No Cooperation with Commies and Fellow Travellers, Ideologies Are Exhausted, Bipartisanship, No Utopias. These are incomplete, and there are few new prophets. It has been said that our liberal and socialist predecessors were plagued by vision without program, while our own generation is plagued by program without vision. All around us there is astute grasp of method, technique—the committee, the ad hoc group, the lobbyist, that hard and soft sell, the make, the projected image—but, if pressed critically, such expertise is incompetent to explain its implicit ideals. It is highly fashionable to identify oneself by old categories, or by naming a respected political figure, or by explaining "how we would vote" on various issues.

Theoretic chaos has replaced the idealistic thinking of old—and, unable to reconstitute theoretic order, men have condemned idealism itself. Doubt has replaced hopefulness—and men act out a defeatism that is labeled realistic. The decline of utopia and hope is in fact one of the defining features of social life today. The reasons are various: the dreams of the older left were perverted by Stalinism and never recreated; the congressional stalemate makes men narrow their view of the possible; the specialization of human activity leaves little room for sweeping thought; the horrors of the twentieth century, symbolized in the gas-ovens and concentration camps and atom bombs, have blasted hopefulness. To be idealistic is to be considered apocalyptic, deluded. To have no serious aspirations, on the contrary, is to be "tough minded".

In suggesting social goals and values, therefore, we are aware of entering a sphere of some disrepute. Perhaps matured by the past, we have no sure formulas, no closed theories—but that does not mean values are beyond discussion and tentative determination. A first task of any social movement is to convenience people that the search for orienting theories and the creation of human values is complex but worthwhile. We are aware that to avoid platitudes we must analyze the concrete conditions of social order. But to direct such an analysis we must use the guideposts of basic principles. Our own social values involve conceptions of human beings, human relationships, and social systems.

We regard *men* as infinitely precious and possessed of unfulfilled capacities for reason, freedom, and love. In affirming these principles we are aware of countering perhaps the dominant conceptions of man in the twentieth century: that he is a thing to be manipulated, and that he is inherently incapable of directing his own affairs. We oppose the depersonalization that reduces human beings to the status of things—if anything, the brutalities of the twentieth century teach that means and ends are intimately related, that vague appeals to "posterity" cannot justify the mutilations of the present. We oppose, too, the doctrine of human incompetence because it rests essentially on the modern fact that men have been "competently" manipulated into incompetence—we see little reason why men cannot meet with increasing skill the complexities and responsibilities of their situation, if society is organized not for minority, but for majority, participation in decision-making.

Men have unrealized potential for self-cultivation, self-direction, self-understanding, and creativity. It is this potential that we regard as crucial and to which we appeal, not to the human potentiality for violence, unreason, and submission to authority. The goal of man and society should be human independence: a concern not with image of popularity but with finding a meaning in life that is personally authentic: a quality of mind not compulsively driven by a sense of powerlessness, nor one which unthinkingly adopts status values, nor one which represses all threats to its habits, but one which has full, spontaneous access to present and past experiences, one which easily unites the fragmented parts of personal history, one which openly faces problems which are troubling and unresolved: one with an intuitive awareness of possibilities, an active sense of curiosity, an ability and willingness to learn.

This kind of independence does not mean egoistic individualism—the object is not to have one's way so much as it is to have a way that is one's own. Nor do we deify man—we merely have faith in his potential.

Human relationships should involve fraternity and honesty. Human interdependence is contemporary fact; human brotherhood must be willed however, as a condition of future survival and as the most appropriate form of social relations. Personal links between man and man are needed, especially to go beyond the partial and fragmentary bonds of function that bind men only as worker to worker, employer to employee, teacher to student, American to Russian.

Loneliness, estrangement, isolation describe the vast distance between man and man today. These dominant tendencies cannot be overcome by better personnel management, nor by improved gadgets, but only when a love of man overcomes the idolatrous worship of things by man. As the individualism we affirm is not egoism, the selflessness we affirm is not self-elimination. On the contrary, we believe in generosity of a kind that imprints one's unique individual qualities in the relation to other men, and to all human activity. Further, to dislike isolation is not to favor the abolition of privacy; the latter differs from isolation in that it occurs or is abolished according to individual will. Finally, we would replace power and personal uniqueness rooted in possession, privilege, or circumstance by power and uniqueness rooted in love, reflectiveness, reason, and creativity.

As a social system we seek the establishment of a democracy of individual participation, governed by two central aims: that the individual share in those social decisions determining the quality and direction of his life; that society be organized to encourage independence in men and provide the media for their common participation. In a participatory democracy, the political life would be based in several root principles:

- that decision-making of basic social consequence be carried on by public groupings;
- that politics be seen positively, as the art of collectively creating an acceptable pattern of social relations;
- that politics has the function of bringing people out of isolation and into community, thus being a necessary, though not sufficient, means of finding meaning in personal life;
- that the political order should serve to clarify problems in a way instrumental to their solution; it should provide outlets for the expression of personal grievance and aspiration; opposing views should be organized so as to illuminate choices and facilitate the attainment of goals;

channels should be commonly available to relate men to knowledge and to power so that private problems—from bad recreation facilities to personal alienation—are formulated as general issues.

The economic sphere would have as its basis the principles:

- that work should involve incentives worthier than money or survival. It should be educative, not stultifying; creative, not mechanical; self-directed, not manipulated, encouraging independence, a respect for others, a sense of dignity and a willingness to accept social responsibility, since it is this experience that has crucial influence on habits, perceptions and individual ethics;
- that the economic experience is so personally decisive that the individual must share in its full determination;
- that the economy itself is of such social importance that its major resources and means of production should be open to democratic participation and subject to democratic social regulation.

Like the political and economic ones, major social institutions—cultural, education, rehabilitative, and others—should be generally organized with the well-being and dignity of man as the essential measure of success.

In social change or interchange, we find violence to be abhorrent because it requires generally the transformation of the target, be it a human being or a community of people, into a depersonalized object of hate. It is imperative that the means of violence be abolished and the institutions—local, national, international—that encourage nonviolence as a condition of conflict be developed.

These are our central values, in skeletal form. It remains vital to understand their denial or attainment in the context of the modern world.

The Students

In the last few years, thousands of American students demonstrated that they at least felt the urgency of the times. They moved actively and directly against racial injustices, the threat of war, violations of individual rights of conscience and, less frequently, against economic manipulation. They succeeded in restoring a small measure of controversy to the campuses after the stillness of the McCarthy period. They succeeded, too, in gaining some concessions from the people and institutions they opposed, especially in the fight against racial bigotry.

The significance of these scattered movements lies not in their success or failure in gaining objectives—at least not yet. Nor does the significance lie in the intellectual "competence" or "maturity" of the students involved—as some pedantic elders allege. The significance is in the fact the students are breaking the crust of apathy and overcoming the inner alienation that remain the defining characteristics of American college life.

If student movements for change are rarities still on the campus scene, what is commonplace there? The real campus, the familiar campus, is a place of private people, engaged in their notorious "inner emigration." It is a place of commitment to business-as-usual, getting ahead, playing it cool. It is a place of mass affirmation of the Twist, but mass reluctance toward the controversial public stance. Rules are accepted as "inevitable", bureaucracy as "just circumstances", irrelevance as "scholarship", selflessness as "martyrdom", politics as "just another way to make people, and an unprofitable one, too."

Almost no students value activity as a citizen. Passive in public, they are hardly more idealistic in arranging their private lives: Gallup concludes they will settle for "low success, and won't risk high failure." There is not much willingness to take risks (not even in business), no setting of dangerous goals, no real conception of personal identity except one manufactured in the image of others, no real urge for personal fulfillment except to be almost as successful as the very successful people. Attention is being paid to social status (the quality of shirt collars, meeting people, getting wives or husbands, making solid contacts for later on); much too, is paid to academic status (grades, honors, the med school rat-race). But neglected generally is real intellectual status, the personal cultivation of the mind.

"Students don't even give a damn about the apathy," one has said. Apathy toward apathy begets a privately-constructed universe, a place of systematic study schedules, two nights each week for beer, a girl or two, and early marriage; a framework infused with personality, warmth, and under control, no matter how unsatisfying otherwise.

Under these conditions university life loses all relevance to some. Four hundred thousand of our classmates leave college every year.

But apathy is not simply an attitude; it is a product of social institutions, and of the structure and organization of higher education itself. The extracurricular life is ordered according to in loco parentis theory, which ratifies the Administration as the moral guardian of the young. The accompanying "let's pretend" theory of student extracurricular affairs validates student government as a training center for those who want to spend their lives in political pretense, and discourages initiative from more articulate, honest, and sensitive students. The bounds and style of controversy are delimited before controversy begins. The university "prepares" the student for "citizenship" through perpetual rehearsals and, usually, through emasculation of what creative spirit there is in the individual.

The academic life contains reinforcing counterparts to the way in which extracurricular life is organized. The academic world is founded in a teacher-student relation analogous to the parent-child relation which characterizes in loco parentis. Further, academia includes a radical separation of student from the material of study. That which is studied, the social reality, is "objectified" to sterility, dividing the student from life—just as he is restrained in active involvement by the deans controlling student government. The specialization of function and knowledge, admittedly necessary to our complex technological and social structure, has produced and exaggerated compartmentalization of study and understanding. This has contributed to an overly parochial view, by faculty, of the role of its research and scholarship; a discontinuous and truncated understanding, by students, of the surrounding social order; a loss of personal attachment, by nearly all, to the worth of study as a humanistic enterprise.

There is, finally, the cumbersome academic bureaucracy extending throughout the academic as well as extracurricular structures, contributing to the sense of outer complexity and inner powerlessness that transforms so many students from honest searching to ratification of convention and, worse, to a numbness of present and future catastrophes. The size and financing systems of the university enhance the permanent trusteeship of the administrative bureaucracy, their power leading to a shift to the value standards of business and administrative mentality within the university. Huge foundations and other private financial interests shape underfinanced colleges and universities, not only making them more commercial, but less disposed to diagnose society critically, less open to dissent. Many social and physical scientists, neglecting the liberating heritage of higher learning, develop "human relations" or "morale-producing" techniques for the corporate economy, while others exercise their intellectual skills to accelerate the arms race.

Tragically, the university could serve as a significant source of social criticism and an initiator of new modes and molders of attitudes. But the actual intellectual effect of the college experience is hardly distinguishable from that of any other communications channel—say, a television set—passing on the stock truths of the day. Students leave college somewhat more "tolerant" than when they arrived, but basically unchallenged in their values and political orientations. With administrators ordering the institutions, and faculty the curriculum, the student learns by his isolation to accept elite rule within the university, which prepares him to accept later forms of minority control. The real function of the educational system—as opposed to its more rhetorical function of "searching for truth"—is to impart the key information and styles that will help the student get by, modestly but comfortably, in the big society beyond.

The Society Beyond

Look beyond the campus, to America itself. That student life is more intellectual, and perhaps more comfortable, does not obscure the fact that the fundamental qualities of life on the campus reflect the habits of society at large. The fraternity president is seen at the junior manager levels; the sorority queen has gone to Grosse Pointe; the serious poet burns for a place, any place, or work; the once-serious and never serious poets work at the advertising agencies. The desperation of people threatened by forces about which they know little and of which they can say less; the cheerful emptiness of people "giving up" all hope of changing things; the faceless ones polled by Gallup who listed "international affairs" fourteenth on their list of "problems" but who also expected thermonuclear war in the next few years; in these and other forms, Americans are in withdrawal from public life, from any collective effort at directing their own affairs.

Some regard this national doldrums as a sign of healthy approval of the established order—but is it approval by consent or manipulated acquiescence? Others declare that the people are withdrawn because compelling issues are fast disappearing—perhaps there are fewer breadlines in America, but is Jim Crow gone, is there enough work and work more fulfilling, is world war a diminishing threat, and what of the revolutionary new peoples? Still others think the national quietude is a necessary consequence of the need for elites to resolve complex and specialized problems of modern industrial society—but, then, why should business elites help decide foreign policy, and who controls the elites anyway, and are they solving mankind's problems? Others, finally, shrug knowingly and announce that full democracy never worked anywhere in the past—but why lump qualitatively different civilizations together, and how can a social order work well if its best thinkers are skeptics, and is man really doomed forever to the domination of today?

There are no convincing apologies for the contemporary malaise. While the world tumbles toward the final war, while men in other nations are trying desperately to alter events, while the very future qua future is uncertain—America is without community, impulse, without the inner momentum necessary for an age when societies cannot successfully perpetuate themselves by their military weapons, when democracy must be viable because of its quality of life, not its quantity of rockets.

The apathy here is, first subjective—the felt powerlessness of ordinary people, the resignation before the enormity of events. But subjective apathy is encouraged by the objective American situation—the actual structural separation of people from power, from relevant knowledge, from pinnacles of decision-making. Just as the university influences the student way of life, so do major social institutions create the circumstances in which the isolated citizen will try hopelessly to understand his world and himself.

The very isolation of the individual—from power and community and ability to aspire—means the rise of a democracy without publics. With the great mass of people structurally remote and psychologically hesitant with respect to democratic institutions, those institutions themselves attenuate and become, in the fashion of the vicious circle, progressively less accessible to those few who aspire to serious participation in social affairs. The vital democratic connection between community and leadership, between the mass and the several elites, has been so wrenched and perverted that disastrous policies go unchallenged time and again....

Anti-Communism

An unreasoning anti-communism has become a major social problem for those who want to construct a more democratic America. McCarthyism and other forms of exaggerated and conservative anti-communism seriously weaken democratic institutions and spawn movements contrary to the interests of basic freedoms and peace. In such an atmosphere even the most intelligent of Americans fear to join political organizations, sign petitions, speak out on serious issues. Militaristic policies are easily "sold" to a public fearful of a democratic enemy. Political debate is restricted, thought is standardized, action is inhibited by the demands of "unity" and "oneness" in the face of the declared danger. Even many liberals and socialists share static and repetitious participation in the anti-communist crusade and often discourage tentative, inquiring discussion about "the Russian question" within their ranks—often by employing "stalinist", "stalinoid", "trotskyite" and other epithets in an oversimplifying way to discredit opposition.

Thus much of the American anti-communism takes on the characteristics of paranoia. Not only does it lead to the perversion of democracy and to the political stagnation of a warfare society, but it also has the unintended consequence of preventing an honest and effective approach to the issues. Such an approach would require public analysis and debate of world politics. But almost nowhere in politics is such a rational analysis possible to make.

It would seem reasonable to expect that in America the basic issues of the Cold War should be rationally and fully debated, between persons of every opinion—on television, on platforms and through other media. It would seem, too, that there should be a way for the person or an organization to oppose communism without contributing to the common fear of associations and public actions. But these things do not happen; instead, there is finger-pointing and comical debate about the most serious of issues. This trend of events on the domestic scene, towards greater irrationality on major questions, moves us to greater concern than does the "internal threat" of domestic communism. Democracy, we are convinced, requires every effort to set in peaceful opposition the basic viewpoints of the day; only by conscious, determined, though difficult, efforts in this direction will the issue of communism be met appropriately....

Towards American Democracy

Every effort to end the Cold War and expand the process of world industrialization is an effort hostile to people and institutions whose interests lie in perpetuation of the East-West military threat and the postponement of change in the "have not" nations of the world. Every such effort, too, is bound to establish greater democracy in America. The major goals of a domestic effort would be:

1. America must abolish its political party stalemate....
2. Mechanisms of voluntary association must be created through which political information can be imparted and political participation encouraged....
3. Institutions and practices which stifle dissent should be abolished, and the promotion of peaceful dissent should be actively promoted....
4. Corporations must be made publicly responsible....
5. The allocation of resources must be based on social needs. A truly "public sector" must be established, and its nature debated and planned....
6. America should concentrate on its genuine social priorities: abolish squalor, terminate neglect, and establish an environment for people to live in with dignity and creativeness....

Alternatives to Helplessness

The goals we have set are not realizable next month, or even next election—but that fact justifies neither giving up altogether nor a determination to work only on immediate, direct, tangible problems. Both responses are a sign of helplessness, fearfulness of visions, refusal to hope, and tend to bring on the very conditions to be avoided. Fearing vision, we justify rhetoric or myopia. Fearing hope, we reinforce despair.

The first effort, then, should be to state a vision: what is the perimeter of human possibility in this epoch? This we have tried to do. The second effort, if we are to be politically responsible, is to evaluate the prospects for obtaining at least a substantial part of that vision in our epoch: what are the social forces that exist, or that must exist, if we are to be at all successful? And what role have we ourselves to play as a social force?

1. In exploring the existing social forces, note must be taken of the Southern civil rights movement as the most heartening because of the justice it insists upon, exemplary because it indicates that there can be a passage out of apathy.

This movement, pushed into a brilliant new phase by the Montgomery bus boycott and the subsequent nonviolent action of the sit-ins and Freedom Rides has had three major results: first, a sense of self-determination has been instilled in millions of oppressed Negroes; second, the movement has challenged a few thousand liberals to new social idealism; third, a series of important concessions have been obtained, such as token school desegregation, increased Administration help, new laws, desegregation of some public facilities.

But fundamental social change—that would break the props from under Jim Crow—has not come. Negro employment opportunity, wage levels, housing conditions, educational privileges—these remain deplorable and relatively constant, each deprivation reinforcing the impact of the others. The Southern states, in the meantime, are strengthening the fortresses of the status quo, and are beginning to camouflage the fortresses by guile where open bigotry announced its defiance before. The white-controlled one-party system remains intact; and even where the Republicans are beginning under the pressures of industrialization in the towns and suburbs, to show initiative in fostering a two-party system, all Southern state Republican Committees (save Georgia) have adopted militant segregationist platforms to attract Dixiecrats.

Rural dominance remains a fact in nearly all the Southern states, although the reapportionment decision of the Supreme Court portends future power shifts to the cities. Southern politicians maintain a continuing aversion to the welfare legislation that would aid their people. The reins of the Southern economy are held by conservative businessmen who view human rights as secondary to property rights. A violent anti-communism is rooting itself in the South, and threatening even moderate voices. Add the militaristic tradition of the South, and its irrational regional mystique and one must conclude that authoritarian and reactionary tendencies are a rising obstacle to the small, voiceless, poor, and isolated democratic movements.

The civil rights struggle thus has come to an impasse. To this impasse, the movement responded this year by entering the sphere of politics, insisting on citizenship rights, specifically the right to vote. The new voter registration stage of protest represents perhaps the first major attempt to exercise the conventional instruments of political democracy in the struggle for racial justice. The vote, if used strategically by the great mass of now-unregistered Negroes theoretically eligible to vote, will be decisive factor in changing the quality of Southern leadership from low demagoguery to decent statesmanship.

More important, the new emphasis on the vote heralds the use of political means to solve the problems of equality in America, and it signals the decline of the short-sighted view that "discrimination" can be isolated from related social problems. Since the moral clarity of the civil rights movement has not always been accompanied by precise political vision, and sometimes not every by a real political consciousness, the new phase is revolutionary in its implication. The intermediate goal of the program is to secure and insure a healthy respect and realization of Constitutional liberties. This is important not only to terminate the civil and private abuses which currently characterize the region, but also to prevent the pendulum of oppression from simply swinging to an alternate extreme with a new unsophisticated electorate, after the unhappy example of the last Reconstruction. It is the ultimate objectives of the strategy which promise profound change in the politics of the nation. An increased Negro voting race in and of itself is not going to dislodge racist controls of the Southern power structure; but an accelerating movement through the courts, the ballot boxes, and especially the jails is the most likely means of shattering the crust of political intransigency and creating a semblance of democratic order, on local and state levels.

Linked with pressure from Northern liberals to expunge the Dixiecrats from the ranks of the Democratic Party, massive Negro voting in the South could destroy the vise-like grip reactionary Southerners have on the Congressional legislative process.

2. The broadest movement for peace in several years emerged in 1961–62. In its political orientation and goals it is much less identifiable than the movement for civil rights: it includes socialists, pacifists, liberals, scholars, militant activists, middle-class women, some professionals, many students, a few unionists. Some have been emotionally single-issue: Ban the Bomb. Some have been academically obscurantist. Some have rejected the System (sometimes both systems). Some have attempted, too, to "work within" the System. Amidst these conflicting streams of emphasis, however, certain basic qualities appear. The most important is that the "peace movement" has operated almost exclusively through peripheral institutions—almost never through mainstream institutions. Similarly, individuals interested in peace have nonpolitical social roles that cannot be turned to the support of peace activity. Concretely, liberal religious societies, anti-war groups, voluntary associations, ad hoc committees have been the political unit of the peace movement, and its human movers have been students, teacher, housewives, secretaries, lawyers, doctors, clergy. The units have not been located in spots of major social influence, the people have not been able to turn their resources fully to the issues that concern them. The results are political ineffectiveness and personal alienation.

The organizing ability of the peace movement thus is limited to the ability to state and polarize issues. It does not have an institution or the forum in which the conflicting interests can be debated. The debate goes on in corners; it has little connection with the continuing process of determining allocations of resources. This process is not necessarily centralized, however much the peace movement is estranged from it. National policy, though dominated to a large degree by the "power elites" of the corporations and military, is still partially founded in consensus. It can be altered when there actually begins a shift in the allocation of resources and the listing of priorities by the people in the institutions which have social influence, e.g., the labor unions and the schools. As long as the debates of the peace movement form only a protest, rather than an opposition viewpoint within the centers of serious decision-making, then it is neither a movement of democratic relevance, nor is it likely to have any effectiveness except in educating more outsiders to the issue. It is vital, to be sure, that this educating go on (a heartening sign is the recent proliferation of books and journals dealing with peace and war from newly-developing countries); the possibilities for making politicians responsible to "peace constituencies" becomes greater.

But in the long interim before the national political climate is more open to deliberate, goal-directed debate about peace issues, the dedicated peace "movement" might well prepare a local base, especially by establishing civic committees on the techniques of converting from military to peacetime production. To make war and peace relevant to the problems of everyday life, by relating it to the backyard (shelters), the baby (fall-out), the job (military contracts)—and making a turn toward peace seem desirable on these same terms—is a task the peace movement is just beginning, and can profitably continue.

3. Central to any analysis of the potential for change must be an appraisal of organized labor. It would be ahistorical to disregard the immense influence of labor in making modern America a decent place in which to live. It would be confused to fail to note labor's presence today as the most liberal of mainstream institutions. But it would be irresponsible not to criticize labor for losing much of the idealism that once made it a driving movement. Those who expected a labor upsurge after the 1955 AFL-CIO merger can only be dismayed that one year later, in the Stevenson-Eisenhower campaign, the AFL-CIO Committee on Political Education was able to obtain solicited $1.00 contributions from only one of every 24 unionists, and prompt only 40% of the rank-and-file to vote.

As a political force, labor generally has been unsuccessful in the postwar period of prosperity. It has seen the passage of the Taft-Hartley and Landrum-Griffin laws, and while beginning to receiving slightly favorable National Labor Relations Board rulings, it has made little progress against right-to-work laws. Furthermore, it has seen less than adequate action on domestic problems, especially unemployment.

This labor "recession" has been only partly due to anti-labor politicians and corporations. Blame should be laid, too, to labor itself for not mounting an adequate movement. Labor has too often seen itself as elitist, rather than mass-oriented, and as a pressure group rather than as an 18-million member body making political demands for all America. In the first instance, the labor bureaucracy tends to be cynical toward, or afraid of, rank-and-file involvement in the work of the union. Resolutions passed at conventions are implemented only by high-level machinations, not by mass mobilization of the unionists. Without a significant base, labor's pressure function is materially reduced since it becomes difficult to hold political figures accountable to a movement that cannot muster a vote from a majority of its members.

There are some indications, however, that labor might regain its missing idealism. First, there are signs within the movement: of worker discontent with the economic progress, of collective bargaining, of occasional splits among union leaders on questions such as nuclear testing or other Cold War issues. Second, and more important, are the social forces which prompt these feelings of unrest. Foremost is the permanence of unemployment, and the threat of automation, but important, too, is the growth of unorganized ranks in white-collar fields with steady depletion in the already-organized fields. Third, there is the tremendous challenge of the Negro movement for support from organized labor: the alienation from and disgust with labor hypocrisy among Negroes ranging from the NAACP to the Black Muslims (crystallized in the formation of the Negro American Labor Council) indicates that labor must move more seriously in its attempts to organize on an interracial basis in the South and in large urban centers. When this task was broached several years ago, "jurisdictional" disputes prevented action. Today, many of these disputes have been settled—and the question of a massive organizing campaign is on the labor agenda again.

These threats and opportunities point to a profound crisis: either labor continues to decline as a social force, or it must constitute itself as a mass political force demanding not only that society recognize its rights to organize but also a program going beyond desired labor legislation and welfare improvements. Necessarily this latter role will require rank-and-file involvement. It might include greater autonomy and power for political coalitions of the various trade unions in local areas, rather than the more stultifying dominance of the international unions now. It might include reductions in leaders' salaries, or rotation from executive office to shop obligations, as a means of breaking down the hierarchical tendencies which have detached elite from base and made the highest echelons of labor more like businessmen than workers. It would certainly mean an announced independence of the center and Dixiecrat wings of the Democratic Party, and a massive organizing drive, especially in the South to complement the growing Negro political drive there.

A new politics must include a revitalized labor movement; a movement which sees itself, and is regarded by others, as a major leader of the breakthrough to a politics of hope and vision. Labor's role is no less unique or important in the needs of the future than it was in the past, its numbers and potential political strength, its natural interest in the abolition of exploitation, its reach to the grass roots of American society, combine to make it the best candidate for the synthesis of the civil rights, peace, and economic reform movements.

The creation of bridges is made more difficult by the problems left over from the generation of "silence". Middle class students, still the main actors in the embryonic upsurge, have yet to overcome their ignorance, and even vague hostility, for what they see as "middle class labor" bureaucrats. Students must open the campus to labor through publications, action programs, curricula, while labor opens its house to students through internships, requests for aid (on the picket-line, with handbills, in the public dialogue), and politics. And the organization of the campus can be a beginning—teachers' unions can be argued as both socially progressive, and educationally beneficial university employees can be organized—and thereby an important element in the education of the student radical.

But the new politics is still contained; it struggles below the surface of apathy, awaiting liberation. Few anticipate the breakthrough and fewer still exhort labor to begin. Labor continues to be the most liberal—and most frustrated—institution in mainstream America.

4. Since the Democratic Party sweep in 1958, there have been exaggerated but real efforts to establish a liberal force in Congress, not to balance but to at least voice criticism of the conservative mood. The most notable of these efforts was the Liberal Project begun early in 1959 by Representative Kastenmeier of Wisconsin. The Project was neither disciplined nor very influential but it was concerned at least with confronting basic domestic and foreign problems, in concert with several liberal intellectuals.

In 1960 five members of the Project were defeated at the polls (for reasons other than their membership in the Project). Then followed a "post mortem" publication of the Liberal Papers, materials discussed by the Project when it was in existence. Republican leaders called the book "further out than Communism." The New Frontier administration repudiated any connection with the statements. Some former members of the Project even disclaimed their past roles.

A hopeful beginning came to a shameful end. But during the demise of the Project, a new spirit of Democratic Party reform was occurring: in New York City, Ithaca, Massachusetts, Connecticut, Texas, California, and even in Mississippi and Alabama where Negro candidates for Congress challenged racist political power. Some were for peace, some for the liberal side of the New Frontier, some for realignment of the parties—and in most cases they were supported by students.

Here and there were stirrings of organized discontent with the political stalemate. Americans for Democratic Action and the *New Republic*, pillars of the liberal community, took stands against the President on nuclear testing. A split, extremely slight thus far, developed in organized labor on the same issue. The Rev. Martin Luther King, Jr. preached against the Dixiecrat-Republican coalition across the nation.

5. From 1960 to 1962, the campuses experienced a revival of idealism among an active few. Triggered by the impact of the sit-ins, students began to struggle for integration, civil liberties, student rights, peace, and against the fast-rising right wing "revolt" as well. The liberal students, too, have felt their urgency thwarted by conventional channels: from student governments to Congressional committees. Out of this alienation from existing channels has come the creation of new ones; the most characteristic forms of liberal-radical student organizations are the dozens of campus political parties, political journals, and peace marches and demonstrations. In only a few cases have students built bridges to power: an occasional election campaign; the sit-ins, Freedom Rides, and voter registration activities; some relatively large Northern demonstrations for peace and civil rights; and infrequently, through the United States National Student Association whose notable work has not been focused on political change.

These contemporary social movements—for peace, civil rights, civil liberties labor—have in common certain values and goals. The fight for peace is one for a stable and racially integrated world; for an end to the inherently volatile exploitation of most of mankind by irresponsible elites; and for freedom of economic, political and cultural organization. The fight for civil rights is also one for social welfare for all Americans; for free speech and the right to protest; for the shield of economic independence and bargaining power; for a reduction of the arms race which takes national attention and resources away from the problems of domestic injustice. Labor's fight for jobs and wages is also one against exploitation of the Negro as a source of cheap labor; for the right to petition and strike; for world industrialization; for the stability of a peacetime economy instead of the instability of the war economy; for expansion of the welfare state. The fight for a liberal Congress is a fight for a platform from which these concerns can issue. And the fight for students, for internal democracy in the university, is a fight to gain a forum for the issues.

But these scattered movements have more in common: a need for their concerns to be expressed by a political party responsible to their interests. That they have no political expression, no political channels, can be traced in large measure to the existence of a Democratic Party which tolerates the perverse unity of liberalism and racism, prevents the social change wanted by Negroes, peace protesters, labor unions, students, reform Democrats, and other liberals. Worse, the party stalemate prevents even the raising of controversy—a full Congressional assault on racial discrimination, disengagement in Central Europe, sweeping urban reform, disarmament and inspection, public regulation of major industries; these and other issues are never heard in the body that is supposed to represent the best thoughts and interests of all Americans.

An imperative task for these publicly disinherited groups, then, is to demand a Democratic Party responsible to their interests. They must support Southern voter registration and Negro political candidates and demand that Democratic Party liberals do the same (in the last Congress, Dixiecrats split with Northern Democrats on 119 of 300 roll-calls, mostly on civil rights, area redevelopment and foreign aid bills; the breach was much larger than in the previous several sessions). Labor should begin a major drive in the South. In the North, reform clubs (either independent or Democratic) should be formed to run against big city regimes on such issues as peace, civil rights, and urban needs. Demonstrations should be held at every Congressional or convention seating of Dixiecrats. A massive research and publicity campaign should be initiated, showing to every housewife, doctor, professor, and worker the damage done to their interests every day a racist occupies a place in the Democratic Party. Where possible, the peace movement should challenge the "peace credentials" of the otherwise-liberals by threatening or actually running candidates against them.

The University and Social Change

There is perhaps little reason to be optimistic about the above analysis. True, the Dixiecrat-GOP coalition is the weakest point in the dominating complex of corporate, military and political power. But the civil rights and peace and student movements are too poor and socially slighted, and the labor movement too quiescent, to be counted with enthusiasm. From where else can power and vision be summoned? We believe that the universities are an overlooked seat of influence.

First, the university is located in a permanent position of social influence. Its educational function makes it indispensable and automatically makes it a crucial institution in the formation of social attitudes. Second, in an unbelievably complicated world, it is the central institution for organizing, evaluating, and transmitting knowledge. Third, the extent to which academic resources presently is used to buttress immoral social practice is revealed, first, by the extent to which defense contracts make the universities engineers of the arms race. Too, the use of modern social science as a manipulative tool reveals itself in the "human relations" consultants to the modern corporation, who introduce trivial sops to give laborers feelings of "participation" or "belonging", while actually deluding them in order to further exploit their labor. And, of course, the use of motivational research is already infamous as a manipulative aspect of American politics. But these social uses of the universities' resources also demonstrate the unchangeable reliance by men of power on the men and storehouses of knowledge: this makes the university functionally tied to society in new ways, revealing new potentialities, new levers for change. Fourth, the university is the only mainstream institution that is open to participation by individuals of nearly any viewpoint.

These, at least, are facts, no matter how dull the teaching, how paternalistic the rules, how irrelevant the research that goes on. Social relevance, the accessibility to knowledge, and internal openness these together make the university a potential base and agency in a movement of social change.

1. Any new left in America must be, in large measure, a left with real intellectual skills, committed to deliberativeness, honesty, reflection as working tools. The university permits the political life to be an adjunct to the academic one, and action to be informed by reason.
2. A new left must be distributed in significant social roles throughout the country. The universities are distributed in such a manner.
3. A new left must consist of younger people who matured in the postwar world, and partially be directed to the recruitment of younger people. The university is an obvious beginning point.
4. A new left must include liberals and socialists, the former for their relevance, the latter for their sense of thoroughgoing reforms in the system. The university is a more sensible place than a political party for these two traditions to begin to discuss their differences and look for political synthesis.
5. A new left must start controversy across the land, if national policies and national apathy are to be reversed. The ideal university is a community of controversy, within itself and in its effects on communities beyond.
6. A new left must transform modern complexity into issues that can be understood and felt close-up by every human being. It must give form to the feelings of helplessness and indifference, so that people may see the political, social and economic sources of their private troubles and organize to change society. In a time of supposed prosperity, moral complacency and political manipulation, a new left cannot rely on only aching stomachs to be the engine force of social reform. The case for change, for alternatives that will involve uncomfortable personal efforts, must be argued as never before. The university is a relevant place for all of these activities.

But we need not indulge in allusions: the university system cannot complete a movement of ordinary people making demands for a better life. From its schools and colleges across the nation, a militant left might awaken its allies, and by beginning the process towards peace, civil rights, and labor struggles, reinsert theory and idealism where too often reign confusion and political barter. The power of students and faculty united is not only potential; it has shown its actuality in the South, and in the reform movements of the North.

The bridge to political power, though, will be built through genuine cooperation, locally, nationally, and internationally, between a new left of young people, and an awakening community of allies. In each community we must look within the university and act with confidence that we can be powerful, but we must look outwards to the less exotic but more lasting struggles for justice.

To turn these possibilities into realities will involve national efforts at university reform by an alliance of students and faculty. They must wrest control of the educational process from the administrative bureaucracy. They must make fraternal and functional contact with allies in labor, civil rights, and other liberal forces outside the campus. They must import major public issues into the curriculum—research and teaching on problems of war and peace is an outstanding example. They must make debate and controversy, not dull pedantic cant, the common style for educational life. They must consciously build a base for their assault upon the loci of power.

As students for a democratic society, we are committed to stimulating this kind of social movement, this kind of vision and program in campus and community across the country. If we appear to seek the unattainable, as it has been said, then let it be known that we do so to avoid the unimaginable.

CHAPTER 18

Malcolm X Rejects American Pluralism

"We don't go for segregation. We go for separation."

In 1903, W. E. B. Du Bois wrote in *The Souls of Black Folk* that he looked to a day when it would be possible to be a black man and an American at the same time (see Chapter 3). Sixty years later, in 1963, Du Bois had moved to Ghana and abandoned his dream. He now considered himself an African, not an American. By this time, the modern civil rights movement was at high tide. Its central tenet, that an African American could and should *be* an American, was held by millions. In August 1963, Dr. Martin Luther King, Jr., delivered his iconic "I Have a Dream" speech at the March on Washington for Jobs and Freedom, in which he defined the African American experience as "deeply rooted in the American dream."[1] The March's primary objective was to offer support to a civil rights bill introduced by President John F. Kennedy that guaranteed equal access to public accommodations, employment, and education. The bill was designed to bring blacks into the mainstream of national life and allow them to claim the benefits of American citizenship while retaining a distinctive racial identity, thus realizing Du Bois' 1903 goals.

But as King, Kennedy, and others struggled for those goals in 1963, Du Bois himself no longer shared them. His death on the eve of the March on Washington, in that sense, was freighted with symbolism. And despite the March's huge audience—estimated at 250,000—there were still substantial numbers of African Americans who did not believe in King's dream. One of the most prominent was Malcolm X, Minister of New York's Temple Number Seven of the Nation of Islam (NOI), and the group's leading spokesman, who had denounced the March on Washington as the "Farce on Washington."[2] Malcolm believed that a black man could never be an American, nor should he try to be one. Malcolm argued that blacks were unique among America's immigrants for having come to the country involuntarily. "We didn't land on Plymouth Rock," he intoned repeatedly. "Plymouth Rock landed on us."[3] All his people had to show for three centuries in America, Malcolm maintained, were two unacceptable options: a segregated life as a marginalized and impoverished second-class citizen, or an "integrated" one that came at the cost of authentic black identity. Rejecting both options, Malcolm turned his back on the pluralist ideal that King and the young Du Bois so prized. Malcolm also spurned Randolph Bourne's "cosmopolitanism" (see Chapter 4), fearing that even this most open of social arrangements would still force blacks to surrender themselves to an invasive white identity.

Malcolm was a "race man" who conducted his American conversations through the language of racialized exclusivity and difference. He viewed the United States not as a nation of individuals but of groups. His message was intentionally discomforting and provocative. It had none of the redemptive qualities of King's, in which whites could be freed from centuries of racial guilt through Judeo-Christian brotherhood and adherence to the colorblind individualism of America's founding texts—the Declaration of Independence, the Constitution, the Emancipation Proclamation, and the Gettysburg Address. Malcolm demanded that whites repay blacks what they were owed. There would be no reconciliation between races, only cold justice between the separate and equal, obtained, in Malcolm's words, "by any means necessary." King's philosophy of nonviolent action against evil was in Malcolm's view the epitome of folly. "If someone puts his hand on you," Malcolm said, "send him to the cemetery."[4]

By insisting that it was impossible to be authentically black in a white-dominated society, Malcolm X raised the question of whether the American pluralist experiment was workable on any level. Could Americans ever be judged solely as individuals— in King's famous words, "by the content of their character"? *Should* they be? Or was the price in lost racial and ethnic distinctiveness too high? By arguing that one could either be "black" or "American," but not both, Malcolm X took the conversation over American identity in a troubling new direction.

It was not difficult to understand why Malcolm referred to the American dream as the "American nightmare." He grew up the hard way. Born Malcolm Little in 1925 in Omaha, Nebraska, and raised in Lansing, Michigan, his father Earl was a vocal black nationalist who drew the ire of white supremacists in both cities. In 1931, Earl was found dying on a Lansing trolley track. His death was officially ruled a suicide but was almost certainly the work of the Black Legion, a white racist organization similar to the Ku Klux Klan. Malcolm's mother never recovered from the trauma of her husband's death. She sank into mental illness and was institutionalized, leaving Malcolm and his siblings to be separated and assigned to foster homes.

Young Malcolm was a good student, but it was difficult for most whites living in Lansing during the late 1930s to imagine an educated, professional future for even the most promising black youngsters. When he told his eighth-grade teacher he aspired to be a lawyer, Malcolm was told to become a carpenter instead. Careers as attorneys, the teacher advised him, were for white people. Disillusioned and angry, Malcolm left school and drifted. In 1941 he moved to Boston to live with his half-sister. He soon became a street hustler, selling drugs, procuring prostitutes, and committing armed robberies. Ashamed of his appearance, he sought to straighten his hair to look less "black." He also pursued liaisons with white women as a way of lessening his racial shame. At this point in his life, Malcolm considered anyone and anything connected with "whiteness" desirable. In addition to his criminal activities, Malcolm worked at a series of low-level jobs—busboy, shoe shiner, drug store soda jerker—in which he learned to flatter whites, debasing himself for their amusement and approval.

In his *Autobiography*, Malcolm described this period as one of degradation, alienation, and ignorance. Filled with racial self-loathing, he was "dead—mentally dead."[5] Malcolm no longer valued education. "Every word I spoke was hip or profane," he recalled. "I would bet that my working vocabulary wasn't two hundred words."[6] Malcolm both feared and envied whites. He deferred to them in public even while planning to rob their homes after dark. Finally, in 1946, Malcolm received what he later viewed as a gift: He was caught. Convicted of a series of robberies, Malcolm was sentenced to ten years in prison.[7]

There, he changed the direction of his life. First, Malcolm decided to resume the education he had abandoned when he left school. He started by reading and copying every word in the dictionary, a laborious undertaking that refamiliarized him with the English language. He then began to read history, literature, philosophy, and science, hiding his books from patrolling guards after the prison lights were turned off at night. One day during a prison visit, Malcolm's brother Reginald mentioned a religious group he had recently joined called the NOI. Reginald told Malcolm that the NOI, popularly known as the Black Muslims, taught black men to *be* men: strong, independent, self-sufficient, proud, and disciplined.

The NOI demanded respect from whites. Its theology adapted traditional Islam to the specific circumstances of black life in white America. The NOI taught that blacks, who were the chosen people, originally inhabited the world. But a traitorous black created the white race in an act of vengeance, and whites soon established themselves as masters. In time, however, blacks would regain their rightful position of dominance and displace the "white devils." Malcolm was deeply affected by the NOI's ideas. They appeared to speak directly to his own experience as a black man in the United States and offer the possibility of a new beginning.

Malcolm began corresponding with Elijah Muhammad, the leader of the NOI, who he came to regard as a father figure and prophet. By the time he was released from prison in 1952, Malcolm had become a Black Muslim. He also took a new name, "Malcolm X," having discarded "Little" as a "slave" name and replaced it with an "X" that stood for his unknown African surname. Malcolm X quickly rose through the NOI ranks. After brief stops in Detroit, Boston, and Philadelphia, Malcolm came to New York as the minister of the NOI's flagship ministry in Harlem, Temple Number Seven. There, he became the group's most prominent spokesman, delivering fiery sermons, speaking on street corners, and promoting the NOI in the media and through public appearances. Thanks largely to Malcolm, the Black Muslims grew from approximately 500 members in 1952, the year he was released from prison, to an estimated 30,000 by the early 1960s.[8] Malcolm's prominence quickly grew to eclipse that of Muhammad himself, a development that would eventually lead to friction between the two men.

As he built the NOI's membership in the 1950s and early 1960s, Malcolm was a magnet for controversy. Indeed, he seemed to welcome it. At a time when the idea of an integrated American society was an article of faith among liberal Northern whites and the professional and business class of African Americans, Malcolm's was an insistent dissenting voice. Malcolm maintained that race was the essential and defining characteristic of every human being. There was a way to "be" black and a way to "be" white, and no valid identity in between. Any form of "mixing" would be detrimental to both races. "'Integration,'" Malcolm asserted, "ultimately would destroy the white race...and destroy the black race."[9] He cited the Holocaust as an example of the detrimental consequences of integration. Malcolm believed that German Jews, by striving to assimilate into the dominant culture, lost their group strength and made themselves vulnerable to attack by the Nazis. Malcolm viewed the Jews' fate as a cautionary tale for his own people: "history's most tragic result of a mixed, therefore diluted and weakened, ethnic identity."[10] The Holocaust's lesson to America's black community was that only unity and group solidarity would protect against white oppression. Integration was a sham and a trap.

Malcolm coupled this idea with one of racial "authenticity." Nothing made him angrier than blacks who in his opinion sought to "act white." These included supporters of integration, who assumed that association with whites conferred enhanced status and offered opportunities for advancement within white American society. Mindful of his own racial shame as a younger man, Malcolm dismissed these posers as "black bodies with white hearts."[11] He spat contemptuously at middle-class "Negroes" who supported King, using terms like "bourgeoisie" and "intellectual" as epithets. Malcolm believed that only the poor blacks of the nation's ghettos were "authentic." The true "souls of black folk," he maintained, were to be found here. During this race-obsessed period of Malcolm's career, it is doubtful that he believed that blacks who favored integration were "black" at all.

Malcolm became known as a man who, in the words of one supporter, "said out loud.... what African-American people had been saying out loud forever behind closed doors."[12] He delighted in debating black civil rights leaders on the merits of integration and nonviolence, using a combination of logic, rhetoric, and ridicule to win audiences to his side. Malcolm also enjoyed visiting college campuses for lectures, and by the early 1960s, he was one of the most sought-after speakers in the country. On January 23, 1963, Malcolm traveled to Michigan State University in East Lansing, Michigan, a short distance from where he had grown up, to deliver one such speech.

He began, as he usually did, by shocking his largely white audience. "So we don't even profess to speak as an American," he told them, referring to himself and Elijah Muhammad. "We are speaking as—I am speaking as a Black man."[13] As an authentic black man, Malcolm refused to let whites define him. He insisted on defining himself. Malcolm also was determined to startle the whites in his audience who assumed that pro-integrationist black "leaders" represented the entire black community. "Some Negroes," Malcolm said bitingly, "don't want a Black man to speak for them. That type of Negro doesn't even want to be Black. He's ashamed of being Black."[14] Malcolm cleverly put the onus on his black opponents, and King in particular, to prove their own racial authenticity. The black man, living in America as an alien, never had "his own." He always had to borrow what belonged to whites. "And the poor so-called Negro," Malcolm told his Michigan State hosts, "doesn't have his own name, doesn't have his own language, doesn't have his own culture, doesn't have his own history. He doesn't have his own country."[15]

The only way to make "his own" a reality, Malcolm argued, was voluntary separation, which he distinguished from forced segregation. "We don't go for segregation," he said. "We go for separation. Separation is when you have your own. You control your own economy; you control your own politics; you control your own society; you control your own everything. You have yours and you control yours; we have ours and we control ours."[16] To this end, Malcolm demanded that the federal government set aside a portion of the United States for exclusive black habitation and "give us everything we need to start our own civilization."[17]

Malcolm's Michigan State audience listened to him with a combination of anger and fascination. He was challenging virtually all of their assumptions about their country. He was telling them that America was a closed society, that it was incapable of growth and change, and that its founding principles—equality and freedom—were myths. Malcolm's message was that blacks had no future in America, nor did they want one, despite the public pronouncements of civil rights "leaders" like King. The young Du Bois had been wrong: It was not possible to live as both a black man and as an American. Blacks who wished to be "American" were traitors to their race. Malcolm sneered at them: "And knowing that America is a white country, he knows he can't be Black and be an American too. So he never calls himself Black. He calls himself an American Negro—a Negro in America. And usually he'll deny his own race, his own color, just to be a second-class American."[18]

Malcolm's prognosis, then, was bleak and unsparing. He offered his Michigan State listeners no way out. He had no dream of an American promised land that blacks and whites could reach together. His vision was of irreconcilable colors and cultures. During the question period following his lecture, Malcolm parried the crowd with cold equanimity, refusing to budge an inch. He left a startled, chastened audience in his wake as he traveled back to New York.

But only a few months after his Michigan State appearance, Malcolm's certainties would unravel, propelling him in new and unexpected directions. He discovered that Elijah Muhammad, the man who had rescued Malcolm from a life of crime and degradation and given him a new identity as a proud black man, had betrayed the principles of the NOI. Black Muslims were required to adhere to a strict code of personal conduct. They were not permitted to drink alcohol, use drugs, consume pork products, attend theatres or nightclubs, or commit adultery. Protection of black women was a particularly important NOI tenet. Black Muslims were obsessed with the image of the lustful white slave master and determined to offer black women the respect they deserved. Marital infidelity was viewed as an unforgivable sin. Thus, when Malcolm learned that the married Muhammad had fathered a number of children out of wedlock with his secretaries, he was outraged. A meeting with the NOI leader in April 1963 at which Muhammad attempted to justify his behavior angered Malcolm even more.

The episode forced a showdown. Malcolm had a much higher national profile than the reclusive and insular NOI leader, and Muhammad had long resented his notoriety. Muhammad came upon a golden opportunity to attack his rival in November 1963, immediately after the assassination of President Kennedy. Asked to comment, Malcolm called the murder an example of "the chickens coming home to roost," referring to white America's historic culture of violence.[19] After the remark attracted widespread attention, Muhammad "silenced" Malcolm for ninety days, effectively suspending him from the NOI. By March of 1964, Malcolm had left the organization permanently.

The last year of Malcolm X's life has always fascinated historians. An outcast from the Black Muslims, who had marked him for death, he now enjoyed a new sense of freedom and possibility. Malcolm traveled to Africa, where he met with leaders of the continent's anti-colonial movements, including Kwame Nkrumah of Ghana and Julius Nyerere of Tanzania. These visits allowed him to connect the struggles of his people at home with those on the African continent. Malcolm imagined a worldwide movement of nonwhites against racism and oppression, aided by the United Nations, which could hear and adjudicate charges of human rights violations against the United States.

Malcolm also became a traditional Sunni Muslim and made the "Hajj" to Mecca in Saudi Arabia—a pilgrimage every follower of Islam is asked to make at least once. In Mecca, he encountered Muslims of all races, including whites. Malcolm saw the wrong-headedness of the NOI's belief that all whites were "devils," and renounced it. He realized that "white man" meant "specific attitudes and actions toward the black man," and not an all-determining skin color.[20] Henceforth, Malcolm announced, he would not "speak against the sincere, well-meaning, good white people. I have learned that there *are* some."[21] While he remained a black nationalist and expected sympathetic whites to work for racial justice exclusively in their own communities, the mere fact that he would entertain the idea of collaborating with them at all spoke to the distance he had traveled from NOI ideology in a few short months.

Years earlier, a white college student had traveled to New York after hearing Malcolm speak on her campus to ask him what she could do about the conditions he had described. "Nothing," Malcolm had replied. Devastated, the young woman burst into tears. Recalling that incident, Malcolm now said that he wished he had given her more encouragement and hope. Since leaving the Black Muslims, he had seen instances of whites fighting against racism, and Malcolm now knew that some degree of interracial cooperation was possible. "I did many things as a (Black) Muslim that I'm sorry for now," he said. "I was a zombie then...It cost me twelve years."[22]

Malcolm formed two new organizations after his departure from the NOI. The Muslim Mosque, Inc., represented an effort to introduce traditional Sunni Islam to the Harlem community as an alternative to the NOI. The Organization of Afro-American Unity (OAAU) was a black nationalist group that in contrast to the Black Muslims was secular in orientation. Its goal was to bring together all Americans of African descent—Malcolm was now willing to use the term "American" to describe himself—for mass action.

Malcolm was unsure of the direction this "action" would take. It might even include electoral politics, at which Malcolm had scoffed during his Black Muslim years, but now began to consider more seriously. Perhaps African Americans could use mass voting power to achieve their goals just as white ethnic groups had in the past. After all, Malcolm reasoned, "U.S. politics is ruled by special-interest blocs and lobbies. What group has a more urgent special interest, what group needs a bloc, a lobby, more than the black man?"[23] Malcolm also hoped to connect the OAAU to the struggles of black people worldwide. He envisioned the group as the American chapter of the Organization of African Unity, whose proceedings he had observed during his time in Africa. Even as he began to come to terms with America, then, Malcolm was also looking beyond it to a global community of nonwhite peoples in which African Americans could view themselves as part of a worldwide majority. In one form or another, their time was coming.

In the last weeks of his life, Malcolm also reached out to his philosophical rival Martin Luther King, Jr. In February 1965, Malcolm traveled to Selma, Alabama, where King was conducting a voter registration drive. Malcolm spoke with King's wife Coretta, telling her, "I didn't come (to Selma) to make (King's) job more difficult. I thought that if the white people understood what the alternative was that they would be willing to listen to Dr. King."[24] The sarcasm and bravado of the man who had ridiculed the "Farce on Washington" just eighteen months earlier was gone, replaced by a more sober appreciation of the complexities of black identity in the United States and the many different roads that led toward racial justice. Back in New York after his Selma visit, Malcolm said to a journalist: "I'm man enough to tell you that I can't put my finger on exactly what my philosophy is now, but I'm flexible."[25] Three days later, on February 21, 1965, NOI-sponsored assassins shot Malcolm to death as he was addressing an OAAU meeting in Harlem.

The suddenness of his death and the relative brevity of his post-NOI career have lent Malcolm an air of mystery and uncertainty. How would Malcolm have evolved had he lived? It is doubtful that he would have embraced King's nonviolent interracialism, as some more optimistic historical observers have suggested; the roots of his anger ran too deep. It is also unlikely he would have continued to espouse a philosophy of implacable racial separatism, from which he was beginning to distance himself during the last year of his life. One can, however, envision Malcolm building the OAAU into an organization of influence, and becoming a powerful and respected African American spokesman and leader.[26] Malcolm and the OAAU could have mobilized African Americans as a major interest group in American political, social, and economic life. His tactics could have been, as he said just before his death, "flexible": lobbying, demonstrations, boycotts, legal action, global outreach, and electioneering. In this way, Malcolm might have become, if not a cosmopolitan in the mold of Randolph Bourne (see Chapter 4), at the least a pluralist resembling the young W. E. B. Du Bois (see Chapter 3). Malcolm X could have successfully merged Du Bois' double selves into an African and American identity that acknowledged the claims of both.

But it is also possible that Malcolm would never have come to grips with his life as a black man in the United States. He never showed any particular interest in the democratic process. The NOI, of course, had been dominated by a single man—Elijah Muhammad—around whom a cult of personality had formed and whom Malcolm regarded as infallible until their falling-out in 1963. Malcolm also lauded the autocratic African rulers he met, never questioning their governing methods. In his *Autobiography* Malcolm quoted with approval the remarks of a "passionately political African" he encountered on a flight to Nigeria in 1964: "...(T)here is no *time* for voting!... The people don't know what the vote means! It is the job of the enlightened leaders to raise the people's intellect."[27] Undoubtedly Malcolm intended to preside over the OAAU in the same imperial manner.

Nor did Malcolm appear to value religious tolerance. When he returned from Mecca with a new perspective on whites after observing them practicing Islam, he was merely substituting one prejudice for another. Could Malcolm ever be completely comfortable in a secular America where all faiths were treated equally? He offered no indication that he would be.

Finally, there was the issue of inclusion. Even after leaving the NOI, Malcolm never stopped believing that blacks had qualities that made them unique and that set them apart from whites. Thus their "success" as Americans—in education, employment, and income—would actually be failure, because it would come at the expense of their unique black "essence." Malcolm might well have concluded that despite political, economic, and social progress over the years, it was indeed impossible to be authentically "black" and "American" at once, and that Du Bois' dream had not been worth pursuing. Democracy, tolerance, secularism, inclusion—whether or not the United States has lived up to these ideals, they are defining American values. Would Malcolm have been able to embrace them? If he could not, the impact of his life would have been greatly diminished. But of course we will never know for sure. The brevity of Malcolm's days allows our historical imagination free rein. We can end his story any way we wish.

Malcolm X's *Autobiography*, which he wrote with the author Alex Haley, was published a few months after his death. A critical sensation, it went on to become one of the top ten best-selling nonfiction works of the twentieth century.[28] This alone has assured Malcolm a place in the American popular imagination. A 1992 Spike Lee-directed film biography established Malcolm as a cultural icon, a visual image, and even a fashion statement.[29] But Malcolm X was more than a figure on a wall poster or a T-shirt. His true legacy lies in his ability to disquiet those who accept unreflectively the values of American pluralism. At the time of his death, Malcolm was less sure of the answer to the question "can a man be both black and American?" than he had been during his years in the NOI. This too is part of his legacy. Malcolm X's complex, unfinished life mirrors the ongoing conversation over the nature of American identity in his century and ours.

Questions for Consideration and Conversation

1. Until the last months of his life, Malcolm X did not consider himself an "American." Why?
2. Why did Malcolm reject the American pluralism of the younger W. E. B. Du Bois (Chapter 3) and the cosmopolitanism of Randolph Bourne (Chapter 4)? Would Malcolm have identified with Charles Kikuchi (Chapter 9)?
3. How did Malcolm's outlook change during the last year of his life?
4. What are the implications of Malcolm's idea that America is a nation of groups and not individuals?
5. Was Malcolm's insistence on racial "authenticity" itself an example of racism?
6. How did Malcolm distinguish "segregation" and "separation"? Are you convinced?
7. "The brevity of Malcolm's days allows our historical imagination free rein. We can end his story any way we wish." End it.

Endnotes

1. See Clayborne Carson and Kris Shepard, eds., *A Call to Conscience: The Landmark Speeches of Dr. Martin Luther King, Jr.* (New York: Warner Books, 2001), 81–89.
2. Malcolm X, with Alex Haley, *The Autobiography of Malcolm X* (New York: Grove Press, 1965), 278.
3. Ibid., 201.
4. Malcolm X, "Message to Grassroots," October 10, 1963, http://teachingamericanhistory.org/library/index
5. Malcolm X, *Autobiography*, 125.
6. Ibid., 134.
7. Ibid., 151.
8. http://www.malcolmx.com/about/bio.html
9. Malcolm X, *Autobiography*, 276.
10. Ibid., 277.
11. Ibid., 244.
12. Sonia Sanchez, quoted in Henry Hampton and Steve Fayer, *Voices of Freedom: An Oral History of the Civil*

Rights Movement from the 1950s through the 1980s (New York: Bantam Books, 1990), 254.

13. Malcolm X, "Twenty Million Black People in a Political, Economic, and Mental Prison," in Bruce Perry, ed., *Malcolm X: The Last Speeches* (New York: Pathfinder, 1989), 27.
14. Ibid., 28.
15. Ibid., 33.
16. Ibid., 38–39.
17. Ibid., 50.
18. Ibid., 35.
19. Malcolm X, *Autobiography*, 301.
20. Ibid., 333.
21. Ibid., 367.
22. Ibid., 429.
23. Ibid., 314.
24. Coretta Scott King, quoted in Hampton and Fayer, *Voices of Freedom*, 221–22.
25. Malcolm X, *Autobiography*, 428.
26. In reality, the OAAU did not recover from Malcolm's death and never attracted a mass following.
27. Malcolm X, *Autobiography*, 349.
28. See *Time*, June 8, 1998, 108.
29. The film spawned a fashion line of garments emblazoned with a large "X."

MALCOLM X, TWENTY MILLION BLACK PEOPLE IN A POLITICAL, ECONOMIC, AND MENTAL PRISON (1963)

Source: Bruce Perry, ed., *Malcolm X: The Last Speeches.* New York: Pathfinder, 1989, pp. 25–57.

It should be pointed out at the outset that I represent the Honorable Elijah Muhammad, whose followers are known as the Muslims here in America and actually are the fastest growing group—fastest growing religious group—among Black people anywhere in the Western Hemisphere. And it is our intention to try and spell out what the philosophy and aims and motivations of the Honorable Elijah Muhammad happen to be and his solution to this very serious problem that America finds herself confronted with.

And I might point out, too, that if you don't think that the problem is serious, then you need only to listen to the attorney general, Robert F. Kennedy. In almost every speech he's been involved in, especially during the past few months and even today, he has pointed out that the race problem is America's most serious domestic problem. And since the problem is so serious, it's time to take some serious steps to get to the factors that create this problem.

And again I want to thank the African Students Association and the campus NAACP for displaying the unity necessary to bring a very controversial issue before the students here on campus. The unity of Africans abroad and the unity of Africans here in this country can bring about practically any kind of achievement or accomplishment that Black people want today.

When I say the Africans abroad and the Africans here in this country—the man that you call Negro is nothing but an African himself. Why, some of them have been brainwashed into thinking that Africa is a place with no culture, no history, no contribution to civilization or science. So many of these Negroes, they take offense when they're identified with their homeland. But today we want to point out the different types of Negroes that you have to deal with. Then once you know there's more than one type, then you won't come up with just one type solution.

And to point out how timely the invitation is or was—I don't want to read newspapers to you, but in the Detroit News dated Thursday, January 17, it told about the Interfaith Council of Religion that was held in Chicago last week. And the topic of their conversation was the race problem here in America. And it pointed out that all of the time that they spent and money that they spent, actually they didn't get to the meat of the issue. And in this particular copy of the paper, on page three, the chaplain at Wayne State University actually criticized the efforts of these Protestants, Catholics, and Jews in Chicago last week for failing to bring spokesmen to that conference who really would speak for Black people and spell out issues that were not being spelled out by the others.

And I just want to read a recommendation that he made. Mr. [Malcolm] Boyd believes that the conference might have accomplished much good if the speakers had included a white supremacist and a Negro race leader, preferably a top man in the American Black Muslim movement. He said that a debate between them would undoubtedly be bitter, but it would accomplish one thing. It would get some of the real issues out into the open. And I think that the man is right. Most of the so-called Negroes that you listen to on the race problem usually don't represent any following of Black people. Usually they are Negroes who have been put in that position by the white man himself. And when they speak they're not speaking for Black people, they're saying exactly what they know the white man who put them in that position wants to hear them say.

So again, I think that it was very progressive and objective on the part of these two sponsoring groups to give us an opportunity to tell you how Black people really think and how Black people really feel and how dissatisfied Black people have become—increasingly so—with the conditions that our people find ourselves in here in this country.

Now in speaking as a—professing to speak for Black people by representing the Honorable Elijah Muhammad, you want to know who does he represent. Who does he speak for? There are two types of Negroes in this country. There's the bourgeois type who blinds himself to the condition of his people, and who is satisfied with token solutions. He's in the minority. He's a handful. He's usually the handpicked Negro who benefits from token integration. But the masses of Black people who really suffer the brunt of brutality and the conditions that exist in this country are represented by the leadership of the Honorable Elijah Muhammad.

So when I come in here to speak to you, I'm not coming in here speaking as a Baptist or a Methodist or a Democrat or a Republican or a Christian or a Jew or—not even as an American. Because if I stand up here—if I could stand up here and speak to you as an American we wouldn't have anything to talk about. The problem would be solved. So we don't even profess to speak as an American. We are speaking as—I am speaking as a Black man. And I'm letting you know how a Black man thinks, how a Black man feels, and how dissatisfied Black men should have been 400 years ago. So, and if I raise my voice you'll forgive me or excuse me, I'm not doing it out of disrespect. I'm speaking from my heart, and you get it exactly as the feeling brings it out.

When I pointed out that there are two kinds of Negroes—some Negroes don't want a Black man to speak for them. That type of Negro doesn't even want to be Black. He's ashamed of being Black. And you'll never hear him refer to himself as Black. Now that type we don't pretend to speak for. You can speak for him. In fact you can have him. [Laughter]

But the ones that the Honorable Elijah Muhammad speaks for are those whose pattern of thinking, pattern of thought, pattern of behavior, pattern of action is being changed by what the Honorable Elijah Muhammad is teaching throughout America. These are that mass element, and usually when you hear the press refer to the Honorable Elijah Muhammad, they refer to him as a teacher of hate or an advocator of violence or—what's this other thing?—Black supremacist.

Actually this is the type of propaganda put together by the press, thinking that this will alienate masses of Black people from what he's saying. But actually the only one whom that type of propaganda alienates is this Negro who's always up in your face begging you for what you have or begging you for a chance to live in your neighborhood or work on your job or marry one of your women. Well that type of Negro naturally doesn't want to hear what the Honorable Elijah Muhammad is talking about. But the type that wants to hear what he's saying is the type who feels that he'll get farther by standing on his own feet and doing something for himself towards solving his own problem, instead of accusing you of creating the problem and then, at the same time, depending upon you to do something to solve the problem.

So you have two types of Negro. The old type and the new type. Most of you know the old type. When you read about him in history during slavery he was called "Uncle Tom." He was the house Negro. And during slavery you had two Negroes. You had the house Negro and the field Negro. The house Negro usually lived close to his master. He dressed like his master. He wore his master's secondhand clothes. He ate food that his master left on the table. And he lived in his master's house—probably in the basement or the attic—but he still lived in the master's house. So whenever that house Negro identified himself, he always identified himself in the same sense that his master identified himself.

When his master said, "We have good food," the house Negro would say, "Yes, we have plenty of good food." "We" have plenty of good food. When the master said that "we have a fine home here," the house Negro said, "Yes, we have a fine home here." When the master would be sick, the house Negro identified himself so much with his master he'd say, "What's the matter boss, we sick?" His master's pain was his pain. And it hurt him more for his master to be sick than for him to be sick himself. When the house started burning down, that type of Negro would fight harder to put the master's house out than the master himself would.

But then you had another Negro out in the field. The house Negro was in the minority. The masses—the field Negroes were the masses. They were in the majority. When the master got sick, they prayed that he'd die. [Laughter] If his house caught on fire, they'd pray for a wind to come along and fan the breeze.

If someone came to the house Negro and said, "Let's go, let's separate," naturally that Uncle Tom would say, "Go where? What could I do without boss? Where would I live? How would I dress? Who would look out for me?" That's the house Negro. But if you went to the field Negro and said, "Let's go, let's separate," he wouldn't even ask you where or how. He'd say, "Yes, let's go." And that one ended right there.

So today you have a twentieth-century-type of house Negro. A twentieth-century Uncle Tom. He's just as much an Uncle Tom today as Uncle Tom was 100 or 200 years ago. Only he's a modern Uncle Tom. That Uncle Tom wore a handkerchief around his head. This Uncle Tom wears a top hat. He's sharp. He dresses just like you do. He speaks the same phraseology, the same language. He tries to speak it better than you do. He speaks with the same accents, same diction. And when you say, "your army," he says, "our army." He hasn't got anybody to defend him, but anytime you say "we" he says "we." "Our president," "our government," "our Senate," "our congressmen," "our this and our that." And he hasn't even got a seat in that "our" even at the end of the line. So this is the twentieth-century Negro. Whenever you say "you," the personal pronoun in the singular or in the plural, he uses it right along with you. When you say you're in trouble, he says, "Yes, we're in trouble."

But there's another kind of Black man on the scene. If you say you're in trouble, he says, "Yes, you're in trouble." [Laughter] He doesn't identify himself with your plight whatsoever.

And this is the thing that the white people in America have got to come to realize. That there are two types of Black people in this country. One who identifies with you so much so he will let you brutalize him and still beg you for a chance to sit next to you. And then there's one who's not interested in sitting next to you. He's not interested in being around you. He's not interested in what you have. He wants something of his own. He wants to sit someplace where he can call his own. He doesn't want a seat in your restaurant where you can give him some old bad coffee or bad food. He wants his own restaurant. And he wants some land where he can build that restaurant on, in a city that it can go in. He wants something of his own.

And when you realize that this type of thinking is existing and developing fastly or swiftly behind the teachings of the Honorable Elijah Muhammad among the so-called Negroes, then I think that you'll also realize that this whole phony effort at integration is no solution. Because the most you can do with this phony effort toward integration is to put out some token integration. And whereas this Uncle Tom will accept your token effort, the masses of Black people in this country are no more interested in token integration than they would be if you offered them a chance to sit inside a furnace somewhere. The only one who'll do that is this twentieth-century Uncle Tom. And you can always tell him because he wants to be next to you. He wants to eat with you. He wants to sleep with you. He wants to marry your woman, marry your mother, marry your sister, marry your daughter. And if you watch him close enough he's even after your wife.

This type has blind faith—in your religion. He's not interested in any religion of his own. He believes in a white Jesus, white Mary, white angels, and he's trying to get to a white heaven. When you listen to him in his church singing, he sings a song, I think they call it, "Wash me white as snow." He wants to be—he wants to be turned white so he can go to heaven with a white man. It's not his fault; it's actually not his fault. But this is the state of his mind. This is the result of 400 years of brainwashing here in America. You have taken a man who is black on the outside and made him white on the inside. His brain is white as snow. His heart is white as snow. And therefore, whenever you say, this is ours, he thinks he's white the same as you, so what's yours he thinks is also his. Even right on down to your woman.

Now many of them will take offense at my implying that he wants your woman. They'll say, "No, this is what Bill Bowen, Talmadge, and all of the White Citizens' Councils say." They say that to fool you. If this is not what they want, watch them. And if you find evidence to the contrary, then I'll take back my words. But all you have to do is give him the chance to get near you, and you'll find that he is not satisfied until he is sitting next to your woman, or closer to her than that.

And this type of Negro, usually he hates Black and loves white. He doesn't want to be Black, he wants to be white. And he'll get on his bended knees and beg you for integration, which means he would rather live—rather than live with his own kind who love him, he'll force himself to live in neighborhoods around white people whom he knows don't mean him any good. And again I say, this is not his fault. He is sick. And as long as America listens to this sick Negro, who is begging to be integrated into American society despite the fact that the attitude and actions of whites are sufficient proof that he is not wanted, why then you are actually allowing him to force you into a position where you look just as sick as he looks.

If someone holds a gun on a white man and makes him embrace me—put his hand, arm, around me—this isn't love nor is it brotherhood. What they are doing is forcing the white man to be a hypocrite, to practice hypocrisy. But if that white man will put his arm around me willingly, voluntarily, of his own volition, then that's love, that's brotherhood, that's a solution to the problem.

Likewise, as long as the government has to get out here and legislate to force Negroes into a white neighborhood or force Negroes into a white school or force Negroes into white industry—and make white people pretend that they go for this—all the government is doing is making white people be hypocrites. And rather than be classified as a bigot, by putting a block, the average white person actually would rather put up a hypocritical face, the face of a hypocrite, than to tell the Black man, "No, you stay over there and let me stay over here." So that's no solution.

As long as you force people to act in a hypocritical way, you will never solve their problem. It has to be—the Honorable Elijah Muhammad teaches us that a solution has to be devised that will be satisfactory, completely satisfactory to the Black man and completely satisfactory to the white man. And the only thing that makes white people completely satisfied and Black people completely satisfied, when they're in their right mind, is when the Black man has his own and the white man has his own. You have what you need; we have what we need. Then both of us have something, and even the Bible says, "God bless the child that has his own." And the poor so-called Negro doesn't have his own name, doesn't have his own language, doesn't have his own culture, doesn't have his own history. He doesn't have his own country. He doesn't even have his own mind. And he thinks that he's Black 'cause God cursed him. He's not Black 'cause God cursed him. He's Black because—rather he's cursed because he's out of his mind. He has lost his mind. He has a white mind instead of the type of mind that he should have.

So, when these so-called Negroes who want integration try and force themselves into the white society, which doesn't solve the problem—the Honorable Elijah Muhammad teaches us that that type of Negro is the one that creates the problem. And the type of white person who perpetuates the problem is the one who poses as a liberal and pretends that the Negro should be integrated, as long as he integrates someone else's neighborhood. But all these whites that you see running around here talking about how liberal they are, and we believe everybody should have what they want and go where they want and do what they want, as soon as a Negro moves into that white liberal's neighborhood, that white liberal is—well he moves out faster than the white bigot from Mississippi, Alabama, and from someplace else.

So we won't solve the problem listening to that Uncle Tom Negro, and the problem won't be solved listening to the so-called white liberal. The only time the problem is going to be solved is when a Black man can sit down like a Black man and a white man can sit down like a white man. And make no excuses whatsoever with each other in discussing the problem. No offense will stem from factors that are brought up. But both of them have to sit down like men, on one side and on the other side, and look at it in terms of Black and white. And then take some kind of solution based upon the factors that we see, rather than upon that which we would like to believe.

And when I said that this Negro wants to force his way into the white man's family, this integrationist-minded Negro wants to force his way into the white man's family, some don't believe that. Some take issue with that. But you take all of the integrationists, all of those who are used to finance the program of the integrationists, the average so-called Negro celebrity, put all of them in one pile. And as fast as you name them off, you'll find that every one of them is married either to a white woman or a white man. From Lena Horne, Eartha Kitt, Sammy Davis, and you could name 'em all night long, they—although they say that this is not what we want—that's what they've done. That's what they have. And we don't—the Black masses don't want what Lena Horne wants or what Sammy Davis wants or what who's-his-name, the rest of them want.

Usually you'll find that before Sammy Davis and Lena Horne and Eartha Kitt and Harry Belafonte become involved in a mixed marriage you could go into the Negro community, any one across the country, and find those stars with records on the jukeboxes in the Negro community. You can't walk into a Negro community today and find anybody that the Negro community knows is involved in a mixed marriage with their records being popular in the Negro community. Subconsciously a Negro doesn't have any respect or regard or confidence, nor can he be moved by, another Black man, a Black man who marries a white woman or a Black woman who marries a white man.

And when they put out that picture to you that all of us want your woman, no, just that twentieth-century Uncle Tom. He wants her. But, then when you fulfill—think you're going to solve your problem by pleasing him, you're only making the problem worse. You have to go back and listen to the problem as it is presented by the masses of Black people, not by these handpicked, handful of Uncle Toms who benefit from token integration.

Also this type of so-called Negro, by being intoxicated over the white man, he never sees beyond the white man. He never sees beyond America. He never looks at himself or where he fits into things on the world stage. He only can see himself here in America, on the American stage or the white stage, where the white man is in the majority, where the white man is the boss. So this type of Negro always feels like he's outnumbered or he's the underdog or he's the minority. And it puts him in the role of a beggar—a cowardly, humble, Uncle Tomming beggar on anything that he says is—that should be his by right.

Whereas there is—he wants to be an American rather than to be Black. He wants to be something other than what he is. And knowing that America is a white country, he knows he can't be Black and be an American too. So he never calls himself Black. He calls himself an American Negro—a Negro in America. And usually he'll deny his own race, his own color, just to be a second-class American. He'll deny his own history, his own culture. He'll deny all of his brothers and sisters in Africa, in Asia, in the East, just to be a second-class American. He denies everything that he represents or everything that was in his past, just to be accepted into a country and into a government that has rejected him ever since he was brought here.

For this Negro is sick. He has to be sick to try and force himself amongst some people who don't want him, or to be accepted into a government that has used its entire political system and educational system to keep him relegated to the role of a second-class citizen. Therefore he spends a lifetime begging for acceptance into the same government that made

slaves of his people. He gives his life for a country that made his people slaves and still confines them to the role of second-class citizens. And we feel that he wastes his time begging white politicians, political hypocrites, for civil rights or for some kind of first-class citizenship.

He is like a watchdog or a hound dog. You may run into a dog—no matter how vicious a dog is, you find him out in the street, he won't bite you. But when you get him up on the porch, he will growl, he'll take your leg. Now that dog, when he's out in the street, only his own life is threatened, and he's never been trained to protect himself. He's only been trained by his master to think in terms of what's good for his master. So when you catch him in the street and you threaten him, he'll go around you. But when you come up on the—through the gate when he's sitting on the master's porch, then he'll bare his fangs and get ready to bite you. Not because you're threatening him, but because you threaten his master who has trained him not to protect himself but to protect the property of the master.

And this type of twentieth-century Uncle Tom is the same way. He'll never attack you, but he'll attack me. I can run into him out on the street and blast him; he won't say a word. But if I look like I'm about to blast you in here, he'll open up his mouth and put up a better defense for you than you can put up for yourself. Because he hasn't been trained to defend himself. He has only been trained to open up his mouth in defense of his master. He hasn't been educated, he's been trained. When a man is educated, he can think for himself and defend himself and speak for himself. But this twentieth-century Uncle Tom Negro never opens up his mouth in defense of a Black man. He opens up his mouth in defense of the white man, in defense of America, in defense of the American government. He doesn't even know where his government is, because he doesn't know that he ever had one. He doesn't know where his country is, because he doesn't know that he ever had one.

He believes in exactly what he was taught in school. That when he was kidnapped by the white man, he was a savage in the jungle someplace eating people and throwing spears and with a bone in his nose. And the average American Negro has that concept of the African continent. It is not his fault. This is what has been given to him by the American educational system.

He doesn't realize that there were civilizations and cultures on the African continent at a time when the people in Europe were crawling around in the caves, going naked. He doesn't realize that the Black man in Africa was wearing silk, was wearing slippers—that he was able to spin himself, make himself at a time when the people up in Europe were going naked.

He doesn't realize that he was living in palaces on the African continent when the people in Europe were living in caves. He doesn't realize that he was living in a civilization in Africa where science had been so far advanced, especially even the astronomical sciences, to a point where Africans could plot the course of the stars in the universe when the people up in Europe still thought the earth was round, the planet was round—or flat.

He doesn't realize the advancement and the high state of his own culture that he was living in before he was kidnapped and brought to this country by the white man. He knows nothing about that. He knows nothing about the ancient Egyptian civilization on the African continent. Or the ancient Carthaginian civilization on the African continent. Or the ancient civilizations of Mali on the African continent. Civilizations that were highly developed and produced scientists. Timbuktu, the center of the Mali Empire, was the center of learning at a time when the people up in Europe didn't even know what a book was. He doesn't know this, because he hasn't been taught. And because he doesn't know this, when you mention Africa to him, why he thinks you're talking about a jungle.

And I went to Africa in 1959 and didn't see any jungle. And I didn't see any mud huts until I got back to Harlem in New York City. [Laughter and applause]

So you're familiar with that type of Negro. And the Black man that you're not familiar with is the one that we would like to point out now.

He is the new—he is the new type. He is the type that the white man seldom ever comes in contact with. And when you do come in contact with him, you're shocked, because you didn't know that this type of Black man existed. And immediately you think, well here's one of those Black supremacists or racists or extremists who believe in violence and all of that kind of—well that's what they call it.

This new type of Black man, he doesn't want integration; he wants separation. Not segregation, separation. To him, segregation, as we're taught by the Honorable Elijah Muhammad, means that which is forced upon inferiors by superiors. A segregated community is a Negro community. But the white community, though it's all white, is never called a

segregated community. It's a separate community. In the white community, the white man controls the economy, his own economy, his own politics, his own everything. That's his community. But at the same time while the Negro lives in a separate community, it's a segregated community. Which means its regulated from the outside by outsiders. The white man has all of the businesses in the Negro community. He runs the politics of the Negro community. He controls all the civic organizations in the Negro community. This is a segregated community.

We don't go for segregation. We go for separation. Separation is when you have your own. You control your own economy; you control your own politics; you control your own society; you control your own everything. You have yours and you control yours; we have ours and we control ours.

They don't call Chinatown in New York City or on the West Coast a segregated community, yet it's all Chinese. But the Chinese control it. Chinese voluntarily live there, they control it. They run it. They have their own schools. They control their own politics, control their own industry. And they don't feel like they're being made inferior because they have to live to themselves. They choose to live to themselves. They live there voluntarily. And they are doing for themselves in their community the same thing you do for yourself in your community. This makes them equal because they have what you have. But if they didn't have what you have, then they'd be controlled from your side; even though they would be on their side, they'd be controlled from your side by you.

So when we who follow the Honorable Elijah Muhammad say that we're for separation, it should be emphasized we're not for segregation; we're for separation. We want the same for ourselves as you have for yourself. And when we get it, then it's possible to think more intelligently and to think in terms that are along peaceful lines. But a man who doesn't have what is his, he can never think always in terms that are along peaceful lines.

This new type rejects the white man's Christian religion. He recognizes the real enemy. That Uncle Tom can't see his enemy. He thinks his friend is his enemy and his enemy is his friend. And he usually ends up loving his enemy, turning his other cheek to his enemy. But this new type, he doesn't turn the other cheek to anybody. He doesn't believe in any kind of peaceful suffering. He believes in obeying the law. He believes in respecting people. He believes in doing unto others as he would have done to himself. But at the same time, if anybody attacks him, he believes in retaliating if it costs him his life. And it is good for white people to know this. Because if white people get the impression that Negroes all endorse this old turn-the-other-cheek cowardly philosophy of Dr. Martin Luther King, then whites are going to make the mistake of putting their hands on some Black man, thinking that he's going to turn the other cheek, and he'll end up losing his hand and losing his life in the try.

So it is always better to let someone know where you stand. And there are a large number of Black people in this country who don't endorse any phase of what Dr. Martin Luther King and these other twentieth-century religious Uncle Toms are putting in front of the public eye to make it look like this is the way, this is the behavior, or this is the thought pattern of most of our people.

Also this new type, you'll find, he doesn't look upon it as being any honor to be in America. He knows he didn't come here on the Mayflower. He knows he was brought here in a slave ship. But this twentieth-century Uncle Tom, he'll stand up in your face and tell you about when his fathers landed on Plymouth Rock. His father never landed on Plymouth Rock; the rock was dropped on him [Laughter] but he wasn't dropped on it.

So this type doesn't make any apology for being in America, nor does he make any apology for the problem his presence in America presents for Uncle Sam. He knows he was brought here in chains, and he knows he was brought here against his will. He knows that the problem itself was created by the white man and that it was created because the white man brought us here in chains against our will. It was a crime. And the one who committed that crime is the criminal today who should pay for the crime that was committed. You don't put the crime in jail, you put the criminal in jail. And kidnapping is a crime. Slavery is a crime. Lynching is a crime. And the presence of 20 million Black people in America against their will is a living witness, a living testimony of the crime that Uncle Sam committed, your forefathers committed, when our people were brought here in chains.

And the reason the problem can't be solved today is you try and dress it up and doctor it up and make it look like a favor was done to the Black man by having brought the Black man here. But when you realize that it was a crime that was committed, then you approach the solution to that problem in a different light and then you can probably solve it. And as long as you think Negroes are running around here of the opinion that you're doing them a favor by letting them have some of this and letting them have some of that, why naturally every time you give a little bit more justice or freedom to the Black man, you stick out your chest and say, "See, we're solving the problem."

You're not doing the Black man any favor. If you stick a knife in my back, if you put it in nine inches and pull it out six inches, you haven't done me any favor. If you pull it all the way out, you haven't done me any favor. And this is what you have to realize. If you put a man in jail against his will—illegally, he's not guilty—you frame him up, and then because he resents what you've done to him, you put him in solitary confinement to break his spirit, then after his spirit is broken, you let him out a little bit and give him the general run of the prison, you haven't done him any favor. If you let him out of prison completely, you haven't done him any favor, because you put him in there unjustly and illegally in the first place.

Now you have 20 million Black people in this country who were brought here and put in a political, economic, and mental prison. This was done by Uncle Sam. And today you don't realize what a crime your forefathers have committed. And you think that when you open the door a few cracks, and give this little integration-intoxicated Negro a chance to run around in the prison yard—that's all he's doing—that you're doing him a favor. But as long as he has to look up to someone who doesn't represent him and doesn't speak for him, that person only represents the warden, he doesn't represent some kind of president or mayor or governor or senator or congressman or anything else.

So this new type—the fact has to be faced that he exists. Especially since he's in the house. And he didn't come here because it was his will. So you have to take the blame for his being here. And once you take the blame, then it's more easy. It's easier for you to approach the problem more sensibly and try and get a solution. And the solution can never be based upon hypocrisy. The Honorable Elijah Muhammad says that this solution has to be based upon reality. Tokenism is hypocrisy. One little student in the University of Mississippi, that's hypocrisy. A handful of students in Little Rock, Arkansas, is hypocrisy. A couple of students going to school in Georgia is hypocrisy.

Integration in America is hypocrisy in the rawest form. And the whole world can see it. All this little tokenism that is dangled in front of the Negro and then he's told, "See what we're doing for you, Tom."

Why the whole world can see that this is nothing but hypocrisy. All you do is make your image worse; you don't make it better.

So again, this new type, as I say, he rejects the white man's Christian religion. You find in large numbers they're turning toward the religion of Islam. They are becoming Muslims, believing in one God, whose proper name is Allah, in Muhammad as his apostle, in turning toward Mecca, praying five times a day, fasting during Ramadan, and all the other principles that are laid out by the religion of Islam. He's becoming a Muslim and just as—I think it was Dr. Billy Graham who made a crusade through Africa and came back and said that Islam is sweeping through Africa, outnumbering Christianity in converts eleven to one, which means every time one African becomes a Christian, eleven of them become a Muslim. And then that one who became a Christian, he forgets it and goes on and be a Muslim, too.

So that—and Bishop Pike pointed out the same thing in Look magazine in December 1960 and then Time magazine, heaven forbid that I should mention that magazine, [Laughter and applause] but Time magazine mentioned it, two weeks ago, that Islam is sweeping throughout Africa. And just as it is sweeping throughout the Black people of Africa, it is sweeping throughout the Black people right here in America. Only the one who's teaching it here in America is the Honorable Elijah Muhammad. He is the religious leader, the religious teacher. He is the one who is spreading the religion of Islam among the slaves, ex-slaves, here in America.

You have Muslims who have come to this country from the Muslim world. There are probably 200,000 Muslims in this country from the Muslim world, who were born in the Muslim world. And all of them combined have never been able to convert a hundred Americans to the religion of Islam. Yet it is the nature of Islam to propagate the faith, to spread the faith, to make everyone bear witness that there's no God but Allah and Muhammad is his apostle.

And if you find all of the Muslims of the Muslim world who come here, unable or incapable of turning the American people toward Allah and toward Mecca and toward Islam, and then this little Black man from the cotton fields of Georgia is able to stand up and get Black people by the hundreds of thousands to turn toward Mecca five times a day and give praise to Allah and come together in unity and harmony, why you'd have to be out of your mind to think the people of the Muslim world don't recognize the wonderful religious and spiritual accomplishment that's being achieved here among the so-called Negroes by the Honorable Elijah Muhammad.

And I take time to mention that because the propagandists try and convey the picture that we're not Muslims, we're not religiously motivated, and that we are in no way identified or recognized or connected with our people of the Muslim world. Well if they didn't recognize us, we wouldn't care. We're not particularly looking for recognition. We're looking for recognition from Allah, from God, and if Allah accepts you as a Muslim, you're accepted. It's not left to somebody walking around here on this earth. But those people over there would be out of their minds, when they find themselves unable to spread the religion of Islam and then they see this little Black man here in America spreading it, why they'd be out of their mind to reject him. And you'll find if you take the time to look, that you don't find any Muslim today who rejects another Muslim.

You might find some who come over here, who operate stores or some kind of little business in the white neighborhood, the Christian neighborhood, and they want to get along with all the white people, with all the Christians.

They might say some words to please you. But they're only trying to get your money.

So the followers of the Honorable Elijah Muhammad look to him and what he teaches, his program and his message, as our only solution. And they see separation as our only salvation.

We don't think as Americans any more, but as a Black man. With the mind of a Black man, we look beyond America. And we look beyond the interests of the white man. The thinking of this new type of Negro is broad. It's more international. This integrationist always thinks in terms of an American. But you find the masses of Black people today think in terms of Black. And this Black thinking enables them to see beyond the confines of America. And they look all over the world. They look at the happenings in the international context.

By this little integrationist Negro thinking locally, by his thinking and desires being confined to America, he's limited. He's the underdog. He's a minority. But the masses of Black people who have been exposed to the teachings of the Honorable Elijah Muhammad, their thinking is more international. They look on this earth and they see that the majority of the people on this earth are dark. And by seeing that the majority of the people on this earth are dark, they don't regard themselves as a minority in America, but rather they regard themselves as part of that vast, dark majority.

So therefore, when you run into that type of Black man, he doesn't speak as an underdog. He doesn't speak like you outnumber him, or he doesn't speak like there's any harm that you can do to him. He speaks as one who outnumbers you. He sees that the dark world outnumbers the white world. That the odds have turned today and are in his favor, are on his side. He sees that the people of this earth are on his side. That time is on his side. That history is on his side. And most important of all, he sees that God is on his side toward getting him some kind of solution that's immediate, and that's lasting, and that is no way connected or concerned or stems from the goodwill or good conscience in any way, shape, 'soever of the man who created—who committed the crime and created the problem in the first place.

I would like to point out, quickly and briefly—no I won't, I think my time is up.

Voice: Just about.

Well Dr. here says my time is up, and I'm telling him his time is short. [Laughter] So I think what's good for the goose is good for the gander.

Discussion Period

[Following an extended comment by someone in the audience, there were questions from the floor.]

Question: Do you consider Elijah Muhammad as a prophet or as a leader?

Malcolm X: We never refer to the Honorable Elijah Muhammad as a prophet. He never refers to himself as that, and he teaches us that the world has no need for prophets today. But he's a leader, he's a leader of the Black people here in this country against the oppression and exploitation that our people have suffered for 400 years. And we need a leader from among ourselves, because our people back home never came and tried to relieve us of the suffering that we've undergone.

Question: I'm a white man—

Malcolm X: You're not a white man.

Question: If I was a white man, do you accept him to attend your mosque, to worship God with you?

Malcolm X: If the—all of the Muslims in this country from Egypt and elsewhere

have not been successful in getting the white man to turn toward the religion of Islam and they are born in the Muslim world, well we find we'd be wasting our time trying to convert the white man ourself. Mr. Muhammad is primarily concerned with the condition of the Black man in this country.

Now if the other Muslims who come here from abroad want to set up some kind of mosque and let the white man in it and teach him how to be a Muslim and get him to say, "No God but Allah," then they can do that. But they shouldn't criticize us for not doing it, because they haven't succeeded in doing it.

Question: Will you accept me in your mosque?

Malcolm X: Sir, you're not white.

Question: I'm asking you if a white man, many people are white men and they are Muslim too.

Malcolm X: I answered you. Mr. Muhammad's concern is not with the white man. His concern is with the Black man....Islam means to submit to the will of one God whose personal and proper name is Allah. What you forget, if you're in the Muslim world practicing Islam, you're not faced with the same problem of Black people who have been kidnapped from the Muslim world and have been deprived of Islam.

[Question unintelligible]

Malcolm X: You have to ask the white man that. He's the one who segregates us. Segregation is done by him. You have to ask him that question....Sir, I just want to add some light to your question.

We are brothers. Mr. Muhammad's youngest son attends al-Azhar, and his brother-in-law, in Egypt too. We are brothers, I was in Egypt. I lived in Egypt, I stayed in Egypt, and I was among brothers and I felt the spirit of brotherhood. But an Egyptian who comes to America should realize the problem confronted by Black people in this country. And when you see us being chased by a dog, the best thing for you to do is wait until the dog stops chasing us and then ask us some questions. Especially when you should have come a long time ago and helped your little brothers whip the dog. [Applause]

[Question unintelligible]

Malcolm X: There are many different ways to understand politics. Number one, we're not a political group. We are not politically inclined or motivated nor are our political aims in any way connected with the Honorable Elijah Muhammad. But when you study the science of politics, or study it as it's practiced in the UN at the international level, you'll find usually on questions you have those who say yes, those who say no, those who don't say anything.

Those who don't say anything usually are the neutrals. And by abstaining they have just as much political power, if not more so, than those who take an active part in all situations. Where the Negro in America is concerned, he's been without the ballot so long, today when he gets the ballot, he's ballot-happy. He's like the man to whom you give a gun, and he just starts shooting to let everybody know he's got a gun. He doesn't aim at anything.

Well, we believe in shooting, too. But we first believe that we should have a target and then when that target gets within our reach, then we'll put the bullet where it belongs. Or the ballot where it belongs. Whatever you call it, where it belongs. We don't see at this point where the Black man gains anything in politics.

Let me just give you an example. In the last presidential election, whites were evenly divided between Kennedy and Nixon. It was the Negro who went for Kennedy, 80 percent, and put Kennedy in the White House. And they went for him based upon the promises—false promises, by the way—that he made. Well, facts are facts. He said he [Applause]—I think everybody has a right to his opinion. [Laughter] And

I'm quite certain those who are familiar with Kennedy's promises to the Negro know what he said he could do with the stroke of his pen. And he was in office for two years before he found where his fountain pen was [Laughter and applause] where the Negro was concerned. [Applause]

And the excuse that he used was that he first had to change the attitude of southern segregationists. Now he didn't tell you that when he asked you to vote for him. But once he got in, then he had to tell you what problems he was facing. He didn't want to take a stand against the southern segregationists. But he did take a stand against U.S. Steel, which is the strongest corporation on this earth. He threw down the gauntlet. He threw down the gauntlet to Cuba. He has thrown down the gauntlet to anybody he desires. But when it comes to the Negro, he's always got an alibi that puts him off until a little while later. This is why we don't believe in any white politicians or anything like that can solve our problem. We'll get together among ourselves, with these students who go to these colleges and get equipped and solve the problem for ourselves....

[Question unintelligible]

Malcolm X: Whenever you send 15,000 troops and spend six or seven million dollars just to put one Negro in the midst of some yapping wolves, you haven't done that Negro nor the masses of Black people any favor, nor have you solved the problem. If it's legal and just and right for Meredith to be at the University of Mississippi according to Robert Kennedy, the attorney general, and all of the others, then every other Black man in Mississippi has just as much right to be there. So if you're going to spend all that money and all that manpower putting one in there, why not just go in and take the criminals who are responsible for keeping the masses out, and take them down off their posts and then open the doors to everybody. That would be a solution, but they're not going to do that. They always want to use methods that push one Negro at a time, then they use him to turn around and tell the masses, "You see, we're solving the problem." And the problem is still unsolved....

The Honorable Elijah Muhammad says the only way to solve the problem of the so-called Negro is complete separation in the United States.... The Honorable Elijah Muhammad says, every effort on the part of the government up till now to solve this problem by bringing about a just, equitable situation between whites and Blacks mixed up together here in this house has failed. Has failed absolutely. So he says that since you can't give the Negro justice in your house, let us leave this house and go back home.

Now at the same time that he says let us go back home to our own people and our own homeland, the government itself is the leading opposer toward any mass element of Black people becoming orientated in the direction of home. They put forth the effort to stop this. So what he says is, since you can't give it to us here mixed up in your house, and you don't want us to go home back to our own people, then the only alternative is to separate the house. Give us part of this country and let us live in that part. [Laughter]

You've asked me to explain. Now you want me to proceed? You may think its funny, but one of these days you won't. [Applause] ... He says that in this section that will be set aside for Black people, that the government should give us everything we need to start our own civilization. They should give us everything we need to exist for the next twenty-five years. And when you stop and consider the—you shouldn't be shocked, you give Latin America $20 billion

and they never fought for this country. They never worked for this country. You send billions of dollars to Poland and to Hungary, they're Communist countries, they never contributed anything here. [Applause]

This is what you should realize. The greatest contribution to this country was that which was contributed by the Black man. If I take the wages, just a moment, if I take the wages of everyone here, individually it means nothing, but collectively all of the earning power or wages that you earned in one week would make me wealthy. And if I could collect it for a year, I'd be rich beyond dreams. Now, when you see this, and then you stop and consider the wages that were kept back from millions of Black people, not for one year but for 310 years, you'll see how this country got so rich so fast. And what made the economy as strong as it is today. And all that, and all of that slave labor that was amassed in unpaid wages, is due someone today. And you're not giving us anything when we say that it's time to collect.

[Question unintelligible]

Malcolm X: Up until a few years ago, the whole dark world, which was then the majority, was ruled by Europe—the white man, who was actually a minority.

And realizing that they were only ruled because of the scientific effort put forth to divide and conquer by the European whites, all of the people black, brown, red, and yellow in Africa got together in what was known as the Bandung Conference. They realized that they had religious differences, economic differences, educational differences, even cultural differences. And they agreed to submerge all of their differences because they had one thing in common—oppression, exploitation. And they had an oppressor in common, an exploiter in common—the European. Once they realized they had this in common, they had a common enemy and they reached the agreement not to fight among themselves anymore.

And just by being able to submerge their own differences and come together in a spirit of unity, the Bandung Conference produced the condition by which all of the nations in Africa that are independent today were able to secure their independence. And so they have come into the UN. Now they are in a position they can outvote the white man. And it has actually created an accomplishment.

Whereas in the past you had European, white Christians always at the helm in the UN, today the black, brown, red, and yellow people of Africa and Asia so greatly outnumber the white man, they can't get a white, Christian European elected to any position of power. Usually, the secretariat and the president's chair stays in the hands of an African, an Asian, a Muslim, a Hindu, or a Christian. This is what unity is able to do.

And here in America, the Negro, the so-called Negroes, all we have to do is forget our differences. Usually whites cite things to try and divide us, and then use us one against the other. They try and use the NAACP against the Muslims, Muslims against CORE; they try and keep them all fighting one another. And as we fight one another, they continue to rule. So what the Honorable Elijah Muhammad says is what you and I should do is forget all of our differences and put first things first. Get at the one who's holding both of us down and we can talk to each other later on.

[Question unintelligible]

Malcolm X: The South African whites are, number one, on a continent where they don't belong and have no business there and won't be there that much longer. [Laughter and applause] The Black people in South Africa outnumber the whites there about eleven to one. [Applause] The Blacks in South Africa outnumber the whites. Enough to

get rid of them when the time comes. Now, their type of separation is not the type of separation that we're looking for. We're looking for a separation in which we have our own. We can either go back home and practice it or we can stay here and practice it. But we are not going to sit around with this integration hypocrisy that whites are talking about which will take another hundred years. The only thing you can bring about in the morning is complete separation. It has no connection or comparison whatsoever with that which is being practiced in South Africa.

South African apartheid is segregation. It's not separation. And they are afraid to let those Africans build up a society of their own in which they will become equal or just as powerful politically, economically, and otherwise as the whites are in their parts. They don't want that. No, no comparison whatsoever. Theirs is something of the past, it's outmoded and it's on its way out. Ours is riding on the wave of the future....

[Question unintelligible]

Malcolm X: If you can't receive justice in a man's house, that man deprives you of justice, he should let you leave. And if he doesn't want you to leave his house, yet he can't give you justice in the house, he'll end up losing the whole house himself. This is what America is faced with.

[Question unintelligible]

Malcolm X: No, the Fruit—you asked another question within that—the Fruit of Islam are the brothers who have been reformed, rehabilitated; who don't drink, don't smoke, don't commit fornication or adultery, don't become involved in any kind of crime. Who learn how to respect their women—to respect the Black woman, who has never had any respect or protection in this society. These are the brothers who have actually reformed themselves and they set an example of what the religion of Islam will do for others of the so-called Negroes. And these brothers will give you respect when you respect them.

[Question unintelligible]

Malcolm X: No, they don't comprise a small army. But an army in this sense—army only means a lot of people. They don't comprise an army in the sense that they are looking for violence. But you will find this: that a Muslim brother, whenever he's attacked, he'll defend himself.

[Question unintelligible]

Malcolm X: No, I'll answer the last question first. No, there's no such thing as a sincere white liberal—listen I'm giving you my answer. You can hiss all night, that's what the snake did in the Garden of Eden. [Laughter and applause]

Usually you'll find, sir, that in any integrated group that the so-called Negro has, if you examine its composition, where the whites are concerned, they end up leading it, they end up ruling it, they end up controlling it.

I'll give you an example. The NAACP is one of the leading organizations that Negroes have. It has been in existence for fifty-four years, and the Black people in the NAACP have never had enough power in there to elect a Black man as the national president. They have an election every year. Which means they have had an election fifty-four times in fifty-four years. And every time, they've had to elect a white man. The man who is the president of it now, Arthur Spingarn, has been president of it for twenty-four consecutive years.

Now if—I'm not knocking the NAACP—but if the NAACP—I'm just, uhm, analyzing it. [Laughter] If the NAACP in fifty-four years cannot get a Black man qualified to be its national president, then it leads me to believe either they are failing to create and develop the proper leadership caliber among the Black people in it, or else they are practicing the same

discrimination that they accuse the white man of.

Where CORE is concerned—the Urban League is another famous Negro organization that's integrated. It has a white president. It has never had a Black president. CORE has a Negro national director; but he's a Negro who's married to a white woman. James Farmer, he's married to a white woman and that almost makes him a white man. Although they have a Black—they have a white president also. It's true—Farmer, in 1945, divorced his Black wife and married a white woman.

[Question unintelligible]

Malcolm X: In the UN with the Lebanese or Arabs—in the UN you have the Afro-Asian-Arab bloc. Now a lot of Arabs might like for you to think that they are white, but whenever you see them involved in the international picture, they are lined up with the dark world. Those who are making progress are lined up with the dark world. Afro-Asian-Arab. They can come around here and pose as white. But when they get back home, they're not white....

[Question unintelligible]

Malcolm X: You never heard me today refer to myself as a Black Muslim. This is what the press says. We call ourselves Muslim. Just a moment. We call ourselves Muslim—we don't call ourselves Black Muslims. This is what the newspapers call us. This is what Dr. Eric Lincoln calls us. We are Muslims. Black, brown, red, and yellow.

[Question unintelligible]

Malcolm X: Now you say that we come here and use Islam for political purposes because we reject the white man. When the Algerians refused to integrate with the French, did that make, mean that they weren't Muslims? When the Arabs refused to integrate with the Israelis, does that mean they're not Muslims? When the Pakistanis refused to integrate with the Hindus, does that mean they're not Muslims? No, just a moment. The Algerians have the right to reject the French, who exploited them. The Arabs have the right to reject the Israelis, whom they feel exploit them. The Pakistanis have the right to reject the Hindus, whom they feel exploit them. The Algerians are still Muslims. The Arabs are still Muslims and the Pakistanis are still Muslims. There are 20 million Black people in this country who have been here for 400 years. And who have suffered the worst form of abuse ever perpetrated on a people in the twentieth century. Now when we accept Islam as our religion, that doesn't mean that we are religiously wrong to reject the man who has exploited us and colonized us here in this country.

[Question unintelligible]

Malcolm X: It's not wrong to expect justice. It's not wrong to expect freedom. It's not wrong to expect equality. If Patrick Henry and all of the Founding Fathers of this country were willing to lay down their lives to get what you are enjoying today, then it's time for you to realize that a large, ever-increasing number of Black people in this country are willing to die for what we know is due us by birth.

The white man is being given a favor, when you give him a chance today to solve a problem that stems from a crime that he committed himself. You ask me—like I'm committing a crime or asking for something that's ethically wrong or morally wrong when we seek a solution to this problem right now. A problem that has the government all tied up all over this earth. What you need to realize, you from India, you from Iraq, you from Egypt, and you from right here in America, and we who are enslaved—that a crime has been committed against the Negro. Some of you from over there, you knew we were over here and never come over here to help us, and now when

we stand up and are ready to help ourselves, don't come with your criticism. Help us.

[Question unintelligible]

Malcolm X: Would you think that I was wrong if I asked: how are you going to integrate? If the Supreme Court says integrate, and they can't do it, and that's the highest court—we're not rejecting anything. We reserve—I said no, he asked me was I rejecting, were we rejecting violence or were we rejecting peaceful methods. We don't reject any methods. We leave—we reserve the right to use whatever method that will bring about a solution to the problem and then when—and the reason that I haven't— Sir, I don't think you would give me credit. If you have a lamb inside of a wolf's den and you need to get that lamb out of the clutches of that wolf, you don't stand up and tell the lamb, how are you going to take him, or where you're going to take him, while he's still in the clutches of the wolf, or while he's still under the jurisdiction of the wolf....

[Question unintelligible]

Malcolm X: As you say, [Uncle] Tom always was a good actor. And where the white man thinks we're dangerous to him, Tom is more dangerous to the white man than anyone, because Tom has him fooled.

The white man knows where we stand; but Tom today is waking up the same as anybody else. Well, you won't get any argument out of me. It is true that many Negroes in prominent positions who have been known Uncle Toms in the past today are waking up, and their allegiances and other aims are very much camouflaged still, as they were then....

[Question unintelligible]

Malcolm X: We'll do it the same way the Jews got what they wanted. They got their own state, their own country. No, they got it, and yeah, well you're right, it was given to them by

England and Truman. But, sir, no the Jews are the ones who usually represent themselves as white liberals. More so probably than any other segment of this society. Now if the Jews are genuinely liberal and they want to help the Negro, then they should show the Negro how to use the same kind of strategy and tactics to solve his problem that they used to solve their problems. And you'll find that all over this country, wherever the Jews have been segregated and Jim Crowed, they haven't sat-in, they haven't been sit-in or Freedom Riders, they usually go and use the economic weapon. They bought Atlantic City, and now they can go there. They bought Miami Beach and now they can go there. [Laughter and applause]

CHAPTER 19

Vietnam Traps Lyndon Johnson

*"I can't get out, and I can't finish it with what I have got.
And I don't know what the hell to do!"*

The month of July 1965 should have been one of the most satisfying of Lyndon Johnson's life. A man of driving ambition, he had risen from a rural Texas backwater to the most powerful office in the world. His road to the White House had been bumpy and winding. Johnson had come within a few votes of losing a U.S. Senate primary election in 1948 that would have derailed his political career. A massive heart attack in 1955 had almost killed him. Elected vice president in 1960, he was marginalized in the administration of President John F. Kennedy to the point of near-invisibility. But Kennedy's assassination on November 22, 1963, had made "LBJ" president, albeit under the most tragic of circumstances. He won a smashing reelection victory over Republican Barry Goldwater in November 1964, carrying 44 states and outpolling his opponent by a margin of almost 16 million votes.

Now, in July 1965, as a popular president whose Democratic Party enjoyed solid majorities in both houses of Congress, Johnson had launched the most ambitious program of economic and social reform since the New Deal and the most transformative agenda of civil rights legislation since Reconstruction. Johnson was a Southerner, but he was sensitive to the effects of racial discrimination and inequality, and resolved to use his presidency to do something about them. As a young New Deal congressman, he had been one of Franklin D. Roosevelt's most enthusiastic supporters, a passionate advocate for an expanded federal role in improving the lives of ordinary Americans. The youthful Johnson believed, in fact, that the New Deal did not go far enough. In July 1965, President Johnson was determined to complete FDR's unfinished agenda.

Johnson would do so through a massive program he called the Great Society. Its centerpiece was the War on Poverty, which included job training programs, aid to education, medical assistance for the indigent, and increased social service expenditures. The president had not stopped there. The Medicare Act, which would for the first time in the nation's history provide health insurance to the elderly, was working its way through Congress. In addition, having already secured passage of the Civil Rights Act of 1964, prohibiting all forms of discrimination in public accommodations and hiring (see Chapter 18 on Malcolm X), Johnson now set his sights on a sweeping Voting Rights Act that would enable African Americans to at last enjoy full citizenship rights. It too was close to passage.

In July 1965, then, Lyndon Johnson should have been savoring his accomplishments and successes. Instead, he was gloomy and pessimistic, almost despairing. The reason was Vietnam, a small country half a world away. Johnson never imagined that this Southeast Asian nation would occupy so much of his time and energy. He had intended his presidency to be one of domestic achievement; foreign affairs had always been an afterthought. Yet here was Vietnam, pushing up against his dreams of an America free from poverty and racism, constraining his actions and resources. In July 1965, Johnson could already see the walls crashing in. As the nation's Chief Executive, he was privy to information others did not see. While his Democratic Party allies celebrated his domestic triumphs, Johnson feared the worst: Vietnam could ruin his presidency.

How did it come to this? And how do we know so much about Johnson's state of mind in July 1965? Richard Nixon was not the only president to tape White House conversations. LBJ's Oval Office recordings reveal much about this complicated, contradictory personality, in turn kind and cruel, confident and insecure, idealistic and cynical. They show Johnson agonizing over a Vietnam conflict that is spinning out of control and offer both a glimpse into the mind of a powerful decision maker and a window onto the most important decision of his career.

To understand how Vietnam came to consume Lyndon Johnson's presidency, we must go back to the origins of the Cold War in the immediate aftermath of World War II, a time when it was possible that the young Johnson, then a Texas congressman, could not even locate Vietnam on a map. President Harry Truman, who had succeeded Roosevelt in April 1945, had adopted a policy of "containment" toward the Soviet Union, which he and his advisers viewed as relentlessly expansionist and implacably hostile. After World War II, the Soviets established puppet regimes in East Germany and the eastern European states on its borders, sought to subvert pro-American governments in nations such as Greece and Turkey, and even attempted to come to power through legal communist parties in France and Italy. Everywhere, it seemed, communism was on the march, and Truman shared Whittaker Chambers' fear that unless the United States made a strong countervailing stand, it would be on the losing side (see Chapter 11).

The "containment" strategy attempted to parry every Soviet thrust with countervailing political, economic, cultural, and if necessary, military power. The president gave containment virtual worldwide application when he declared in his 1947 "Truman Doctrine" address that "it must be the policy of the United States to support free peoples who are resisting attempted subjugation by armed minorities."[1] This meant that Vietnam, despite its distant location and relatively small size, assumed a position of major importance for American policymakers. France, a crucial U.S. Cold War ally, had been Vietnam's colonial master from the nineteenth century until World War II, when the Japanese invaded the country. After the war, the French moved to reestablish their control. Standing in their way was Ho Chi Minh, a popular local leader whose ideology combined Marxism and intense Vietnamese nationalism.

Ho Chi Minh had fought his entire life to free Vietnam from foreign influence and secure its independence. While Ho was a communist, he was not a puppet of the Soviet Union, or for that matter, neighboring China, which had fallen to Marxist rebels led by Mao Tse-tung in 1949. Ho accepted military and economic assistance from his two allies, but he made political decisions based on his own nation's interests. This distinction, however, was lost on Truman and his advisers. They regarded Ho as an agent of the Soviet Union and China, and thus an enemy in the escalating Cold War. Ho had to be defeated because communism needed to be contained everywhere in the world. Failure anywhere, even in a nation that did not directly threaten American security interests, would represent a loss of "credibility" and "face" among its allies and treaty partners. Vietnam thus had a symbolic power that extended far beyond its borders. Lyndon Johnson may not have paid the Cold War much mind as a congressman and senator in the 1940s and 1950s, but as a loyal Democrat he accepted the containment doctrine without question. He entered the presidency in 1963 so firmly committed to its perspectives and assumptions that he could not imagine any workable alternative.

Thus it came to be that while Johnson could see an onrushing train of disaster in Vietnam he could not bring himself to turn aside.

The United States needed France in its Cold War competition with the Soviet Union, and France wanted its Vietnamese colony back. This was enough to impel Truman and his successor in the White House, Dwight Eisenhower, to spend billions of dollars between 1945 and 1954 to support France's increasingly futile efforts to defeat Ho Chi Minh militarily and retain control over Vietnam. When that effort ended in defeat with the surrender of France's main colonial army to Ho's forces at Dien Bien Phu in May 1954, the United States stepped in to take France's place. Later that year, at a peace conference in Geneva, Switzerland, it was agreed that Vietnam would be temporarily partitioned. Ho would control the north, while below the 17th parallel, South Vietnam would be an American sphere of influence. Elections to reunify the country were scheduled for 1956.

They were never held. American officials quickly realized that Ngo Dinh Diem, their handpicked choice as South Vietnamese president, would be no match for the popular Ho in a free election. Diem was a stiff and remote aristocrat who had lived abroad while Ho was fighting the French for his country's independence. Diem was also a devout Catholic in a predominantly Buddhist nation, estranging him even further from the average Vietnamese citizen. Rather than see Vietnam unified under Ho's Marxist regime, the United States refused to participate in elections, arguing that they could not be fair if conducted under communist auspices. The country remained divided.

Over the next two decades, Ho and his successors fought relentlessly to make Vietnam a single nation. By 1959, an insurgent movement had formed in South Vietnam to oppose the Diem government, which had balked at crucial land reform and was riddled with cronyism and corruption. Ho moved to use the insurgency for his own purposes, and the next year it was officially named the National Liberation Front (NLF) under his leadership and control. The NLF launched guerrilla attacks on government installations in the cities and soon controlled much of South Vietnam's abundant countryside, where 90% of its population lived. In time, American troops would give NLF fighters the nickname "Vietcong," a contraction of the words "Vietnam Communist." The NLF/Vietcong used a combination of largesse and intimidation to dominate large sections of rural South Vietnam, aided by the Diem government's many failings. Ho also sent units of North Vietnam's regular army to the South, where it engaged Diem's often demoralized army.

President Eisenhower attempted to prop up Diem without committing a significant number of American ground troops. During the 1950s, the United States sent South Vietnam some $127 million in direct economic aid, as well as about 1500 "advisers" charged with training its army and strengthening its domestic institutions.[2] The process of nation building was difficult, however, with the intransigent Diem seemingly more interested in personal gain and absolute power than in improving the lives of his people. But Diem's reliable anticommunism meant that neither Eisenhower nor John F. Kennedy, who became president in 1961, could safely jettison him. As the only alternative to Ho Chi Minh and a Marxist Vietnam, he was "the best we've got," in Kennedy's rueful words.[3]

With the Diem regime in danger of falling to the communists in 1962, JFK stepped up his efforts to save it. He sent more advisers to the country, bringing their total to 9,000 by the end of the year.[4] Kennedy also instituted a "strategic hamlet" program, under which a number of South Vietnamese villages were combined in one area and placed under American protection. Neither this initiative nor the increased number of advisers stemmed the NLF tide, and by the end of 1962, 300,000 Vietcong occupied South Vietnam. Making matters worse, Diem continued to resist reform measures despite Kennedy's entreaties. The final straw came during the spring and summer of 1963, when Diem launched a harsh crackdown on Buddhist critics of his regime, ordering mass arrests, raids on houses of worship, and beatings of demonstrators. When a number of Buddhists publicly burned themselves to death in protest, Diem responded dismissively. This was too much even for JFK. Anti-communist or not, Diem had to go. On November 1, 1963, a group of South Vietnamese generals, acting with the tacit encouragement of the Kennedy Administration, deposed Diem and—against JFK's wishes—murdered him. Three weeks later Kennedy himself was murdered, and Johnson inherited Vietnam and its burdens.

The new president was acutely aware of the shadow cast by his predecessor. Kennedy, with his elite background and air of charisma, made Johnson appear provincial and oafish by comparison. Ivy League–educated Kennedy aides would snicker at the vice president from Southwest Texas State Teachers College. Johnson harbored deep insecurities about his worth in relation to the glittering Kennedy circle. Perhaps as a form of compensation, Johnson asked virtually all of JFK's top officials to stay on, including the late president's brother, Attorney General Robert Kennedy, whom Johnson disliked and distrusted. These men had been the architects of Kennedy's Vietnam policy, which LBJ also resolved to continue. Kennedy, in the words of historian George Herring, had "accepted, without critical analysis, the assumption that a non-Communist Vietnam was vital to America's global interests."[5] Now Johnson did as well. The weight of prior decisions made by Truman, Eisenhower, and Kennedy hung over the new Johnson presidency. LBJ believed they predetermined his course.

Like his White House predecessors, Johnson used what he perceived as the "lessons" of recent history to dictate his actions in Vietnam. For LBJ, there were three such "lessons." First, there was the "lesson" of Munich. In 1938, at a conference in that city, British prime minister Neville Chamberlain attempted to appease German dictator Adolf Hitler by permitting him to annex the Sudetenland section of Czechoslovakia. The very next year, the Nazi leader invaded Poland and began World War II. From these events, Johnson drew the "lesson" that totalitarians—in this case Ho Chi Minh—had to be confronted.

Then there was the "lesson" of China. When that country fell to Mao Tse-tung's communist forces in 1949, Republicans scapegoated President Truman and the Democratic Party for having "lost" China. The resulting anticommunist hysteria that swept the nation made the rise of the red-baiting senator Joseph McCarthy possible and allowed him to brand Democrats generally as "soft on communism." The Democratic Party proceeded to lose presidential elections in 1952 and 1956. China's "lesson," as far as Johnson was concerned, was never to allow Vietnam to fall to communism, or the consequences for his party would be severe.

Finally, there was the "lesson" of Korea. In June 1950, Marxist North Korea invaded South Korea, a U.S. ally. Acting decisively, President Truman committed American ground troops to defending the South. After a back-and-forth struggle that included hostilities with China and cost some 33,000 American lives, an armistice was signed in 1953 that preserved South Korea's independence. Korea taught Johnson that allies of the United States had to be defended against aggressor states even if they were thousands of miles away in Asia, but not so vigorously as to prompt an attack by China—which by the early 1960s had developed nuclear weapons.

The "lessons" of Munich, China, and Korea, then, determined Lyndon Johnson's course in Vietnam. History, of course, is a useful guide to understanding the present and planning for the future. But history is an art and not a science. The variability of human experience makes the literal application of its "lessons" dangerous. Ho Chi Minh was not Adolf Hitler. China dwarfed Vietnam in its impact on America's vital interests. South Koreans were willing to fight for their country's independence against the invaders from the North. History never reproduces identical circumstances. Johnson's failure to appreciate this truth was the great tragedy of his presidency.

In March 1964, four months after Johnson assumed office, the NLF controlled approximately 40% of the territory of South Vietnam and about half its population. Unless they were dislodged, the South would fall. Johnson believed he had no choice but to increase the American presence there. On August 4, 1964, he received the opportunity he hoped for when two U.S. reconnaissance ships reported an attack by North Vietnamese gunboats in international waters. In response, LBJ sent Congress the Gulf of Tonkin Resolution, named after the site of the incident, which authorized the president to take "all necessary measures to repel any armed attack against the forces of the United States and to prevent further aggression."[6] It passed the House of Representatives unanimously and the Senate by a vote of 88 to 2. In reality, however, on the night of August 4 the American ships were in North Vietnamese waters and conducting espionage activities. Further investigation raised questions of whether the reported attacks had taken place at all. In his eagerness to win its approval, Johnson had not informed Congress of these complicating factors. He would employ the Gulf of Tonkin Resolution as a blanket authorization for his actions in Vietnam for the rest of his presidency.

In March 1965, with South Vietnam once again in imminent danger of collapse, Johnson authorized the massive "Rolling Thunder" bombing campaign against Vietcong and North Vietnamese targets, the largest in history up to that time. In April, he ordered 40,000 additional troops to the country in response to the demands of his commanding general, William Westmoreland. By June, Westmoreland was asking for 150,000 more troops and Johnson was at a crossroads. The White House recordings show him increasingly desperate, reaching out to aides, congressional allies, and even his wife Lady Bird, as he searched for an answer—any answer—to the question of what to do about Vietnam.

None of his options were attractive. If he escalated the war with a large infusion of men and material, as Westmoreland and his Joint Chiefs of Staff advised, he ran the risk of angering Congress, siphoning resources away from his Great Society programs, and bringing China into the war on the side of North Vietnam. If he committed only enough troops to hold the line against the Vietcong and North Vietnamese, as his Secretary of Defense Robert McNamara counseled, he would only delay an inevitable South Vietnamese—and American—defeat. If he withdrew his forces, as Undersecretary of State George Ball recommended, he would be attacked by Republicans for "surrendering" to communism and would signal to America's treaty allies across the globe that its word could not be relied upon. "I can't get out, and I can't finish it with what I have got," he had told Lady Bird in March 1965. "And I don't know what the hell to do!"[7]

Gradually, Johnson moved toward the middle ground, as so many presidents do when faced with a major decision. He knew that if he gave Westmoreland all the troops he wanted, the general would soon be back asking for more. "(I)f they get a hundred and fifty (thousand)," he told Senate Majority Leader Mike Mansfield on June 8, "they'll have to have another hundred and fifty. And then they'll have to have *another* hundred and fifty."[8] But Johnson also knew how badly the war was going and how close South Vietnam was to collapse. "(We) think (the North Vietnamese) are winning," he told Mansfield. "Now if *we* think they're winning, you can imagine what *they* think."[9] Johnson hoped, as he told Senator Birch Bayh of Indiana on June 15, "to deter them and wear them out, without losing a lot of people."[10] But he had little faith in that strategy. "We killed twenty-six thousand Vietcong this year," he complained to Dwight Eisenhower during a conversation with the former president on July 2. "Three hundred yesterday.... Two hundred and fifty of them the day before. But they just keep coming in from North Vietnam."[11]

Johnson was also concerned about the fates of two pieces of domestic legislation close to his heart. The Medicare and Voting Rights bills were before Congress that month. Shifting attention to Vietnam might jeopardize them. Thus, whatever he decided to do about the war, he needed to do it without fanfare. This meant no major presidential speech to Congress; no announcement of a national emergency or state of war; no call-ups of Army reserve units; no increase in taxes to pay for increased Vietnam spending; and no request for a new congressional authorization to replace the Gulf of Tonkin Resolution.

By late July, LBJ had made his decision. He would give Westmoreland more troops, but not as many as the general wanted—50,000 right away, with more to follow incrementally during the rest of the year. It would be done quietly. "I can't just sit there and let (American troops) be murdered," Johnson told Mansfield on July 27. "So I've got to put enough there to hold them and protect them. And...if we don't heat it up ourselves, and we don't dramatize it, we don't play it up and say we're appropriating billions and we're sending millions and all (those) men, I don't think that you (will) get the Russians....or the Chinese worked up about it."[12] The next day, during a routine press conference, Johnson announced almost casually that 50,000 new troops would be sent to Vietnam, with the possibility of reinforcements in the future as the military situation demanded.

On July 30, with former President Truman at his side, LBJ signed the Medicare Act. On August 6, standing in the Capitol Rotunda before a bust of Abraham Lincoln, he signed the Voting Rights Act. Johnson hoped that these laws would help build his legacy, and of course they have. But Johnson's July 28 announcement on Vietnam would be his defining legacy. By the end of 1965, LBJ had sent another 50,000 military personnel to the country, bringing the total of U.S. servicemen there to 175,000.[13] Two years later that number had risen to 431,000, and in early 1968, over half a million.[14] The massive draft calls necessary to sustain such manpower levels radicalized college campuses and fueled an antiwar movement that would topple the Johnson presidency and alter the direction of American political culture (see Chapter 17 on SDS).

By 1967, Johnson was spending $2 billion per month on Vietnam, and the Great Society programs he so cherished were drawing criticism from a resurgent Republican right and even elements of the Democratic Party. An escalated ground war and saturation bombings had killed hundreds of thousands of the enemy, but still they fought on, pouring troops and material down the so-called "Ho Chi Minh Trail" just outside Vietnam's borders in nominally "neutral" Laos and Cambodia. With 200,000 North Vietnamese youths becoming draft-eligible each year, that nation was able to replenish its losses and keep soldiers in the field, where both regular army units and the Vietcong proved resourceful, elusive, and unyielding. Despite billions of dollars in U.S. military assistance, the South Vietnamese never developed an army capable of fighting independently, forcing American troops to fight "their" war for them. While the political situation in the South finally stabilized in 1965 with the installation of General Nguyen Van Thieu as president—a position he would hold until his country fell to the North Vietnamese in 1975—governmental corruption and repression continued. Efforts at land reform stalled in the countryside and food shortages and black markets plagued the cities. South Vietnam was simply not a viable nation.

The final blow to Johnson's presidency came in January 1968 when North Vietnamese and Vietcong forces launched a massive offensive timed to coincide with the Tet Lunar New Year observance. It overran South Vietnam's major cities and even reached the grounds of the American embassy in Saigon. While U.S. and South Vietnamese forces retook the cities and inflicted heavy casualties on the enemy, the offensive shocked an American public that had been led to believe the war was winding down and, in the words of Westmoreland, there was "some light at the end of the tunnel."[15]

After the Tet Offensive, poll support for the war plummeted, with more Americans opposing it than favoring it for the first time since American involvement began.

Walter Cronkite, the CBS news anchor known as "Uncle Walter" for his integrity and honesty, exclaimed, "What the hell is going on? I thought we were winning the war!"[16] When Johnson heard of this remark, he said, "if I've lost Cronkite, I've lost Middle America."[17] The success of antiwar presidential candidate Eugene McCarthy in the February 1968 New Hampshire Democratic primary and the entry of LBJ's nemesis Robert Kennedy into the race in mid-March reflected the hardening divisions among Democrats over the war and foretold an intraparty bloodbath if Johnson insisted on running for reelection. On the evening of March 31, 1968, the president went before the American people in a nationally televised address on Vietnam and announced a bombing reduction, the initiation of peace negotiations with the North Vietnamese, and his decision not to seek another term in office. Just as Johnson feared in July 1965, Vietnam had wrecked his presidency.

In November 1968, Americans elected Republican Richard Nixon to succeed Johnson in the hope that he could find a way out of the Vietnam quagmire. Nixon did, but at the cost of some 20,000 additional lives, bringing the total of Americans killed in the war to over 58,000.[18] Nixon's attempts to end the war, in his words, "with honor," included a "Vietnamization" program that shifted primary military responsibilities to the South Vietnamese; the 1970 invasion of neighboring Cambodia to attack North Vietnamese and Vietcong sanctuaries; and the furious, saturation-level "Christmas bombing" of December 1972. Here, Nixon took advantage of American détente with China to attack North Vietnam's capital of Hanoi and its major port in Haiphong, targets that Johnson had been afraid to strike.

None of Nixon's measures significantly affected North Vietnam's will to fight. Even Ho Chi Minh's death in September 1969 did not alter its resolve. The January 1973 peace treaty that finally extricated the United States from Vietnam left much of the South under the control of North Vietnamese and Vietcong forces. It was only a matter of time before hostilities commenced again. When they did in the spring of 1975, the South Vietnamese army collapsed abjectly and fell in weeks to a North Vietnamese offensive. On May 1, Northern troops marched into the Southern capital of Saigon, posthumously fulfilling Ho Chi Minh's dream of a united Vietnam. Saigon was immediately renamed Ho Chi Minh City.

Lyndon Johnson died in January 1973. In a final touch of irony, his death came one day before President Nixon's announcement that the United States and North Vietnam had agreed to a treaty ending America's direct military involvement in the war. LBJ had already lived through a nightmare. Reelected in 1964 in an epic landslide, he was driven out of office four years later. Thanks to Vietnam, a war he knew from the outset he could not win, Johnson's vision of a Great Society free from need and want would not be fulfilled. Thanks also to Vietnam, the United States was more divided than it had been since the Civil War. The conflict fractured America's political and social unity. It separated parents from children, students from teachers, and young from old (see Chapter 17 on Students for a Democratic Society). It exacerbated already existing racial tensions (see Chapter 18 on Malcolm X). It helped create an angry, frustrated "silent majority," as well as an alienated counterculture, facing off against each other in a "culture war" that would last for decades and continue into the twenty-first century. It stretched the American economy to its breaking point, causing inflation, depressing the value of the dollar, and setting the stage for the recession and stagnation of the 1970s.

Finally, Vietnam raised questions regarding America's world role and its conduct of the Cold War. Was there an alternative to the "containment" strategy that had pushed Lyndon Johnson down the road to defeat in Vietnam? Did the "lessons" of Munich, China, and Korea impel the United States to intervene in regions like Southeast Asia? Should communism be confronted everywhere in the world?

Did foreign governments merit American support simply because they were anticommunist? What were the limits of American "credibility" when confronting Marxism abroad? What were the limits of American power generally? While men like Whittaker Chambers (see Chapter 11) and organizations like Students for a Democratic Society (see Chapter 17) offered their own answers to these questions, only presidents were in a position to confront them with the force of national authority. In Chapter 21, we will see how President Ronald Reagan turned the conversation over these questions in a new direction, moving past the idea of containing communism and instead envisioning its elimination.

Questions for Consideration and Conversation

1. Why did Lyndon Johnson feel he "had" to hold the line in Vietnam? How was he a prisoner of decisions previous American presidents had made?

2. How did American policymakers misapprehend Ho Chi Minh? Why was he so hard to understand?

3. How did Johnson use what he perceived as the historical "lessons" of the recent past to determine his policy in Vietnam? Do you think this was an appropriate use of history?

4. Imagine Johnson sitting down with Tom Hayden (Chapter 17) in 1965 and attempting to justify his decision to escalate the war in Vietnam. What would he say? What would Hayden say?

5. What were Johnson's Vietnam policy options as of June 1965? Why were all of them fraught with peril?

6. Why did LBJ feel he had to announce his decision to send large numbers of American troops to Vietnam in such a muted, almost offhand way? How did this eventually come to wreck his presidency?

7. How would Ronald Reagan (Chapter 21) evaluate Johnson's decisions on Vietnam? Samuel Huntington (Chapter 23)?

Endnotes

1. Truman Doctrine Address, quoted in William H. Chafe, *The Unfinished Journey: America Since World War II*, 6th ed. (New York: Oxford University Press, 2007), 63.

2. George C. Herring, *America's Longest War: The United States and Vietnam, 1950–1975*, 2nd ed. (New York: Knopf, 1986), 56, 59.

3. John F. Kennedy, quoted in Ibid., 85.

4. Ibid., 86.

5. Ibid., 106.

6. Gulf of Tonkin Resolution, quoted in Thomas D. Langston, *Lyndon Baines Johnson* (Washington, DC: CQ Press, 2002), 188.

7. Lyndon B. Johnson, quoted in Michael Beschloss, *Reaching for Glory: Lyndon Johnson's Secret Tapes, 1964–1965* (New York: Simon & Schuster, 2001), 216.

8. Lyndon B. Johnson, quoted in Ibid., 345.

9. Ibid., 346.

10. Ibid., 355.

11. Ibid., 384.

12. Ibid., 412–13.

13. David Kaiser, *American Tragedy: Kennedy, Johnson, and the Origins of the Vietnam War* (Cambridge, MA: Harvard University Press, 2000), 478.

14. Ibid., 490; Herring, *America's Longest War*, 152.

15. William Westmoreland, quoted in Larry Berman, *Lyndon Johnson's War: The Road to Stalemate in Vietnam* (New York: W.W. Norton, 1989), 120.

16. Walter Cronkite, quoted in Don Oberdorfer, *Tet! The Turning Point in the Vietnam War* (Baltimore, MD: The Johns Hopkins University Press, 1971), 158.

17. Lyndon B. Johnson, quoted in Robert Dallek, *Flawed Giant: Lyndon Johnson and His Times, 1961–1973* (New York: Oxford University Press, 1998), 506.

18. Herring, *America's Longest War*, 256.

EXCERPTS FROM WHITE HOUSE TAPES (1965)

Source: Michael Beschloss, *Reaching for Glory: Lyndon Johnson's Secret Tapes, 1964–1965.* New York: Simon & Schuster, 2001, pp. 216, 238–39, 279–80, 344–53, 354–62, 364–66, 376–77, 381–84, 407–13.

Lady Bird Johnson

Sunday, March 7, 1965, Tape-recorded Diary

LADY BIRD: In talking about the Vietnam situation [during dinner], Lyndon summed it up quite simply— "I can't get out, and I can't finish it with what I have got. And I don't know what the hell to do!"

Drew Pearson

Tuesday, March 23, 1965, 11:35 A.M.

LBJ: I don't believe I can walk out.... If I did, they'd take Thailand.... They'd take Cambodia....They'd take Burma....They'd take Indonesia....They'd take India.... They'd come right back and take the Philippines....I'd be another Chamberlain and...we'd have another Munich. The aggressors feed on blood....I'm *not* coming *home! They* may get another President, but I'm not going to pull out. Now, the second thing is negotiation....I've said in forty different speeches I'll go anywhere, I'll do anything...in an honorable way to promote peace at any time....Okay. Now let's see whether I need to go to Hanoi or not. Let's see whether I need to go to Peiping or not. My last intelligence from Peiping sums it up pretty well...."Mao Tse-tung says that Emperor Johnson must know that he cannot win at the conference table what he has lost on the battlefield." Now, so far that's pretty strong for China.

PEARSON: It sure is.

LBJ: They denounced Russia yesterday morning for...not coming in and raising more hell themselves. So Hanoi—I got a most recent report that says they think that the South is crumbling. They will not talk negotiation...until we pull back to San Francisco. Until we get out. Until they take over South Vietnam. Then they'll be glad to talk....

So the third thing is the LeMay viewpoint. I can take my bombs, and I can take my nuclear weapons, as Barry [Goldwater] says. I can defoliate, and I can clear out that brush where I can see anybody coming down that line, and I can wipe out Hanoi, and I can wipe out Peiping....But I think that would start World War III....I'd have seven, eight hundred million, and I'd have a land war in Asia. I think I'd have to send three or four hundred thousand men there....I haven't bombed any cities. I haven't killed any women and children. I have said I would be "appropriate and fitting and measured."...The people of South Vietnam forces do have some tear gas and nausea bombs....Every police chief in the United States has them...Rather than shooting people, you give them something that will upset their stomach or make their eyes blink. Hell, they used them in Selma a week ago.... All this big propaganda they are making about gas? It's not poison gas....It's the same kind of gas Chief Murray's got right here if the Negroes started moving into the White House and they told them to stop. And it's the same kind used by...military police everyplace. Matter of fact, we got them down there right now in case the state troopers and the rest of them take us on in Alabama....

PEARSON: Yeah.

LBJ: ...When Kennedy didn't have it in Mississippi, they just raised unshirted hell, and he had to...fly them in, day and night, so they could protect our people.... When the mob gets in action, a hundred thousand people coming at you, turn it loose....These boys—the propagandists and the Communists—are working pretty full string. They keep us, all the time, fighting with our own people, trying to explain that we are not warmongers. Trying to explain to the Goldwaters and to the Nixons—and even to the Lodges and to Rockefeller—why we are not dropping bombs up there....And I have to explain to them....Let's do like I do with my daughter Luci. Let's try to reason with them. Let's be patient....I'll make any sacrifice to keep people from being killed. Just like I didn't want to go into Montgomery and Selma. I did everything a human could to *avoid* it....[Governor Wallace] came up here. I spent three hours with him....He said that he would do it. Then he wouldn't do it because he "didn't have money." So I was left with no choice.

LBJ: How did you like that speech before the Congress?

PEARSON: Which one?

LBJ: Before the Congress in joint session on civil rights?

PEARSON: Oh, that was terrific.

LBJ: Thank you. Bye!

Philip Potter

Washington Bureau Chief, Baltimore Sun
Saturday, April 17, 1965, 9:01 A.M.

LBJ: [This] Asian situation...is the number-one problem on my desk. I'm trying, with everything I've got, day and night. A good many people don't know and can't know all the things that we're trying to do. Because it would considerably weaken us. But I can assure you that the Churches and the Indians don't want peace as much as I do.

POTTER: I'm sure of that.

LBJ: ...Pearson comes out with his suggestion that we have a cease-fire....He says, "Don't bomb three or four days, and see if you can't work out...some kind of an agreement." And I said.... "[If we] just did nothing, can you, Mr. Russia, indicate to me that they would quit?...Could you indicate, Mr. British, that they would quit? Could you indicate, Mr. France, that they would quit?...That I wouldn't lose everything I'd done?" No! No! None of them can give you anything!

POTTER: I understand.

LBJ: ...They wouldn't quit. They would really move in then and try to take our planes out of Danang. Or they would hit our Pleiku compound....We think we have made phenomenal progress. The report I got from out there yesterday was just unbelievable. Looks like almost a new day, although I...don't want to be too much optimistic, because I always get thrown for a loss when I do.

POTTER: Yes, sir.

LBJ: ...[The Senate] Foreign Relations [Committee] really has no great strong leadership....Fulbright philosophizes. He's a great liberal, but he's against wage-and-hour. And he's a gre-e-eat man, but he wants Armed Services to take over all the military assistance. He just doesn't want to take on anything that's real tough.

Lady Bird Johnson

Sunday, April 18, 1965, Tape-recorded Diary

LADY BIRD: We talked about the short nights Lyndon has been having for several months. He asked to be waked up whenever there was an operation going out. He won't leave it alone. He said, "I want to be called every time somebody dies." He can't separate himself from it. Actually, I don't want him to, no matter how painful. In Washington, he seldom gets to sleep until about two.

Mike Mansfield

Tuesday, June 8, 1965, 5:05 P.M.

LBJ: I don't see exactly the medium for pulling out [of Vietnam].... [But] I want to talk to you....Rusk doesn't know that I'm thinking this. McNamara doesn't know I'm thinking this. Bundy doesn't. I haven't talked to a human. I'm over here in bed. I just tried to take a nap and get going with my second day, and I couldn't. I just decided I'd call you. But I think I'll say to the Congress that General Eisenhower thought we ought to go in there and do here what we...did in Greece and Turkey, and...President Kennedy thought we ought to do this....But all of my military people tell me...that we cannot do this [with] the commitment [of American forces] we have now. It's got to be materially increased. And the outcome is not really predictable at the moment.... I would say...that...our seventy-five thousand men are going to be in great danger unless they have seventy-five thousand more....

    I'm no military man at all. But...if they get a hundred and fifty [thousand Americans], they'll have to have another hundred and fifty. And then they'll have to have *another* hundred and fifty. So, the big question then is: What does the Congress want to do about it?...I know what the military wants to do. I really know what Rusk and McNamara want to

do....And I think I know what the country wants to do *now*. But I'm not sure that they want to do that *six months* from now. I want you to give me your best thinking on it. See how we ought to handle it, if we handle it at all....We have...some very bad news on the government [in Saigon].... Westmoreland says that the offensive that he has anticipated, that he's been fearful of, is now on. And he wants people as quickly as he can get them.

MANSFIELD: [Fulbright] is tremendously disturbed about the situation in Vietnam.

LBJ: Well, we *all* are.

MANSFIELD: I know, but I mean, *really*....He just feels it's too little and too late....

LBJ: ...Unless you can guard what you're doing, you can't do anything. We can't build an airport, by God, much less build an REA line. And it takes more people to guard us in building an airport than it does to build the airport.... That's why we had to limit it to just three or four REA projects, and one little dam....

MANSFIELD: Yeah, but some people seem to think that we're just building it for the Vietcong to take over.

LBJ: It could very well be. But I have the feeling from the way Bill Fulbright talked...that the feeling on the Hill was that we ought to be doing more of that, and that might be a better answer than the bombs.

MANSFIELD: ...There's a feeling of apprehension and suspense up here that's pretty hard to define....

LBJ: Well, we have it here....Do you have any thoughts about the approach that we might make to the Congress—whether one is wise, and if so, how?

MANSFIELD: If you make another approach to the Congress, I think really the roof will blow off this time, because people who have remained quiet will no longer remain silent.... I think you'd be in for some trouble. The debate would spread right out.

LBJ: I think you might near *got* to have the debate, though, hadn't you?

MANSFIELD: Yes, sir.

LBJ: Do you think that we ought to send all these troops without a debate?

MANSFIELD: No, sir. I think that we've got too many in there now. And we've been bombing the North without any appreciable results....

LBJ: What do we do about [Westmoreland's] request for more men?...If it assumes the proportions that I can see it assuming, shouldn't we say to the Congress, "What do you want to do about it?"

MANSFIELD: I would hate to be the one to say it because, as you said earlier, it's seventy-five thousand, then it's a hundred and fifty thousand, then it's three hundred thousand. Where do you stop?

LBJ: You don't....To me, it's shaping up like this, Mike—you either get out or you get *in*....We've tried all the neutral things. And we think they are winning. Now, *if we* think they're winning, you can imagine what *they* think.

MANSFIELD: They *know* they're winning.

LBJ: And if they know that, you can see that they're not anxious to find any answer to it.... We seem to have tried everything that we know to do. I stayed here for over a year when they were urging us to bomb before I'd go beyond the line. I have stayed away from [bombing] their industrial targets and their civilian population, although they urge you to do it.

MANSFIELD: Yeah, but Hanoi and Haiphong are spit clean, and have been for months. You bomb them, you get nothing. You just build up more hatred. You get these people tied more closely together because they are tied by blood, whether from the North or the South.

LBJ: I think that's true. I think that you've done nearly everything that you can do, except make it a complete white man's war.

MANSFIELD: If you do that, then you might as well say goodbye to all of Asia and to most of the world.

LBJ: That's probably...right. Therefore, where do you go?

MANSFIELD: You don't go ahead....You don't pull out. You try to do something to consolidate your position in South Vietnam. And that may take more troops. It certainly will take more [South] Vietnamese [soldiers].

LBJ: They're getting more of them in, Mike, but...they're deserting just like flies!

MANSFIELD: When McNamara speaks about three hundred thousand American troops against Giap's thirty-one divisions in North Vietnam, that's the absolute minimum.

LBJ: Yes, he knows that.

MANSFIELD: When he speaks about a hundred and sixty thousand being increased, with respect to the [South] Vietnamese army, he knows he isn't telling the truth. Because they're not coming....

LBJ: ...He thinks he's telling the truth, because the [Saigon] government assures him they'll stop them. But they can't do it.... That's what Taylor told us this morning. I don't know quite how to approach this, Mike, so far as the Congress is concerned, before we make up our mind. When we take it much further than you and McCormack, you know what I get into—discussions and so forth.... Do you have any feeling whether it would be better to let [Taylor] go up before Foreign Relations and

Armed Services, or would it be better to just have some of the representative ones of them here?...

MANSFIELD: ...If you start picking out a selected few, you're asking for trouble, because others will feel they've been left out and they'll get grumpy. To put it mildly.

LBJ: Would your thought then be that it would be best to ask Russell and Fulbright to have a joint hearing with him, and do the same on the House side? We'll have this all in the papers then.

MANSFIELD: If you see a few, it's going to get in the papers. I mean, how could you pick out three or four or five and not expect it to leak?

LBJ: ...Do you have any feeling about Taylor coming out?...

MANSFIELD: ...I have more feeling about Lodge going in, to tell you the truth.... Lodge is not well loved on the Hill, and he was tied in somewhere with Diem. That was the big mistake.

LBJ: [*defensive:*] They like [Lodge] better out there than anybody we've had....And...my people tell me that he is less likely to get us in an Asian war than Taylor....He'd like to talk it out, rather than fight it out. And that's pretty appealing these days. [*chuckles*] He's experienced, and he has the language...and he gets along pretty well with the Catholics [and] the Buddhists. To start all over with a new man is pretty rough.

MANSFIELD: That's true. It has to be done, I guess.

LBJ: No, it doesn't. We can do anything that looks better. We've had Rusk and McNamara and Bobby Kennedy and all of them offer to go—and Mac Bundy. But I don't believe any of them are in either Lodge's or Taylor's class.... Lodge...goes [for] this economic stuff that Bill [Fulbright] is talking [about] all the time....Fulbright

kept shoving Lodge [on me] the other night...and demanding we do it, and I kind of indicated, "All right, we'll try some of this, if you want us to."

Robert McNamara

Thursday, June 10, 1965, 6:40 P.M.

McNAMARA: The Chiefs met for two hours this afternoon.... They discussed two plans—essentially the Westmoreland plan and the... Taylor-McNamara plan. And they came out unanimously in favor of the Westmoreland plan.... At tomorrow's meeting, you might simply want to hear the pros and cons of the matter and just leave it undecided. Then, after it appears you've given it ample thought, send your decision down.

LBJ: All right. Had you given any thought to letting Goodpaster present these things to Eisenhower too and get his ideas?...I don't see that he's overeager....He's emphasizing the economic and the morale...pretty strongly, and looks to me like they're playing on him pretty strong on the television. Do you watch television?

McNAMARA: I see it sometimes....

LBJ: I'm going to make them get you one of these sets in your office where you can turn them all three [networks] on....

McNAMARA: There's a little danger here, Mr. President. Eisenhower's a great one to simply support...the commander's recommendations....

LBJ: ...Has anyone [assessed] the disadvantages of the division's location and the danger of entrapment?

McNAMARA: Yes, and therefore they've modified the plan....They [will] keep it down on the coast....

LBJ: Then it gets down to a question of numbers. You're talking about one division....Are we talking about an eighteen-thousand-man division?

McNAMARA: ...Westmoreland recommended ten additional battalions over and above the thirteen you've already authorized, which would have a strength of something [like] forty-five thousand men. I would recommend five battalions with the strength of about twenty-five thousand men. So, we're talking about...the difference of twenty thousand people. But they're all combat people. And it's quite a difference in risk....Really this is the difference. And this is a hard one to argue out with the Chiefs, because in the back of my mind, I have a very definite limitation on commitment [on U.S. ground troops] in mind. I don't think the Chiefs do. In fact, I *know* they don't.

LBJ: Do you think that this is just the next step with them up the ladder?

McNAMARA: Yes. They hope they don't have to go any further. But Westmoreland outlines in his cable the step beyond it. And he doesn't say that's the last.

LBJ: I don't guess anybody knows.

McNAMARA: I don't think anybody knows.... But I'm inclined to think that unless we're really willing to go to a full potential land war, we've got to slow down here and try to halt, at some point, the ground troop commitment.

LBJ: I've got to see Reston in the morning. He is very concerned about the "narrowing of the basic decisions of government." Now, our old friends [Robert Kennedy and his clique] are feeding [him] some stuff [saying] it's too concentrated. In a matter of a decision like this this morning, Mac [Bundy] says that the decisions and recommendations are made by these same people [that made them under Kennedy]—the field people, the Joint Chiefs, the McNamaras and the Vances, and the Rusks, and the Balls, the Bill Bundys and the Mac Bundys and the President....Do you have any people in your outfit that...feel that they made decisions [under Kennedy] that they're not in on now?

McNAMARA: No....

LBJ: ...The only one I know that might not be is the Attorney General. And he's not my brother! *[laughs]*

LBJ: Is Taylor going up to see the committee in the morning?

McNAMARA: Yes....

LBJ: ...I think that the line he ought to take is...that there has been a constant [Vietcong] buildup, and the buildup came really before the bombing....We may have made it more difficult. But they keep coming [into South Vietnam]. And...you've got to do something about it....They're going to keep putting their stack in, and moving new chips into the pot. We've either got to do one of two things. We've got to tuck tail and run, or we've got to have somebody...tell us that "the Indians are coming" and protect us....That puts [Congress] in the position of either tucking tail and running or giving us what we need....

I would just say, "I know the President is troubled [about] this....But...they've got a pistol at our temple, and we've got to react. And the only way we can react is to put a pistol at *their* temple." Now...we know that with two pistols at temples, one of them's liable to go off. But it doesn't seem that we're ready to tuck tail and run....We waited as long to bomb as a human could....We made every diplomatic initiative and overture that we know to make....And a good many that we didn't believe in....[Now] they've got to go through this monsoon season. We don't believe that we ought to...leave these fifty thousand boys there without some help....

[The Senators] just got the living hell scared out of them.... [Mansfield] came down with two memos in an hour [saying,] "Oh, my God, don't send any resolution up here!" They don't want to *vote* against doing it. They just want to talk and *whine* about it....I just chucked it back to him. I said,..."I don't want to do anything that doesn't represent the reasonable unanimity of this country. We ought to have these things settled at the water's edge. Then...we ought to be one nation united. I'm willing to let you write the ticket. If you'll write it. I thought you wrote it with the SEATO treaty. I thought you wrote it when you approved the...appropriation and the [Tonkin Gulf] action. But if you...want to tuck tail and run...you can just pass a joint resolution."...That jarred him, but it hasn't jarred him enough...to keep him from whining. He ran to Aiken....They had breakfast, and Aiken comes out...and says that Johnson is going to put us on the spot and get off the hook himself. Did you read that?

McNAMARA: Oh, sure I did.

LBJ: *[laughs]* Of course I would like to do that. But...in submitting it, I think I'm just making more trouble for myself....Did you notice how quick Russell got away from us?

McNAMARA: Yeah, sure did.

LBJ: ...I think Taylor's got to say,..."Here's the [Gulf of Tonkin] which says 'to deter aggression.'...In order to do that, I've got to have these men. If there's anyone who thinks we oughtn't to, he ought to introduce a resolution repealing it."...I think it would be

disastrous to the country. I'd object to it as a citizen. But the Congress is the policy-making branch of the government, and they've got a right to pass on it....Now, tell me...the position...that our friend [Robert Kennedy] took on what happened to our [bombing] pause. Did we do it wrong? Didn't do it the right day?

McNAMARA: No, he didn't rake that over.

LBJ: Did he show any...appreciation of the fact that we had heeded the suggestion and tried it?

McNAMARA: Yeah....I think that he would say that...it didn't work, but it was wise to have done it. But now the line [he takes] is...we have an unlimited liability here that we're accepting: "Advancing toward world war....We haven't told the people why....Sleight of hand constantly."...So I said to him, "Do you think we ought to go to Congress with a resolution...[and] debate [it]?" [He said,] "Yeah, I probably would...The President ought to go on TV and explain what it is we're doing, how far we're going to go."

LBJ: I can't do that, can I?

McNAMARA: No, no, you can't.

LBJ: Do you know how far we're going to go?

McNAMARA: No.

LBJ: Or do the Joint Chiefs know? *What human being knows?* I would imagine if they wiped out a thousand boys tomorrow, we might go a hell of a lot further than we'd do if they just wiped out four.

McNAMARA: Sure....There's going to be uncertainty here. It *is* risky. That's the nature of the problem. I do think there can be more said about how many troops...we've decided to have, and what their role would be. This could be explained...much the way you're talking about Max [Taylor] explaining tomorrow that there's been this continued

Vietcong buildup and we have to respond to it....

LBJ: Well, I wouldn't say that we *have* to respond. I'd say there's been this constant buildup, and we *must protect* ourselves as best we *can*.... Now, this is not a war-lord here. This is Mr. Johnson and Mr. Taylor...and General Westmoreland, who has been out there a good long time and hasn't tried to invade the North. And *they* think that in the light of the developments, this is essential to protect our people. Now, we don't say that putting these people in is going to win [the war], but we say if you *don't* put them in, you're going to lose substantially what you have....This is...a holding action....We're trying to be prudent....Now, not a damn human thinks that fifty thousand or a hundred thousand or a hundred and fifty thousand are going to end that war.

McNAMARA: That's right.

LBJ: And we're not getting out. But we're trying to hold what we *got*. And...we're losing, at the rate we're going....He could say we've tried to be as peaceful as we can, and we've had our bombings limited....But the cold hard facts are that...they're taking extra territory. They killed six hundred last week, compared to a normal hundred....We want to come in there and do everything we can [so] that the [South] Vietnamese...will have enough people to resist it. When they can't resist it and they're overran, why, we got to carry in men to help them.

Lady Bird Johnson

Thursday, June 10, 1965, Tape-recorded Diary

Lady Bird: It was a late night for Lyndon.... Eleven o'clock when he came home to dinner....Sometimes it makes me almost angry because he's spending himself so. But I don't know a better thing in the world to spend himself for....From my small viewpoint, it just looks like the problems of the world are so much more insoluble than those of these United States. We can work on these here and make a dent—a rather wonderful dent.

Birch Bayh

Tuesday, June 15, 1965, 1:20 P.M.

LBJ: None of us want to do what the Joint Chiefs of Staff say you ought to do to win—and that's "go in and bomb the hell out of them." I'm...refusing to do that. On the other hand, if we walked out of [Vietnam], we would bust every treaty we got. Forty-four nations would say that United States couldn't be depended on for anything. Whether it's Tokyo or Berlin or NATO or any of the rest of them—SEATO, CENTO. So we can't walk out—and we can't walk in...with heavy bombs and atomic weapons....We're trying to deter them and wear them out, without losing a lot of people. Now, we've lost four hundred, but we've lost a hundred and sixty thousand casualties since World War II....

I held off as long and long and long as I could [on the bombing] because I knew the [American] people would raise hell. I knew it didn't look good. It didn't have a peace image. But it has done what we thought it ought to do....It's hard as hell for them to get any more men down [into South Vietnam]....They get to a bridge and the damn bridge is out. So then they've got to...get a ferry and...unload their truck...and take it by pieces [to] the other side. Then they...go four miles...to another bridge that's out....

[The bombing] has got them all scared to death. They…hide and get in their caves.…We hope that by that war of nerves, over…several months, they'll finally say, "Let's talk." As it is now, they spit in our face. When I gave them the [bombing] pause and told them I wouldn't do anything for a week if they talk, they just spit in our face. They wouldn't even open the letter telling them that. They're arrogant as hell. I don't blame them. I defeated Goldwater [by] 15 million [votes]. Now why would I want to give Goldwater half my Cabinet? They're winning. Why would they want to talk? All the talk would do is get them to give up something they're going to win.

BAYH: …The thing that gripes me…is that these so-called intellectuals, the people that are supposed to have all the brains, are…clear out in left field. They just can't conceive of what you have to do there.

LBJ: That's right. I said…yesterday [to] a group of intellectuals, "What would you have me do that I'm not doing?"…They said, "Stop your bombing." I said,…"The only way you can get a political solution…is to have some pressure on them. The only pressure I've got is the bombing. I don't instigate any incidents. They go and kill us. They're gone before we can even get waked up to bury our dead."…They said, "Maybe you ought to…[go to] the United Nations."…[But the United Nations] ordered the North Vietnamese to come in there last August, up to the Security Council. And the North Vietnamese said, *"Fuck you!"*

LBJ: Eighty-five percent of the people in this country are for what we're doing in the Dominican Republic and Vietnam. And the polls so show it.…Eight or ten

are against it. But they're the ones that are raising hell. Now, we read the Communist bulletins. Their orders go out to do it. This Du Bois youth thing. It's doing all these colleges. They've got a sit-in tomorrow. They're all led by Communist people. Hoover's got people after them all the time. But if I get out and go talking about the Communists, they say, "Oh, he's a McCarthy!"… But…they're stirring up this agitation.…The Chinese got their folks working. The Russians got their folks working. This Russian Ambassador—hell, he's talking to all of our Senators! After he has lunch with one of our Senators, it takes me *two weeks* to get the fellow to where he doesn't think I'm a warmonger again!

BAYH: …They're using the propaganda from our own Senators against us.

LBJ: Oh, yeah.…They get one speech by Morse…and print it in leaflets. Drop it out to all of our people. Then they come back and say that the country is so divided.… This morning some article…said 85 percent of the Senators in the United States Senate were really undercover against Johnson's position. I believe 85 percent of them are *for* it.

BAYH: That's right.

LBJ: But the alternatives! Do I want to go [with] LeMay and bomb Peking? If I do, I'll get thirty-five, forty divisions the next morning.…Do I want to get out like Morse? No! Do I want to just sit there and get hit like I did for several months? I don't think I ought to ask an American boy to get shot at and not shoot back. So…I tell them to defend themselves.…We've got to put men in there. Because they're…going to…build up their forces and try to run us out during the monsoon season.…

So it's going to be real rough for the next ninety days. We hope at the end of that period, we'll wear them down some. . . . They hope they can wear *us* out. And I really believe they'll last longer than we do. One of their boys gets down in a rut and he stays there for two days without water, food, or anything and never moves. Waiting to ambush somebody. Now an American, he stays there about twenty minutes and, God damn, he's got to get him a cigarette!

Robert McNamara

Wednesday, June 16, 1965, 12:55 P.M.

LBJ: Then how are you going to say you'll do in the future what's necessary?

McNAMARA: I'm not going to say a thing beyond this. And then the questions will come. . . . "Aren't you going to send some more? Aren't you considering it?" And I'm going to say that . . . the President has said we will do what's necessary to assist the South Vietnamese . . . to preserve their independence, and will not do anything more than is absolutely necessary to achieve that objective.

LBJ: . . . When will they be in there? About the 15th of July?

McNAMARA: Yeah, between the 15th and 25th.

Robert McNamara

Thursday, June 17, 1965, 3:25 P.M.

LBJ: What do I say about that when I'm asked?

McNAMARA: . . . I don't think, Mr. President, any defense bill in recent years has ever gone through the Appropriations Committee with as little change. It's absolutely fantastic. . . .

LBJ: Yeah, but they say that you ought to have more.

McNAMARA: The answer is we don't need more.

LBJ: They say you got more men going out.

McNAMARA: . . . The number of men we have is the number of men we planned for in the budget. We have to feed the men, house them, equip them . . . whether they are in the United States or in South Vietnam . . .

LBJ: Well, in light of the President's decision to escalate the war—

McNAMARA: I don't know that you *made* any decision to escalate the war. In any case, this question . . . frequently comes up—do we need more in the budget for '66? And the answer is, "Not now." We may later, depending upon what happens in the next thirteen months . . .

LBJ: Now, McGovern says that "the war is taking a very dangerous new turn with a commitment of large land forces to a combat mission. These guerrillas have lived twenty years off the countryside. . . . Their strength is they are part of the people and the terrain in which they fight, and how long will it take for some people to realize that bombing Hanoi or Peking will have little or no effect on the guerrilla forces fighting a thousand miles away in the jungle?"

McNAMARA: If bombing won't have any effect and the added men are undesirable, what in the hell do we do? Get out? . . .

LBJ: The Senator said instead of continuing bombing, we [should] have taken advantage of the forthcoming Afro-Asian conference . . . to encourage discussion with the Vietcong leaders.

McNAMARA: Now, this is the new tack. First, you didn't say what the objective was. Then we wouldn't tell them what the strategy was. Then we should have stopped bombing, and had the pause. Then we should have been ready for negotiation. Now the theme is . . . we haven't talked to the Vietcong. This is becoming more and more the dominant theme and criticism. And I think we're going to have to answer that.

LBJ: And how are we?

McNAMARA: ...The answer is that they are a creature of the North Vietnamese, and the North Vietnamese...are the ones that we're trying to deal with....

LBJ: Would you say it's just like asking the Vietcong and Vietnam to negotiate with Mississippi? *[laughs]*

McNAMARA: Yeah, I think so....I just wanted to tell you, unless you see some reason not to, I'm planning to have dinner with Jackie [Kennedy] tonight in New York. I can do something on that front, if I can't on Bobby. I confess to failure on the latter, but I have been able to do a little on the other.

LBJ: I sure hope so.... Confidentially...after your second drink, when you think that you can have some influence, I would sure urge her to keep Dick Goodwin down here to help us. I think [he's] getting some encouragement to move...away.

William Fulbright

Thursday, June 17, 1965, 7:45 P.M.

LBJ: We've got thirty B-52s that have just unloaded their bombs on a square mile in South Vietnam [where] there's...a concentration of Vietcong that has been giving us all this trouble....I didn't want you hearing about it on the radio and think that I had started a new war....They asked me in my press conference today...about...your friend Joe Clark—your protégé: "Joe Clark says that you'll never get anywhere unless you negotiate with the Vietcong." I said Senator Clark's a very able Senator. He wanted to get on [the] Foreign Relations [Committee] a long time, all the time I was leader, and I've observed he's

recently become a member of the Committee. *[laughs]* I wanted it known he'd become a member after I left. But it's right and it's his duty to give his thought.

LBJ: If you will look at my press conference and find anything good to observe, I'd like to have [you say so], because I'm tired of reading these AP dispatches about "Fulbright, the voice of Johnson in the Congress, differed with him."...[Even] if you don't find anything except a little reference down there to the state of Arkansas, say, "I embrace it."

Gerald Ford

Thursday, June 17, 1965, 7:50 P.M.

LBJ: Sorry about your boy.

FORD: His sister slammed the car door on his finger....It's pretty badly cut up.

LBJ: Sounds like he's got a Democratic sister!

FORD: *[laughs]* I hope not.

LBJ: I'm sitting here with Tom Dewey. He's listening to us talk....We sent thirty B-52s over a square mile area in...South Vietnam...[against a] concentration of Vietcong.... There will be some excitement on the television and radio.... But...that's the only way we could get them....I sent Goodpaster up...to go over it with General Eisenhower. He thought that it ought to be done. He also felt we ought to approve Westmoreland's request for these troops...to protect his bases....

FORD: ...The one question that I hoped we could sit down and talk about before we go any further is: How much are we going to use the ground forces?...

LBJ: Only when and if and as necessary to protect our national interest. Presently we have...about...thirteen thousand of combat on the ground. We'll move those up...to seventy to seventy-five. Out of that, I would guess we'll get another eight or ten thousand combat. Now, [when] those combats...go out, we'll try to keep them [at a] distance where they can't lob their mortars in for three miles. We'll constantly be on patrol....When [the South Vietnamese] get in trouble...they'll call us. We'll come to their rescue. They did that last week. Westmoreland said,..."I'm going to authorize it. You want to cancel it?"...I said, "Hell no, I'm not going to cancel it." I just hate to see twelve hundred American boys involved. But this is no Sunday school picnic....I can't tell a commander on the ground that he's got to let his people get wiped out or let his allies get wiped out. That's why we're out there....

FORD: I fully agree....The only thing [is] if we're going to do more offensively on the ground, then I think we all ought to sit down and talk about it.

LBJ: I'll be glad to do that. If I can stay out of the papers. I don't want to tell either the North Vietnamese or...China. And I haven't been to a meeting yet that they don't get something out about what happened....You don't send a general out and a bunch of damn troops and tell him that "you got to get them killed."...

FORD: I agree with you a thousand percent.

LBJ: ...Westmoreland went out there from West Point because he's the best general we had....They ask this damn fool McCloskey,..."Has Westmoreland got authority to keep our American boys from getting killed?" Answer is yes. "When did Johnson give him that authority?" This damn fool says, "I don't know, but I'm sure he got it."...So

then the headline read, JOHNSON ENTERS NEW PHASE/COMBAT WAR IN VIETNAM. When I looked at the damn paper, I called up and said, "Who's smoking *marijuana* around here?"...I [told Reedy], "Here's a statement. I want you to put it in your eleven o'clock briefing. 'No order has been issued. There's no change in the situation.' "...Then they wrote the story:..."The government's right hand doesn't know what the left hand's doing. And Johnson is a dictator."

FORD: ...Don't worry about that kind of thing.

LBJ: I'm not worrying. I'm explaining to you so that you're on this team. It's your country. And a good many of these boys, I'm told, are *Republicans*. I don't think they use good judgment in their party. But...they're out there fighting, and I think you ought to know the facts.

FORD: I agree exactly with what you did with the B-52s....As I have done in the past, you know, I sit shoulder to shoulder with you.

LBJ: I know that. I'm proud of you, and your country's proud of you. The only thing I regret is that you're going to pick up some Republican seats [in Congress in 1966] as a result of that kind of a forward-looking policy. I won't be happy [about] that, unless they're like you....But I think you ought to get a muzzle on Laird and make him quit telling me that I can't have ground troops I need to protect my own airplanes. Because I can't bomb like he wants to if the goddamned Vietcong are destroying my airplanes on the ground....Would you consider letting me trade Morse to you for Laird?

FORD: *[laughs]*

LBJ: Take care of your boy, and I'm sorry to bother you, Jerry.

Robert McNamara

Monday, June 21, 1965, 12:15 P.M.

LBJ: I think that you ought to spend some time with your friend Mr. Kennedy. I don't want this repeated to him. But...I think that he's functioning in this Vietnam field and Dominican field a little bit overtime. With he and some of his stooges very much against us....His general feeling is that we should not have asked for the $700 million appropriation....He wanted to demonstrate his independence. And while he wouldn't vote against it, he [made] the speech he did....

Certain Senators tell me that they talk to him in the cloakroom, and that they hear little snide remarks about the situation.... Bobby's going to be in the background, because he operates...that way. But they're going to be asking for a new congressional debate [on Vietnam]....Tell him that...we don't think it would be wise, but that we have asked Fulbright if he thinks we ought to have a new resolution [of support]. And we've asked Mansfield,...Dirksen, and...Russell. They are the men in this field in the Senate....I think you [also] ought to talk to him about the new [bombing] pause that's being proposed....We're afraid that if we do pause, we [get] hell knocked out of us....

McNAMARA: Oh, I don't think now is the time.

LBJ: I just think that we ought to talk to him about it, because this is where most of our real trouble's coming from....The real flare-up came on this statement on this $700 million....We don't object to McGovern and Church....We have never asked one Senator not to speak. And we haven't asked him. We put on a pause. Let's see what else he thinks ought to be done. [But] I think that it's very

potentially dangerous to our general cause on Vietnam.

In time, it's going to be like the Yale professors said. It's going to be difficult for us to very long prosecute effectively a war that far away from home with the divisions we have here—and particularly the potential divisions. That's really had me concerned for a month. I'm very depressed about it. Because I see no program from either Defense or State that gives me much hope of doing anything, except just praying and gasping to hold on during monsoon and hope they'll quit.

I don't believe they're *ever* going to quit. And I don't see...: that we have any...plan for a victory—militarily or diplomatically....You and Dean [Rusk] have got to sit down and try to see if there's any people that we have in those departments that can give us any program or plan or hope. If not, we got to...have you...go out there and take one good look at it and say to these new people, "Now you changed the government about the last time. And this is it. Call the Buddhists and the Catholics and the generals and everybody together and say we're going to do our best. And be sure they're willing to let new troops come in. Be sure they're not going to resent them. If not, why, you-all can run over us and have a government of your own choosing. But we just can't take these changes all the time."

That's the Russell plan. Russell thinks we ought to take one of these changes [of government] to get out of there. I don't think we can get out of there with our [SEATO] treaty like it is and with what all we've said. I think it would just lose us face in the world. I just shudder to think what [other countries] would say.... You...better talk to your military people.... Say ... the President wants some kind of plan that gives us some hope of victory.

LBJ: [The North Vietnamese] just laugh at us. Ho Chi Minh and Chou En-lai both have made statements on this [Harold] Wilson mission, telling him to go to hell.

McNAMARA: No indication they want to talk now. That's clear.

LBJ: I think Wilson will just screw up things more when he comes over here.... Couldn't we say,... "We're very anxious to work on this thing if you have any chance of seeing them at all. But if you don't, don't ... just make a big speech dividing our country." ...

McNAMARA: I don't think you can keep him out of here.... It would be awfully difficult for you to say, "You can't come here, unless you're going to be accepted in Hanoi and Peking."

Robert McNamara

Wednesday, June 30, 1965, 7:35 P.M.

LBJ: You've got to sit down and talk to Bobby. He's getting ready to tour Latin America. And you've got to sell the liberal bloc [in the Senate] on "You cannot run out [of] there [in Vietnam] and you can't stay there without [more] people. You've got to back these men." So that he doesn't get off on a tangent again.

McNAMARA: ... I'll get ahold of him tonight.

LBJ: You just got to have a serious talk with him. Go over the figures and ... facts. Tell him that ... you presented [the situation in Vietnam] ... to Eisenhower ... and that you just can't find anybody who thinks we ought to leave these boys out there and do nothing. And we can't give up. I don't see anything to do except give them what they need, Bob. Do you?

McNAMARA: Mr. President, I'm very much of that frame of mind. I must tell you I don't think others in your

government are.... But Cy [Vance] and I feel very strongly on that point. We want you to be sure that you see the full risk of this. It is a very heavy risk. But that's my vote.

LBJ: I don't believe it is as big a risk as walking out.

McNAMARA: Neither do we.

LBJ: Now, what are the alternatives?

McNAMARA: ... The alternative is to go in in a half-assed way.

LBJ: I think we'll get wrecked doing that.

McNAMARA: I went through the Bay of Pigs, and I'm responsible in part for that. And we were wrong not because we did what we did. We were wrong because we failed.

LBJ: That's right.

Robert McNamara

Friday, July 2, 1965, 8:41 A.M.

LBJ: I'm pretty depressed reading all these proposals. They're tough, aren't they?

McNAMARA: They are.... But we're at a point of a fairly tough decision, Mr. President.... We purposely made no effort to compromise any of our views....

LBJ: Two or three things that I want you to explore. First, assuming we do everything we can, to the extent of our resources, can we really have any assurance that we win? I mean, assuming we have all the big bombers and all the powerful payloads and everything else, can the Vietcong come in and tear us up and continue this thing indefinitely, and never really bring it to an end? ... Second, ... can we really, without getting any further authority from the Congress, have ... sufficient, overwhelming [domestic] support to ... fight successfully? .... You know the friend you talked to about the pause [Robert Kennedy]. You know the Mansfields. You know the Clarks. And those men carry a good deal of weight. And this fellow we talked to the other day here at lunch (Everett Dirksen) has a good deal of weight....He's got cancer, in my judgment. I've never told anybody, but I saw him yesterday coughing several times.

McNAMARA: He doesn't look good.

LBJ: He went home that very day and he hasn't been back since. Had a stomach upset. He can't carry on much for us. We have to rely on the younger crowd....The McGoverns and the Clarks and the other folks....If you don't ask them, I think you'd have a long debate about not having asked them, with this kind of a commitment. Even though there's some record behind us, we know ourselves, in our own conscience, that when we asked for this resolution, we had no intention of committing this many ground troops. We're doing so now, and we know it's going to be bad. And the question is, Do we just want to do it out on a limb by ourselves? I don't know whether those [Pentagon] men have ever [calculated] whether we can win with the kind of training we have, the kind of power, and...whether we can have a united support at home.

McNAMARA: ...If we do go as far as my paper suggested, sending numbers of men out there, we ought to call up Reserves. You have authority to do that without additional legislation. But...almost surely, if we called up Reserves, you would want to go to the Congress to get additional authority....Yes, it also might lead to an extended debate and divisive statements. I think we could avoid that. I really think if we were to go to the Clarks and the McGoverns and the Churches and say to them, "Now, this is our situation. We cannot win with our existing commitment. We must increase it if we're going to

win, and [with] this limited term that we define [and] limited way we define 'win,' it requires additional troops. Along with that approach, we are...continuing this political initiative to probe for a willingness to negotiate a reasonable settlement here. And we ask your support."...I think you'd get it....And that's a vehicle by which you both get the authority to call up the Reserves and also tie them into the whole program.

LBJ: That makes sense.

McNAMARA: I don't know that you want to go that far. I'm not pressing you to. It's my judgment you should, but my judgment may be in error here....

LBJ: Does Rusk generally agree with you?

McNAMARA: ...He very definitely does. He's a hard-liner on this, in the sense that he doesn't want to give up South Vietnam under any circumstances. Even if it means going to general war. Now, he doesn't think we ought to go to general war. He thinks we ought to try to avoid it. But if that's what's required to hold South Vietnam, he would go to general war. He would say, as a footnote, "Military commanders always ask for all they need. For God's sakes, don't take what they request as an absolute, iron-clad requirement." I don't disagree with that point...I do think...that this request for thirty-four U.S. battalions and ten non-U.S., a total of forty-four battalions, comes pretty close to the minimum requirement....

LBJ: When you put these people in and you really do go all out [and] you call up your Reserves and everything else, can you do anything to restore your communication and your railroads and your roads?...

McNAMARA: Yes, I think so.... By the end of the year, we ought to have that railroad...and...the major highways opened.... The problem is you can't send an engineering company into an area...unless you send combat troops with them. And we just don't have the combat troops to do that....

LBJ: What has happened out there in the last forty-eight hours? Looks like we killed six or seven hundred of them.

McNAMARA: Yeah, we killed a large number, I'd say, over the last three or four days...At least five hundred.

LBJ: ...Can they continue losses like that?

McNAMARA: ...Of the numbers that are killed by [U.S.] Air Force actions, and a great bulk of these people are killed that way, I would think that 75 percent are probably not from what we call the...guerrilla force.

Dwight Eisenhower

Friday, July 2, 1965, 11:02 A.M.

LBJ: I'm having a meeting this morning with my top people.... McNamara recommends really what Westmoreland and Wheeler do—a quite expanded operation, and one that's really going to kick up some folks like Ford. He says that he doesn't want to use ground troops. He thinks we ought to do it by bombing. We can't even protect our bases without the ground troops, according to Westmoreland. And we've got all the Bobby Kennedys and the Mansfields and the Morses against it. But [Westmoreland] recommends an all-out operation. We don't know whether we can beat them with that or not. The State Department comes in and recommends a rather modified one through the monsoon season, to see how effective we are with our B-52 strikes and with our other strikes.... Westmoreland has urged...about double what we've got there now. But if we do that, we've got to call up the Reserves and get authority from Congress...That will really serve notice that we're in a land operation over there. Now, I guess it's your view that we ought to do that. You don't think that we can just have a holding operation, from a military standpoint, do you?

EISENHOWER: ...You've got to go along with your military advisers, because otherwise you are just going to continue to have these casualties indefinitely.... My advice is, do what you have to do. I'm sorry that you have to go to the Congress...but I guess you would be calling up the Reserves.

LBJ: Yes, sir. We're out of them, you see.... And if they move on other fronts, we'll have to increase our strength, too....[The State Department says] we ought to avoid bombing Hanoi until we can see through the monsoon season whether, with these forces there, we can make any progress...before we go out and execute everything. Of course, McNamara's people recommend taking all the harbors....Mining and blowing the hell out of it.... They go all out. State Department people say they're taking too much chance on bringing China in and Russia in.... They [want] to try...during the monsoon season to hold what [we've] got, and to really try to convince Russia that if she doesn't bring about some kind of understanding, we're going to have to give them the works. But they believe that she doesn't really want an all-out war.

EISENHOWER: ...[For them to] agree to some kind of negotiation...[you must say,] "Hell, we're going to end this and win this thing.... We don't intend to fail."....

LBJ: You think that we can really beat the Vietcong out there?

EISENHOWER: ...This is the hardest thing [to decide,] because we can't finally find out how many of these Vietcong have been imported down there and how many of them are just rebels.

LBJ: We killed twenty-six thousand [Vietcong] this year....Three hundred yesterday....Two hundred and fifty of them the day before. But they just keep coming in from North Vietnam....How many they're going to pour in from China, I don't know....

EISENHOWER: ...I would go ahead and...do it as quickly as I could.

LBJ: ...You're the best chief of staff I've got....I've got to rely on you on this one.

Richard Russell

Monday, July 26, 1965, 5:46 P.M.

LBJ: Westmoreland says that we ought to take out everything simultaneously. He's just really a firefighter. He's an old South Carolina boy, and I guess he's been out there messing with them long enough, and he's getting fed up with it.... Wheeler and the Joint Chiefs are real tough on taking out Six and Seven immediately. They'd be glad to take out everything in the whole of Southeast Asia. But they *really* want to take these out.... McNamara thinks you've got to take them out, and the quicker the better. If you don't, you'll send a false signal to Russia that she can do this with impunity...and pretty soon we'll have no planes in the air...because they'll knock them out.... Notwithstanding what people think...[McNamara] holds down the military a good deal....Most [people] think he's a hawk and that he's always raising hell to go to war.

RUSSELL: ...I think he's got the military to where they're somewhat circumscribed from expressing themselves freely.

LBJ: ...I've had [the military] over here for hours....Some of them are awfully irresponsible. They'll just scare you. They're ready to put a million men in right quick....Rusk thinks that we ought to go...and take these sites out. Ball and Goldberg and Humphrey kind of wobbled on both sides....We think that the Russians are manning [the sites]....We don't want anybody to know that....

RUSSELL: No, I'd say they were manned by North Vietnamese....I think the Russians have got people there showing them how to shoot them. But I would never mention that.

LBJ: We don't want to put them behind the wall where they got to fight back....That's why I'm trying to hold down this play....We told [the Russians] what our defense budget was. We said, "Ours is $2 billion lower. You lower yours." And they did. When we cut out this nuclear production...last year, you wondered why it hadn't been cut out before. It was running out of our ears when I first came in as President. They cut down theirs. Now...I don't want to...say, "I'm just going to have a hell of a lot of billions of dollars." Because...[North] Vietnam is trying to pull [China and Russia] back together....Any big, dramatic announcement on my part will throw them together....So five minutes from now, they're coming in here to decide what to do about the SAM site. The weight of opinion is pretty solidly on taking out Six and Seven tonight....

RUSSELL: I'd take...every one out....And I'd at least take out one other that I knew exactly where it was.

LBJ: If you do, that gets you in the Hanoi area. That gets you in civilians. That gets…the world upset. I just can't do that on these others. They're not bothering me and my targets.…[Six and Seven] are right in line with all the targets I've got that's worth a damn. I can't send my boys up there without knocking them down. The Hanoi ones don't bother me too much.…If [you hit those other sites], you're going to hit the goddamn capital. You'll have [Russia and China] in the war in fifteen minutes…when you go to bombing Hanoi. I think [the North Vietnamese] are trying to trap us into doing that.

RUSSELL: Our CIA thinks they moved a lot of the government out of Hanoi.

LBJ: …We'll debate that later. This one is right up now.

RUSSELL: I'd say yes, get them tonight, if I could. But I'd hate like hell to try to get them and miss them.

LBJ: We think we're likely to miss them.…They may just have slips of ground that look like a landing strip and have mobile ones that they move in just like a trailer and move out.…Now…on this other thing, I think I'm going to work out a deal where I give Westmoreland what he needs in about three increments. Thirty or forty thousand each. Send a division right away from down at your Fort Benning.…Give [us]…that division right quick, and then do it in two or three increments between now and the first of December.

RUSSELL: You have one damn good soldier out there named Walter Brown Russell, Jr.…

LBJ: Is he in that crowd?

RUSSELL: Yes, sir.…

LBJ: He knows he's going, does he?

RUSSELL: Oh, yeah. They all know it. They're just sitting there waiting for it…

LBJ: We don't think we'll ask for much money [from Congress] because we don't want to blow this thing up.

RUSSELL: I'm with you on that.…I didn't see a bit of need of pressing so damn hard.

LBJ: We don't think we'll need any legislation. We'll tell them to get the Reserve plans ready…if next year we do. Then I'm going to do everything I can with this Jew up at the United Nations, and everywhere in the world, to find a way to get out without saying so. But if I can't do that, January I'll have to decide on the Reserves. But I don't think I'll call them up now. I think it's too dramatic. I think it commits me where I can't get out. And it puts me out there further than I want to get right at the moment. Now, does that make sense to you?

RUSSELL: Yes. Except it adds to old Ho Chi Minh's argument that we ain't going to stay in there. That we're going to pull out. It may ease the pressure that we…hoped Russia would put on to get him out.

LBJ: What do you think?

RUSSELL: Call up the Reserves. They understand that language. They understood it in Berlin.…

LBJ: If I extend the enlistments, if I put a hundred thousand out there, they'll understand it. I'm afraid they'll understand it too much. I don't have to have the Reserves to do that. And I'm going to step up my draft calls. Double them.

RUSSELL: You shouldn't send many more than a hundred thousand over there, Mr. President.

LBJ: No, I'm not. I'm not going to try to send more.…I'm just going to send a little less, maybe.

RUSSELL: You've been living with it every minute. I just live with it at night.

LBJ: I never worked on anything as hard in my life. I've had every human—

RUSSELL: It's just nearly driven me mad. I guess it's the only thing I've ever hit in my life I didn't have some quick answer to. But I haven't got one to this....

LBJ: ...I want to [brief]...the [congressional] leaders first. Then the Foreign Relations and Foreign Affairs and Armed Services [Committees]....Do you think I ought to send a message to Congress or just make a statement? I'm not going to need any appropriation or any legislation...[for] my decision out there. Couldn't I just give a statement and say, "I'm going to send thirty thousand within the next few days and thirty thousand more, and it will be a total of a hundred thousand additionally that will be added. And if I do need anything, I'll call you back."...I don't want to dramatize it and throw Russia—

RUSSELL: ...If that's the way you're going to play it, I'd play it down.

LBJ: You wouldn't have a Joint Session [of Congress]?

RUSSELL: I wouldn't cut down on the actual fighting, because those people over there are playing for keeps.

LBJ: Oh, I'm putting a *hundred* thousand in there. *Gosh*, I've moved a hundred and fifty thousand in the last ninety *days!*

RUSSELL: Has all the First Division got there yet?

LBJ: I don't know. All I know is I've got eighty thousand there, and I've got a hundred thousand that I'm going to authorize.

RUSSELL: I don't know. It has a mighty good psychological effect to call up some Reserves....

LBJ: Yeah, but it upsets the hell out of [the North Vietnamese]. They'll immediately go to...pressing... for commitments now that they are not getting from Russia. I don't want to force them.

RUSSELL: ...God knows,...and the thing that scares me worse is that these damn [South] Vietnamese are going to say, "Here is your war. Go ahead and take it!" And they'll quit fighting. That's what I've been looking for then to do. That little old mustached fellow [General Ky] was on the television. He indicated that *we* ought to fight the war and *his* troops ought to pacify the villages in the rear. God, that scared the hell out of me! If they're going to try to fight *that* kind of war, I'm in favor of getting *out* of there. If they're not going to really fight. The Koreans fought every inch of the way....Even when they were taking staggering losses, they were increasing their units....These people are letting theirs run *down*. They're not making any real effort over there now.

LBJ: ...You don't think that I ought to have a Joint Session, do you?

RUSSELL: No, if I wasn't going to call up any Reserves...I wouldn't....I think I'd just do it on television.

Mike Mansfield

Tuesday, July 27, 1995, 2: 43 P.M.

MANSFIELD: Bill Fulbright came to me and suggested that it might be a good idea for him, Dick Russell, John Sherman Cooper, George Aiken, and John Sparkman to come down and see you...on the present Vietnamese situation.

LBJ: ...I've talked to practically all of them. All I think would come out of it would be a story in the paper about the worrying and the mess and the difficulty and their whining. I've been out on the boat with Bill [Fulbright]. I've had him down for breakfast....We're going to see them all tomorrow morning in great detail. The fact is, there is no easy way....Bill's never going to be much of a leader. He's going to find things to worry him and concern him. His stuff he puts out of his meetings on Dominican Republic hurt us down there. *[sarcastically:]* He's really worried about things in Vietnam. I sit down with him and he agrees with me when I get through, and I think he will in the morning, when we get through....

I'm going to tell you everything that I know this afternoon.... I'm taking the soft line of the deal. A good many of my Cabinet, and a good many other people, think that [since] Kennedy called up the Reserve in '61 [and] in the Cuban Missile Crisis, we ought to go all the way....I'm not doing that. I'm following more or less your memorandum. I'm saying to them that I want Rusk and Goldberg and you and Clark Clifford and Abe Fortas, all the folks who really don't want to be in a land war there...to do all they can, around the clock. For Rusk to just lock himself up with the greatest experts he can—the Kissingers, the Bohlens, anybody that he can think of...and try to find a way to get out....I would tell [Fulbright] that we don't want to move into Hanoi, where either Russia or China will have to do more than she's doing now, if we can avoid it....

Number two, we don't see how we can run out [of Vietnam].... Number three, we don't think that we can leave these boys there inadequately protected at these bases....Now...we're...giving [the military], in our own way, what they say they have to have. But we're not [letting] them...go with any new adventures. And we're hoping...to get through the monsoon season....Hoping that maybe the other thing will work. If it doesn't, then by January, you may have to appropriate and appropriate and appropriate. And you may have to do other things. But I'm doing my best to hold this thing in balance just as long as I can.

I can't run out. I'm not going to run in. I can't just sit there and let them be murdered. So I've got to put enough there to hold them and protect them. And...if we don't heat it up ourselves, and we don't dramatize it, we don't play it up and say we're appropriating billions and we're sending millions and all [those] men, I don't think that you [will] get the Russians...or the Chinese worked up about it. That's what we are hoping.

CHAPTER 20

Jo Freeman Redefines the American Woman

"Bitch is Beautiful."

W hen the editors of *Life* magazine published their women's issue in 1956, they had tried to render a representative view of the lives of American women while at the same time containing any ideas of radical or evolutionary social change. As mentioned in Chapter 14, the degree to which the editors were successful remains an open question. Nevertheless, the daily life of the issue's iconic upper middle-class housewife, Marge Sutton, no doubt made sense to some of the magazine's readers. Just ten years later, however, the women featured in the magazine appeared to belong to a bygone era. In the mid-1960s, a new women's movement quickly and dramatically redefined the American woman and gender relations in the United States. Through their words and by their actions, by the 1970s, feminists had largely succeeded in breaking down the intellectual frameworks that prescribed stifling social roles for women and was fast creating new economic, political, and social opportunities for women.

The women's liberation movement of the 1960s directly challenged the 1950s version of domesticity as well as older feminist ideals. There were, however, historical similarities with the work of women rights advocates of previous eras. Perhaps the most important parallel related to the antebellum women's movement. Like women's rights activists who developed their ideas and organizations as a result of their work for abolitionism, many feminists in the 1960s drew inspiration from the civil rights movement. In particular, their connection with the Student Nonviolent Coordinating Committee (SNCC), which was founded in 1960, had a profound effect upon what later became known as second-wave feminism.

During the Freedom Summer of 1964, white women in the North and the South joined SNCC workers in a voter registration campaign. About 800 white northern students went to Mississippi alone. Fighting for political rights in the South did more than advance the cause of racial equality; it opened the doors to a wider social movement. By engaging in public actions, white women were breaking down core elements of white Southern society. For generations, white supremacy had been predicated upon the protection of the "southern lady" from black men. During the Freedom Summer, white and black young men and women mingled freely, shattering mores and stereotypes. In this way, racial equality also meant transforming sex roles. Working for SNCC also gave women opportunities to learn about organizing, participate in a movement dedicated to equality, and grapple with ideologies of liberation.

Women's experiences in other organizations such as Students for a Democratic Society (SDS), which was established in the same year as SNCC, shaped the women's liberation movement. SDS and SNCC shared tenets such as an emphasis on participatory democracy, a commitment to civil rights, criticism of the war in Vietnam, and a desire for a more just and equitable society. Together the two groups comprised the center of what became known as "the Movement." Women participated in all major SDS activities including various Economic Research and Action Project (ERAP) activities in cities across the North. Although not all the ERAP programs amounted to much, women in Cleveland and Boston led two of the most successful ones.

As much as women's positive experiences in the Movement were formative in the development of the 1960s feminist movement, their problems, setbacks, and negative confrontations were major catalysts as well. Not all was well in the Movement. In late 1964, five white women—Ruby Davis, Smith Robinson, Mary King, Casey Hayden, and Mary Varela—who had been working with SNCC in Mississippi, penned a summary listing their grievances. They complained that they had been relegated to supporting roles, most often as secretaries. All Movement leaders were male. "Girls," as they were labeled, had more to offer the civil rights movement. Their talent, energy, and leadership abilities were being wasted. The authors of this position paper, who declined to sign their names to it fearing retribution, hoped that a serious discussion of male supremacy would come from its distribution. That did not happen. When civil rights activists finally discussed the paper, it was belittled and denounced. Infamously, Stokely Carmichael mocked it, saying, "The only position for women in SNCC is prone."[1]

Women in SDS suffered similarly. In 1965, Casey Hayden and Mary King published another paper. This time their target was SDS's leadership. They again criticized the limits on women's roles within the Movement, the lack of the ability to get their ideas heard, and the unwillingness of men to take up their causes. Again, they called for discussion and dialogue. Again, they faced a hostile reaction. By 1967, a break was seemingly inevitable as women who had witnessed and been victimized by sexism within the Movement and who wished to add a fight against male supremacy to the 1960s battles against racism and imperialism realized that they needed their own movement. In early summer 1967, a group of SDS women produced another key document titled "Liberation of Women." They framed their demands to "free women to participate in other meaningful activities" and to "relieve our brothers of the burden of male chauvinism" within the larger context of world revolutions and struggles between capitalism, socialism, and the Third World. "As we analyze the positions of women in capitalist society and especially in the United States," they wrote, "we find that women are in a colonial relationship to men and we recognize ourselves as part of the Third World."[2] They called for women's independence, the transformation of the family to end "the autocratic and paternalistic role of men," and easy access to the means for women to control reproduction.[3]

The largely unsympathetic reaction by men in SDS convinced many women that they needed their own organizations to fight for women's liberation. A significant fracture came on Labor Day in 1967 during the National Conference for New Politics, held in Chicago. The raucous affair quickly exposed the divisions between blacks and whites and men and women. Two activists there, Shulamith Firestone and Jo Freeman, attempted to have the conference pass a resolution allocating 51% of the convention's votes and committees to women since they represented 51% of the population. Their resolution condemned the mass media for stereotyping women as sex objects and auxiliaries of men. They also demanded that the convention support the notion that women must have complete control over their bodies. The Firestone-Freeman resolution was not even given a hearing. A few months after the conference, Firestone, Freeman, and other women in their Chicago group of feminists published their manifesto, "To the

Women of the Left," in New Left Notes. It was a clarion call for a women's liberation movement. The second wave of feminism had arrived.

Within months of the publication of "To the Women of the Left" in New Left Notes, women across the nation began joining groups to discuss women's liberation and ways to create equality. Rarely did these groups work in concert with one another. In fact, there were deep divisions among the new feminists. The "great divide," as historian Alice Echols has called it, was over the issue of politics and the New Left movement.[4] On one side were the politicos who believed that fighting against women's oppression was part of the larger battle against capitalism. Radical feminists rejected that position. To them, gender was more important than class. They offered sharp criticisms of family structure, marriage, love, heterosexuality, and laws that subsumed women's freedoms and choices to those of men. Radical feminists also launched attacks upon an older generation of women activists, including members of the National Organization for Women (NOW), founded in 1966, who sought accommodation within the existing power structure. At times, these factions within the women's movement worked together. In 1968, women from across the feminist spectrum collaborated in protesting the Miss America Pageant. One hundred women liberationists descended on Atlantic City on September 7 to engage in picketing and guerilla street theater. In a "Freedom Trash Can," they burned the symbols of women's pacification such as high-heeled shoes, bras, girdles, and hair curlers, as well as the periodicals of oppression—*Playboy*, *Cosmopolitan*, and *Ladies Home Journal*. Despite making national headlines, the event ultimately served to widen the growing gulf between politicos who thought the protest's central message concerned the capitalist commodification of beauty and feminists who thought that they were battling male chauvinism.

The fights within the women's liberation movement took their toll. As second-wave feminism evolved in the late 1960s and early 1970s, radical feminists, who had been in the minority, ascended. Some embraced cultural feminism, which emphasized female culture and community over relations with men and politics. Some of the women who had been at the center of the creation of the movement now found themselves out of place. For instance, in 1968, Jo Freeman left the politico-oriented Westside group in Chicago and began writing about her experiences. Without her voice, within a few years the Westside group drifted toward radical feminism. Freeman kept engaged in the women's liberation movement, becoming one of its most prominent thinkers. Among her most significant articles were "The Tyranny of Structurelessness," "Thrashing," and "The Bitch Manifesto." The latter was not only representative of the women's liberation movement but a window into a moment in time when women were dramatically reshaping American society.

"The Bitch Manifesto" is a biting and irreverent critique of American society reminiscent of the feminists of the 1910s. Although it was clear that second-wave feminists were blazing their own trail and that they had significant differences with their predecessors, women such as Crystal Eastman (see Chapter 5) would have liked Jo Freeman, although Eastman would not have wanted to be her. That would have been too much for Eastman's 1920s-era sensibilities. Eastman would not have dared to call herself a "Bitch," as Freeman did. But just as African Americans admired Malcolm X for articulating what they would only say in private (see Chapter 18), Eastman might have thought well of the outspoken Freeman. She would have approved of the way Freeman transformed the word "bitch" from a slur to a label of power and revolution.

Jo Freeman was the product of a post–World War II American culture that, even in the 1950s, was broadening in ways Eastman could only have imagined (see Chapter 14 on the American woman of the 1950s; Chapter 12 on Allen Ginsberg; and Chapter 13 on Elvis Presley). As a result, Freeman was in a position to turn her words into realities, and in a little more than a decade, overturn centuries of established belief about the nature, desires, and capabilities of women. Born in 1945, she was raised as the daughter of a schoolteacher in the Los Angeles area. She entered the University of California at Berkeley in 1961, and soon was caught up in its atmosphere of political and cultural rebellion. By the time she graduated in 1965, a number of overlapping student movements had swept the campus. The Free Speech Movement defied the Berkeley administration's ban on university political activity. Anti–Vietnam War protests followed on the heels of the August 1964 Gulf of Tonkin Resolution committing the United States to an expanded combat presence (see Chapter 17 on SDS and Chapter 19 on Lyndon Johnson). Berkeley also became a center of civil rights activism, with its students helping lead drives for desegregation and voting rights in the South and equal access to housing and jobs in the North. Freeman participated in all of these, sitting in at university administration buildings demanding free political expression on campus, demonstrating against the Vietnam War, and picketing racially discriminatory San Francisco Bay area employers. Like members of SDS (see Chapter 17), Freeman dreamed of a transformative "New Left" that would attack racism, poverty, imperialism, and bureaucracy. But she discovered that the egalitarian impulses of male leftists did not extend to women. In fact, radical men seemed to replicate the prejudices of the American establishment whose values they claimed to oppose. She discovered firsthand that few women held positions of leadership in the antiwar, civil rights, or Free Speech movements. And she was angered that women were often regarded as little more than support personnel: secretaries, cooks, messengers, and, on occasion, sex objects. Freeman's involvement in the Movement as well as her growing dissatisfaction with women's place in it led her to attend the 1967 National Conference for New Politics in Chicago, one of the largest New Left meetings of the decade. There, her and Firestone's experiences with the male-dominated convention led to outrage. Both Freeman and Firestone walked out of the convention early, marking their break with the Movement.

Freeman decided to apply the New Left's egalitarian rhetoric to women as an oppressed class. Searching out a group of like-minded females, she helped form the Westside, an organization that through discussion, writing, and activism sought to liberate women from male control and authority. Westside's newsletter, "Voice of the Women's Liberation Movement," was one of the first of its kind, and the Westside women were among the first to use the phrase "women's liberation movement."[5] Although she did not abandon her commitment to the causes of civil rights, free speech, and peace, Freeman now viewed them primarily through the lens of gender. She identified first and foremost as a woman.

Freeman entered the University of Chicago as a political science graduate student in 1968, and the school became her base as she sought to realize her vision of a new American woman demanding and enjoying full equality with men. Freeman found herself on both sides of the politico versus feminist debate. She was committed to change through politics. But she also critiqued modern American society. Unlike Eastman, who accepted marriage as an institution, albeit in modified form (see Chapter 5), Freeman rejected any relationship with men that disadvantaged women. Marriage as practiced in the United States, in her view, was a form of "patriarchy," a legalized dominion of males over females. For centuries, men had determined the direction of women's lives. Education? Job? Dress? Demeanor? Childbearing? Marriage itself? Women controlled none of these basic life choices. Freeman decided it was time they did.

She knew that acts of self-assertion would be costly. Men would respond to the new woman with anger and ridicule. They would marginalize her and attempt to read her out of the company of "true" women. One of the words they might employ to stigmatize strong and assertive women was "bitch." With its connotations of hysteria and rage, "bitch" was an indispensable tool of male power. No woman wanted to be labeled a "bitch." But Freeman understood that words were flexible and malleable. "Bitch" could take on new meanings in more sympathetic hands. "Like the term 'nigger,'" she argued, "'bitch' serves the social function of isolating and discrediting a class of people who do not conform to the socially accepted patterns of behavior."[6] But as others did with the N-word as well as "black," Freeman sought to reframe the connotation of "bitch." Clearly drawing on the African American civil rights movement, Freeman wrote that "a woman should be proud to declare she is a bitch, because Bitch is Beautiful."[7] The very qualities of independence, confidence, and pride she wished to encourage in the new woman made her a "bitch." The word was thus not an insult but a compliment.

In this spirit, Freeman composed "The Bitch Manifesto" in the fall of 1968. Writing as "Joreen," the name by which she was known in the women's movement, she defined "Bitch" in deliberately provocative terms: "aggressive, assertive, domineering, overbearing, strong-minded, spiteful, hostile, direct, blunt, candid, obnoxious, thick-skinned, hard-headed." Bitches were physically uninhibited. They "move their bodies freely rather than restrain, refine and confine their motions in the proper feminine manner." Bitches deferred to no one, especially men. They "seek their identity strictly through themselves and what they do. They are subjects, not objects…(They) believe they are capable of doing anything they damn well want to. If something gets in their way, well, that's why they become Bitches."[8] Above all, Bitches "rudely violate conceptions of proper sex role behavior."[9] Previous generations of women were inhibited by accusations of "acting like men." Not Bitches. They followed the direction of their instincts, inclinations, and ambitions. They refused to let their lives be determined by biology, convention, or history. Bitches were not helpers, appendages, trophies, dependents, or children. They were free human beings.

As such, Freeman knew that Bitches constituted "a threat to the social structures which enslave women and the social values which justify keeping them in their place."[10] She anticipated a furious backlash from men fearful of losing their traditional privileges and prerogatives. But Bitches could not give up or give in. Only by being themselves could they win. "Bitches," Freeman wrote, "were the first women to go to college, the first to break through the Invisible Bar of the professions, the first social revolutionaries, the first labor leaders, the first to organize other women. Because they were not passive beings and acted on their resentment at being kept down, they dared to do what other women would not."[11]

Here, Freeman could have been describing Crystal Eastman, who was attacked in "respectable" circles for being all of these things. But Bitches possessed resources Eastman never enjoyed. Post–World War II prosperity had given them a more secure economic position and greater educational opportunities. Freeman herself was the product of a middle-class upbringing and had graduated from college. In addition, the very existence of the New Left, with all of its dismissiveness toward women, offered a model for political organization that Freeman and her sisters could emulate. "BITCH," the group that "Joreen" hoped her manifesto would inspire, never materialized. But thousands of like-minded women came together in small communities of shared interest to read, discuss, bond, organize, lobby, advocate, and demonstrate. NOW replicated these patterns of activism across the United States. As a result, by the end of the twentieth century, the qualities that Freeman associated with "Bitch" would be viewed as positive signs of strength and achievement.

Jo Freeman received her Ph.D. from the University of Chicago in 1973 and went on to a career as a feminist writer and activist. In 1983, she earned a law degree at New York University, following in the footsteps of Crystal Eastman. Like her predecessor, Freeman worked to use the law as an instrument of social change. Active in NOW, she supports pro-choice candidates for political office and defends against legal challenges to abortion rights. Crystal Eastman did not live to see her dreams bear fruit. Jo Freeman did. "The Bitch Manifesto" helped create an America with room for women who shared Jo Freeman's values, outlook, and life path. Henceforth, they would be known not as "bitches," but as feminists—or simply as women.

Questions for Consideration and Conversation

1. Why do you think male members of SNCC and SDS, who professed to be committed to the idea of "equality" for all Americans, found it so difficult to apply their principles to women?
2. In 1967, a group of female SDS members complained of their "colonial relationship to men." Evaluate this claim.
3. Why do you think Crystal Eastman (Chapter 5) would not have wanted to "be" Jo Freeman, but would have liked her?
4. Can you make any connections between the sentiments expressed in *Life*'s "American Woman" essays (Chapter 14) and "The Bitch Manifesto"?

5. How did Freeman attempt to redefine the term "bitch"? Do you think she succeeded?
6. How did SDS and the New Left, despite the sexism within their ranks, help propel the modern women's movement?
7. "The Bitch Manifesto" was written by a white, middle-class woman. What relevance does it have to poor women? African American women?

Endnotes

1. Sara Evans, *Personal Politics: The Roots of Women's Liberation in the Civil Rights Movement & the New Left* (New York: Vintage, 1979), 87.
2. Ibid., 240.
3. Ibid., 241.
4. Alice Echols, *Daring to Be Bad: Radical Feminism in America, 1967–1975* (Minneapolis: University of Minnesota, 1989), 51–101.
5. Ibid., 53.
6. Jo Freeman, "The Bitch Manifesto," in Shulamith Firestone and Anne Koedt, eds., *Notes from the Second Year* (New York: Radical Feminism, 1970), 5.
7. Ibid., 6.
8. Ibid., 5.
9. Ibid., 6.
10. Ibid., 6.
11. Ibid., 9.

JO FREEMAN, THE BITCH MANIFESTO (1968)

Source: Shulamith Firestone and Anne Koedt, eds., *Notes from the Second Year: Women's Liberation: Major Writing of the Radical Feminists.* New York: Radical Feminism, 1970, pp. 5–9.

> . . . man is defined as a human being and woman is defined as a female. Whenever she tries to behave as a human being she is accused of trying to emulate the male . . .
>
> **Simone de Beauvoir**

BITCH is an organization which does not yet exist. The name is not an acronym. It stands for exactly what it sounds like.

BITCH is composed of Bitches. There are many definitions of a bitch. The most complimentary definition is a female dog. Those definitions of bitches who are also homo sapiens are rarely as objective. They vary from person to person and depend strongly on how much of a bitch the definer considers herself. However, everyone agrees that a bitch is always female, dog or otherwise.

It is also generally agreed that a Bitch is aggressive, and therefore unfeminine (ahem). She may be sexy, in which case she becomes a Bitch Goddess, a special case which will not concern us here. But she is never a "true woman."

Bitches have some or all of the following characteristics.

1. Personality. Bitches are aggressive, assertive, domineering, overbearing, strong-minded, spiteful, hostile, direct, blunt, candid, obnoxious, thick-skinned, hard-headed, vicious, dogmatic, competent, competitive, pushy, loud-mouthed, independent, stubborn, demanding, manipulative, egoistic, driven, achieving, overwhelming, threatening, scary, ambitious, tough, brassy, masculine, boisterous, and turbulent. Among other things. A Bitch occupies a lot of psychological space. You always know she is around. A Bitch takes shit from no one. You may not like her, but you cannot ignore her.

2. Physical. Bitches are big, tall, strong, large, loud, brash, harsh, awkward, clumsy, sprawling, strident, ugly. Bitches move their bodies freely rather than restrain, refine and confine their motions in the proper feminine manner. They clomp up stairs, stride when they walk and don't worry about where they put their legs when they sit. They have loud voices and often use them. Bitches are not pretty.

3. Orientation. Bitches seek their identity strictly through themselves and what they do. They are subjects, not objects. They may have a relationship with a person or organization, but they never marry anyone or anything; man, mansion, or movement. Thus Bitches prefer to plan their own lives rather than live from day to day, action to action, or person to person. They are independent cusses and believe they are capable of doing anything they damn well want to. If something gets in their way; well, that's why they become Bitches. If they are professionally inclined, they will seek careers and have no fear of competing with anyone. If not professionally inclined, they still seek self-expression and self-actualization. Whatever they do, they want an active role and are frequently perceived as domineering. Often they do dominate other people when roles are not available to them which more creatively sublimate their energies and utilize their capabilities. More often they are accused of domineering when doing what would be considered natural by a man.

A true Bitch is self-determined, but the term "bitch" is usually applied with less discrimination. It is a popular derogation to put down uppity women that was created by man and adopted by women. Like the term "nigger," "bitch" serves the social function of isolating and discrediting a class of people who do not conform to the socially accepted patterns of behavior.

BITCH does not use this word in the negative sense. A woman should be proud to declare she is a Bitch, because Bitch is Beautiful. It should be an act of affirmation by self and not negation by others. Not everyone can qualify as a Bitch. One does not have to have all of the above three qualities, but should be well possessed of at least two of them to be considered a Bitch. If a woman qualifies in all three, at least partially, she is a Bitch's Bitch. Only Superbitches qualify totally in all three categories and there are very few of those. Most don't last long in this society.

The most prominent characteristic of all Bitches is that they rudely violate conceptions of proper sex role behavior. They violate them in different ways, but they all violate them. Their attitudes towards themselves and other people, their goal orientations, their personal style, their appearance and way of handling their bodies, all jar people and make them feel uneasy. Sometimes it's conscious and sometimes it's not, but people generally feel uncomfortable around Bitches. They consider them aberrations. They find their style disturbing. So they create a dumping ground for all who they deplore as bitchy and call them frustrated women. Frustrated they may be, but the cause is social not sexual.

What is disturbing about a Bitch is that she is androgynous. She incorporates within herself qualities traditionally defined as "masculine" as well as "feminine". A Bitch is blunt, direct, arrogant, at times egoistic. She has no liking for the indirect, subtle, mysterious ways of the "eternal feminine." She disdains the vicarious life deemed natural to women because she wants to live a life of her own.

Our society has defined humanity as male, and female as something other than male. In this way, females could be human only by living vicariously thru a male. To be able to live, a woman has to agree to serve, honor, and obey a man and what she gets in exchange is at best a shadow life. Bitches refuse to serve, honor or obey anyone. They demand to be fully functioning human beings, not just shadows. They want to be both female and human. This makes them social contradictions. The mere existence of Bitches negates the idea that a woman's reality must come thru her relationship to a man and defies the belief that women are perpetual children who must always be under the guidance of another.

Therefore, if taken seriously, a Bitch is a threat to the social structures which enslave women and the social values which justify keeping them in their place. She is living testimony that woman's oppression does not have to be, and as such raises doubts about the validity of the whole social system. Because she is a threat she is not taken seriously. Instead, she is dismissed as a deviant. Men create a special category for her in which she is accounted at least partially human, but not really a woman. To the extent to which they relate to her as a human being, they refuse to relate to her as a sexual being. Women are even more threatened because they cannot forget she is a woman. They are afraid they will identify with her too closely. She has a freedom and an independence which they envy and challenges them to forsake the security of their chains. Neither men nor women can face the reality of a Bitch because to do so would force them to face the corrupt reality of themselves. She is dangerous. So they dismiss her as a freak.

This is the root of her own oppression as a woman. Bitches are not only oppressed as women, they are oppressed for not being like women. Because she has insisted on being human before being feminine, on being true to herself before kowtowing to social pressures, a Bitch grows up an outsider. Even as girls, Bitches violated the limits of accepted sex role behavior. They did not identify with other women and few were lucky enough to have an adult Bitch serve as a role model. They had to make their own way and the pitfalls this uncharted course posed contributed to both their uncertainty and their independence.

Bitches are good examples of how women can be strong enough to survive even the rigid, punitive socialization of our society. As young girls it never quite penetrated their consciousness that women were supposed to be inferior to men in any but the mother/helpmate role. They asserted themselves as children and never really internalized the slave style of wheedling and cajolery which is called feminine. Some Bitches were oblivious to the usual social pressures and some stubbornly resisted them. Some developed a superficial feminine style and some remained tomboys long past the time when such behavior is tolerated. All Bitches refused, in mind and spirit, to conform to the idea that there were limits on what they could be and do. They placed no bounds on their aspirations or their conduct.

For this resistance they were roundly condemned. They were put down, snubbed, sneered at, talked about, laughed at and ostracized. Our society made women into slaves and then condemned them for acting like slaves. Those who refused to act like slaves they disparaged for not being true women. It was all done very subtly. Few people were so direct as to say that they did not like Bitches because they did not play the sex role game.

In fact, few were sure why they did not like Bitches. They did not realize that their violation of the reality structure endangered the structure. Somehow, from early childhood on, some girls didn't fit in and were good objects to make fun of. But few people consciously recognized the root of their dislike. The issue was never confronted. If it was talked about at all, it was done with snide remarks behind the young girl's back. Bitches were made to feel that there was something wrong with them; something personally wrong.

Teenage girls are particularly vicious in the scapegoat game. This is the time of life when women are told they must compete the hardest for the spoils (i.e. men) which society allows. They must assert their femininity or see it denied. They are very unsure of themselves and adopt the rigidity that goes with uncertainty. They are hard on their competitors and even harder on those who decline to compete. Those of their peers who do not share their concerns and practice the arts of charming men are excluded from most social groupings. If she didn't know it before, a Bitch learns during these years that she is different.

As she gets older she learns more about why she is different. As Bitches begin to take jobs, or participate in organizations, they are rarely content to sit quietly and do what they are told. A Bitch has a mind of her own and wants to use it. She wants to rise high, be creative, assume responsibility. She knows she is capable and wants to use her capabilities. This is not pleasing to the men she works for, which is not her primary goal.

When she meets the hard brick wall of sex prejudice she is not compliant. She will knock herself out batting her head against the wall because she will not accept her defined role as an auxiliary. Occasionally she crashes her way through. Or she uses her ingenuity to find a loophole, or creates one. Or she is ten times better than anyone else competing with her. She also accepts less than her due. Like other women her ambitions have often been dulled for she has not totally escaped the badge of inferiority placed upon the "weaker sex." She will often espouse contentment with being the power behind the throne—provided that she does have real power—while rationalizing that she really does not want the recognition that comes with also having the throne. Because she has been put down most of her life, both for being a woman and for not being a true woman, a Bitch will not always recognize that what she has achieved is not attainable by the typical woman. A highly competent Bitch often deprecates herself by refusing to recognize her own superiority. She is wont to say that she is average or less so; if she can do it, anyone can.

As adults, Bitches may have learned the feminine role, at least the outward style but they are rarely comfortable in it. This is particularly true of those women who are physical Bitches. They want to free their bodies as well as their minds and deplore the effort they must waste confining their physical motions or dressing the role in order not to turn people off. Too, because they violate sex role expectations physically, they are not as free to violate them psychologically or intellectually. A few deviations from the norm can be tolerated but too many are too threatening. It's bad enough not to think like a woman, sound like a woman or do the kinds of things women are supposed to do. To also not look like a woman, move like a woman or act like a woman is to go way beyond the pale. Ours is a rigid society with narrow limits placed on the extent of human diversity. Women in particular are defined by their physical characteristics. Bitches who do not violate these limits are freer to violate others. Bitches who do violate them in style or size can be somewhat envious of those who do not have to so severely restrain the expansiveness of their personalities and behavior. Often these Bitches are tortured more because their deviancy is always evident. But they do have a compensation in that large Bitches have a good deal less difficulty being taken seriously than small women. One of the sources of their suffering as women is also a source of their strength.

The trial by fire which most Bitches go through while growing up either makes them or breaks them. They are strung tautly between the two poles of being true to their own nature or being accepted as a social being. This makes them very sensitive people, but it is a sensitivity the rest of the world is unaware of. For on the outside they have frequently grown a thick defensive callous which can make them seem hard and bitter at times. This is particularly true of those Bitches who have been forced to become isolates in order to avoid being remade and destroyed by their peers. Those who are fortunate enough to have grown up with some similar companions,

understanding parents, a good role model or two and a very strong will, can avoid some of the worse aspects of being a Bitch. Having endured less psychological punishment for being what they were they can accept their differentness with the ease that comes from self-confidence.

Those who had to make their way entirely on their own have an uncertain path. Some finally realize that their pain comes not just because they do not conform but because they do not want to conform. With this comes the recognition that there is nothing particularly wrong with *them*—they just don't fit into this kind of society. Many eventually learn to insulate themselves from the harsh social environment. However, this too has its price. Unless they are cautious and conscious, the confidence gained in this painful manner—with no support from their sisters—is more often a kind of arrogance. Bitches can become so hard and calloused that the last vestiges of humanity become buried deep within and almost destroyed.

Not all Bitches make it. Instead of callouses, they develop open sores. Instead of confidence they develop an unhealthy sensitivity to rejection. Seemingly tough on the outside, on the inside they are a bloody pulp, raw from the lifelong verbal whipping they have had to endure. These are Bitches who have gone Bad. They often go around with a chip on their shoulders and use their strength for unproductive retaliation when someone accepts their dare to knock it off. These Bitches can be very obnoxious because they never really trust people. They have not learned to use their strength constructively.

Bitches who have been mutilated as human beings often turn their fury on other people—particularly other women. This is one example of how women are trained to keep themselves and other women in their place. Bitches are no less guilty than non-Bitches of self-hatred and group-hatred and those who have gone Bad suffer the worse of both these afflictions. All Bitches are scapegoats and those who have not survived the psychological gauntlet are the butt of everyone's disdain. As a group, Bitches are treated by other women much as women in general are treated by society—all right in their place, good to exploit and gossip about, but otherwise to be ignored or put down. They are threats to the traditional woman's position and they are also an outgroup to which she can feel superior. Most women feel both better than and jealous of Bitches. While comforting themselves that they are not like these aggressive, masculine freaks, they have a sneaking suspicion that perhaps men, the most important thing in their lives, do find the freer, more assertive, independent Bitch preferable as a woman.

Bitches, likewise, don't care too much for other women. They grow up disliking other women. They can't relate to them, they don't identify with them, they have nothing in common with them. Other women have been the norm into which they have not fit. They reject those who have rejected them. This is one of the reasons Bitches who are successful in hurdling the obstacles society places before women scorn these women who are not. They tend to feel those who can take it will make it. Most women have been the direct agents of much of the shit Bitches have had to endure and few of either group have had the political consciousness to realize why this is. Bitches have been oppressed by other women as much if not more than by men and their hatred for them is usually greater.

Bitches are also uncomfortable around other women because frequently women are less their psychological peers than are men. Bitches don't particularly like passive people. They are always slightly afraid they will crush the fragile things. Women are trained to be passive and have learned to act that way even when they are not. A Bitch is not very passive and is not comfortable acting that role. But she usually does not like to be domineering either—whether this is from natural distaste at dominating others or fear of seeming too masculine. Thus a Bitch can relax and be her natural non-passive self without worrying about mascerating someone only in the company of those who are as strong as she. This is more frequently in the company of men than of women but those Bitches who have not succumbed totally to self-hatred are most comfortable of all only in the company of fellow Bitches. These are her true peers and the only ones with whom she does not have to play some sort of role. Only with other Bitches can a Bitch be truly free.

These moments come rarely. Most of the time Bitches must remain psychologically isolated. Women and men are so threatened by them and react so adversely that Bitches guard their true selves carefully. They are suspicious of those few whom they think they might be able to trust because so often it turns out to be a sham. But in this loneliness there is a strength and from their isolation and their bitterness come contributions that other

women do not make. Bitches are among the most unsung of the unsung heroes of this society. They are the pioneers, the vanguard, the spearhead. Whether they want to be or not this is the role they serve just by their very being. Many would not choose to be the groundbreakers for the mass of women for whom they have no sisterly feelings but they cannot avoid it. Those who violate the limits, extend them; or cause the system to break.

Bitches were the first women to go to college, the first to break thru the Invisible Bar of the professions, the first social revolutionaries, the first labor leaders, the first to organize other women. Because they were not passive beings and acted on their resentment at being kept down, they dared to do what other women would not. They took the flak and the shit that society dishes out to those who would change it and opened up portions of the world to women that they would otherwise not have known. They have lived on the fringes. And alone or with the support of their sisters they have changed the world we live in.

By definition Bitches are marginal beings in this society. They have no proper place and wouldn't stay in it if they did. They are women but not true women. They are human but they are not male. Some don't even know they are women because they cannot relate to other women. They may play the feminine game at times, but they know it is a game they are playing. Their major psychological oppression is not a belief that they are inferior but a belief that they are not. Thus, all their lives they have been told they were freaks. More polite terms were used of course, but the message got through. Like most women they were taught to hate themselves as well as all women. In different ways and for different reasons perhaps, but the effect was similar. Internalization of a derogatory self-concept always results in a good deal of bitterness and resentment. This anger is usually either turned in on the self—making one an unpleasant person—or on other women—reinforcing the social cliches about them. Only with political consciousness is it directed at the source—the social system.

The bulk of this Manifesto has been about Bitches. The remainder will be about BITCH. The organization does not yet exist and perhaps it never can. Bitches are so damned independent and they have learned so well not to trust other women that it will be difficult for them to learn to even trust each other. This is what BITCH must teach them to do. Bitches have to learn to accept themselves as Bitches and to give their sisters the support they need to be creative Bitches. Bitches must learn to be proud of their strength and proud of themselves. They must move away from the isolation which has been their protection and help their younger sisters avoid its perils. They must recognize that women are often less tolerant of other women than are men because they have been taught to view all women as their enemies. And Bitches must form together in a movement to deal with their problems in a political manner. They must organize for their own liberation as all women must organize for theirs. We must be strong, we must be militant, we must be dangerous. We must realize that Bitch is Beautiful and that we have nothing to lose. Nothing whatsoever.

This manifesto was written and revised with the help of several of my sisters, to whom it is dedicated.

CHAPTER 21

Ronald Reagan Confronts Marxism and Big Government

"Mr. Gorbachev, open this gate! Mr. Gorbachev, tear down this wall!"

Ronald Wilson Regan (1911–2004) is now the undisputed patron saint of the Republican Party and the modern conservative movement, having eclipsed his party rivals: Abraham Lincoln, Theodore Roosevelt, and Dwight Eisenhower. Whatever influence these last three have had upon American life, it is no longer a concern of those who claim a home within the Grand Old Party (GOP). To some, that transformation seemed sudden and perhaps tragic. But to others and importantly to Reagan himself, his successful struggles to remake the GOP into a conservative party and to put himself atop of it were the results of four decades of political work to roll back Franklin D. Roosevelt's New Deal and to defeat the Soviet Union in the Cold War. In many ways, it was also the product of a decades-long conversation with the American people.

Reagan's childhood predicted little of his later triumphs. Born in 1911, the second son of a shoe salesman and his wife, he grew up in small towns in Illinois. At the urging of his mother, Reagan escaped the insular nature of the rural Midwest and the pains of living with his impoverished, alcoholic father by devoting himself to school, particularly drama and sports. A bright student who was an avid reader and thoughtful writer, he excelled scholastically and eventually earned his way to Eureka College, located about 130 miles southwest of Chicago. By then, Reagan already displayed his legendary genial composure, warm charm, and charisma. His peers elected him class president. A rebel of sorts, Reagan even led his classmates on a student strike, which resulted in a change in campus leadership as well as a new student code of behavior and a reversal of budget-saving maneuvers that adversely affected students.

Reagan graduated in 1932 with a degree in economics and sociology. His interest in politics was rather undeveloped. Like so many Americans, he inherited his politics from his parents. Reagan was a Democrat. His affinity for the party of Thomas Jefferson only grew as Franklin Roosevelt entered the White House to save America from the Great Depression. Reagan was enamored with FDR's ability to exude confidence and raise public morale even in the darkest days of the economic disaster. Those direct appeals to citizens through the relatively new medium of radio left an indelible impression.

Reagan's first job after college was as a radio announcer in Iowa, covering sporting events. In 1937, after following the Chicago Cubs to spring training in California, Reagan took a screen test for Warner

Brothers Studios and landed a film contract. From 1937 to 1965, he starred in dozens of films. Most were forgettable but some like *Knute Rockne—All American* (1940) have become a part of America's cultural heritage. After World War II, during which Reagan served stateside making movies for the Army Air Corps, Reagan's Hollywood career flagged. It was then that he turned to other means of making a living. He became the president of the Screen Actors Guild (SAG), joined General Electric (GE) as one of their chief spokesmen, and became active in politics.

Smart, engaging, and humble, Reagan achieved more success in the public sphere of politics than he ever did as an actor. As SAG president, he became an exemplar of responsible unionism, as opposed to the confrontational—if not radical—social unionism of some industrial labor organizations. Although Reagan remained a Democrat in name through the 1960 presidential election, he supported Dwight Eisenhower in 1952 and again in 1956. In 1960, Reagan led the Democrats for Nixon forces in opposition to John F. Kennedy. His conservatism blossomed while under the employ of GE. Being a GE spokesman involved more than hawking their home products. It was Reagan's job to talk with the company's employees about politics and economics. He was the bulldog of GE vice president Lemuel Boulware, who had devised a scheme to defeat unions by winning worker loyalty, drawing them away from the union. The key to success was Reagan's plant visit. He pressed the flesh on the shop floor and gave a down-home, captivating speech about the dangers of big government, the necessity of low taxes, and the lurking fear of Socialism and Communism from within and without the United States. Married with a tough, anti-union stance, Boulwarism, as it became known, was tremendously successful. By the end of the 1950s, GE had bested its union. An added bonus for Boulware was that Reagan had developed into a right-wing ideologue with the common touch. He was not merely useful for the corporation, but by 1960, he was instrumental to the new, rapidly developing conservative movement. When Reagan left GE in 1962, he was primed to become a major political player.

Americans first discovered Ronald Reagan the politician during the 1964 presidential campaign. A week before the election, he appeared on television and gave an extraordinary address. His "Time for Choosing" speech—"The Speech" as it later became known—energized voters who rallied to Barry Goldwater. It was not enough to save the new-era conservative from complete disaster, but it did propel Reagan further into the political sphere. Two years later, he used much of the same conversational style of politicking to win the gubernatorial contest in California, unseating a heavily favored Democratic incumbent. Reagan was the master communicator, in person and on television. Talking to voters was like talking with workers from his GE days. Be brief, be folksy, and be funny. He was the master of the one-liner that put a rhetorical dagger into the heart of the opposition. He blamed Democrats for everything from budget woes to urban riots to student uprisings to cultural shifts. Famously he said of hippies—which he claimed were a byproduct of liberal social policies—that they acted like Tarzan, looked like Jane, and smelled like Cheetah.

Although he ran from the political right, Reagan ruled closer to the center, approving tax increases, increasing state educational spending, and signing the nation's most liberal abortion law. Playing the middle won him re-election. The successful two-term governor left office in 1975 with the clear intention of running for president in America's bicentennial year. During his party's primary, he appealed to voters as the conservative, right-wing alternative to Gerald R. Ford and the Nixon legacy. In fact, many new conservatives had welcomed President Richard M. Nixon's demise as he was not an advocate for small government. Worse, a modern Republican in some ways, Nixon had enhanced worker and consumer safety programs, refined equal employment opportunities, and increased environmental regulations. Right-wingers like Reagan opposed Nixon's settlement in Vietnam. Nixon's final apostasy came in the form of diplomacy. He took heretical steps to ease tensions between the United States and its Communist rivals, namely China and the Soviet Union. Although Reagan did not win his primary battle with Ford, it was a minor setback, one that in fact made him the strongest GOP political contender for the 1980 election.

Reagan's 1980 campaign was brilliant. Blaming the Democrats for a terrible economy, he conveyed his messages simply, asking voters if they were better off after four years under President Jimmy Carter. Reagan built upon Nixon's southern strategy of pulling southern working-class whites away from the Democratic Party. In direct appeals to groups like the Moral Majority and the Christian Coalition, he wooed Christian evangelicals to his camp by offering them the chance to eliminate legalized abortion and to insert prayer in public schools. He promised to get tough on Communism, pledging to restore America's military superiority. Reagan routed Carter. That conversation that Reagan began with American citizens in the 1950s had finally paid the ultimate dividend. And, as Reagan continued it during his presidency, it supplied the rhetorical power to rally voters behind his political agenda and to explain away his administration's shortcomings and failures.

Reagan's 1981 inaugural address had no surprises. It was a quintessential restatement of the ideas and ideology that he had been relating to the American people for thirty years. But, he was in a position to make good on his promises to shrink government, to cut taxes, to transform programs designed to aid the poor and the disadvantaged, and to defeat what Reagan eventually labeled the evil empire. At each step, the Great Communicator utilized television and radio—along with a few public appearances—to gather and maintain support for his agenda. Continuing that conversation was especially critical since many of Reagan's efforts were extraordinarily controversial. But Reagan adeptly soothed public fears and muffled protest and outrage at his actions. Thus, without much dissent, rebuke, or backlash, he was able to, for example, smash the strike of the Professional Air Traffic Controllers Organization; slash taxes for wealthy individuals and corporations; cut funding for education and antipoverty programs; reduce the effectiveness of civil rights and labor agencies; and remove all sorts of regulations to protect the environment, consumer safety, small businesses, and workers. Critics complained about the new direction in American politics to no avail. Until 1987, even various scandals and over hundred investigations, indictments, and convictions for administrative wrongdoing had little effect. It was tantamount to shouting in the wilderness. As one Democrat put it, Reagan was the Teflon president: Nothing stuck to him. The most dramatic breech of ethics—the Iran-Contra Affair which was fully revealed in 1987—was something different that demonstrated the limits of Reagan's presidency as well the boundaries of rhetorical credulity.

A master of domestic politics, Reagan had great difficulty initially finding his way on the international scene. For decades, he had relished the chance to cow the Russians and their lackeys. But his singular pursuit of the Reagan Doctrine, which lent aid and comfort to all states and movements fighting Communists, proved often to be too blunt an instrument for dealing with global conflicts as well as opportunities. As he pledged, the U.S. military grew at an unprecedented rate in the 1980s, adding not only personnel but also new equipment and new programs such as the Strategic Defense Initiative (dubbed the "Star Wars" defense plan) and the deployment of new stealth aircraft. Reagan authorized the unleashing of the Central Intelligence Agency to arm and train anti-Communist militias in Latin America and the Middle East. But the Reagan Doctrine was not nuanced enough to deal with Middle Eastern crises over religion and oil politics. For instance, when Iraq invaded Iran in 1980, the United States quickly backed Iraq's strongman, Saddam Hussein, knowing full well that he was a bloodthirsty dictator, who had already illegally used chemical weapons against Iran. In Lebanon, Reagan's policies resulted in the deployment of U.S. Marines into a warzone with incredibly tragic results; and his foreign policy initiatives bollixed him into creating a shadow federal government under the direction of White House staffer Oliver North for the purpose of selling arms to Iran and using the proceeds to illegally fund anti-Communist rebels in Latin America, known as the Contras. When news of the scheme first appeared in 1986, Reagan tried to explain to a shocked citizenry. This time, and perhaps for the first time, his words failed him. The Great Communicator's approval ratings plummeted. During the last years of his presidency, Reagan recovered to a considerable degree by seeking a lasting peace with the Soviets. In a series of meetings, diplomatic negotiations, and historic treaties, President Reagan and Russian leader Mikhail Gorbachev dramatically improved relations, culminating in 1989 in the demolition of the Berlin Wall, that concrete symbol of the divisions between the United States and its allies and the Soviets and theirs. In a speech two years previous at Brandenburg Gate commemorating the Berlin's sesquiseptcentennial, Reagan had seemingly found a way to converse with Americans, Germans, and all who cared to tune in. He captured their imaginations by speaking of freedom, security, peace, and an end to political divisions. It's that Reagan that Americans often remember, and not the blundering one attempting to explain hostage deals or black ops or illegal deals with hostile foreign countries. In November 1994, more than three years out of office, Reagan ended his conversation with America with a brief letter. He revealed that he had contracted Alzheimer's disease and that he was moving to the sunset of his life.

Below are six of Reagan's most celebrated speeches. Spanning a quarter century, they demonstrate his skill as a rhetorician, illustrate the development of his ideology, and indicate the changes that he made to American political culture. They can be separated into two groups. The first chronicles Reagan's conversation with America as he ascended into the White House. The second batch continues that train of thought while adding Reagan's engagement with the Soviet Union, culminating with his famous Brandenburg speech.

After the 1960 presidential election, Ronald Reagan began to widen his political audience from mainly GE workers to the general electorate. In doing so, he revamped his basic shop floor speech. In it, he raised the specter of an insidious Communist takeover, trying to rouse Americans from their stupor. "We are at war," he intoned, "and we are losing that war simply because we don't, or won't, realize that we are in it." This conflict, he explained, was not happening on military battlefields, because the Communists knew that they could not defeat American forces, unless "we yielded to a massive peace campaign and disarmed." Rather, the plan was to burrow into existing American institutions and instigate Socialist programs slowly so that one day capitalism and freedom would be snuffed out. This "encroaching control" had to be stopped. Reagan outlined a handful of examples of this glacial process, detailing his growing fears of government-paid medicine, social security, and educational reform (including integration). He implored his listeners to join him "to do something about it!." The "main battleground" was taxation. Cutting off the money supply to government would force it to stop spending on social(ist) programs. Thus, the war was not some Communist boogieman in Europe or Asia; the war was against the federal government itself.

The "Encroaching Control" speech set Reagan apart from and ahead of other Republican politicians, save one: Barry Goldwater, who ran for president in 1964 as the standard bearer for the new conservative movement with its heated anti-Communist and anti-government rhetoric. For Goldwater, the campaign against Lyndon B. Johnson went poorly. Just days before the election, the Republican Party paid for a primetime speech by Ronald Reagan, who called on Americans to vote for Goldwater. Perhaps singlehandedly, Reagan's speech—titled "A Time for Choosing" but commonly referred to as "The Speech"—briefly revitalized Goldwater's camp, bringing in new volunteers and money. Reagan began by stating that despite American prosperity the nation was in dire trouble, caused by the slow descent toward socialism. "The issue of this election," he proclaimed, was "whether we believe in our capacity for self-government or whether we abandon the American Revolution and confess that a little intellectual elite in a far-distant capitol can plan our lives for us better than we can plan them ourselves." Liberals had been willing dupes or worse in the steady march toward more government control, which sought to destroy freedom under the guises of government-run agricultural, urban renewal, and social security programs. These programs had not reduced poverty. On the contrary, liberals maintained more programs and money was needed to combat the ever-growing need. Further, Reagan insisted that the system bred welfare cheats who were willing to sacrifice their families, marriages, and jobs for a government handout. Who could save America from this illegitimate imposition of socialism? "Barry Goldwater thinks he can." Ultimately, the choice was the voters': to "reserve for our children this, the last best hope of man on earth," or to "sentence them to take the last step into a thousand years of darkness." Reagan had faith that the voters would join him. Stealing a line from his former idol, he boldly stated, "You and I have a rendezvous with destiny."

Although Reagan's "A Time for Choosing" speech failed in its direct goal, it catapulted the former actor far into national politics like no other speech save William Jennings Bryan's "Cross of Gold" address at the 1896 Democratic convention. It provided the rhetorical basis for his commanding electoral victory over Democratic incumbent Jimmy Carter in 1980. In his first inaugural, a more somber President Reagan spoke of reawakening and a "new beginning," harkening a new era of smaller government, lower taxes, and the unrelenting pursuit of the "enemies of freedom." Reagan pledged not to do away with government but to "curb the size and influence" and eliminate "unnecessary and excessive growth." Only with this pernicious intervention and intrusion removed could the "industrial giant" reawaken. "So, with all the creative energy at our command," Reagan intoned, "let us begin an era of national renewal. Let us renew our determination, our courage, and our strength. And, let us renew our faith and our hope."

In the modern era, it has been common for presidents to refer to religion in their inaugurals. However, Reagan's references to faith as well as to "the happiness and the liberty of the millions yet unborn" were intended to energize the new element of the Republican base: evangelical Christians. While president, he cemented the ties to those "God-fearing, dedicated, noble men and women" who believe that "freedom prospers only where the blessings of God are avidly sought and humbly accepted" and where institutions "foster and nourish values like concern for others and respect for the rule of law under God." In a famous speech in 1983 before the National Association of Evangelicals, he attacked those he called "modern-day" secularists who used their government positions to take the prerogatives of parents in the name of family planning. He called for a return of "Judeo-Christian" principles and a series of policy initiatives including parental notification for birth control and abortion and the legalization of prayer in public schools. Harkening to his inaugural, President Reagan told his audience to take heart and not get discouraged at the slow pace of reform. "There's a great spiritual awakening in America, a renewal of the traditional values that have been the bedrock of America's goodness and greatness." No doubt, his listeners were encouraged when he stated that "there is sin and evil in the world, and we are enjoying by Scripture and the Lord Jesus to oppose it with all our might."

After talking about the "phenomenology of evil" and the "doctrine of sin," Reagan launched into the final section of his speech, reminding these evangelicals that sin was confined to the borders of the United States. And, in a world of depravity, "America has kept alight the torch of freedom." He urged all Americans to see totalitarian powers, specifically the Soviet Union, for what they were: darkness in the world. Reagan pledged to oppose "the aggressive impulses of an evil empire" while at the same time seeking to negotiate a settlement to reduce both sides' nuclear arsenals.

This was not the first time that Reagan had called totalitarianism evil. In 1982, in a speech before the British Parliament, President Reagan spoke of the threat of global nuclear war and promised to fight those forces around the world "who seek subversion and conflict" in order to "further their barbarous assault on the human spirit." The allied world democracies, Reagan boldly stated, must not "wither in a quiet, deadening accommodation with totalitarian evil." Rather, in a restatement of what became known as the Reagan Doctrine, he called for continued pressure on Communist governments by backing "brave freedom-fighters" in Central America and elsewhere so that in the end "freedom is not the sole prerogative of a lucky few, but the inalienable and universal right of all human beings." Rhetorically at least, this was not simply a matter for the military and intelligence agencies. "The objective I propose is quite simple to state," Reagan continued, "to foster the infrastructure of democracy, the system of a free press, unions, political parties, universities, which allows a people to choose their own way to develop their own culture, to reconcile their own differences through peaceful means." Ultimately, this "march of freedom and democracy...will leave Marxism-Leninism on the ash-heap of history as it has left other tyrannies which stifle the freedom and muzzle the self-expression of the people."

Although some historians and political pundits have credited Reagan's jingoistic, brash, belligerent rhetoric for bringing and keeping the Soviets at the negotiating tables during his presidency, Mikhail Gorbachev's role cannot be underestimated. Until his rise to power in 1985, Reagan's relationship with the Soviet Union's leaders was tenuous at best. Despite continuing the nuclear disarmament work begun under the Carter administration, Reagan had made very little headway. And, there were moments when all diplomatic ties were lost. Gorbachev's commitment to talks and treaties revived hopes for peace so much so that by 1987 momentum seemed to be building for an epoch change. Reagan and those working under him understood that this was their chance and pressed the initiative. In June 1987, Reagan appeared in West Berlin at the Brandenbugh Gate to celebrate the city's 750th anniversary. It was there that he reaffirmed his and the American people's love and devotion to Germany and Berlin. As he had done before—most clearly in his 1982 speech before Parliament—he denounced the wall that dissected the city. "As long as this scar of a wall is permitted to stand," he said, "it is not the German question alone that remains open, but the question of freedom for all mankind." But seizing the moment, Reagan used this platform to call for its demolition. "General Secretary Gorbachev, if you seek peace, if you seek prosperity for the Soviet Union and Eastern Europe, if you seek liberalization: Come here to this gate! Mr. Gorbachev, open this gate! Mr. Gorbachev, tear down this wall!." Reagan's speech did so well what his policies and actions sometimes failed to do—which was to lift the spirits of those whose movements whether they be anti-Communist or anti-government drew strength from his administration. A little over two years later, Germans on both sides of the wall broke through, reuniting a people that had been separated for generations.

It is difficult to say to what degree Reagan's words influenced the reunification of Berlin. Given the direction of Gorbachev's policies, it may have happened anyway. But, as with the new conservative movement in the United States, there is no doubt that Reagan's conversational rhetoric had a transformative impact on some and gave rise to a new political climate that created consequential opportunities for those who wanted to topple Communist governments, for those who sought to roll back or even eliminate the New Deal state, for those who sought to inculcate their evangelical Christian views into American public policy and life, and for those who desired to create political economy without the concerns of unionists or civil rights activists. The Great Communicator helped to fashion a political language and a framework for understanding that continues to influence the twenty-first century debates on a whole range of political and social issues from taxation to civil rights to the decline in the American social fabric.

Questions for Consideration and Conversation

1. Why do you think so many Americans find Reagan's personal story appealing and compelling?
2. Why did Reagan switch political parties?
3. How did Reagan use his acting skills for GE and as president?
4. Which one of these speeches appeals the most to you and why? Which one appeals the least to you?
5. How did Reagan infuse his political rhetoric with language that drew social and political conservatives to him?
6. Compare and contrast Reagan's conservative rhetoric with the left-leaning rhetoric of the Students for a Democratic Society (Chapter 17). Are there any similarities? What are the differences?

RONALD REAGAN, ENCROACHING CONTROL (1961)

Source: Transcript from http://www.starkiller-online.net/wiki/index.php?title=Encroaching_Control

[I]t must seem presumptuous to many of you, it would be strange if it didn't, that a member of my profession and my industry should attempt to speak to you on the serious subjects that face the people of the world today....

Last November, the communist parties of 81 countries held a convention in Moscow and again they reaffirmed this principle of Marx that it was war to the death. In a 20,000 word manifesto issued as a result of that convention, they called on communists all over the world in countries where there were non-communist governments to work for the destruction of their own governments by treason and subversion. Only in one phase, the one we fear most, are we ahead in this conflict and that is, if the communists should resort to armed force. Thanks to the dedicated patriotism and realistic thinking of our men in uniform, we would win the shooting war. But this isn't too disturbing to the men in the Kremlin because they actually only counted on armed conflict in one

eventuality. By their own words, they said, if the Americans should stupidly yield to a massive peace offensive and submit to disarmament and we could shortcut our regular program, our strategy, with armed conflict that would be of no risk to ourselves then we would resort to force. Lenin, in 1923, said, "We will take Eastern Europe, we will organize the hordes of Asia and we won't have to take the United States. We will surround it and that last bastion of capitalism will fall into our outstretched hand like overripe fruit." Well, they've taken Eastern Europe. They are organizing the hordes of Asia around the red colossus of China and today I'm sure many of us suspect we are being prepared for the bitter cup of capitulation in Laos that will be watered down only slightly by a few face-saving devices. Cuba is a Russian beach head 90 miles off our Florida coast and more telling that even that, 250,000 communist professional organizers are scattered up and down the length and breadth of Latin America.

Discussing other weapons and their effectiveness against us, Bulganin said "We can't appeal to the American working man, he's too well fed. But when, through inflation, America has priced herself out of the world markets, and unemployment follows, then we will settle our debt with the United States." Part of the American apathy is probably due to our reluctance to believe there can be any menace in a communist party so few in numbers here in our country. That only if it becomes a mass party with millions of people supporting it does it become something we should pay attention to and should worry about. And yet we ignore the fact that this was exactly the premise upon which Lenin took power within the ranks of the socialist followers. Lenin, determined the idea that the communist party never would be a large party. That it would be a hard, small, professional cadre. That only those people who had proven themselves would be allowed membership and this small professional cadre would, as he said, manipulate and use the masses when they were needed and he referred to us as the masses, we were the willing idiots. The communists are supremely confident of victory. They believe that you and I, under the constant pressure of the Cold War, will one by one give up our democratic traditions and principles and customs. Only temporarily, of course, but only temporarily we will turn to totalitarian tactics and methods just for the purpose of opposing the enemy. And then they cynically believe we will one day awake to find that we have, in adopting these tactics, become so much like the enemy that the causes for conflict have disappeared between us. Three and a half months before his last visit to this country, Nikita Khrushchev said, "We can't expect the American people to jump from capitalism to communism but we can assist their elected leaders in giving them small doses of socialism until one day they will awaken to find they have communism." Well this isn't exactly a new thought. As a matter of fact, the struggle we're in isn't new at all, no matter our confusion it's the same age-old struggle of mankind since his climb from the swamps. The struggle of those who believe that a few have the right to rule the many as against those who believe in individual liberty. James Madison speaking before the Virginia convention in 1788 said, "Since the general civilization of mankind, I believe there are more instances of the abridgement of the freedom of the people by gradual and silent encroachment of those in power, than by violent and sudden usurpation." Others, not realizing perhaps, that one day they would be serving the communist cause also subscribe to this belief and decided to use it. A socialist clergyman, writing in 1927, in *The New Leader*, the socialist magazine of that day, called for a new strategy of the American socialist party. He said they must infiltrate government and put men in government jobs and then he said we must work for government ownership of power, government control of railroads and banking and key industries. And he said we'll call our program, Encroaching Control. A short time ago, Norman Thomas, six times candidate for president on the socialist party ticket, gave a critique on the success of this program when he said the American people will never knowingly vote for socialism, but under the name of liberalism the American people will adopt every fragment of the socialist program.

They've appealed not to the worst, but to the best in us. To our sense of fair play, our willingness to compromise, and compromise is a noble thing when it involves two people of diametrically opposed views, willing to meet in some middle ground where they can coexist together. But compromise in the field of legislation has been developed into a technique of foot-in-the-door legislation. Get any part of a proposed government program enacted into law and then, with the principle of government participation in that field established, work particularly during each election year to expand that to the ultimate aim that one day government must become a big brother to us all. Traditionally, one of the methods first used in imposing statism on a people has been government paid medical care. It's the easiest to disguise as a humanitarian project and none of us wants to be in the position of opposing medical aid to the sick. Today, in our country, the most expensive government medical program in the world is our own Veteran's Administration hospital program. Now, none of us disagree with the idea that a man wounded in the service of his country is entitled to the finest of medical and hospital care that we can possibly afford and give him. But today three out of four veteran's administration beds are filled with patients suffering diseases or injuries neither originated by nor aggravated by military service. Indeed there are only 40,000 service connected disabilities in the whole United States, and yet every annual budget contains millions of dollars for veteran's hospital building the expansion of present facilities. Counting the twenty-three million of us who are veterans and the recent liberalization of our benefits and those other government programs already enacted, today one out of four American citizens is entitled to some form of government paid medical or hospital care. Now it is proposed that all people of Social Security age should come under a program of such comprehensive government care. On an emotional basis, we are presented with a picture of our senior citizens, millions of them, needing medical care, unable to finance it. But somehow in this plea, the proponents of this measure fail to, or seem strangely reluctant, to meet the facts face-to-face. In the last decade, 127 million Americans have come under the protection of some form of private medical or hospital insurance. This includes some two-thirds of the people of Social Security age, seventy percent of the total population. And if the same rate continues, by 1970, the coverage will amount to ninety percent of our population. As nearly as we can determine, the real problem concerns about ten percent of our senior citizens who have medical needs and who do not have the means to finance them. To that end, the last session of Congress adopted a program known as the Kerr-Mills bill. To make funds available through the states to provide medical care for that ten percent. Now, without even waiting to see if that program will work, we find that the proponents of this other program, the once defeated Forand Bill, are pleading that the only you can meet the problem of these ten percent is an overall compulsory program forcing all people into compulsory government insurance above age 65 whether they need it or not. We're justified, I believe, in accepting that this federal aid to medical . . . to a medical program actually is simply an excuse to bring about socialized medicine. As a matter of fact, ex-Congressman Forand by his own words says, "If we can only break through and get our foot inside the door then we can expand the program after that." Walter Reuther has announced that it is no secret that the organization that he represents favors a complete program of national health insurance for all the population. *New America*, the socialist magazine, has said, "The Forand Bill will not be paid for on insurance principles according to factors of estimated risk. It will be paid for through the tax mechanisms of Social Security. Once the bill is passed, this nation will be provided with a mechanism for socialized medicine." Well, he has mentioned the tax mechanism of Social Security. In 1935, Social Security called for a three percent contribution of $3000 of annual income. Today it calls for six percent of $4800 of annual income. And if the

expansions now proposed are voted, including this medical program, by 1969 it will call for eleven percent of $5000 of income and again it is no secret that the proponents of this measure are openly advocating that there should be no limit that Social Security taxes and dues should be based on gross income with no ceiling. Social Security was never intended to supplant private savings, insurance or pension plans of unions or industries. It actually was supposed to form a basis for a savings program so that destitution wouldn't follow unemployment by reason of death, disability or old age. But the temptation during election years to some politicians was too great. In 1943, the actuarial experts of Social Security estimated that by 1957, the total outgo in benefit payments would be $1,200,000,000. But by 1957, the total outgo was over $7,000,000,000. In 1959, we started paying out more than we're taking in. Today, the people drawing Social Security benefits will collect $65,000,000,000 more than they paid in. And those of us who are participating in the program and paying into it now are unfunded to an amount between 300 and 600 billion dollars. This program has been presented to us as an insurance program and indeed that term is used over and over again and we are told and led to believe that we and our employers are contributing to a fund and that some day we will call upon that fund on our own money to tide us over our non-earning years. But this isn't the tone of the testimony uttered by the experts of Social Security recently in a lawsuit before the United States Supreme Court. In that lawsuit, the experts of Social Security said it is not an insurance program. It does not have to be based on actuarial principles because it has at its beck and call the tax mechanism of the country. It then went on to say that Social Security dues are a tax for the general use of the government and the payment of this tax does not automatically entitle any citizen to the payment of Social Security benefits. It then goes on to say that these benefits are a welfare program at the behest of Congress and that Congress can curtail or cancel these benefit payments any time it sees fit.

And what of our sons? What of the young men who in these next few years will come into the nation's workforce? He will pay, in annual Social Security taxes, he and his employer, an amount which if he had at his disposal to invest in private insurance would provide him with a policy that would pay him almost double the benefits he will get from Social Security. But this isn't the only cost in personal freedom. Recently, the press reported the case of a religious group in this country has, as a tenet of its faith, the belief that it cannot participate in any pension or welfare program of government. The government stepped in, confiscated their property, sold their cattle at auction to enforce their payment of Social Security taxes. The foot in the door of education has been the $900 million National Defense Education Act of 1958. The excuse, once again, was the Cold War, Russia had put a Sputnik into the heavens, obviously something must be wrong with our education system. And so we are presented with a picture of overcrowded classrooms, of destitute teachers and of bankrupt school districts. But again let's face the facts. Ninety-nine and one half percent of the school districts in the United States have not even approached the limit of their bonded indebtedness. An increase of 35% of students in the last ten years has been matched with a 134% increase in spending at the local level. We have increased, in this decade, 10 million of the number of students educated in our public schools. We have matched this with a building program of classroom space for 15 million students. 500 colleges in America today can take an additional 200,000 students, without even adding a chair or desk, let alone another classroom. We're told that we must, on a crash program, build 60,000 classrooms a year for the next 10 years. But they forget to tell us we've been building for the last 5 years, 68,000 classrooms a year and if we continue at that rate, by 1970 we will have a surplus of classroom space in this country. Of course we want our teachers adequately paid. We believe they are entitled to the finest that we can afford and we've been doing something about it. Perhaps not as much as we should, but in the last few years the average salary of teachers has gone up from $3100 a year to $5300. The truth is there is not one shred of evidence has been presented that there is a necessity for any federal aid to our traditional local and state educational program. The aim, the aim alone is federal control. They deny this in proposing the legislation, but two and a half billion dollar program now that is advocated by the largest spending lobby in Washington D.C. But what do we hear in other utterances? The director of public education of the state of Washington spoke out in protest publicly against the problem of his state. For two years, in trying to fit itself to the rigid requirements of the director, the national director of education under the present act and he said this is federal control by indirection. All

the more dangerous because it pretends to be a federal handout. The former president of the National Education Association spoke publicly on the probable need for temporary federal control of the school system in order to bring about integration in the South. The former chairman of the president's youth fitness committee has said much as we would like to keep our traditional system of local management of the schools we can no longer afford it. We must, in order to meet Russia on equal terms, adopt a same kind of nationalized program they have. The Health, Education and Welfare Department has quadrupled its staff. It today is working to create a system of national curriculum and a set of national policies for education because they look forward to the day when we will have a federal school system. In short, the proponents of this measure believe that the only way we can properly educate our young, is to take the control of teachers and subjects and curriculum out of the hands of the parents and put it in the hands of a bureau in Washington, D.C....

Here is the main battleground. Two years ago, I had the experience of going to Washington representing the motion picture industry before the House Ways and Means Committee, to advocate the adoption of a tax reform program. This was an experience similar to going over Niagara Falls in a barrel...the hard way, upstream.

[laughter and applause]

In a month of unprecedented hearings, practically every segment of the American economy appeared before that program and 100% of those appearing demanded some kind of tax reform. But it was obvious there was little sympathy on the part of the majority of that committee with our views so it was a surprise when a few months later they decided to hold additional hearings on tax reform. This time, no volunteers. They would hand pick and invite a few selected witnesses and so a group mainly of campus economists appeared before the committee and they to talked tax reform. But they talked a tax reform which would see that the government got additional revenue, a greater share of the national income. They said this could be done by closing some of the loop-holes whereby you and I were avoiding our just share of taxation. And some of these loop-holes were the very legitimate deductions without which the whole hodge-podge system would have long since proven unworkable. They were that you and I should not be allowed to deduct our real estate tax or the interest on our mortgages or loans before computing income tax. We shouldn't be allowed to deduct charitable and education contributions at 100%. Those of the liberal persuasion today are lobbying for a tax reform measure now before Congress, a tax reform measure which may come to us piecemeal, not all in one piece. But this tax reform measure actually will be presented with a reduction of rates but so many loop-holes would be closed that the advocates openly say the government, if they adopt this program, will get $18 billion more than they are now getting. And then they just as openly say by coincidence we happen to have $18 billion worth of welfare programs we want the government to adopt. These same people tell us we're not smart enough to spend our money for the things we should buy, that the function of government should be to take our money from us through taxation and buy for us the welfare programs that our intelligence will not or, our lack of intelligence will not permit us to buy. They say they refute, before a Senate committee one of them as a spokesman said they refute the idea that the least government is the best government. And when we suggest to them the danger of more deficit spending, when they tell us that only local and state debt is bad, but the federal debt is meaningless, they tell us that we are sacrificing our security on the false altar of a balanced budget. Well, ladies and gentleman, they very source of our strength is our individual liberty and our free economy. And there is no security anyplace in the free world if there isn't fiscal stability within the United States. Of course the federal debt is meaningless, it's incomprehensible. I've taken to drawing a picture for myself. If I had here in my hand a 4-inch stack of $1000 bills, I'd be a millionaire. But if we had in front of us the national debt, piled up in $1000 bills, the pile would be more than 18 miles high. And this is only the part that shows above the surface like an iceberg. Actually in legislation already enacted into law our government is obligated to more than $750 billion. This added to the local and state debt and the private debt of our citizens amounts to a figure more than double the market value of every tangible asset and every foot of real estate in the United States.

Today, with no one using the term socialism to describe encroaching control, we find one out of seven of the workforce on the public payroll. In 15 years, a 50% increase in public employees has been matched by a 170% increase in their payroll. One-fourth of our people now entitled to government-paid medical care, socialized medicine if you please. One-fifth of our industry owned and operated by government. Senator Byrd has estimated that today 40 million American citizens receive some form of direct cash payment from the federal government. We have a tax system that in direct contravention to the Constitution is not designed solely to raise revenue, but is openly and admittedly used to regulate and control the economy and the level the earnings of our citizens, aiming again at that mediocrity which is the utopian dream of the socialists. Here is where we must expend the main effort. Don't forsake the other issues that I have mentioned but as Justice Oliver Wendell Holmes said, "Strike for the jugular. Reduce taxes and spending. Keep government poor, and remain free." Write to your Congressman and demand a tax reform immediately which will reduce the percentage of the national income the government is taking in taxes. Write to your Congressman and tell him you want an end to deficit spending, that you want the same control of the federal government's right to borrow that we exert here at the local community and at the state level. Tell him further, with an eye on our children, that you want, as part of the annual budget a regular payment on that national debt. And if your Congressman is one who writes back and says he, too, is for economy, but we must reduce government spending before we reduce taxes, you write back and tell him this is a dishonest theory. Because no government in history has ever voluntarily reduced itself in size. Government doesn't tax to get the money it needs, government will always find a need for the money it gets. There can be only one end to the war we are in. We can't just out-wait it and hope by not looking, that it will go away. Wars like this one end in victory or defeat. One of the foremost authorities on communism in the world today, a former medical missionary, has said that we have ten years, not ten years in which to make a decision, we have ten years to decide the verdict because within this decade, the world will become either all free or all slave. Our Founding Fathers, here in this country, brought about the only true revolution that has ever taken place in man's history. Every other revolution simply exchanged one set of rulers for another set of rulers. But only here did that little band of men so advanced beyond their time that the world has never seen their like since, evolve the idea that you and I have within ourselves the God-given right and the ability to determine our own destiny. But freedom is never more than one generation away from extinction. We didn't pass it on to our children in the bloodstream. The only way they can inherit the freedom we have known is if we fight for it, protect it, defend it and then hand it to them with the well thought lessons of how they in their lifetime must do the same. And if you and I don't do this, then you and I may well spend our sunset years telling our children and our children's children what it once was like in America when men were free.

Thank You.

RONALD REAGAN, A TIME FOR CHOOSING (1964)

Source: Ronald Reagan Presidential Library, "Chronology of Ronald Reagan's Presidency, 1979–89," http://www.reagan.utexas.edu/archives/reference/preschrono.html

...

I have spent most of my life as a Democrat. I recently have seen fit to follow another course. I believe that the issues confronting us cross party lines. Now, one side in this campaign has been telling us that the issues of this election are the maintenance of peace and prosperity. The line has been used, "We've never had it so good."

But I have an uncomfortable feeling that this prosperity isn't something on which we can base our hopes for the future. No nation in history has ever survived a tax burden that reached a third of its national income. Today, 37 cents out of every dollar earned in this country is the tax collector's share, and yet our government continues to spend 17 million dollars a day more than the government takes in. We haven't balanced our budget 28 out of the last 34 years. We've raised our debt limit three times in the last twelve months, and now our national debt is one and a half times bigger than all the combined debts of all the nations of the world. We have 15 billion dollars in gold in our treasury; we don't own an ounce. Foreign dollar claims are 27.3 billion dollars. And we've just had announced that the dollar of 1939 will now purchase 45 cents in its total value.

As for the peace that we would preserve, I wonder who among us would like to approach the wife or mother whose husband or son has died in South Vietnam and ask them if they think this is a peace that should be maintained indefinitely. Do they mean peace, or do they mean we just want to be left in peace? There can be no real peace while one American is dying some place in the world for the rest of us. We're at war with the most dangerous enemy that has ever faced mankind in his long climb from the swamp to the stars, and it's been said if we lose that war, and in so doing lose this way of freedom of ours, history will record with the greatest astonishment that those who had the most to lose did the least to prevent its happening. Well I think it's time we ask ourselves if we still know the freedoms that were intended for us by the Founding Fathers....

This is the issue of this election: Whether we believe in our capacity for self-government or whether we abandon the American revolution and confess that a little intellectual elite in a far-distant capitol can plan our lives for us better than we can plan them ourselves.

You and I are told increasingly we have to choose between a left or right. Well I'd like to suggest there is no such thing as a left or right. There's only an up or down—[up] man's old—old-aged dream, the ultimate in individual freedom consistent with law and order, or down to the ant heap of totalitarianism. And regardless of their sincerity, their humanitarian motives, those who would trade our freedom for security have embarked on this downward course.

In this vote-harvesting time, they use terms like the "Great Society," or as we were told a few days ago by the President, we must accept a greater government activity in the affairs of the people. But they've been a little more explicit in the past and among themselves; and all of the things I now will quote have appeared in print. These are not Republican accusations. For example, they have voices that say, "The cold war will end through our acceptance of a not undemocratic socialism." Another voice says, "The profit motive has become outmoded. It must be replaced by the incentives of the welfare state."

Or, "Our traditional system of individual freedom is incapable of solving the complex problems of the 20th century." Senator Fullbright has said at Stanford University that the Constitution is outmoded. He referred to the President as "our moral teacher and our leader," and he says he is "hobbled in his task by the restrictions of power imposed on him by this anti-quated document." He must "be freed," so that he "can do for us" what he knows "is best." And Senator Clark of Pennsylvania, another articulate spokesman, defines liberalism as "meeting the material needs of the masses through the full power of centralized government."

Well, I, for one, resent it when a representative of the people refers to you and me, the free men and women of this country, as "the masses." This is a term we haven't applied to ourselves in America. But beyond that, "the full power of centralized government"—this was the very thing the Founding Fathers sought to minimize. They knew that governments don't control things. A government can't control the economy without controlling people. And they know when a government sets out to do that, it must use force and coercion to achieve its purpose. They also knew, those Founding Fathers, that outside of its legitimate functions, government does nothing as well or as economically as the private sector of the economy....

Now—so now we declare "war on poverty," or "You, too, can be a Bobby Baker." Now do they honestly expect us to believe that if we add 1 billion dollars to the 45 billion we're spending, one more program to the 30-odd we have—and remember, this new program doesn't replace any, it just duplicates existing programs—do they believe that poverty is suddenly going to disappear by magic? Well, in all fairness I should explain there is one part of the new program that isn't duplicated. This is the youth feature. We're now going to solve the dropout problem, juvenile delinquency, by reinstituting something like the old CCC camps [Civilian Conservation Corps], and we're going to put our young people in these camps. But again we do some arithmetic, and we find that we're going to spend each year just on room and board for each young person we help 4,700 dollars a year. We can send them to Harvard for 2,700! Course, don't get me wrong. I'm not suggesting Harvard is the answer to juvenile delinquency.

But seriously, what are we doing to those we seek to help? Not too long ago, a judge called me here in Los Angeles. He told me of a young woman who'd come before him for a divorce. She had six children, was pregnant with her seventh. Under his questioning, she revealed her husband was a laborer earning 250 dollars a month. She wanted a divorce to get an 80 dollar raise. She's eligible for 330 dollars a month in the Aid to Dependent Children Program. She got the idea from two women in her neighborhood who'd already done that very thing.

Yet anytime you and I question the schemes of the do-gooders, we're denounced as being against their humanitarian goals. They say we're always "against" things—we're never "for" anything.

Well, the trouble with our liberal friends is not that they're ignorant; it's just that they know so much that isn't so.

Now—we're for a provision that destitution should not follow unemployment by reason of old age, and to that end we've accepted Social Security as a step toward meeting the problem.

But we're against those entrusted with this program when they practice deception regarding its fiscal shortcomings, when they charge that any criticism of the program means that we want to end payments to those people who depend on them for a livelihood. They've called it "insurance" to us in a hundred million pieces of literature. But then they appeared before the Supreme Court and they testified it was a welfare program. They only use the term "insurance" to sell it to the people. And they said Social Security dues are a tax for the general use of the government, and the government has used that tax. There is no fund, because Robert Byers, the actuarial head, appeared before a congressional committee and admitted that Social Security as of this moment is 298 billion dollars in the hole. But he said there should be no cause for worry because as long as they have the power to tax, they could always take away from the people whatever they needed to bail them out of trouble. And they're doing just that.

A young man, 21 years of age, working at an average salary—his Social Security contribution would, in the open market, buy him an insurance policy that would guarantee 220 dollars a month at age 65. The government promises 127. He could live it up until he's 31 and then take out a policy that would pay more than Social Security. Now are we so lacking in business sense that we can't put this program on a sound basis, so that people who do require those payments will find they can get them when they're due—that the cupboard isn't bare?

Barry Goldwater thinks we can.

At the same time, can't we introduce voluntary features that would permit a citizen who can do better on his own to be excused upon presentation of evidence that he had made provision for the non-earning years? Should we not allow a widow with children to work, and not lose the benefits supposedly paid for by her deceased husband? Shouldn't you and I be allowed to declare who our beneficiaries will be under this program, which we cannot do? I think we're for telling our senior citizens that no one in this country should be denied medical care because of a lack of funds. But I think we're against forcing all citizens, regardless of need, into a compulsory government program, especially when we have such examples, as was announced last week, when France admitted that their Medicare program is now bankrupt. They've come to the end of the road.

In addition, was Barry Goldwater so irresponsible when he suggested that our government give up its program of deliberate, planned inflation, so that when you do get your Social Security pension, a dollar will buy a dollar's worth, and not 45 cents worth?...

No government ever voluntarily reduces itself in size. So governments' programs, once launched, never disappear.

Actually, a government bureau is the nearest thing to eternal life we'll ever see on this earth....

Our Democratic opponents seem unwilling to debate these issues. They want to make you and I believe that this is a contest between two men—that we're to choose just between two personalities....

We cannot buy our security, our freedom from the threat of the bomb by committing an immorality so great as saying to a billion human beings now enslaved behind the Iron Curtain, "Give up your dreams of freedom because to save our own skins, we're willing to make a deal with your slave masters." Alexander Hamilton said, "A nation which can prefer disgrace to danger is prepared for a master, and deserves one." Now let's set the record straight. There's no argument over the choice between peace and war, but there's only one guaranteed way you can have peace—and you can have it in the next second—surrender.

Admittedly, there's a risk in any course we follow other than this, but every lesson of history tells us that the greater risk lies in appeasement, and this is the specter our well-meaning liberal friends refuse to face—that their policy of accommodation is appeasement, and it gives no choice between peace and war, only between fight or surrender. If we continue to accommodate, continue to back and retreat, eventually we have to face the final demand—the ultimatum. And what then—when Nikita Khrushchev has told his people he knows what our answer will be? He has told them that we're retreating under the pressure of the Cold War, and someday when the time comes to deliver the final ultimatum, our surrender will be voluntary, because by that time we will have been weakened from within spiritually, morally, and economically. He believes this because from our side he's heard voices pleading for "peace at any price" or "better Red than dead," or as one commentator put it, he'd rather "live on his knees than die on his feet." And therein lies the road to war, because those voices don't speak for the rest of us.

You and I know and do not believe that life is so dear and peace so sweet as to be purchased at the price of chains and slavery. If nothing in life is worth dying for, when did this begin—just in the face of this enemy? Or should Moses have told the children of Israel to live in slavery under the pharaohs? Should Christ have refused the cross? Should the patriots at Concord Bridge have thrown down their guns and refused to fire the shot heard 'round the world? The martyrs of history were not fools, and our honored dead who gave their lives to stop the advance of the Nazis didn't die in vain. Where, then, is the road to peace? Well it's a simple answer after all.

You and I have the courage to say to our enemies, "There is a price we will not pay." "There is a point beyond which they must not advance." And this—this is the meaning in the phrase of Barry Goldwater's "peace through strength." Winston Churchill said, "The destiny of man is not measured by material computations. When great forces are on the move in the world, we learn we're spirits—not animals." And he said, "There's something going on in time and space, and beyond time and space, which, whether we like it or not, spells duty."

You and I have a rendezvous with destiny.

We'll preserve for our children this, the last best hope of man on earth, or we'll sentence them to take the last step into a thousand years of darkness.

We will keep in mind and remember that Barry Goldwater has faith in us. He has faith that you and I have the ability and the dignity and the right to make our own decisions and determine our own destiny.

Thank you very much.

RONALD REAGAN, FIRST INAUGURAL ADDRESS (1981)

Source: The Public Papers of President Ronald W. Reagan. Ronald Reagan Presidential Library, http://www.reagan.utexas.edu/archives/speeches/1981/12081a.htm

Mr. President, I want our fellow citizens to know how much you did to carry on this tradition. By your gracious cooperation in the transition process, you have shown a watching world that we are a united people pledged to maintaining a political system which guarantees individual liberty to a greater degree than any other, and I thank you and your people for all your help in maintaining the continuity which is the bulwark of our Republic.

The business of our nation goes forward. These United States are confronted with an economic affliction of great proportions. We suffer from the longest and one of the worst sustained inflations in our national history. It distorts our economic decisions, penalizes thrift, and crushes the struggling young and the fixed-income elderly alike. It threatens to shatter the lives of millions of our people.

Idle industries have cast workers into unemployment, causing human misery and personal indignity. Those who do work are denied a fair return for their labor by a tax system which penalizes successful achievement and keeps us from maintaining full productivity.

But great as our tax burden is, it has not kept pace with public spending. For decades, we have piled deficit upon deficit, mortgaging our future and our children's future for the temporary convenience of the present. To continue this long trend is to guarantee tremendous social, cultural, political, and economic upheavals.

You and I, as individuals, can, by borrowing, live beyond our means, but for only a limited period of time. Why, then, should we think that collectively, as a nation, we are not bound by that same limitation?

We must act today in order to preserve tomorrow. And let there be no misunderstanding—we are going to begin to act, beginning today....

Well, this administration's objective will be a healthy, vigorous, growing economy that provides equal opportunity for all Americans, with no barriers born of bigotry or discrimination. Putting America back to work means putting all Americans back to work. Ending inflation means freeing all Americans from the terror of runaway living costs. All must share in the productive work of this "new beginning" and all must share in the bounty of a revived economy. With the idealism and fair play which are the core of our system and our strength, we can have a strong and prosperous America at peace with itself and the world.

So, as we begin, let us take inventory. We are a nation that has a government—not the other way around. And this makes us special among the nations of the Earth. Our Government has no power except that granted it by the people. It is time to check and reverse the growth of government which shows signs of having grown beyond the consent of the governed.

It is my intention to curb the size and influence of the Federal establishment and to demand recognition of the distinction between the powers granted to the Federal Government and those reserved to the States or to the people. All of us need to be reminded that the Federal Government did not create the States; the States created the Federal Government.

Now, so there will be no misunderstanding, it is not my intention to do away with government. It is, rather, to make it work—work with us, not over us; to stand by our side, not ride on our back. Government can and must provide opportunity, not smother it; foster productivity, not stifle it.

If we look to the answer as to why, for so many years, we achieved so much, prospered as no other people on Earth, it was because here, in this land, we unleashed the energy and individual genius of man to a greater extent than has ever been done before. Freedom and the dignity of the individual have been more available and assured here than in any other place on Earth. The price for this freedom at times has been high, but we have never been unwilling to pay that price....

We have every right to dream heroic dreams. Those who say that we are in a time when there are no heroes just don't know where to look. You can see heroes every day going in and out of factory gates. Others, a handful in number, produce enough food to feed all of us and then the world beyond. You meet heroes across a counter—and they are on both sides of that counter. There are entrepreneurs with faith in themselves and faith in an idea who create new jobs, new wealth and opportunity. They are individuals and families whose taxes support the Government and whose voluntary gifts support church, charity, culture, art, and education. Their patriotism is quiet but deep. Their values sustain our national life.

I have used the words "they" and "their" in speaking of these heroes. I could say "you" and "your" because I am addressing the heroes of whom I speak—you, the citizens of this blessed land. Your dreams, your hopes, your goals are going to be the dreams, the hopes, and the goals of this administration, so help me God....

In the days ahead I will propose removing the roadblocks that have slowed our economy and reduced productivity. Steps will be taken aimed at restoring the balance between the various levels of government. Progress may be slow—measured in inches and feet, not miles—but we will progress. Is it time to reawaken this industrial giant, to get government back within its means, and to lighten our punitive tax burden. And these will be our first priorities, and on these principles, there will be no compromise....

And as we renew ourselves here in our own land, we will be seen as having greater strength throughout the world. We will again be the exemplar of freedom and a beacon of hope for those who do not now have freedom.

To those neighbors and allies who share our freedom, we will strengthen our historic ties and assure them of our support and firm commitment. We will match loyalty with loyalty. We will strive for mutually beneficial relations. We will not use our friendship to impose on their sovereignty, for our own sovereignty is not for sale.

As for the enemies of freedom, those who are potential adversaries, they will be reminded that peace is the highest aspiration of the American people. We will negotiate for it, sacrifice for it; we will not surrender for it—now or ever....

This is the first time in history that this ceremony has been held, as you have been told, on this West Front of the Capitol. Standing here, one faces a magnificent vista, opening up on this city's special beauty and history. At the end of this open mall are those shrines to the giants on whose shoulders we stand....

Beyond those monuments to heroism is the Potomac River, and on the far shore the sloping hills of Arlington National Cemetery with its row on row of simple white markers bearing crosses or Stars of David. They add up to only a tiny fraction of the price that has been paid for our freedom.

Each one of those markers is a monument to the kinds of hero I spoke of earlier. Their lives ended in places called Belleau Wood, The Argonne, Omaha Beach, Salerno and halfway around the world on Guadalcanal, Tarawa, Pork Chop Hill, the Chosin Reservoir, and in a hundred rice paddies and jungles of a place called Vietnam.

Under one such marker lies a young man—Martin Treptow—who left his job in a small town barber shop in 1917 to go to France with the famed Rainbow Division. There, on the western front, he was killed trying to carry a message between battalions under heavy artillery fire.

We are told that on his body was found a diary. On the flyleaf under the heading, "My Pledge," he had written these words: "America must win this war. Therefore, I will work, I will save, I will sacrifice, I will endure, I will fight cheerfully and do my utmost, as if the issue of the whole struggle depended on me alone."

The crisis we are facing today does not require of us the kind of sacrifice that Martin Treptow and so many thousands of others were called upon to make. It does require, however, our best effort, and our willingness to believe in ourselves and to believe in our capacity to perform great deeds; to believe that together, with God's help, we can and will resolve the problems which now confront us.

And, after all, why shouldn't we believe that? We are Americans. God bless you, and thank you.

Ronald Reagan, Address to Members of the British Parliament (1982)

Source: The Public Papers of President Ronald W. Reagan. Ronald Reagan Presidential Library, http://www.reagan.utexas.edu/archives/speeches/1982/60882a.htm

Speaking for all Americans, I want to say how very much at home we feel in your house. Every American would, because this is, as we have been so eloquently told, one of democracy's shrines. Here the rights of free people and the processes of representation have been debated and refined....

Well, from here I will go to Bonn and then Berlin, where there stands a grim symbol of power untamed. The Berlin Wall, that dreadful gray gash across the city, is in its third decade. It is the fitting signature of the regime that built it.

And a few hundred kilometers behind the Berlin Wall, there is another symbol. In the center of Warsaw, there is a sign that notes the distances to two capitals. In one direction it points toward Moscow. In the other it points toward Brussels, headquarters of Western Europe's tangible unity. The marker says that the distances from Warsaw to Moscow and Warsaw to Brussels are equal. The sign makes this point: Poland is not East or West. Poland is at the center of European civilization. It has contributed mightily to that civilization. It is doing so today by being magnificently unreconciled to oppression.

Poland's struggle to be Poland and to secure the basic rights we often take for granted demonstrates why we dare not take those rights for granted. Gladstone, defending the Reform Bill of 1866, declared, "You cannot fight against the future. Time is on our side." It was easier to believe in the march of democracy in Gladstone's day—in that high noon of Victorian optimism.

We're approaching the end of a bloody century plagued by a terrible political invention—totalitarianism. Optimism comes less easily today, not because democracy is less vigorous, but because democracy's enemies have refined their instruments of repression. Yet optimism is in order, because day by day democracy is proving itself to be a not-at-all-fragile flower. From Stettin on the Baltic to Varna on the Black Sea, the regimes planted by totalitarianism have had more than 30 years to establish their legitimacy. But none—not one regime—has yet been able to risk free elections. Regimes planted by bayonets do not take root....

America's time as a player on the stage of world history has been brief. I think understanding this fact has always made you patient with your younger cousins—well, not always patient. I do recall that on one occasion, Sir Winston Churchill said in exasperation about one of our most distinguished diplomats: "He is the only case I know of a bull who carries his china shop with him." [Laughter]

But witty as Sir Winston was, he also had that special attribute of great statesmen—the gift of vision, the willingness to see the future based on the experience of the past. It is this sense of history, this understanding of the past that I want to talk with you about today, for it is in remembering what we share of the past that our two nations can make common cause for the future.

We have not inherited an easy world. If developments like the Industrial Revolution, which began here in England, and the gifts of science and technology have made life much easier for us, they have also made it more dangerous. There are threats now to our freedom, indeed to our very existence, that other generations could never even have imagined.

There is first the threat of global war. No President, no Congress, no Prime Minister, no Parliament can spend a day entirely free of this threat. And I don't have to tell you that in today's world the existence of nuclear weapons could mean, if not the extinction of mankind, then surely the end of civilization as we know it. That's why negotiations on intermediate-range nuclear forces now underway in Europe and the START talks—Strategic Arms Reduction Talks—which will begin later this month, are not just critical to American or Western policy; they are critical to mankind. Our commitment to early success in these negotiations is firm and unshakable, and our purpose is clear: reducing the risk of war by reducing the means of waging war on both sides.

At the same time there is a threat posed to human freedom by the enormous power of the modern state. History teaches the dangers of government that overreaches—political control taking precedence over free economic growth, secret police, mindless bureaucracy, all combining to stifle individual excellence and personal freedom....

Historians looking back at our time will note the consistent restraint and peaceful intentions of the

West. They will note that it was the democracies who refused to use the threat of their nuclear monopoly in the forties and early fifties for territorial or imperial gain. Had that nuclear monopoly been in the hands of the Communist world, the map of Europe—indeed, the world—would look very different today. And certainly they will note it was not the democracies that invaded Afghanistan or suppressed Polish Solidarity or used chemical and toxin warfare in Afghanistan and Southeast Asia.

If history teaches anything it teaches self-delusion in the face of unpleasant facts is folly. We see around us today the marks of our terrible dilemma—predictions of doomsday, antinuclear demonstrations, an arms race in which the West must, for its own protection, be an unwilling participant. At the same time we see totalitarian forces in the world who seek subversion and conflict around the globe to further their barbarous assault on the human spirit. What, then, is our course? Must civilization perish in a hail of fiery atoms? Must freedom wither in a quiet, deadening accommodation with totalitarian evil?...

Well, this is precisely our mission today: to preserve freedom as well as peace. It may not be easy to see; but I believe we live now at a turning point.

In an ironic sense Karl Marx was right. We are witnessing today a great revolutionary crisis, a crisis where the demands of the economic order are conflicting directly with those of the political order. But the crisis is happening not in the free, non-Marxist West, but in the home of Marxist-Leninism, the Soviet Union. It is the Soviet Union that runs against the tide of history by denying human freedom and human dignity to its citizens. It also is in deep economic difficulty. The rate of growth in the national product has been steadily declining since the fifties and is less than half of what it was then.

The dimensions of this failure are astounding: A country which employs one-fifth of its population in agriculture is unable to feed its own people. Were it not for the private sector, the tiny private sector tolerated in Soviet agriculture, the country might be on the brink of famine. These private plots occupy a bare 3 percent of the arable land but account for nearly one-quarter of Soviet farm output and nearly one-third of meat products and vegetables. Overcentralized, with little or no incentives, year after year the Soviet system pours its best resource into the making of instruments of destruction. The constant shrinkage of economic growth combined with the growth of military production is putting a heavy strain on the Soviet people. What we see here is a political structure that no longer corresponds to its economic base, a society where productive forces are hampered by political ones.

The decay of the Soviet experiment should come as no surprise to us. Wherever the comparisons have been made between free and closed societies—West Germany and East Germany, Austria and Czechoslovakia, Malaysia and Vietnam—it is the democratic countries what are prosperous and responsive to the needs of their people. And one of the simple but overwhelming facts of our time is this: Of all the millions of refugees we've seen in the modern world, their flight is always away from, not toward the Communist world. Today on the NATO line, our military forces face east to prevent a possible invasion. On the other side of the line, the Soviet forces also face east to prevent their people from leaving.

The hard evidence of totalitarian rule has caused in mankind an uprising of the intellect and will. Whether it is the growth of the new schools of economics in America or England or the appearance of the so-called new philosophers in France, there is one unifying thread running through the intellectual work of these groups—rejection of the arbitrary power of the state, the refusal to subordinate the rights of the individual to the super state, the realization that collectivism stifles all the best human impulses....

And then one day those silent, suffering people were offered a chance to vote, to choose the kind of government they wanted. Suddenly the freedom-fighters in the hills were exposed for what they really are—Cuban-backed guerrillas who want power for themselves, and their backers, not democracy for the people. They threatened death to any who voted, and destroyed hundreds of buses and trucks to keep the people from getting to the polling places. But on election day, the people of El Salvador, an unprecedented 1.4 million of them, braved ambush and gunfire, and trudged for miles to vote for freedom.

They stood for hours in the hot sun waiting for their turn to vote. Members of our Congress who went there as observers told me of a women who was wounded by rifle fire on the way to the polls, who refused to leave the line to have her wound treated until after she had voted. A grandmother, who had been told by the guerrillas she would be killed when she returned from the polls, and she told the guerrillas, "You can kill me, you can kill my family, kill my neighbors, but you can't kill us all."

The real freedom-fighters of El Salvador turned out to be the people of that country—the young, the old, the in-between.

Strange, but in my own country there's been little if any news coverage of that war since the election. Now, perhaps they'll say it's—well, because there are newer struggles now.

On distant islands in the South Atlantic young men are fighting for Britain. And, yes, voices have been raised protesting their sacrifice for lumps of rock and earth so far away. But those young men aren't fighting for mere real estate. They fight for a cause—for the belief that armed aggression must not be allowed to succeed, and the people must participate in the decisions of government—[applause]—the decisions of government under the rule of law. If there had been firmer support for that principle some 45 years ago, perhaps our generation wouldn't have suffered the bloodletting of World War II.

In the Middle East now the guns sound once more, this time in Lebanon, a country that for too long has had to endure the tragedy of civil war, terrorism, and foreign intervention and occupation. The fighting in Lebanon on the part of all parties must stop, and Israel should bring its forces home. But this is not enough. We must all work to stamp out the scourge of terrorism that in the Middle East makes war an ever-present threat.

But beyond the trouble spots lies a deeper, more positive pattern. Around the world today, the democratic revolution is gathering new strength. In India a critical test has been passed with the peaceful change of governing political parties. In Africa, Nigeria is moving into remarkable and unmistakable ways to build and strengthen its democratic institutions. In the Caribbean and Central America, 16 of 24 countries have freely elected governments. And in the United Nations, 8 of the 10 developing nations which have joined that body in the past 5 years are democracies.

In the Communist world as well, man's instinctive desire for freedom and self-determination surfaces again and again. To be sure, there are grim reminders of how brutally the police state attempts to snuff out this quest for self-rule—1953 in East Germany, 1956 in Hungary, 1968 in Czechoslovakia, 1981 in Poland. But the struggle continues in Poland. And we know that there are even those who strive and suffer for freedom within the confines of the Soviet Union itself. How we conduct ourselves here in the Western democracies will determine whether this trend continues.

No, democracy is not a fragile flower. Still it needs cultivating. If the rest of this century is to witness the gradual growth of freedom and democratic ideals, we must take actions to assist the campaign for democracy.

Some argue that we should encourage democratic change in right-wing dictatorships, but not in Communist regimes. Well, to accept this preposterous notion—as some well-meaning people have—is to invite the argument that once countries achieve a nuclear capability, they should be allowed an undisturbed reign of terror over their own citizens. We reject this course.

As for the Soviet view, Chairman Brezhnev repeatedly has stressed that the competition of ideas and systems must continue and that this is entirely consistent with relaxation of tensions and peace.

Well, we ask only that these systems begin by living up to their own constitutions, abiding by their own laws, and complying with the international obligations they have undertaken. We ask only for a process, a direction, a basic code of decency, not for an instant transformation....

The objective I propose is quite simple to state: to foster the infrastructure of democracy, the system of a free press, unions, political parties, universities, which allows a people to choose their own way to develop their own culture, to reconcile their own differences through peaceful means.

This is not cultural imperialism, it is providing the means for genuine self-determination and protection for diversity. Democracy already flourishes in countries with very different cultures and historical experiences. It would be cultural condescension, or worse, to say that any people prefer dictatorship to democracy. Who would voluntarily choose not to have the right to vote, decide to purchase government propaganda handouts instead of independent newspapers, prefer government to worker-controlled unions, opt for land to be owned by the state instead of those who till it, want government repression of religious liberty, a single political party instead of a free choice, a rigid cultural orthodoxy instead of democratic tolerance and diversity?...

We in America now intend to take additional steps, as many of our allies have already done, toward realizing this same goal. The chairmen and other leaders of the national Republican and Democratic Party organizations are initiating a study with the bipartisan American political foundation to determine how the United States can best contribute as a nation to the global campaign for democracy now gathering force. They will have the cooperation of congressional leaders of both parties, along with representatives of business, labor, and other major institutions in our society. I look forward to receiving their recommendations and to working with these institutions and the Congress in the common task of strengthening democracy throughout the world.

It is time that we committed ourselves as a nation—in both the pubic and private sectors—to assisting democratic development....

Well, the emergency is upon us. Let us be shy no longer. Let us go to our strength. Let us offer hope. Let us tell the world that a new age is not only possible but probable.

During the dark days of the Second World War, when this island was incandescent with courage, Winston Churchill exclaimed about Britain's adversaries, "What kind of a people do they think we are?" Well, Britain's adversaries found out what extraordinary people the British are. But all the democracies paid a terrible price for allowing the dictators to underestimate us. We dare not make that mistake again. So, let us ask ourselves, "What kind of people do we think we are?" And let us answer, "Free people, worthy of freedom and determined not only to remain so but to help others gain their freedom as well."

Sir Winston led his people to great victory in war and then lost an election just as the fruits of victory were about to be enjoyed. But he left office honorably, and, as it turned out, temporarily, knowing that the liberty of his people was more important than the fate of any single leader. History recalls his greatness in ways no dictator will ever know. And he left us a message of hope for the future, as timely now as when he first uttered it, as opposition leader in the Commons nearly 27 years ago, when he said, "When we look back on all the perils through which we have passed and at the mighty foes that we have laid low and all the dark and deadly designs that we have frustrated, why should we fear for our future? We have," he said, "come safely through the worst."

Well, the task I've set forth will long outlive our own generation. But together, we too have come through the worst. Let us now begin a major effort to secure the best—a crusade for freedom that will engage the faith and fortitude of the next generation. For the sake of peace and justice, let us move toward a world in which all people are at last free to determine their own destiny.

Thank you.

RONALD REAGAN, REMARKS AT THE ANNUAL CONVENTION OF THE NATIONAL ASSOCIATION OF EVANGELICALS (1983)

Source: The Public Papers of President Ronald W. Reagan. Ronald Reagan Presidential Library, http://www.reagan.utexas.edu/archives/speeches/1983/30883b.htm

Those of you in the National Association of Evangelicals are known for your spiritual and humanitarian work. And I would be especially remiss if I didn't discharge right now one personal debt of gratitude. Thank you for your prayers. Nancy and I have felt their presence many times in many ways. And believe me, for us they've made all the difference....

I want you to know that this administration is motivated by a political philosophy that sees the greatness of America in you, her people, and in your families, churches, neighborhoods, communities— the institutions that foster and nourish values like concern for others and respect for the rule of law under God.

Now, I don't have to tell you that this puts us in opposition to, or at least out of step with, a prevailing attitude of many who have turned to a modern-day secularism, discarding the tried and time-tested values upon which our very civilization is based. No matter how well intentioned, their value system is radically different from that of most Americans. And while they proclaim that they're freeing us from superstitions of the past, they've taken upon themselves the job of superintending us by government rule and regulation. Sometimes their voices are louder than ours, but they are not yet a majority.

An example of that vocal superiority is evident in a controversy now going on in Washington. And since I'm involved, I've been waiting to hear from the parents of young America. How far are they willing to go in giving to government their prerogatives as parents?

Let me state the case as briefly and simply as I can. An organization of citizens, sincerely motivated and deeply concerned about the increase in illegitimate births and abortions involving girls well below the age of consent, sometime ago established a nationwide network of clinics to offer help to these girls and, hopefully, alleviate this situation. Now, again, let me say, I do not fault their intent. However, in their well-intentioned effort, these clinics have decided to provide advice and birth control drugs and devices to underage girls without the knowledge of their parents.

For some years now, the Federal Government has helped with funds to subsidize these clinics. In providing for this, the Congress decreed that every effort would be made to maximize parental participation. Nevertheless, the drugs and devices are prescribed without getting parental consent or giving notification after they've done so. Girls termed "sexually active"—and that has replaced the word "promiscuous"—are given this help in order to prevent illegitimate birth or abortion.

Well, we have ordered clinics receiving Federal funds to notify the parents such help has been given. One of the Nation's leading newspapers has created the term "squeal rule" in editorializing against us for doing this, and we're being criticized for violating the privacy of young people. A judge has recently granted an injunction against an enforcement of our rule. I've watched TV panel shows discuss this issue, seen columnists pontificating on our error, but no one seems to mention morality as playing a part in the subject of sex.

Is all of Judeo-Christian tradition wrong? Are we to believe that something so sacred can be looked upon as a purely physical thing with no potential for emotional and psychological harm? And isn't it the parents' right to give counsel and advice to keep their children from making mistakes that may affect their entire lives?

Many of us in government would like to know what parents think about this intrusion in their family by government. We're going to fight in the courts. The right of parents and the rights of family take precedence over those of Washington-based bureaucrats and social engineers.

But the fight against parental notification is really only one example of many attempts to water down traditional values and even abrogate the original terms of American democracy. Freedom prospers when religion is vibrant and the rule of law under God is acknowledged. When our Founding Fathers passed the first amendment, they sought to protect churches from government interference. They never intended to construct a wall of hostility between government and the concept of religious belief itself.

The evidence of this permeates our history and our government....

Last year, I sent the Congress a constitutional amendment to restore prayer to public schools. Already this session, there's growing bipartisan support for the amendment, and I am calling on the Congress to act speedily to pass it and to let our children pray.

Perhaps some of you read recently about the Lubbock school case, where a judge actually ruled that it was unconstitutional for a school district to give equal treatment to religious and nonreligious student groups, even when the group meetings were being held during the students' own time. The first amendment never intended to require government to discriminate against religious speech.

Senators Denton and Hatfield have proposed legislation in the Congress on the whole question of prohibiting discrimination against religious forms of student speech. Such legislation could go far to restore freedom of religious speech for public school students. And I hope the Congress considers these bills quickly. And with your help, I think it's possible we could also get the constitutional amendment through the Congress this year.

More than a decade ago, a Supreme Court decision literally wiped off the books of 50 States statutes protecting the rights of unborn children. Abortion on demand now takes the lives of up to 1.5 million unborn children a year. Human life legislation ending this tragedy will some day pass the Congress, and you and I must never rest until it does. Unless and until it can be proven that the unborn child is not a living entity, then its right to life, liberty, and the pursuit of happiness must be protected.

You may remember that when abortion on demand began, many, and, indeed, I'm sure many of you, warned that the practice would lead to a decline in respect for human life, that the philosophical premises used to justify abortion on demand would ultimately be used to justify other attacks on the sacredness of human life—infanticide or mercy killing. Tragically enough, those warnings proved all too true. Only last year a court permitted the death by starvation of a handicapped infant.

I have directed the Health and Human Services Department to make clear to every health care facility in the United States that the Rehabilitation Act of 1973 protects all handicapped persons against discrimination based on handicaps, including infants. And we have taken the further step of requiring that each and every recipient of Federal funds who provides health care services to infants must post and keep posted in a conspicuous place a notice stating that "discriminatory failure to feed and care for handicapped infants in this facility is prohibited by Federal law." It also lists a 24-hour, toll-free number so that nurses and others may report violations in time to save the infant's life.

In addition, recent legislation introduced in the Congress by Representative Henry Hyde of Illinois not only increases restrictions on publicly financed abortions, it also addresses this whole problem of infanticide. I urge the Congress to begin hearings and to adopt legislation that will protect the right of life to all children, including the disabled or handicapped.

Now, I'm sure that you must get discouraged at times, but you've done better than you know, perhaps. There's a great spiritual awakening in America, a renewal of the traditional values that have been the bedrock of America's goodness and greatness.

One recent survey by a Washington-based research council concluded that Americans were far more religious than the people of other nations; 95 percent of those surveyed expressed a belief in God and a huge majority believed the Ten Commandments had real meaning in their lives. And another study has found that an overwhelming majority of Americans disapprove of adultery, teenage sex, pornography, abortion, and hard drugs. And this same study showed a deep reverence for the importance of family ties and religious belief.

I think the items that we've discussed here today must be a key part of the Nation's political agenda. For the first time the Congress is openly and seriously debating and dealing with the prayer and abortion issues—and that's enormous progress right there. I repeat: America is in the midst of a spiritual awakening and a moral renewal. And with your Biblical keynote, I say today, "Yes, let justice roll on like a river, righteousness like a never-failing stream."

Now, obviously, much of this new political and social consensus I've talked about is based on a positive view of American history, one that takes pride in our country's accomplishments and record. But we must never forget that no government schemes are going to perfect man. We know that living in this world means dealing with what philosophers would call the phenomenology of evil or, as theologians would put it, the doctrine of sin.

There is sin and evil in the world, and we're enjoined by Scripture and the Lord Jesus to oppose it with all our might. Our nation, too, has a legacy of evil with which it must deal. The glory of this land has been its capacity for transcending the moral evils of our past. For example, the long struggle of minority citizens for equal rights, once a source of disunity and civil war, is now a point of pride for all Americans. We must never go back. There is no room for racism, anti-Semitism, or other forms of ethnic and racial hatred in this country.

I know that you've been horrified, as have I, by the resurgence of some hate groups preaching bigotry and prejudice. Use the mighty voice of your pulpits and the powerful standing of your churches to denounce and isolate these hate groups in our midst. The commandment given us is clear and simple: "Thou shalt love thy neighbor as thyself."

But whatever sad episodes exist in our past, any objective observer must hold a positive view of American history, a history that has been the story of hopes fulfilled and dreams made into reality. Especially in this century, America has kept alight the torch of freedom, but not just for ourselves but for millions of others around the world.

And this brings me to my final point today. During my first press conference as President, in answer to a direct question, I pointed out that, as good Marxist-Leninists, the Soviet leaders have openly and publicly declared that the only morality they recognize is that which will further their cause, which is world revolution. I think I should point out I was only quoting Lenin, their guiding spirit, who said in 1920 that they repudiate all morality that proceeds from supernatural ideas—that's their name for religion—or ideas that are outside class conceptions. Morality is entirely subordinate to the interests of class war. And everything is moral that is necessary for the annihilation of the old, exploiting social order and for uniting the proletariat.

Well, I think the refusal of many influential people to accept this elementary fact of Soviet doctrine illustrates an historical reluctance to see totalitarian powers for what they are. We saw this phenomenon in the 1930's. We see it too often today.

This doesn't mean we should isolate ourselves and refuse to seek an understanding with them. I intend to do everything I can to persuade them of our peaceful intent, to remind them that it was the West that refused to use its nuclear monopoly in the forties and fifties for territorial gain and which now proposes 50-percent cut in strategic ballistic missiles and the elimination of an entire class of land-based, intermediate-range nuclear missiles.

At the same time, however, they must be made to understand we will never compromise our principles and standards. We will never give away our freedom. We will never abandon our belief in God. And we will never stop searching for a genuine peace. But we can assure none of these things America stands for through the so-called nuclear freeze solutions proposed by some.

The truth is that a freeze now would be a very dangerous fraud, for that is merely the illusion of peace. The reality is that we must find peace through strength.

I would agree to a freeze if only we could freeze the Soviets' global desires. A freeze at current levels of weapons would remove any incentive for the Soviets to negotiate seriously in Geneva and virtually end our chances to achieve the major arms reductions which we have proposed. Instead, they would achieve their objectives through the freeze.

A freeze would reward the Soviet Union for its enormous and unparalleled military buildup. It would prevent the essential and long overdue modernization of United States and allied defenses and would leave our aging forces increasingly vulnerable. And an honest freeze would require extensive prior negotiations on the systems and numbers to be limited and on the measures to ensure effective verification and compliance. And the kind of a freeze that has been suggested would be virtually impossible to verify. Such a major effort would divert us completely from our current negotiations on achieving substantial reductions....

It was C. S. Lewis who, in his unforgettable "Screwtape Letters," wrote: "The greatest evil is not done now in those sordid 'dens of crime' that Dickens loved to paint. It is not even done in concentration camps and labor camps. In those we see its final result. But it is conceived and ordered (moved, seconded, carried and minuted) in clear, carpeted, warmed, and well-lighted offices, by quiet men with white collars and cut fingernails and smooth-shaven cheeks who do not need to raise their voice."

Well, because these "quiet men" do not "raise their voices," because they sometimes speak in soothing tones of brotherhood and peace, because, like other dictators before them, they're always making "their final territorial demand," some would have us accept them at their word and accommodate ourselves to their aggressive impulses. But if history teaches anything, it teaches that simple-minded appeasement or wishful thinking about our adversaries is folly. It means the betrayal of our past, the squandering of our freedom.

So, I urge you to speak out against those who would place the United States in a position of military and moral inferiority. You know, I've always believed that old Screwtape reserved his best efforts for those of you in the church. So, in your discussions of the nuclear freeze proposals, I urge you to beware the temptation of pride—the temptation of blithely declaring yourselves above it all and label both sides equally at fault, to ignore the facts of history and the aggressive impulses of an evil empire, to simply call the arms race a giant misunderstanding and thereby remove yourself from the struggle between right and wrong and good and evil.

I ask you to resist the attempts of those who would have you withhold your support for our efforts, this administration's efforts, to keep America strong and free, while we negotiate real and verifiable reductions in the world's nuclear arsenals and one day, with God's help, their total elimination.

While America's military strength is important, let me add here that I've always maintained that the struggle now going on for the world will never be decided by bombs or rockets, by armies or military might. The real crisis we face today is a spiritual one; at root, it is a test of moral will and faith....

I believe we shall rise to the challenge. I believe that communism is another sad, bizarre chapter in human history whose last pages even now are being written. I believe this because the source of our strength in the quest for human freedom is not material, but spiritual. And because it knows no limitation, it must terrify and ultimately triumph over those who would enslave their fellow man. For in the words of

Isaiah: "He giveth power to the faint; and to them that have no might He increased strength....But they that wait upon the Lord shall renew their strength; they shall mount up with wings as eagles; they shall run, and not be weary...."

Yes, change your world. One of our Founding Fathers, Thomas Paine, said, "We have it within our power to begin the world over again." We can do it, doing together what no one church could do by itself.

God bless you, and thank you very much.

RONALD REAGAN, REMARKS AT THE BRANDENBURG GATE (1987)

Source: The Public Papers of President Ronald W. Reagan. Ronald Reagan Presidential Library, http://www.reagan.utexas.edu/archives/speeches/1987/061287d.htm

Our gathering today is being broadcast throughout Western Europe and North America. I understand that it is being seen and heard as well in the East. To those listening throughout Eastern Europe, I extend my warmest greetings and the good will of the American people. To those listening in East Berlin, a special word: Although I cannot be with you, I address my remarks to you just as surely as to those standing here before me. For I join you, as I join your fellow countrymen in the West, in this firm, this unalterable belief: Es gibt nur ein Berlin. [There is only one Berlin.]

Behind me stands a wall that encircles the free sectors of this city, part of a vast system of barriers that divides the entire continent of Europe. From the Baltic, south, those barriers cut across Germany in a gash of barbed wire, concrete, dog runs, and guardtowers. Farther south, there may be no visible, no obvious wall. But there remain armed guards and checkpoints all the same—still a restriction on the right to travel, still an instrument to impose upon ordinary men and women the will of a totalitarian state. Yet it is here in Berlin where the wall emerges most clearly; here, cutting across your city, where the news photo and the television screen have imprinted this brutal division of a continent upon the mind of the world. Standing before the Brandenburg Gate, every man is a German, separated from his fellow men. Every man is a Berliner, forced to look upon a scar.

President von Weizsacker has said: "The German question is open as long as the Brandenburg Gate is closed." Today I say: As long as this gate is closed, as long as this scar of a wall is permitted to stand, it is not the German question alone that remains open, but the question of freedom for all mankind. Yet I do not come here to lament. For I find

in Berlin a message of hope, even in the shadow of this wall, a message of triumph.

In this season of spring in 1945, the people of Berlin emerged from their air raid shelters to find devastation. Thousands of miles away, the people of the United States reached out to help. And in 1947 Secretary of State—as you've been told—George Marshall announced the creation of what would become known as the Marshall plan. Speaking precisely 40 years ago this month, he said:

"Our policy is directed not against any country or doctrine, but against hunger, poverty, desperation, and chaos."...

In West Germany and here in Berlin, there took place an economic miracle, the Wirtschaftswunder. Adenauer, Erhard, Reuter, and other leaders understood the practical importance of liberty—that just as truth can flourish only when the journalist is given freedom of speech, so prosperity can come about only when the farmer and businessman enjoy economic freedom. The German leaders reduced tariffs, expanded free trade, lowered taxes. From 1950 to 1960 alone, the standard of living in West Germany and Berlin doubled.

Where four decades ago there was rubble, today in West Berlin there is the greatest industrial output of any city in Germany-busy office blocks, fine homes and apartments, proud avenues, and the spreading lawns of park land. Where a city's culture seemed to have been destroyed, today there are two great universities, orchestras and an opera, countless theaters, and museums. Where there was want, today there's abundance—food, clothing, automobiles—the wonderful goods of the Ku'damm. From devastation, from utter ruin, you Berliners have, in freedom, rebuilt a city that once again ranks as one of the greatest on Earth. The

Soviets may have had other plans. But, my friends, there were a few things the Soviets didn't count on Berliner herz, Berliner humor, ja, und Berliner schnauze. [Berliner heart, Berliner humor, yes, and a Berliner schnauze.]

[Laughter]

In the 1950's, Khrushchev predicted: "We will bury you." But in the West today, we see a free world that has achieved a level of prosperity and well-being unprecedented in all human history. In the Communist world, we see failure, technological backwardness, declining standards of health, even want of the most basic kind-too little food. Even today, the Soviet Union still cannot feed itself. After these four decades, then, there stands before the entire world one great and inescapable conclusion: Freedom leads to prosperity. Freedom replaces the ancient hatreds among the nations with comity and peace. Freedom is the victor.

And now the Soviets themselves may, in a limited way, be coming to understand the importance of freedom. We hear much from Moscow about a new policy of reform and openness. Some political prisoners have been released. Certain foreign news broadcasts are no longer being jammed. Some economic enterprises have been permitted to operate with greater freedom from state control. Are these the beginnings of profound changes in the Soviet state? Or are they token gestures, intended to raise false hopes in the West, or to strengthen the Soviet system without changing it? We welcome change and openness; for we believe that freedom and security go together, that the advance of human liberty can only strengthen the cause of world peace.

There is one sign the Soviets can make that would be unmistakable, that would advance dramatically the cause of freedom and peace. General Secretary Gorbachev, if you seek peace, if you seek prosperity for the Soviet Union and Eastern Europe, if you seek liberalization: Come here to this gate! Mr. Gorbachev, open this gate! Mr. Gorbachev, tear down this wall!

I understand the fear of war and the pain of division that afflict this continent—and I pledge to you my country's efforts to help overcome these burdens. To be sure, we in the West must resist Soviet expansion. So we must maintain defenses of unassailable strength. Yet we seek peace; so we must strive to reduce arms on both sides. Beginning 10 years ago, the Soviets challenged the Western alliance with a grave new threat, hundreds of new and more deadly SS-20 nuclear missiles, capable of-striking every capital in Europe. The Western alliance responded by committing itself to a counter-deployment unless the Soviets agreed to negotiate a better solution; namely, the elimination of such weapons on both sides. For many months, the Soviets refused to bargain in earnestness. As the alliance, in turn, prepared to go forward with its counter-deployment, there were difficult days—days of protests like those during my 1982 visit to this city—and the Soviets later walked away from the table.

But through it all, the alliance held firm. And I invite those who protested then—I invite those who protest today—to mark this fact: Because we remained strong, the Soviets came back to the table. And because we remained strong, today we have within reach the possibility, not merely of limiting the growth of arms, but of eliminating, for the first time, an entire class of nuclear weapons from the face of the Earth. As I speak, NATO ministers are meeting in Iceland to review the progress of our proposals for eliminating these weapons. At the talks in Geneva, we have also proposed deep cuts in strategic offensive weapons. And the Western allies have likewise made far-reaching proposals to reduce the danger of conventional war and to place a total ban on chemical weapons.

While we pursue these arms reductions, I pledge to you that we will maintain the capacity to deter Soviet aggression at any level at which it might occur. And in cooperation with many of our allies, the United States is pursuing the Strategic Defense Initiative—research to base deterrence not on the threat of offensive retaliation, but on defenses that truly defend; on systems, in short, that will not target populations, but shield them. By these means we seek to increase the safety of Europe and all the world. But we must remember a crucial fact: East and West do not mistrust each other because we are armed; we are armed because we mistrust each other. And our differences are not about weapons but about liberty. When President Kennedy spoke at the City Hall those 24 years ago, freedom was encircled, Berlin was under siege. And today, despite all the pressures upon this city, Berlin stands secure in its liberty. And freedom itself is transforming the globe....

In Europe, only one nation and those it controls refuse to join the community of freedom. Yet in this age of redoubled economic growth, of information and innovation, the Soviet Union faces a choice: It must make fundamental changes, or it will become obsolete. Today thus represents a moment of hope. We in the West stand ready to cooperate with the East to promote true openness, to break down barriers that separate people, to create a safer, freer world.

And surely there is no better place than Berlin, the meeting place of East and West, to make a start. Free people of Berlin: Today, as in the past, the United States stands for the strict observance and full implementation of all parts of the Four Power Agreement of 1971. Let us use this occasion, the 750th anniversary of this city, to usher in a new era, to seek a still fuller, richer life for the Berlin of the future. Together, let us maintain and develop the ties between the Federal Republic and the Western sectors of Berlin, which is permitted by the 1971 agreement.

And I invite Mr. Gorbachev: Let us work to bring the Eastern and Western parts of the city closer together, so that all the inhabitants of all Berlin can enjoy the benefits that come with life in one of the great cities of the world. To open Berlin still further to all Europe, East and West, let us expand the vital air access to this city, finding ways of making commercial air service to Berlin more convenient, more comfortable, and more economical. We look to the day when West Berlin can become one of the chief aviation hubs in all central Europe.

With our French and British partners, the United States is prepared to help bring international meetings to Berlin. It would be only fitting for Berlin to serve as the site of United Nations meetings, or world conferences on human rights and arms control or other issues that call for international cooperation. There is no better way to establish hope for the future than to enlighten young minds, and we would be honored to sponsor summer youth exchanges, cultural events, and other programs for young Berliners from the East. Our French and British friends, I'm certain, will do the same. And it's my hope that an authority can be found in East Berlin to sponsor visits from young people of the Western sectors....

As I looked out a moment ago from the Reichstag, that embodiment of German unity, I noticed words crudely spray-painted upon the wall, perhaps by a young Berliner, "This wall will fall. Beliefs become reality." Yes, across Europe, this wall will fall. For it cannot withstand faith; it cannot withstand truth. The wall cannot withstand freedom.

And I would like, before I close, to say one word. I have read, and I have been questioned since I've been here about certain demonstrations against my coming. And I would like to say just one thing, and to those who demonstrate so. I wonder if they have ever asked themselves that if they should have the kind of government they apparently seek, no one would ever be able to do what they're doing again.

Thank you and God bless you all.

CHAPTER 22

Robert Putnam Decries the Solitary Bowler

"Whatever happened to civic engagement?"

In U.S. history, there are only a handful of intellectually pioneering and socially groundbreaking books, speeches, and articles. During the last two decades of the twentieth century, perhaps, no other essay was as influential as Robert D. Putnam's "Bowling Alone: America's Declining Social Capital." Published in 1995, the article quickly captured the attention and imagination of Americans, set bold political and social agendas, and reshaped Americans' understanding of themselves, their past, and their aspirations for the future. At the same time, Putnam's thesis about the decay of society unleashed a vigorous debate among pundits and plebeians alike. Was the United States in decline? Was democracy at risk? Had Americans become strangers in their own country? And, if it were all true, who was to blame?

The tremendous popularity and culture cache of Putnam's article—and later book by the same name—has much to do with historical contexts, both nationally and internationally. Politicians, academics, and activists had been talking about social declension for many years before Putnam. In some ways, this is not unusual. In the Western world, social observers have been complaining about the fall of culture for hundreds of years. But Putnam tapped squarely into the post-Vietnam, post-Watergate American zeitgeist. Whether on the political right or the left, Americans believed that they lived in times of diminishing returns in terms of the economy, politics, education, and basic law-abiding civility. During Reagan Era of the 1980s, conservatives such as Charles Murray and Diane Ravitch launched searing attacks upon various public policies and institutions, which they maintained were bringing American potential down. Similarly, liberal commentators decried the fraying of the New Deal and the loss of solidarity among the working class. Nothing told the tale more, they claimed, than the demise of organized labor, whose numbers were dipping toward dissolution. International events only heightened American anxiety. By the early 1990s, several of the former Soviet bloc states were struggling to invent democratic institutions as well as civil societies separate from the government and the economic market. Many in Europe and western Asia looked to the United States for leadership only to find that Americans were living off a democratic and free market myth and a reputation that seemed to no longer hold true.

Putnam, Dillon Professor of International Affairs and Director of the Center for Intuitional Affairs at Harvard University, spent years researching civil society in the United States and agreed with the gloomy critics. His work led him to one inexorable conclusion. "There is striking evidence," he wrote, "that the vibrancy of American civil society has notably declined over the past several decades." The trend was even more troubling since this vibrant civil society had been a national tradition, if not obsession. In the 1830s, Alexis de Tocqueville visited from France and discovered the American passion for gregariousness: "Americans of all ages, conditions, and all dispositions constantly unite together. Not only do they have commercial and industrial associations to which all belong but also a thousand other kinds, religious, moral, serious, futile, very general and very specialized, large and small."[1] These associations provided the connective social tissue that allowed American democracy, which was still in its infancy, to flourish and grow. According to social scientists, the same held true at the end of the twentieth century. Further, Putnam and other researchers argued that civic associations had only grown in importance, becoming a key condition (as well as an essential leading indicator) of the health of American communities in terms of employment, crime, substance abuse, political participation, and education. In short, the more social engagement and connectivity, the smarter, happier, healthier, safer, and wealthier we all are.

Had he returned one hundred and sixty years later, Tocqueville would have been aghast at the changes. In his 1995 article, Putnam chronicled them briefly, adding to the theoretical underpinnings of his observations the notion of social capital. Akin to physical capital and human capital, social capital "refers to features of social organization such as networks, norms, and social trust that facilitate coordination and cooperation for mutual benefit." Social capital, Putnam explains, fosters trust and reciprocity that are so essential in dealing with community-wide problems and opportunities. The deficit in social capital produces the converse: mistrust, atomism, greed, and conflict. In several crucial areas of American life in the 1990s, civic engagement and the resulting social capital were down. In the political sphere, voter turnout had declined dramatically since the early 1960s at all levels of government. Further, far fewer Americans attended public meetings. Millions of Americans had removed themselves from the political process. When asked, they told researchers that they no longer trusted politicians or the institution of government itself. Other areas of American life showed similar deterioration and distrustfulness. Putnam reported that the number of churchgoers had dwindled substantially. Union membership had plummeted. Some social groups such as the Federation of Women's Clubs and the League of Women Voters had begun to worry about long-term survival. No matter what association or segment Putnam examined the pattern remained the same. The United States was no longer a nation of joiners, activists, and volunteers. For Putnam, nothing typified the situation more than an odd example: league bowling was becoming a thing of the past and was being replaced by "solo bowling." Millions of kelgers still practiced their sport. In fact, generally more people rolled balls toward pins than pulled levers in voting booths. But that was not the point. "Whether or not bowling beats balloting in the eyes of most Americans," Putnam wrote, "bowling teams illustrate yet another vanishing form of social capital."

What caused the decline? Putnam maintained that the problem did not appear overnight. Rather, since the 1960s—a point that delighted conservatives—there had been a steady erosion of social capital and civic engagement. Although in this short essay, Putnam only fingered possible culprits, four stood out. Changes in demographics and the labor force, specifically more women working, might have something to do with it. Residential mobility such as the movement of Americans to Sunbelt states and into the suburbs might have contributed as well. Finally, Putnam suggested that the rapid growth of electronic and computer-based forms of leisure were sapping the will of many Americans to go out and engage the world. "The new 'virtual reality' helmets that we will soon don to be entertained in total isolation," he wrote somewhat in jest, "are merely the latest extension of this trend." Stopping short of any prescription to remedy this epidemic of social disconnection, Putnam called for more research and new public policies that promote rather than encourage investment in social capital.

Putnam's article set off a firestorm of debate about the merits of his thesis as well as the evidence to support it. Five years later, he answered his critics and rallied supporters by providing a fuller accounting of the shortfall in American social capital.

His five-hundred page book, which shares the title of his essay, fully examines the problem of falling participation rates in politics and voluntary associations, from parent–teacher organizations to fraternal orders to charity groups. Further, Putnam refined his analysis to state that not all areas of the nation suffer equally. In particular, Northern states fair better than Southern states. As such, he offers plenty of evidence that in certain areas of the country that have more social capital people are "smarter, healthier, safer, richer, and better able to govern a just and stable democracy."[2] In the book, he also deals concretely with counterexamples, causality, and an ambitious agenda that might reverse the trends. Putnam notes that there is evidence that not all civic engagement is a social plus. Groups such as violent extremist organizations have done by far more harm than good to American democracy. Additionally, among some demographic cohorts such as those born after the X Generation, participation rates—especially in terms of volunteering—have risen considerably. But overall, Putnam maintains that four factors have caused a general collapse of community: (1) the increase in the number of working Americans; (2) suburban sprawl; (3) television and other electronic distractions; and (4) the generation change from the selfless "civic generation" of the 1930s and 1940s—which had united in the crucible of economic disaster and war to help one another—to the more egotistical generation of the Baby Boomers and Gen X-ers. Putnam does not suggest a return to the America of the 1930s, but rather he calls for public policies that promote tolerance, that ease the pressures on working Americans, that encourage more bridging social capital between groups and people, and that help Americans build safer, better educated, and kinder communities. "In the end," he wrote, "institutional reform will not work—indeed, it will not happen—unless you and I, along with our fellow citizens, resolve to become reconnected with our friends and neighbors."[3]

Many scholars and social commentators have taken issue with Putnam's "bowling alone" thesis. Some accepted the basic premise that social capital and civil engagement had declined, but disagreed with the meaning of the trends. It seemed incontrovertible that certain historic clubs had atrophied since the 1960s. But many pointed out the rise of others. Putnam had been quick to dismiss what he labeled as "tertiary associations" such as the Sierra Club or brand loyalty groups. "For the vast majority of their members," he wrote, "the only act of membership consists in writing a check for dues or perhaps occasionally reading a newsletter." But to many members of these so-called tertiary organizations from Apple Macintosh fans to Harley-Davidson aficionados, the social connections are real and palpable. Critics charged that Putnam's willingness to dismiss this evidence of rising memberships as well as his readiness to explain away recent upticks in volunteering and charitable donations weakened his case. Perhaps it is only natural that associations come and go. Further, Putnam may have misinterpreted his celebrated example. The image of the lonely, disconsolate bowler that adorned the cover of his book is a powerful one. We can all sympathize with that solitary man making strikes and spares in an empty bowling alley. But according to some, the evidence did not support this. Researchers at Northwestern and Indiana University investigated American keglers and found that while indeed fewer bowlers organized leagues, bowling was a healthy sport and industry. In 2003, there were 5,800 businesses where people could bowl and nearly 120,000 lanes. It was then a $4 billion enterprise. Each year, about one out of every three Americans reported bowling at least once, and significantly, they tended to bowl in groups of five or six. Is this a sign of social decay? People may have rearranged their social networks, but they still had them. People weren't bowling alone; they were still bowling with their friends and having fun with the relatively new inventions of cosmic bowling, rock 'n' roll bowling, and Xtreme bowling.

Did Putnam overstate his case? Two surveys indicated that indeed he might have. One of Putnam's central arguments was that as social capital has declined people have become more suspicious of everyone, especially their elected officials and the bureaucrats that run the government. Assuming that this is true, one might have expected a low return on the 2000 U.S. Census. Just the opposite happened. Americans sent in their forms and talked with census workers at a higher rate than 1990. Putnam was "stunned" and could not immediately explain the phenomenon.[4] Similarly, a survey of the Americans, born between the late 1970s and the late 1990s, indicated that they were more likely to volunteer and engage in the political sphere. As a group, they were less cynical, more optimistic, and more likely to adhere to social norms than any generation since that much-heralded long civic generation of the 1930s and 1940s. This Y Generation or Millennial Generation has remained socially active, and few are able to account for it. Not even the ubiquity of electronic devices has stopped these young Americans, who appear ready to use the Internet and its virtual environment such as Second Life and Warcraft for the creation of social capital and for civic engagement as much as for entertainment.

Finally, there were those who maintained that Putnam was simply wrong. Thomas Rotolo of Washington State University and John Wilson of Duke University carefully examined the long civic generation and compared their volunteer behavior with the generations that followed and found no statistically significant differences. In other words, their research did not support Putnam's thesis of declension. A more systematic refutation came from Everett Carl Ladd, whose eponymous report contradicted Putnam's. Ladd was not fazed by the passing of groups like the Parent-Teachers Association (PTA) or fraternal organizations like the Elks. They have been supplanted by newer groups with expanded or updated missions. Take for example the fall of the nationally affiliated Parent-Teachers Associations. PTA memberships have fallen dramatically. But these formal organizations were often replaced by less formal but nonetheless as effective parent groups. As Ladd pointed out, parents were not less involved in the lives of their students. Rather, they were if anything too enmeshed in the lives of their children. Later critics called these adults "helicopter" parents, and their stories provided a counterpoise to the solo bowlers. But if Putnam had run past his evidence, Ladd opened himself up to charges of being a Pangloss, stating that everything in American society was normal and copasetic. That certainly did not ring true with many Americans who long had the uneasy feeling that something was wrong with their communities and the nation as a whole. The United States did not seem so united anymore.

All that changed on September 11, 2001. The terrorists aimed to strike a blow not only to American political, economic, and military might but also sow the seeds of discord and disillusion. Generally speaking, quite the opposite happened. Even before the flames were extinguished, Americans began donating blood and money, volunteering to help the families of victims, and returned to places of worship to commune with neighbors as much as to seek answers and solace. Within a month after the attacks, financial donations topped $1 billion. One out of every three New Yorkers—who were once lampooned and stereotyped for their callousness—donated blood. Was this a momentary reaction to the horror of the worst attack on the United States? Or, was this the beginning of a new and improved social trend? Fifteen years after he published his pioneering study, Robert D. Putnam along with his Harvard University colleague Thomas H. Sander offered an answer: The 9/11 Generation was different and more civically engaged.

Putnam still maintains that his "bowling alone" thesis accurately represented the conditions at the end of the twentieth century. Nothing the critics had said had made him rethink or reconsider his position. In all facets of social life, Americans had become increasingly withdrawn in that period between Watergate and the end of the millennium. He did, however, concede that the one hopeful trend he described was perhaps more important than he realized: "an increase in youth volunteering that potentially heralded broader generational engagement."[5] Writing in the late 1990s,

Putnam had viewed the evidence of youthful engagement with some skepticism, and for good reason. Some of the rise in volunteering was a result of high-school graduation requirements. Additionally, as college admissions and the professional job markets have become more competitive, juniors and seniors at the high school and college levels have packed their lives and résumés with civic engagement. On September 10, 2001, all this social activity may have seemed less deep and meaningful. But twenty-four hours later, civic engagement among young Americans became the precondition for a rising trend.

The so-called 9/11 Generation seems to be not only more socially engaged but also more interested in politics and public policy. More than their parents, they are willing to attend political meetings and to vote. In 2008, presidential hopeful Barack Obama and his leadership team aptly took advantage of this youth movement. They also utilized young people's penchant for Internet-based social connections. In stark contrast to his opponent, the Obama campaign had an impressive presence on popular Web pages; it constantly updated supporters using email and texting; it had an interactive iPhone app; it was integrated into eighteen popular video games from Madden '09 to NASCAR '09 to NBA Live '08; and it was the first presidential political camp to make extensive use of Facebook, which went live in 2004, and Twitter (2006). This electronic technology did not isolate Obama's citizen backers, but instead helped them find each other and build a momentum that carried their candidate into the White House.

Putnam's and Sander's exuberance over the 9/11 Generation is tempered by the yawning gap between the civic participation rates of affluent and poor Americans. On one side of the divide, the economically and politically advantaged young men and women—who are more than often white—are strongly connected to their communities, families, and places of worship. By contrast, the poor, especially those who belong to historically disadvantaged groups, "slipped farther into disengagement every year."[6] Making matters worse, the poorest of the poor lack access to the computer technology that seems to have such a vital role in rebuilding social capital in the United States. Even so, Putnam and Sander remain "agnostic about whether Internet social entrepreneurs have found the right mix of virtual and real strands to replace traditional social ties."[7] Moreover, it remains to be seen if the division between "haves" and "have-nots," which is now so prevalent in American life, can be bridged. Likely, it will take the old-time social capital rather than the new computer-intensive kind to transform society in this precarious post-9/11 world.

Questions for Consideration and Conversation

1. Do you agree with Putnam that the vibrancy of American society was in decline in the 1980s and early 1990s? Do you think he was examining the right things to draw this conclusion?

2. Putnam uses generational differences to help explain why things became so disintegrated in the 1980s and 1990s. How do you think older generations maintained social ties and built social capital? How does your generation maintain its ties? Which way do you think is better?

3. Putnam touches briefly on the future of social interaction and the possible roles for technology. Do you think

that our social media has increased interconnectedness or has further ruined the fabric of American society?

4. What are the political implications of a weak, disintegrated society?

5. Re-examine the chapters relating to the student movement (Chapter 17), civil rights movement (Chapter 18), and the feminist movement (Chapter 20). Do you think that these movements have flourished in this "bowling alone" period of American society? To be successful, is it necessary for social movements to exist in periods of high social interconnectedness?

Endnotes

1. Alexis de Tocqueville, *Democracy in America and Two Essays on America* (New York: Penguin Group, 2003), 596.
2. Robert D. Putnam, *Bowling Alone: The Collapse and Revival of American Community* (New York: Simon and Schuster, 2000), 290.
3. Ibid., 414.
4. Steven A. Holmes, "Defying Forecasts, Census Response Ends Declining Trend," *New York Times*, September 20, 2000.
5. Thomas H. Sander and Robert D. Putnam, "Still Bowling Alone?: The Post-9/11 Split," *Journal of Democracy*, 21, no. 1 (January 2010), 10.
6. Ibid., 14.
7. Ibid., 15.

ROBERT PUTNAM, BOWLING ALONE: AMERICA'S DECLINING SOCIAL CAPITAL (1995)

Source: Robert D. Putnam, "Bowling Alone: America's Declining Social Capital," *Journal of Democracy*, 6 (January 1995), pp. 65–78.

Many students of the new democracies that have emerged over the past decade and a half have emphasized the importance of a strong and active civil society to the consolidation of democracy. Especially with regard to the postcommunist countries, scholars and democratic activists alike have lamented the absence or obliteration of traditions of independent civic engagement and a widespread tendency toward passive reliance on the state. To those concerned with the weakness of civil societies in the developing or postcommunist world, the advanced Western democracies and above all the United States have typically been taken as models to be emulated. There is striking evidence, however, that the vibrancy of American civil society has notably declined over the past several decades.

Ever since the publication of Alexis de Tocqueville's *Democracy in America*, the United States has played a central role in systematic studies of the links between democracy and civil society. Although this is in part because trends in American life are often regarded as harbingers of social modernization, it is also because America has traditionally been considered unusually "civic" (a reputation that, as we shall later see, has not been entirely unjustified).

When Tocqueville visited the United States in the 1830s, it was the Americans' propensity for civic association that most impressed him as the key to their unprecedented ability to make democracy work. "Americans of all ages, all stations in life, and all types of disposition," he observed, "are forever forming associations. There are not only commercial and industrial associations in which all take part, but others of a thousand different types—religious, moral, serious, futile, very general and very limited, immensely large and very minute.... Nothing, in my view, deserves more attention than the intellectual and moral associations in America."

Recently, American social scientists of a neo-Tocquevillean bent have unearthed a wide range of empirical evidence that the quality of public life and the performance of social institutions (and not only in America) are indeed powerfully influenced by norms and networks of civic engagement. Researchers in such fields as education, urban poverty, unemployment, the control of crime and drug abuse, and even health have discovered that successful outcomes are more likely in civically engaged communities. Similarly, research on the varying economic attainments of different ethnic groups in the United States has demonstrated the importance of social bonds within each group. These results are consistent with research in a wide range of settings that demonstrates the vital importance of social networks for job placement and many other economic outcomes.

Meanwhile, a seemingly unrelated body of research on the sociology of economic development has also focused attention on the role of social networks. Some of this work is situated in the developing countries, and some of it elucidates the peculiarly successful "network capitalism" of East Asia. Even in less exotic Western economies, however, researchers have discovered highly efficient, highly flexible "industrial districts" based on networks of collaboration among workers and small entrepreneurs. Far from being paleoindustrial anachronisms, these dense interpersonal and interorganizational networks undergird ultramodern industries, from the high tech of Silicon Valley to the high fashion of Benetton.

The norms and networks of civic engagement also powerfully affect the performance of representative government. That, at least, was the central conclusion of my own 20-year, quasi-experimental study of subnational governments in different regions of Italy. Although all these regional governments seemed identical on paper, their levels of effectiveness varied dramatically. Systematic inquiry showed that the quality of governance was determined by longstanding traditions of civic engagement (or its absence). Voter turnout, newspaper readership, membership in choral societies and football clubs—these were the hallmarks of a successful region. In fact, historical analysis suggested that these networks of organized reciprocity and civic solidarity, far from being an epiphenomenon of socioeconomic modernization, were a precondition for it.

No doubt the mechanisms through which civic engagement and social connectedness produce such results—better schools, faster economic development, lower crime, and more effective government—are multiple and complex. While these briefly recounted findings require further confirmation and perhaps qualification, the parallels across hundreds of empirical studies in a dozen disparate disciplines and subfields are striking. Social scientists in several fields have recently suggested a common framework for understanding these phenomena, a framework that rests on the concept of *social capital*. By analogy with notions of physical capital and human capital—tools and training that enhance individual productivity— "social capital" refers to features of social organization such as networks, norms, and social trust that facilitate coordination and cooperation for mutual benefit.

For a variety of reasons, life is easier in a community blessed with a substantial stock of social capital. In the first place, networks of civic engagement foster sturdy norms of generalized reciprocity and encourage the emergence of social trust. Such networks facilitate coordination and communication, amplify reputations, and thus allow dilemmas of collective action to be resolved. When economic and political negotiation is embedded in dense networks of social interaction, incentives for opportunism are reduced. At the same time, networks of civic engagement embody past success at collaboration, which can serve as a cultural template for future collaboration. Finally, dense networks of interaction probably broaden the participants' sense of self, developing the "I" into the "we," or (in the language of rational-choice theorists) enhancing the participants' "taste" for collective benefits.

I do not intend here to survey (much less contribute to) the development of the theory of social capital. Instead, I use the central premise of that rapidly growing body of work—that social connections and civic engagement pervasively influence our public life, as well as our private prospects—as the starting point for an empirical survey of trends in social capital in contemporary America. I concentrate here entirely on the American case, although the developments I portray may in some measure characterize many contemporary societies.

Whatever Happened to Civic Engagement?

We begin with familiar evidence on changing patterns of political participation, not least because it is immediately relevant to issues of democracy in the narrow sense. Consider the well-known decline in turnout in national elections over the last three decades. From a relative high point in the early 1960s, voter turnout had by 1990 declined by nearly a quarter; tens of millions of Americans had forsaken their parents' habitual readiness to engage in the simplest act of citizenship. Broadly similar trends also characterize participation in state and local elections.

It is not just the voting booth that has been increasingly deserted by Americans. A series of identical questions posed by the Roper Organization to national samples ten times each year over the last two decades reveals that since 1973 the number of Americans who report that "in the past year" they have "attended a public meeting on town or school affairs" has fallen by more than a third (from 22 percent in 1973 to 13 percent in 1993). Similar (or even greater) relative declines are evident in responses to questions about attending a political rally or speech, serving on a committee of some local organization, and working for a political party. By almost every measure, Americans' direct engagement in politics and government has fallen steadily and sharply over the last generation, despite the fact that average levels of education—the best individual-level predictor of political participation—have risen sharply throughout this period. Every year over the last decade or two, millions more have withdrawn from the affairs of their communities.

Not coincidentally, Americans have also disengaged psychologically from politics and government over this era. The proportion of Americans who reply that they "trust the government in Washington" only "some of the time" or "almost never" has risen steadily from 30 percent in 1966 to 75 percent in 1992.

These trends are well known, of course, and taken by themselves would seem amenable to a strictly political explanation. Perhaps the long litany of political tragedies and scandals since the 1960s (assassinations, Vietnam, Watergate, Irangate, and so on) has triggered an understandable disgust for politics and government among Americans, and that in turn has motivated their withdrawal. I do not doubt that this common interpretation has some merit, but its limitations become plain when we examine trends in civic engagement of a wider sort.

Our survey of organizational membership among Americans can usefully begin with a glance at the aggregate results of the General Social Survey, a scientifically conducted, national-sample survey that has been repeated 14 times over the last two decades. Church-related groups constitute the most common type of organization joined by Americans; they are especially popular with women. Other types of organizations frequently joined by women include school-service groups (mostly parent-teacher associations), sports groups, professional societies, and literary societies. Among men, sports clubs, labor unions, professional societies, fraternal groups, veterans' groups, and service clubs are all relatively popular.

Religious affiliation is by far the most common associational membership among Americans. Indeed, by many measures America continues to be (even more than in Tocqueville's time) an astonishingly "churched" society. For example, the United States has more houses of worship per capita than any other nation on Earth. Yet religious sentiment in America seems to be becoming somewhat less tied to institutions and more self-defined.

How have these complex crosscurrents played out over the last three or four decades in terms of Americans' engagement with organized religion? The general pattern is clear: The 1960s witnessed a significant drop in reported weekly churchgoing—from roughly 48 percent in the late 1950s to roughly 41 percent in the early 1970s. Since then, it has stagnated or (according to some surveys) declined still further. Meanwhile, data from the General Social Survey show a modest decline in membership in all "church-related groups" over the last 20 years. It would seem, then, that net participation by Americans, both in religious services and in church-related groups, has declined modestly (by perhaps a sixth) since the 1960s.

For many years, labor unions provided one of the most common organizational affiliations among American workers. Yet union membership has been falling for nearly four decades, with the steepest decline occurring between 1975 and 1985. Since the mid-1950s, when union membership peaked, the unionized portion of the nonagricultural work force in America has dropped by more than half, falling from 32.5 percent in 1953 to 15.8 percent in 1992. By now, virtually all of the explosive growth in union membership that was associated with the New Deal has been erased. The solidarity of union halls is now mostly a fading memory of aging men.

The PTA has been an especially important form of civic engagement in twentieth-century America because parental involvement in the educational process represents a particularly productive form of social capital. It is, therefore, dismaying to discover that participation in parent-teacher organizations has dropped drastically over the last generation, from more than 12 million in 1964 to barely 5 million in 1982 before recovering to approximately 7 million now.

Next, we turn to evidence on membership in (and volunteering for) civic and fraternal organizations. These data show some striking patterns. First, membership in traditional women's groups has declined more or less steadily since the mid-1960s. For example, membership in the national Federation of Women's Clubs is down by more than half (59 percent) since 1964, while membership in the League of Women Voters (LWV) is off 42 percent since 1969.

Similar reductions are apparent in the numbers of volunteers for mainline civic organizations, such as the Boy Scouts (off by 26 percent since 1970) and the Red Cross (off by 61 percent since 1970). But what about the possibility that volunteers have simply switched their loyalties to other organizations? Evidence on "regular" (as opposed to occasional or "drop-by") volunteering is available from the Labor Department's Current Population Surveys of 1974 and 1989. These estimates suggest that serious volunteering declined by roughly one-sixth over these 15 years, from 24 percent of adults in 1974 to 20 percent in 1989. The multitudes of Red Cross aides and Boy Scout troop leaders now missing in action have apparently not been offset by equal numbers of new recruits elsewhere.

Fraternal organizations have also witnessed a substantial drop in membership during the 1980s and 1990s. Membership is down significantly in such groups as the Lions (off 12 percent since 1983), the Elks (off 18 percent since 1979), the Shriners (off 27 percent since 1979), the Jaycees (off 44 percent since 1979), and the Masons (down 39 percent since 1959). In sum, after expanding steadily throughout most of this century, many major civic organizations have experienced a sudden, substantial, and nearly simultaneous decline in membership over the last decade or two.

The most whimsical yet discomfiting bit of evidence of social disengagement in contemporary America that I have discovered is this: more Americans are bowling today than ever before, but bowling in organized leagues has plummeted in the last decade or so. Between 1980 and 1993 the total number of bowlers in America increased by 10 percent, while league bowling decreased by 40 percent. (Lest this be thought a wholly trivial example, I should note that nearly 80 million Americans went bowling at least once during 1993, *nearly a third more than voted in the 1994 congressional elections* and roughly the same number as claim to attend church regularly. Even after the 1980s' plunge in league bowling, nearly 3 percent of American adults regularly bowl in leagues.) The rise of solo bowling threatens the livelihood of bowling-lane proprietors because those who bowl as members of leagues consume three times as much beer and pizza as solo bowlers, and the money in bowling is in the beer and pizza, not the balls and shoes. The broader social significance, however, lies in the social interaction and even occasionally civic conversations over beer and pizza that solo bowlers forgo. Whether or not bowling beats balloting in the eyes of most Americans, bowling teams illustrate yet another vanishing form of social capital.

Countertrends

At this point, however, we must confront a serious counterargument. Perhaps the traditional forms of civic organization whose decay we have been tracing have been replaced by vibrant new organizations. For example, national environmental organizations (like the Sierra Club) and feminist groups (like the National Organization for Women) grew rapidly during the 1970s and 1980s and now count hundreds of thousands of dues-paying members. An even more dramatic example is the American Association of Retired Persons (AARP), which grew exponentially from 400,000 card-carrying members in 1960 to 33 million in 1993, becoming (after the Catholic Church) the largest private organization in the world. The national administrators of these organizations are among the most feared lobbyists in Washington, in large part because of their massive mailing lists of presumably loyal members.

These new mass-membership organizations are plainly of great political importance. From the point of view of social connectedness, however, they are sufficiently different from classic "secondary associations" that we need to invent a new label—perhaps "tertiary associations." For the vast majority of their members, the only act of membership consists in writing a check for dues or perhaps occasionally reading a newsletter. Few ever attend any meetings of such organizations, and most are unlikely ever (knowingly) to encounter any other member. The bond between any two members of the Sierra Club is less like the bond between any two members of a gardening club and more like the bond between any two Red Sox fans (or perhaps any two devoted Honda owners): they root for the same team and they share some of the same interests, but they are unaware of each other's existence. Their ties, in short, are to common symbols, common leaders, and perhaps common ideals, but not to one another. The theory of social capital argues that associational membership should, for example, increase social trust, but this prediction is much less straightforward with regard to membership in tertiary associations. From the point of view of social connectedness, the Environmental Defense Fund and a bowling league are just not in the same category.

If the growth of tertiary organizations represents one potential (but probably not real) counterexample to my thesis, a second countertrend is represented by the growing prominence of nonprofit organizations, especially nonprofit service agencies. This so-called third sector includes everything from Oxfam and the Metropolitan Museum of Art to the Ford Foundation and the Mayo Clinic. In other words, although most secondary associations are nonprofits, most nonprofit agencies are not secondary associations. To identify trends in the size of the nonprofit sector with trends in social connectedness would be another fundamental conceptual mistake.

A third potential countertrend is much more relevant to an assessment of social capital and civic engagement. Some able researchers have argued that the last few decades have witnessed a rapid expansion in "support groups" of various sorts.

Robert Wuthnow reports that fully 40 percent of all Americans claim to be "currently involved in [a] small group that meets regularly and provides support or caring for those who participate in it." Many of these groups are religiously affiliated, but many others are not. For example, nearly 5 percent of Wuthnow's national sample claim to participate regularly in a "self-help" group, such as Alcoholics Anonymous, and nearly as many say they belong to book-discussion groups and hobby clubs.

The groups described by Wuthnow's respondents unquestionably represent an important form of social capital, and they need to be accounted for in any serious reckoning of trends in social connectedness. On the other hand, they do not typically play the same role as traditional civic associations. As Wuthnow emphasizes,

> Small groups may not be fostering community as effectively as many of their proponents would like. Some small groups merely provide occasions for individuals to focus on themselves in the presence of others. The social contract binding members together asserts only the weakest of obligations. Come if you have time. Talk if you feel like it. Respect everyone's opinion. Never criticize. Leave quietly if you become dissatisfied.... We can imagine that [these small groups] really substitute for families, neighborhoods, and broader community attachments that may demand lifelong commitments, when, in fact, they do not.

All three of these potential countertrends—tertiary organizations, nonprofit organizations, and support groups—need somehow to be weighed against the erosion of conventional civic organizations. One way of doing so is to consult the General Social Survey.

Within all educational categories, total associational membership declined significantly between 1967 and 1993. Among the college-educated, the average number of group memberships per person fell from 2.8 to 2.0 (a 26-percent decline); among high-school graduates, the number fell from 1.8 to 1.2 (32 percent); and among those with fewer than 12 years of education, the number fell from 1.4 to 1.1 (25 percent). In other words, at *all* educational (and hence social) levels of American society, and counting *all* sorts of group memberships, *the average number of associational memberships has fallen by about a fourth over the last quarter-century.* Without controls

for educational levels, the trend is not nearly so clear, but the central point is this: *more Americans than ever before are in social circumstances that foster associational involvement (higher education, middle age, and so on), but nevertheless aggregate associational membership appears to be stagnant or declining.*

Broken down by type of group, the downward trend is most marked for church-related groups, for labor unions, for fraternal and veterans' organizations, and for school-service groups. Conversely, membership in professional associations has risen over these years, although less than might have been predicted, given sharply rising educational and occupational levels. Essentially the same trends are evident for both men and women in the sample. In short, the available survey evidence confirms our earlier conclusion: American social capital in the form of civic associations has significantly eroded over the last generation.

Good Neighborliness and Social Trust

I noted earlier that most readily available quantitative evidence on trends in social connectedness involves formal settings, such as the voting booth, the union hall, or the PTA. One glaring exception is so widely discussed as to require little comment here: the most fundamental form of social capital is the family, and the massive evidence of the loosening of bonds within the family (both extended and nuclear) is well known. This trend, of course, is quite consistent with—and may help to explain our theme of social decapitalization.

A second aspect of informal social capital on which we happen to have reasonably reliable time-series data involves neighborliness. In each General Social Survey since 1974 respondents have been asked, "How often do you spend a social evening with a neighbor?" The proportion of Americans who socialize with their neighbors more than once a year has slowly but steadily declined over the last two decades, from 72 percent in 1974 to 61 percent in 1993. (On the other hand, socializing with "friends who do not live in your neighborhood" appears to be on the increase, a trend that may reflect the growth of workplace-based social connections.)

Americans are also less trusting. The proportion of Americans saying that most people can be trusted fell by more than a third between 1960, when 58 percent chose that alternative, and 1993, when only 37 percent did. The same trend is apparent in all educational groups; indeed, because social trust is also correlated with education and because educational levels have risen sharply, the overall decrease in social trust is even more apparent if we control for education.

Our discussion of trends in social connectedness and civic engagement has tacitly assumed that all the forms of social capital that we have discussed are themselves coherently correlated across individuals. This is in fact true. Members of associations are much more likely than nonmembers to participate in politics, to spend time with neighbors, to express social trust, and so on.

The close correlation between social trust and associational membership is true not only across time and across individuals, but also across countries. Evidence from the 1991 World Values Survey demonstrates the following:

1. Across the 35 countries in this survey, social trust and civic engagement are strongly correlated; the greater the density of associational membership in a society, the more trusting its citizens. Trust and engagement are two facets of the same underlying factor—social capital.

2. America still ranks relatively high by cross-national standards on both these dimensions of social capital. Even in the 1990s, after several decades' erosion, Americans are more trusting and more engaged than people in most other countries of the world.

3. The trends of the past quarter-century, however, have apparently moved the United States significantly lower in the international rankings of social capital. The recent deterioration in American social capital has been sufficiently great that (if no other country changed its position in the meantime) another quarter-century of change at the same rate would bring the United States, roughly speaking, to the midpoint among all these countries, roughly equivalent to South Korea, Belgium, or Estonia today. Two generations' decline at the same rate would leave the United States at the level of today's Chile, Portugal, and Slovenia.

Why Is U.S. Social Capital Eroding?

As we have seen, something has happened in America in the last two or three decades to diminish civic engagement and social connectedness. What could that "something" be? Here are several possible explanations, along with some initial evidence on each.

The movement of women into the labor force. Over these same two or three decades, many millions of American women have moved out of the home into paid employment. This is the primary, though not the sole, reason why the weekly working hours of the average American have increased significantly during these years. It seems highly plausible that this social revolution should have reduced the time and energy available for building social capital. For certain organizations, such as the PTA, the League of Women Voters, the Federation of Women's Clubs, and the Red Cross, this is almost certainly an important part of the story. The sharpest decline in women's civic participation seems to have come in the 1970s; membership in such "women's" organizations as these has been virtually halved since the late 1960s. By contrast, most of the decline in participation in men's organizations occurred about ten years later; the total decline to date has been approximately 25 percent for the typical organization. On the other hand, the survey data imply that the aggregate declines for men are virtually as great as those for women. It is logically possible, of course, that the male declines might represent the knock-on effect of women's liberation, as dishwashing crowded out the lodge, but time-budget studies suggest that most husbands of working wives have assumed only a minor part of the housework. In short, something besides the women's revolution seems to lie behind the erosion of social capital.

Mobility: The "re-potting" hypothesis. Numerous studies of organizational involvement have shown that residential stability and such related phenomena as homeownership are clearly associated with greater civic engagement. Mobility, like frequent re-potting of plants, tends to disrupt root systems, and it takes time for an uprooted individual to put down new roots. It seems plausible that the automobile, suburbanization, and the movement to the Sun Belt have reduced the social rootedness of the average American, but one fundamental difficulty with this hypothesis is apparent: the best evidence shows that residential stability and homeownership in America have risen modestly since 1965, and are surely higher now than during the 1950s, when civic engagement and social connectedness by our measures was definitely higher.

Other demographic transformations. A range of additional changes have transformed the American family since the 1960s—fewer marriages, more divorces, fewer children, lower real wages, and so on. Each of these changes might account for some of the slackening of civic engagement, since married, middle-class parents are generally more socially involved than other people. Moreover, the changes in scale that have swept over the American economy in these years—illustrated by the replacement of the corner grocery by the supermarket and now perhaps of the supermarket by electronic shopping at home, or the replacement of community-based enterprises by outposts of distant multinational firms may perhaps have undermined the material and even physical basis for civic engagement.

The technological transformation of leisure. There is reason to believe that deep-seated technological trends are radically "privatizing" or "individualizing" our use of leisure time and thus disrupting many opportunities for social-capital formation. The most obvious and probably the most powerful instrument of this revolution is television. Time-budget studies in the 1960s showed that the growth in time spent watching television dwarfed all other changes in the way Americans passed their days and nights. Television has made our communities (or, rather, what we experience as our communities) wider and shallower. In the language of economics, electronic technology enables individual tastes to be satisfied more fully, but at the cost of the positive social externalities associated with more primitive forms of entertainment. The same logic applies to the replacement of vaudeville by the movies and now of movies by the VCR. The new "virtual reality" helmets that we will soon don to be entertained in total isolation are merely the latest extension of this trend. Is technology thus driving a wedge between our individual interests and our collective interests? It is a question that seems worth exploring more systematically.

What Is to Be Done?

The last refuge of a social-scientific scoundrel is to call for more research. Nevertheless, I cannot forbear from suggesting some further lines of inquiry.

- We must sort out the dimensions of social capital, which clearly is not a unidimensional concept, despite language (even in this essay) that implies the contrary. What types of organizations and networks most effectively embody—or generate—social capital, in the sense of mutual reciprocity, the resolution of dilemmas of collective action, and the broadening of social identities? In this essay I have emphasized the density of associational life. In earlier work I stressed the structure of networks, arguing that "horizontal" ties represented more productive social capital than vertical ties.

- Another set of important issues involves macrosociological crosscurrents that might intersect with the trends described here. What will be the impact, for example, of electronic networks on social capital? My hunch is that meeting in an electronic forum is not the equivalent of meeting in a bowling alley—or even in a saloon—but hard empirical research is needed. What about the development of social capital in the workplace? Is it growing in counterpoint to the decline of civic engagement, reflecting some social analogue of the first law of thermodynamics—social capital is neither created nor destroyed, merely redistributed? Or do the trends described in this essay represent a deadweight loss?

- A rounded assessment of changes in American social capital over the last quarter-century needs to count the costs as well as the benefits of community engagement. We must not romanticize small-town, middle-class civic life in the America of the 1950s. In addition to the deleterious trends emphasized in this essay, recent decades have witnessed a substantial decline in intolerance and probably also in overt discrimination, and those beneficent trends may be related in complex ways to the erosion of traditional social capital. Moreover, a balanced accounting of the social-capital books would need to reconcile the insights of this approach with the undoubted insights offered by Mancur Olson and others who stress that closely knit social, economic, and political organizations are prone to inefficient cartelization and to what political economists term "rent seeking" and ordinary men and women call corruption.

- Finally, and perhaps most urgently, we need to explore creatively how public policy impinges on (or might impinge on) social-capital formation. In some well-known instances, public policy has destroyed highly effective social networks and norms. American slum-clearance policy of the 1950s and 1960s, for example, renovated physical capital, but at a very high cost to existing social capital. The consolidation of country post offices and small school districts has promised administrative and financial efficiencies, but full-cost accounting for the effects of these policies on social capital might produce a more negative verdict. On the other hand, such past initiatives as the county agricultural-agent system, community colleges, and tax deductions for charitable contributions illustrate that government can encourage social-capital formation. Even a recent proposal in San Luis Obispo,

California, to require that all new houses have front porches illustrates the power of government to influence where and how networks are formed.

The concept of "civil society" has played a central role in the recent global debate about the preconditions for democracy and democratization. In the newer democracies this phrase has properly focused attention on the need to foster a vibrant civic life in soils traditionally inhospitable to self-government. In the established democracies, ironically, growing numbers of citizens are questioning the effectiveness of their public institutions at the very moment when liberal democracy has swept the battlefield, both ideologically and geopolitically. In America, at least, there is reason to suspect that this democratic disarray may be linked to a broad and continuing erosion of civic engagement that began a quarter-century ago. High on our scholarly agenda should be the question of whether a comparable erosion of social capital may be under way in other advanced democracies, perhaps in different institutional and behavioral guises. High on America's agenda should be the question of how to reverse these adverse trends in social connectedness, thus restoring civic engagement and civic trust.

CHAPTER 23

Samuel Huntington Imagines a Post-9/11 World

"Conflict between civilizations will be the latest phase in the evolution of conflict in the modern world."

On September 10, 2001, the *New York Times'* front page heralded the most important news of the day. It was a mixed bag of the serious and the superficial: fears of an economic recession, crises in New York City's public schools, that city's upcoming mayoral election, and tennis great Pete Sampras' defeat at the hands of twenty-year-old Australian Lleyton Hewitt. Just two days later, the same newspaper—just like every other newspaper in the world—told the stories of horror, sadness, and anger related to the worst attacks on the United States since World War II. The news itself was hard enough: thousands dead, the World Trade Center destroyed, the Pentagon terribly damaged, and three airliners and their passengers incinerated. The nation was in economic, if not social and political, turmoil. However, people needed help to make sense of the 9/11 attacks. Who was responsible? Why had they done this? What did it mean for life in the twenty-first century?

As the dead were buried, the fires put out, and the dust settled, many turned to the ideas of Samuel P. Huntington (1927–2008), a political theorist at Harvard University, to understand what had happened. Huntington—who wrote his first path-breaking book in the 1950s and who had been an advisor to several presidents—was no neophyte. In 1993, Huntington published one of the most controversial and most widely debated scholarly articles. In "The Clash of Civilizations?" published in the policy journal *Foreign Affairs*, he had predicted that in the post–Cold War world "the clash of civilizations [a phrase borrowed from another political commentator Bernard Lewis] will dominate global politics." In the months after the attacks, Americans and many around the world came to agree: 9/11 was the start of a global cultural clash between the West and Islam.

When Huntington was writing his article in the early 1990s, his dark and pessimistic vision seemed out of place. At the end of the twentieth century and the dawn of the 21st, Americans felt triumphant. The Cold War—that ideological, economic, political, diplomatic, and military conflict between the Soviet Union and its allied nations and the United States and its allies that defined the period from 1946 to 1990—was over. The U.S. economy was flush; unemployment was low and personal incomes were up. Politics reflected American self-satisfaction. In the 2000 presidential election, the key issues were domestic and related to how to handle the federal government's budget surplus and how to reduce taxes. Some political theorists such as Francis Fukuyama (b. 1952) even saw utopian possibilities. In a famous and much-discussed book published a year before Huntington's article, Fukuyama argued that the post–Cold War world was witnessing the "end of history." He did not imply an "end of times," but rather an end to the ideological, political, and economic strife that had propelled history along and raged since the fall of the Roman Empire. At every turn as feudalism gave way to monarchism and as monarchism gave way to republicanism, oligarchy, communism, and fascism, there had been great upheaval, wars, tremendous loss of life, and a resetting of the international order. But now that the Soviet Union had disappeared, democracy, the free market, and the Western humanist values no longer had competition and were poised to spread everywhere, creating a kind of universal culture and civilization. The world's political and economic evolution, Fukuyama and his adherents predicted, was at an end.

Huntington, Fukuyama's former teacher, could not have disagreed more. Both Huntington and Fukuyama correctly sensed that the 1990s marked a turning point in world history. However, Huntington foresaw that as global ideological conflicts recessed "great divisions among humankind" would surface (or resurface) and that "the dominating source of conflict will be cultural." In other words, the clash of political "isms" would be replaced by a clash of civilizations and "the fault lines between civilizations would be the battle lines of the future." Thus, history was not dead, but it would be shaped by the peoples and governments of Western and non-Western civilizations. And, conflict, not peaceful co-existence, would reign. "Conflict between civilizations," he famously envisaged, "will be the latest phase in the evolution of conflict in the modern world."

In his essay, Huntington provided a definition and taxonomy of world civilizations. A civilization is the highest cultural grouping of people who share a general history; language; system of government; religion; and ideas about gender, sexuality, family and the like. On the planet, civilizations have come and gone. Huntington identified eight current major ones: Western, Confucian (which he later labeled Sinic), Japanese, Islamic, Hindu, Slavic-Orthodox, Latin American, and African.

Huntington maintained that cultural identities and differences are real and intrinsic, and not an academic invention. Moreover, they were at the root of conflict in the post–Cold War world. Why conflict and not cooperation? Why can we all just get along? Huntington offered a range of answers. He asserted that cultural differences are the products of centuries of human development; they will not quietly disappear. Rather, as the world becomes a smaller place by means of migration, international trade, and electronic communication, cultural differences will be highlighted. As Huntington elucidated, "the interactions among peoples of different civilizations enhance the civilization-consciousness of people that, in turn, invigorates differences and animosities stretching or thought to stretch back deep in history." These animosities will be further enhanced by highly political fundamentalist movements in religion, which will seek among other things to confront and challenge the West. Thus, tolerance of other views and other peoples both within civilizations and among them will decrease. Huntington also asserted that these religious movements will enhance the trend toward separating civilizations, establishing what he calls "fault lines" between them. These are not ideological divisions. In the Cold War, the litmus test for nations as well as individuals was: which side are you on? Were you pro-capitalist or pro-Communist? Now the essential questions are: to what civilization do you belong? What is your cultural identity?

Huntington forecasted how the civilizations will work together or will fight. He identified a central conflict—perhaps *the* conflict—between Western and Islamic civilizations. This clash is not new, having a chronology extending 1,300 years. But, "it could become more virulent." Huntington used as his example the recent history of the 1991 Gulf War against Saddam Hussein. Although the West had come to the defense of a Muslim country (as well as its oil interests in the region), the war "left some Arabs feeling proud that Saddam Hussein had attacked Israel and stood up to the West." Rather than create any alliances in the Middle East, that war had invigorated anti-West sentiment, sharpened the divisions between Muslims and Christians, encouraged Islamic fundamentalists, and sparked new fights between these civilizations. "Islam," Huntington famously commented, "has bloody borders."

In the future, Huntington stated, countries along the fault lines between civilizations will have to decide to which bloc they subscribe. This kin-country syndrome will help determine political, economic, and military partners as well as the outcomes of the clashes. Huntington saw this as one of the crucial lessons from the fighting in the former Yugoslavia in the 1990s, when Western nations "rallied behind their corelgionists," as did Muslim countries. Yet, nothing is predetermined. There are some countries such as Turkey and Mexico that have divided loyalties, being uncertain about cultural alignment. These "torn" nations are vital to the larger clashes, which Huntington ultimately boiled down to the West versus the Rest. Should Russia, for example, not identify with the West, then it may well become an adversary in global politics and economics. In this way, potentially torn countries could also become military opponents.

Huntington again provided examples from recent history to illustrate his West-versus-the-Rest notion. The West is certainly integrated in terms of political, economic, and military cooperation. The North Atlantic Treaty Organization, the European Community, and the International Monetary Fund represent well the global interests of the United States, England, France, Germany, and other kin countries. Similarly the Economic Cooperation Organization, which includes Iran, Pakistan, Turkey, Azerbaijan, Kazakhstan, Kyrgyzstan, Turkmenistan, Tajikistan, Uzbekistan, and Afghanistan, have united on a "cultural and religion" basis to counter the West. Given the political, economic, and military dominance of the Western countries, non-Westerns have also formed regional and cross-cultural alliances. For instance, in the late 1980s and early 1990s, there developed what Huntington calls a "Confucian-Islamic connection." China exported components for chemical and nuclear weapons to Iraq, Libya, and Pakistan. This proliferation as well as this cultural connection has sparked fears among the leaders of the Western civilization, causing a new Western emphasis on arms control, aimed not at achieving parity as during the Cold War but rather prevention. In Huntington's view, the military escalation in China, Iraq, Libya, North Korea, and Algeria is about finding a way to challenge and perhaps defeat the West. Non-Western nations, he explained, "absorbed, to the full, the truth of the response of the Indian defense minister when asked what lesson he learned from the Gulf War: 'Don't fight the United States [and its European allies] unless you have nuclear weapons'."

In the final analysis, the clash of civilizations is a slow movement toward a global conflict. It's worth quoting Huntington at length. In the future, "successful political, security, and economic international institutions are more likely to develop within civilizations than across civilizations; conflicts between groups in different civilizations will be more frequent, more sustained and more violent than conflicts between groups in the same civilizations; violent conflicts between groups in different civilizations are the most likely and most dangerous source of escalation that could lead to global wars; the paramount axis of world politics will be the relations between 'the West and the Rest'." Assuming that all this is true, Huntington advised two courses of action, one short-term and one long-term. In the short run, the West should cultivate cultural allies and maintain military superiority. Long-term survival in the clash of civilizations will require tolerance, understanding, and compromise between civilizations. "For the relevant future, there will be no universal civilization, but instead a world of different civilizations, each of which will have to learn to coexist with the others." In other words, in the end, civilizations will have to get along and work together or endlessly clash and perhaps risk being destroyed.

Huntington's article generated an amazing and acrimonious reaction. Almost immediately, policymakers, politicians, and pundits began comparing it with George F. Kennan's 1948 "X" article about the containment of the Soviet Union, which also appeared in *Foreign Affairs*. At first, the stormy debate surrounding Huntington's clash of civilizations hypothesis (he did after all put a question mark after his title) was largely an academic one. *Foreign Affairs* led the way with a special issue of the journal containing five reactions and a response from Huntington himself. Fouad Ajami, a professor of Middle Eastern Studies at the Johns Hopkins University, provided the lead critique, which was a systematic rebuke to Huntington's argument. First, Ajami charged that Huntington operated with an unnuanced view of culture and civilizations, which are far messier "creatures" than he gave credit.[1] Further, Ajami complained that Huntington ignored the fact that nation states, not civilizations, are the reigning international entities. Finally, and most significantly and most fundamentally, "Huntington is wrong": He "underestimated the tenacity of modernity and secularism in places that acquired these ways against great odds."[2] In other words, modernism has won out in countries such as India and Turkey and in entire regions such as the Middle East. "The phenomenon we have dubbed as Islamic fundamentalism," wrote Ajami, "is less a sign of resurgence than of panic and bewilderment."[3] He maintained that there is no "sinister" connection between China and the Muslim world, bent on raising the military capabilities of Iran, Pakistan, and other non-Western nations. Muslim nations simply were not cooperating in that fashion. Huntington's kin-country syndrome was nothing but "delusion."[4] In short, there was no growing danger between civilizations since states, not civilizations, controlled international events, and "states avert their gaze from blood ties when they need to."[5] Realpolitik, not cultural imperatives, governed international destinies.

The other commentators in *Foreign Affairs* offered a range of criticisms that added depth to Ajami's words. The veteran diplomat Jeane F. Kirpatrick, who was then a professor of government at Georgetown University and a senior fellow at the American Enterprise Institute, thought Huntington had gotten the basics wrong. She objected to his notions of culture and civilization. Since when was Latin America its own civilization, apart from the West? Sure, Indian people had transformed Spanish culture in Central, South, and parts of North America. But hadn't African cultures transformed the United States in similar ways? She also urged a more nuanced interpretation of the rhetoric of the non-Western world, differentiating for example between political extremists who happen to be Muslim and Muslim fundamentalism. Put another way, Kirpatrick suggested that Westerners make a distinction between religious and cultural goals and political ones.

Robert L. Bartley, the editor of the *Wall Street Journal*, criticized Huntington's clash of civilizations thesis for being too pessimistic, adding that Huntington's vision did not "sound like a pleasant 21st century."[6] Like Ajami and Fukuyama, Bartley saw "powerful forces toward world integration" not only in terms of economics but also in terms of popular culture and even language. "The world's language is English," Bartley asserted assuredly.[7] The future was not bleak. Rather, "economic development leads to demands for democracy and individual (or familial) autonomy; instant worldwide communications reduces the power of oppressive governments; the spread of democratic states diminishes the potential for conflict."[8]

Foreign Affairs gave Huntington a chance to defend his argument. Nothing his peers said made him rethink anything. His response, titled "If Not Civilizations, What?", was an unrepentant defense of his post–Cold War paradigm. Again, he argued that the notion of a universal global civilization was fantasy. He then offered page after page of new evidence culled from the recent newspapers showing that the clash of civilizations not only existed but also had grown more intense. For Huntington, this litany made him more pessimistic and left him wondering if the United States would survive the clash of civilizations. Whatever the outcome, he proclaimed that "history has not ended."[9] Rather "faith and family, blood and belief, are what people identify with and what they will fight and die for."[10]

Samuel Huntington's articles and his subsequent 1996 book, titled *The Clash of Civilizations and the Remaking of the World Order* (note that the question mark had disappeared), carried enormous cultural and political weight in the 1990s, and not just in the United States. To politicians and pundits in Europe, Africa, Asia, and the Middle East, his thesis made sense and provided a simple but powerful framework for analysis. But no amount of scholarly or political debate provided as much convincing proof as the attacks of September 11, 2001. Those horrific acts of terror perpetrated by nineteen Islamic radicals from Middle Eastern countries gave, as Fouad Ajami put it, "more of history's compliance than [Huntington] could ever have imagined."[11] In fact, Ajami later recanted his former position as well as his critique. Only a clash of civilizations could explain Islam's war with the West.[12]

Since 2001, there have been no major new paradigms to replace "the clash of civilizations." Like Kennan did generations earlier, Huntington has set a framework for understanding world events. Some scholars have argued that Huntington's characterizations of culture and civilization—particularly as they relate to Islam—are too facile. But rather than unseat Huntington's dominant position, they tend to give it more nuance, explaining in clearer detail how Muslims and Christians differ or how the variation in Asian cultures provides opportunities for the West to establish some cross-cultural alliances. And yet, for all the continuing debate and refinement about the clash between civilizations, most have ignored Huntington's missives about the fights within civilizations. A few have charged that he homogenized Islamic cultures and glossed over the civil wars raging in various countries. This banter made Huntington, who was a quiet, mild-mannered academic, caustic. Such comments on his work were "totally wrong!" he once screamed at a reporter.[13] Indeed, both in his article and in the larger book, Huntington was always careful to mention and explain the significance of intra-civilizational conflicts, especially within the Muslim world. But, Westerners have not seemingly heard his cautionary words about the cultural clash within the West. Likewise, Fouad Ajami worries "whether the West will remain true to itself and its mission." "It is no fault of Samuel Huntington's," Ajami has recently written, "that we have not heeded his darker, and possibly truer, vision."[14]

Questions for Consideration and Conversation

1. Huntington painted a dark future for the post–Cold War world. In what ways has that future come about? In what was has it not?
2. Huntington predicted more conflict than cooperation. Yet, the world seems more interconnected than ever. How can one reconcile the growing global dependency with the rise in conflicts?
3. What role does religion play in the clashes of civilizations?
4. Assuming Huntington is right—that there is currently a great clash of civilizations—what can the United States do to mitigate or even eliminate that conflict?
5. Can you use Huntington's thesis to explain the recent political turmoil in Egypt, Libya, and Syria? Does that clash of civilizations still provide a model of explanation for what is going on in the Middle East?
6. How do our contemporary "clashes" in the world compare to those of the Cold War, particularly Vietnam (Chapter 19)?

Endnotes

1. Fouad Ajami, "The Summoning: 'But They Said, We Will Not Hearken'," *Foreign Affairs* 72 (September–October, 1993), 2.
2. Ibid., 3.
3. Ibid.
4. Ibid., 7.
5. Ibid., 9.
6. Robert L. Bartley, "The Case for Optimism: The West Should Believe in Itself," *Foreign Affairs*, 72 (September–October, 1993), 15.

7. Ibid., 16.

8. Ibid., 17.

9. Samuel F. Huntington, "If Not Civilizations, What?: Paradigms of the Post-Cold War World," *Foreign Affairs* 72 (September–October, 1993), 194.

10. Ibid., 194.

11. Fouad Ajami, "The Clash," *New York Times*, January 6, 2008.

12. See Fouad Ajami, "Huntington and His Discontents," *Wall Street Journal*, December 30, 2008.

13. Joel Achenbach, "The Clash: Two Professors, Two Academic Theories, One Big Difference," *Washington Post Sunday Magazine* (December 16, 2001), W17.

14. Fouad Ajami, "The Clash," *New York Times*, January 6, 2008.

SAMUEL HUNTINGTON, THE CLASH OF CIVILIZATIONS? (1993)

Source: Samuel P. Huntington, *The Clash of Civilizations and the Remaking of World Order.* New York: Simon & Schuster, 1993, pp. 19–21, 28–29, 125–39, 155–63, 308–11, 319–21.

Introduction: Flags and Cultural Identity

On January 3, 1992 a meeting of Russian and American scholars took place in the auditorium of a government building in Moscow. Two weeks earlier the Soviet Union had ceased to exist and the Russian Federation had become an independent country. As a result, the statue of Lenin which previously graced the stage of the auditorium had disappeared and instead the flag of the Russian Federation was now displayed on the front wall. The only problem, one American observed, was that the flag had been hung upside down. After this was pointed out to the Russian hosts, they quickly and quietly corrected the error during the first intermission.

The years after the Cold War witnessed the beginnings of dramatic changes in peoples' identities and the symbols of those identities. Global politics began to be reconfigured along cultural lines. Upside-down flags were a sign of the transition, but more and more the flags are flying high and true, and Russians and other peoples are mobilizing and marching behind these and other symbols of their new cultural identities.

On April 18, 1994 two thousand people rallied in Sarajevo waving the flags of Saudi Arabia and Turkey. By flying those banners, instead of U.N., NATO, or American flags, these Sarajevans identified themselves with their fellow Muslims and told the world who were their real and not-so-real friends.

On October 16, 1994 in Los Angeles 70,000 people marched beneath "a sea of Mexican flags" protesting Proposition 187, a referendum measure which would deny many state benefits to illegal immigrants and their children. Why are they "walking down the street with a Mexican flag and demanding that this country give them a free education?" observers asked. "They should be waving the American flag." Two weeks later more protestors did march down the street carrying an American flag—upside down. These flag displays ensured victory for Proposition 187, which was approved by 59 percent of California voters.

In the post–Cold War world flags count and so do other symbols of cultural identity, including crosses, crescents, and even head coverings, because culture counts, and cultural identity is what is most meaningful to most people. People are discovering new but often old identities and marching under new but often old flags which lead to wars with new but often old enemies....

The central theme of this book is that culture and cultural identities, which at the broadest level are civilization identities, are shaping the patterns of cohesion, disintegration, and conflict in the post–Cold War world. The five parts of this book elaborate corollaries to this main proposition.

Part I: For the first time in history global politics is both multipolar and multicivilizational; modernization is distinct from Westernization and is producing neither a universal civilization in any meaningful sense nor the Westernization of non-Western societies.

Part II: The balance of power among civilizations is shifting: the West is declining in relative influence; Asian civilizations are expanding their economic, military, and political strength; Islam is exploding demographically with destabilizing consequences for Muslim countries and their neighbors; and non-Western civilizations generally are reaffirming the value of their own cultures.

Part III: A civilization-based world order is emerging: societies sharing cultural affinities cooperate with each other; efforts to shift societies from one civilization to another are unsuccessful; and countries group themselves around the lead or core states of their civilization.

Part IV: The West's universalist pretensions increasingly bring it into conflict with other civilizations, most seriously with Islam and China; at the local level fault line wars, largely between Muslims and non-Muslims, generate "kin-country rallying," the threat of broader escalation, and hence efforts by core states to halt these wars.

Part V: The survival of the West depends on Americans reaffirming their Western identity and Westerners accepting their civilization as unique not universal and uniting to renew and preserve it against challenges from non-Western societies. Avoidance of a global war of civilizations depends on world leaders accepting and cooperating to maintain the multicivilizational character of global politics.

A Multipolar, Multicivilizational World

In the post–Cold War world, for the first time in history, global politics has become multipolar *and* multicivilizational. During most of human existence, contacts between civilizations were intermittent or nonexistent. Then, with the beginning of the modern era, about A.D. 1500, global politics assumed two dimensions. For over four hundred years, the nation states of the West-Britain, France, Spain, Austria, Prussia, Germany, the United States, and others—constituted a multipolar international system within Western civilization and interacted, competed, and fought wars with each other. At the same time, Western nations also expanded, conquered, colonized, or decisively influenced every other civilization. During the Cold War global politics became bipolar and the world was divided into three parts. A group of mostly wealthy and democratic societies, led by the United States, was engaged in a pervasive ideological, political, economic, and, at times, military competition with a group of somewhat poorer communist societies associated with and led by the Soviet Union. Much of this conflict occurred in the Third World outside these two camps, composed of countries which often were poor, lacked political stability, were recently independent, and claimed to be nonaligned.

In the late 1980s the communist world collapsed, and the Cold War international system became history. In the post–Cold War world, the most important distinctions among peoples are not ideological, political, or economic. They are cultural. Peoples and nations are attempting to answer the most basic question humans can face: Who are we? And they are answering that question in the traditional way human beings have answered it, by reference to the things that mean most to them. People define themselves in terms of ancestry, religion, language, history, values, customs, and institutions. They identify with cultural groups tribes, ethnic groups, religious communities, nations, and, at the broadest level, civilizations. People use politics not just to advance their interests but also to define their identity. We know who we are only when we know who we are not and often only when we know whom we are against.

Nation states remain the principal actors in world affairs. Their behavior is shaped as in the past by the pursuit of power and wealth, but it is also shaped by cultural preferences, commonalities, and differences. The most important groupings of states are no longer the three blocs of the Cold War but rather the world's seven or eight major civilizations, Non-Western societies, particularly in East Asia, are developing their economic wealth and creating the basis for enhanced military power and political influence. As their power and self-confidence increase, non-Western societies increasingly assert their own cultural values and reject those "imposed" on them by the West. The "international system of the twenty-first century," Henry Kissinger has noted, "... will contain at least six major powers—the United States, Europe, China, Japan, Russia, and probably India—as well as a multiplicity of medium-sized and smaller countries," Kissinger's six major powers belong to five very different civilizations, and in addition there are important Islamic states whose strategic locations, large populations, and/or oil resources male them influential in world affairs. In this new world, local politics is the politics of ethnicity; global politics is the politics of civilizations. The rivalry of the superpowers is replaced by the clash of civilizations.

In this new world the most pervasive, important, and dangerous conflicts will not be between social classes, rich and poor, or other economically defined groups, but between peoples belonging to different cultural entities. Tribal wars and ethnic conflicts will occur within civilizations. Violence between states and groups from different civilizations, however, carries with it the potential for escalation as other states and groups from these civilizations rally to the support of their "kin countries." The bloody clash of clans in Somalia poses no threat of broader conflict. The bloody clash of tribes in Rwanda has consequences for Uganda, Zaire, and Burundi but not much further. The bloody clashes of civilizations in Bosnia, the Caucasus, Central Asia, or Kashmir could become bigger wars. In the Yugoslav conflicts, Russia provided diplomatic support to the Serbs, and Saudi Arabia, Turkey, Iran, and Libya provided funds and arms to the Bosnians, not for reasons of ideology or power politics or economic interest but because of cultural kinship. "Cultural conflicts," Vaclav Havel has observed, "are increasing and are more dangerous today than at any time in history," and Jacques Delors agreed that "future conflicts will be sparked by cultural factors rather than economics or ideology." And the most dangerous cultural conflicts are those along the fault lines between civilizations.

In the post–Cold War world, culture is both a divisive and a unifying force. People separated by ideology but united by culture come together, as the two Germanys did and as the two Koreas and the several Chinas are beginning to. Societies united by ideology or historical circumstance but divided by civilization either come apart, as did the Soviet Union, Yugoslavia, and Bosnia, or are subjected to intense strain, as is the case with Ukraine, Nigeria, Sudan, India, Sri Lanka, and many others. Countries with cultural affinities cooperate economically and politically. International organizations based on states with cultural commonality, such as the European Union, are far more successful than those that attempt to transcend cultures. For forty-five years the Iron Curtain was the central dividing line in Europe. That line has moved several hundred miles east. It is now the line separating the peoples of Western Christianity, on the one hand, from Muslim and Orthodox peoples on the other.

The philosophical assumptions, underlying values, social relations, customs, and overall outlooks on life differ significantly among civilizations. The revitalization of religion throughout much of the world is reinforcing these cultural differences. Cultures can change, and the nature of their impact on politics and economics can vary from one period to another. Yet the major differences in political and economic development among civilizations are clearly rooted in their different cultures. East Asian economic success has its source in East Asian culture, as do the difficulties East Asian societies have had in achieving stable democratic political systems. Islamic culture explains in large part the failure of democracy to emerge in much of the Muslim world. Developments in the postcommunist societies of Eastern Europe and the former Soviet Union are shaped by their civilizational identities. Those with Western Christian Heritages are making progress toward economic development and democratic politics; the prospects for economic and political development in the Orthodox countries are uncertain; the prospects in the Muslim republics are bleak.

The West is and will remain for years to come the most powerful civilization. Yet its power relative to that of other civilizations is declining. As the West attempts to assert its values and to protect its interests, non-Western societies confront a choice. Some attempt to emulate the West and to join or to "bandwagon" with the West. Other Confucian and Islamic societies attempt to expand their own economic and military power to resist and to "balance" against the West. A central axis of post–Cold War world politics is thus the interaction of Western power and culture with the power and culture of non-Western civilizations.

In sum the post–Cold War world is a world of seven or eight major civilizations. Cultural commonalities and differences shape the interests antagonisms and associations of States. The most important countries in the world come overwhelmingly from different civilizations. The local conflicts most likely to escalate into broader wars are those between groups and states from different civilizations. The predominant patterns of political and economic development differ from civilization to civilization. The key issues on the international agenda involve differences among civilizations. Power is shifting from the long predominant West to non-Western civilizations. Global politics has become multipolar and multicivilization....

Groping for Groupings: The Politics of Identity

Spurred by modernization, global politics is being reconfigured along cultural lines. Peoples and countries with similar cultures are coming together. Peoples and countries with different cultures are coming apart. Alignments defined by ideology and superpower relations are giving way to alignments defined by culture and civilization. Political boundaries increasingly are redrawn to coincide with cultural ones: ethnic, religious, and fault lines between civilizations are becoming the central lines of conflict in global politics....

The 1990s have seen the eruption of a global identity crisis. Almost everywhere one looks people have been asking, "Who are we?" "Where do we belong?" and "Who is not us?" These questions are central not only to peoples attempting to forge new nation states, as in the former Yugoslavia, but also much more generally. In the mid-1990s the countries where questions of national identity were actively debated included, among others: Algeria, Canada, China, Germany, Great Britain, India, Iran, Japan, Mexico, Morocco, Russia, South Africa, Syria, Tunisia, Turkey, Ukraine, and the United States. Identity issues are, of course, particularly intense in cleft countries that have sizable groups of people from different civilizations.

In coping with identity crisis, what counts for people are blood and belief, faith and family. People rally to those with similar ancestry, religion, language, values, and institutions and distance themselves from those with different ones. In Europe, Austria, Finland, and Sweden, culturally part of the West, had to be divorced from the West and neutral during the Cold War; they are now able to join their cultural kin in the European Union. The Catholic and Protestant countries in the former Warsaw Pact, Poland, Hungary, the Czech Republic, and Slovakia, are moving toward membership in the Union and in NATO, and the Baltic states are in line behind them. The European powers make it clear that they do not want a Muslim state, Turkey, in the European Union and are not happy about having a second Muslim state, Bosnia, on the European continent. In the north, the end of the Soviet Union stimulates the emergence of new (and old) patterns of association among the Baltic republics and between them, Sweden, and Finland. Sweden's prime minister pointedly reminds Russia that the Baltic republics are part of Sweden's "near abroad" and that Sweden could not be neutral in the event of Russian aggression against them.

Similar realignments occur in the Balkans. During the Cold War, Greece and Turkey were in NATO, Bulgaria and Romania were in the Warsaw Pact, Yugoslavia was nonaligned, and Albania was an isolated sometime associate of communist China. Now these Cold War alignments are giving way to civilizational ones rooted in Islam and Orthodoxy. Balkan leaders talk of crystallizing a Greek-Serb-Bulgarian Orthodox alliance. The "Balkan wars," Greece's prime minister alleges, "...have brought to the surface the resonance of Orthodox ties....this is a bond. It was dormant, but with the developments in the Balkans, it is taking on some real substance. In a very fluid world, people are seeking identity and security. People are looking for roots and connections to defend themselves against the unknown." These views were echoed by the leader of the principal opposition party in Serbia: "The situation in southeastern Europe will soon require the formation of a new Balkan alliance of Orthodox countries, including Serbia, Bulgaria, and

Greece, in order to resist the encroachment of Islam." Looking northward, Orthodox Serbia and Romania cooperate closely in dealing with their common problems with Catholic Hungary. With the disappearance of the Soviet threat, the "unnatural" alliance between Greece and Turkey becomes essentially meaningless, as conflicts intensify between them over the Aegean Sea, Cyprus, their military balance, their roles in NATO and the European Union, and their relations with the United States. Turkey reasserts its role as the protector of Balkan Muslims and provides support to Bosnia. In the former Yugoslavia, Russia backs Orthodox Serbia, Germany promotes Catholic Croatia, Muslim countries rally to the support of the Bosnian government, and the Serbs fight Croatians, Bosnian Muslims, and Albanian Muslims. Overall, the Balkans have once again been Balkanized along the religious lines. "Two axes are emerging," as Misha Glenny observed, "one dressed in the garb of Eastern Orthodoxy, one veiled in Islamic raiment" and the possibility exists of an "ever-greater struggle for influence between the Belgrade/Athens axis and the Albanian/Turkish alliance."...

Will political and economic alignments always coincide with those of culture and civilization? Of course not. Balance of power considerations will at times lead to cross-civilizational alliances, as they did when Francis I joined with the Ottomans against the Hapsburgs. In addition, patterns of association formed to serve the purposes of states in one era will persist into a new era. They are, however, likely to become weaker and less meaningful and to be adapted to serve the purposes of the new age. Greece and Turkey will undoubtedly remain members of NATO but their ties to other NATO states are likely to attenuate. So also are the alliances of the United States with Japan and Korea, its de facto alliance with Israel, and its security ties with Pakistan. Multicivilizational international organizations like ASEAN [Association of Southeast Asian Nations] could face increasing difficulty in maintaining their coherence. Countries such as India and Pakistan, partners of different superpowers during the Cold War, now redefine their interests and seek new associations reflecting the realities of cultural politics. African countries which were dependent on Western support designed to counter Soviet influence look increasingly to South Africa for leadership and succor.

Why should cultural commonality facilitate cooperation and cohesion among people and cultural differences promote cleavages and conflicts?...

The civilizational "us" and the extracivilizational "them" is a constant in human history. These differences in intra- and extracivilizational behavior stem from:

1. feelings of superiority (and occasionally inferiority) toward people who are perceived as being very different;
2. fear of and lack of trust in such people;
3. difficulty of communication with them as a result of differences in language and what is considered civil behavior;
4. lack of familiarity with the assumptions, motivations, social relationships and social practices of other people.

In today's world, improvements in transportation and communication have produced more frequent, more intense, more symmetrical, and more inclusive interactions among people of different civilizations. As a result their civilizational identities become increasingly salient. The French, Germans, Belgians and Dutch increasingly think of themselves as European. Middle East Muslims identify with and rally to the support of Bosnians and Chechens. Chinese throughout East Asia identify their interests with those of the mainland. Russians identify with and provide support to Serbs and other Orthodox peoples. These broader levels of civilizational identity mean deeper consciousness of civilizational differences and of the need to protect what distinguishes "us" from "them."...

Culture and Economic Cooperation

The early 1990s heard much talk of regionalism and the regionalization of world politics. Regional conflicts replaced the global conflict on the world's security agenda. Major powers, such as Russia, China, and the United States, as well as secondary powers, such as Sweden and Turkey, redefined their security interests in explicitly regional terms. Trade within regions expanded faster than trade between regions, and many foresaw the emergence of regional economic blocs, European, North American, East Asian, and perhaps others.

The term "regionalism," however, does not adequately describe what was happening. Regions are geographical not political or cultural entities. As with the Balkans or the Middle East, they may be riven by inter- and intracivilization conflicts. Regions are a basis for cooperation among states only to the extent that geography coincides with culture. Divorced from culture, propinquity does not yield commonality and may foster just the reverse. Military alliances and economic associations require cooperation among their members, cooperation depends on trust, and trust most easily springs from common values and culture. As a result, while age and purpose also play a role, the overall effectiveness of regional organizations generally varies inversely with the civilizational diversity of their membership. By and large, single civilization organizations do more things and are more successful than multicivilizational organizations. This is true of both political and security organizations, on the one hand, and economic organizations, on the other....

The relation of culture to regionalism is clearly evident with respect to economic integration. From least to most integrated, the four recognized levels of economic association among countries are:

1. free trade area;
2. customs union;
3. common market;
4. economic union.

The European Union has moved furthest down the integration road with a common market and many elements of an economic union. The relatively homogeneous Mercosur and the Andean Pact countries in 1994 were in the process of establishing customs unions. In Asia the multicivilizational ASEAN only in 1992 began to move toward development of a free trade area. Other multicivilizational economic organizations lagged even further behind. In 1995, with the marginal exception of NAFTA, no such organization had created a free trade area much less any more extensive form of economic integration.

In Western Europe and Latin America civilizational commonality fosters cooperation and regional organization. Western Europeans and Latin Americans know they have much in common. Five civilizations (six if Russia is included) exist in East Asia. East Asia, consequently, is the test case for developing meaningful organizations not rooted in common civilization. As of the early 1990s no security organization or multilateral military alliance, comparable to NATO, existed in East Asia. One multicivilizational regional organization, ASEAN, had been created in 1967 with one Sinic, one Buddhist, one Christian, and two Muslim member states, all of which confronted active challenges from communist insurgencies and potential ones from North Vietnam and China.

ASEAN is often cited as an example of an effective multicultural organization. It is, however, an example of the limits of such organizations. It is not a military alliance. While its members at times cooperate militarily on a bilateral basis, they are also all expanding their military budgets and engaged in military buildups, in striking contrast to the reductions West European and Latin American countries are making. On the economic front, ASEAN was from the beginning designed to achieve "economic cooperation rather than economic integration," and as a result regionalism has developed at a "modest pace," and even a free trade area is not contemplated until the twenty-first century. In 1978 ASEAN created the Post Ministerial Conference in which its foreign ministers could meet with those from its "dialogue partners"; the United States, Japan, Canada, Australia, New Zealand, South Korea, and the European Community. The PMC, however, has been primarily a forum for bilateral conversations and has been unable to deal with "any significant security issues." In 1993 ASEAN spawned a still larger arena, the ASEAN Regional Forum, which included its members and dialogue partners, plus Russia, China, Vietnam, Laos, and Papua New Guinea, As its name implies, however, this organization was a place for collective talk not collective action. Members used its first meeting in July 1994 to "air their views on regional security issues," but controversial issues were avoided because, as one official commented, if they were raised, "the participants concerned would begin attacking each other." ASEAN and its offspring evidence the limitations that inhere in multicivilizational regional organizations.

Meaningful East Asian regional organizations will emerge only if there is sufficient East Asian cultural commonality to sustain them. East Asian societies undoubtedly share some things in common which differentiate them from the West. Malaysia's prime minister, Mahathir Mohammad, argues that these commonalities provide a basis for association and has promoted formation of the East Asian Economic Caucus on these grounds. It would include the ASEAN countries, Myanmar, Taiwan, Hong Kong, South Korea, and, most important, China and Japan. Mahathir argues that the EAEC is rooted in a common culture. It should be thought of "not just as a geographical group, because it is in East Asia, but also as a cultural group. Although East Asians maybe Japanese or Koreans or Indonesians, culturally they have certain similarities.... Europeans flock together and Americans flock together. We Asians should flock together as well." Its purpose, as one of his associates said, is to enhance "regional trade among countries with commonalities here in Asia."...

Trade expansion follows economic integration, and during the 1980s and early 1990s intraregional trade became increasingly more important relative to interregional trade. Trade within the European Community constituted 50.6 percent of the community's total trade in 1980 and grew to 58.9 percent by 1989. Similar shifts toward regional trade occurred in North America and East Asia. In Latin America, the creation of Mercosur and the revival of the Andean Pact stimulated an upsurge in intra-Latin American trade in the early 1990s, with trade between Brazil and Argentina tripling and Colombia-Venezuela trade quadrupling between 1990 and 1993. In 1994 Brazil replaced the United States as Argentina's principal trading partner. The creation of NAFTA was similarly accompanied by a significant increase in Mexican-U.S. trade. Trade within East Asia also expanded more rapidly than extraregional trade, but its expansion was hampered by Japan's tendency to keep its markets closed. Trade among the countries of the Chinese cultural zone (ASEAN, Taiwan, Hong Kong, South Korea, and China), on the other hand, increased from less than 20 percent of their total in 1970 to almost 30 percent of their total in 1992, while Japan's share of their trade declined from 23 percent to 13 percent. In 1992 Chinese zone exports to other zone countries exceeded both their exports to the United States and their combined exports to Japan and the European Community.

As a society and civilization unique to itself, Japan faces difficulties developing its economic ties with East Asia and dealing with its economic differences with the United States and Europe. However strong the trade and investment links Japan may forge with other East Asian countries, its cultural differences from those countries, and particularly from their largely Chinese economic elites, preclude it from creating a Japanese-led regional economic grouping comparable to NAFTA or the European Union. At the same time, its cultural differences with the West exacerbate misunderstanding and antagonism in its economic relations with the United States and Europe. If, as seems to be the case, economic integration depends on cultural commonality, Japan as a culturally lone country could have an economically lonely future.

In the past the patterns of trade among nations have followed and paralleled the patterns of alliance among nations. In the emerging world, patterns of trade will be decisively influenced by the patterns of culture. Businessmen make deals with people they can understand and trust; states surrender sovereignty to international associations composed of like-minded states they understand and trust. The roots of economic cooperation are in cultural commonality.

The Structure of Civilizations

In the Cold War, countries related to the two super-powers as allies satellites clients, neutrals, and non-aligned. In the post–Cold War world, countries relate to civilizations as member states, core states, lone countries, cleft countries and torn Countries. Like tribes and nations, civilizations have political structures. A *member state* is a country fully identified culturally with one civilization as Egypt is with Arab-Islamic civilization and Italy is with European-Western civilization. A civilization may also include people who share in and identify with its culture, but who live in states dominated by members of another civilization. Civilizations usually have one or more places viewed by their members as the principal source or sources of the civilization's culture. These sources are often *loci* ted within the *core state* or states of the civilization, that is, its most powerful and culturally central state or states.

The number and role of core states vary from civilization to civilization and may change over time. Japanese civilization is virtually identical with the single Japanese core state. Sinic, Orthodox, and Hindu civilizations each have one overwhelmingly dominant core state, other member states, and people affiliated with their civilization in states dominated by people of a different civilization (overseas Chinese, "near abroad" Russians, Sri Lankan Tamils). Historically the West has usually had several core states; it has now two cores, the United States and a Franco-German core in Europe, with Britain an additional center of power adrift between them. Islam, Latin America, and Africa lack core states. This is in part due to the imperialism of the Western powers, which divided among themselves Africa, the Middle East, and in earlier centuries and less decisively, Latin America.

The absence of an Islamic core state poses major problems for both Muslim and non-Muslim societies.... With respect to Latin America, conceivably Spain could have become the core state of a Spanish-speaking or even Iberian civilization but its leaders consciously chose to become a member state in European civilization, while at the same time maintaining cultural links with its former colonies. Size, resources, population military and economic capacity, qualify Brazil to be the leader of Latin America, and conceivably it could become that. Brazil, however, is to Latin America what Iran is to Islam. Otherwise well-qualified to be a core state, subcivilizational differences (religious with Iran, linguistic with Brazil) make it difficult for it to assume that role. Latin America thus has several states, Brazil, Mexico, Venezuela, and Argentina, which cooperate in and compete for leadership. The Latin American situation is also complicated by the fact that Mexico has attempted to redefine itself from a Latin American to a North American identity and Chile and other states may follow. In the end, Latin American civilization could merge into and become one subvariant of a three-pronged Western civilization.

The ability of any potential core state to provide leadership to sub-Saharan Africa is limited by its division into French-speaking and English-speaking countries. For a while Côte d'Ivoire was the core state of French-speaking Africa. In considerable measure, however, the core state of French Africa has been France, which after independence maintained intimate economic, military, and political connections with its former colonies. The two African countries that are most qualified to become core states are both English-speaking. Size, resources, and location make Nigeria a potential core state, but its intercivilizational disunity, massive corruption, political instability, repressive government, and economic problems have severely limited its ability to perform this role, although it has done so on occasion. South Africa's peaceful and negotiated transition from apartheid, its industrial strength, its higher level of economic development compared to other African countries, its military capability, its natural resources, and its sophisticated black and white political leadership all mark South Africa as clearly the leader of southern Africa, probably the leader of English Africa, and possibly the leader of all sub-Saharan Africa.

A *lone country* lacks cultural commonality with other societies. Ethiopia, for example, is culturally isolated by its predominant language, Amharic, written in the Ethiopic script; its predominant religion, Coptic Orthodoxy; its imperial history; and its religious differentiation from the largely Muslim surrounding peoples. While Haiti's elite has traditionally relished its cultural ties to France, Haiti's Creole language, Voodoo religion, revolutionary slave origins, and brutal history combine to make it a lone country. "Every nation is unique," Sidney Mintz observed, but "Haiti is in a class by itself." As a result, during the Haitian crisis of 1994, Latin American countries did not view Haiti as a Latin American problem and were unwilling to accept Haitian refugees although they took in Cuban ones. "[I]n Latin America," as Panama's president-elect put it, "Haiti is not recognized as a Latin American country. Haitians speak a different language. They have different ethnic roots, a different culture. They are very different altogether."

Haiti is equally separate from the English-speaking black countries of the Caribbean. Haitians, one commentator observed, are "just as strange to someone from Grenada or Jamaica as they would be to someone from Iowa or Montana." Haiti, "the neighbor nobody wants," is truly a kinless country.

The most important lone country is Japan. No other country shares its distinct culture, and Japanese migrants are either not numerically significant in other countries or have assimilated to the cultures of those countries (e.g., Japanese-Americans) Japan's loneliness is further enhanced by the fact that its culture is highly particularistic and does not involve a potentially universal religion (Christianity, Islam) or ideology (liberalism, communism) that could be exported to other societies and thus establish a cultural connection with people in those societies.

Almost all countries are heterogeneous in that they include two or more ethnic, racial, and religious groups. Many countries are divided in that the differences and conflicts among these groups play an important role in the politics of the country. The depth of this division usually varies over time. Deep divisions within a country can lead to massive violence or threaten the country's existence. This latter threat and movements for autonomy or separation are most likely to arise when cultural differences coincide with differences in geographic location. If culture and geography do not coincide, they may be made to coincide through either genocide or forced migration.

Countries with distinct cultural groupings belonging to the same civilization may become deeply divided with separation either occurring (Czechoslovakia) or becoming a possibility (Canada). Deep divisions are, however, much more likely to emerge within a *cleft country* where large groups belong to different civilizations. Such divisions and the tensions that go with them often develop when a majority group belonging to one civilization attempts to define the state as its political instrument and to make its language, religion, and symbols those of the state, as Hindus, Sinhalese, and Muslims have attempted to do in India, Sri Lanka, and Malaysia.

Cleft countries that territorially bestride the fault lines between civilizations face particular problems maintaining their unity. In Sudan, civil war has gone on for decades between the Muslim north and the largely Christian south. The same civilizational division has bedeviled Nigerian politics for a similar length of time and stimulated one major war of secession plus coups, rioting, and other violence. In Tanzania, the Christian animist mainland and Arab Muslim Zanzibar have drifted apart and in many respects become two separate countries, with Zanzibar in 1992 secretly joining the Organization of the Islamic Conference and then being induced by Tanzania to withdraw from it the following year. The same Christian-Muslim division has generated tensions and conflicts in Kenya. On the horn of Africa, largely Christian Ethiopia and overwhelmingly Muslim Eritrea separated from each other in 1993. Ethiopia was left, however, with a substantial Muslim minority among its Oromo people. Other countries divided by civilizational fault lines include: India (Muslims and Hindus), Sri Lanka (Sinhalese Buddhists and Tamil Hindus), Malaysia and Singapore (Chinese and Malay Muslims), China (Han Chinese, Tibetan Buddhists, Turkic Muslims), Philippines (Christians and Muslims), and Indonesia (Muslims and Timorese Christians).

The divisive effect of civilizational fault lines has been most notable in those cleft countries held together during the Cold War by authoritarian communist regimes legitimated by Marxist-Leninist ideology. With the collapse of communism, culture replaced ideology as the magnet of attraction and repulsion, and Yugoslavia and the Soviet Union came apart and divided into new entities grouped along civilizational lines: Baltic (Protestant and Catholic), Orthodox, and Muslim republics in the former Soviet Union; Catholic Slovenia and Croatia; partially Muslim Bosnia-Herzegovina; and Orthodox Serbia-Montenegro and Macedonia in the former Yugoslavia. Where these successor entities still encompassed multicivilizational groups, second-stage divisions manifested themselves, Bosnia-Herzegovina was divided by war into Serbian, Muslim, and Croatian sections, and Serbs and Croats fought each other in Croatia. The sustained peaceful position of Albanian Muslim Kosovo within Slavic Orthodox Serbia is highly uncertain, and tensions rose between the Albanian Muslim minority and the Slavic Orthodox majority in Macedonia. Many former Soviet republics also bestride civilizational fault lines, in part because the Soviet government shaped boundaries so as to create divided republics, Russian Crimea going to Ukraine, Armenian Nagorno-Karabakh to Azerbaijan. Russia has several, relatively small, Muslim minorities, most notably in the North Caucasus and the Volga region. Estonia, Latvia, and Kazakhstan have substantial Russian minorities, also produced in considerable measure by Soviet policy. Ukraine is divided between the Uniate nationalist Ukrainian-speaking west and the Orthodox Russian-speaking east.

In a cleft country major groups from two or more civilizations say, in effect, "We are different peoples and belong in different places." The forces of repulsion drive them apart and they gravitate toward civilizational magnets in other societies. A *torn country*, in contrast, has a single predominant culture which places it in one civilization but its leaders want to shift it to another civilization. They say, in effect, "We are one people and belong together in one place but we want to change that place." Unlike the people of cleft countries, the people of torn countries agree on who they are but disagree on which civilization is properly their civilization. Typically, a significant portion of the leaders embrace a Kemalist strategy and decide their society should reject its non-Western culture and institutions, should join the West, and should both modernize and Westernize. Russia has been a torn country since Peter the Great, divided over the issue of whether it is part of Western civilization or is the core of a distinct Eurasian Orthodox civilization. Mustafa Kemal's country is, of course, the classic torn country which since the 1920s has been trying to modernize, to Westernize, and to become part of the West. After almost two centuries of Mexico defining itself as a Latin American country in opposition to the United States, its leaders in the 1980s made their country a torn country by attempting to redefine it as a North American society. Australia's leaders in the 1990s, in contrast, are trying to delink their country from the West and make it a part of Asia, thereby creating a torn-country-in-reverse. Torn countries are identifiable by two phenomena. Their leaders refer to them as a "bridge" between two cultures, and observers describe them as Janus-faced. "Russia looks West—and East"; "Turkey; East, West, which is best?"; "Australian nationalism: Divided loyalties"; are typical headlines highlighting torn country identity problems....

Civilizations and Order

In the emerging global politics, the core states of the major civilizations are supplanting the two Cold War superpowers as the principal poles of attraction and repulsion for other countries. These changes are most clearly visible with respect to Western, Orthodox, and Sinic civilizations. In these cases civilizational groupings are emerging involving core states, member states, culturally similar minority populations in adjoining states, and, more controversially, people of other cultures in neighboring states. States in these civilizational blocs often tend to be distributed in concentric circles around the core state or states, reflecting their degree of identification with and integration into that bloc. Lacking a recognized core state, Islam is intensifying its common consciousness but so far has developed only a rudimentary common political structure.

Countries tend to bandwagon with countries of similar culture and to balance against countries with which they lack cultural commonality. This is particularly true with respect to the core states. Their power attracts those who are culturally similar and repels those who are culturally different. For security reasons core states may attempt to incorporate or to dominate some peoples of other civilizations, who, in turn, attempt to resist or to escape such control (China vs. Tibetans and Uighurs; Russia vs. Tatars, Chechens, Central Asian Muslims). Historical relationships and balance of power considerations also lead some countries to resist the influence of their core state. Both Georgia and Russia are Orthodox countries, but the Georgians historically have resisted Russian domination and close association with Russia. Vietnam and China are both Confucian countries, yet a comparable pattern of historical enmity has existed between them. Over time, however, cultural commonality and development of a broader and stronger civilizational consciousness could bring these countries together, as Western European countries have come together.

During the Cold War, what order there was the product of superpower dominance of their two blocs and superpower influence in the Third World. In the emerging world, global power is obsolete, global community a distant dream. No country, including the United States, has significant global security interests. The components of order in today's more complex and heterogeneous world are found within and between civilizations. The world will be ordered on the basis of civilizations or not at all. In this world the core states of civilizations are sources of order within civilizations and, through negotiations with other core states, between civilizations.

A world in which core states play a leading or dominating role is a spheres-of-influence world. But it is also a world in which the exercise of influence by the core state is tempered and moderated by the common culture it shares with member states of its civilization. Cultural commonality legitimates the leadership and order-imposing role of the core state for both member states and for the external powers and institutions. It is thus futile to do as U.N. Secretary General Boutros Boutros-Ghali did in 1994 and promulgate a rule of "sphere of influence keeping" that no more than one-third of the U.N. peacekeeping force should be provided by the dominant regional power. Such a requirement defies the geopolitical reality that in any given region where there is a dominant state peace can be achieved and maintained only through the leadership of that state. The United Nations is no alternative to regional power, and regional power becomes responsible and legitimate when exercised by core states in relation to other members of their civilization.

A core state can perform its ordering function because member states perceive it as cultural kin. A civilization is an extended family and, like older members of a family, core states provide their relatives with both support and discipline. In the absence of that kinship, the ability of a more powerful state to resolve conflicts in and impose order on its region is limited. Pakistan, Bangladesh, and even Sri Lanka will not accept India as the order provider in South Asia and no other East Asian state will accept Japan in that role in East Asia.

When civilizations lack core states the problems of creating order within civilizations or negotiating order between civilizations become more difficult. The absence of an Islamic core state which could legitimately and authoritatively relate to the Bosnians, as Russia did to the Serbs and Germany to the Croats, impelled the United States to attempt that role. Its ineffectiveness in doing so derived from the lack of American strategic interest in where state boundaries were drawn in the former Yugoslavia, the absence of any cultural connection between the United States and Bosnia, and European opposition to the creation of a Muslim state in Europe. The absence of core states in both Africa and the Arab world has greatly complicated efforts to resolve the ongoing civil war in Sudan. Where core states exist, on the other hand, they are the central elements of the new international order based on civilizations.

Bounding the West

During the Cold War the United States was at the center of a large, diverse, multicivilizational grouping of countries who shared the goal of preventing further expansion by the Soviet Union. This grouping, variously known as the "Free World," the "West," or the "Allies," included many but not all Western societies, Turkey, Greece, Japan, Korea, the Philippines, Israel, and, more loosely, other countries such as Taiwan, Thailand, and Pakistan. It was opposed by a grouping of countries only slightly less heterogeneous, which included all the Orthodox countries except Greece, several countries that were historically Western, Vietnam, Cuba, to a lesser degree India, and at times one or more African countries. With the

end of the Cold War these multicivilizational, cross-cultural grouping fragmented. The dissolution of the Soviet system, particularly the Warsaw Pact, was dramatic. More slowly but similarly the multicivilizational "Free World" of the Cold War is being reconfigured into a new grouping more or less coextensive with Western civilization. A bounding process is underway involving the definition of the membership of Western international organizations.

The core states of the European Union, France and Germany, are circled first by an inner grouping of Belgium, Netherlands, and Luxembourg, all of which have agreed to eliminate all barriers to the transit of goods and persons; then other member countries such as Italy, Spain, Portugal, Denmark, Britain, Ireland, and Greece; states which became members in 1995 (Austria, Finland, Sweden); and those countries which as of that date were associate members (Poland, Hungary, Czech Republic, Slovakia, Bulgaria, and Romania). Reflecting this reality, in the fall of 1994 both the governing party in Germany and top French officials advanced proposals for a differentiated Union. The German plan proposed that the "hard core" consist of the original members minus Italy and that "Germany and France form the core of the hard core." The hard core countries would rapidly attempt to establish a monetary union and to integrate their foreign and defense policies. Almost simultaneously French Prime Minister Edouard Balladur suggested a three-tier Union with the five pro-integrationist states forming the core, the other current member states forming a second circle, and the new states on the way to becoming members constituting an outer circle. Subsequently French Foreign Minister Alain Juppé elaborated this concept proposing "an outer circle of 'partner' states, including Eastern and Central Europe; a middle circle of member states that would be required to accept common disciplines in certain fields (single market, customs union, etc.); and several inner circles of 'reinforced solidarities' incorporating those willing and able to move faster than others in such areas as defense, monetary integration, foreign policy and so on." Other political leaders proposed other types of arrangements, all of which, however, involved an inner grouping of more closely associated states and then outer groupings of states less fully integrated with the core state until the line is reached separating members from nonmembers.

Establishing that line in Europe has been one of the principal challenges confronting the West in the post–Cold War world. During the Cold War Europe as a whole did not exist. With the collapse of communism, however, it became necessary to confront and answer the question: What is Europe? Europe's boundaries on the north, west, and south are delimited by substantial bodies of water, which to the south coincide with clear differences in culture. But where is Europe's eastern boundary? Who should be thought of as European and hence as potential members of the European Union, NATO, and comparable organizations?

The most compelling and pervasive answer to these questions is provided by the great historical line that has existed for centuries separating Western Christian peoples from Muslim and Orthodox peoples. This line dates back to the division of the Roman Empire in the fourth century and to the creation of the Holy Roman Empire in the tenth century. It has been in roughly its current place for at least five hundred years. Beginning in the north, it runs along what are now the borders between Finland and Russia and the Baltic states (Estonia, Latvia, Lithuania) and Russia, through western Belarus, through Ukraine separating the Uniate west from the Orthodox east, through Romania between Transylvania with its Catholic Hungarian population and the rest of the country, and through the former Yugoslavia along the border separating Slovenia and Croatia from the other republics. In the Balkans, of course, this line coincides with the historical division between the Austro-Hungarian and Ottoman empires. It is the cultural border of Europe, and in the post–Cold War world it is also the political and economic border of Europe and the West.

The civilizational paradigm thus provides a clear-cut and compelling answer to the question confronting West Europeans: Where does Europe end? Europe ends where Western Christianity ends and Islam and Orthodoxy begin. This is the answer which West Europeans want to hear, which they overwhelmingly support sotto voce, and which various intellectuals and political leaders have explicitly endorsed. It is necessary, as Michael Howard argued, to recognize the distinction, blurred during the Soviet years, between Central Europe or *Mitteleuropa* and Eastern Europe proper. Central Europe includes "those lands which once formed part of Western Christendom; the old lands of the Hapsburg Empire, Austria, Hungary and Czechoslovakia, together with Poland and the eastern marches of Germany. The term 'Eastern Europe' should be reserved for those regions which developed under the aegis of the Orthodox Church: the Black Sea communities of Bulgaria and Romania which only emerged from Ottoman domination in the nineteenth century, and the 'European' parts of

the Soviet Union." Western Europe's first task, he argued, must "be to reabsorb the peoples of Central Europe into our cultural and economic community where they properly belong: to reknit the ties between London Paris, Rome, Munich, and Leipzig, Warsaw, Prague and Budapest." A "new fault line" is emerging, Pierre Behar commented two years later, "a basically cultural divide between a Europe marked by western Christianity (Roman Catholic or Protestant), on the one hand, and a Europe marked by eastern Christianity and Islamic traditions, on the other." A leading Finn similarly saw the crucial division in Europe replacing the Iron Curtain as "the ancient cultural fault line between East and West" which places "the lands of the former Austro-Hungarian empire as well as Poland and the Baltic states" within the Europe of the West and the other East European and Balkan countries outside it. This was, a prominent Englishman agreed, the "great religious divide...between the Eastern and Western churches: broadly speaking, between those peoples who received their Christianity from Rome directly or through Celtic or German intermediaries, and those in the East and Southeast to whom it came through Constantinople (Byzantium)."

People in Central Europe also emphasize the significance of this dividing line. The countries that have made significant progress in divesting themselves of the Communist legacies and moving toward democratic politics and market economies are separated from those which have not by "the line dividing Catholicism and Protestantism, on the one hand, from Orthodoxy, on the other." Centuries ago, the president of Lithuania argued, Lithuanians had to choose between "two civilizations" and "opted for the Latin world, converted to Roman Catholicism and chose a form of state organization founded on law." In similar terms, Poles say they have been part of the West since their choice in the tenth century of Latin Christianity against Byzantium. People from Eastern European Orthodox countries, in contrast, view with ambivalence the new emphasis on this cultural fault line. Bulgarians and Romanians see the great advantages of being part of the West and being incorporated into its institutions; but they also identify with their own Orthodox tradition and, on the part of the Bulgarians, their historically close association with Russia and Byzantium.

The identification of Europe with Western Christendom provides a clear criterion for the admission of new members to Western organizations. The European Union is the West's primary entity in Europe and the expansion of its membership resumed in 1994 with the admission of culturally Western Austria, Finland, and Sweden. In the spring of 1994 the Union provisionally decided to exclude from membership all former Soviet republics except the Baltic states. It also signed "association agreements" with the four Central European states (Poland, Hungary, Czech Republic, and Slovakia) and two Eastern European ones (Romania, Bulgaria). None of these states, however, is likely to become a full member of the EU until sometime in the twenty-first century, and the Central European states will undoubtedly achieve that status before Romania and Bulgaria, if, indeed, the latter ever do. Meanwhile eventual membership for the Baltic states and Slovenia looks promising, while the applications of Muslim Turkey, too-small Malta, and Orthodox Cyprus were still pending in 1995. In the expansion of EU membership, preference clearly goes to those states which are culturally Western and which also tend to be economically more developed. If this criterion were applied, the Visegrad states (Poland, Czech Republic, Slovakia, Hungary), the Baltic republics, Slovenia, Croatia, and Malta would eventually become EU members and the Union would be coextensive with Western civilization as it has historically existed in Europe.

The logic of civilizations dictates a similar outcome concerning the expansion of NATO. The Cold War began with the extension of Soviet political and military control into Central Europe. The United States and Western European countries formed NATO to deter and, if necessary, defeat further Soviet aggression. In the post–Cold War world, NATO is the security organization of Western civilization. With the Cold War over, NATO has one central and compelling purpose: to insure that it remains over by preventing the reimposition of Russian political and military control in Central Europe. As the West's security organization NATO is appropriately open to membership by Western countries which wish to join and which meet basic requirements in terms of military competence, political democracy, and civilian control of the military.

American policy toward post–Cold War European security arrangements initially embodied a more universalistic approach, embodied in the Partnership for Peace, which would be open generally to European and, indeed, Eurasian countries. This approach also emphasized the role of the Organization on Security and Cooperation in Europe. It was reflected in the remarks of President Clinton when he visited Europe in January 1994: "Freedom's boundaries now should be defined by new behavior, not by old history. I say to all…who would draw

a new line in Europe; we should not foreclose the possibility of the best future for Europe—democracy everywhere, market economies everywhere, countries cooperating for mutual security everywhere. We must guard against a lesser outcome." A year later, however, the administration had come to recognize the significance of boundaries defined by "old history" and had come to accept a "lesser outcome" reflecting the realities of civilizational differences. The administration moved actively to develop the criteria and a schedule for the expansion of NATO membership, first to Poland, Hungary, the Czech Republic, and Slovakia, then to Slovenia, and later probably to the Baltic republics.

Russia vigorously opposed any NATO expansion, with those Russians who were presumably more liberal and pro-Western arguing that expansion would greatly strengthen nationalist and anti-Western political forces in Russia. NATO expansion limited to countries historically part of Western Christendom, however, also guarantees to Russia that it would exclude Serbia, Bulgaria, Romania, Moldova, Belarus, and Ukraine as long as Ukraine remained united. NATO expansion limited to Western states would also underline Russia's role as the core state of a separate, Orthodox civilization, and hence a country which should be responsible for order within and along the boundaries of Orthodoxy.

The usefulness of differentiating among countries in terms of civilization is manifest with respect to the Baltic republics. They are the only former Soviet republics which are clearly Western in terms of their history, culture, and religion, and their fate has consistently been a major concern of the West. The United States never formally recognized their incorporation into the Soviet Union, supported their move to independence as the Soviet Union was collapsing, and insisted that the Russians adhere to the agreed-on schedule for the removal of their troops from the republics. The message to the Russians has been that they must recognize that the Baltics are outside whatever sphere of influence they may wish to establish with respect to other former Soviet republics. This achievement by the Clinton administration was, as Sweden's prime minister said, "one of its most important contributions to European security and stability" and helped Russian democrats by establishing that any revanchist designs by extreme Russian nationalists were futile in the face of the explicit Western commitment to the republics.

While much attention has been devoted to the expansion of the European Union and NATO, the cultural reconfiguration of these organizations also raises the issue of their possible contraction. One non-Western country, Greece, is a member of both organizations, and another, Turkey, is a member of NATO and an applicant for Union membership. These relationships were products of the Cold War. Do they have any place in the post–Cold War world of civilizations?

Turkey's full membership in the European Union is problematic and its membership in NATO has been attacked by the Welfare Party. Turkey is, however, likely to remain in NATO unless the Welfare Party scores a resounding electoral victory or Turkey otherwise consciously rejects its Ataturk heritage and redefines itself as a leader of Islam. This is conceivable and might be desirable for Turkey but also is unlikely in the near future. Whatever its role in NATO, Turkey will increasingly pursue its own distinctive interests with respect to the Balkans, the Arab world, and Central Asia.

Greece is not part of Western civilization, but it was the home of Classical civilization which was an important source of Western civilization. In their opposition to the Turks, Greeks historically have considered themselves spearcarriers of Christianity. Unlike Serbs, Romanians, or Bulgarians, their history has been intimately entwined with that of the West. Yet Greece is also an anomaly, the Orthodox outsider in Western organizations. It has never been an easy member of either the EU or NATO and has had difficulty adapting itself to the principles and mores of both. From the mid-1960s to the mid-1970s it was ruled by a military junta, and could not join the European Community until it shifted to democracy. Its leaders often seemed to go out of their way to deviate from Western norms and to antagonize Western governments. It was poorer than other Community and NATO members and often pursued economic policies that seemed to flout the standards prevailing in Brussels. Its behavior as president of the EU's Council in 1994 exasperated other members, and Western European officials privately label its membership a mistake.

In the post–Cold War world, Greece's policies have increasingly deviated from those of the West. Its blockade of Macedonia was strenuously opposed by Western governments and resulted in the European Commission seeking an injunction against Greece in the European Court of Justice. With respect to the conflicts in the former Yugoslavia, Greece separated itself from the policies pursued by the principal Western powers, actively supported the Serbs, and blatantly violated the U.N. sanctions levied against them. With

the end of the Soviet Union and the communist threat, Greece has mutual interests with Russia in opposition to their common enemy, Turkey. It has permitted Russia to establish a significant presence in Greek Cyprus, and as a result of "their shared Eastern Orthodox religion," the Greek Cypriots have welcomed both Russians and Serbs to the island. In 1995 some two thousand Russian-owned businesses were operating in Cyprus; Russian and Serbo-Croatian newspapers were published there; and the Greek Cypriot government was purchasing major supplies of arms from Russia. Greece also explored with Russia the possibility of bringing oil from the Caucasus and Central Asia to the Mediterranean through a Bulgarian-Greek pipeline bypassing Turkey and other Muslim countries. Overall Greek foreign policies have assumed a heavily Orthodox orientation. Greece will undoubtedly remain a formal member of NATO and the European Union. As the process of cultural reconfiguration intensifies, however, those memberships also undoubtedly will become more tenuous, less meaningful, and more difficult for the parties involved. The Cold War antagonist of the Soviet Union is evolving into the post–Cold War ally of Russia....

The West in the World

A world in which cultural identities—ethnic, national, religious, civilizational—are central, and cultural affinities and differences shape the alliances, antagonisms, and policies of states has three broad implications for the West generally and for the United States in particular.

First, statesmen can constructively alter reality only if they recognize and understand it. The emerging politics of culture, the rising power of non-Western civilizations, and the increasing cultural assertiveness of these societies have been widely recognized in the non-Western world. European leaders have pointed to the cultural forces drawing people together and driving them apart. American elites, in contrast, have been slow to accept and to come to grips with these emerging realities. The Bush and Clinton administrations supported the unity of the multi-civilizational Soviet Union, Yugoslavia, Bosnia, and Russia, in vain efforts to halt the powerful ethnic and cultural forces pushing for disunion. They promoted multicivilizational economic integration plans which are either meaningless, as with APEC, or involve major unanticipated economic and political costs, as with NAFTA and Mexico. They attempted to develop close relationships with the core states of other civilizations in the form of a "global partnership" with

Russia or "constructive engagement" with China, in the face of the natural conflicts of interest between the United States and those countries. At the same time, the Clinton administration failed to involve Russia wholeheartedly in the search for peace in Bosnia, despite Russia's major interest in that war as Orthodoxy's core state. Pursuing the chimera of a multi-civilizational country the Clinton administration denied self-determination to the Serbian and Croatian minorities and helped to bring into being a Balkan one-party Islamist partner of Iran. In similar fashion the U.S. government also supported the subjection of Muslims to Orthodox rule, maintaining that "Without question Chechnya is part of the Russian Federation."

Although Europeans is universally acknowledge the fundamental significance of the dividing line between Western Christendom, on the one hand, and Orthodoxy and Islam, on the other, the United States, its secretary of state said, would "not recognize any fundamental divide among the Catholic, Orthodox, and Islamic parts of Europe." Those who do not recognize fundamental divides, however, are doomed to be frustrated by them. The Clinton administration initially appeared oblivious to the shifting balance of power between the United States and East Asian; societies and hence time and again proclaimed goals with respect to trade human rights, nuclear proliferation, and other issues which it was incapable of realizing. Overall the U.S. government has had extraordinary difficulty adapting to an era in which global politics is shaped by cultural and civilizational tides.

Second, American, foreign policy thinking also suffered from a reluctance to abandon, alter, or at times even reconsider policies adapted to meet Cold War needs. With some this took the form of still seeing a resurrected Soviet Union as a potential threat. More generally people tended to sanctify Cold War alliances and arms control agreements. NATO must be maintained as it was in the Cold War. The Japanese-American Security Treaty is central to East Asian security. The ABM treaty is inviolate. The CFE treaty must be observed. Obviously none of these or other Cold War legacies should be lightly cast aside. Neither, however, is it necessarily in the interests of the United States or the West for them to be continued in their Cold War form. The realities of a multicivilizational world suggest that NATO should be expanded to include other Western societies that wish to join and should recognize the essential meaninglessness of having as members two states each of which is the other's worst enemy and both of which lack cultural

affinity with the other members. An ABM treaty designed to meet the Cold War need to insure the mutual vulnerability of Soviet and American societies and thus to deter Soviet-American nuclear war may well obstruct the ability of the United States and other societies to protect themselves against unpredictable nuclear threats or attacks by terrorist movements and irrational dictators. The U.S.-Japan security treaty helped deter Soviet aggression against Japan. What purpose is it meant to serve in the post–Cold War era? To contain and deter China? To slow Japanese accommodation with a rising China? To prevent further Japanese militarization? Increasingly doubts are being raised in Japan about the American military presence there and in the United States about the need for an unreciprocated commitment to defend Japan. The Conventional Forces in Europe agreement was designed to moderate the NATO-Warsaw Pact confrontation in Central Europe, which has disappeared. The principal impact of the agreement now is to create difficulties for Russia in dealing with what it perceives to be security threats from Muslim peoples to its south.

Third, cultural and civilizational diversity challenges the Western and particularly American belief in the universal relevance of Western culture. This belief is expressed both descriptively and normatively. Descriptively it holds that peoples in all societies want to adopt Western values, institutions, and practices. If they seem not to have that desire and to be committed to their own traditional cultures, they are victims of a "false consciousness" comparable to that which Marxists found among proletarians who supported capitalism. Normatively the Western universalist belief posits that people throughout the world should embrace Western values, institutions, and culture because they embody the highest, most enlightened, most liberal, most rational, most modern, and most civilized thinking of humankind.

In the emerging world of ethnic conflict and civilizational clash, Western belief in the universality of Western culture suffers three problems: it is false; it is immoral; and it is dangerous. That it is false has been the central thesis of this book, a thesis well summed up by Michael Howard: the "common Western assumption that cultural diversity is a historical curiosity being rapidly eroded by the growth of a common, western-oriented, Anglophone world-culture, shaping our basic values...is simply not true." A reader not by now convinced of the wisdom of Sir Michael's remark exists in a world far removed from that described in this book.

The belief that non-Western peoples should adopt Western values, institutions, and culture is immoral because of what would be necessary to bring it about. The almost-universal reach of European power in the late nineteenth century and the global dominance of the United States in the late twentieth century spread much of Western civilization across the world. European globalism, however, is no more. American hegemony is receding if only because it is no longer needed to protect the United States against a Cold War–style Soviet military threat. Culture, as we have argued, follows power. If non-Western societies are once again to be shaped by Western culture, it will happen only as a result of the expansion, deployment, and impact of Western power. Imperialism is the necessary logical consequence of universalism. In addition, as a maturing civilization, the West no longer has the economic or demographic dynamism required to impose its will on other societies and any effort to do so is also contrary to the Western values of self-determination and democracy. As Asian and Muslim civilizations begin more and more to assert the universal relevance of their cultures, Westerners will come to appreciate more and more the connection between universalism and imperialism.

Western universalism is dangerous to the world because it could lead to a major intercivilizational war between core states and it is dangerous to the West because it could lead to defeat of the West. With the collapse of the Soviet Union, Westerners; see their civilization in a position of unparalleled dominance, while at the same time weaker Asian, Muslim, and other societies are beginning to gain strength....

The Commonalities of Civilization

Some Americans have promoted multiculturalism at home; some have promoted universalism abroad; and some have done both. Multiculturalism at home threatens the United States and the West; universalism abroad threatens the West and the world. Both deny the uniqueness of Western culture. The global monoculturalists want to make the world like America. The domestic mulitculturalists want to make America like the world. A multicultural America is impossible because a non-Western America is not American. A multicultural world is unavoidable because global empire is impossible. The preservation of the United States and the West requires the renewal of Western identity. The security of the world requires acceptance of global multiculturality.

Does the vacuousness of Western universalism and the reality of global cultural diversity lead inevitably and irrevocably to moral and cultural relativism? If universalism legitimates imperialism, does relativism legitimate repression? Once again, the answer to these questions is yes and no. Cultures are relative; morality is absolute. Cultures, as Michael Walzer has argued, are "thick"; they prescribe institutions and behavior patterns to guide humans in the paths which are right in a particular society. Above, beyond, and growing out of this maximalist morality, however, is a "thin" minimalist morality that embodies "reiterated features of particular thick or maximal moralities." Minimal moral concepts of truth and justice are found in all thick moralities and cannot be divorced from them. There are also minimal moral "negative injunctions, most likely, rules against murder, deceit, torture, oppression, and tyranny." What people have in common is "more the sense of a common enemy [or evil] than the commitment to a common culture." Human society is "universal because it is human, particular because it is a society." At times we march with others; mostly we march alone. Yet a "thin" minimal morality does derive from the common human condition, and "universal dispositions" are found in all cultures. Instead of promoting the supposedly universal features of one civilization, the requisites for cultural coexistence demand a search for what is common to most civilizations. In a multicivilizational world, the constructive course is to renounce universalism, accept diversity, and seek commonalities....

Modernization has generally enhanced the material level of Civilization throughout the world. But has it also enhanced the moral and cultural dimensions of Civilization? In some respects this appears to be the case. Slavery torture, vicious abuse of individuals, have become less and less acceptable in the contemporary world. Is this, however, simply the result of the impact of Western civilization other cultures and hence will a moral reversion occur as Western power declines? Much evidence exists in the 1990s for the relevance of the "sheer chaos" paradigm of world affairs: a global breakdown of law and order, failed states and increasing anarchy in many parts of the world a global crime wave, transnational mafias and drug cartels, increasing drug addiction in many societies, a general weakening of the family, a decline in trust and social solidarity in many countries, ethnic, religious, and civilizational violence and rule by the gun prevalent in much of the world. In city after city—Moscow, Rio de Janeiro, Bangkok, Shanghai, London, Rome, Warsaw, Tokyo, Johannesburg, Delhi, Karachi, Cairo, Bogota, Washington—crime seems to be soaring and basic elements of Civilization fading away. People speak of a global crisis in governance. The rise of transnational corporations producing economic goods is increasingly matched by the rise of transnational criminal mafias, drug cartels, and terrorist gangs violently assaulting Civilization. Law and order is the first prerequisite of Civilization and in much of the world—Africa Latin America, the former Soviet Union, South Asia, the Middle East—it appears to be evaporating while also under serious assault in China, Japan, and the West. On a worldwide basis Civilization seems in many respects to be yielding to barbarism, generating the image of an unprecedented phenomenon, a global Dark Ages, possibly descending on humanity.

In the 1950s Lester Pearson warned that humans were moving into "an age when different civilizations will have to learn to live side by side in peaceful interchange, learning from each other, studying each other's history and ideals and art and culture, mutually enriching each others' lives. The alternative, in this overcrowded little world, is misunderstanding, tension, clash, and catastrophe." The futures of both peace and Civilization depend upon understanding and cooperation among the political, spiritual, and intellectual leaders of the world's major civilizations. In the clash of civilizations, Europe and America will hang together or hang separately. In the greater clash, the global *real* clash, between Civilization and barbarism, the world's great civilizations, with their rich accomplishments in religion, art, literature, philosophy, science technology morality, and compassion, will also hang together or hang separately. In the emerging era, clashes of civilizations are the greatest threat to world peace, and an international order based on civilizations is the surest safeguard against world war.

AFTERWORD

"History is indeed an argument without end."

—Pieter Geyl

I n 1877, the United States was a nascent industrial capitalist nation with deep class divisions. Just over a decade removed from a devastating civil war, it still bore the scars of sectional strife. Its racial landscape was fractured, as African Americans struggled desperately to rescue newly won constitutional rights from a vengeful white counterrevolution. Half of its population—women—did not have the right to vote. White Protestants wielded a preponderance of political, economic, and social power. Outside the Western Hemisphere, its governmental influence, military weight, and diplomatic presence were modest and limited.

The better part of a century-and-a-half later, what would a hypothetical visitor from 1877 see? By the twenty-first century, having passed through an industrial stage during which it was the world's preeminent producer of manufactured goods, the United States had entered a "postindustrial" period featuring services, media, technology, and information as new commodities and exports. America remained a capitalist nation with a market-oriented economy, but our visitor from 1877 would be impressed at the extent to which the federal government was involved in the daily lives of Americans. An 1877-era American, of course, would have been unaware of the New Deal. His contacts with the national government were in all likelihood confined to the United States Post Office, and he could only guess at the prospective impact of the recently ratified Fourteenth (1868) and Fifteenth (1870) Amendments to the Constitution establishing federal citizenship and voting rights. Transported to the twenty-first-century United States, he would probably believe, with much justification, that he was visiting another country.

Moreover, our time traveler would marvel at the extent to which the United States had become a middle-class nation—over half of Americans so classified themselves in a 2008 survey—and at the diminution in raw class tensions that accompanied this demographic shift.[1] Extremes of wealth and poverty still existed in the United States, of course, and labor and management still faced off over wages, hours, and benefits—but nothing approached the Great Upheaval of 1877, when the nation teetered on the brink of a violent workers' revolution. Early twenty-first-century Americans appeared much closer to fulfilling the founding fathers' vision of a broad-based society of small and moderate property holders than their 1877 counterparts.

They were also, of course, much closer to fulfilling the ideals of the Declaration of Independence. In 1877 the promise of racial justice embodied in the Fourteenth and Fifteenth Amendments, the 1875 Civil Rights Act outlawing discrimination in public accommodations, and the Civil War itself was unrealized, a casualty of white supremacist Southern "Redeemers" and their Northern abettors. But thanks to the civil rights movement and its legislative triumphs—the Civil Rights (1964) and Voting Rights (1965) Acts as well as the Fair Housing Act (1968) and the Americans with Disabilities Act (1990)—Americans enjoyed more political equality in the twenty-first century United States. In addition, members of minority groups had joined with millions of whites to elect the nation's first black president, a development that our 1870s-era guest would have found mind-boggling.

The sectional bitterness that had played such a major role in American society and politics in 1877 had also dissipated by the early twenty-first century. The same civil rights revolution that had largely fulfilled Du Bois' dream of merging the "double selves" of America's black population (see Chapter 3) helped reintegrate the South into the nation's sociocultural mainstream. While the twenty-first-century South remained a distinct American region, it had absorbed a national system of mores and values. For better or worse—and to some contemporary observers disturbed at the trend toward standardized tastes and practices, it was the latter—Southerners consumed the same Big Macs, shopped at the same Wal-Marts, and watched the same versions of *Dancing With the Stars* as other Americans. The South of 1877, seething over military defeat and belligerently protective of a separate and unique "way of life," was no more.

Gone as well was the political, social, and economic disenfranchisement of American women, yet another development that would shock our emissary from 1877. That women had exercised the right to vote since 1920 would be surprise enough, but their active participation in virtually every aspect of American society—as professionals, in business, in media, as elected officials—would truly give this unreconstructed Victorian pause, as his certainties about the "natural" and "proper" role of the American woman crumbled before his eyes.

The ethnocultural diversity of the twenty-first-century United States would also startle our observer from the 1870s. Between 1880 and 1924, some twenty-five million men, women, and children, the vast majority non-Protestants, entered the country, vastly altering the American cultural landscape. Then, between 1965 and the first decade of the twenty-first century, another movement of immigrants, primarily from Latin America, Asia, and Africa, came to the United States, some under authority of the Immigration and Nationality Act of 1965, others without legal sanction. By 2007, there were over thirty-eight million foreign-born individuals in the United States.[2] Taken together, these two great in-migrations transformed the meaning of "American" identity. They produced a nation with a diverse array of ethnic affiliations, religious practices, and racial allegiances, one that would be so unrecognizable to our 1877 time traveler that he might again wonder if he was in America at all.

Finally, our amazed nineteenth-century tourist would behold a twenty-first-century America that, after fighting and winning two world wars as well as a Cold War against its main ideological rival, had not only engaged with the world community but also stood astride it as its preeminent military, geopolitical, economic, and cultural power. Our visitor had been absent for the twentieth century, which was, in the famous words of *Time* publisher Henry Luce, the "American Century." Here, in a new century, was its inheritance.

We now return our dazed historical guest to his own era, having confirmed what we knew intuitively: The United States is a vastly different place in the early twentieth century than it was in 1877. Perhaps, however, not as different as we think. Throughout this volume, the same basic questions have traveled across time, circulating among our historical subjects. Circumstances, conditions, and, of course, personalities have differed. But our American conversations over the years have been much about the same things. What, for example, does it mean to be "equal" in America? Our striking railroad worker from 1877 and the 1920s individualist Herbert Hoover spoke to this question from different eras. W. E. B. Du Bois, in the 1900s, and Malcolm X, in the 1960s, did the same. What is American "freedom"? Charles Kikuchi and Ronald Reagan never met, nor did Crystal Eastman and Jo Freeman, but all sought to capture its meaning in their own times and places.

And so it was, and is, with the other great questions of the American conversation. What should the role of the federal government be in American political, social, and economic life? Is America a "capitalist" nation? A "Christian" nation? A nation of individuals or groups? What are America's world obligations? What are the limits of its powers? Who is an "American"? What does being an "American" mean? What is "American" identity? History has been described as "an argument without end," and between 1877 and the dawn of the twenty-first century the American conversation was this and more, passing across the years, unceasing and unresolved.[3] We will bequeath it to our children and to those who come after them. It is made up of insistent questions that vex and challenge us no matter when or where we live. Try as we may, we will never answer them definitively. Does this mean we have failed? Quite the contrary. America—as an idea, a place, a nation, a culture, and a symbol—is never complete, never at rest, and never merely the sum of its parts. Our American conversations—our arguments without end—offer their own rewards, if not in absolute certainty, then in understanding, insight, and humanity. "America" remains maddeningly elusive, but we must never stop pursuing it. May your American conversations be without end.

Endnotes

1. http://pewsocialtrends.org/assets/pdf/MC-Middle-class-report.pdf
2. Demetrious G. Papademetriou and Aaron Terrazas, "Immigrants in the United States and the Current Economic Crisis," Migration Policy Institute, April 2009, http://www.migrationinformation.org/feature/display.cfm?id=723
3. Pieter Geyl, *Napoleon: For and Against* (New Haven: Yale University Press, 1949), 16.

FURTHER READING

CHAPTER 1

Bellesiles, Michael A. *1877: America's Year of Living Violently*. New York: New Press, 2010.

Bruce, Robert V. *1877: Year of Violence*. Chicago: Ivan R. Dee, Inc., 1959.

Foner, Philip Sheldon. *The Great Labor Uprising of 1877*. New York: Pathfinder Press, 1977.

Stowell, David O., ed. *The Great Strikes of 1877*. Urbana: University of Illinois Press, 2008.

CHAPTER 2

Avrich, Paul. *The Haymarket Tragedy*. Princeton, NJ: Princeton University Press, 1984.

Bridge, James Howard. *The Inside History of the Carnegie Steel Company: A Romance of Millions*. Pittsburgh: University of Pittsburgh Press, 1991.

Carnegie, Andrew. *The Gospel of Wealth and Other Timely Essays*. Garden City, NY: Doubleday, 1933.

Green, James. *Death in the Haymarket: A Story of Chicago, the First Labor Movement, and the Bombing that Divided Gilded Age America*. New York: Pantheon Books, 2006.

Krass, Peter. *Carnegie*. New York: John Wiley & Son, 2002.

Krause, Paul. *The Battle for Homestead, 1880–1892: Politics, Culture, and Steel*. Pittsburgh: University of Pittsburgh Press, 1992.

Livesay, Harold. *Andrew Carnegie and the Rise of Big Business*. Edited by Oscar Handlin. Boston: Little, Brown, 1975.

Nasaw, David. *Andrew Carnegie*. New York: Penguin Press, 2006.

Serrin, William. *Homestead: the Glory and Tragedy of an American Steel Town*. New York: Vintage Books, 1993.

CHAPTER 3

Anderson, Elijah., ed. *The Study of African American Problems: W. E. B. Du Bois's Agenda, Then and Now*. Thousand Oaks, CA: Sage Publications, 2000.

Du Bois, W.E.B. *The Souls of Black Folk*. New York: Vintage Books/Library of America, 1990 (orig. Pub. 1903).

Du Bois, Shirley Graham. *His Day Is Marching On: A Memoir of W.E.B. Du Bois*. Philadelphia: Lippincott, 1971.

Lewis, David L. *W.E.B. Du Bois: Biography of a Race, 1868–1919*. New York: Henry Holt, 1993.

Lewis, David L. *W.E.B. Du Bois: The Fight for Equality and the American Century, 1919–1963*. New York: Henry Holt, 2000.

Marable, Manning. *W.E.B. Du Bois, Black Radical Democrat*. Boston: Twayne, 1986.

Moore, Jacqueline. *Booker T. Washington, W.E.B. Du Bois, and the Struggle for Racial Uplift*. Wilmington, Delaware: Scholarly Resources, 2003.

Zamir, Shamoon. *Dark Voices: W.E.B. Du Bois and American Thought, 1888–1903*. Chicago: University of Chicago Press, 1995.

CHAPTER 4

Blake, Casey Nelson. *Beloved Community: The Cultural Criticism of Randolph Bourne, Van Wyck Brooks, Waldo Frank & Lewis Mumford*. Chapel Hill: University of North Carolina Press, 1990.

Clayton, Bruce. *Forgotten Prophet: The Life of Randolph Bourne*. Baton Rouge: Louisiana State University Press, 1984.

Dorreboom, Iris. *The Challenge of Our Time. Woodrow Wilson, Herbert Croly, Randolph Bourne and the Making of Modern America*. Atlanta, GA: Rodopi, 1991.

Moreau, John Adam. *Randolph Bourne: Legend and Reality*. Washington, DC: Public Affairs Press, 1966.

Vaughan, Leslie J. *Randolph Bourne and the Politics of Cultural Radicalism*. Lawrence: University Press of Kansas, 1997.

CHAPTER 5

Cook, Blanche, ed. *Crystal Eastman on Women and Revolution*. New York: Oxford University Press, 1978.

Douglas, Ann. *Terrible Honesty: Mongrel Manhattan in the 1920s*. New York: Farrar, Straus and Giroux, 1995.

Schoen, June. *The New Woman: Feminism in Greenwich Village, 1910–1920*. New York: Quadrangle Books, 1972.

Stansell, Christine. *American Moderns: Bohemian New York and the Creation of a New Century*. New York: Metropolitan Books, 2000.

CHAPTER 6

Barber, William J. *From New Era to New Deal: Herbert Hoover, the Economists and American Economic Policy, 1921–1933*. Cambridge and New York: Cambridge University Press, 1985.

Clements, Kendrick A. *The Life of Herbert Hoover: Imperfect Visionary, 1918-1928*. New York: Palgrave Macmillan, 2010.

Fausold, Martin L. *The Presidency of Herbert C. Hoover*. Lawrence, KS: University Press of Kansas, 1985.

Hoff-Wilson, Joan. *Herbert Hoover, Forgotten Progressive*. Boston: Little, Brown, 1975.

Hoover, Herbert. *American Individualism*. Garden City, NY: Doubleday, Page & Company, 1922.

Nash, George H. *The Life of Herbert Hoover*. New York: W. W. Norton, 1983.

Nash, Lee, ed. *Understanding Herbert Hoover: Ten Perspectives*. Stanford, CA: Hoover Institution Press, Stanford University, 1987.

Smith, Richard Norton. *An Uncommon Man: The Triumph of Herbert Hoover*. New York: Simon and Schuster, 1984.

CHAPTER 7

Caplow, Theodore, et al. *Middletown Families: Fifty Years of Change and Continuity*. Minneapolis: University of Minnesota Press, 1982.

Condran, John G., et al. *Working in Middletown: Getting a Living in Muncie, Indiana*. Indiana Committee for the Humanities, 1986.

Geelhoed, E. Bruce. *Muncie: The Middletown of America*. Chicago: Arcadia Publishing, 2000.

Lynd, Robert S., and Helen Merrell Lynd. *Middletown: A Study in Contemporary American Culture*. New York: Harcourt, Brace, and Company, 1929.

Lynd, Robert S., and Helen Merrell Lynd. *Middletown in Transition: A Study in Cultural Conflicts*. New York: Harcourt, Brace, and Company, 1937.

CHAPTER 8

Agee, James. *Let Us Now Praise Famous Men, a Death in the Family, & Shorter Fiction*. New York: Library of America, 2005.

Galassi, Peter. *Walker Evans & Company*. Distributed by Harry N. Abrams. New York: The Museum of Modern Art, 2000.

Gordon, Linda. *Dorothea Lange: A Life Beyond Limits*. London and New York: W.W. Norton & Co., 2009.

Lange, Dorothea. *Dorothea Lange*. Millerton, NY: Aperture, 1981.

Mahridge, Dale, and Michael Williamson. *And Their Children After Them: The Legacy of* Let Us Now Praise Famous Men: *James Agee, Walker Evans, and the Rise and Fall of Cotton in the South*. New York: Seven Stories Press, 2008.

Mellow, James R. *Walker Evans*. New York: Basic Books, 1999.

Rathbone, Belinda. *Walker Evans: A Biography*. Boston; New York: Houghton Mifflin, 1995.

CHAPTER 9

Briones, Matthew M. *Jim and Jap Crow: A Cultural History of 1940s Interracial America*. Princeton, NJ: Princeton University Press, 2012.

Conrat, Richard, and Maisie Conrat. *Executive Order 9066: The Internment of 110,000 Japanese Americans*. Introduction by Edison Uno. Photographs by Dorothea Lange and others. Cambridge, MA: MIT PRESS for the California Historical Society, 1972.

Daniels, Roger. *Concentration Camps USA: Japanese Americans and World War II (Berkshire Studies in History)*. Hinsdale, IL: Dryden Press, 1971.

Daniels, Roger. *Prisoners Without Trial: Japanese Americans in World War II*. New York: Hill and Wang, 2004.

Gordon, Linda, and Gary Okihiro, eds. *Impounded: Dorothea Lange and the Censored Images of Japanese American Internment*. New York: W.W. Norton, 2006.

Okihiro, Gary. *Whispered Silences. Japanese Americans and World War II*. Photographs by Joan Meyers. Seattle: University of Washington Press, 1996.

Robinson, Greg. *By Order of the President: FDR and the Internment of Japanese Americans*. Cambridge, MA: Harvard University Press, 2001.

Tanforan Journals of Charles Kikuchi. Edited and with an Introduction by John Modell. Urbana: University of Illinois Press, 1973.

CHAPTER 10

Claridge, Laura. *Norman Rockwell: A Life*. New York: Random House, 2001.

Hennessey, Maureen Hart, and Anne Knutson, eds. *Norman Rockwell: Pictures for the American People*. New York: H.N. Abrams, 1999. See Maureen Hart Hennessey, "The Four Freedoms," 94–102; and Laurie Norton Moffatt, "The People's Painter, " 23–27.

Mendoza, George. *Norman Rockwell's Patriotic Times*. Foreword by Ronald Reagan. New York: Viking, 1985.

Meyer, Susan E. *Norman Rockwell's People*. New York: Harrison House, 1987. Distributed by Crown Publishers.

Murray, Stuart. *Norman Rockwell's Four Freedoms: Images That Inspire a Nation*. Stockbridge, MA: Berkshire House, 1993.

Rockwell, Norman. *My Adventures as an Illustrator*. Garden City, NY: Doubleday & Company, 1960.

Rockwell Norman. *Norman Rockwell: A Sixty Year Retrospective*. With a Text by Thomas S. Buechner. New York: Abrams, 1972.

CHAPTER 11

Chambers, Whittaker. *Witness*. New York: Random House, 1952.

Hiss, Alger. *In the Court of Public Opinion*. New York: Knopf, 1957.

Jacoby, Susan. *Alger Hiss and the Battle for History*. New Haven: Yale University Press, 2009.

Kimmage, Michael. *The Conservative Turn: Lionel Trilling, Whittaker Chambers, and the Lessons of Anti-Communism*. Cambridge, MA: Harvard Univeristy Press, 2009.

Navasky, Victor S. *Naming Names*. New York: Penguin, 1981.

Schrecker, Ellen. *Many Are the Crimes: McCarthyism in America*. Boston: Little, Brown, 1998.

Shelton, Christina. *Alger Hiss: Why He Chose Treason*. New York: Threshold Editions, 2012.

Tanenhaus, Sam. *Whittaker Chambers: A Biography*. New York: Random House, 1997.

Weinstein, Allen. *Perjury: The Hiss-Chambers Case*. 2nd edition. New York: Random House, 1997.

White, G. Edward. *Alger Hiss's Looking Glass Wars: The Covert Life of a Soviet Spy*. New York: Oxford University Press, 2004.

CHAPTER 12

Ginsberg, Allen. *Howl and Other Poems*. San Francisco: City Lights Books, 1956.

Morgan, Bill. *I Celebrate Myself: The Somewhat Private Life of Allen Ginsberg*. New York: Viking Penguin, 2006.

Morgan, Bill, and David Stanford, eds. *Jack Kerouac and Allen Ginsberg: The Letters*. New York: Viking, 2010.

Raskin, Jonah. *American Scream: Allen Ginsberg's Howl and the Making of the Beat Generation*. Berkeley: University of California Press, 2004.

Shinder, Jason, ed. *The Poem that Changed America: "Howl" Fifty Years Later*. New York: Farrar, Straus, and Giroux, 2006.

CHAPTER 13

Bertrand, Michael T. *Race, Rock, and Elvis*. Urbana: University of Illinois Press, 2004.

Guralnick, Peter. *Last Train to Memphis: The Rise of Elvis Presley*. Boston: Little, Brown, and Company, 1994.

Guralnick, Peter. *Carless Love: The Unmaking of Elvis Presley*. Boston: Little, Brown, and Company, 1999.

Mason, Bobbie Ann. *Elvis Presley*. New York: Viking, 2003.

CHAPTER 14

Friedan, Betty. *The Feminine Mystique*. New York: W.W. Norton, 1963.

Harvey, Brett. *The Fifties: A Women's Oral History*. New York: HarperCollins, 1993.

Kaledin, Eugenia. *Mothers and More: American Women in the 1950s*. Boston: Twayne Publishers, 1984.

May, Elaine Tyler. *Homeward Bound: American Families in the Cold War Era*. New York: Basic Books, 1988.

Meyerowitz, Joanne J., ed. *Not June Cleaver: Women and Gender in Postwar America, 1945–1960*. Philadelphia: Temple University Press, 1994.

CHAPTER 15

Baughman, James L. *Same Time, Same Station: Creating American Television, 1948–1961*. Baltimore: Johns Hopkins University Press, 2007.

Edgerton, Gary R. *The Columbia History of American Television*. New York: Columbia University Press, 2007.

Postman, Neil. *Amusing Ourselves to Death: Public Discourse in the Age of Show Business*. New York: Viking, 1985.

Spigel, Lynn. *Make Room for TV: Television and the Family Ideal in Postwar America*. Chicago: University of Chicago Press, 1992.

Watson, Mary Ann. *The Expanding Vista: American Television in the Kennedy Years*. New York: Oxford University Press, 1990.

CHAPTER 16

Bourdon, David. *Warhol*. New York: H.N. Abrams, 1989.

Doyle, Jennifer, Jonathan Flatley, and Jose Esteban Munoz. *Pop Out: Queer Warhol*. Durham: Duke University Press, 1996.

Foster, Hal. *The First Pop Age: Painting and Subjectivity in the Art of Hamilton, Lichtenstein, Warhol, Richer, and Ruscha*. Princeton, NJ: Princeton University Press, 2011.

Koestenbaum, Wayne. *Andy Warhol*. New York: Viking, 2001.

Warhol, Andy. *The Philosophy of Andy Warhol: From A to B and Back Again*. New York: Harcourt Brace Jovanovich, 1977.

Warhol, Andy, and Pat Hackett. *POPism: The Warhol Sixties*. London: Penguin Books, 2007.

CHAPTER 17

Gitlin, Todd. *The Sixties: Years of Hope, Days of Rage*. New York: Bantam Books, 1987.

Hayden, Tom. *The Port Huron Statement: The Visionary Call of the 1960s Revolution*. New York: Thunder's Mouth Press, 2005.

Isserman, Maurice. *If I Had a Hammer: The Death of the Old Left and the Birth of the New Left*. Urbana: University of Illinois Press, 1993.

Miller, James. *"Democracy Is in the Streets": From Port Huron to the Siege of Chicago*. New York: Simon and Schuster, 1987 (contains Port Huron Statement).

Pekar, Harvey and Paul Buhle. *Students for a Democratic Society: A Graphic History*. New York: Hill and Wang, 2009.

Sale, Kirkpatrick. *SDS*. New York: Vintage Books, 1974.

CHAPTER 18

Clarke, John Henrik. *Malcolm X: The Man and His Times*. Edited, with an Introduction by John Henrik Clarke. Assisted by A. Peter Bailey and Earl Grant. New York: Macmillan, 1969.

Dyson, Michael Eric. *Making Malcolm: The Myth and Meaning of Malcolm X*. New York: Oxford University Press, 1995.

Gallen, David. *Malcolm X: As They Knew Him*. New York: Ballantine Books, 1996.

Hampton, Henry, and Steve Fayer, eds. *Voices of Freedom: An Oral History of the Civil Rights Movement from the 1950s through the 1980s.* New York: Bantam Books, 1990, pp. 241–66.

X, Malcolm. *The Autobiography of Malcolm X.* With the assistance of Alex Haley. New York: Ballantine Books, 1990 (orig. pub. 1965).

Marable, Manning. *Malcolm X: A Life of Reinvention.* New York: Viking, 2011.

Perry, Bruce. *Malcolm: The Life of a Man That Changed Black America.* Barrytown, NY: Station Hill Press, 1991.

Perry, Bruce, ed. *Malcolm X: The Last Speeches.* New York: Pathfinder, 1989.

CHAPTER 19

Berman, Larry. *Planning a Tragedy: The Americanization of the War in Vietnam.* New York: W.W. Norton, 1982.

Berman, Larry. *Lyndon Johnson's War: The Road to Stalemate in Vietnam.* New York: Norton, 1989.

Beschloss, Michael. *Reaching for Glory: Lyndon Johnson's White House Tapes, 1964–1965.* New York: Simon & Schuster, 2001.

Dallek, Robert. *Lone Star Rising: Lyndon Johnson and His Times, 1908–1960.* New York: Oxford University Press, 1991.

Dallek, Robert. *Flawed Giant: Lyndon Johnson and His Times, 1961–1973.* New York: Oxford University Press, 1998.

Herring, George C. *America's Longest War: The United States and Vietnam, 1950–1975.* New York: Wiley, 1979.

Kaiser, David. *American Tragedy: Kennedy, Johnson, and the Origins of the Vietnam War.* Cambridge, MA: Belknap Press of Harvard University Press, 2000.

VanDeMark, Brian. *Into the Quagmire: Lyndon Johnson and the Escalation of the Vietnam War.* New York: Oxford University Press, 1995.

Woods, Randall B. *LBJ: Architect of American Ambition.* New York: Free Press, 2006.

CHAPTER 20

Cohen, Marcia. *The Sisterhood: The True Story of the Women Who Changed the World.* New York: Simon & Schuster, 1988.

DuPlessis, Rachel Blau, and Ann Snitow, eds. *The Feminist Memoir Project: Voices from Women's Liberation.* New York: Three Rivers Press, 1998.

Echols, Alice. *Daring to Be Bad: Radical Feminism in America, 1967–1975.* Minneapolis: University of Minnesota Press, 1989.

Evans, Sara. *Personal Politics: The Roots of Women's Liberation in the Civil Rights Movement and the New Left.* New York: Knopf, 1979.

Firestone, Shulamith. *The Dialectic of Sex: The Case for Feminist Revolution.* New York: William Morrow and Company, 1970.

Firestone, Shulamith, and Ann Koedt, eds. *Notes from the Second Year: Women's Liberation: Major Writing of the Radical Feminists.* New York: Radical Feminism, 1970 (contains Bitch Manifesto).

Freeman, Jo. *The Politics of Women's Liberation: A Case Study of an Emerging Social Movement and Its Relation to the Policy Process.* New York: McKay, 1975.

Freeman, Jo. *At Berkeley in the '60s: The Education of an Activist, 1961–1965.* Bloomington, IN: Indiana University Press, 2004.

Koedt, Anne, Ellen Levine, and Anita Rapone, eds. *Radical Feminism.* New York: Quadrangle Books, 1973, pp. 50–59 (contains Bitch Manifesto).

Rupp, Leila J., and Verta A. Taylor. *Survival in the Doldrums: The American Women's Rights Movement, 1945 to the 1960s.* New York: Oxford University Press, 1987.

Stansell, Christine. *The Feminist Promise, 1792 to the Present.* New York: Random House/Modern Library, 2010.

CHAPTER 21

Brownlee, W. Elliot, and Hugh Davis Graham. *The Reagan Presidency: Pragmatic Conservatism and Its Legacies.* Lawrence: University of Press of Kansas, 2003.

Diggins, John Patrick. *Ronald Reagan: Fate, Freedom, and the Making of History.* New York: W.W. Norton, 2007.

Evans, Thomas W. *The Education of Ronald Reagan: The General Electric Years and the Story of His Conversion to Conservatism.* New York: Columbia University Press, 2006.

Fraser, Steve and Gary Gerstle. *The Rise and Fall of the New Deal Order, 1930–1980*. Princeton: Princeton University Press, 1989.

Wilentz, Sean. *The Age of Reagan: A History, 1974–2008*. New York: HarperCollins, 2008.

CHAPTER 22

Putnam, Robert D. *Bowling Alone: The Collapse and Revival of American Community*. New York: Simon & Schuster, 2001.

Putnam, Robert D. *Better Together: Restoring the American Community*. New York: Simon & Schuster, 2004.

Rotolo, Thomas, and John Wilson. "What Happened to the 'Long Civic Generation'?: Explaining Cohort Differences in Volunteerism." *Social Forces* 82 (March 2004): 1091–1121.

Wilson, James Q. "Bowling with Others." *Commentary* 66 (October 2007): 30–33.

CHAPTER 23

Ajami, Fouad. "The Summoning: 'But They Said, We Will Not Hearken'." *Foreign Affairs* 72 (September/October 1993): 2–9.

Bartley, Robert L. "The Case for Optimism: The West Should Believe in Itself." *Foreign Affairs* 72 (September/October 1993): 15–18.

Binyan, Liu. "Civilization Grafting: No Culture Is an Island." *Foreign Affairs* 72 (September/October 1993): 19–21.

Fukuyama, Francis. *The End of History and the Last Man*. New York: Free Press, 1992.

Huntington, Samuel P. "If Not Civilizations, What? Paradigms of the Post-Cold War World." *Foreign Affairs* 72 (November/December 1993): 186–194.

Huntington, Samuel P. "The Clash of Civilizations?" *Foreign Affairs* 72 (Summer 1993): 22–49.

Huntington, Samuel P. *The Clash of Civilizations and the Remaking of World Order*. New York: Simon & Schuster, 1996.

Kirkpatrick, Jeane J. "The Modernizing Imperative: Tradition and Change." *Foreign Affairs* 72 (September/October 1993): 22–26.

Mahbubani, Kishore. "The Dangers of Decadence: What the Rest Can Teach the West." *Foreign Affairs* 72 (September/October 1993): 10–14.